SO-AHU-548

# Play and Child Development

FOURTH EDITION

**JOE L. FROST**

*University of Texas, Emeritus*

**SUE C. WORTHAM**

*University of Texas at San Antonio, Emerita*

**STUART REIFEL**

*University of Texas, Austin*

Boston  Columbus  Indianapolis  New York  San Francisco  Upper Saddle River
Amsterdam  Cape Town  Dubai  London  Madrid  Milan  Munich  Paris  Montreal  Toronto
Delhi  Mexico City  São Paulo  Sydney  Hong Kong  Seoul  Singapore  Taipei  Tokyo

**Vice President and Editorial Director:** Jeffery W. Johnston
**Senior Acquisitions Editor:** Julie Peters
**Vice President, Director of Marketing:** Margaret Waples
**Senior Marketing Manager:** Chris Barry
**Senior Managing Editor:** Pamela Bennett
**Senior Project Manager:** Mary M. Irvin
**Production Project Manager:** Debbie Ryan

**Senior Art Director:** Jayne Conte
**Cover Designer:** Karen Salzbach
**Cover Art:** Fotolia
**Composition:** PreMediaGlobal
**Full Service Project Management:** Chitra Ganesan
**Printer/Binder:** STP Courier
**Cover Printer:** STP Courier
**Text Font:** Palatino 10/12

Every effort has been made to provide accurate and current Internet information in this book. However, the Internet and information posted on it are constantly changing, so it is inevitable that some of the Internet addresses listed in this textbook will change.

Photo Credits: Francis G. Mayer/Corbis, p. 1; Detail Athenia Red Figure Vase, reproduced by permission of Hirmer Fotoarchiv München, p. 5; Annie Pickert/Pearson, pp. 11, 27, 134, 399; EyeWire Collection/Getty Images–Photodisc–Royalty Free, p. 19; Scott Cunningham/Merrill, p. 20; Todd Yarrington/Merrill, pp. 34, 42; David Mager/Pearson Learning Photo Studio, p. 42; Anne Vega/Merrill, pp. 46, 113, 115, 345; Vanessa Davies © Dorling Kindersley, p. 51; Fotolia, LLC–Royalty Free, pp. 60, 69, 96, 107, 163, 164, 181, 224, 356, 360, 365, 392, 396, 410, 440: (top right, bottom left); Shirley Zeiberg/PH College, p. 91; Ruth Jenkinson © Dorling Kindersley, p. 120; Charles Gatewood/PH College, p. 130; Krista Greco/Merrill, pp. 159, 263; Laimute Druskis/PH College, p. 176; Shutterstock, pp. 194, 249, 284, 363, 366, 371; Larry Fleming/PH College, p. 201; National Palace Museum, Taiwan, Republic of China, p. 214; Michal Heron/PH College, p. 219; Laura Bolesta/Merrill, p. 234; BananaStock Ltd, p. 245; Ben Molyneux/Alamy, p. 265; Andy Brunk/Merrill, p. 269; From American Playgrounds, by E. B. Mero (Boston: American Gymnasia Co., 1908), p. 288; Courtesy of Rusty Keeler, Planet Earth Playscapes, p. 298; Courtesy of Redeemer Lutheran School, Austin, Texas, pp. 299, 300, 304, 308; Courtesy of Dr. Rick Worch, Bowling Green State University, pp. 311, 314, 315; Barbara Schwartz/Merrill, p. 320; Scott Cunningham/Merrill, p. 328; Anthony Magnacca/Merrill, p. 336; Getty Images Inc/Jupiter Images/Comstock, p. 379; David J. Phillip/AP Wide World Photos, p. 393; provided by Joe L. Frost, pp. 421, 423, 445, 455; Image Source/Alamy, pp. 407, 410 (bottom right); I love images/Alamy, p. 410 (top left); Charles O. Cecil/Alamy, p. 457.

Copyright © 2012, 2008, 2005, 2001 **by Pearson Education, Inc.** All rights reserved. Printed in the United States of America. This publication is protected by Copyright and permission should be obtained from the publisher prior to any prohibited reproduction, storage in a retrieval system, or transmission in any form or by any means, electronic, mechanical, photocopying, recording, or likewise. To obtain permission(s) to use material from this work, please submit a written request to Pearson Education, Inc., Permissions Department, One Lake Street, Upper Saddle River, New Jersey 07458 or you may fax your request to 201-236-3290.

**Library of Congress Cataloging-in-Publication Data**

Frost, Joe L.
  Play and child development / Joe L. Frost, Sue C. Wortham, Stuart Reifel. — 4th ed.
    p. cm.
  Includes index.
  ISBN-13: 978-0-13-259683-1
  ISBN-10: 0-13-259683-0
 1. Play—Social aspects.  2. Child development.  I. Wortham, Sue Clark, 1935-
II. Reifel, Robert Stuart.  III. Title.
  HQ782.F75 2011
  305.231—dc22

                                            2011011996

10 9 8 7 6 5 4 3 2 1

www.pearsonhighered.com

ISBN 10: 0-13-259683-0
ISBN 13: 978-0-13-259683-1

*We dedicate this book to our families and to Brandon, who support our work and endure our mood swings—lovingly and patiently.*

# Preface

*Play and Child Development* is designed for students who have a need to understand the fascinating and complex world of children's play. Building on a rich research base, each topic is presented to enhance the comprehension of upper division students who wish to deepen their understanding of children. Although the depth of presentation is better suited to advanced students, beginning students will find ample linkages to how play research has implications for practice in a range of professional settings.

 **NEW TO THIS EDITION**

- A complete new chapter on technology and play (Chapter 11).
  - Current research on children's use of computers and technology in a historical perspective.
  - Research with younger children and implications for caretakers.
  - New standards and research on the implication of technology play on children's development.
- New sections on observing and assessing play in the classroom and coverage of the Tools of the Mind curriculum and the Creative Curriculum.
- New research in neuroscience relevant to understanding the benefits of play, the consequences of play deprivation, and the influence of play on brain development. Linkages between brain development, exercise, sleep, diet, trauma, emotional disorders, and competent-child behavior. (See Chapter 3.)

- Discussion of new literature on how adults acquire an understanding of play, as well as new material on play theory.
- Updated information on the value of play at different ages, as well as new resources on developmental play.
- New feature boxes addressing the benefits of block play, guidelines for adult/child interaction in play, and other topics.
- New research on how different disabilities are understood, along with a comprehensive chart of types of disabilities. Expanded discussion on the role of technology in assisting children with disabilities.
- More on the therapeutic benefits of play, training that teachers can receive to use play therapy techniques, and the use of group therapy.
- Expanded information about natural habitats, settings, and gardens to complement conventional playgrounds and a renewed focus on nature.
- New emphasis on freeing children to play in more challenging environments.
- New literature on play/work programs and their implications for U.S. child-care centers and schools.

 **ORGANIZATION OF THIS TEXT**

To understand any human activity such as play, it is necessary to explore that activity as it has evolved over time. **Chapter 1** frames the history of play in terms of philosophy, practices in different eras, and the values that underlie children's activities. Through the past century, research on children's play has contributed to theories about play and its role in development. As we look at our efforts to make sense of play, we see a variety of rhetorics for play and a wider variety of theories to make sense of it.

In **Chapter 2**, various play theories are presented as tools for understanding different aspects of children's development, including communications and language, cognition and learning, social relationships, and creativity. New literature on how adults acquire an understanding of play should help students add theory to their personal views of play, including classroom play practices. This chapter introduces a number of theories that dominated play scholarship throughout the 20th century, as well as a number of emerging theories that are leading us into the 21st century. Chapter 2 also provides a framework for deciding which theory may be most useful for professionals who support play.

During the 20th century, additional tools emerged from research in several disciplines. **Chapter 3** details the work of behavioral scientists who, during the 1960s, introduced the notion of the plasticity of the human brain with particular reference to very young children. This set the stage for national attention to early development in playful contexts. This edition identifies linkages between brain development, exercise, sleep, diet, trauma, emotional disorders, and competent child behavior. Appropriate roles of teachers and other adults who work closely with children are identified.

Three chapters address play and child development with updated information on the value of play at different ages and new resources on developmental play. The first, **Chapter 4**, discusses the first three years of development with information on how to implement play with infants and toddlers as well as the changing role of toys. The preschool years are discussed in **Chapter 5**, which has expanded information on block play and new perceptions of the role of solitary play. These chapters also illustrate using group games to combine play

and cognitive learning. **Chapter 6** contains information about school-age play in light of increasing academic expectations and contrasting views of the importance of recess.

Issues of culture and gender are addressed in **Chapter 7**. Because so many societies are multicultural at this time, there are always questions about the traditions, meanings, relationships, and communications that may vary with different groups of people. Gender differences in play are universal and apparent from many studies. A discussion of theories of gender development introduces a description of the continuing debate on the nature and nurture of play. Studies, although not resolving the debate, illustrate girl/boy differences in social patterns, toys used, and texts dramatized in play.

Over recent decades, a number of approaches have evolved that address the integration of play into curriculum and the roles of teachers. In **Chapter 8**, we examine the dominant approaches, ranging from hands-off play to broadly and narrowly focused play intervention. Play is not all that children need, but knowledge is constructed through play, and, through sensitive adult intervention, play and work become complementary activities. A section on creating classroom play environments and indoor safety is presented in this edition. New features include boxed content that address the benefits of block play, guidelines for adult/child interaction in play, the value of board games, and cautions about literacy play.

Because play is an important ingredient of indoor as well as outdoor activities, **Chapter 9** focuses on the creation and use of special, magical, creative outdoor play environments, including both natural and built. This section is intended to counter the growing pattern of cookie-cutter, standardized playgrounds in U.S. child-care centers, schools, and public parks by focusing on comprehensive environments featuring natural elements such as sand, water, tools, materials for construction, nature areas, and special places. Discussion topics include built and natural play and learning environments in schools, parks, neighborhoods, and in special destinations such as children's zoos, museums, summer camps, and nature centers.

**Chapter 10** focuses on the questions of how children with disabilities or special needs engage in play and what adaptations need to be made to adult roles and the environment to expand play. This chapter has been rewritten to reflect changes in the literature as to how different disabilities are named and understood, including a comprehensive chart of types of disabilities and information on the role of technology in assisting people with disabilities.

**Chapter 11** on technology and play is totally new to this edition. Current research on children's use of computers and other forms of technology are placed in historical perspective. Research on technology and play is increasing to keep up with new technology developments. Much of what we know about the effects of technology play on child development is based on older children's play and play activities, but research with younger children is expanding and implications for teachers and caretakers are gradually emerging. Readers are guided to new standards and research and alerted to the serious concerns that many have for the implications of technology play for children's development.

The natural therapeutic qualities of play lend even greater emphasis to the importance of play for child development. As seen in **Chapter 12**, play therapy has its roots in the psychoanalytic tradition, but, over the years, theorists and practitioners modified the practical applications of this tradition to develop several approaches. The fundamental tenets of child-centered play therapy are rooted in the beliefs that children play out their phobias, feelings, and emotions and that play has natural healing powers. This edition is revised to take into account the rapidly growing body of research showing that play itself is therapeutic, that teachers can be trained to employ play therapytechniques, and group therapy can be meaningfully employed in school where many children are experiencing adjustment and traumatic disorders.

The analysis of child safety in public places in **Chapter 13** is unique in play texts, perhaps because of the prevailing view that accidents and injuries are inherent in growing up. Safety experts and a growing body of safety research conclude that accidents can be prevented, especially those that expose children to risks of permanent injury or death. This edition examines problems fundamental to the continuing expansion of and inconsistencies within and among state and national playground safety guidelines, regulations, and standards. Also discussed are other related factors contributing to the decline of recess and spontaneous play.

Finally, in **Chapter 14,** the term *play leadership* is interchanged with *playwork* to reflect the successful playwork programs in Europe. This chapter promotes the concept that all adults who supervise children at play—parents, aides, teachers, youth workers—need certain skills. Good play leaders respect children and play. In this edition, recent literature on play/work programs is introduced with implications for practice in U.S. child-care centers and schools. The growing health and development issues resulting from play deprivation resulted in even greater emphasis on training playworkers or play leaders to interact with children in out-of-school contexts such as neighborhood or city parks and nature centers.

## ACKNOWLEDGMENTS

The authors wish to acknowledge and express appreciation to those who helped prepare this book. To Miai Kim, Yi-Jeng Chen, Holly Carrell Moore, Marcia Molinar, Shelley Nicholson, John Sutterby, and Bhakti Pandya for chapter resources; David Kushner and X. Christine Wang for intellectual guidance; to Rusty Keeler who assisted with photographs; to Alita Zaepfel and Stephen Flynn who helped with manuscript preparation, computer foul-ups and various tasks; and to the many students who contributed in countless ways. We also thank our colleagues at other universities who provided valuable, extensive analyses and suggestions for improving the manuscript: LaVonne Carlson, University of Minnesota; Aviva Dorfman, University of Michigan, Flint; Sherry L. Forrest, Craven University; Vickie E. Lake, Florida State University; and Sandra J. Stone, Northern Arizona University. We also wish to thank Julie Peters and Mary Irvin, the skillful editors at Pearson and Chitra Ganesan at PreMedia Global who guided us through the writing and editorial process.

# Brief Contents

# Contents

# 1 Play's History

## IDEAS, BELIEFS, AND ACTIVITIES

*The remarkable endurance of play and games across centuries, generations, cultures, and countries is quite a story. Both natural and man-made playgrounds change with geography, time, and necessity. Technology, culture, and interest change children's toy choices, but their games, laws, and seasons for playing them endure in modified fashion.*

(Frost, 2010, p. 61)

We all grow up playing. We play the games that are familiar parts of our cultures. Play endures, even as it appears to change over time. Take, for example, peekaboo. A toddler pokes his head around the edge of an open doorway. We don't think about it. We just say, "Peekaboo!" The toddler laughs, and so do we. It is fun. It is natural. It is something that people just do. Play is so much a part of our lives as human beings that we often fail to reflect on the range of our play activities and on what those activities mean for us. In this text, we provide a basis for reflecting on what play is for humans—in particular young developing humans. We hope to enable you to reflect in more depth about the role of play in our lives. What other games, like peekaboo, do we play, and why do we play them? What does play like peekaboo, patty-cake, pretend cops and robbers, Crazy Eights, and MORGs (multiplayer online role-playing games) contribute to children's development? Children play in many ways and for many reasons. There are multiple meanings for play and multiple forms of activities that we call play. This book provides a guide for what we know about play and how we can think about it.

Some suggest that play is necessary for children and is based on their imagination. For more than a century, we have believed that imaginary play stimulates thinking and is good for children (Archer, 1910). Others suggest children may pretend in a manner that reflects the experiences they have had; play becomes an imitation of life that serves to educate children. Scholars and researchers provide many ways for us to think about play as it is connected to development, emotions, motivation, cognition, socialization, culture, and learning. For example, Bruner and Sherwood (1976) tell us that that peekaboo begins to teach children social rules about how to interact with others. In the following chapters, we will see how play tells us a great deal about who we are as human beings and how scholars have many ways of addressing our understanding of play.

Children's play is a complex variety of activities. Peekaboo gives way to pretend, which over time is replaced by soccer and computer games as common play activities in our culture. Many layers of meaning are associated with play. Do we assume that play is an innate, biological phenomenon, or is it a reflection of the child's *culture?* When we think of play, are we focusing on social, cognitive, motor, or cultural aspects of *development?* Are we conscious of some play, as when we plan play activities for children's birthday parties or when we support their participation in sports? Or are there unconscious attributes to play, things that we don't bother to think about, like when we play peekaboo or send children outdoors just to play? We must continually revisit play activities to analyze and understand what they mean to us. We can also look at research to see what it can teach us about children and play. Play activities are complex, and how we make sense of them, with research and from our own experience, is complex and challenging. You can play peekaboo without thinking about it, but we intend to show you that there is more to play than just fun. Scholarship about play is a tool to help us think about children in complex ways, the way Bruner and Sherwood (1976) help us see peekaboo as interactive, with rules, language, and suspense, as well as fun. This book is designed to build on your experiences with play, to think about play.

We begin our book with this chapter on the history of play as a set of ideas, showing the ancient origins of play's complexity. How we make sense of human activity like play is complicated by the fact that our "thought has operated over the centuries" (Spariosu,1989, p. 12). Our current thinking about play has been shaded by history, by the centuries of thought about play that precede our own (Frost, 2010). One function of the study of history is to help us understand the evolution of our ideas over the centuries, to better situate our current thinking and beliefs. This chapter shows some of the historical origins of our contemporary ideas about play.

The activity of play may have both rational and prerational meanings for us. When we reflect on play (or research it), we are making play into a rational activity. Prerational play has it roots in ancient experience that may still be with us, perhaps in fun activities that helped us relate and communicate with one another. Prerational play may be unconscious (that is, we do it without awareness), and it may become conscious (that is, we are aware of it and know we are doing it) (Spariosu, 1989). We can play peekaboo without thinking; that makes it a prerational activity. When we start to think about peekaboo, we make it a conscious activity (we do it on purpose; we may know why we are doing it), and we may begin studying it; we start to have reasons for play. Play, as an activity that may have prehistoric roots for human beings (Bateson, 1995/2000), has been part of human experience prior to the onset of rational, reasoned (reflective, scholarly) thought. (Studies of nonhuman, especially primate, play suggest the likelihood of play being a precursor to rationality; see Bekoff & Byers, 1998.) Human beings probably played before we evolved the civilizing institutions of philosophy, science, or teaching. The history of play will show us how our thinking about play has changed over the centuries, as well as how play activities have changed.

Our lives are full of play. We have organized sports in our schools and out of them, including soccer for preschoolers and more traditional Little League, gymnastics, and skating programs. There are playgrounds in city parks, facilities for play in shopping malls, and a burgeoning world of play made available through personal computers. Children's play is thoroughly woven into the fabric of our daily lives, in very visible and organized ways. We are aware of all this play. But how can we think about it? What are our reasons for playing?

Beyond the play recreation that we provide for children, we also base many services for children and families on beliefs about the centrality of play for healthy development and education. Play is described as the foundation for learning and mental health in families (Hellerdorn, Van Der Kooij, & Sutton-Smith, 1994), including family intervention programs designed to counter the influences of poverty (Levenstein, 1998). Play is also a cornerstone for **developmentally appropriate practice (DAP)**, guidelines for the education of young children in group settings (Copple & Bredekamp, 2009). We, as a society, have acknowledged play as more than recreation; we have built it into some of our social institutions. In this day and age, we engage in some play consciously and for a purpose, for example, when we join a soccer team or go to the theater with friends. We have built play into our lives, creating social institutions for its expression. Play, for human beings, is a set of cultural practices of which we are fully conscious. Play is a part of our rational thinking (i.e., reflection, research), how we plan and think about how we live, especially with regard to the lives of children.

With all the visible forms of play that we encounter, whether in schools, parks, malls, or cyberspace, we still overlook or ignore many play activities. Adults tend to ignore teasing games or pretend that offends propriety (Opie, 1993; Opie & Opie, 1997; Reifel, 1986). Adults once overlooked play about violence, although it is now receiving more attention (Beresin, 1989; Carlsson-Paige & Levin, 1987, 1995; Goldstein, 1995). And play on sexual themes may be dismissed by many as "just play," thereby relegating it to the world of the invisible. For all the ways we are more rational about play, there are also many ways that we are prerational; many aspects of play have not been studied. Some forms of play are part of our lives, although we do not truly pay attention to them.

Play is changing over time (Frost, 2010). We must remember that some forms of play may have meaning for us on a prerational level, based on ancient patterns of play that remain nonconscious to us. Such is the power of pretense for humans, who can, without thought, shift from the here and now to an imaginary world when playing with a preschooler; it comes to us naturally, and we don't need to think about it. Other aspects of play have fully rational meanings for us. The centrality of organized sports in schools, for example, highlights play as part of institutionalized, rational experience, from the scheduling of physical education courses into the curriculum to the planning of sport seasons for soccer, basketball, and swimming (e.g., Halliman, 1996). History tells us the story of what occurred. Play has not always been viewed as something worth documenting. Therefore, our understanding of the history of play is complicated by the fact that we do not have rich details describing what people actually did while they played in all eras. Mergen (1995) points out that play can be understood in terms of memories, in terms of relics, and also from our understandings generated by historians. Historians look not at actions but at documents of actions (e.g., the images on vases or paintings) or documents about actions (e.g., records of sports competitions or reflections by participants on playing). They look at relics or objects that were acted upon (clay dolls, miniature bows and arrows), and they look at a full range of documents that may help them understand the phenomenon of play. The painting that introduces this chapter shows a mid–19th-century play scene, with a child on what must have been a handcrafted rocking horse. This gives us one piece of information on how some children played nearly 200 years ago.

One way to understand the history of play is by following a number of strands in the historical literature on play. One strand in this literature highlights our historical understanding of play in general. This understanding gives us laws and definitions of play in terms of activities in which all human beings may participate. The emergence of children's play as a subset of this broader view of play gains historical significance as writers begin to focus specifically on what children do (and, as some eventually argued, ought to do) as they play

(Frost, 2010). A second strand that we should think about has to do with the distinction between what we know about play activities as opposed to what we know about how play was described in the literature. As we see later in this chapter, it is only with the post-Enlightenment Romantic era that we begin to see evidence of what play can be for children and an elaboration of what its significance may be for children's education and development. And it is only after the Romantic era that we begin to see efforts to document activities that we should understand in terms of their playful elements. The post-Darwinian enterprise of conducting observations as part of a controlled scientific effort altered the shape of how we understand play.

This chapter describes the history of children's play. To acknowledge the complexity of play, we will see how the history of thought about play (philosophy, concepts, and beliefs) has changed over time. We can also see ideas that are best dismissed. We will also see that play emerged in the 19th century as a rational phenomenon for considering the education and development of children. With play established as a rational tenet of early education, our thinking about play transformed because of evolutionary theory and the introduction of science to the study of children and education. These strands of history of play contribute to how we make sense of play, how we plan for it, how we participate in it, and whether we advocate for it as an important part of children's lives.

## PHILOSOPHY AND IDEAS OVER THE YEARS

### The Ancients and Play

In the cult of Artemis girls were sometimes placed in the service of the goddess for longer periods, during which they underwent puberty initiation rites. Once again the rites characteristically involved the formation of dancing groups, as well as foot-races, processions to altars and other sacred objects, and the sacrifice of an animal as a substitute for the human victim demanded by Artemis in myth. (Lonsdale, 1993, p. 170)

Play has been part of philosophical discourse since the time of the ancient Greeks. Plato (427–347 B.C.), Socrates (470–399 B.C.), Aristotle (384–322 B.C.), and Xenophanes (6th century B.C.) all explored the meaning of play as part of their frameworks for understanding human expression and thought (Spariosu, 1989). For example, in *The Republic* (c.360 B.C.; 1993) and *The Laws* (c. 360 B.C.; 1975), Plato wrote of the importance of freedom for learning, and he specifically mentioned playing at building in childhood to perfect knowledge that will be used later in life (Wolfe, 2002). Based on ancient religious practices, a number of forms of play were described that helped make sense of ancient lives (Lonsdale, 1993). How can we understand the human condition? *Agon, mimesis*, and *chaos* provided three routes for understanding, and they all provide a basis for how we continue to think about play (Spariosu, 1989).

**Agon**, or conflict, represented one way to consider play. The ancient Greek gods were understood to play with humans on earth, to provide challenges that might take the form of war, politics, or other forms of strife that would put humans into physical or social competition with one another. Those who won the competition, who mastered a conflict such as winning a footrace, were seen as blessed by the gods. Ancient Greeks created sport versions of real conflict in which they could determine who was to be blessed. For example, instead of fighting a real war, there would be games in which competitors threw lances (javelins), heaved stones (shot puts), shot arrows (archery), and engaged in other forms of physical competition, all to see which individual or community had the gods' support. The competitive striving of sport was one avenue for ascertaining who was gifted with divine power. Competitive play, in the form of sport or games, continues to be a major part of how we think about play to this day.

**Mimesis** included any number of representational forms that stemmed from actions designed to mimic the gods as a form of adoration. Acting in ways that were thought to be pleasing to the gods, possibly by doing what the gods were imagined to do, such as dancing, was seen as bringing humans closer to the gods and possibly creating divine favor for the actors. Scenarios where the gods were depicted as orchestrating human actions evolved into theater (plays), rituals (religious rites), and other forms of dramatic or symbolic depiction. Mimesis, or mimicry, might be imitative, interpretive, or expressive, but in all cases it involved acting out of the ordinary. Imaginative or dramatic enactment by adults or

Ancient Greek players used masks in mimesis to take on new roles.

children is still seen to be at the core of contemporary symbolic play and recreation.

**Chaos**, or the order and disorder of nature, provided a third route for ancient peoples to relate to the gods and make sense of humans' role in the world. How can we learn to relate to the randomness of the gods' actions? One way is to try to predict what they want. Perhaps by throwing bones on the ground or reading patterns of entrails we can see a pattern intended for us. Belief that divine order can emerge from randomness involves a trust in **chance**, a belief that from all the possible things that could occur, a godly intervention will mark the player's path. The belief is that tossing bones (rolling dice), exposing images (drawing playing cards), and drawing lots all reveal to the player that he or she is selected by the gods. Games of chance (with or without divine associations) are a third form of play that continues to this day, whether in the form of gambling, drawing straws, or flipping coins to decide who will have the first turn in a game.

> Thus we see a small boy wearing a helmet and holding a spear performing a weapon dance, a training qualification rite for ephebes [citizens]. (Lonsdale, 1993, p. 131)

The ancient Greeks argued about the meanings of these activities and refined their philosophies in relationship to them. The religious connections made between play and human actions are clear, and we can see that some of the ways we think about play (the power and skill of agon, the pretense of mimesis, the luck of chaos) are still with us culturally, at least intuitively. The forms of play the ancients discussed applied both to adult and child's play. What we do not see is a clear rationale for considering the play of children, whether the weapon dance is just a religious ritual or whether it is socialization or practice for actual adult roles. The play actions of children outside of ritual activities were not recorded, so we have little idea what comprised children's play in these ancient times.

## Enlightenment and Romantic Thought on Play

Ideas about play, and children's play in particular, received more attention during the historic eras when thinkers such as John Locke, Immanuel Kant, and Friedrich von Schiller began to reconsider the human mind. Rational thought, rather than a focus on religion and belief, became the major concern of philosophers. What we know and how we know it, whether in the realms of science, morals, or the arts, became issues for reflection. Play was considered as part of this analysis in varying ways: as a foundation for rationality, as the roots of the irrational or spiritual, or in some cases it was just mentioned in passing. Again, we will see that play was discussed in the most general terms, and we have little evidence for understanding what people actually did when they played. We will begin to see the play of children being separated from adult play. And we will see that the increasing emphasis on play and rationality does not preclude a continued connection between ideas of play and the divine or spiritual. Finally, we will see that links between play and rational thought eventually led to the creation of detailed descriptions of what play ought to be for children; play is elevated by educator/philosophers, such as Friedrich Froebel, to a type of activity, with specific play objects that were thought to shape the mind and spirit.

**The Rational Man: Locke and the Tabula Rasa**    The 17th-century British philosopher John Locke (1632–1704) is frequently credited with providing a basis for psychological behaviorism. Locke's interest in the origins of reason led him to speculate that each human being is born as an intellectual blank slate, or *tabula rasa*, on which our sense impressions are inscribed. Human thought results from experiences we have, not from any mystical or spiritual internal processes. What we know is what we learn. Locke's thoughts about the mind and how it is formed contributed to education and child rearing in his own day and long after. Play is not often associated with Locke, but as his 1693 writing on *Some Thoughts Concerning Education* indicates, he was aware of play as an important part of childhood experience.

> Recreation is as necessary, as Labour, or Food [*sic*]. But because there can be no Recreation without Delight, which depends not always on Reason, but oftener on Fancy, it must be permitted Children not only to divert themselves, but to do it after their own fashion. (Locke, 1693/1968, p. 211)

Locke saw play as a necessary part of childhood. Children are players by nature, pursuing their imaginative fancy for the pleasure that it brings. Although such experiences were not understood to contribute to rationality and the mind, Locke saw them as contributing to children's health and spirit. Although not good for the mind per se, play did have a role in improving attitude, aptitude, and physical well-being. Locke was among the first to specify that play with particular toys, carefully supervised by adults, was desirable for children.

**Kant: Categorical Imperative, Play, and Aesthetics**   Immanuel Kant (1724–1804) was an Enlightenment thinker with important ideas that still influence us. He drew on many ancient Greek concepts for his philosophical framework, including many of those ancient ideas about play (agon, mimesis, and chaos), but his primary concern was with how we know things (Spariosu, 1989). Kant's writings on reason, the use of science to create knowledge, and the ways the mind categorically treats knowledge continue with us to this day through the research of Jean Piaget and others (Piaget, 1932/1965, 1970).

What does play have to do with knowledge, within this philosophical perspective? For adult human beings, the imagination, or free play of the mind, is the *context* in which knowledge and reason operate. Imaginings are those things that we strive to make sense of, thereby creating the need for knowledge. Play, in this sense, drives us to pursue knowledge. Kant did not stop here. He also attributed to play the basis for the arts and morality. Because spiritual and moral matters are not concrete and cannot be objectively determined, it is left to the play of the imagination to guide us to understand the more ephemeral aspects of humanity.

By rooting adult imagination in play, Kant argued for a more cognitive, or mental, view of play. Play goes on in the head. He never linked his idea of play to activities (other than, perhaps, artistic creation), so we have no clues as to what play would look like. Rational play is clearly placed in the mental world as opposed to the world of activity. And Kant's world is an adult world, where he never deals with children and their play. It would be left to those who came after him to apply these ideas to children's play.

**Schiller: The Roots of Creativity in Play**
Philosophical thought about the role of play and human experience took a large step forward in the Enlightenment with Friedrich von Schiller (1759–1805). In the late 18th century, his philosophical work identified play as a key part of who we are as human beings, and he wrote specifically about play as an expenditure of exuberant energy. Schiller's philosophical concerns were related to the role of play with all human beings, not just with children. As we will see, it was later philosophers and educators who refined his ideas with regard to children. For Schiller, work consumes our human energy to meet our physical needs; we work to survive, and that work consumes energy. Any energy we may have left over is dedicated to play. Human beings use this play for exploring creativity, for transcending the reality of life in work. This makes play a symbolic activity that goes beyond the here and now (Schiller, 1795/1965).

Within Schiller's framework are notions of physical play as well as symbolic play. Physical play can take the form of sport or festival that involves the use of excess physical energy;

therefore, one strand of play within his thinking dealt with physical actions. Far more important to Schiller, however, were the aspects of play that took the form of symbolic or dramatic activity and were most frequently expressed through the arts. Any excess mental energy we may have on completion of our labors can be used for creation of aesthetic or pleasing activities that allow us to move beyond the rote activities of labor, to think on a higher level. Play is our route to higher-level spiritual thought. In this view, play allows humans to transcend their condition. Play becomes emancipatory and a source of hope. Schiller's message resonated with the revolutionary times in which he lived. It is also the root of contemporary thought linking play with creativity, including current beliefs in the connection between play and imagination.

From the Enlightenment, we get a progression of ideas from philosophers about play. John Locke saw play as natural for children, contributing to their spirits and well-being. Immanuel Kant attributed to play an important role in higher thought; play was the mental activity from which rationality emerged, especially as a basis for aesthetic expression. Friedrich von Schiller took this view one step further, theorizing that play was excess energy from which all creative, artistic, and spiritual activities grow. Philosophical beliefs evolved during this era, but they fell short of articulating or describing the actual play of children.

**Shaping Rational Man: Froebel on Play in the Kindergarten**    As discussed earlier, Schiller had a great influence on intellectuals and artists during the Romantic era. His poetry inspired the composer Ludwig van Beethoven to include Schiller's poem, "Ode to Joy," in his Ninth Symphony. He also influenced the thought of the German educator Friedrich Froebel (1782–1852), a student of the innovative Swiss educator Johann Pestalozzi (1746–1827). Among Pestalozzi's innovations were a commitment to universal, democratic education and an

understanding of the educational needs of younger learners, drawing on some aspects of Jean-Jacques Rousseau's (1712–1778) *Emile* (1762/1972) and Comenius's *The Great Didactic* (1896). Instead of learning by means of rote memorization, Pestalozzi showed how children learn naturally from their encounters with real things, so-called *object lessons.* Learning by doing was a radical concept that was put into practice in Pestalozzi's Swiss school (Wolfe, 2002).

Froebel interpreted Pestalozzi's ideas and practices based on a number of his own learning experiences. He spent time as a youth working as a woodsman, and he studied physical science before serving as curator of a natural museum's crystal collection. These experiences combined with his study of Romantic philosophy, including Schiller and Rousseau, and ideas about humankind's relationship to nature, the innate goodness of learning from nature, and self-initiated learning. Schiller proposed the natural role of play as excess or **surplus energy**, as humankind's route to higher, more spiritual thought. Froebel combined these principles to formulate not just an activity-based curriculum, with objects inspired by physical science, but a play-based curriculum (Brosterman, 1997).

Given the pivotal role of Froebel's educational thought in the history of children's play, it seems worthwhile to explore his curriculum on a number of levels. What did he believe play was? How can we reconcile the co-occurrence of so-called natural (i.e., not tainted by society) activity and educational (a necessarily social) activity? How can we enable activity that captures the spiritual qualities characteristic of higher forms of thought? How should we think about such play activities as a curriculum, whereby children play their way to understanding? Froebel did not provide explicit answers to all these questions, but he did draw connections between philosophical beliefs and practical actions, in particular with the play materials and activities he included in his curriculum (Shapiro, 1983).

*Gifts and Occupations*   In terms of play, one of the most interesting of Froebel's contributions was his interpretation of philosophical beliefs about play. Froebel saw the surplus aesthetic energy that Schiller described as an avenue for the natural education of children. He translated beliefs about play into educational practices by means of play objects that would be manipulated in ways that supposedly lead to educational insights. These objects, or gifts, and their related activities were situated in a natural setting, where children were to be nourished like flowers in a garden—the children's garden, or, in German, *kindergarten.* A closer look at Froebel's revolutionary form of educational play will raise questions about how natural this view of play really is.

Froebel designed gifts and occupations to allow children to experience a universal spirituality, an understanding of a humanist God's universe and one's place in that universe (Froebel, 1826/1902). That universe could be understood in terms of the physical world (nature), mathematics (how we know nature), and art (aesthetics or beauty) (Brosterman, 1997). By means of play activities, children would encounter the forms of nature, knowledge, and beauty that would reveal the "Divine Unity" of the world and our place in that unity (Froebel, 1826/1902). As he explains, "The baker cannot bake if the miller grinds him no meal; the miller can grind no meal if the farmer brings him no corn; . . . she could not work in this inner harmony if God did not place in her power and material, and if His love did not guide everything to its fulfillment. . . . It is doubtless with these ideas that the children are brought up, who are playing at baking and feasting on bread" (Froebel, 1844/1897, p. 148). Thus Froebel's ambitions for play were lofty, including everyday life experiences and divine beliefs.

What were the gifts and occupations designed to meet these high aspirations? Froebel developed his system of education over a period of decades, but he did not make clear distinctions between gifts and occupations. Versions of his publications describe a range of play materials included in the kindergarten (Brosterman, 1997). Figure 1.1 lists play objects from his *Education of Man* (1826/1902).

**FIGURE 1.1**   Froebel's Gifts and Occupations

**Gifts**

| | |
|---|---|
| **First gift:** | Six small yarn balls, one each in a primary or secondary color |
| **Second gift:** | A small wood ball, wood cylinder, and wood cube |
| **Third gift:** | A small wooden cube, composed of eight component cubes |
| **Fourth gift:** | A small wooden cube, composed of eight rectangular blocks |
| **Fifth gift:** | A larger wooden cube, composed of 27 cubes |
| **Sixth gift:** | A comparably sized wooden cube, composed of 27 rectangular blocks |
| **Seventh gift:** | Wooden tablets (squares, half squares, triangles, half triangles, third triangles) [parquetry shaped blocks] |
| **Eighth gift:** | Wooden sticks (lines) and metal curves (circles, half circles, quadrants) |
| **Ninth gift:** | Points (beans, seeds, pebbles, holes in paper) |
| **Tenth gift:** | Peas (or pellets) construction, with sticks |

**Occupations**

Plastic clay (solids)
Paper folding (surfaces)
Weaving (lines)
Drawing (lines)
Stringing beads (points)
Painting (surfaces)

What did it mean to play in Froebel's kindergarten? From the gifts and occupations listed in Figure 1.1, it may seem that children might play just as they do in today's early childhood classrooms. The blocks, clay modeling, painting, and colored balls sound familiar; they are common playthings that might be on the open shelves of play centers in child-care centers or kindergartens. But there may be great differences between traditional kindergarten practices and contemporary ones because of very different beliefs about what play is (Kuschner, 2001). A look at some of Froebel's writings may illustrate those differences.

*Natural Education, at Mother's Knee*   Some of Froebel's earliest educational writing is in *Mother's Songs, Games, and Stories* (1844/1897). Froebel thought that child's play was symbolic and developmental, and codified play was the foundation of education. From a review of the play activities he described, it is clear that what he saw as good, natural play for children were the games that mothers played with their young children, symbolically reflecting very specific cultural practices and values. Games like Beckoning the Chickens or Beckoning the Pigeons (pp. 26–29), in which the toddler is encouraged to simulate the mother's actions aimed at summoning and feeding birds, are good examples. These pretend activities for the child are clearly based on assumptions about participation in a very specific form of agrarian community, where cultural practices such as animal care were central to life and custom. Likewise, Froebel's natural game of patty-cake (1844/1897, p. 147) reflects a simulation of the (then) culturally meaningful act of baking bread; the child was asked to participate in the actions performed by the baker or mother as she mixed, kneaded, and baked a loaf of bread. Froebel goes to great lengths to affirm that such games were natural for the child and mother while at the same time claiming that "it is a link in the great chain of life's inner dependence" with society (and thereby culture) at large (p. 148).

We could continue with an analysis of the entire volume of *Mother's Songs, Games, and Stories* to see a limitless set of culturally specific play activities, such as finger games (e.g., The Shopman and the Girl, p. 102; The Carpenter, p. 76) and action-accompanied songs (e.g., The Fish in the Brook, p. 30; Mowing Grass, p. 24). These play activities all involve some sort of pretense seen as natural; specific cultural experiences are the "what" of the pretense. Many of us grew up playing some of these games because Froebel's beliefs and practices of mother–child play were passed on to us.

How are we to be educationally natural, from Froebel's point of view? The answer is play. "The plays of childhood are the germinal leaves of all later life" (1826/1902, p. 55). The naturally creative actions of children are the basis for education. What are the natural play activities that Froebel points to as naturally educative? He identifies a number of play activities that form the core of the kindergarten curriculum: the ball (for simulating the relationship of objects in the world to one another and for representing our connection to one another through games); building blocks (construction materials to simulate worldly structures); sticks (for pattern creation to simulate letters); and "pricking sheets" (pp. 285–287) for creating patterns and sewing (sewing or lacing cards), paper folding and cutting, and a number of other simulative manipulatives. Add to these the songs and games that mothers play with children, and we have a picture of Froebel's beliefs about what is natural in childhood.

Kindergarten play materials are a good deal less obviously tied to cultural customs than are his Shopman finger plays and the Fish in the Brook song. There is something more abstract and educational about building with blocks as compared with imitating a weather vane. Yet the educational use of manufactured balls or paper for folding and sewing, available from new manufacturing advancements, illustrates how culturally based all of Froebel's educational

Modern block play reflects Froebel's influence on our play practices.

play really was. The materials Froebel selected were very much reflective of the industrializing society and culture of which he was a part.

Froebel codified and institutionalized certain ideas and practices that have been passed on to us (although not necessarily intact) in his books. It is doubtful that any contemporary practitioner of early childhood education would call herself or himself a Froebelian, but go into any classroom and you will witness residue of his influence: block play, ball games, finger plays, circle time, and any number of other play activities that we can trace directly to him. When we think about play, we think about these activities. Also present in teacher thinking are any number of Froebel-linked ideas, such as the naturally unfolding/developing child and the spiritual, innate goodness of the child.

As a student of Pestalozzi, Froebel saw the importance of education in shaping the rational and spiritual child. Good, thoughtful people were created by education, so a purposeful program was needed to create conditions where those ends could be reached. With Froebel, we see a shift from mere thought about practice and play to specific prescriptions about what practice should be. He began with the world of play ideas and translated the ideas into activities, and he prescribed what play should be for it to serve the ends of education. Play would no longer be abstract (only for philosophers) and intuitive (practiced without thinking). German immigrants were impressed with Froebel's ideas and brought them in 1856 to the United States, where they became extremely popular.

By linking play and education, Froebel saw the benefit of particular play settings (his garden) for the education of children. He made play less a part of *nature* and more a part of *nurture.* Play may take place anywhere, but educational play occurs in particular, planned settings. This effort to make play more rational, or conscious to us, suggests the idea that specific forms of children's play are *not* natural, like those found in many North American middle-class homes, where education and schooling are significant parental concerns and the context is richly arranged with concrete play materials to engage and guide children. The material and symbolic nature of this particular play becomes a meaningful entry point for understanding particular family socialization patterns. Froebel made part of such play rational to us while ignoring its cultural roots. His beliefs also reflected assumptions about what is natural for children, assumptions that would be explored later in his century.

Ideas about play and education were merging with cultural play practices. In America, children in the early colonies and the young United States engaged in a range of play. Colonial children had their toys and games, as did slave and Native American children, as well as settlers on the frontier. Some of their play had parental support, for spiritual and educational purposes, whereas other play was unsupervised. The competing pull of natural play and play that was nurtured by adult support continued throughout the early history of the United States (Chudacoff, 2010; Daniels, 1995; David, 1968; Frost, 2010: Hale, 1980).

## On the Nature of Play: Scientific Approaches

The rich history of philosophical musing about play, from the ancient Greeks to the Romantic thinkers, gave way to a new perspective inspired by the revolutionary work of Charles Darwin (Schwartzman, 1978; Spariosu, 1989; Sutton-Smith, 1997). Although Darwin himself was not much interested in play, his work on evolutionary science had a tremendous impact on how scholars subsequently thought about play. His writings about natural selection and species' survival contributed to a scientific look

at play, as opposed to the earlier philosophical speculations. Those earlier speculations were not entirely lost, but in the post-Darwin era, they were reinterpreted and given new meanings. For example, the late 19th-century philosopher Herbert Spencer (1820–1903) revisited Schiller's notion of play as surplus energy and converted it into a psychological version of Darwin's ideas about adaptation. In this modified theory, surplus energy fuels instincts that assist natural selection, play fighting is associated with the need for social dominance, coordinated games are associated with the need for social interaction, and artistic/aesthetic play enhances symbolic skills. Schiller's philosophical beliefs were refocused on specific human activities that were consistent with emergent thought about human adaptation.

Darwin's evolutionary theory influenced a number of 19th-century scholars of play, including Spencer, G. Stanley Hall, Karl Groos, and, bridging into the 20th century, John Dewey. The scientific view of play contributed to theoretical and research-based views of play that are described in detail in Chapter 2. The following sections address the historical progress of the play concept prior to the advent of a systematic, empirical study of play.

**Hall on Recapitulation**    Just as Herbert Spencer had adapted earlier thinking about play in light of Darwin's theory of evolution, G. Stanley Hall (1844–1924) found his own way of interpreting (or misinterpreting) evolution in his theoretical understanding of children and their development. Hall, a psychology professor at Clark University and founder of the Child Study Movement in the United States, was dedicated to creating a scientific approach to understanding child development. Like other behavioral scientists of his time, he was influenced by Darwin and by the experimental scientific methods created in the latter half of the 19th century. The purpose of these scientific methods was to move beyond philosophical belief and speculation toward a body of knowledge based on observation and experimentation. Philosophical ideas were to be given their due, but the proof of any idea was in its testing. Efforts to create a scientific, predictable understanding of children were increasing at this time because of the dramatic growth of public education, with the accompanying need for teachers to understand the children they were teaching.

Hall wrote on many aspects of human growth, including childhood play. Basing some of his scholarship on a misconception of Darwin, he articulated what he referred to as a "recapitulation theory" of play and development. The metaphor he used is of interest given the influence he had during his life and with the students who followed him. The essence of **recapitulation theory** is that each organism recreates the evolution of the species during its development. In utero and after birth, the biological and cultural progress of the entire species is played out in how the individual organism grows. In utero, he theorized that the human fetus changes from a single-cell organism to a fish, amphibian, reptile, and finally mammal. Such theorizing had its appeal when it could explain the simple observations of biological development available at that time; of course, contemporary science shows us that the complete complement of any human phenotype is fully present in the DNA of any fetus.

Hall, with the scientific tools available to him, carried his recapitulation metaphor to the development of human behavior. As the biology of each organism had been understood to repeat the evolution of species, so did the behavioral development of each individual repeat the cultural evolution of humankind (as understood at that time). This theory predicted that observing any child would reveal a developmental sequence, which would represent significant steps in the evolution of *Homo sapiens* (see Table 1.1).

By going through all of the play stages included in the recapitulation theory, children would, in essence, get the primitive past of the human species out of their system. They would

**TABLE 1.1**   Hall's Recapitulation Theory of Play

| Evolutionary Stage | Play Forms |
| --- | --- |
| Animal | Climbing, swinging |
| Savage | Tag, hide-and-seek, hunting games |
| Nomad | Pet care |
| Agricultural/settlement | Digging in sand, playing with dolls |
| Tribal | Team games |

then be able to focus on the higher-level mental and social skills expected of civilized human beings. Adult play, in the form of games such as baseball or football, was seen as an instinctual offshoot of residual, pre-civilized times. Play had its purposes in contemporary child development, but it had to do with overcoming our uncivilized biological roots; play did not build toward a future but was seen to allow us to get rid of the past.

It is easy to dismiss the recapitulation theory on any number of grounds. It does not reflect Darwin's theory of evolution, with its emphasis on populations and adaptation. Nor does it reflect an accurate picture of cultural history, with its sequence of stages that grossly simplifies the progress of civilization. And, most telling, the stages of play predicted by the theory have not been validated by observation; child play does not progress as Hall's theory tells us it should. Despite these significant flaws, recapitulation theory continues to impact us because it does something novel: It tells us we can look for progressing stages in child play and development. Hall and his followers (like Archer, 1910) had the facts wrong and misinterpreted any number of theories, but he provided a principle for tracking the behavioral progress of children. This principle has shaped much of the research that has been done since his time, including the work of 20th-century play researchers such as Mildred Parten, Jean Piaget, and Kenneth Rubin.

Hall's play theory is significant for us, not because of what it tells us substantively or theoretically about play; he was clearly in error in his beliefs about what play is. His theory is significant because it has provided us with a way of thinking about children's play in terms of progressive stages that children pass through on their roads to maturity, albeit not the stages he identified. Hall gave us a way of thinking that remains with most of us to this day.

**Groos and Practice Play**    A more faithful and plausible interpretation of Darwin's theory of evolution was explored by the naturalist Karl Groos (1861–1946). Groos was a scholar with broad interests, including aesthetics, ethology, and psychology. Among his writings were two classic books on play, *The Play of Animals* (1898) and *The Play of Man* (1901). Although philosophical speculation is still present in his theory, Groos had the insight to see play as a contributor to evolutionary adaptation.

His argument reduces to a number of basic points. The so-called lower animals, those that have not evolved over the course of history, do not play; we have no evidence to support the belief that insects, fish, snakes, or toads play. Plenty of evidence indicates that species that have evolved to higher levels, including mammals and especially great apes, do play a great deal. It is also apparent that species that have evolved to these so-called higher levels demonstrate much more play with their juvenile members; puppies play more than mature dogs, and human children play more than adults. These observations suggested to Groos that play serves an adaptive purpose, that it functions to contribute to the survival of the species. He identified this function as **preexercise**, or practice.

Groos's idea about play makes more sense when we remember that the species he thought of as having evolved to higher levels, particularly humans, have a relatively longer period of immaturity in their lifespans. Immature insects, in their pupal forms, are immobile, and when most snakes or fish are hatched, they may be smaller than adults but are fully responsible for their own survival. Mammals, in contrast, are born immature and need periods of care and weaning prior to moving into their adult roles. We humans consider nearly the first 20 years of our lives as a period of immaturity, when babies are nurtured, children are schooled, and adolescents are socialized into the culture. This period of immaturity is marked by the predominance of play, and the longer the period of immaturity, the more play. Thus Groos saw play during immaturity as the opportunity to practice those things that would prove adaptive for the species during adulthood.

The sorts of things that might be practiced would vary from species to species. We can easily imagine that a kitten chasing and pouncing on a ball or leaf is developing those very skills that an adult cat will use to prey on mice; the kitten is preexercising catlike hunting skills that allow cats to feed and survive. The juvenile chase games of baboons practice the social hierarchies that precede the adult social structures necessary for social cohesion, protection, and propagation of the species. Juvenile baboon play provides a service for what comes after.

It is more complicated to imagine how human childhood play might serve this Darwinian adaptive function. Groos identified two types of human play that he saw as functional: experimental play and socionomic play. Experimental play provides sensory and motoric practice, including object manipulation, construction, and games with rules. Such play should preexercise adult self-control. Socionomic play provides practice for interpersonal skills, including chase and rough-and-tumble games, social and family (dramatic) play, and imitation. Groos was aware of beliefs about play serving as a basis for symbolic and creative endeavors, but he limited his view of practice play to self-control and social skills.

Groos, with his theory on practice play, provided an important rationale for valuing play (see Bruner, 1972). At the same time, he limited his argument to a small number of play domains that he saw as adaptive. Perhaps the biggest strength in his ideas comes from the way he argues that play is necessary and useful for adult human life, as opposed to views like Hall's, in which play was reduced to a set of activities that needed to be worked through by the growing child to allow later development. There are also many weaknesses in Groos's view, not least of which is the difficulty of testing it scientifically.

## The Modern Era of Children's Play

The 19th century began with a set of inspirational beliefs about play. Schiller's philosophical writing, in particular, highlighted the importance of play as a source of human creativity and higher thought. The growth of popular education, especially the revolutionary curriculum designed by Froebel, translated these beliefs into play activities intended to develop and educate young children. Prerational beliefs about play as mimesis (Spariosu, 1989) were translated into symbolic play that served educational and developmental ends. By mid-century, new scientific theory from the biologist Charles Darwin shifted discourse on play away from the spiritual and symbolic toward the biological. Agon and chaos (Spariosu, 1989) were acknowledged as possible contributors to human adaptation, although the role of culture was not yet understood. Beliefs and ideas about play were becoming more rational, but the lack of evidence about what play is and how it functions for children kept our understanding of play activities on a prerational, speculative level.

At the start of the 20th century, values and beliefs about play varied widely, and there were disagreements about play's particular role in development and education. Maria Montessori presented one point of view. Equally widespread was the commitment to study children, making use of the new tools of science that Hall, his students, and others were creating. The study of children inevitably led to research on play. Many of these threads of research, beliefs, and values came together in the writings of John Dewey, one of the foremost educational philosophers of the 20th century.

**Montessori and the Absorbent Mind**   Maria Montessori (1870–1952) was an inspired educator who has contributed to professional and parental ideas about young children's growth and needs. The first woman to receive a medical degree in Italy as well as a PhD in anthropology, Montessori had a rich and varied career in pediatrics, psychiatry, and what we call special education today. Her view of child development and education was well articulated in a number of books, many of which continue to be in print. Perhaps more importantly, she established schools for children, called Houses for Children (Casas dei Bambini), first in Rome, then around the world. In these Houses for Children, the activities were designed to meet the needs of urban, impoverished children who needed education to assist their development by allowing them to organize their environments. Activities were based on beliefs in the child's spiritual goodness, internal motivation, and propensity to act constructively in a free, properly planned environment (Lillard, 2005; Montessori, 1913, 1917, 1964, 1995; Wolfe, 2002).

Montessori's approach to education was impressive in its philosophical and pedagogical richness. Play was not central to her view of education and development, although two aspects of Montessori's program seemed to relate to play. First, the teacher (or directress, as she was called) of a children's house prepared a planned environment, where children freely chose their involvement with Montessori materials. As children developed, they chose more purposefully, no longer playing with materials but preparing for lessons that refined the senses and created order. Acting freely was important and necessary, but the purposes of education and development were reached only when children put their play impulses on hold to receive demonstrations from the directress. The directress observed the children closely, to see when they were ready for lessons.

Second, the planned environment in a Montessori school was rich with miniature or child-size materials. Furniture and materials were designed with great care for developmental needs and competence. Small pitchers and glasses and miniature mops, brooms, and buckets all suggested to the outsider that the children were engaging with toys. Such was not the case. Children did not play, in the sense of pretending, with these materials. Miniature objects in a Montessori school were designed to help the child master real-world skills, with objects crafted to their size; the child did not pretend to pour or clean but refined motor skills in order to really pour and clean. A child pretending with any of these materials was seen as not yet ready to benefit from using them.

Her writing and schools made Montessori famous early in the last century. G. Stanley Hall, Arnold Gesell, John Dewey, and Jean Piaget were among those who knew of her work, although not all agreed with her approach (Wolfe, 2002). Montessori schools existed worldwide, and in the United States they exist as private schools and Head Start centers (consistent with their original design, for low-income children). Although some saw play in her approach, others sensed that play was incidental to Montessori's beliefs and curriculum.

**Dewey on Science in Planned Contexts**
John Dewey (1859–1952) was a leading American philosopher who continues to have influence on academic and professional thought. He was interested in creating a pragmatic point of view in the service of society, which in his time was changing rapidly because of immigration and industrialization. It could be argued that the quick changes Dewey saw were no less pronounced than our current waves of immigration and increasing technology.

As a critic of public education, Dewey established a laboratory school at the University of Chicago, where he taught before moving to Columbia University. Among the beliefs that he elaborated were using research as a tool for studying practice, to understand how and why practice worked; that education is based on the experiences of students; and that the values of democracy and freedom need to be infused into education. In his writings and laboratory, Dewey attempted to refine those beliefs.

To what educational end might play contribute, especially the aim of education for participation in a democratic society? Dewey wrote about play in two ways: (a) play as providing a more generalized internalizing of knowledge by younger children and (b) play as the free, intrinsically interesting exploration of society and nature. Dewey's writings serve as a framework of sorts for guiding how and what we think about play as an educative activity. In some of his earliest educational and psychological writing on play, he addressed the nursery school child's experience and the centrality of play for helping the child make ideas his or her own: "The child does not get hold of any impression or any idea until he has *done* it" (p. 195). "He acts the idea *out* before he takes it *in*" (p. 196). Intrinsically motivated, freely chosen, communicative pretense was described as *the* primary educative experience for the preschool child. Play actions, as communicative efforts, were described as the way children form ideas. The experience of pretend play allows children to actively make meaningful what is most important to them (i.e., their interests), but symbolic enactment also necessarily builds the shared symbol systems and community that go with them. It is a good deal less clear how this view of play, as pretend, relates to the education of school-age children (Dewey, 1896/1972).

*Play*, as a term relevant to older children, was more fully discussed 20 years later by Dewey (1916) in *Democracy and Education* when he presented additional notions of play, especially his distinction of work and play. Again, freedom and intrinsic motivation were seen as defining elements of play, as a means of exploring personal and shared interests. At this point, Dewey noted that work is undifferentiated from play for younger children (p. 239), whereas older children presumably have more distinct notions about the different purposes of work and play (King, 1982).

If school-age children's play is somewhat different than the pretend play of preschoolers, then what is play during that developmental stage (or what should it be)? What *are* free and intrinsically motivating activities for elementary school–age children? Dewey gave us only the most general ideas, about exploring outdoors (Rivkin, 1997) and playgrounds (Frost, 1992). He did not give us enough of his thinking about play, especially at the elementary-school level, on which to build. He seemed to acknowledge that despite common component dispositions to play (such as freedom, intrinsic motivation, social engagement), we are dealing with a different play phenomenon for preschoolers (pretend) and elementary children (exploration). In terms of the educative aims of play, both of these senses of play are a model or foundation for free participation in a community of people with shared interests.

Dewey wrote eloquently of the inseparability of means and ends. To practice freedom, one must experience freedom. The same must be true for formation of any social community. Play seems to embody those experiences of freedom, but it seems that there are any number of forms of play that Dewey did not describe or anticipate: illicit play, scapegoating, peer culture, and exclusionary pretend and games. Children can be mean and antidemocratic when they play, as Sutton-Smith (1997) has argued. Dewey was working from a set of beliefs about what play was, influenced by Romantic and Enlightenment thinkers. He did not have an extensive database on play in its many forms. What he was able to do was articulate his belief in the freedom inherent in play and weave that belief into his view of education.

Today, Dewey is more typically cited in support of the philosophy regarding the child-centered curriculum. His specific notions about play are ignored as scholars rely on more contemporary theorists, such as Vygotsky (1978), with whom Dewey has a certain degree of agreement regarding play. In Dewey's view, play is a form of activity that for young children *is* their form of thought, and play is a freely chosen activity. Dewey's freedom has implications for social and societal relationships.

Dewey specified his relevant context in terms of democratic society; the values of democracy have their roots in the choices of play. He also gave schools, as institutions that shape the minds and beliefs of citizens, a challenge to include play and study by means of play as part of the curriculum for a democratic society. How must we think about play differently, to support it and make it a better educational tool for promoting democratic relationships? This is a question that was not asked by Froebel, Hall, or earlier thinkers who shaped our beliefs about play. Dewey also shifted thinking about play from the evolutionary, biological thinking of Darwin and Groos toward beliefs about play as a social institution.

As a pragmatic philosopher, Dewey bridged the era when scholars elaborated their beliefs and the contemporary era when scientists tested their beliefs. Dewey built systematic inquiry into his philosophy, challenging his followers to test their ideas in the laboratory of life. If we create play customs in classrooms, then we should study those customs to understand how they work. Children's play was gaining more legitimacy as a scholarly interest, and what follows in this book is a record of that scholarship. And as we came to know more about play, scholars in a variety of disciplines, including history, studied it.

**Academic Child Development in the Early 20th Century**  The growing field of scientific child study in universities and colleges combined with the growth of kindergarten education and the emergence of the nursery school movement to stimulate research and academic writing on children's play in the first half of the 20th century. Ideas about play in the kindergarten were being tested and refined in light of newer theories of development (Kuschner, 2001). Nursery school laboratories were beginning to provide play-based settings for describing children's growth in rigorous ways. Ideas about play and development became increasingly differentiated during this period, and the issue of play as an indicator of child interests emerged.

Froebel's vision of the child as a natural player, using gifts and occupations to learn about forms of beauty, life, and knowledge, was still popular in some circles. Others were adapting his activities to a child study movement notion of "the whole child." Prominent educators such as Patty Smith Hill were among those who wanted to adapt a playful kindergarten to more of the needs of children and the school curriculum (Wolfe, 2002). She, and many others, attempted to incorporate Dewey's thinking about studying children in school as a way to understand their education. Using kindergartens, and then nursery schools, as laboratories for studying children's education became important (Burk & Burk, 1920; Hall, 1911; Jersild & Fite, 1939).

Laboratory schools, still influenced by a version of the Froebelian idea of play as the primary avenue for learning for young children, were settings where play was described and researched. Prominent texts on child psychology and development asserted, "We have already pointed out that much of the child's learning takes place during play" (Jersild, 1933, p. 431) while describing the child in terms of motor, language, social, emotional, cognitive (i.e., "understanding"), and imaginative development. Classroom play was seen as the norm for young children, where optimal learning occurred in all aspects of development. Some effort was made to describe laboratory play settings that were considered optimal (Hill & Langdon, 1930; Jersild, 1933, 1942, 1946; Jersild & Fite, 1939; Morgan, 1935).

Much of the research and writing produced during this period tended to describe play development in terms of children's chronological age. The sorts of writing that had existed 50 years before, such as Froebel's mystical writing about children's nature and Montessori's writing about the spiritual child, were being replaced by normative descriptions of children at different ages. (Most of the children being described were White and from university communities.) The dominant impression was that children could be understood in terms of how they play at different ages, and their play could be understood in terms of aspects of development (motor, language, social, emotional, cognitive, etc.). The convergence of play, learning, and development of the whole child was standard in textbooks and research. An age and stage understanding of play provided a guide for teachers and parents as they looked to age norms as a way of understanding the progress that children were making. Such an age and stage approach to understanding children perhaps had the unanticipated consequence of suggesting that aging by itself (i.e., maturation) was enough to ensure developmental progress. The role of social context and support for play (i.e., the nurture of play) took a back seat to the assumed nature of play (that which the child brings with him or her while playing) (Gesell, 1934, 1939; Jersild, 1933; Parten, 1932; Rasmussen, 1920; Thomas, 1996).

Issues of culture and context were not totally ignored, although they are almost afterthoughts in the description of the child study movement of the whole child as player. One way that the educational context appeared was in the recurring emphasis on play as an avenue for understanding children's interests. Dewey had proposed education as a developmental process where we pursue our individual and socially shared interests. Child development researchers, building on Hall's survey approach, saw the study of children's play as an important way of understanding children's interests and the context of their development. By looking at

Children's play interests lead to learning.

children's play, teacher/ researchers could learn about children's interests and prepare the curriculum to build on children's intrinsic interests. Play was not just a natural process; it was a window to the things that motivated children. Children's play interests were an important feature of child psychology in the 1930s and 1940s, but had virtually disappeared as a topic 30 years later (Jersild, 1933, 1942, 1946; Jersild, Telford, & Sawrey, 1975). It reappeared nearly a half-century later (Gopnik, 2010).

The abstractions of 19th-century thought about play were being refined and replaced in the early 20th century. Development of the whole child, as a physical, social, thinking being (who, to a lesser degree, operates in a culture), had become our way of thinking about play; play was seen as how children learn and develop. Scientifically established age norms replaced Romantic ideas, and debates about the freedom and meaning of play began (e.g., Burk & Burk, 1920; Kuschner, 2001). Although age and stage descriptions of the development of play became firmly entrenched, there was still some acknowledgment that observations of play should not discount the social setting within which they take place.

**Huizinga on Cultural Change**  During the early 20th century, children's play emerged as a topic of study. Continuing today, researchers focus on aspects of play and development or on play itself. Play scholars may view children's play as part of the larger picture of human play (e.g., Caillois, 1961; Figler & Whitaker, 1991; Reifel, 1999; Spariosu, 1989; Sutton-Smith,

1997). The Dutch historian Johan Huizinga (1872–1945) attempted an ambitious cultural history of play, parts of which have been very influential for children's play scholars.

In his 1938 book *Homo Ludens: A Study of the Play-Element in Culture*, Huizinga brought together descriptions of a broad range of anthropological, sociological, and artistic activities from around the world. His purpose was to demonstrate "that civilization arises and unfolds in and as play" (Huizinga, 1938, foreword). Play, of both children and adults, serves social and cultural functions: forming social groups, creating distinct communities within society, creating social status among groups and individuals, enabling social cohesion, transforming culture, displaying social oppositions, and reaffirming social concerns. Musical performance, adult festivals, sport, and children's play are all part of this analysis, all part of what makes civilization exist and change. (See Henricks, 1988, for a critique of these functions.)

Play, as seen by Huizinga, has great power over who we are as members of society. It defines our social position, supports our values, and contributes to our identities as

## FIGURE 1.2    Huizinga's Characteristics of Play

1. Play is voluntary.
2. Play is not ordinary or real.
3. Play is secluded or limited.
4. Play creates order, is order.
5. Play tends to surround itself with secrecy.

members of the group. Even more powerfully, play does not merely replicate existing social and cultural standards. Because of the social dynamic created by play, it is a force for challenging and advancing society. The play of social strife and resolution is not metaphoric; it has real consequences. Most researchers of children's play acknowledge the characteristics of play that he devised (see Figure 1.2) (Bergen, 1988; Spodek & Saracho, 1988).

The qualities of play that he saw as descriptive and transformative for society have become useful definitions for what play is, including its voluntary nature (we must choose to play); its non-ordinariness (pretend is not real); the seclusion or delimitation of play (it takes place in particular places such as a playing field or is private like computer games); its orderliness (there are rules inherent in most play); and its secrecy (we keep key information from non-players). Duncan (1988) argues that too much of Huizinga's understanding of play is based on competitive or conflict forms of play. In spite of possible biases in Huizinga's work, these characteristics have been adapted for child play scholarship, whether in the form of descriptive dispositions to play or the refinement of other theoretical constructs (Rubin, Fein, & Vandenberg 1983; Spodek & Saracho, 1988).

**Materials for Play**    The study of the history of play has been made difficult by the lack of extensive documentation of play activities and, to some degree, by the lack of play objects that tell us about how people played in the past. Growth of the toy industry, caused by the technology and wealth of the industrial revolution

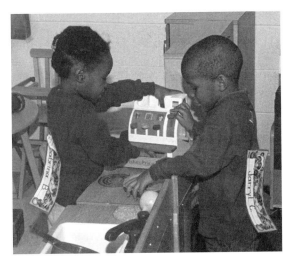

Many believe that children practice in play those skills they will need later in life.

in the 19th century, contributed to new forms of play research: the study of toys. Cross (1997) describes the transition from locally crafted playthings to the mass market of toys in the United States. The tradition of craftspeople (often from Germany; see also Brosterman, 1997) preparing limited numbers of dolls and building sets for the few families who could afford them was replaced by the trend of less expensive machine-made toys for the general public. Such toys became more available, in part due to new institutions such as five-and-dime stores and catalog shopping. Growth in this new market sparked debates during the 20th century about what toys were good or bad, the appropriateness of certain toys for boys and girls, parental roles in play, and social class and race. Cross documents these debates in both academic publications and popular magazines. Do manufactured toys shape a child's future, as a type of preexercise? Do toys affect personality and character? To what extent do manufactured toys expand or suppress children's imaginations (Lamb & Brown, 2006)? These debates have been going on for a century, prior to concerns about whether Barbie dolls damage girls' body images or G.I. Joe action figures make boys more violent.

The role of manufactured toys in play, particularly the growth of electronic and online games, continues to be of interest for play researchers. (See Chapter 11.) As new technology creates new play objects, new questions arise about how children are playing and what that play means for them (Verenikina, Harris, & Lysaght, 2003).

## EMERGING ISSUES

A gaggle of hilarious boys gathered around, almost drunk with jollity, wanting to know what I had written down. "It's War this morning," they said, waving their plastic pistols. One of them was wearing the top part of a camouflaged battledress. (Opie, 1993, p. 60)

Industrial and technological society creates a new context within which play has new meanings. War play is no longer seen as a ritual for citizenship, as it had been in ancient times; contemporary scholars see toy guns and war play through a number of lenses, as a kind of mass market by the toy industry, as promoting aggression, or simply as a noisy nuisance. Communities where play takes place have changed, and parental supervision is not what it once was; suburban neighborhoods and mobile professionals provide more change in children's lives than stability. Television and other electronic media contribute to play, providing ideas to mimic and objects for play; every new summer movie has a shelf of toys that represents it (at the local fast-food restaurant or at the mall) and online electronic activities that are beginning to be studied. Toys are available in a wider variety of places; having popular playthings (consumerism), rather than making things, is the norm. As we move further into the 21st century, we need to look for play in new places, at new play objects, and at contexts that force us to refocus our lenses on play (Frost, 2010; Reifel & Sutterby, 2009). Following are a number of topics that are drawing attention in our current era. These issues are of such importance that they are revisited in later chapters.

Our understanding of the importance of play as physical activity for children appears to have run into competing contemporary forces: schools that ban recess, parents who fear to let their children explore their neighborhoods, child obesity associated with lack of active play, and the allure of sedentary electronic media. In many states, schools have eliminated recess from the school day, either fearing liability for student injury or believing that the time spent on recess is better spent on academic learning. This belief survives, in spite of research on the educational benefits of recess for academic performance (e.g., Pellegrini, 2005). A major issue we face is whether free-play recess will continue in our schools. Reconceptualizing recess as something other than a traditional break for students (and teachers) will involve looking through the range of lenses that we present in this book.

Recess is not the only concern of many educators and parents. Some are disturbed by a contemporary trend to emphasize academic learning, as opposed to the sorts of developmental learning that has been associated with play for the past century and a half (Elkind, 2007a, 2007b). Do young children need to learn particular academic skills as preparation for success at school and later in life? Learning for children should not be separated from play, but it should emerge from play. There is no reason to hurry children into learning; they will become learners by playing. Pressure to learn skills, unassociated with play, puts stress on children that "mis-educates" them (Elkind, 1987). The broad developmental benefits of free play, tied to imagination, creativity, social relationships, and learning, may become lost with a narrow focus on school success.

Measurable school skills associated with high-stakes testing (i.e., pass the test or repeat the grade) now preoccupy many educators and parents. Play is not testable, so it is often eliminated from school activity, in spite of research that demonstrates the many benefits associated with play. Debates about high-stakes testing have led many professional organizations to take positions urging caution about standardized testing, whether they explicitly support play or not (Association for Childhood Education International [ACEI], 2001; National Association for the Education of Young Children [NAEYC], 2005a). Throughout this book, we present a perspective of children that views them as much more than reflections of standardized tests. We encourage readers to think of children in this complex way.

In spite of data on health risks associated with childhood obesity, schools and families continue to restrict the amount of children's physical activity (Brown, Sutterby, & Thornton, 2006). At this point in history, parents and schools are deeply concerned with academic productivity, often to the detriment of other aspects of the developing child. Parental and school supports for active play are changing, as are the types of play and toys that we provide children. Active play (and healthier diets) is emerging as a major issue related to child obesity and its associated health concerns.

No other era in history has provided the range of electronic play opportunities for children, including online games and virtual settings for socialization. This emerging realm of play is described in Chapter 11. We are only beginning to understand what play may become in this era of online play for young and older players.

History provides some perspective on these emerging conditions in which play continues to be important. In ways that we have not anticipated, popular culture, new technology, academic expectations, and family practices all are contributing to new forms of play and new ways that we need to understand children's play. Themes that have withstood millennia will be useful, but they must be interpreted and added to in light of new circumstances. The complexity of play, as reflected by its history and the multitude of ideas we have about it, seems to call for multiple ways of viewing it. In Chapter 2, we present multiple views of play, framed as lenses we can use to observe and to reflect on the meanings of what we see children doing.

## SUMMARY

Core concepts about play—mimesis, agon, and chaos—have a venerable history in Western thought. The imitative, competitive or aggressive, and random qualities of play remain commonalities as we participate in play, whether as adults or children. Over the past 2,000 years, we have become more aware of these qualities and moved them from the prerational to the fully rational parts of our minds, where we can fully think about them. The ancient Greeks emphasized more competitive play; their games were imitations of conflict. They also valued the imitative in their religious rites and theater. The innate, natural quality of play was assumed. But it was not until the 18th century that we began to value the rational, creative, and imagination-provoking qualities of mimesis.

The Enlightenment began to link play with the mind and thinking, as a source of creativity. Kant and Schiller made play a key element of their philosophies, allowing subsequent thinkers to apply those ideas to children and child development. Other thinkers, such as Locke, at least acknowledged the value of play for recreation and identifying aptitudes. Froebel, building on ideas from Schiller, Rousseau, and Pestalozzi, made his form of play rational. He took the pre-rational cultural customs of German life and made them into a tool for shaping the spiritual, creative, and intellectual lives of children. Froebel was one of the first thinkers in history to translate ideas about children's play into practice. His popular ideas helped shape thinking about play in the United States and elsewhere.

Developments in natural science, especially Darwin's theory of evolution, provided new ways to think about play as a natural phenomenon. From the mid-19th century to the beginning of the 20th century, it was assumed that play is a biological mechanism, a part of what we are as human beings. Psychologists such as Hall saw play as a necessary stage that children must go through, repeating the biological development of the species, before they can transcend our primitive history. Images of play as imitation predominated. Groos interpreted child play as practice for what was to come, a form of preparation for helping the species adapt. The biological bases of play continue to interest scholars, but the lasting contribution of these thinkers was the idea of stage theory for play. This influence continues in educational programs for young children and in the child development research that guides our understanding of play.

More recent history has seen not only the mimesis of play, in the form of pretend, but also the agon of play return as a topic of interest. Conflict, and its resolution in the service of democratic principles, were part of Dewey's play legacy, in addition to his interest in active pretend play. From a different perspective, Huizinga pointed to the socially generative functions of play, based not only on symbolic action (as during festivals) but also on the social stratification of play (as with team formation). He made us aware of how we might be using play to transform our culture; he made the unconscious conscious. These scholars also pointed to the emergence of evidence, or research findings, in our efforts to know more about play, whether in the world of children or in society as a whole.

The imaginary, the challenging, and the purely fanciful come together in contemporary studies of the history of play. Play has become a predominant element in our materialistic society. The study of toys and the play that goes with them seems to return to questions about our historically rooted philosophical beliefs. Our ideas about play change, but history shows us that play changes over time. New issues related to play emerge, such as whether we should have recess during the school day, how sedentary play relates to child obesity, and what the multitude of new electronic games might do for (or to) children. And how do our current cultural conditions alter any of those questions? The answers to these questions, although based in historical beliefs, may depend on which theoretical lenses we use to inspect play (Sutton-Smith, 1995).

 **KEY TERMS**

| | |
|---|---|
| Agon | Mimesis |
| Chance | Preexercise |
| Chaos | Recapitulation theory |
| Developmentally | Surplus energy |
| appropriate | |
| practice (DAP) | |

 **STUDY QUESTIONS**

1. How did the ancient Greeks think about play?
2. What was the role of religious belief in ancient Greek play?
3. What are the characteristics of agon, mimesis, and chaos?
4. How did the Enlightenment alter how people thought about play?
5. How did various Enlightenment philosophers (e.g., Locke, Kant) see play as contributing to rational thought?
6. How did various Romantic philosophers (e.g., Schiller, Froebel) see play as contributing to a rational spirit?
7. In what ways are play and creativity linked?

8. How did the following researchers/theorists contribute to how we think about play: Locke, Kant, Schiller, Froebel, Groos, Hall, Huizinga, Dewey, and Vygotsky? What were their specific contributions?

9. How did Darwin's theory of evolution alter thoughts and beliefs about play?

10. Contrast two biologically based theories of the development of play. How does play serve different developmental ends from these points of view?

11. What basic beliefs did Dewey have about play and its role in education? How did he propose to verify that his beliefs were correct?

12. How does this historical era influence how we think about play and how we look at play? Why does 20th-century play look different from 19th-century play?

13. With a friend, observe children playing. Compare your beliefs about what the children are doing as they play. What are the historical origins of the beliefs you have?

14. Why is it useful to understand the history of play (a) for understanding a particular play activity such as block play and (b) for gaining insight into how we think about play in general?

15. How might video game play create new opportunities for creativity and socializing? What are possible dangers?

## REFERENCES

Archer, R. A. (1910). Spontaneous constructions and primitive activities of children analogous to those of primitive man. *American Journal of Psychology, 21*, 114–150.

Association for Childhood Education International (ACEI). (2001). ACEI position paper on standardized testing (by Vito Perrone). Retrieved June 2006, from http://www .acei.org/onstandard.htm

Bateson, G. (2000). *Steps to an ecology of mind*. Chicago: University of Chicago Press. (Original work published 1955)

Bekoff, M., & Byers, J. A. (Eds.). (1998). *Animal play: Evolutionary, comparative, and ecological perspectives*. Cambridge: Cambridge University Press.

Beresin, A. R. (1989). Toy war games and the illusion of two-sided rhetoric. *Play & Culture, 2*, 218–224.

Bergen, D. (1988). *Play as a medium for learning and development*. Portsmouth, NH: Heinemann.

Brosterman, N. (1997). *Inventing kindergarten*. New York: Abrams/Times Mirror.

Brown, P.-S., Sutterby, J., & Thornton, C. (2006). Combating childhood obesity with physical play opportunities. Retrieved July 2006, from http:// ptotoday.com/play4. html

Bruner, J. S. (1972). The nature and uses of immaturity. *American Psychologist, 27*, 686–708.

Bruner, J. S., & Sherwood, V. (1976). Peekaboo and the learning of rule structures. In J. S. Bruner, A. Jolly, & K. Sylva (Eds.), *Play: Its role in development and evolution* (pp. 277–285). New York: Basic.

Burk, F., & Burk, C. F. (1920). *A study of the kindergarten problem in the public kindergartens of Santa Barbara, California, 1898–1899*. New York: Teachers College, Columbia University.

Caillois, R. (1961). *Man, play, and games*. New York: Free Press.

Carlsson-Paige, N., & Levin, D. E. (1987). *The war play dilemma*. New York: Teachers College Press.

Carlsson-Paige, N., & Levin, D. E. (1995). Can teachers resolve the war-play dilemma? *Young Children, 50*, 62–63.

Chudacoff, H. P. (2010). *Children at play: An American history*. New York: New York University Press.

Comenius, J. A. (1896). *The great didactic*. London: Black.

Copple, C., & Bredekamp, S. (Eds.). (2009). *Developmentally appropriate practice in early childhood programs serving children from birth through age 8* (3rd ed.). Washington, DC: National Association for the Education of Young Children.

Cross, G. (1997). *Kids' stuff: Toys and the changing world of American childhood*. Cambridge, MA: Harvard University Press.

Daniels, B. C. (1995). *Puritans at play: Leisure and recreation in Colonial New England*. New York: St. Martin's Press.

David, J. (Ed.). (1968). *Growing up Black: From slave days to the present—25 African-Americans reveal the trials and triumphs of their childhoods*. New York: Avon Books.

Dewey, J. (1896). Imagination and expression. In *John Dewey: The Early Works, 1882–1898: Vol. 5. 1895–1898* (pp. 192–201). Carbondale: Southern Illinois University Press. (Original work published 1972, Feffer & Simons)

Dewey, J. (1916). *Democracy and education*. New York: Free Press.

Duncan, M. C. (1988). Play discourse and the rhetorical turn: A semiological analysis of *Homo ludens*. *Play & Culture, 1*, 28–42.

Elkind, D. (1987). *Miseducation: Preschoolers at risk*. New York: Knopf.

Elkind, D. (2007a). *The hurried child: 25th anniversary edition*. Cambridge, MA: Perseus.

Elkind, D. (2007b). *The power of play*. Cambridge, MA: Da Capo Lifelong Books.

Figler, S., & Whitaker, G. (1991). *Sport and play in American life*. Dubuque, IA: Brown.

Froebel, F. (1897). *Mother's songs, games, and stories* (F. & E. Lord, Trans.). London: Rice. (Original work published 1844.)

Froebel, F. (1902). *Education of man* (W. N. Hailmann, Trans.). New York: Appleton. (Original work published 1826)

Frost, J. L. (1992). *Play and playscapes.* Albany, NY: Delmar.

Frost, J. L. (2010). *A history of children's play and play environments: Toward a contemporary child-saving movement.* New York: Routledge.

Gesell, A. (1934). *An atlas of infant behavior.* New Haven, CT: Yale University Press.

Gesell, A. (1939). *Biographies of child development.* New York: P. B. Hoeber.

Goldstein, J. (1995). Aggressive toy play. In A. D. Pellegrini (Ed.), *The future of play theory* (pp. 127–147). Albany: State University of New York Press.

Gopnik, A. (2010). *The philosophical baby: What children's minds tell us about truth, love, and the meaning of life.* New York: Farrar, Straus & Giroux.

Groos, K. (1898). *The play of animals.* New York: Appleton.

Groos, K. (1901). *The play of man.* New York: Appleton.

Hale, E. E. (1908). *A New England boyhood.* New York: Grosset & Dunlap.

Hall, G. S. (1911). *Educational problems* (Vol. 1). New York: Appleton.

Halliman, P. K. (1996). *Let's play as a team!* Nashville, TN: Ideals Children's Books.

Hellerdorn, J., Van Der Kooij, R., & Sutton-Smith, B. (1994). *Play and intervention.* Albany: State University of New York Press.

Henricks, T. S. (1988). Huizinga's legacy for sports studies. *Sociology of Sport Journal, 5*(1), 37–49.

Hill, P. S., & Langdon, G. (1930). Nursery school procedures at Teachers College. *Revue internationale de l'enfant, 9*(53), 398–407.

Huizinga, J. (1950). *Homo ludens: A study of the play-element in culture.* Boston: Beacon. (Original work published 1938).

Jersild, A. T. (1933). *Child psychology.* New York: Prentice-Hall.

Jersild, A. T. (1942). *Child psychology* (Rev. ed.). New York: Prentice-Hall.

Jersild, A. T. (1946). *Child psychology* (3rd ed.). New York: Prentice-Hall.

Jersild, A. T., & Fite, M. D. (1939). *The influence of nursery school experience on children's social adjustments.* New York: Teachers College, Columbia University.

Jersild, A. T., Telford, C. W., & Sawrey, J. M. (1975). *Child psychology* (7th ed.). New York: Prentice-Hall.

King, N. R. (1982). Work and play in the classroom. *Social Organization, 46,* 110–113.

Kuschner, D. (2001). The dangerously radical concept of free play. In S. Reifel & M. Brown (Eds.), *Advances in early education and day care: Vol. 11. Early education and care, and reconceptualizing play* (pp. 275–293). Oxford, UK: JAI/Elsevier Science.

Lamb, S., & Brown, M. L. (2006). *Packaging girlhood: Rescuing our daughters from marketers' schemes.* New York: St. Martin's Press.

Levenstein, P. (1988). *Mother-child home program.* Columbus: Ohio State University Press.

Lillard, A. (2005). *Montessori: The science behind the genius.* New York: Oxford University Press.

Locke, J. (1968). *Some thoughts on education.* Cambridge: Cambridge University Press. (Original work published 1693)

Lonsdale, S. (1993). *Dance and ritual play in Greek religion.* Baltimore, MD: Johns Hopkins University Press.

Mergen, B. (1995). Past play: Relics, memory, and history. In A. D. Pellegrini (Ed.), *The future of play theory* (pp. 257–274). Albany: State University of New York Press.

Montessori, M. (1913). *Pedagogical anthropology.* New York: F. A. Stokes.

Montessori, M. (1917). *The advanced Montessori method: Vol. 1. Spontaneous activity in education.* New York: F. A. Stokes.

Montessori, M. (1964). *The Montessori method.* New York: Schocken.

Montessori, M. (1995). *The absorbent mind.* New York: Henry Holt.

Morgan, J. J. B. (1935). *Child psychology.* New York: Farrar & Rinehart.

National Association for the Education of Young Children (NAEYC). (2005a). *Learning to read and write: Developmentally appropriate practices.* Retrieved June 2006, from http://www.naeyc.org about/positions/pdf/PSREAD98.PDF

Opie, I. (1993). *The people in the playground.* New York: Oxford University Press.

Opie, I., & Opie, P. (1997). *Children's games with things.* New York: Oxford University Press.

Parten, M. (1932). Social participation among preschool children. *Journal of Abnormal and Social Psychology, 27,* 243–262.

Pellegrini, A. D. (2005). *Recess: Its role in education and development.* Mahwah, NJ: Erlbaum.

Piaget, J. (1965). *The moral judgment of the child.* New York: Free Press. (Original work published 1932)

Piaget, J. (1970). *Structuralism.* New York: Basic.

Plato. (1975). *The laws.* Harmondsworth: Penguin.

Plato. (1993). *The republic.* Oxford, UK: Oxford University Press.

Rasmussen, V. (1920). *Child psychology.* London: Gyldendal.

Reifel, S. (1986). Play in the elementary school cafeteria. In B. Mergen (Ed.), *Cultural dimensions of play, games, and sport* (pp. 29–36). West Point, NY: Leisure Press.

Reifel, S. (Ed.). (1999). *Play and culture studies: Vol. 2. Play contexts revisited.* Stamford, CT: Ablex.

Reifel, S., & Sutterby J. (2009). Play theory and practice in contemporary classrooms. In S. Feeney, A. Galper, & C. Seefeldt (Eds.), *Continuing issues in early childhood education* (3rd ed., pp. 238–257). Upper Saddle River, NJ: Prentice Hall/Merrill.

Rivkin, M. (1997). *The great outdoors: Restoring children's right to play outdoors*. Washington, DC: National Association for the Education of Young Children.

Rousseau, J.-J. (1972). *Emile* (A. Bloom, Trans.). London: Basic. (Original work published 1911)

Rubin, K. H., Fein, G. G., & Vandenberg, B. (1983). In P. H. Mussen (Ed.), *Handbook of child psychology: Vol. 7. Social- ization, personality, and social development* (4th ed., pp. 693–774). New York: Wiley.

Schiller, F. (1965). *On the aesthetic education of man*. New York: Ungar. (Original work published 1795)

Schwartzman, H. (1978). *Transformations: The anthropology of children's play*. New York: Plenum.

Shapiro, M. (1983). *Child's garden*. University Park: Pennsyl- vania State University Press.

Spariosu, M. (1989). *Dionysus reborn: Play and the aesthetic dimension in modern philosophical and scientific discourse*. Ithaca, NY: Cornell University Press.

Spodek, B., & Saracho, O. (1988). The challenge of educa- tional play. In D. Bergen (Ed.), *Play as a medium for learning and development* (pp. 9–22). Portsmouth, NH: Heinemann.

Sutton-Smith, B. (1995). Conclusion: The persuasive rhetorics of play. In A. D. Pellegrini (Ed.), *The future of play theory* (pp. 275–295). Albany: State University of New York Press.

Sutton-Smith, B. (1997). *The ambiguity of play*. Cambridge, MA: Harvard University Press.

Thomas, R. M. (1996). *Comparing theories of child development* (4th ed.). Pacific Grove, CA: Brooks/Cole.

Verenikina, I., Harris, P., & Lysaght, P. (2003). Child's play: Computer games, theories of play and children's development. *Proceedings of the international federation for information processing working group 3.5 open conference on young children and learning technologies* (Vol. 34, pp. 99–106). Sydney, AU: ACM International.

Vygotsky, L. S. (1978). *Mind in society: The development of higher psychological processes*. Cambridge, MA: Harvard University Press.

Wolfe, J. (2002). *Learning from the past: Historical voices in early childhood education*. Mayerthorpe, Alberta: Piney Branch Press.

# 2 Theory as Lenses on Children's Play

*SOME STUDY the body, some study behavior, some study thinking, some study groups or individuals, some study experience, some study language—and they all use the word* play *for these quite different things. Furthermore their play theories, which are the focus of this present work, rather than play itself, come to reflect these various diversities and make them even more variable.*

(Sutton-Smith, 1997, p. 6)

We all know what play is; we grow up playing, and we know what play means to us. So, what is play theory, and why should it matter to us? Why bother to confuse ourselves, and spoil the fun, by adding theory? The fact is that we cannot escape theory, in the sense that we are always using it. As parents, teachers, or others who may have an interest and participate in play, we bring to play experiences our own understandings of what play is and what it means to play. We might look at the photo introducing this chapter and see children having fun, or cooperating, or developing fine motor skills, or exploring ideas. Chapter 1 reviewed historical ideas about play, including a number of theories. Those ideas allow us to see play as part of our thinking about biology, nurture, aesthetics, and social relationships. In this chapter, we explore the reasons scholars devise to explain play, including current theories, views of theory and beliefs about play, a number of theories that have proved to be useful for understanding children's play, and current issues that are shaping our theoretical understanding of children's play.

As Sutton-Smith's (1997) opening quote suggests, there are many ways of thinking about play, as well as many play activities to think about. We think of a baby shaking his rattle, a girl playing hopscotch, an adult playing tennis, and we can call all these activities play. Yet we must think about these activities differently. We do not associate the same sort of skill, strategy, and purposefulness with shaking a rattle as we do when we think of tennis, and hopscotch brings to mind an entirely different set of ideas. Reflecting about play, however, is not so simple. Theory is one tool that can help us decide how to think about play, what to observe or listen to, and how to understand its meaning.

What ideas do we have when we think about play activities, and how do we make sense of them? When we think of play, do we think of hopscotch and tennis? Do we think about play more often when we think of children, adults, or other species of animals? Do we think about play when we turn on the computer, or do those thoughts occur to us only some of the time? Vygotsky (1984) suggests that as we grow up we develop spontaneous concepts, based on what we do without reflection; when our mothers told us to "Go play," we didn't think about it, we just did it. He contrasts spontaneous concepts to scientific (or academic) thinking that we acquire through schooling, where we must make conscious how we are thinking about something; this text book is an academic tool to give you ways to conceptualize play. What does research tell us about these activities? Theory is part of our thinking, and it guides research on play. It tells us how hopscotch and tennis share common play attributes (e.g., they are both games) and how they differ (children play hopscotch, either alone or with playmates; adults play tennis with others). It tells us who plays what (e.g., children play house, and adults play card games like bridge; we play fetch with dogs but not with cats or other people). It informs us that computers are popular game venues for children, but that adults use computers for both work and play.

The sections that follow are intended to help us understand theories that have been promoted by 20th-century play scholars (Rubin, Bukowski, & Parker, 1998). We will see how theories contribute to commonly shared conceptions about play (e.g., that it promotes children's cognitive, social, creative, motor, and moral development), but we will also see how each of us, as we engage in play, have our own theories about play. We will explore how our beliefs about play combine with scholarly theory to provide us with ways of thinking about play in our particular contexts. Our experiences, informed by research and theory, allow us to generate our own ways of thinking about play and looking at play. We will see play theories as helpful lenses we can use, to see and to think about children's play.

## WHY STUDY THEORIES?

Whenever we think about something, judge it, or form a belief about it, we are by definition in a world of theory. We may not be aware we are theorizing, but we are. Theory may be a more formally derived set of empirically verified academic principles (Williams, 1996) or a conception that may build on spontaneous experience. Others see theory as a conceptual lens for developing and communicating meanings and understandings (Beyer & Bloch, 1996; Chafel & Reifel, 1996). There are many ways to think about what a theory is. We might use theory to help us understand ordinary and extraordinary aspects of our lives, like play. Play is part of child rearing and classroom practice, so it is something that we think and theorize about. We need to think about what play means for children as they are playing; every time children play, it means something for them. We need to think about how to plan the settings in which they play; the context in which children play shapes that play and gives it unique meaning. We need to think about how we will participate with them as they play; adults are part of the play context for children. To do all these things, we must know how others have thought about play, as well as what the children we observe are telling us as they play; we can make sense of our own play experiences by understanding how others have made sense of theirs.

We will see in this chapter how each theory provides a lens through which we can look at play. Depending on our reasons for observing play, we may best be served by having a variety of theoretical lenses at our disposal.

## CURRENT THEORIES OF PLAY

There is a variety of academic ways to think about play. We think about it in terms of how we have fun. We think about games we play. We think about children as they pretend. We think about things we do when we are not

working or doing the things we must do. How might scholars' scientific ideas and research about play help us understand more about what we see when children are playing?

In *The Ambiguity of Play,* Sutton-Smith (1997; see also 1999) reviews numerous studies on play from far-ranging disciplines. He looks at research from biology, anthropology, literary studies and performance, risky and vicarious play, along with the pretend and games that we see in our daily observations of children. He identifies seven broad **rhetorics,** in the sense that fields of scholarship adopt belief systems, underlying ideologies, and the values of those who participate in such scholarship. Although rhetorics may be associated more with a discipline or disciplines and related epistemologies, they inevitably have broader cultural meanings. Table 2.1 summarizes these rhetorics.

A particular problem for researchers and childhood specialists is how we think about play. What activities do we define as play for children, and what activities are not play? Many people think children's play is good for them, that it promotes learning, that it creates social competence. Some argue that play is the way we learn to solve problems, whether cognitive (Bruner, Jolly, & Sylva, 1976) or social (Sutton-Smith, Gerstmyer, & Meckley, 1988). We make sweeping assertions about play, but as Table 2.1 illustrates, there are many forms of play and many ways of thinking about it. When children play house, is it pretend, leisure, fantasy, or nonsense? Are children learning about "house," each other, or just fooling around? When children watch television, are they experiencing leisure, imagining, or just wasting time? When children play soccer, is it an athletic, leisure, or game experience? Or, are all of these perspectives in some sense true? We need theory as a tool to help us think about what we mean when we talk about play, especially when we make assertions about how important play is or claim that play is allowing us to meet educational or developmental purposes.

**TABLE 2.1**    Rhetorics of Play and Their Respective Disciplines and Theorists

| Rhetoric | Discipline | Play Form(s) | Scholars | Child Play Research |
|----------|-----------|--------------|----------|---------------------|
| Progress | Biology, psychology, education | Pretend, games | Erikson, Piaget, Vygotsky | Smilansky (1968) |
| Fate | Mathematics | Gambling | Abt, Fuller | |
| Power | Sociology | Athletics | Spariosu, Huizinga | Yeatman & Reifel (1997) |
| Identity | Anthropology | Festivals, parties | Turner | Fine (1983) |
| Imaginary | Art, literature | Fantasy | Bateson, Bakhtin | Dyson (1997) |
| Self | Psychiatry | Leisure | Csikszentmihalyi | Kelly-Byrne (1989) |
| Frivolity | Pop culture | Nonsense | Stewart, Welsford | Opie & Opie (1959) |

*Source:* Adapted from Sutton-Smith (1997, p. 215).

Educational and developmental literature refers to play in many ways that conceal what is meant by the term *play*. Most scholarship on children's play has kept theory, ideology, or philosophy implicit, making some meanings presented in the research literature seem obscure. Although early childhood education and play have an affinity that dates back hundreds of years (the educational uses of play can be traced to Comenius [1896] in the 17th century; see Chapter 1 of this text), it is not always clear what activities are implied or what ends are being met. This problem continues today, in the way theory about play is included in the National Association for the Education of Young Children's developmentally appropriate practice (DAP) guidelines (Bredekamp & Copple, 1997; Copple & Bredekamp, 2009). The assumption seems to be that play is good for children and that children benefit from play in a number of ways. (That assumption is, in fact, one of the foundations of this book.) This perspective appears to reflect Sutton-Smith's rhetoric of Progress, within which he discusses play as an avenue for learning or development (Fein, 1999; Reifel, 1999; Reifel & Sutterby, 2009; Rivkin, 1999; Samaras, 1999).

Given all these views on what play may be, we need theory to help us sort out the complexity of play as we plan, observe, and participate in activities we call play. We want to make sure that we are not talking about different things,

conceptually, by resorting to a vague term that glosses over what we really mean by "play." We want to build on our spontaneous understandings of play, with solid scientific evidence. Becoming aware of our beliefs and purposes is necessary as a step in our selection and use of play theory. Researchers must use this step as they study activities that we recognize as play and by practitioners as they engage children in play activities. A number of theories have proved useful as lenses through which we can look at play to understand more about children's play.

## DOMINANT CONTEMPORARY THEORIES

Let's look at an early childhood play interaction as one avenue for understanding how dominant contemporary theories guide what we look for and what we see when we are viewing play.

The interaction began during a regularly scheduled free play time as Anna joined Zoe at a[n] easel supplied with newsprint, green, orange, and purple paints, and brushes.

*Anna:*    I'm makin' pumpkin.

*Zoe:*    Me, too. [singing, humming]

*Zoe:*    Wanna call this a pumpkin?

| | |
|---|---|
| *Anna:* | Yeah. |
| | .... |
| *Zoe:* | Yeah, make a Halloween picture. |
| | [a verbal exchange of opinions with peers who passed by] |
| *Julie:* | Well, a pumpkin doesn't look like that. |
| *Zoe:* | I know but I'm just making it the way I want. |
| *Julie:* | Did you know Zoe's makin' a pumpkin the wrong way? |
| | .... |
| *Zoe:* | Let's make a big blump and then finger paint. |
| *Anna:* | OK. I'm just gonna keep on finish painting. |
| | .... |
| *Anna:* | I'm a witch so I make purple stew. |
| *Zoe:* | Oh, I make green stew. |
| *Anna:* | I'm a witch cuz I make purple stew. |
| *Anna:* | Hehehehe. We are witches, we are making [chanting] |
| *Zoe:* | We are witches, we are witches. |

Moving further into their imaginary Halloween frame, the girls exchange loud and excited "Boo's!" as they squat down and jump up, peeking around the sides of the easel.

| | |
|---|---|
| *Anna:* | I have another idea that we can do [chanting] |
| | I have a black cat, her name is Black Cat. |
| *Zoe:* | [chanting, inaudible] |
| *Anna:* | I have a black cat, her name is Black Cat. |
| *Zoe:* | [Laughter] I have a black cat! And my name is Black Cat. (Reifel & Yeatman, 1993, pp. 356–360) |

Perhaps the most significant theoretical assertions that shape how we think about play today can be traced to Charles Darwin's (1859) revolutionary theory on the biological and environmental adaptation of species (Schwartzman, 1978; Spariosu, 1989; Sutton-Smith, 1997). Some play theorists write about biological or environmental influences they see as relevant to play; other theorists keep those assumptions implicit. In the following sections, we will see how nature and nurture appear in a number of theoretical perspectives, including the work of Freud and the psychoanalysts who followed him, communications scholars, cognitive specialists, social theorists, and, finally, work that attempts to synthesize some of these points of view. At each step along the way, we will revisit Anna and Zoe to see what theory can tell us about what they are doing as they play.

## Psychoanalysis: Emotional Motives for Play

Within a matter of decades after Darwin's (1859) *Origin of Species* appeared, the medical doctor Sigmund Freud (1856–1939) began to interpret human behavior in terms of its biological and cultural influences. Basic to Freud's theory is how nature and nurture contribute to the structure of personality, including ego, id, and superego. We are born with biological drives (the id, including such drives as hunger, social contact, and sexuality), but society limits or guides the degree to which we can pursue those drives. For example, we may want to eat cookies all the time because we desire them, but parents and teachers limit the number of cookies we may eat and the times when we may eat them. As we internalize those social limitations, we develop our superego, or conscience, to provide an internal representation of society's rules; we reach a point when we can tell ourselves when and how we can indulge our desires. The interplay of forces (internal id; external social restrictions) shapes who we are as a person, or our ego. Freud argues that much of this dynamic happens subconsciously or unconsciously; what we know consciously is only a small part of what we are processing in our minds (Freud, 1918). This is a key foundation for thinking of play as a rhetoric of Self (Sutton-Smith, 1997, 1999).

This theory of personality attempts to describe what motivates us (our drives), how our morality is formed (our superego), and how we emerge as human beings. Parents serve as our first contact with society, letting us know when we may eat, sleep, and pursue our interests, as well as letting us know how we should act. Teachers, playmates, and other agents of society provide additional limits on what we may or may not do. Imbalance in the forces that shape us (too much biological drive; inappropriate social restrictions) can lead to mental illness. Our personal histories, in whatever forms they may take, contribute to who we are. The balance of nature and nurture reveals itself in personality formation.

Play has an important role in normal development, as a mechanism in childhood for resolving past pressures a child feels when drives are being curbed by societal expectations. Play also has a therapeutic role; it serves as an avenue for dealing with experiences that have proved to be maladaptive. For most children, play provides a psychologically safe context where what is desired can be obtained, in the world of fantasy. If mother will not allow cookies between meals, then we can play tea party and pretend to have cookies. Play, in the form of fantasy or pretense, is a reflection of children's efforts to deal with those things that are out of their control (i.e., the adult world) that are placing limits on their desires. Childhood play for most children is a pressure valve that allows desires to be acted on symbolically through pretend actions that adults and others tend to ignore and not take seriously. In play, children can get away with all sorts of things that they cannot get away with in reality: Children can boss around others (they would be punished by adults if they tried it in real life); they can consume all they want (adults ration consumables in real life); and they can control everything that adults control in reality (when they sleep and get up, when they come and go,

how they relate to others). Fantasy play allows children to begin to deal with reality on their own terms, and they deal with those aspects of reality that are most important to them. Play, from a psychoanalytic perspective, is an important part of early personality formation. The rhetorics of Self and the Imaginary come together here (Erikson, 1941, 1963; Freud, 1909, 1922/1959; Peller, 1954; Singer & Singer, 1977, 1992; Sutton-Smith, 1997, 1999; Winnecott, 1971).

Therapeutically, play is a window into the concerns of the child. Psychoanalysts were among the first to use play as part of child therapy. For those children who are perceived as suffering from psychological problems, therapeutic play sessions provide the analyst with an avenue for understanding the child's problems. More importantly, play is the means by which children can take charge of their problems and find routes for mastery and wellness (Axline, 1969; Erikson, 1963, 1972; A. Freud, 1964; Klein, 1955). Chapter 10, on play therapy, presents these psychoanalytic ideas up to date.

Freud's followers refined his theory of personality development and play. Erik Erikson is perhaps one of his best-known students. His *Childhood and Society* (1963) provides a more detailed analysis of early personality formation from a psychoanalytic perspective and highlights play as a key feature of early socialization. In other writings, Erikson points to play as a number of things: a reflection of the child's past, musings about the present, or explorations about what is to come. In all cases, Erikson continues the Freudian idea of nature (biology) dealing with nurture (social relationships, culture) through play.

A different perspective is provided by Lili Peller (1954). Peller argues that, in some cases, what we see in play is not just a reflection of the child dealing with reality; the child may be dealing with the ways he or she wishes reality would be. When a child hugs a doll, it may not be a reflection of the child having been hugged by an adult; it may be that the child wants to be hugged by an adult. Peller points to the difficulty of interpreting the meaning of play actions from a psychoanalytic perspective. Reality and fantasy must be seen from the point of view of each child's developmental history and from the child's personal meanings.

Play is an important theoretical concept that comes with Freudian connotations. It is one of the important developmental activities that allow us to become who we are as human beings. It allows us to deal with society's rules and to find out who we are. And, in those cases when we are having difficulties, it allows us to heal. We may have difficulty believing in some of the pieces of Freud's theory (e.g., childhood sexuality; drives as a source of motivation), but a number of features of his theory appear to stay with us:

- Play tells us about who the child uniquely is, as a constructor of his or her life history.
- Children resolve problems as they play.
- Feelings, or affect, is an important part of play.
- Who we are as individuals (i.e., our self-concept) is shaped in play.
- Our developmental or life histories are important for understanding who we are.

Clearly, when Julie challenges Zoe about the appearance of her painted pumpkin, Zoe has feelings about the challenge. Zoe opts to turn her painted pumpkin into a "big blump" that she can finger-paint over; when her initial painting is found to be wanting, she reverts to a less mature stage of painting, where representation does not matter. Her play provides a safe place where she can continue playing with Anna on a level that cannot be challenged by others. In play, Zoe makes things the way she wants them to be, and in play she resolves her hurt feelings.

More than most of the other theories that are described here, psychoanalytic theory reminds us of the totality of the child, including feelings and motives (Biber, 1984). It gives us lenses to

see each child as a biography that is being written. Zoe copes with challenges. It is not until we hear from Bruner (1990) that meaningful activity in narrative form reemerges as a topic of developmental interest.

## Communications and Play

**Bateson on Play Frames**   When children play, they communicate in many ways. When play is social, children must communicate with each other so that everyone knows what is happening. When children play alone, they are also communicating, although the signals may not be clear or obvious. The communicative aspects of play have become increasingly interesting to play researchers, but the nature and nurture of play communications are not always acknowledged. (Christie, Enz, & Vukelich, 1997; Garvey, 1993; Goncu, 1993; Schwartzman, 1978; see Chapter 7)

One of the earliest and most profound theories that connects play and communication is Gregory Bateson's theory of play and fantasy (1955/2000). An anthropologist, Bateson was interested in questions of adaptation and misadaptation (particularly mental illness) and developed his theory after observing otters playing in the surf. His insight was that many actions that would be taken seriously in reality are not taken seriously when individuals are engaged in play; when animals play fight, their nips are not mistaken for the bites that would occur in real fights. "I saw two young monkeys *playing, i.e.,* engaged in an interactive sequence of which the unit actions or signals were similar to but not the same as those of combat" (Bateson, 1955/2000, p. 179). When a 5-year-old girl asks whether we want to go to a tea party, adults do not expect to be less hungry when we are done; and if a young boy asks whether we want to fly with him to the moon, we do not call NASA. Bateson argues that all organisms that play (human or not) have adapted signals that allow us to know when an action is intended to be real or not. Dogs that are play

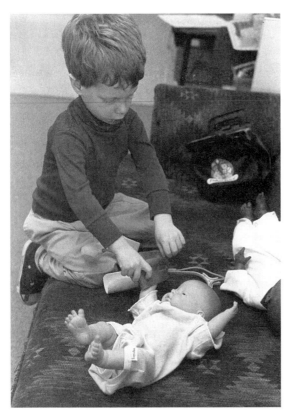

The social roles that children take as they play can be understood in terms of any number of theories.

fighting wag their tails so playmates will know that their nips are not bites. Humans develop both verbal and nonverbal signals to communicate their intent. "[P]lay, could only occur if the participant organisms were capable of some degree of meta-communication, *i.e.*, of exchanging signals which would carry the message 'this is play'" (Bateson, 1955/2000, p. 179).

Bateson's argument about play signals has evolutionary, philosophical, cognitive, and social aspects. In terms of human evolution, with the onset of play we were able to begin to communicate about the nonpresent (i.e., what was or what will be, rather than what is; what is happening elsewhere). This evolutionary leap in communications allowed our minds to evolve, creating cognitive processes for dealing with the nonliteral or imaginary; we became capable of thinking about things other than what we were doing. Such thinking leads to abstraction and the ability to theorize. As humans evolved, play was important because it allowed us to act both in and out of context and to know the difference; play is a tool for decontextualization. This is a form of the rhetoric of the Imaginary (Sutton-Smith, 1997, 1999).

The key to Bateson's theory is his notion of the **play frame.** The frame is that which we signal when we indicate to others that we want to shift from reality to imaginary. For Bateson, the imaginary is a map and reality is the terrain, which can be mapped. When we play house, our table-setting and baby-dressing actions are the map, and real-life housekeeping is the terrain; when we play the computer game Sim City, the computer screen images are our map, and city planning is our terrain. The frame might be seen as knowledge, or scripts (Bretherton, 1989; Goffman, 1974; Nelson, 1989). What makes the frame important is that it is not real, not present, which means that effort must be made to indicate that it is being created as what it is to be. Anna and Zoe agree on play about pumpkins (a "Halloween picture"), witches, and ghosts, all of which relate to Halloween. It is perhaps no surprise that many frames children select as they play relate to events in their worlds. Bateson gives us a way of beginning to relate those worldly experiences to what children negotiate in their play; Halloween means (at least) pumpkins, witches, and ghosts for these girls. Thus signals and elaborated communications are necessary for human play to take place.

Socially, it becomes important to take roles and to learn to make use of signals. To be in the same frame, players must agree to be in the same imaginary world, and they must know what to do there. Childhood play allows children to develop role flexibility, so they can move in and out of the many roles they will eventually take in life. Perhaps our adult ability to take on many roles (e.g., spouse, parent, employee, neighbor) is based on the way we took roles as players. For Bateson, particular roles matter less than the facility to move in and out of roles; we do not play cowboys when we are children in order to grow up to become cowboys. And cognitively, the ways we explore the nonliteral worlds within frames may allow our minds to move beyond the here and now, to worlds of theory and abstraction.

Human beings communicate and play to varying degrees. At the extreme end of adult maladaption (e.g., schizophrenia), the frame between real and not real is lost, and communication lacks meaning to those of us for whom the frames are clear. Whether play could ever remedy such problems is questionable. Cultural differences in play may be a function of the roles and frames that are legitimate within a culture (see Chapter 7). Within the realm of typical humans, research has revealed a number of useful communicative signals theorized by Bateson. Catherine Garvey has done much to document the language of play communication, as described next.

**Garvey on Play Talk**   As a psychologist interested in language of children, Garvey (1993) has done a number of studies describing transitions into and out of pretend play frames. Her observations and analyses of preschoolers (primarily girls) as they pretend have revealed the sorts of communicative efforts that Bateson predicted, with spoken language serving as a vehicle for indicating the play frame and its meanings. When most young children (especially girls) engage with one another, they use the types of talk that Garvey identified (see Figure 2.1).

When observing and listening to children play, it is apparent that children are signaling one another as theory suggests. They frequently

---

**FIGURE 2.1**   Garvey's Language Tools for Social Play

Preparatory Talk ("Let's play"; "These dolls are mine")

Explicit Directions for Pretend
    Transformation of self ("Pretend I'm a doctor")
    Transformation of other ("You be a patient")
    Transformation of joint roles ("Let's be nurses")
    Transformation of action for self ("I need to make some medicine")
    Transformation of action for other ("Pretend you broke your leg")
    Transformation of joint actions ("Let's pretend we're saving lives")
    Transformation of object ("This clay can be our medicine")
    Transformation of environment ("Under the table can be our hospital")
    Transformation of nothing to something (Child holds up empty hand while
        approaching another child and says, "This is a needle so I can give you a shot")

Within Pretend Talk (enactment talk)
    "Take all your medicine."
    "Let the nurse give you your shot."

Negation of Pretend
    "I don't want a shot. I'm leaving."
    "I don't want to play anymore."

Play Signals
    Altered tone of voice (e.g., high-pitched when speaking like a baby)
    Giggles while acting or speaking
    Winks

*Source:* Adapted from Garvey (1993).

invite others to "pretend," and they often indicate exactly what frame is relevant to the play. Anna did so when she said, "I'm makin' pumpkin," and Zoe signaled, "Me, too." They elaborate their Halloween frame by signaling that "I am a witch," and that, as a witch, Anna has transformed her paint into "purple stew" (probably a witch's brew). We can also hear Anna and Zoe make use of enactment talk, when they talk as the witches they are pretending to be: "Hehehehe. We are witches." When listening for Garvey's types of play talk, we can hear the children negotiate and refine their play frame, then move into the frame to enact it. When the frame becomes boring or threatening, they may terminate it or alter it, as Zoe did when Julie criticized her painted pumpkin; Anna explicitly alters the frame when she says, "I have another idea that we can do" and suggests the ghost peekaboo game. Many students have been able to replicate Garvey's framework for pretend play, especially for girls (who tend to be more verbal in general than boys). The decontextualized language implied by Garvey's framework has proved to be useful as a way of understanding the foundations of literacy (Christie et al., 1997; Reifel, 1995).

Garvey's version of Bateson's theory is useful, but there are still areas where research has not followed this theory. It is less helpful for understanding nonverbal play, games, and some aspects of pretend. For example, boys play just as much as girls do, but without as many of the language signals that girls use (Scales & Cook-Gumperz, 1993). What signals are the boys using? How do boys come to know that a certain gesture or sound indicates it is time to be a superhero? This code has not yet been cracked. And the frames that children elect to pretend have not been studied, in spite of our culture's efforts to promote particular frames for play. We could know much more about gender stereotypes implied by certain frames. Bateson's idea that fantasy contributes to role flexibility also deserves further attention. In any case, we have naturally evolved the propensity to communicate in different ways by means of play, as Anna and Zoe show us with their signals about what they are playing. This refines the rhetoric of the Imaginary (Sutton-Smith, 1997, 1999). How culture nourishes such play and communication is described in detail in Chapter 7.

## Cognitive Views

**Vygotsky on Play as a Zone of Proximal Development** Lev Semenovich Vygotsky (1896–1934) was a Russian student of psychology, philosophy, linguistics, social sciences, and the arts. His systematic work in psychology, education, and psychopathology, begun in 1924, was cut short by his untimely death of tuberculosis at the age of 38. The Western world did not have ready access to his work until the mid-1950s, because it was suppressed by Soviet guardians of "proper Marxian interpretation" (Bruner in Vygotsky, 1962). As a researcher interested in materialist influences on psychology, he advanced an approach to social constructivism that has become influential in many Western countries.

With respect to the role of play in the development of young children, Vygotsky (1966) was concerned with two fundamental issues: first, the origin and genesis of play and how it develops and, second, whether play is the predominant activity of young children. He concluded that play is not the predominant activity during the preschool years, but it is the leading source of development. As Vygotsky (1978, pp. 96–97) says, "The child sees one thing but acts differently in relation to what he sees. Thus, a condition is reached in which the child begins to act independently of what he sees." Play frees the child's thinking from concrete experience, allowing for higher levels of thinking. Play is therefore a form of Progress (Sutton-Smith, 1997, 1999).

Vygotsky was critical of the usual definitions of play. He rejected the view that play could be defined on the basis of the pleasure it gives to the child. Many activities give the child keener pleasure than play does, and some games do not afford pleasure at all, particularly organized games (athletic sports) with unpleasant outcomes. (This, of course, begs the question currently debated among play professionals: Are organized games play?) Vygotsky was inclined to focus on broader, more general meanings of play—namely, the child's needs, inclinations, incentives, and motives to act or play.

In *Mind and Society* (Vygotsky, 1978), the chapter "The Role of Play in Development" sketches some of the key elements of play as a contributor to mental development. Play, primarily pretend play, serves a key developmental function for mental development for a number of reasons. As play develops, a conscious realization of purpose emerges, as when Anna and Zoe agree on what it means to play Halloween. Play is purposeful, as seen in games in which children can win or lose, and the purpose decides the winner. The intent or object of winning is recognized in advance of playing the game; and the more demanding the rules ("Well, a pumpkin doesn't look like that"), the more intense the play becomes. As children develop, play without purpose or rules results in increasingly dull, unappealing activity. For school-age children, the separation of play and work (i.e., compulsory activity based on rules) is possible, and play is increasingly of the athletic type. As development evolves from imaginary play to games and work, play permeates reality and is continued in school instruction and work. Play evolves but does not die.

For the young child, special needs and incentives arise that are spontaneously expressed in play. The child desires immediate gratification, but many needs cannot be immediately realized (e.g., no young child wants to wait a few days for a birthday party). "[P]lay is invented at the point when unrealizable tendencies appear in development" (Vygotsky, 1966, p. 7). Indeed, if all needs could be gratified immediately, there would be no play. Therefore, the explanation of why children play is the "imaginary, illusory realization of unrealizable desires" (p. 7).

In explaining play or distinguishing it from other forms of activity, Vygotsky (1966) proposes that in play the child creates an imaginary situation that is, in fact, rule-based play. There is no such thing as play without rules laid down in advance by real-life behavior. For example, if the child is "nurturing" a child, she is obeying the rules of maternal behavior, rules that are not noticed by the child in real life. In imaginary play, there are rules that govern roles the child will play, so the child's play is free, but this is an illusory freedom. Here, Vygotsky conflicts with those, including Piaget, who propose that rules emerge after the preschool period, primarily in organized games or games with rules. Vygotsky goes further to propose that all games with rules contain imaginary situations (play), just as all imaginary play contains rules.

Vygotsky (1978) maintains that it is impossible for a child younger than age 3 to play with an imaginary situation. The child must be liberated from situational or concrete constraints (e.g., playing with real or concrete objects) to play with an imaginary situation. Play objects (i.e., toys, or **pivots** in Vygotsky's language) are one key factor in liberating children from the concrete; orange, green, and purple paint and brushes are pivots that create opportunities for Halloween play for Anna and Zoe. The preschool child (ages 3–5) begins to separate thought from objects during play, and so a stick becomes a gun or a rag becomes a doll. Play serves as a transitional stage for disconnecting thought from objects. At the point when the rag becomes a doll, meaning begins to dominate the object. Play becomes the context for acquiring culturally sanctioned meanings (like Halloween for Anna and Zoe), by way of the pivots for meaning that children encounter.

At school age, play is converted to internal processes: internal speech, logical memory, and abstract thought. The child can now play with meanings derived from objects. The meaning of rag can be transferred to a doll, and the child can act as though the rag is a doll. He or she is no longer constrained to concrete situations. Anna and Zoe have enough internalized ideas about Halloween that they can play the peekaboo ghost game without having any objects that suggest ghosts (although the presence of the easel may suggest peekaboo in general). Play is connected to pleasure, so children subject themselves to rules because they promise greater gratification than acting on impulses does. The inner self-restraint and self-determination established through obeying rules help shape the child's standards of action and morality in later years. However, Vygotsky warns that the real world is not a play world, and one cannot live in search of pleasure (as in play) or subordinate oneself to the kind of rules existing in play.

Vygotsky (1966) proposes that a **zone of proximal development (ZPD)** exists—a range of tasks between those the child can handle independently and those at the highest level she can master through play or with the help of adults or more competent peers. Thus three factors are seen as creating levels of the ZPD above the normal independent or lower levels. Play is a source of development and creates a ZPD. In play, the child performs above his usual behavior, as though he were a head taller than himself (Vygotsky, 1978, p. 102). The upper levels of the ZPD are also promoted by social interactions with adults and more competent peers who create situations that challenge or require the child to think and act beyond her independent level. Adults and competent peers can effectively **scaffold** the child's learning, helping her achieve ever-higher levels of development of thought and action. The play–development relationship is similar to the instruction–development relationship, but the activities and consequences of play are much broader than those provided by peers and adults, making it the "highest level of preschool development" (1966, p. 16). No one was present to assist Zoe as she tried to paint a pumpkin, but Julie's criticism of her painting may begin to create a ZPD in which Zoe will attempt to improve her painting.

The lens on play Vygotsky provides has only recently been studied. Many find his argument that play is a developmental zone, in which the child can do more than she can under normal circumstances, to be persuasive and supportive of play as an educational activity, such as language and speech development and self-regulation (Berk & Winsler, 1995; Bodrova, 2008; Bodrova & Leong, 1996, 1998b, 2006, 2007; Diamond et al, 2007; Elias & Berk, 2002; Gregory, Kim, & Whiren, 2003; Whitebread, 2010). Critical aspects of his theory, in particular the pivotal roles of objects and culture for pre school play, are currently under investigation (Chin & Reifel, 2000; Lin & Reifel, 1999; Reifel & Yeatman, 1993).

**Piaget on Play as Assimilation**    Jean Piaget (1896–1980) was a Swiss scholar who has variously been described as a psychologist, logician, biologist, or genetic epistemologist (Elkind, 1968). Piaget's interests in cognition took shape based on philosophical foundations (an assumption that innate mental structures were an inevitable result of experience, a post-Kantian structuralism; Piaget, 1970) and on observations of his three children, who were subjects for his early studies of the development of intelligent behavior. The child as knowledge constructor approaches the environment in terms of the mental structures already developed. These are incorporated into existing schemata or patterns of behavior through assimilation and accommodation. **Assimilation** is the action of the child on surrounding objects, whereas the converse action, **accommodation,** is the action of the environment (objects) on the child (Piaget, 1966). Adaptation is the equilibrium between assimilation and accommodation. Play is essentially assimilation (action on objects) or the primacy of assimilation over accommodation. A continuation of accommodation for its own sake is described as imitation (repeating actions already learned) (Piaget, 1962).

*Play, Dreams and Imitation in Childhood* (Piaget, 1962) is perhaps the most incisive and thorough analysis of linkages between play and intellectual development; certainly it is Piaget's seminal work on play. It is this work that has allowed researchers and educators to argue that play has a central role in children's cognitive

**FIGURE 2.2** Piaget's Concept of Play as Cognitively Assimilating Experience

Stage 1: Functional (exploratory, sensorimotor) activity (e.g., grasping a rattle; repeatedly dropping a toy on the ground)

Stage 2: Symbolic play (representing experience)
Construction (a special category, between sensorimotor and symbolic games; e.g., building with blocks; modeling clay)
Sociodramatic play (e.g., pretending to feed a doll; role playing in a pretend doctor's office)

Stage 3: Games with rules (e.g., marbles; tag)

development. However, in this volume, he describes play as essentially assimilation:

> In every act of intelligence is an equilibrium between assimilation and accommodation, while imitation is a continuation of accommodation for its own sake, it may be said conversely that play is essentially assimilation, or the primacy of assimilation over accommodation. (1962, p. 87)

Play, then, follows development rather than causing it (Sutton-Smith, 1966). All activities during the first months of life, except feeding and emotions (fear, anger, etc.), are play, which Piaget calls "practice" or "functional play." When the child repeats actions or operations previously learned (grasping for the sake of grasping; shaking hanging toys repeatedly), she is performing actions that are ends in themselves and have no external aim. Symbolic play, like Anna and Zoe's pretend, occurs during the preoperational period, when construction and dramatic play symbolically reflect the thoughts the child is developing. As the child enters the concrete operational period of thought, games with rules, like Anna and Zoe's peekaboo ghost game, become the play form that reflects that level of cognition (see Figure 2.2).

Piaget drew close linkages between forms or types of play and stages of development. Contemporary research indicates that with respect to drawing accurate conclusions about the nature and development of play, these links are questionable and perhaps inaccurate. He proposed that the only form of play occurring during the sensorimotor period is functional or practice play. Zoe's finger-painting could be

seen as a form of practice play. Practice play begins after the child has learned (i.e., developed schemata) for grasping, swinging, throwing, and so forth, and repeats her behavior for the mere joy of mastery and feelings of power in subduing reality. The child initially modifies existing mental structures (accommodation) to develop swinging or throwing schemata and later advances to the level of subordinating (repeating and mastering) the behavior (assimilation). From then on, practice play, accompanied by "functional pleasure," occurs. At any stage of development, it is probably the case that we will see a predominant form of play, as outlined by Piaget, but any child at any age may be able to play at any of the levels he describes (Van Hoorn, Scales, Nourot, & Alward, 2011); we see Anna and Zoe pretending, constructing with paint, manipulating the paint with their senses, and playing a game with rules, but at their ages we are most likely to see repetitive pretend and construction. The arc of Piaget's thinking has been influential in any number of studies describing the cognitive progression that can be seen in a child's play (e.g., Fein, 1975; Nicholich, 1977; Watson & Fisher, 1977; Watson & Jackowitz, 1984). It is probably incorrect to associate a particular play activity with a particular age, but we can typically see a progression in the complexity of most children's play as they develop. (See Figure 2.3 for a descriptive progression in symbolic pretend play based on research inspired by Piaget.) Piaget helps us see the mental transformations associated with Anna and Zoe's play desires, including their role transformations of themselves

**FIGURE 2.3**   Pretend: The First 8 Years

---

**Single pretend transformation toward self** (with toys that resemble real objects; e.g., the child hugs a toy doll or toy animal; the child pretends to eat toy food.)

**Other object is pretend agent** (object is treated as if it acts, with toys that resemble real objects; e.g., the child has a toy doll or toy animal act as if it is eating toy food.)

**Single pretend transformation** (with toys that have no resemblance to real objects; e.g., the child creates a bed out of building blocks; the child forms a pancake from Play-Doh.)

**Pretend role** (with toys associated with a role that resemble real objects; e.g., a child pretends to be a cook with toy food; a child pretends to be a firefighter with a toy fire hat and a toy truck.)

**Multiple pretend role transformations** (with toys that resemble real-world objects; e.g., a child takes roles such as doctor, patient, and nurse while playing with dolls or toy animals.)

**Pretend role** (without the support of toys that resemble real objects; with blocks or Play-Doh, a child creates a pretend setting by constructing the objects needed; e.g., children pretend to be farmers by building a farm from blocks and forming animals with Play-Doh.)

**Multiple pretend roles** (with toys that resemble real-world objects; a group of children negotiates roles such as a doctor, patient, and nurse in the presence of doctor's office toys.)

**Multiple pretend roles** (without toys that resemble real objects; e.g., children create a pretend setting with blocks or Play-Doh and designate pretend roles to enact.)

---

*Source*: Adapted from Fein (1975), Nicholich (1977), Watson and Fischer (1977), and Watson and Jackowitz (1984).

("I'm a witch." "My name is Black Cat.") and the object transformations they need for their play ("I am makin' pumpkin." "I make purple stew.").

Given the current critical examination of the accuracy and relevance of Piagetian theory for early childhood education (Smolucha & Smolucha, 1998), certain cautions and clarifications are needed. Piaget warned that the age at which intellectual abilities appear is approximate and varies with individual children. The fact that he attached approximate ages to stages of development led to misunderstanding about his intent regarding individual differences in children. The stage theory that Piaget articulated provides a set of lenses for identifying types of play with particular age groups, and perhaps his greatest weakness was proposing that children cannot progress beyond the stage within which they are operating. Theorists from around the world have challenged his view. Another weakness in his approach is his view of the individual child at play. Piaget analyzes individual cognitive development as reflected in play, whereas much play is social, requiring an analysis of

what occurs in a group context (Reifel & Yeatman, 1993). We revisit these criticisms later.

**Bruner on Problem Solving**   In *Play: Its Role in Development and Evolution*, Jerome Bruner (1915- ) and colleagues collected landmark articles on many aspects of play, including Bruner's own classic survey on "The Nature and Uses of Immaturity" (1972). Sections in the book included "The Evolutionary Context," "Play and the World of Objects and Tools," "Play and the Social World," and "Play and the World of Symbols." By bringing together diverse writings on play in this one volume, Bruner was able to demonstrate the predominant themes in play research and the theories associated with them. The overriding theme was that play allows development to occur in many domains, including problem solving, cooperative and competitive social interactions, sex roles, cultural acquisition, language, and creativity. His interest in play, as a developmental foundation for problem solving and thinking, was represented by his own work on cognitive and social play. For example, Anna and Zoe painting at the easel creates opportunities for solving problems about depiction, relating socially, and dealing with criticism.

Bruner (1972) values play as an immature activity that allows children to explore and master abilities they will need in their adult worlds. Play allows children to act in ways that minimize consequences, allowing errors to be made before there are real consequences. It also allows actions to be combined in ways that might never occur under normal circumstances; we can learn to relate subroutines to larger tasks by means of play. Play is a context for using objects as tools to solve problems, and when adults are involved, there is potential for teaching social conventions and symbols. The skills acquired in play also require *decontextualization,* or the transition, from "knowing how" to "knowing that"; like Bateson (1955/ 2000) and Vygotsky (1978), Bruner sees play as a transition from action (which reflects knowing how) to meaning (which reflects knowing that). Play requires that we psychologically separate actions from the contexts in which they normally take place, and that psychological separation makes the mind operate in new ways; the Halloween play of Anna and Zoe takes ideas about the holiday out of context where they are practiced into the context of peer play. Bruner places play in the realm of nature (what he calls "biologically rooted modes") that is shaped by culture (i.e., rituals, like Halloween). Play is a way we have evolved to learn to use tools to problem solve, and play is the setting where social meanings are constructed; for Anna and Zoe, they are constructing meanings about Halloween as well as about social relations such as friendship and disagreement. Play is clearly one way of understanding evolutionary and developmental progress (Sutton-Smith, 1997, 1999).

By 1990 in *Acts of Meaning,* Bruner had placed much of this thinking in the service of narrative. Human efforts, including play, are directed toward creating meaning. Narrative is one form that meaning can take. Although Bruner has not elaborated his current theoretical position with the earlier work on play, it may be fair to infer that one of the social problems that gets solved by means of play is how we come to understand our experiences. This strand of theory, although based on cultural and cognitive rather than biological assumptions, appears to mirror the lens of psychoanalytic thought about play.

## Social Play

Many people automatically assume that play is a social activity, something one does with friends, like playing house. This common assumption persists in spite of the fact that we have abundant evidence that a good deal of childhood play time is spent alone, with a child engaged in solitary pretend, computer games, television viewing, or other activities that could be done with others but, as often as not, are done solo. Our theoretical picture of play as a social activity may be biased by the fact that much research is done in classrooms, where group play is more likely to occur. Studies of children's play at home and outside of schools reemerged as a source of understanding about children's lives (e.g., Haight & Miller, 1993; Kelly-Byrne, 1989).

Interest in social play has increased, not only in terms of how peers play with each other but also regarding other social influences on play (e.g., Smilansky, 1968, 1990). The roles of adults in children's play has reemerged as a theoretical concern, whether the adults are parents, teachers, play facilitators, or therapists. Beyond questions of social interaction influences on play, there are questions of the social meaning for media (computers, television, cinema) and children's culture for play. The meaning of social play today differs from earlier versions of the topic. To understand these various social lenses on play, we look at traditional theory (Parten's developmental stages) about play relationships and then review current thinking on play culture and social constructivism (Corsaro, 1985, 2003; Meckley, 1995; Opie & Opie, 1959, 1969, 1997).

Children begin to experience social hierarchies as they play.

**Parten on Social Participation** Mildred Parten (1932, 1933) conducted a classic study on the development of social relationships in group settings for children. Her interest was in the genetic sociology of the classroom, or what transitions children make as they become social participants in group activities. Her assumptions appear to fall on the nature end of the nature–nurture continuum, with a belief that social relations are more innate or genetic than shaped by the environment. Although her framework for observing children as they interact is frequently equated by researchers with play in its various forms (see Howes, 1987b, 1992; Rubin et al., 1983), her theory applies to all social contacts that might occur in groups, including eating snacks, washing hands, or participating in any event where children might enter and leave a group. Her main point is that for any child, we see a developmental progression in the type of social involvement that a child exhibits, and the onset of each type is roughly linked with age. Figure 2.4 presents the developmental progression.

The sweep of Parten's theory suggests that from age 2 on, children make the transition from being nonsocial (uninvolved), to socially aware (onlooker observes others; solitary acts like others while not near them), to close proximity (acts in parallel with others, as Anna and Zoe demonstrate when they both paint

**FIGURE 2.4**    Parten's Genetic Sociology of Social Participation

| | |
|---|---|
| **Uninvolved:** | The child is active and mobile but seemingly aimless; there is no sense of others' play. |
| **Onlooker:** | The child attends to others' play, may speak with players, but does not participate. |
| **Solitary:** | The child plays alone, with own toys; typical of 2- to 3-year-olds. |
| **Parallel:** | The child plays beside or near others, but not with them—no sharing, including play goals. |
| **Associative:** | The child plays with others, conversing, but purposes of play may not be similar. |
| **Cooperative:** | Goals of play are shared and negotiated; tasks and roles relate to play's purpose; group sense is marked by turn-taking, common goal, product, or game. |

*Source*: Adapted from Parten (1932).

pumpkins on their separate sides of the easel), and finally to interactive (associates with others while not sharing a joint purpose, then sharing a joint purpose, as when Anna and Zoe decide to play witches or when they play peekaboo). We see the child developing from pre- or aso-cial toward a stage when an experience is socially shared. This change typically occurs in the preschool years, so that children are cooper-ative with peers by age 5 or 6.

It is worth remembering that these stages are useful for describing play and any other social event. We might see onlooker (Julie observing Zoe), parallel activity (Anna and Zoe painting on opposite sides of the easel), or cooperative interactions at the snack table, as well as when children pretend to play house or build with blocks. Parten's stages are not just play stages, but because much of what young children do is play, many associate her stages primarily with play. Parten did not equate play and social participation.

Note that the validity of Parten's stages has been confirmed by numerous researchers. Current research has demonstrated the develop-mental progression that she described, although some studies have indicated that today's children, who have been entering group care in the form of child care at earlier ages, may be progressing through these stages at an earlier pace; we might see parallel or cooperative interactions with 2- or 3-year-olds, if those children have been in child care since they were infants (Howes, 1987b). It is also true that children who as preschoolers may not have been exposed to groups of peers demon-strate the same developmental progression at the time when they first encounter peers, but they may go through the stages more quickly.

Parten did not try to account for individual differences in her social theory. She did not attempt to deal with the idea that some chil-dren may prefer to play alone, even if they have the skills to play cooperatively. So the develop-mental progression that Parten's theory sets forth provides a general framework for considering how children interact with peers, including those

times when they are playing. Her theory does not provide a lens for understanding individual children's reasons for wanting to play, or not, with others in their groups. How the social environment might nurture or support social relations is beyond the scope of her theory. (Takhvar & Smith, 1990)

**Peer Culture and Play**   Parten and her work represent more of the biological influences on social play theory; social play naturally emerges as the child grows. Contrasting cul-tural influences are well represented by writers who come from anthropologic, sociologic, and folkloric traditions (e.g., Corsaro, 1985; Opie, 1993; Opie & Opie, 1969, 1997; Schwartzman, 1978). These theorists question the biological inevitability of social play, arguing that play is a context in which social relations and mean-ings (i.e., culture) are constructed. Growth in this realm of thought about play has been dra-matic over the past 15 years. In some cases, researchers build on classical social science the-ory (e.g., Bateson, 1955/2000; Goffman, 1974; Mead, 1934); in other cases, theory emerges from empirical findings (e.g., Corsaro, 1985; Opie, 1993; Opie & Opie, 1969, 1997).

There are many notions of peer culture, but most seem to assume that children, as they interact, create communities of participants who share common values, interests, and ritu-als. These communities are most frequently formed based on play activities, in which par-ticipants learn who shares their interests (such as in Halloween or in other cultural events), who has skills (like who can paint well), and who can be counted on to make the right things happen (who criticizes whom, and who does not). Some of the earliest efforts to document and describe this phenomenon were the Opies studies, *The Lore and Language of School-children* (1959) and *Children's Games in the Street and Playground* (1969). The Opies revealed that play exists in an astonishing range of forms, most of which serve children's social purposes (see Figure 2.5). Those purposes include fun but

**FIGURE 2.5** Types of Peer Culture Play

**Wit and Repartee/Nonsense**

*Kindergartener girl*

I'm gonna tell on you,
That you put ants in my pants
And made me do a boogie dance.

*Kindergartener*

Look left;
Look right;
Look everywhere.
Na Na Na Na Na Na!
Your pants are falling down.

*2nd Grader*

Look up, look down. Look all around.
Your pants are falling down.

*Kindergartener*

Skunk in the barnyard: P.U.!
Somebody ate it: that's you!

*Kindergartener group*

Bubble gum, bubble gum, in a dish.
How many pieces do you wish?
One, two, three, four.

**Guile**

*2nd Grader*

Are you a P.T.?
If yes: Then you're a pregnant teacher.
If no: Then you are not a pretty teacher.
Are you an S.K.?
If yes: Then you're a stupid kid.
If no: Then you are not a smart kid.

**Jeers and Torments**

*2nd Grader*

Say I.
I
Your mommie had a baby at the FBI.
Whoever looks at ____ is a nerd [has cooties, etc.]

**Riddles**

*2nd Grader*

What's green and flies through the air?
Super pickle.

*3rd Grader*

Why do you salute the refrigerator?
Because it's General Electric.

*Kindergartener*

What goes up white and comes down yellow?
An egg.

*2nd Grader*

What's green and red and goes 30 miles an hour?
A frog in a blender.

*2nd Grader*

Knock! Knock!
Who's there?
Banana.
Banana who?
Knock! Knock!
Who's there?
Banana.
Banana who?
Knock! Knock!
Who's there?
Orange.
Orange who?
Orange you glad I didn't say banana?

**Pranks**

*2nd Grader*

Child left his seat to get something. Prankster ran quickly to the vacant seat, took the lunch tray, and moved it to a new location. The returning child missed the tray and had to search for it.

**Pretend**

*Kindergartener boys*

Sneak Matchbox cars into cafeteria and pretend to race during lunch.

*2nd Grader*

Blow bubbles through a straw into chocolate milk, to make a "milkshake."

*All ages*

Make little "pills" out of wads of white bread, then take "medicine."

*2nd Grader*

Chew around the edges of graham crackers to form toy "guns" that they shoot at one another.

*Kindergartener boys*

Use bananas from lunchboxes as "phones" to have conversation.

*3rd Grader group*

When a cafeteria monitor limited to three the number of boys at each table, one of the boys asked, "How do girls eat?" All the children began to eat their lunches "the way girls do," lifting little fingers as they brought food to their mouths, taking delicate little bites, and raising the pitch of their voices and giggling. Then they all pretended to be boys.

*Source*: Adapted from Opie and Opie (1959, 1969), Reifel (1986).

also function to create cohesive social systems that operate with rules that are meaningful to children themselves. Children will use games and chants to keep others in line or to exclude them from the group. Adults are outsiders, if not anathema, to these forms of play; adults might ruin it.

Such peer cultures develop on streets and playgrounds and may lead to activity of which the larger culture disapproves (i.e., gang activity). Cultures also develop under adults' noses, in preschool and elementary classrooms (Corsaro, 1985; Meckley, 1995; Miller, Fernie, & Kantor, 1992; Reifel, 1986; Scales, 1996). Children pretend or play games in ways that most adults ignore (as long as there is no disruption to adult-sanctioned activity), establishing shared meanings that create in-groups, out-groups, and hierarchies of influence in classrooms. In some cases, we choose to see such play as the basis for forming friendships (Corsaro, 1985; Howes, 1992). In most cases, such play is overlooked entirely. Sutton-Smith (1984) has noted that this play can be cruel to those who are excluded or scapegoated.

Corsaro (1985) has formalized one understanding of peer culture with his sociolinguistic analysis of talk during play. He theorizes that language during play serves social functions for creating play groups, including children's efforts to exclude others from play. Like Garvey (1993) has done for pretend communications, Corsaro identifies types of talk that can be heard during play, talk that leads to hierarchical group formation (see Figure 2.6).

Patterns of **play talk** reveal who has power in the group and what is the relative social status of players, such as Zoe's relative subordinate status with peers. Zoe is informed by Julie that the painted pumpkin does not look like a pumpkin, and Zoe answers Anna very ofen. Instead of reflecting social status, play is seen as the context where social status, social power, and shared values are created. These creations may be adaptive for humans who must learn to work together, but they may be maladaptive for those who are excluded from play. Developmentalists have studied the long-term effects of such exclusion for decades (e.g., Kemple, 1991; Moore, 1967).

As a part of children's culture, play becomes an activity with significance in its own right. Instead of an activity in which we can witness individual children's various forms of development, it is seen as an activity that creates development. The trouble with peer culture theory is that it begins to raise questions about the values inherent in play (Sutton-Smith, 1997). Play per se is no longer just a benign activity that may contribute to Progress; it can now be seen as a context for creation of both good (social cohesion, role exploration, sense-making, and exploration

**FIGURE 2.6**   Corsaro on Social Play Talk

**Imperatives:** commands, warnings (make play happen; common from superordinate player to subordinate)

**Informative statements:** acknowledge or provide information (clarify what is going on; common with all players, but more so for subordinate to superordinate and from one superordinate to another)

**Request for permission:** ask to engage (from subordinate to superordinate)

**Request for joint action:** refer to another speaker's suggestion (from superordinate to superordinate)

**Answers:** respond to a directive (more common from subordinates)

**Information requests:** ask for clarification (more common from superordinates)

**Directive questions:** give indirect orders

**Tag questions:** make statement with "OK?" or "Right?" (from superordinate to superordinate)

**Greetings:** say "Hi" (most common among children of the same status)

**Baby talk:** human or animal forms (more subordinates)

of meanings) and bad (social rejection, prejudice, and bullying). The meaning of play activities, however defined, takes on new significance when we think about the cumulative meaning of play, filtered through a theory of child culture.

One way of seeing this theoretical perspective in practice is through the work of Alice Meckley (1995), who observed preschoolers at play over a 5-month period and documented their pretend actions, playmates, social status, and other features of what they did during play time. The same play would repeat itself from day to day but with different players taking roles. She found that play ideas (themes, topics) seemed to transfer over time from more popular to less popular children and that less popular children took desirable roles after popular children were done with them. All children were creating social meanings as they played, but what they played (and when) was influenced by the status of players in the classroom peer culture. We have a picture of play that is very much shaped by the social environment.

## Creativity in Play

The assumption that play is linked with the arts, aesthetics, and creativity emerged years ago with Enlightenment scholars such as Schiller (1795/1965) (see Chapter 1). Current researchers have pursued that assumption by studying the relationship of childhood play with different aspects of creativity. Just as play has been defined in different ways by different theorists, so has creativity. Researchers in this tradition have considered creativity in terms of originality and fluidity; flow experience; intelligence; or educational programming. Clearly, the Imaginary is central to much of this scholarship (Csikszentmihalyi, 1977, 1979, 1990; Csikszentmihalyi & Csikszentmihalyi, 1995; Edwards, Gandini, & Forman, 1998; Gardner, 1983, 1993, 1999; Gardner & Hatch, 1989; Guilford, 1957; Sutton-Smith, 1997, 1999).

Creativity can take many forms, which means that play can be associated with any number of variables. Theorists such as Guilford assume that creativity takes the form

Peer play can support creative social and language development, building a foundation for literacy.

of individuals finding original solutions to problems or challenges, acting in a fluid and flexible manner; Anna and Zoe find lots of ways to use the paint and the easel to create different forms of play. A child who uses a towel to create a roof for a block building might be considered creative from this point of view. Others, such as Csikszentmihalyi, consider the subjective experience of the individual; if an activity, such as playing computer games, transports the player psychologically to a state where time and the environment are irrelevant, then the player might be engaged in creative flow. Anna and Zoe can be seen in creative flow when they pretend to be witches and when they play their peekaboo game. Creativity can also be understood theoretically as a form of intelligence, as Gardner (1983, 1993, 1999) has done; in addition to traditional forms of intelligence (language, math), other creative activities such as musical and visual expression may be part of an individual's potential.

Some educational programs, such as the Reggio Emilia School in Italy, may build their entire curriculum around creativity. The arts and other forms of expression are encouraged, although a particular theory of creativity is not identified within the program. The play of children, as guided by teachers and the environment, is assumed to be creative. This sort of expressiveness is valued in that program, as it is by many educators in other parts of the world (e.g., Isenberg & Jalongo, 2006). (see Chapter 8).

## EMERGING THEORIES OF PLAY

Over the past decade, a number of new theories related to play, or combinations of theories, have appeared in the literature. These theories have attempted to explain some aspect of human development, social relations, or play in particular contexts. For example, Fromberg (1998, 1999) and others have begun to apply complexity, or **chaos theory,** and hermeneutics to group play.

Working from principles that have been applied to geology, physics, psychology, and many other branches of science, these authors are attempting to understand the various contributors to play equilibrium or play's oscillating balance. One thing triggers another, through the lens of chaos theory, and regular patterns emerge from the interplay of social relationships, ideas, materials, and guidance in the play setting. At this point, complexity theory has not been tested (VanderVen, 1998, 2004; Waldrop, 1992).

Hermeneutic analysis of play has been suggested by philosophers and anthropologists, who see play as meaningful human text. We learn to read play texts within any number of overlapping and intersecting frames of meaning, rather than using a particular theory or point of view for interpretation. VanderVen (2004) laid out the multiplicities of children's play as a complex text; Reifel, Hoke, Pape, and Wisneski (2004) used the approach to explore the multiple meanings of classroom play. Reifel (2007) argues that Vivian Paley (e.g., 2004) and others (e.g., Blaise, 2005) view play as a text that calls for layered, analytic reading. Paley has been doing such thoughtful readings of play in her books on teaching in the kindergarten.

Theory of mind has been linked with play since Leslie's 1987 article, in which he argues that pretend play provides the context in which children begin to understand that others have thoughts, beliefs (true and false), and desires. Play requires children to acquire this **theory of mind,** from which they become aware of the internal mental states of themselves and others. The concerns of this theory are how aspects of play, such as communications about the "as if" of play, are linked to mental representations about social relationships, whether among children or between children and adults. Knowing the difference between what is real and what is pretend involves a variety of cognitive processes that are being explored by these researchers. Most of the work with this theory has been done in laboratory settings, but it deals with issues encountered in many play contexts, including imaginary companions and gestural meaning (Lillard, 1993, 1998a, 1998b, 2000, 2001; Lillard & Witherington, 2004; Richert & Lillard, 2004; Sharon & Woolley, 2004; Suddendorf, 2000; Taylor, Carlson, & Gerow, 2000; Woolley, 1995; Woolley, Boerger, & Markman, 2004; Woolley & Cox, 2007; Woolley & Tullos, 2008; Woolley & Wellman, 1990).

Older concerns are reappearing in new theories about play. The centrality of emotion for play is no longer associated only with psychoanalytic theories. Greta Fein (1989; Fein & Kinney, 1994) has directed her thinking to the feelings that are expressed in play and how those feelings organize play for children. Sawyer (1997, 2003) analyzed communication, metacommunication, and creativity during play, going beyond the work of Bateson, Garvey, and Corsaro. Sawyer argues that play is a form of improvisation, subject to the same rules of social interplay that apply to all generative encounters. He uses sociolinguistic theory to show how early childhood pretend play is not only metacommunicative but also metapragmatic. Children are not just signaling others about what they are playing; they are signaling each other about relationships. Both Fein and Sawyer's ideas rework longstanding views of play with their contemporary lenses.

How can teachers participate in classroom play without interfering with children's play purposes? Lobman (2003a, 2003b, 2005, 2006; Lobman & Lundquist, 2007) deals with teaching as the responsive, engaging activity that meets learners where they are coming from. Building on the idea of improvisation, from music, theater, and comedy, she is exploring how teachers can think and act in ways that help children build pretend relationships and thinking. Listening to children is necessary to hear what they are offering during an interaction. Lobman gives guidance for receiving play offers, trusting, listening, and other tools for relating to classroom players and understanding how they

are learning. Improvisation is a theoretical lens that is also a way of teaching that meets students on their level while relating with them as a player who can enhance play.

New play materials, such as electronic, video, and online games, seem to be calling on new conceptualizations of play. Thinking about electronic games (and doing research on them) raises totally new ideas about context and playful participation, as elaborated in Chapter 11 (Facer, Sutherland, Furling, & Furlong, 2001; Gee, 2003; Kohler, 2004; Verenikina, Harris, & Lysaght, 2003).

Emerging theories of children's play do not reflect only abstract ideas and concerns. Many new theories are tied to play as it is practiced in classrooms and homes and on playgrounds. Several attempts to make the prerational into something rational (Spariosu, 1989) begin with children's play activities and seek theory to aid understanding. A number of these efforts combine existing theories to interpret children's actions. For example, Meckley (1995) draws on Vygotsky, Mead, and other social theorists to make sense of the roles and rules of children's play. Reifel and Yeatman (1993; Yeatman & Reifel, 1997) combine the theories of Bateson and Vygotsky to create a model for understanding children's creation of meanings around pivots in classroom play. As teacher-scholars such as Scales (1996), Reynolds and Jones (1997), Jones and Cooper (2006), and Paley (1981, 1992, 2004) provide more description of play with their thoughtful theoretical analyses, we are left with new combinations of lenses to enhance our understanding.

## PLAY THROUGH DIFFERENT LENSES

Play has theoretical significance from the point of view of any number of disciplines and scholars (Rubin, Bukowski, & Parker, 1998; Sutton-Smith, 1997, 1999). In previous sections, we demonstrated how a number of theoretical perspectives provide us with different lenses for understanding play. Psychoanalysis gives us a view of play as critical for balancing the conflicting pressures that result when our biological drives meet social constraints. The emotions of players motivate them and are treated by means of play therapy. Communications theory marks play as crucial for establishing signal systems, frames of reference, and all those social and cognitive skills that are required for communications. Cognitive theory gives us a number of alternative lenses: Play reflects developing cognition (Piaget), play is a tool for problem solving (Bruner), or play is a zone to promote mental development (Vygotsky). The biological and environmental are given varying weights in these cognitive views. Socially, we can see play as an innate, unfolding process (Parten) or as a context for generating social structure and meaning (in peer culture). Play can also be linked to creativity in its many theoretical forms, reflecting a belief that goes back hundreds of years. Each of these lenses can show us a different perspective on Anne and Zoe's play, including their relationships, how they are communicating, their thinking, what they are thinking about, and how they are relating to the world around them. Each of these theoretical views points to the importance of play, but they do not share common assumptions about the role or function of play. As Figure 2.7 illustrates, important thinkers attribute slightly different meanings to play, whether it deals with play's functions (personality integration, problem solving,

**FIGURE 2.7** Key Theoretical Statements on Play

### Psychoanalysis: Emotional Motives for Play

"In Mary's case, her play disruption and her play satiation, if seen in the framework of all the known circumstances, strongly suggest that a variety of past and future, real and imagined events had been incorporated into a system of mutually aggravating dangers." (Erikson, 1963, p. 232)

### Communications and Play

### Bateson on Play Frames

"'This is play' looks something like this: 'These actions in which we now engage do not denote what those actions *for which they stand* would denote.'" (Bateson, 1955/2000, p. 180)

### Cognitive Views of Play

### Vygotsky on Play as a Zone of Proximal Development

"In play thought is separated from objects and action arises from ideas rather than from things: a piece of wood begins to be a doll and a stick becomes a horse. Action according to rules begins to be determined by ideas and not by objects themselves." (Vygotsky, 1978, p. 97)

### Piaget on Play as Assimilation

"Symbolic play, then, is only one form of thought, linked to all the others by its mechanism, but having as its sole aim satisfaction of the ego, i.e., individual truth as opposed to collective and impersonal truth." (Piaget, 1962, p. 167)

### Bruner on Problem Solving

"Play appears to serve several centrally important functions. First, it is a means of minimizing the consequences of one's actions and of learning, therefore, in a less risky situation." (Bruner, 1976, p. 38)

### Social Play

"'First-years against second-years, OK?' 'I know, let's play Om Pom [hide and seek].' Two girls approached a third and said with almost oriental politeness, 'Melanie, may we play Stuck in the Mud, please?'" (Opie, 1993, p. 21)

abstract thought, social group formation), as a reflection of or contributor to development, as a process within an individual or a group, or related to ideas or relationships. They tell us to look at play, but they tell us to look for different things (or to listen for different things) when we see play. It is as if we were using a different lens to see what is there, and each lens allows us to see something different in the same activity.

## BELIEFS AND PHILOSOPHY

All of the lenses on play that we have described in this chapter add to the understandings about play that you bring with you, based on your own background experiences. Recent research illustrates how prospective teachers build on their spontaneous beliefs about play, as they begin to use academic theories to construct thinking about play. Studying play theories and conducting academic fieldwork where you observe play are part of how you move beyond thinking about play as fun, creative, or free, to a point where you can use reliable tools for understanding children's development and education (Klugman, 1996; Sherwood & Reifel, 2010). People who deal with play daily must create their own ways of thinking about play, possibly based on scholarly theories (Gross, 2003) or years of professional experience (Jones & Cooper, 2006; Paley, 2004). Are you a parent hoping for the happiness and stimulation of your child? Are you a teacher aiming to educate young children? Are you a therapist hoping to help a child master psychological challenges? Each of these aims is associated with different adult roles and assumptions about what children are experiencing when they play. It is likely that particular theories may be more or less relevant as each of those questions is answered. In the following sections, we make sense of play theories based on who we are and how we will use them.

## Views of Classroom Play

At the beginning of this chapter, we suggested that one way that educators, parents, or other professionals relate to play is in terms of their spontaneous thinking and beliefs, as well as any scientific theories they may have learned. One trouble with this point is that our beliefs are complex and, at times, conflicting (Bennett, Wood, & Rogers, 1997). One thing this chapter might help you do is to look at play in the classroom in terms of various aspects of children's development, as they relate to the curriculum. Sorting out beliefs can be confusing when they may blend with ways of thinking about children and (for example) education. To value play as a means of forming meaning, for instance, has implications for the theories we turn to in order to make sense of play, as well as for the research findings we look to as validation for our practices. Parents, in contrast, may have more of an interest in their children's play as a basis for exploring family interests and recreation. Therapists have a commitment to healing their patients, so their theoretical view takes that fact into account. These are all ways we as concerned adults relate to play, and we are not yet detailing the complexities of children's play itself.

To put theory (or theories) into practical context, we explore how it plays a role in a particular context: the early childhood classroom. The details of practice can show up in any number of ways to which we need to relate, including the play materials we include in our classrooms, how they are arranged, and the real-world experiences we provide with the intent of stimulating play (Reifel & Yeatman, 1993). The basic beliefs that guide us are another consideration, such as the valuing of a free society (Cuffaro, 1995; Dewey, 1916); people should participate in activities of their own choice, within which mistakes can be made, rules generated, and conflicts resolved.

Another belief might be that we learn (or understand) what we do from our own efforts. Any meaningful activity becomes meaningful by virtue of what we bring to it. Indeed, we construct our knowledge, based on our participation in the experiences of life (Dewey, 1938; Vygotsky, 1978). When children choose their classroom play activities, they create a sense of ownership for their actions. As they communicate about those actions with others, they become clearer about what they are doing and how they are relating to others. The social laboratory of play allows children to create and refine their interests by acting, through play, in a community of learners.

A related belief that ties together the two core principles thus far is the importance of expression. It is only through expression, whether saying, drawing, building, enacting, or representing by any other means, that we can truly construct knowledge. We can freely participate in any number of experiences, but it is only in our efforts to communicate those experiences to others (i.e., to express them) that our meanings can take shape. Without communication, we can have no clarification, correction, or elaboration. We need play theory to help us understand children in this context.

An additional core belief that helps focus thinking about play is that cultural context is essential for giving meaning to experience. Our cultures give us the physical and social environments that we experience. They also give us beliefs and customs that provide essential meanings to life. Culture also gives us our language(s) for socially sharing experience. Our cultures, including our own backgrounds, as well as those of children and their families, become critical sources for meaningful experiences.

How do these principles help us delimit the complexity of play? They help us establish priorities for what we do in the classroom. For example, in the area of early writing, Dyson (1997) argues that imaginary topics created by friends during play are important bases for early composition. Depending on how those values are featured in our thinking, we need to select theoretical lenses to focus on them.

The unique educational purposes of classroom play, as opposed to children's play at

A playful classroom allows children to choose based on their needs and interests.

home or in their neighborhoods, requires specialized play theory. Context must be understood if we are to understand classroom play. For example, a contextual model including the play theories of Bateson (1955/2000, on the play frame) and Vygotsky (1978, on meaningful play pivots to create zones of proximal development) might call our attention to the play materials and what the children are playing with those materials. No matter what her beliefs are, the early childhood teacher will be selecting meaningful play materials (i.e., pivots) with which children will create meaningful pretend frames. Paley (2004) writes about her beliefs in the relationship between pretend play and literacy. She observes how children play with one another to sort out their developing ideas of character, plot, and personal relationships, all of which tie into creation of literature and appreciating it. The writings of Garvey (1993) and Corsaro (1985), among others, provide necessary dimensions that help us see communicative play interactions where children express character, plot, and other aspects of literacy. To understand more about the expressive qualities of play, post-Piagetian researchers, such as Fein (1975) and Watson and Jackowitz (1984), are informative; they describe the development of expressive transformations that children make with the pivots we provide them. Again, theoretical writing gives us the lenses with which we can see what is happening during play.

**Creating a Playful Classroom**   When we plan to include play in our classrooms, we bring our beliefs and reasons. Based on some of the values articulated earlier in this section, some of the reasons we might have for classroom play might be (1) learning to make choices and dealing with the ramifications of those choices and (2) communicating and expressing ideas. How can we know that children are having playful experiences related to these reasons? Teachers need to keep in mind (i.e., reflect on) the dimensions of their models, to assess, for example, whether children are making responsible choices and expressing themselves. Having such theory-based reflection helps focus on important valued beliefs and directs us to observe these features of play that are most relevant to our purposes (Hirsh-Pasek, Golinkoff, Berk, & Singer, 2009; Van Hoorn, Nourot, Scales, & Alward, 2011).

**Embracing Flexibility**   There are many possible differing configurations of elements that can vary from school to school and community to community. How might the model of play look different, for example, if literacy was the core belief underlying the educator's thinking? First, a different set of theories and research may guide our thinking. Second, the environment might look very different, with more books, play materials for words and writing, and props such as phone books, menus, and magazines in dramatic play centers. Also, we would expect that time would be spent exploring these materials, including guiding and questioning children about their use during play. If teachers observe that children are exploring certain meanings, like children's explorations of the idea of bridges, then there would seem to be reason to value children's interests and make sense of ways to expand their understandings. The same argument could be made when there is reason to consider emotions, spatial understanding, creativity, or any other phenomenon we might elevate to high value. Clearly, a teacher relates to play very differently when a core value is literacy, emotion, or spatial understanding, calling on different lenses for interpreting play (Christie, 1994; Christie et al., 1997; Cox, 1996; Dyson, 1997; Fein, 1989; Golbeck, 1995; Isenberg & Jalongo, 2006; Miller, Fernie, & Kantor, 1992; Paley, 2004; Reifel, 1984; Vygotsky, 1978).

A teacher must be willing to revisit her thinking about play, observe children carefully, relate observations to research-based constructs, and, when research does not tell us all it could about what occurs in classrooms, be willing to become an action researcher to expand the database (Chafel & Reifel, 1996; Paley, 2004; Williams, 1996). It is through reflection that the teacher has numerous ways to relate to play theory.

**Research Implications: Teacher Beliefs**   Beliefs about play are an important foundation for the theories we choose and our educational practices. In their study of teacher thinking about play, Bennett et al. (1997) found that when asked to reflect on their own classroom play practices, a range of teachers, from novice to experienced, had dynamic theories of what play is and what roles it might have in the classroom. Observing is important, and filtering observations through our own thinking, including beliefs and theory, is necessary. That filtering has its foundation in the beliefs we bring with us to our professional education (Klugman, 1996; Sherwood & Reifel, 2010).

Academic knowledge about play is a necessary basis for guiding such observations and interpretations. Seeing girls painting pumpkins at the easel (Reifel & Yeatman, 1993), for example, can be seen as a Piagetian construction play form (Piaget, 1962), a symbolic transformation by means of low-resemblance materials (Watson & Jackowitz, 1984), an associative social play form (Parten, 1932), a part of a Halloween script (Bretherton, 1989; Nelson & Seidman, 1984), or a meaningful pivot for generating pretense (Vygotsky, 1978). Can one play action be all these things? Yes. But many theories of play become our lenses for observation and reflection.

## ISSUES SHAPING PLAY THEORY

From our basic definition of theory to the survey of theories as they inform us of children's play, it is clear that ideas about play are central to our understanding of children and how children grow. Perspectives differ on these matters, but most practitioners, if not most researchers, are eclectic in the way they draw on theory to understand play. As we look at play more closely, to help us in our work with children and to further our research, we find that several issues may shape future views or rhetorics of play. The context of play is becoming a consideration for our theory of play. What makes play activities meaningful, for participants and observers, may be the context itself. Theories that recognize context are being developed (e.g., Fromberg, 1998; Fromberg & Bergen, 2006; Meckley, 1995; Reifel & Yeatman, 1993).

### Interdisciplinarity

Following on Sutton-Smith (1997, 1999) and his argument that play can be understood in terms of disciplinary rhetorics, it appears that multidisciplinary views of play may be necessary. Any one discipline may inadvertently remove a play activity from its context, thereby stripping it of its meaning. We may need to link theories or generate new theories to acknowledge the social, aesthetic, physical, meaningful, virtual qualities of play, as several researchers have done (e.g., Reifel, 1999, 2007; Sawyer, 1997; Scales, 1996).

### Teachers' Thinking About Play

Much of children's play is context specific, and as more play is taking place in settings that have been designed for play and supervised by adults, it may be that adult perceptions of play will become a growing area of play theory. How

---

**SUGGESTIONS FOR USING THEORY IN THE CLASSROOM**

1. Reflect on your own play experience, and remember that it differs from others'.
2. Relate your own thinking about play to academic theories you learn at school and in workshops.
3. Identify theory (or theories) that are appropriate for what you are observing: social, communicative, cognitive, cultural, or other aspects of development.
4. Identify theory (or theories) that will help plan classroom activities and assessment (observation, child products).
5. Remember that theory should help you think about and understand what you are seeing children do, and that no one theory will explain it all.

do participants begin to make sense of play (Klugman, 1996; Sherwood & Reifel, 2010)? How are the multiple perspectives of participants resolved, so that activity becomes and remains meaningful? Contextual theory, perhaps building on some of the theories presented earlier, is needed (Bennett et al., 1997; Kontos & Dunn, 1993; Stremmel, Fu, Patet, & Shah, 1995).

## SUMMARY

Theory helps us think about what we experience. It is a tool for understanding, and it can serve as a lens for viewing the world and making sense of it. Theories of children's play provide diverse lenses shaped by the many disciplines that have contributed to our knowledge of play. Those theories, and the beliefs and assumptions associated with them, form different rhetorics of play (Sutton-Smith, 1997, 1999). Much theory about children's play can be described in terms of a rhetoric of Progress, the assumption that play is a contributing factor to human development.

Any number of contemporary theories provide lenses for our understanding of play. Those theories may emphasize the nature or the nurture of play (i.e., the biological, cultural, or interactive influences of play on development). Psychoanalytic theory emphasizes the emotional, motivational aspects of play and how play allows children to express their feelings. Scholars such as Freud, Erikson, and Peller have refined psychoanalytic theoretical lenses. Bateson and Garvey have given us ways to view play in terms of communications. Children signal one another when they play, and those verbal and nonverbal signals provide theoretical lenses for understanding children's play talk and the pretend frames they create. Cognitive theorists, such as Piaget, Bruner, and Vygotsky, tell us that play links theoretically with our minds. Play may be a way of assimilating knowledge (as Piaget tells us), problem solving (in Bruner's sense), or creating knowledge within a zone of proximal development (in Vygotsky's terms). Depending on the cognitive lens we select, we can see different aspects of thinking in the developing child's play.

Play is often understood to be social. Theorists have provided a number of rational frameworks for understanding the social features of play. Play may be a setting for increasing social participation, as Parten tells us. Or it may be the setting for creation of social structures, where social status is established. Corsaro and social status researchers provide a number of lenses for seeing (and hearing) how play relationships benefit players differently, making some players popular and others less so. Others show us how play is a foundation for children's own culture. Other scholars see play as a creative activity, in which children find original solutions to their problems and explore novelty and the arts. Different theories are needed for all these views of play, and each view provides us with unique lenses for observing and understanding children's play.

Given the selection of contemporary play theories that exist, how do we decide which is true or even useful for us? As the play example presented in this chapter suggests, we can see many theoretical ideas about play in one play event. We argue that children's play theories may be more or less appropriate, depending on the role you will be taking with children. Parents may have one set of concerns about their children's play, but those concerns will probably differ from a play therapist's interests. We explored the special needs of teachers, as planners and observers of play, in this chapter. In the model of classroom play presented, competing values and beliefs help determine which theories will be most relevant for planning the environment, guiding children, and assessing their play. Different theoretical lenses are needed to understand children's play if a teacher is more interested in a particular aspect— social relationships, literacy, or problem solving. The challenge for the teacher is to become familiar with theories, to make sound decisions about classroom play. Teachers may also add to theory with their own research on play in their classrooms. The lenses we need to view play are changing as we create new contexts for play, as the composition of the players changes, and as new research becomes available to us.

## KEY TERMS

| | |
|---|---|
| Accommodation | Rhetoric |
| Assimilation | Scaffold |
| Chaos theory | Theory of mind |
| Pivot | Zone of proximal |
| Play frame |     development (ZPD) |
| Play talk | |

**STUDY QUESTIONS**

1. What is a theory? What is a theory of play?
2. What beliefs about play do you have? Which of those beliefs do you share with others?
3. What discipline are you studying? What rhetoric of play is most likely to be associated with that discipline?
4. In a small group, see whether you can identify examples of children's play that correspond with each of the seven rhetorics of play.
5. With a number of classmates, observe children's play. Try on a number of theoretical lenses as you observe. How does the play look different if you are wearing psychodynamic lenses versus cognitive lenses? (Try thinking of Bruner's ideas about play, and then consider Vygotsky's.) Cognitive lenses versus communication lenses? (Try thinking of Garvey's forms of talk, and then consider Corsaro's.)
6. Compare observations of children that you make with Parten's social participation lens to observations those made with Corsaro's social structure lens. What differences do they tell you about the children you see?
7. In a small group, list your beliefs and values about what is good for children. Identify play theories most closely associated with those beliefs and values. Why are some values higher on your list?
8. Which theory (or theories) seem most reasonable to you? How does that theory align with the beliefs you stated in question 2?
9. In a small group, identify your basic beliefs, values, and theories. What play objects and settings are necessary for your view of play to be put into practice?
10. What play have you seen that does not seem to be described by any of the theories presented in this chapter? What research might help you understand that play better?

## REFERENCES

Axline, V. (1969). *Play therapy.* New York: Ballantine.

Bateson, G. (2000). *Steps to an ecology of mind.* Chicago: University of Chicago Press. (Original work published 1955)

Bennett, N., Wood, L., & Rogers, S. (1997). *Teaching through play: Teachers' thinking and classroom practice.* Philadelphia: Open University Press.

Berk, L. E., & Winsler, A. (1995). *Scaffolding children's learning: Vygotsky and early childhood education.* Washington,

DC: National Association for the Education of Young Children.

Beyer, L., & Bloch, M. (1996). Theory: An analysis (Part 1). In J. Chafel & S. Reifel (Eds.), *Advances in early education and day care: Vol. 8. Theory and practice in early childhood teaching* (pp. 1–40). Greenwich, CT: JAI.

Biber, B. (1984). *Early education and psychological development.* New Haven, CT: Yale University Press.

Blaise, M. (2005). *Playing it straight: Uncovering gender discourses in the early childhood classroom.* New York: Routledge.

Bodrova, E. (2008). Make-believe play versus academic skills: A Vygotskian approach to today's dilemma of early childhood education. *European Early Childhood Education Research Journal, 16*(3), 357–369.

Bodrova, E., & Leong, D. J. (1996). *Tools of the mind: The Vygotskian approach to early childhood education.* Upper Saddle River, NJ: Merrill/Prentice Hall.

Bodrova, E., & Leong, D. J. (1998b). Development of dramatic play in young children and its effects on self-regulation: The Vygotskian approach. *Journal of Early Childhood Teacher Education, 20*, 115–124.

Bedrova, E., & Leong, D. J. (2006). Vygotskian perspectives on teaching and learning early literacy. In D. K. Dickinson & S. B. Neuman (Eds.), *Handbook of Early Literacy Research* (Vol. 2, 243–256). New York: Guilford.

Bedrova, E., & Leong, D. J. (2007). *Tools of the mind: The Vygotskian approach to early childhood education* (2nd Ed.). Upper Saddle River, NJ: Pearson/Merrill Prentice Hall.

Bredekamp, S., & Copple, C. (1997). *Developmentally appropriate practice in early childhood programs* (Rev. ed.). Washington, DC: National Association for the Education of Young Children.

Bretherton, I. (1989). Pretense: The form and function of make-believe play. *Developmental Review, 9*, 383–401.

Bruner, J. S. (1972). The nature and uses of immaturity. *American Psychologist, 27*, 686–708.

Bruner, J. S. (1990). *Acts of meaning.* Cambridge, MA: Harvard University Press.

Bruner, J. S., Jolly, A., & Sylva, K. (Eds.). (1976). *Play: Its role in development and evolution.* New York: Penguin.

Chafel, J., & Reifel, S. (Eds.). (1996). *Advances in early education and day care: Theory and practice in early childhood teaching* (Vol. 8). Greenwich, CT: JAI.

Chin, J. H., & Reifel, S. (2000). Maternal scaffolding of Taiwanese play: Qualitative patterns. In S. Reifel (Ed.), *Play and culture studies: Vol. 3. Play in and out of context.* Stamford, CT: Ablex.

Christie, J. (1994). Literacy play interventions: A review of empirical research. In S. Reifel (Ed.), *Advances in early education and day care* (Vol. 6, pp. 3–24). Greenwich, CT: JAI.

Christie, J., Enz, B., & Vukelich, C. (1997). *Teaching language and literacy: Preschool through the elementary grades.* New York: Addison-Wesley Educational.

Comenius, J. A. (1896). *The great didactic.* London: Black.

Copple, C., & Bredekamp, S. (Eds.). (2009). *Developmentally appropriate practice in early childhood programs serving children from birth through age 8* (3rd Ed.). Washington, DC: National Association for the Education of Young Children.

Corsaro, W. (1985). *Friendship and peer culture in the early years*. Norwood, NJ: Ablex.

Corsaro, W. A. (2003). *"We're friends, right?" Inside kids' culture*. Washington, DC: Joseph Henry Press.

Cox, T. (1996). Teachable moments: Socially constructed bridges. In S. Reifel (Ed.), *Advances in early education and day care: Vol. 8. Theory and practice in early childhood teaching* (pp. 187–200). Greenwich, CT: JAI.

Csikszentmihalyi, M. (1977). *Beyond boredom and anxiety*. San Francisco: Jossey-Bass.

Csikszentmihalyi, M. (1979). The concept of flow. In B. Sutton-Smith (Ed.), *Play and learning*. New York: Gardner.

Csikszentmihalyi, M. (1990). *Flow: The psychology of optimal experience*. New York: Harper & Row.

Csikszentmihalyi, M., & Csikszentmihalyi, I. S. (Eds.). (1995). *Optimal experience*. New York: Cambridge University Press.

Cuffaro, H. (1995). *Experimenting with the world: John Dewey and the early childhood classroom*. New York: Teachers College Press.

Darwin, C. (1859). *On the origin of species by means of natural selection, or the preservation of favoured races in the struggle for life*. London: Murray.

Dewey, J. (1916). *Democracy and education*. New York: Free Press.

Diamond, A., Barnett, S. W., Thomas, J., & Munro, S. (2007). Preschool program improves cognitive control. *Science, 318*(5855), 1387–1388.

Dyson, A. H. (1997). *Writing superheroes: Contemporary childhood, popular culture, and classroom literacy*. New York: Teachers College Press.

Elias, C., & Berk, L. (2002). Self-regulation in young children: Is there a role for sociodramatic play? *Early Childhood Research Quarterly, 17*, 216–238.

Elkind, D. (1968). Editor's introduction. In J. Piaget, *Six psychological studies* (pp. v–xviii). New York: Vintage.

Erikson, E. H. (1941). Further exploration in play construction: Three spatial variables in their relation to sex and anxiety. *Psychological Bulletin, 38*, 748.

Erikson, E. H. (1963). *Childhood and society* (Rev. ed.). New York: Norton.

Facer, K., Sutherland, R. J., Furling, R., & Furlong, J. (2001). What's the point of using computers? The development of young people's expertise in the home. *New Media & Society, 3*(2), 199–219.

Fein, G. G. (1975). A transformational analysis of pretending. *Developmental Psychology, 11*, 291–296.

Fein, G. G. (1989). Mind, meaning, and affect: Proposals for a theory of pretense. *Developmental Review, 9*, 345–363.

Fein, G. G. (1999). Commentary on Rhetorics Redux. In S. Reifel (Ed.), *Advances in early education and day care:*

*Vol. 10. Foundations, adult dynamics, teacher education and play* (pp. 189–200). Greenwich, CT: JAI.

Fein, G. G., & Kinney, P. (1994). He's a nice alligator: Observations on the affective organization of pretense. In A. Slade & D. P. Wolf (Eds.), *Children at play* (pp. 188–204). Boston: Oxford University Press.

Fine, G. A. (1983). *Shared fantasy: Role-playing games as social worlds*. Chicago: University of Chicago Press.

Freud, A. (1964). *The psychological treatment of children*. New York: Schocken.

Freud, S. (1909). Analysis of a phobia in a five-year-old boy. In *The standard edition of the complete psychological works of Sigmund Freud*. London: Hogarth.

Freud, S. (1918). *Totem and taboo*. New York: New Republic.

Freud, S. (1959). Beyond the pleasure principle. In J. Strachey (Ed.), *The standard edition of the complete psychological works of Sigmund Freud*. London: Institute of Psychoanalysis. (Original work published 1922)

Fromberg, D. P. (1998). Play issues in early childhood education. In C. Seefeldt (Ed.), *Continuing issues in early childhood education* (2nd ed., pp. 190–212). Upper Saddle River, NJ: Merrill/Prentice Hall.

Fromberg, D. P. (1999). A review of research on play. In C. Seefeldt & A. Galper (Eds.), *The early childhood curriculum: Current findings in theory and practice* (3rd ed., pp. 190–212). New York: Teachers College Press.

Fromberg, D.P., & Bergen, D. (2006). *Play from birth to twelve: Contexts, perspectives, and meanings* (2nd Ed.). New York: Routledge.

Gardner, H. (1983). *Frames of mind: The theory of multiple intelligences*. New York: Basic.

Gardner, H. (1993). *Multiple intelligences: The theory in practice*. New York: Basic.

Gardner, H. (1999). *Intelligence reframed: Multiple intelligences for the 21st century*. New York: Basic.

Gardner, H., & Hatch, T. (1989). Multiple intelligences go to school. *Educational Researcher, 18*, 4–10.

Garvey, C. (1993). *Play* (Enlarged ed.). Cambridge, MA: Harvard University Press.

Gee, J. P. (2003). *What video games have to teach us about learning and literacy*. New York: Palgrave/Macmillan.

Goffman, I. (1974). *Frame analysis: An essay on the organization of experience*. Cambridge, MA: Harvard University Press.

Golbeck, S. L. (1995). The social context and children's spatial representations: Recreating the world with blocks, drawings, and models. In S. Reifel (Ed.), *Advances in early education and day care* (Vol. 7, pp. 213–250). Greenwich, CT: JAI.

Goncu, A. (1993). Development of intersubjectivity in the dyadic play of preschoolers. *Early Childhood Research Quarterly, 8*, 99–116.

Gregory, K. M., Kim, A. S., & Whiren, A. (2003). The effect of verbal scaffolding on the complexity of preschool children's block constructions. In D. Lytle (Ed.), *Play and*

*Culture Studies: Vol. 5. Play and educational theory and practice* (pp. 117–133). Westport, CT: Praeger.

Gross, D. L. (2003). An introduction to research in psychology: Learning to observe children play. In D. Lytle (Ed.), *Play and Culture Studies: Vol. 5. Play and educational theory and practice* (pp. 33–41). Westport, CT: Praeger.

Guilford, J. P. (1957). Creative abilities in the arts. *Psychological Review, 64,* 110–118.

Haight, W. L., & Miller, P. J. (1993). *Pretending at home: Early development in a sociocultural context.* Albany: State University of New York Press.

Hirsh-Pasek, K., Golinkoff, R. M., Berk, L. E., & Singer, D. G. (2009). *A mandate for playful learning in preschool: Presenting the evidence.* New York: Oxford University Press.

Howes, C. (1987b). Social competence with peers in young children: Developmental sequences. *Developmental Review, 7,* 252–272.

Howes, C. (1992). *The collaborative construction of pretend: Social pretend play functions.* Albany: State University of New York Press.

Isenberg, J. P., & Jalongo, M. R. (2006). *Creative expression and play in early childhood* (4th ed.). Upper Saddle River, NJ: Prentice Hall.

Jones, E., & Cooper, R. M. (2006). *Playing to get smart.* New York: Teachers College Press.

Kelly-Byrne, D. (1989). *A child's play life: An ethnographic study.* New York: Teachers College Press.

Kemple, K. M. (1991). Preschool children's peer acceptance and social interaction. *Young Children, 40*(5), 47–54.

Klein, M. (1955). The psychoanalytic play technique. *American Journal of Orthopsychiatry, 25,* 223–237.

Klugman, E. (1996). The value of play as perceived by Wheelock College freshmen. In A. L. Phillips (Ed.), *Topics in early childhood education (Vol. 2.): Playing for keeps: Supporting young children's play* (pp. 13–30). St. Paul, MN: Redleaf Press.

Kontos, S., & Dunn, L. (1993). Caregiver practices and beliefs in child care varying in developmental appropriateness and quality. In S. Reifel (Ed.), *Advances in early education and day care: Vol. 5. Perspectives on developmentally appropriate practice* (pp. 53–74). Greenwich, CT: JAI.

Lillard, A. S. (1993). Pretend play skills and the child's theory of mind. *Child Development, 64,* 348–371.

Lillard, A. S. (1998a). Wanting to be it: Children's understanding of intentions underlying pretense. *Child Development, 69,* 979–991.

Lillard, A. S. (1998b). Playing with a theory of mind. In O. N. Saracho & B. Spodek (Eds.), *Multiple perspectives on play in early childhood* (pp. 11–33). Albany: State University of New York.

Lillard, A. S. (2000). Pretending, understanding pretense, and understanding minds. In S. Reifel (Ed.), *Play and culture studies: Vol. 3. Play in and out of context.* Stamford, CT: Ablex.

Lillard, A. S. (2001). Pretend play as Twin Earth. *Developmental Review, 21,* 1–33.

Lillard, A. S., & Witherington, D. S. (2004). Mothers' behavioral modifications during pretense snacks and their possible signal value for toddlers. *Developmental Psychology, 40,* 95–113.

Lin, S.-H., & Reifel, S. (1999). Context and meanings in Taiwanese kindergarten play. In S. Reifel (Ed.), *Play and culture studies* (Vol. 2, pp. 151–176). Stamford, CT: Ablex.

Lobman, C. (2003a). The bugs are coming: Improvisation and early childhood teaching. *Young Children, 58*(3), 18–23.

Lobman, C. (2003b). What should we create today? Improvisational teaching in early childhood classrooms. *International Journal for Early Years Education, 23*(2), 133–145.

Lobman, C. (2005). Improvisation: Postmodern play for early childhood teachers. In S. Ryan & S. Grieshaber (Eds.), *Practical transformations and transformational practices: Globalization, postmodernism, and early childhood education: Vol. 14: Advances in early education and day care* (pp. 243–272). New York: Elsevier/JAI.

Lobman, C. (2006). Improvisation: An analytic tool for examining teacher-child interactions in the early childhood classroom. *Early Childhood Research Quarterly, 21*(4), 455–470.

Lobman, C., & Lundquist, M. (2007). *Unscripted learning: Using improv activities across the K-8 curriculum.* New York: Teachers College Press.

Mead, G. H. (1934). *Mind, self and society.* Chicago: University of Chicago Press.

Meckley, A. (1995). Studying children's social play through a child cultural approach: Roles, rules, and shared knowledge. In S. Reifel (Ed.), *Advances in early education and day care* (Vol. 7, pp. 179–211). Greenwich, CT: JAI.

Miller, S. M., Fernie, D., & Kantor, R. (1992). Distinctive literacies in different preschool contexts. *Play & Culture, 5,* 107–119.

Moore, S. G. (1967). Correlates of peer acceptance in nursery school children. In W. W. Hartup & N. L. Smothergill (Eds.), *The young child: Reviews of research* (Vol. 1, pp. 229–247). Washington, DC: National Association for the Education of Young Children.

Nelson, K. (1989). *Narratives from the crib.* Cambridge, MA: Harvard University Press.

Nelson, K., & Seidman, S. (1984). Playing with scripts. In I. Bretherton (Ed.), *Symbolic play: The development of social understanding* (pp. 45–72). New York: Academic.

Nicholich, L. M. (1977). Beyond sensorimotor intelligence: Assessment of symbolic maturity through analysis of pretend play. *Merrill-Palmer Quarterly, 23,* 89–99.

Opie, I. (1993). *The people in the playground.* New York: Oxford University Press.

Opie, I., & Opie, P. (1959). *The lore and language of schoolchildren.* New York: Oxford University Press.

Opie, I., & Opie, P. (1969). *Children's games in street and playground.* New York: Oxford University Press.

Opie, I., & Opie, P. (1997). *Children's games with things.* New York: Oxford University Press.

Paley, V. G. (1981). *Wally's stories*. Cambridge, MA: Harvard University Press.

Paley, V. G. (1992). *You can't say you can't play*. Cambridge, MA: Harvard University Press.

Paley, V. G. (2004). *A child's work: The importance of fantasy play*. Chicago: University of Chicago Press.

Parten, M. (1932). Social participation among preschool children. *Journal of Abnormal and Social Psychology, 27*, 243–262.

Parten, M. (1933). Social play among preschool children. *Journal of Abnormal & Social Psychology, 28*, 136–147.

Peller, L. (1954). Libidinal phases, ego development, and play. *Psychoanalytic Study of the Child, 9*, 178–198.

Piaget, J. (1962). *Play, drama and imitation in childhood*. New York: Norton.

Piaget, J. (1966). *Psychology of intelligence*. Totowa, NJ: Littlefield, Adams.

Piaget, J. (1970). *Structuralism*. New York: Basic.

Reifel, S. (1984). Block construction: Children's developmental landmarks in representation of space. *Young Children, 40*(1), 61–67.

Reifel, S. (1986). Play in the elementary school cafeteria. In B. Mergen (Ed.), *Cultural dimensions of play, games, and sport* (pp. 29–36). West Point, NY: Leisure Press.

Reifel, S. (1995). Preschool play: Some roots for literacy. In B. Immroth & V. Ash-Geisler (Eds.), *Achieving school readiness: Public libraries and national education goal number one* (pp. 10–30). Chicago: American Library Association.

Reifel, S. (1999). Play research and the early childhood profession. In S. Reifel (Ed.), *Advances in early education and day care: Vol. 10. Foundations, adult dynamics, teacher education and play* (pp. 201–211). Stamford, CT: JAI.

Reifel, S. (2007). Hermeneutic text analysis of play: Exploring meaningful early childhood classroom events. In J. A. Hatch (Ed.), *Early childhood qualitative research*. (pp. 25–42). New York: Routledge.

Reifel, S., Hoke, P., Pape, D., & Wisneski, D. (2004). From context to texts: DAP hermeneutics, and reading classroom play. In S. Reifel & M. Brown (Eds.), *Advances in early education and day care* (Vol. 13). Oxford, UK: JAI/Elsevier Science.

Reifel, S., & Sutterby J. (2009). Play theory and practice in contemporary classrooms. In S. Feeney, A. Galper, & C. Seefeldt (Eds.), *Continuing Issues in Early Childhood Education* (3rd ed., pp. 238–257). Upper Saddle River, NJ: Prentice Hall/Merrill.

Reifel, S., & Yeatman, J. (1993). From category to context: Reconsidering classroom play. *Early Childhood Research Quarterly, 8*, 347–367.

Reynolds, G., & Jones, E. (1997). *Master players: Learning from children at play*. New York: Teachers College Press.

Richert, R. A., & Lillard, A. S. (2004). Observers' proficiency at identifying pretense based on behavioral cues. *Cognitive Development, 19*, 223–240.

Rivkin, M. (1999). Rhetorics redux. In S. Reifel (Ed.), *Advances in early education and day care: Vol. 10. Foundations, adult dynamics, teacher education and play* (pp. 163–168). Stamford, CT: JAI.

Rubin, K. H., Bukowski, W., & Parker, J. G. (1998). Peer interactions, relationships, and groups. In N. Eisenberg (Ed.), *Handbook of child psychology: Social, emotional, and personality* (Vol. 3, 5th ed., pp. 619–700). New York: Wiley.

Rubin, K. H., Fein, G. G., & Vandenberg, B. (1983). In P. H. Mussen (Ed.), *Handbook of child psychology: Vol. 7. Socialization, personality, and social development* (4th ed., pp. 693–774). New York: Wiley.

Samaras, A. P. (1999). Implications of the rhetoric of play as progress for preservice and inservice teachers. In S. Reifel (Ed.), *Advances in early education and day care: Vol. 10. Foundations, adult dynamics, teacher education and play* (pp. 177–188). Stamford, CT: JAI.

Sawyer, K. (1997). *Pretend play as improvisation: Conversation in the preschool classroom*. Hillsdale, NJ: Erlbaum.

Sawyer, R. K. (2003). Levels of analysis in pretend play discourse: Metacommunication in conversational routines. In D. Lytle (Ed.), *Play and educational theory and practice: Vol. 5. Play and Culture Studies* (pp. 137–157). Westport, CT: Praeger.

Scales, B. (1996). Researching the hidden curriculum. In J. Chafel & S. Reifel (Ed.), S. Reifel (Series Ed.) *Advances in early education and day care: Vol. 8. Theory and practice in early childhood teaching* (pp. 237–259). Greenwich, CT: JAI.

Scales, B., & Cook-Gumperz, J. (1993). Gender in narrative and play: A view from the frontier. In S. Reifel (Ed.), *Advances in early education and day care: Volume 5. Perspectives on developmentally appropriate practice* (pp. 167–195). Greenwich, CT: JAI.

Schiller, F. (1965). *On the aesthetic education of man*. New York: Ungar. (Original work published 1795)

Schwartzman, H. (1978). *Transformations: The anthropology of children's play*. New York: Plenum.

Sharon, T., & Woolley, J. D. (2004). Do monsters dream? Young children's understanding of the fantasy/reality distinction. *British Journal of Developmental Psychology, 22*, 293–310.

Sherwood, S.A.S., & Reifel, S. (2010). The multiple meanings of play: Exploring preservice teachers' beliefs about a central element of early childhood education. *Journal of Early Childhood Teacher Education, 31*, 322-343.

Singer, D., & Singer, J. L. (1977). *Partners in play*. New York: Random House.

Singer, D., & Singer, J. L. (1992). *The house of make-believe*. Cambridge, MA: Harvard University Press.

Smilansky, S. (1968). *The effects of sociodramatic play on disadvantaged preschool children*. New York: Wiley.

Smilansky, S. (1990). Sociodramatic play: Its relevance to behavior and achievement in school. In E. Klugman & S. Smilansky (Eds.), *Children's play and learning: Perspectives and policy implications*. New York: Teachers College Press.

Smolucha, L., & Smolucha, F. (1998). The social origins of mind: Post-Piagetian perspectives on pretend play.

In O. N. Saracho & B. Spodek (Eds.), *Multiple perspectives on play in early childhood* (pp. 34–58). Albany: State University of New York.

Spariosu, M. (1989). *Dionysus reborn: Play and the aesthetic dimension in modern philosophical and scientific discourse.* Ithaca, NY: Cornell University Press.

Stremmel, A., Fu, V., Patet, P., & Shah, H. (1995). Images of teaching: Prospective early childhood teachers' constructions of the teacher-learning process of young children. In S. Reifel (Ed.), *Advances in early education and day care,* (Vol. 7, pp. 253–270). Greenwich, CT: JAI.

Suddendorf, T. (2000). A developmental link between the production of gestural representation and understanding of mental states. In S. Reifel (Ed.), *Play and culture studies: Vol. 3. Play in and out of context.* Stamford, CT: Ablex.

Sutton-Smith, B. (1966). Piaget on play: A critique. *Psychological Review, 73,* 104–110.

Sutton-Smith, B. (1984). Introduction. In B. Sutton-Smith & D. Kelly-Byrne (Eds.), *The masks of play.* New York: Leisure Press.

Sutton-Smith, B. (1997). *The ambiguity of play.* Cambridge, MA: Harvard University Press.

Sutton-Smith, B. (1999). The rhetorics of adult and child play theories. In S. Reifel (Ed.), *Advances in early education and day care: Vol. 10. Foundations, adult dynamics, teacher education and play* (pp. 149–162). Stamford, CT: JAI.

Sutton-Smith, B., Gerstmyer, J., & Meckley, A. (1988). Playfighting as folkplay amongst preschool children. *Western Folklore, 47,* 161–176.

Takhvar, M., & Smith, P. K. (1990). A review and critique of Smilansky's classification scheme and the "nested hierarchy" of play categories. *Journal of Research in Childhood Education, 4,* 112–122.

Taylor, M., Carlson, S. M., & Gerow, L. (2000). Imaginary companions: Characteristics and correlates. In S. Reifel (Ed.), *Play and culture studies: Vol. 3. Play in and out of context.* Stamford, CT: Ablex.

VanderVen, K. (1998). Play, Proteus, and paradox: Education for a chaotic and supersymmetric world. In D. Fromberg & D. Bergen (Eds.), *Play from birth to twelve and beyond: Contexts, perspectives, and meanings* (pp. 119–132). New York: Garland.

VanderVen, K. (2004). Beyond fun and games towards a meaningful theory of play: Can a hermeneutic perspective contribute? In S. Reifel & M. Brown (Eds.), *Social contexts of early education, and reconceptualizing play (II): Advances in early education and day care* (Vol. 13, pp. 165–205). Oxford, UK: JAI/Elsevier Science.

Van Hoorn, J., Scales, B., Nourot, P. M., & Alward, K. R. (2007). *Play at the center of the curriculum* (3rd ed.). Upper Saddle River, NJ: Merrill/Prentice Hall.

Van Hoorn, J. M., Nourot, P. M., Scales, B. R., & Alward, K. R. (2011). *Play at the center of the curriculum* (5th Ed.). Upper Saddle River, NJ: Allyn & Bacon/Merrill.

Verenikina, I., Harris, P., & Lysaght, P. (2003). Child's play: Computer games, theories of play and children's development. *Proceedings of the international federation for information processing working group 3.5 open conference on Young children and learning technologies* (Vol. 34, pp. 99–106). Sydney, AU: ACM International.

Vygotsky, L. S. (1962). *Thought and language.* Cambridge, MA: MIT Press.

Vygotsky, L. S. (1966). Play and its role in the mental development of the child. *Soviet Psychology, 12*(6), 62–76.

Vygotsky, L. S. (1978). *Mind in society: The development of higher psychological processes.* Cambridge, MA: Harvard University Press.

Vygotsky, L. S. (1984). *Thought and language.* Cambridge, MA: MIT Press.

Waldrop, M. M. (1992). *Complexity: The emerging science at the edge of order and chaos.* New York: Simon & Schuster.

Watson, M. W., & Fischer, K. W. (1977). A developmental sequence of agent use in late infancy. *Child Development, 48,* 828–836.

Watson, M. W., & Jackowitz, E. R. (1984). Agents and recipient objects in the development of early symbolic play. *Child Development, 55,* 1091–1097.

Whitebread, D. (2010). Play, metacognition and self-regulation. In P. Broadhead, J. Howard & E. Woods (Eds.), *Play and learning in the early years* (pp. 161–176). Thousand Oaks, CA: Sage.

Williams, L. (1996). Does practice lead theory? Teachers' constructs about teaching: Bottom-up perspectives. In S. Reifel (Ed.), *Advances in early education and day care: Vol. 8. Theory and practice in early childhood teaching* (pp. 153–184). Greenwich, CT: JAI.

Winnecott, D. (1971). *Playing and reality.* New York: Basic.

Woolley, J. D. (1995). The fictional mind: Young children's understanding of imagination, pretense, and dreams. *Developmental Review, 15,* 172–211.

Woolley, J. D., Boerger, E. A., & Markman, A. B. (2004). A visit from the Candy Witch: Factors influencing young children's belief in a novel fantastical being. *Developmental Science, 7*(4), 456–468.

Woolley, J. D., & Cox, V. (2007). Development of beliefs about storybook reality. *Developmental Science, 10,* 681–693.

Woolley, J. D., & Tullos, A. (2008). Imagination and fantasy. In M. Haith, & J. Benson (Eds.) *Encyclopedia of infant and early childhood development* (pp. 117–127). New York: Elsevier Press.

Woolley, J. D., & Wellman, H. M. (1990). Young children's understanding of realities, nonrealities, and appearances. *Child Development, 61,* 946–961.

Yeatman, J., & Reifel, S. (1997). Conflict and power in classroom play. *International Journal of Early Childhood Education, 2,* 77–93.

# 3 Neuroscience and Play Deprivation

*. . . the received dogma in neuroscience for a century . . . held that the brain takes its shape for life during our childhood years and does not change its structure thereafter. . . . but that assumption has joined countless others in the trash heap of scientific "givens" that the march of research has forced us to discard.*

(Goleman, 2007, p. xi)

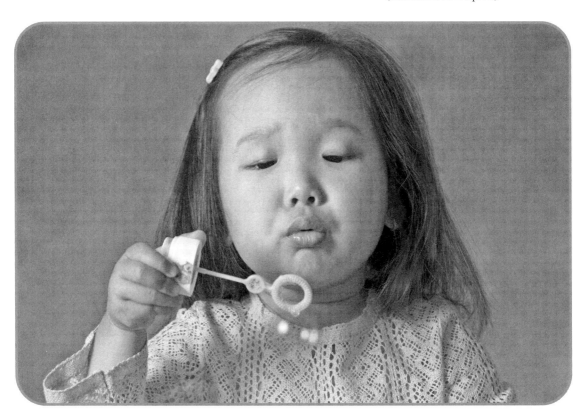

*Virtually every brain system that we know about . . . is importantly shaped by experience. This is what I mean by neuroplasticity.*

(Neville, 2007, p. 75)

*Physical exercise [including free play] acts like a natural wonder drug for the brain. It improves the heart's ability to pump blood . . . burns fat . . . enhances overall brain function . . . encourages the growth of new brain cells [structures] . . . enhances cognitive ability . . . helps alleviate depression . . . calms anxiety . . . eases symptoms of ADD . . . helps prevent disease and dementia . . .*

(Amen, 2010, pp. 66, 67, 109–115)

*There is no evidence . . . that particular educational programs, methods, or techniques are effective for brain development. The evidence is very clear. Play promotes development—and in a number of domains. Based on the research evidence, a new equation is in order: PLAY = LEARNING.*

(Hirsh-Pasek & Golinkoff, 2003, pp. 33, 208)

Research into the functioning of the most complex living organ—the human brain—is resulting in revolutionary insights affecting the fields of child development, education, medicine, and many other disciplines responsible for the health, development and well-being of children. The findings are so compelling and far-reaching that people of all ages and persuasions will be affected, so adults who work with children will need to become brain literate. The author of this chapter taught third grade children the content of this chapter with much success in terms of their interest, retention of content, and ability to relate to practical issues of health, education, and fitness. Future educational programs will be increasingly shaped by brain science.

The conclusions and recommendations herein tap only the surface of exploding knowledge from neuroscience and are in a state of flux as rapidly expanding research with both animal and human subjects emerges. Despite rapid change in understanding, there is sufficient evidence to conclude that research on the human brain will be one of the most influential bases for creating future educational policy for people of all ages.

*"We have learned more about the brain in the past decade than we did in the previous two hundred years. . . . it's currently possible for neuroscientist to observe the development of the brain in real time and without any need for either speculation or dogmatism.*
(Ratey, 2009, pp. 5–6)

Rapidly expanding research on the brain is showing that play plays a far more important role in health, development, and fitness than previously assumed, even by scientists. Since we do not deliberately subject human subjects to health threatening experiments, animal subjects are initially used for much of the research on the complex, invisible brain. *The Playful Brain: Venturing to the Limits of Neuro-science,* by Sergio and Vivien Pellis (2009), is a comprehensive overview of contemporary animal research related to play. Naturally occurring conditions among humans allow complementary research. Although research from both animal and human studies is far from definitive, the amazing findings are sufficiently compelling to warrant increasing study in laboratories around the world.

Ethical concerns about conducting studies with human subjects leaves scientists to speculate about connections between effects of play deprivation in humans and animals. However, the linkages are gradually becoming clearer. Play deprivation in animals is helping inform us about play-deprived humans. We know that too many children are not getting sufficient amounts of free, spontaneous, active, outdoor play, and we know that this contributes to declines in health, fitness, development, and overall well-being. Play deprivation . . . "may be one cause of the current epidemic of hyperkinetic kids with inadequate control over their own impulses" (Panksepp, 2010, p. 271). Research on play and brain may eventually illuminate the brain mechanisms of human play. We must use the vast amount of data collected from animal play to guide our thinking about human play, for some parallels are already evident. For example, Panksepp notes that play-deprived children appear to be more likely to show symptoms of attention deficit hyperactivity disorder. These kids are quieted by such drugs as Ritalin, and the playfulness of rats is dramatically reduced by giving them such drugs.

The Dana Alliance's *2010 Progress Report on Brain Research* (Bloom, et al., 2010) is a fascinating compilation of top scientists research on the genetics of psychiatric disorders with implications for people of all ages. Drawing conclusions for child development and education is a subject of controversy, with some calling for educational programs based on brain research and others declaring it as far too early for such optimistic action. Brain research to date has not demonstrated conclusively that specific educational programs are warranted, but general guidelines are emerging for education, child development, and other disciplines.

Compelling and optimistic evidence is pointing the way to healthier brains and, consequently, healthier bodies, improved cognition, and improved fitness and reduction of disease. In this chapter, we examine research in historical perspective, focusing on brain and play, and suggest implications for early child development subject to modification with time and further study. This chapter illustrates the nature and scope of neuroscience research, explains how children are being deprived of rich, healthy play and play environments, identifies the consequences of play deprivation, and provides practical steps for implementing brain research and amelioration of the consequences of play deprivation. Deprivation of spontaneous, creative play, whatever the cause, may result in stunted or aberrant development, learning, and behavior, but normal, healthy play builds brains, enhances learning, and supports healthy development.

##  NEUROSCIENCE, PLAY, AND CHILD DEVELOPMENT

Neuroscience draws from the disciplines of psychology, neurology, biology, and physiology and is sometimes called *brain science*. With the aid of high-tech brain-imaging technology, neuroscientists around the world are making unprecedented inroads into understanding the role of experience in human development. As early as 1996, the United States had more than 3,000 brain researchers with research resources of over $1 billion, and Japan had drafted a plan to invest $18 billion in brain science over the next two decades and about $1 billion in a state-of-the-art nuclear magnetic resonance (NMR) center for structural biology (Barker, 1996). Because of this unprecedented interest in neuroscience, the 1990s were called the "decade of the brain." The first decade of the 21st century witnessed growth in brain research far eclipsing that of the 1990's and opened up remarkable insights into the nature of the brain and its role in shaping humans and animals throughout the life span.

Neuroscientists are seeing both planned and unanticipated results that are relevant to education and child development. Play, the seemingly frivolous, unimportant behavior with no apparent purpose, has earned new respect as neuroscientists and others see that it is indeed serious business and perhaps equally important as other basic drives like sleep, sex, and food. Indeed, one neuroscientist suggests the existence of a "dedicated circuitry in the brain, equivalent to extensively studied fear and love circuits" (S. Johnson, 2004, p. 125). Yet other researchers suggest that in primates the amount of brain growth between birth and maturity reflects the amount of play in which each species engages (Bekoff, 2001; A. Smith, 2005). In the scientific community, if not in social institutions, play and the people who study it are no longer seen as strange and immature.

## Emergence of Neuroscience

Research in neuroscience is confirming theoretical positions held for several decades that have already been implemented in the most forward early childhood programs. Studies of the role of the human brain in child development gained considerable momentum during the 1960s. A number of scholars concluded from both animal and human studies that infancy and early childhood were optimum periods for development and that the brain is most plastic during these periods and highly influenced by environmental stimulation (Hunt, 1961; Frost, 1968, 1975; Hess & Bear, 1968). Animals (dogs) raised

in isolation from birth were unable to avoid pain (Melzack & Scott, 1957), acquire normal social interactions (Melzack & Thompson, 1956), or perform well on problem-solving tasks (Thompson & Heron, 1954). Similarly, children raised in orphanages with minimal ongoing stimulation suffered emotional deprivation resulting in apathetic, immature behavior during adolescence (Goldfarb, 1953), and in cases of most severe deprivation, 2- to 4-year-olds could not sit alone or walk alone (Dennis, 1960).

In his classic work *Intelligence and Experience,* J. McVicker Hunt, as early as 1961, garnered extensive evidence to conclude that the concept of fixed intelligence was no longer tenable. He viewed intelligence as problem-solving capacity based on hierarchical organization of symbolic representations and information-processing strategies of the brain, derived to a considerable degree from past experiences. He believed that the child's intelligence quotient (IQ) may vary as much as 20 to 40 points as a result of environmental stimulation or lack thereof.

Although Piaget's work has been questioned regarding its authenticity and currency, the serious scholar must acknowledge his brilliant insights into cognition, play, early development, and, in a more remote sense, brain science. Analysis of Piaget's (1945/1951, 1936/1952) work on cognitive structures (e.g., neurons and synapses), which he called schemata, reveals a number of principles relevant to this context. First, the formation of cognitive or brain structures depends on opportunities for use of action sequences. Second, there is continuous development through use and stimulation. Third, accommodation by the child depends on a proper match between existing mental structures and objects and events encountered. Fourth, the greater the variety of situations to which the child must accommodate his cognitive structures, the more differentiated they become, and the more rapid his rate of intellectual development. Fifth, the rate of development appears to be the result of a variety of stimulation during infancy and early childhood.

Research of the 1960s and earlier established the early years as optimum times for intervention and supported a plastic or changeable view as opposed to a fixed view of the brain and cognitive development. The great psychologist, William James, introduced the term "plasticity" in 1890, holding that "organic matter" (brain structures) appeared to be endowed with an extraordinary degree of *plasticity* (*malleable or changeable through experience*). Later, observational studies were sufficiently compelling to influence the development of a range of federally sponsored early childhood intervention programs such as Operation Head Start and the High/Scope Project, both enduring programs demonstrating long-term effects of early intervention in school success, discussed in a later chapter.

Early in the 21st century, there is general agreement among neuroscientists that plasticity is characteristic of virtually all brain systems, including those for language, auditory, visual, and attention, and they are shaped by experience (Begley, 2007). Some appear to be plastic throughout life while others are plastic during limited periods. Plasticity is characteristic of early childhood, but research now shows that it can extend well beyond childhood, if only in a relatively diminished capacity (Swanson, 2010, 80).

Children are born with many more neurons than they will have as adults since density of synapses increase in areas that are used—music, sports, foreign language—and pruned in unused areas The critical process is use it or lose it, but new experience can regenerate declining abilities. Neurogenesis or synapsis generation is a normal process for the developing brain but too many or too few synapses are implicated in several syndromes, including autism (Lesley, 2010). As knowledge about the changeable brain is developed and refined, educators can better create programs and experiences that meet the personal needs and challenges of their students. A crucial key appears to be providing many rich experiences within the present interests and abilities of individual learners.

There is little argument that free, spontaneous, unstructured play is essential for a healthy childhood and a competent adulthood (Frost & Brown, 2008; Brown, 2009). Learning the timing of plasticity, taking into account individual differences, appears to be an important factor for applications to education.

The plasticity of the infant brain (infant plasticity) does not appear to be an advantage in all situations. In 1974, the President's Committee on Mental Retardation sponsored the National Conference on Early Intervention with High Risk Infants and Young Children at the University of North Carolina in Chapel Hill (Frost, 1975; Tjossem, 1976). Here, early plasticity theories were documented with physical evidence. A relatively small amount of damage to the infant brain was found to result in a reduction in volume of the entire hemisphere by more than 30%; similar damage to the adult brain resulted in a reduction of only 20% to 30% (Isaacson, 1954).

Albert Einstein College of Medicine physicians presented evidence at the North Carolina conference that there can be too much stimulation—or too little. Lipton (1974) concluded that no stimulation leads to no elaboration of neurological structure and processes, whereas pushing brain maturation (overstimulation) leads to overdevelopment and later deficits in behavior. In other words, either understimulation or overstimulation seems to result in damage to the child. However, the range of normal stimulation conducive to healthy growth is broad. The implications of such findings are now being examined critically, using brain-imaging technology that provides visible, concrete, quantifiable evidence that is clearer and more convincing than earlier evidence.

Too little play among animals is associated with overreaction to novel encounters with the social and nonsocial world, and too much play is associated with lack of responsiveness to the hazards of the world. The benefits of stress early in life seem to occur with moderate stress. Early play fighting or rough and tumble play, for example, appears to be needed for later competence but such activity is best in moderation (Pellis & Pellis, 2009, 86–87).

The plasticity (commonly called "neuroplasticity") of both young and older brains should not be underestimated. Plasticity requires a dynamically engaged brain, with all neurons firing. "To put it bluntly, if you are only using 10 percent of your brain (as some scholars have claimed), then you are in a vegetative state so close to death that you should hope that your relatives will pull out the plug of the life support machine" (Geake, 2004, p. 71). The brain produces certain chemicals that help protect neurons, including some that allow parts of the brain to take over functions of areas damaged by illness or injury. Reducing calories, selecting certain foods and Vitamin D can aid in neuro-protection and brain cell survival. Deficiency of vitamin D, a vitamin found naturally in very few foods but available through exposure to sunlight and food supplements, is linked to a range of health problems including rickets, cancer, weak bones and muscles, high blood pressure, congestive heart failure, depression, and later memory loss or dementia (Edwards, 2010, 85–88).

## High-Tech Brain Imaging

Sylwester (1995) and Thatcher, Lyon, Rumsey, and Krasnegor (1996) described brain-imaging technology in detail. The technology focuses on three elements of brain organization and operation: chemical composition, electrical transmission and magnetic fields, and distribution of blood through the brain. Even more advanced technology is constantly under development.

Two types of imaging technology are used to study chemical composition: computerized axial tomography (CT scan) and magnetic resonance imaging (MRI). These create graphic three-dimensional images of the anatomy of the brain (or other body parts). The CT scan uses multiple X-rays that respond to the density of areas scanned—dark gray for denser elements (e.g., bones, tumors, and dense tissue) and lighter shades of gray for soft tissue. The MRI provides an image of the chemical composition of the brain by focusing on chemical differences in soft tissue. Fast MRI allows researchers to observe brain activity on television during a subject's cognitive activity.

Positron emission tomography (PET) traces sequential changes in brain energy by monitoring chemical functions, including blood flow, through the brain and other body organs (Chugani, 1994; Sylwester, 1995). This noninvasive technique allows the tracing of brain energy as parts of the brain are activated. Advanced imaging tools and techniques are constantly under development and promise even deeper insight into brain function and implications for child development.

## Organization of the Brain

The function of the brain is based on activities of several billion brain cells, or neurons, and trillions of connections, or synapses, that transmit (receive and send) electrochemical signals (messages). Each single neuron has an axon that sends electrochemical signals to other neurons

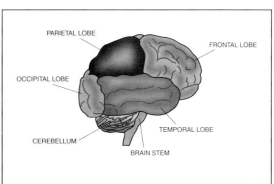

**FRONTAL LOBE**
- Emotions
- Expressive language
- Word associations
- Memory for habits and motor activities
- Problem solving
- Reasoning

**PARIETAL LOBE**
- Integration of different senses
- Location for visual attention
- Location for touch perception
- Manipulation of objects

**OCCIPITAL LOBE**
- Vision

**CEREBELLUM**
- Balance and equilibrium
- Some memory for reflex motor acts

**BRAIN STEM**
- Regulates body functions (e.g., breathing, heart rate, swallowing)
- Reflexes to seeing and hearing (e.g., startle response)
- Controls autonomic nervous system (e.g., sweating, blood pressure, digestion, internal temperature)
- Affects level of alertness

**TEMPORAL LOBE**
- Hearing
- Speech
- Memory acquisition
- Categorization of objects

and contains many small hairlike structures, or dendrites, that receive the signals. When the axon of one neuron connects with the dendrite of another neuron, a synapse is formed. Electrochemical transmission across these structures requires neurotransmitters (chemical catalysts) such as dopamine, serotonin, or endorphins. Neural development, then, is (includes) the proliferation or growth of these key brain elements. For elaboration, see Begley (1996, 2007, 2008), Healy (1997), Shore (1997), Thompson (1997), Hirsh-Pasek and Golinkoff (2003), and Bloom, et al., 2010).

Before an infant is born, considerably more neurons and synapses are developed than the child will need, but most of the surplus neurons have disappeared by the time of birth. As neurons expand, the brain grows in volume and weight. Although the number of synapses increases at a remarkable rate during the first 3 years, the number of neurons remains stable (Shore, 1997). Normal early development is so rapid that the PET scan of a 1-year-old more closely resembles an adult's brain than a newborn's. By age 2, the number of synapses reaches adult levels. By age 3, the child's brain has about 1 quadrillion (1,000 trillion) synapses, or twice the number of an adult's brain, and is two-and-a-half times more active (Shore, 1997). The density of synapses remains supersaturated through the first decade of life, followed by a decline in density. By late adolescence, about half of the brain's synapses have been discarded.

This discarding of synapses is a lifelong process of refining, or pruning, to eliminate those that are not used in favor of those that are created and used through everyday experiences. The early experiences of children play a critical role in determining the wiring of the brain and, it is hypothesized, the range and quality of the child's intellectual abilities. As the child grows, a complex system of synapses or neural pathways is formed. The pathways that are repeatedly activated or used are protected and retained into adulthood.

## Effects of Deprivation on Brain Development

When a child is born, her brain is a mass of neurons, ready to be wired or programmed through use and experience. Some hardwiring is already present to produce breathing and reflexes, regulate body temperature, and control heartbeat. Billions of other neurons are ready to be connected to other neurons, but they must be used for connections to be made and circuitry to be formed. Unused neurons do not survive; the potential synapses or connections are not formed, and the child may never reach her potential. Brain development is truly a use it or lose it process. Although misuse or lack of use may result in loss, individuals can still regain brain functions or create new neurons through experience and exercise. Under therapeutic conditions, many at-risk children manage to thrive. Early experiences determine which neurons are to be used and which are to die and, consequently, whether the child will be brilliant or dull, confident or fearful, articulate or tongue-tied (Begley, 1996).

Much of the violence in the United States may be related to the lack of appropriate attachments of young children to adults. Inappropriate attachments associated with neglect and traumatic stress result in overdevelopment of the brainstem and midbrain, areas that are primitive, hardwired, and not very susceptible to external influence (Perry, 1996). The long-term research of Stroufe and his colleagues (Renken, Egeland, Marvinney, Mangelsdorf, & Stroufe, 1989) and Brown (2009) confirms the link between attachment and violence. Children with primary caregivers who are emotionally unavailable or abusive during the early years are often more aggressive in later childhood and adolescence. Even lingering depression of mothers has adverse effects on young children, particularly those 6 to 18 months old, when mothers fail to provide cognitive stimulation that promotes healthy brain growth (Ounce of Prevention Fund, 1996).

Genetics and experience work together to form the child's intelligence. Early brain development is programmed by nature, which programs the "experience-expectant" behaviors, such as seeing, speaking and certain motor abilities. "Experience-dependent" behaviors, such as using computers, reading, and playing complex games, depend on our unique cultural experiences (Hirsh-Pasek & Golinkoff, 2003). The effects of sensory and motor experience on brain development begin before birth. The neurons that develop in utero begin driving the infant's limbs as early as 7 weeks of gestation (Shore, 1997). Brain development is adversely influenced by environmental influences on the mother—drugs, stress, malnutrition, illness, trauma, abuse—that are passed on to the fetus. Trauma and abuse in the fetus and during infancy continue to have a devastating effect on brain development throughout childhood.

Neglect by parents, social deprivation, stressful living conditions, and lack of appropriate stimulation jeopardize early brain development and may result in immature social and emotional behavior, impulsivity, violence, and dramatic reduction in capacity for later learning. These negative influences are often associated with living in poverty (Ramey & Ramey, 1996) and living in institutions such as orphanages (Frank, Klass, Earls, & Eisenberg, 1996). Poverty exerts strong negative influences on the health, learning, and development of children. Linked to poor diet, lack of medical care, confinement to their indoor cyber play and lack of opportunities common to middle- and upper-income families, the poor suffer the lowest educational levels and the highest rates of obesity and the poorest fitness levels. This pattern is seen across entire geographical regions. Allostatic load, an index of chronic stress, grows more severe with time children are exposed to poverty, resulting in increasing levels of memory deficit in young adults (Evans & Schamberg, 2009). Poverty is associated with altered neurotransmitter activity and suppression of neurogenesis and volume reduction in the hippocampus and prefrontal cortex (Evans & Chamberg, 2009).

In the orphanages of Romania, thousands of children live under cruel and debilitating conditions (ABC News, 1996; Begley, 2008). These conditions resulted from one dictator's plan to double the Romanian population. He outlawed birth control and demanded that women have children, resulting in thousands being placed in institutions. The children were reared under conditions of almost total neglect—some penned in cages and others confined to cribs with little or no stimulation from caretakers. Between 1960 and 1996, more than 3,000 were adopted by Americans.

Many (not all) of these adopted children, particularly those confined to orphanages over extended periods, failed to develop emotionally and intellectually. Some were so severely damaged that one mother described hers as the "child from hell." Some never learned to talk, read, accept love, or even feel pain. Some were violent. After several years of pain and frustration, a support group of American parents of these orphans organized and sought specialized assistance. Scientists at the Denver Children's Hospital conducted PET scans and learned that the children's brains were remarkably different from those of normal children. Although measurable progress resulted from therapy, including play therapy, they never developed like normal children. For many, the therapy came too late. The window of opportunity is open during infancy but appears to narrow for some with each passing year and to close for some very damaged children between ages 8 and 10. By age six, a majority still had major persistent deficits perhaps resulting from biological programming or neural damage from institutional deprivation (Begley, 2007). Both positive and extreme negative experiences in early childhood have their respective consequences.

An interview between the author and the adoptive parents of a Romanian orphan in 2003 revealed that their child (now school age) was developing at a relatively normal rate. They attributed this to their intensive interaction with the child from the beginning and the use of specialized help as needed. Their experience with other families of such children led them to believe that not all parents were able, sufficiently skilled, or inclined to provide such intensive interaction.

## Neuroscience and Play: Connections

What are the linkages between brain development and play during the early childhood years? Let's begin with a few fundamental principles that have considerable support from both neuroscientists and play scholars.

First, *all healthy young mammals play.* Beginning shortly after birth, using built-in neural mechanisms, infant animals and humans engage in their first playful games. Animal infants tend to initiate the early games. Early frivolity is encouraged and mediated by adults, usually the parents or other primary caregivers. Because the human infant's period of helplessness and motor immaturity is relatively long, parents of human infants "must both initiate and give structure and direction to play. . . . That structure acts as a scaffolding for development" (Fagen in Angier, 1992, p. B8).

Second, *the range and complexity of play quickly increase as neurons start hardwiring connections at a remarkable rate.* Simply put, play programs neural structures, and the resulting, increasingly complex, neural structures influence ever more complex play. "An animal plays most vigorously at precisely the time when its brain cells are frenetically forming synaptic connections, creating a dense array of neural links that can pass on electrochemical messages from one neighborhood of the brain to the next" (Angier, 1992, p. B8).

Vigorous, frenetic, play is common in well equipped, challenging playgrounds for young children. The writer observed 2- to 12-year-old children playing over several years on three playgrounds of increasing complexity (Frost, et al., 2004). Levels of play activity were high for all age groups but that of the younger children was more varied, involved more play options, created higher levels of excitement, and, in

general, was more active and frenetic. Observing toddlers during outdoor play in challenging environments is perhaps the closest the typical observer will come to seeing brain development in action. Watch their movements, see their selections of play material, their relatively primitive interactions with other toddlers, their endless trial-and-error diversions, the range of "aha," or discovery, moments, the "out of control" facial expressions, the joy and frustration, the early problem solving breakthroughs, the flights of imagination—an ever-changing symphony of neural construction!

Third, *the early games and frivolity of animals and humans equip them for the skills they will need in later life.* Angier (1992) and Brownlee (1997) describe these games. Games are tailor-made to fit the very different tasks animals and humans will face. Animals practice those skills that assist survival in a dangerous world. Prey animals play escape games, such as mock flight, and carnivores play stalking, pouncing, and capturing games. In so doing, they learn flexibility, inventiveness, and versatility (Brown, 1994). Human infants and young children practice motor, language, and negotiation skills. Across cultures, boys and girls play differently. Boys are more likely to engage in rough-and-tumble and organized games of physical contact and war using miniature war figures and toy weapons. Girls tend to engage in such games as chase, tag, jump rope, and hopscotch and to rehearse motherhood and housekeeping roles with dolls and utensils. Both boys and girls engage in socially and culturally mediated task analysis, problem solving, negotiation, and discourse during their play (Frost, 1992; see Chapter 7).

Fourth, *play is essential for healthy development.* Early childhood experiences exert a dramatic, precise impact on the wiring of the neural circuits, and the formation and selecting out (pruning) of synapses coincides with the emergence of various developmental abilities (Begley, 1997, 2007; Pellis & Pellis, 2009). During the first years of life, playful activity makes a positive difference in brain development and subsequent human functioning. Excessive direct instruction, seclusion, deprivation, and abuse have negative consequences (Nash, 1997; Frost, 2010). Play deprivation resulting from deletion of recess in schools, increased time with computer games and television, playground safety standards, high-stakes testing, and lawsuits are interrelated factors leading to negative developmental consequences for American children (Frost, 2003, 2006a; Frost & Jacobs, 1995; Frost & Brown, 2008; Brown, 2009; Frost, 2010). "Severe maltreatment at an early age can create an enduring negative effect on a child's developing brain" (Society for Neuroscience, 2003).

Knowledge of the brain and implications for health, fitness, development, and well-being have reached sufficient sophistication and lucidity that teachers and students, elementary through university levels can, and should learn about this invisible, complex organ that shapes every individual. The seemingly innocuous, frivolous, inherent play of childhood is deeply involved in healthy learning and continuous development. For example, physical activity, including play, is essential for the development of the prefrontal cortex, located at the front of the brain. The prefrontal cortex is responsible for *executive function,* those qualities that make us most human. It serves as the CEO of many brain functions including planning, sequencing, rehearsing, evaluating, decision making, working memory, and understanding (Ratey, 2008), all having important implications for early childhood curriculum (Meltzer, 2010). Such knowledge is already helping shape educational programs for young children and remains a subject of extensive research (see Meltzer, 2007).

## Neuroscience and Cognitive Development

Brain development and cognitive achievements of very young children are well disguised in the seemingly innocuous cloak of play (Sylwester,

As children explore and manipulate objects, concepts or preconcepts fundamental to later learning are formed.

1995). Essentially, only neuroscientists see physical evidence (brain scans) that reveal the relative consequences of environmental stimulation or neglect. The casual observer does not grasp the profound relationships between achievement and the endless games that the very young play—the patty-cake, peekaboo, dance, and singsong rhythms that are in reality storehouses or machines for programming the brain for language, art, music, math, science, kinesthetic, and interpersonal abilities and intelligence.

Many key brain areas are formed and dedicated, before birth, to general problem-solving areas. Although these systems are interrelated, a distinct brain area is dedicated to processing each function. Seven distinct forms or systems of intelligence exist: linguistic, musical, logical-mathematical, spatial, bodily-kinesthetic, intrapersonal, and interpersonal (Gardner, 1993). An individual can perform exceptionally in one system and poorly in another, depending on complex interactions between genetics and experience. Gardner (1999) added an eighth intelligence, naturalist intelligence, the ability to recognize animals, plants, and other aspects of the natural environment. Some early childhood programs, such as the Montessori approach, emphasize such skills.

The thinking encouraged in classrooms requires the interaction of numerous modules across both the left and right portions of the brain. Rather than attempting to isolate modular thinking in students' brains, teachers should focus on doing the opposite—promoting integrated thinking, acknowledging individual differences, and focusing on a spiral curriculum where important concepts are met repeatedly in different contexts (Geake, 2004). Such practices reflect favorably on the scaffolding and zone of proximal development views of Vygotsky.

The implications of multiple intelligences and neural connectivity are profound. "A major thrust of research in cognitive neuroscience in the next decade will be the mapping of functional connectivity" (Geake, 2004, p. 70). The implications for child rearing and teaching hold much promise for changing the parenting and education. Should we focus on optimizing strengths or remediating weaknesses? Should we value social, cooperative behavior or solitary, competitive behavior? What are the proper roles of parents, teachers, and social institutions in optimizing intelligence? All those responsible for children perform their roles across the developmental domain.

## Neuroscience and Language Development

Language learning begins long before babies are able to speak first words. As early as 6 months, infants develop language magnets that attune their ears to the sounds of their native language (Kuhl in Education Commission of the States, 1996); they have learned the basic phonetic elements of their native language (Blakeslee, 1997). As early as 11 months, infants are losing the ability to distinguish between phonetic sounds not spoken in their presence (Long, 1997).

A growing body of evidence indicates that languages should be taught informally through direct experiences in preschool or in families before entry into school. Vocabulary development is strongly correlated with parents talking with their babies. Through reciprocal talk (parents talking, babies listening and making primitive reactions), parents strengthen the neural pathways essential to language development.

Some researchers at the 1997 White House Conference on Early Child Development concluded that "the number of words an infant hears each day is the single most important predictor of later intelligence, school success and social competence" (Blakeslee, 1997, p. A-14). However, brain research supports earlier studies concluding that there can be too much stimulation or too little stimulation. Merely filling the child with information or scheduling too many activities may lead to overstimulation and/or result in boredom and lack of receptivity. Live language in a warm, emotional context with a caring adult, rather than endless, mindless television, video games, or drilling for high-stakes testing boosts language development (Frost, 2003). Information received in an emotional context is more powerful in stimulating neural development than information alone. Even the tone of voice makes a difference. Perhaps the strongest positive emotion of all, once food and bodily needs are met, is vigorous social engagement (Johnson, 2004). Ideal contexts are rough-and-tumble play, chasing, pretend play, and creating with water, dirt, and other natural materials.

Language appears very early during play experiences. Extensive historical research (Frost, 2010) and extensive program research (Hirsh-Pasek, et al., 2009) show that a whole child approach emphasizing active learning through play and process over product stimulates language development and other forms of development. Children benefit from both free, or unstructured, play, and directed or structured play, but interactions between adults and children during play should be sensitive to children's individual needs.

## Neuroscience and Social Development

Before the availability of high-tech brain-imaging research, the importance of young children's socialization with adults and older children was highlighted by the work of Vygotsky (1966/1976), who proposed that play, and consequently the higher mental functions, evolve from interactions between the child and her caregiver and socialization with older children. Interaction or socialization with others is essential for healthy development. "[T]he single best childhood predictor of adult adaptation is not IQ, not school grades, and not classroom behavior, but rather the adequacy with which the child gets along with other children" (Hartup, 1992).

Children and animals learn social skills through socialization. Animals learn to interpret signals and actions of other animals and to respond appropriately (Brownlee, 1997). Through negotiation during play, they develop mental and emotional mastery and learn cooperation and leadership skills. Children's imaginative or make-believe play is a powerful medium for socialization, allowing them to simplify a complicated world and make otherwise complex and frightening events manageable and comprehensible. Such play also assists the development of cooperation, sharing, negotiating, and problem-solving skills and helps the child get along in an increasingly complex world.

## Neuroscience and Emotional Development

New brain-imaging technologies "have made visible for the first time in human history what has always been a source of deep mystery: exactly how this intricate mass of cells (brain) operates while we think and feel, imagine and dream. . . . This flood of neurobiological data lets us understand . . . the brain's centers for emotion" (Goleman, 1995, p. xi). Scientists propose an "astonishing hypothesis—the idea that our thoughts, sensations, joys and aches consist entirely of physiological activity in the tissues of the brain" (Pinker, 2007, p. 62). Parents and educators need to be aware that emotional intelligence or curriculum lies just below the surface and those emotions deserve attention. Tipping the scale from mild anxiety into stress carries predictable behavioral responses that are bad for learning (Smith, 2005, 259).

The basic wiring that controls emotions develops before birth. After birth, parents play a significant role by mirroring back the child's emotions—his squeals of delight—with hugs and supporting words. Such experiences reinforce the brain's chemical and electrical signals and "wire the brain's calm down circuit" (Begley, 1996, p. 58). Stress also has its effects. Extreme or continuous trauma floods the brain's circuits with neurochemicals such as cortisol, and the more frequently they are stimulated, the easier it is for the circuits to react. Indeed, repeated stress changes the structure of the brain (Begley, 1997). Merely thinking about traumatic experiences or seeing signs related to an incident (e.g., abuse by a parent, a natural disaster) can trigger the flood of neurochemicals and condition the brain to a pattern of high alert.

Texas children who experienced a devastating tornado that killed many relatives and friends and destroyed dozens of homes in 1997 still slept in their clothes, without blankets, a year later so they could be ready to seek cover. Their drawings and paintings still reflected those harrowing experiences, and the mere memory or reminder (clouds and wind) of a storm induced fear. Calm, soothing touch and language by an adult calms these emotions and appears to allow emotion and reason to connect. Recovery efforts for human-created disasters such as genocide in Africa and natural disasters such as the Asian tsunami of 2004, Hurricane Katrina in 2005, and the Haiti earthquakes in 2010 are revealing contexts for seeing firsthand the healing powers of play (see Chapter 10 and Frost, 2005a).

Play is the language of children. Whereas adults talk out their fears and traumatic experiences, children play theirs out. They may lack the words or the cognitive abilities to understand what has happened to them or to resolve their conflicts, but play has therapeutic qualities that allows children to play out their conflicts and to deal with them. "Play gives concrete form and expression to children's inner world. . . . A major function of play is the changing of what may be unmanageable in reality to manageable situations through symbolic representation" (Landreth, 1991, pp. 9–10).

## Neuroscience and Physical Development

At birth, infants are awkward and have little control over their limbs. They cannot sit, stand, crawl, or walk, and they rely on primitive reflexes such as sucking and grasping. These reflexes are rapidly replaced by increasingly complex neural pathways as various regions of the brain develop to accommodate different abilities. Intense sensory and physical stimulation is critical to the growth of synapses in the cerebellum, a region that regulates coordination and muscle control (Angier, 1992). The development of fine- and gross-motor skills develop independently, but both require the formation and myelination (nerve cell coating that insulates against loss of electrical signals) of synapses. The neural circuits that connect the motor cortex of the brain and the muscles are strengthened by repeated motor activities.

If the child's motor neurons are not trained early for a particular athletic skill, there is little chance that the child will be outstanding in that skill. "No world champion skater or golfer took up the sport after 12" (Underwood & Plagens, 1997, p. 15). Tiger Woods, for example, started playing with a golf club at 10 months. Adult neurons do not appear to be plastic enough to allow the required wiring. However, related factors are influential in achieving high levels of motor ability, such as toughness, concentration,

motivation, and ambition. Practicing related skills also appears to carry over to developing new skills. The great football player Walter Payton was in ballet classes as a child; skills learned there encompassing strength, flexibility, and grace may have helped him become a record-holding running back. "Sometimes it is not the obvious experiences that sculpt performance" (Underwood & Plagens, 1997, p. 15). The bottom line is that adults must provide experiences that program the neural structures for the skills to be achieved, and they must do so in a caring, supportive context.

A range of studies demonstrate the influence of physical activity on academic performance. These include enhanced brain function, increased energy levels, improved self-esteem, and relief from boredom. Positive links were reported between physical activity and academic achievement, including mathematics and reading. Regular physical activity can improve cognitive function and increase levels of chemicals in the brain responsible for maintaining neuron health. An intriguing title of one of these papers is "Brain May Also Pump Up from Workout." Scheur and Mitchell (2003). The positive effects of physical activity coupled with nutritious food are seen from infancy through the life span. Restricting caloric intake and losing weight can result in improved memory among the elderly (Witte, et al., 2009). The functional elements of the brain do not act alone, nor do they affect exclusively specific elements. Rather, the brain can be seen as a remarkable ecosystem affecting our every thought, action, and ability.

*When we exercise, particularly if the exercise requires complex motor movement, we're also exercising the areas of the brain involved in the full suite of cognitive functions. We're causing the brain to fire signals along the same network of cells, which solidifies their connections.* (Ratey, 2008, 41)

A wide range of interconnected brain areas are called into action when we play and when we learn. For example, the hippocampus doesn't do much without oversight from the prefrontal cortex. The prefrontal cortex is the boss or the CEO of the brain areas (Ratey, 2008), and it is the chief arbitrator of "executive function," a group of essential mental tasks seen by many leading child development scholars as fundamental organizing tasks for children's child development and educational programs (Hirsh-Pasek, et al., 2009). For many years, leading child development programs have embedded academic activities into play activities, and the evidence for this practice continues to accumulate. These tasks include planning, setting goals, organizing, attending to tasks, self-discipline, self-regulation, making decisions, solving problems, judging, predicting, and a host of other important thinking skills. The prefrontal cortex is among the last brain regions to mature, generally achieving a degree of maturity beyond the teen years. Consequently, the reason that even teens have difficulties making sound decisions, for example, rejecting drugs and making bad decisions when driving cars, are subject to explanation through brain science.

## NEUROSCIENCE AND EDUCATIONAL PRACTICE: BRIDGING THE GAP

Whenever scientific breakthroughs occur, critics, quite appropriately, question their validity and warn against overgeneralization and speculation. Bruer (1997), for example, proposed, "Neuroscience has discovered a great deal about neurons and synapses, but not nearly enough to guide educational practice" (p. 15). Scientists at the Bridging the Gap between Neuroscience and Education workshop, sponsored by the Education Commission of the States (1996), urged the educators in attendance "not to attempt to apply new research findings until further studies confirm and expand them"

(p. vi). Such cautions should, of course, be carefully considered. At that time, it was far too early to reshape American education around brain science, but, 15 years later, scientists were beginning to make preliminary, cautious recommendations for basing elements of child rearing and education on brain science. However, the cautions of the past are still relevant: "The danger with much of the brain-based education literature is that it becomes exceedingly difficult to separate the science from the speculation" (Bruer, 1999, p. 650).

Although researchers themselves are often reluctant to draw implications for the appropriate roles of adults in stimulating healthy development, the collective historical evidence about effects of experience on brain development and behavior is sufficiently compelling to warrant the formulation of tentative implications for child development. Open-mindedness and attention to future research are essential. Just as medicine is now beginning to reap practical benefits from neuroscience, professionals should also study brain research for practical applications in child development and education. (For elaboration see Hirsh-Pasek, et al., 2009). The Committee on Developments in the Science of Learning, sponsored by the National Research Council and the U.S. Department of Education and composed of prominent scientists, conducted a 2-year evaluation (Bransford, Brown, & Cocking, 1999) of new developments in the science of learning and reached the following conclusions:

1. The organization of the brain depends on experience.

2. Instruction and learning are very important for brain development.

3. Different parts of the brain are ready for learning at different times.

4. Development is a biologically driven unfolding process and also an active process of deriving information from experience.

5. Some experiences have the most effect on development during sensitive periods, but

others affect the brain over an extended period.

6. The issue of which research findings have implications for education is still very much open. For example, which experiences and learnings are tied to critical periods, and for which is timing less critical? What dimensions of development and learning are genetically wired, and which are formed through experience?

This landmark document was followed by a second (Donovan, Bransford, & Pellegrino, 1999) that synthesized research on how people learn to draw implications for classroom practice. In this document, Wolfe and Brandt (2000) held that "educators should help direct the search to better understand how the brain learns" (p. 28). Bergen and Coscia (2001) reviewed an extensive array of research on brain and childhood education to conclude that many current educational practices likely have some effect on brain structures and functions, but none of these practices are validated by current brain research. The present chapter does not focus on the classroom practice issue but rather to the implications of neuroscience for early development.

The Society for Neuroscience (2009) is an international organization comprising scientists and educators working together to explore the science of brain function and inform teachers at all levels—early childhood through university—how to teach based on brain science. Their *Neuroscience Core Concepts: The Essential Principles of Neuroscience* is broad in scope, but certain elements are basic for those who work directly with children. For more information, see www.sfn.org/public_education. For example:

1. The brain (nervous system) controls and responds to body function and directs behavior.

2. The structure of the brain is determined by genes and environment throughout the life span. Both structure and function are constantly are constantly changing.

3. Cognition/intelligence results from using all the senses, emotions, instincts, and memories, resulting in language, exploration, problem solving, social competence, ability to predict and plan, and much more.

4. Experience changes the brain. Mental and physical activity challenges and shapes the brain and maintains healthy function and structure. Extreme, abuse, injury, and trauma damage the brain.

Brain research confirms that no two human minds are alike, and a century of research in child development confirms that the role of adults in children's learning should be rooted in understanding, respecting, and providing for individual differences in children. Research across the behavioral sciences makes a strong case against the rigid curriculum standards arising from failed programs such as No Child Left Behind (NCLB) and the equally rigid, one size fits all, developmentally inappropriate standards for K-12 proposed in early 2010 by the National Governor's Association and the Council of Chief State School Officers in 2010 as part of the Race to the Top program intended to replace NCLB.

Neuroscientists are only beginning to learn which experiences wire the brain in which ways, so drawing conclusions from brain research for education and child development is not exact. However, some general conclusions emerging from laboratories across the nation are gaining support. The resulting patterns of intervention are remarkably consistent with what effective parents have always known and done. The following conclusions address parents but may be considered by all adults responsible for the care of children.

## BRAIN RESEARCH AND CHILD DEVELOPMENT

What follows is a summary of some of the conclusions we feel are reasonable to make between brain research and child development:

- Start early. The proper starting time for stimulating healthy brain development is conception, involving two healthy adults. If you wait until your child is in preschool or Head Start to begin, you have already missed the most formative period for some aspects of brain development.

- Spend lots of time playing with children. They need secure attachment or bonding with their parents. Disavow the misguided contention that a little so-called quality time compensates for extended parental absence. Healthy brain development does not take vacations or keep a calendar. There is no downtime. Both dads and moms are needed.

- Be positive, playful, warm, and nurturing. Activity is essential, but there is good activity and bad activity. Good activity supports healthy brain development. Bad activity programs unhealthy brain development, resulting in ability deficits and behavioral aberrations.

- Pay attention to children's social and moral development. Even simple games carry moral overtones such as taking turns, sharing objects, and listening to others. Meeting children's physical and emotional needs does not mean catering to their every whim. Parents, caretakers, and teachers should have clear moral expectations from the beginning, and these should be modeled and enforced. Ensure that toddlers have opportunities to play with other toddlers. This is important for developing social skills—friendships, sharing, negotiating, problem solving, concern for others—and morals. Some moral bases may be hardwired at birth, but patterns of brain chemistry, emerging in early childhood, appear to influence later moral behavior.

    Scientists who study neurotheology are now seeing connections between spirituality and brain structures and activity. "Spiritual experiences are so consistent across cultures, across time and across faiths that it suggests a common core that is likely a reflection of structures and processes in the human brain" (Begley, 2001, p. 53).

- Challenge children, but not beyond their range of abilities. Adults' expectations should be difficult but doable. Infants and toddlers are far more capable than commonly realized, and adults, especially parents, are far more important in their development than generally acknowledged, even by leading professional groups.

- Hug children. Touching has health and therapeutic results. Touch, caress, pat, and cuddle infants. Gently rock them back and forth. People never outgrow their need for physical contact, including hugs. As children develop, engage in gentle wrestling, tugging, tossing, and chasing games. Such activities are essential in programming motor abilities and emotional behavior and in reinforcing related thinking abilities. Adults should be cautious not to shake infants' or toddlers' heads vigorously, for shaken-baby syndrome may include brain damage, developmental delays, or other injury.

- Talk to children. Respond to infants' cooing and babbling. Use "parentese" (baby talk) with babies. Expand your vocabulary as children develop. Listen to children. Early language must be personal—between child and adult—and related to ongoing activity to best stimulate neural development. For positive results, language needs to be used in a positive emotional context.

- Introduce music, art, and dance early. Play soft, soothing music. Introduce children to singsong games during infancy. Introduce musical instruments. Make simple art materials and simple tools available. Cultivate art through simple manipulative activities, and expand to art appreciation activities.

- Substitute play, art, music, family outings, and field trips for television and cyber play. Control television viewing, social networking, and video games. Select programs wisely. Do not use television as a babysitter, as a substitute for family interaction at home, or as a time filler at the child-care center or school. Play, art, and music produce long-term changes in neural structures that influence thinking and reasoning abilities.

- Make homes, child-care centers, and schools drug free. Model drug-free behavior for children. Drugs—including tobacco, alcohol, and misuse of prescription drugs—can have a devastating effect on children's development, *in utero* and later.

- Provide blocks, beads, sand, water, simple tools, pots and pans, dress-up clothes, and other simple and raw materials at age-appropriate times. No child-care setting need be devoid of stimulating materials, for the very young child does not discriminate between simple, inexpensive, natural materials and toys and manufactured, expensive ones. Free, cheap, and natural are good enough, assuming the toys are safe.

- Protect young children from extreme stress and trauma such as scolding, loud persistent noise, isolation, and physical and emotional abuse. The brain is acutely vulnerable to stress and trauma, and the consequences of extended exposure on brain development may be permanent.

- Don't overstimulate children with too many toys, too much meaningless talk, too much noise, or too much activity. Provide plenty of time and interesting, safe places and materials to explore. Special toys or high-tech materials are unlikely to be more effective than talking with the child and making simple toys available. Very young children don't need flash card drills, incessant babbling by a parent, or constant noise to get adequate stimulation

for development (Hirsh-Pasek & Golinkoff, 2003). Indeed, overstimulation and trauma appear to have negative effects on brain development (Lipton, 1974; Shore, 1997; Pellis & Pellis, 2009).

- Read to children, sing with children, and play simple games with children. Do this every day.

- Extend your interest in healthy development to wherever children are present. Ensure that your children have good nutrition and outdoor physical activity at home, child-care centers, and schools. What people eat and how much they exercise affects brain function, ultimately compromising health, learning, and memory. Read food labels with children at school and home and teach them to avoid high calorie, fat, salt, and carbohydrate foods and select unprocessed foods. Visit school cafeterias and work with administrators to ensure that healthy food is served. Good food enhances brains; bad food damages brains. Ensure that children engage in at least an hour each day in outdoor, active play, including free, spontaneous play and semi-structured play for older children.

- Be wary of high-stakes testing leading to overemphasis of test skills over developmental based curricula. Don't accept the growing pattern of deleting recess, playgrounds, physical education, art, and music (the so-called frills) from the school day. Consider another school for your child if such conditions cannot be changed.

- If a child has a birth defect or developmental disorder or has suffered a disabling injury, don't give up. The human brain has an amazing capacity to compensate and, to some degree, regenerate, given proper care and therapy. This has been demonstrated in studies of badly damaged Romanian orphans adopted by American parents.

- Children are primed by biology to acquire certain basic skills of language and thinking that are intricately wired in early childhood. This wiring is the basis for later complex, technical problem solving (e.g., mathematics, computer sciences) that will depend on strong cultural and social support for realization.

- American children spend 6 to 8 hours a day using electronic devices. The Internet is remaking us into its own image. Adults must ensure that children have rich experiences away from the Internet. "We are becoming ever more adept at scanning and skimming, but what we are losing is our capacity for concentration, contemplation, and reflection" (Carr, 2010).

- Certain enduring principles of child development date back through history to some of the world's preeminent thinkers and gained additional respectability through the research of the past century—focusing on the whole child, respecting individual differences in rates and levels of learning, and providing hands-on experiences in a wide range of indoor and outdoor contexts.

- Research on the brain is resulting in new insights and suggestions for teachers and parents at an unprecedented rate. Review new books by prominent scholars such as Ratey, 2008; Pellis & Pellis, 2009; Amen, 2010; and Carr, 2010.

Conventional wisdom says that boys and girls are hardwired differently and are destined to learn and behave differently, but genetics is only the beginning. The brains of infants are very malleable, so the small gender differences at birth are amplified by parents, peers, and teachers who reinforce gender stereotypes. Children themselves play to their modest strengths (Eliot, 2009). Social factors account for much more of the boy–girl differences in behavior than traditionally assumed. Expecting and promoting rough-and-tumble play for boys and imaginative house play with dolls for girls, are examples of stereotyped patterns that children soon learn to respect.

Adults should not give up on children who develop slowly or on children with disabilities. So-called critical periods are not bound hard and fast to a specific time period for the development of many skills. For example, contrary to the notion that the brain is fully developed before puberty, maturation continues into the teens and 20s. The frontal lobes of the brain, responsible for numerous functions (executive functions) such as planning, judgment, and emotional regulation, grow rapidly around puberty, followed by pruning into the 20s (Begley, 2000). In other words, just as there is a period of rapid neural development during infancy, followed by pruning, such phenomena also exist during the preteen and teen years. Some scholars propose that "critical periods" should more aptly be called "sensitive periods." Indeed, researchers are now seeing indications that the capacity to learn may increase into the later years of life.

Different regions of the brain develop on different timetables. The neural network isn't completely installed in most people until they are in their early 20s. Among the last parts to mature are those that make sound judgments and calm unruly emotions (Brownlee, 1999, p. 46). Immature brain development of adolescents appears to help explain why they are vulnerable to risk taking, traumatic experiences, and unhealthy influences (Crenson, 2001, p. A20). The prefrontal cortex, not yet fully developed, is responsible for goal and priority setting, planning, organizing, and impulse inhibition. Possible consequences of immature brain development include a number of profound statistics: Accidents are the leading cause of death among adolescents. They are the group most likely to become crime victims. The large majority of smokers start as teens, and a quarter of all people with HIV contract it during their teen years.

Irresponsibility of adolescents is not the full explanation for their getting themselves into easily avoidable trouble. Regions of the teen brain involved in decision making, behavior control, and impulsivity continue maturing well into their 20s (Sabbagh, 2006). Adults can call on other parts of the brain to support the maturing prefrontal cortex responsible for planning and voluntary behavior, but teen brains are not sufficiently mature to do this. Studies of teens in various cultures (Schlegel & Barry, 1991) indicate that the behavior of American teens is different from in preindustrial cultures. American teens are seen as tumultuous, antisocial behavior is absent in over half the 186 cultures studied by Schlegel and Barry. Sixty percent of the cultures did not have a word for adolescence, for teens spent much of their time with adults, rather than being segregated with their peers as seen in American culture. Environment changes the brain and may underlie the turmoil and troubled behavior of American teens. When adolescents are isolated from adults, they learn from and influence each other. Such findings may have implications for child rearing at various stages.

Lest you attach too much importance to the role of environment on brain maturation and child or adolescent behavior, consider the compelling studies of brain structure and development by Shaw and colleagues (2006). Their 17-year study of 307 children, ages 5 to 19 years, indicates that brain development of highly intelligent children is different from that of more average ability children (measured by IQ tests). The prefrontal cortex thickens more rapidly for highly intelligent children during childhood and has a much longer period of development. Shaw and his colleagues conclude that such studies point to the need for studies in gene variants but also conclude that "the determinants of intelligence will likely prove to be a complex mix of nature and nature."

## EFFECTS OF PLAY DEPRIVATION ON CHILD DEVELOPMENT

Evidence of the effects of play deprivation on child development continues to mount (Brown, 1994, 2009; Frost, 1999, 2010; Frost & Jacobs,

1995). In 1966, a sniper, Charles Whitman, barricaded himself on top of the University of Texas's 27-story tower and shot 44 people.

Governor Connolly retained Stuart Brown, M.D., psychiatrist, and researcher, to study Whitman's childhood in order to help determine motive. Whitman had a history of violence and brutality at the hands of his father and did not engage in normal play as a child (Brown, 1994, 2009). He secluded himself on the playground and was allowed no time to play at home. Following this investigation, Brown helped conduct a study of 26 convicted Texas murderers. He found that 90% showed either the absence of childhood play or abnormal play such as bullying, sadism, cruelty to animals, or extreme teasing. In yet another study of mostly drunk drivers who killed themselves or others while driving, Brown found that 75% had play abnormalities.

The growing view that spontaneous play has declined or is disappearing is frequently debated among proponents of play (Frost, 2006a; Marano, 2004). Some writers contend that modern activities such as sports at an early age and television viewing are displacing spontaneous play (Devereux, 1976; Eifermann, 1971; Postman, 1982). Indeed, Pee Wee, Bantam, and Little League sports (football, soccer, and baseball, respectively) are increasingly involving children as young as 5 years old, and in some instances even younger. Children spend more time watching television than they spend in classrooms (Medrich, Roizen, Rubin, & Buckley, 1982). Presently, the growing popularity of video games and Internet activities, ranging from violent games to chat rooms to adult-style gambling, has directed more of children's time away from spontaneous, traditional play. Yet another factor implicated in the apparent decline of play is the loss of places to play. Once-rural landscapes and wilderness areas are now covered with buildings and populated with vehicles, ever smaller backyards are devoted to adult interests (pools, tennis courts, barbecue areas), and high-rise apartments offer few play places (see Louv, 2005; Nabhan & Trimble, 1994).

Children are not merely losing opportunities for spontaneous play but are being deprived of the richest forms of play, that is, play that transcends and is intense and characterized by risk, obsession, complete absorption, ecstasy, and heightened mental states—transcendental play (Frost, 2003, 2004b, 2010).

> "My earliest recollection of transcendental play dates to the primary school with a small stream running out of the nearby woods and across the schoolyard, gaining vigor and intrigue following the rain. Pulling off shoes and rolling up pants, we waded in and built dams of mud to capture large expanses of water. A rival group, catching the excitement, built a dam upstream and eventually let the water loose in torrents to wash out our downstream dam. This led to frantic activity and collaborative schemes to ultimately build a dam from rocks and limbs that could not be washed out by our competition. We even selected a resourceful third grader to direct the operation! Through trial and error we discovered the value of dense, heavy materials to withstand pressure and of spillways to divert water from our masterpiece of construction." (Frost, 2004)

Drawing from the work of Australian writers, Evans (1992) raised the relevant issue as to whether today's children play less or merely play differently from their predecessors. Factor (1988) argues that adult-inspired activities (e.g., sports) have not obliterated children's traditional play; Palmer (1986) believes that children use television in many creative ways; and Roberts (1980) concludes that the play of children, though ongoing, is not always seen by adults. Also offered are the arguments that children will struggle to play, even under terrible conditions (Factor, 1993). It appears that the nature and extent of children's play may indeed differ from country to country, and such factors must be taken into account when assessing the issue of play deprivation.

Hughes (1998), a playworker in the United Kingdom and director of a project to explore relationships between sectarianism and play in strife-torn Northern Ireland, found that not only does the sectarian conflict have shattering effects on the population as a whole, but it is especially traumatic for children. The carnage and disruption have reduced ranging behavior and the natural diversity of play, creating fear, withdrawal, and manipulation and repression of the outcomes of play. Yes, children struggle to play, even under adverse conditions. However, such play may be radically different from normal play, and the results may be either negative or therapeutic.

There is rational play and irrational play (Sutton-Smith, 1985), normal and abnormal play (Gitlin-Weiner, 1998), or, from the perspectives of healthy child development, good play and bad play (enabling, or constructive, play and disabling, or destructive, play) (Frost, 1987). In adolescence, rough-and-tumble play "is used primarily by bullies victimizing their weaker peers. . . . This form of play is not all good for all children" (Pellegrini, 1998, p. 406). Therapists commonly encounter children whose play is characterized by inflexibility, concreteness, constriction, impulsivity, irrationality, unreliability, inability to sustain play, and inability to distance oneself from previously experienced negative or painful emotions (Gitlin-Weiner, 1998, p. 77). The power of imagination has both destructive and creative impulses (Tuan, 1998). One impulse opens up experiences, broadens possibilities, extends thought and action, generates ideas and diversity, and promotes positive social behavior. The other (addictive, bullying, violence, sadism, animalistic, deviant) narrows possibilities, limits thought and action, and leads to antisocial behavior, channels, and patterns. In sum, good (enabling or constructive) play is creative and promotes positive social behavior; bad (disabling or destructive) play is narrow, unimaginative, uninspired, and cruel (Frost, 1987, p. 166). Play encompasses a broad band of behaviors from the dark, messy, and barbaric (Sutton-Smith, 1981) or irrational play to the rational dimensions of play seen in child-care centers (Sutton-Smith, 1985). From a scholarly perspective, we must study the full range of playful activities—rational/irrational, normal/abnormal, good/bad, constructive/destructive, enabling/disabling—to gain an expansive view of the nature and consequences of play.

Hughes's (1998) employs such distinctions in his analysis of children's play in strife-torn Ireland. "Children in extreme conflict situations, e.g., racial or sectarian conflicts cannot avoid the absorption of that conflict into their play behavior. . . . They imitate the actual physical conflicts, adopt the visual identity of their side, sing the songs, tell the jokes, express the insults and demonize the target of their hatred in much the same way as their extreme adult counterparts" (p. 74).

Play prompted by natural disasters such as tsunamis, hurricanes, terrorism, and war, as well as planned play therapy for domestic abuse, appears to be therapeutic and allows children to play out destructive experiences to understand and deal with them. Adults should use caution in distinguishing the motives of children's play but must draw the line against allowing children to victimize others or to engage in extreme mental or physical abuse in their play.

## ALTERNATIVES TO TRADITIONAL SPONTANEOUS PLAY

The natural forms of children's spontaneous play emerge with time and experience. Across cultures and geographic areas, healthy children engage in similar forms of play, although they may use different play materials. A conference of leading theorists ended their deliberations with the conclusion that "studying nuclear physics is child's play compared to studying child's play" (Sutton-Smith, 1979, p. 294). Each discipline represented at the conference held differing views of the nature and purposes of play, approaching the phenomenon from cultural, sociological, psychological, anthropological, linguistic, and developmental perspectives. However, conference participants generally agreed that there are different forms of play across the age spans, childhood to adulthood, ranging from the relatively simplistic peekaboo play of infants and mothers; across the symbolic, pretend play of early childhood; the organized games of later childhood, the culture of sports; the technology games; the "irrational" (Sutton-Smith, 1985) adult games of gambling, war, and sex; and even "irreverent games" (Sutton-Smith, 1997) of gossip. Almost any human activity can have playful qualities, even those typically classified as entertainment, diversion, work, recreation, or leisure.

Features of traditional, spontaneous play may be present in a wide range of activities that only marginally resemble play. As children develop and gain experience, the orientation of their play changes. For example, sports are sufficiently different from symbolic and constructive play to warrant special and distinct explanations, especially for the organized sports of juveniles and adults. We should also explore the relationships between play and leisure, play and entertainment, play and recreation, and play and work, for it appears that a factor now depriving children of traditional, spontaneous play is adult misunderstanding about the commonalities and distinctions between these related activities.

## Play and Organized Sports

A sport culture emphasizes extrinsic rewards, competition, elitism, and skills specialization (Beal, 1998; Lincoln, 1989; Szala-Meneok, 1994). In addition, formal rules, coaches or referees, and organized contests, all imposed from outside the activity, are usually present. Play may be described as an "inversion of sport." Symbolic inversion has been used to analyze different forms of play and is defined as "any act of expressive behavior which inverts, contradicts, abrogates, or in some fashion presents an alternative to commonly held cultural codes, values, and norms" (Beal, 1998, p. 209; see also Babcock, 1978). Spontaneous child play has many similarities to sports but is commonly different in several key components—namely, intrinsic motivation, lack of imposed rules and authority figures, the option of starting and stopping when desired, and noncompetitiveness.

Beal (1998) uses playful (not competitive) skateboarding as an example of symbolic inversion of sport. Skateboarding, of course, is subject to the rigid rules of competitive sports, but the usual skateboarding activity has no rules, coach, or referee. The players create their own tricks and games; determine how long they will play; contribute their own language, style, and dress; and do not anticipate any extrinsic rewards. In such a play environment, usually in streets, on sidewalks, along concrete canals, or other found places, the players are free to control their own activity, create their own styles and games, and they tend to help and encourage one another. The emphasis is on cooperation and the activity or process itself rather than the outcome. This noncompetitive environment means that there are no losers.

A central variable in distinguishing spontaneous play and sports is the creative element. For example, the make-believe play of early childhood, compared to organized sports, is freer, more open ended, more subject to ongoing modification, more dynamic, less bound by rules—in sum, more creative. Traditional games such as chase and tag are valuable activities for children's cognitive, social, and motor development. Games can stimulate positive socialization and creativity when children are allowed to plan, create, and manage their own games. The consequences of adult pressure from outside the game on children's organized games, including sports, are well known.

## Play and Leisure

Perhaps the most prevalent notion of leisure is free time—free from work, free from imposed constraints and responsibilities, free to do what one pleases. But leisure is more than free time. "It is the experience associated with intrinsically enjoyable activities initiated by the individual" (Kleiber & Barnett, 1980, p. 47). To the extent that the experience is governed or directed by others, it is no longer leisure. Freedom of choice and lack of outside restraints sustain leisure (Kelly, 1976). Leisure is a context in which play, entertainment, and simply messing around can take place.

Two decades ago, sociologists were predicting an era of leisure, but the reality is that a growing number of overscheduled, two-income households are experiencing what some call "the death of leisure." A 1998 study of the diaries of families of 3,600 children by the University of Michigan's Institute for Social Research (Vobejda, 1998) found that free unstructured time left after school, eating, and sleeping has decreased from 40% of a child's time in 1981 to 25% in 1997. With the demise of leisure comes the demise of free, unfettered, spontaneous play.

There is something innate about the spontaneous play of the child—the motivation, tension and joy, the unfettered, creative expression. All healthy children in all cultures play from infancy, although their playthings differ. The child playing in mud has no expectations for results. Her playthings are natural and malleable. The focus of her play has no limits. Leisure—time that is free of responsibilities—makes both activities possible. Which activity has greater potential for growth?

## Play and Entertainment

To be entertained is to be amused, pleased, and diverted from other activities. For the most part, entertainment is more sedentary than play and may require less involvement. Someone else can make the efforts to entertain you, but this is not true of pure, unfettered play. In spontaneous play, the child is involved, making decisions and generating opportunities. The very popular theme parks, video arcades, vacation retreats, and many other pay-for-play places across the United States do indeed amuse or entertain, but most are inferior to the best playgrounds, botanical gardens, children's museums, and a growing number of creative pay-for-play places in promoting imagination, exploration, invention, creativity, and constructive socialization among children. Even Froebel understood that people who think that children are only seeking amusement when they play are committing a grave error, for he proposed that play is the first means of development of the human mind (Baker, 1937, p. 5). Many modern children grow so accustomed to being entertained that they become social misfits, incapable of intelligent, warm human interaction and creative industry.

We wish to stress that there are creative designers in the entertainment industry that put the needs of children first. Some design/production firms speak about the evolution of next-generation "edutainment centers" that feature no rides and no technological gimmicks or virtual reality. Rather, they are based on actual reality and are high touch, offering children a place with the tools to create their own magical worlds and develop their minds, souls, and bodies—a place where kids can just be kids.

## Play and Work

Csikszentmihalyi (1975, 1990) explains play (see Chapter 13) as the experience of flow in a voluntary, autotelic context in which there is no concern for outcomes or real-life applications. In his studies of adults at play and work, Csikszentmihalyi followed Huizinga (1938/1950) and Caillois (1961) in proposing that a spirit of play prevails during play. However, he extended this proposal and agreed with John Dewey (1916) and other contemporaries in concluding that the dichotomy between play and work is largely artificial, and that flow and peak experiences characteristic of play can and may be present in work. In many work roles, flow is defeated by boredom and drudgery.

The significance of Csikszentmihalyi's work is the elimination of a hard-and-fast distinction between play and work and the potential of extending the spiritual, joyful, flow qualities of play, so prevalent in childhood, to the work and games of adults. Of special significance is the potential to recreate sterile, structured, hazardous play and work environments, as in many playgrounds, gambling casinos, factories, and offices, to incorporate the spiritual, joyful, growth-inducing, creative flow qualities of play.

Obviously, we have not made hard and fast distinctions between play and related behaviors. Perhaps it is less important that we have a precise definition than the fact that most people, including children, know when work and play are happening. Our interactions with third-grade students demonstrated that children know the difference between play and work. They concluded that play is fun—you have a choice, it is not planned, and one is free to do what one wants, free to imagine and create, to construct something—that play can lead to a product or a job, and that sometimes work can be play. Research supports these conclusions (Garza, Briley, & Reifel, 1985).

In a study of kindergarten and first- and second-grade children, Wing (1995) found that children have fairly consistent criteria in distinguishing work and play. The single most distinguishing element was whether the activity was obligatory. One *must* work. One *can* play. Other factors included whether the activity was designed and directed by teachers or supervisors, whether there was a specific product, whether someone evaluated the activity, whether the activity required finishing or one could merely quit, whether it was necessary to extend effort and be neat, and whether the activity was easy or hard. The children characterized some activities as "in between"—that is, part play and part work. Overall, children seem to be quite clear about what is play and what is work. Given the distinctions above, the old adage "Play is the work of the child" is clearly misleading. Some contemporary early childhood program developers understand the relationships between play and work and have developed programs that merge play and work activities. Among the best are the High Scope Curriculum (Hohmann & Weikart, 1995) and the program at Reggio Emilia, Italy (Katz, 1994).

## IMPEDIMENTS TO SPONTANEOUS PLAY

Children of the United States and, increasingly, the children of other industrialized nations are losing the freedom to play when and where they choose. Their lives are controlled by the relentless schedules of parents and their own daylight-to-dark schedules, and creative play is displaced by television and pay-for-play entertainment. The current revolution in playground development is resulting in more and better playgrounds, but most are still unimaginative, uninspiring and sterile. Playgrounds alone do not compensate for deprivation of spontaneous play, resulting from urbanization, inaccessibility to natural play places, growing violence, addiction to television and cyber play, and fractured families (Frost, 2010). American children are increasingly deprived of free recess play because of the national No Child Left Behind (NCLB) program emphasizing the emphasis on high-stakes testing, the threat of lawsuits, expanding safety regulations (see Chapter 12), parental fear for children's safety when unsupervised, and the widespread belief that play is irrelevant or less important than academics in the educative process (Frost, 2003, 2006a, 2010).

High-stakes testing is now implemented throughout America's public schools and is affecting children beginning in Head Start (Brandon, 2002; Frost, 2006a; "Head Start Resists Efforts," 2003) despite the fact that a growing number of research studies and professional organizations conclude that such emphasis on testing is harmful, illogical, damages morale, and fails to result in better educated students (Amrein & Berliner, 2002; Association for Childhood Education International [ACEI], 1991; Frost, 2003, 2010; National Association for the Education of Young Children, 1988; Nichols, Glass, & Berliner, 2005; Popham, 2002). (For confirmation, enter "high-stakes testing" on a computer search engine and see reference to more than 2 million websites.) Latino scholars argue that high-stakes testing is especially harmful for poor, minority, non-English-speaking students, and call for fair, impartial assessment, using multiple criteria (Valenzuela, 2005). The negative consequences of high-stakes testing multiply as time on testing grows (Nichols & Berliner, 2007, 2008).

Diane Ravitz, former assistant secretary of education and a proponent of No Child Left Behind, later rejected many of these policies and now concludes they are fundamentally flawed, put us on the wrong track, and are not going to improve public education (Ravitz, 2010).

> High stakes testing is taking the joy out of learning and failing to close achievement gaps. Curriculum is narrowed, teacher and student relationships are undermined, motivation is reduced, teachers are demoralized, and students are bored. School thus becomes uninteresting, punitive, and damaging. (Frost, 2010, p. 231)

Play is made possible and takes place within defined contexts, both physical (as in playgrounds) and symbolic (as in make-believe play)—in the physical or concrete settings and the symbolic playgrounds of the mind. Contemporary research and the brilliant views of Vygotsky and Piaget show that it isn't enough merely to let children play. They need to learn to use tools and create with materials. Given the disappearance of natural play places in urban settings and the reduction and elimination of recess in schools, children need creative playgrounds that feature the lost opportunities. Some of the best urban play environments are "compact countrysides," community gardens, and natural areas of parks.

The availability of pay-for-play places in shopping malls, theme parks, casinos, and vacation destinations gives the false illusion that concern for children's play is alive and well in America. Many of these places substitute high-tech entertainment, pseudo- or actual gambling, junk food, sexual and violent video games, and sedentary activity for spontaneous, vigorous, creative activity and further deprive children of close, intensive, personal interaction with parents, nature, simple tools, and opportunities for positive, imaginative play. Now, cyber play devices, portable and available to most children wherever they go, increasingly dominate their lives. See Chapter 11 and Carr (2010) for elaboration.

The substitution of entertainment, high-stakes testing, and indoor cyber play for creative play and quality interaction with adults in homes and communities is deeply implicated in the growing problems of society. American children rank last among children of industrialized countries on tests of physical fitness. They are the most violent, use more drugs, engage in sex at earlier ages, and, thanks to overdoses of sedentary entertainment, loss of recess, high stakes testing, and junk food, are growing more obese and developing early symptoms of risk for later cardiovascular disease (Center for the Future of Children, 1996; Children's Defense Fund, 1996; Deitz & Gortmaker, 1985; Dennison et al., 1988; Elias, 1995; Frost, 1986, 2003, 2010; Ross & Gilbert, 1985; Sutterby & Frost, 2002).

Levels of obesity in the United States are 12% for ages 2 to 6, 17% for ages 6 to 12 and 17% for ages 12 to 19 (Centers for Disease Control and Prevention, 2010). The primary factors implicated in this are poor diets and lack of physical activity. One gene involved with obesity, the FTO gene, can add to the obesity problem. In a European study of 752 teens in ten countries, the carriers of the FTO gene weighed 7 pounds more than non-carriers, but both groups benefitted from exercising an hour or more a day. The study concluded that adolescents meeting the daily physical activity recommendation of 1 hour a day may overcome the effect of the FTO on obesity (Ruiz, et al., 2010).

In 2008, the Texas Education Agency reported the results of administrating the Cooper Institute's FITNESSGRAM to 2.6 million Texas public-school children. The test includes a 1-mile run, curl-ups, push-ups, shoulder stretches, trunk lift, and skinfold test, and measures aerobic capacity, body composition, strength, endurance, and flexibility. Fitness levels declined with each passing grade level from third grade through 12th grade. Twenty-eight percent of third-grade boys and 32% of third-grade girls achieved the "healthy fitness zone" prescribed for the test. By 12th grade, only 9% of boys and 8% of girls met the health standard (Texas Education Agency, 2008). The lowest-scoring schools were in poverty areas and the highest in higher-income areas. These same schools scoring lowest on the FITNESSGRAM also scored lowest on academic achievement tests, and those scoring highest on the FITNESSGRAM scored highest on academic achievement tests. These findings served a wake-up call for the Texas legislature to counter this crisis that now threatens the health, fitness, and development of children throughout developing countries.

Over a 5-year-period, the California Department of Education (Ratey, 2008) found consistently that students with higher fitness scores also had the higher test scores on achievement tests. Fit kids scored twice as well on academic tests as their unfit peers in 2001 and again scored better in 2002, even among lower-income students, when the tests were repeated. In 2004, a group of 13 noted researchers (Ratey, 2008) reviewed more than 850 studies on the effects of physical activity on schoolchildren. Their review covered a wide range of issues— obesity, cardiovascular fitness, blood pressure, depression, anxiety, self-concept, bone density, and academic performance. Their findings of links between fitness and academic performance mirrored those of the California study, and added benefits for memory, concentration, and classroom behavior. Based on their findings, the researchers recommended that school children participate in 1 hour or more of physical activity each day.

Physical activity—free, spontaneous, unstructured play of recess, in playgrounds, neighborhoods, parks, or in the gym—stimulates biological changes or connections in the brain, resulting in learning and adaptation to novelty and challenge. Such learning and adaptation has carryover benefits for health, fitness, and success in school and beyond—as long as physical activity continues. Cutting physical activity to allow more time for academic activity, such as prepping for tests, does not improve academic achievement over time. Fit bodies are essential for building fit brains. Further, wisely managed physical education and free play programs can be fertile contexts for developing social skills, self-confidence, and freedom from isolation and depression. All this becomes more relevant when considering that overweight children tend to become obese adults. One-third of teens are overweight or obese and two-thirds of older adults are obese or overweight. The time to begin a healthy lifestyle is early—*in utero*—with the health of the mother.

Common but misguided conceptions in the United States are that good parenting is so-called Disney dads showing up occasionally to spend a little quality time with their kids, and that infants and toddlers can be reared just as well by strangers as by parents. The May 12, 1997, article in *Newsweek,* "The Myth of Quality Time"; its special spring/summer 1997 issue on children; and the May 12, 1997, article in *U.S. News and World Report,* "The Lies Parents Tell About Work, Kids, Money, Day Care, and Ambition," illustrate the growing willingness of popular media to discuss the state of parenting in America and highlight the growing body of evidence that parents should spend a lot of constructive time with their kids.

The myth of scheduled quality time is especially pernicious, for a little scheduled quality time has never adequately substituted for genuine, continuous quality time. We cannot merely pencil in time for kids on calendars and expect them to thrive. Kids don't do meetings (Shapiro, 1997); they require lots of time and attention, and their need for close, extensive interaction with parents never goes away. As they enter the teen years, their needs become even more intense. They face a growing array of pressures—sex, drugs, peer influences—at a time when their brain development has not caught up with their need to make decisions—and the need for monitoring and guidance grows.

## SUMMARY

Research in neuroscience demonstrates the power of play and the consequences of play deprivation. This research is buttressed by studies of neglected and abused children and studies of criminals. Children struggle to play even under distressing conditions, yet a growing number are deprived of creative, spontaneous play by loss of recess and neighborhood play, over-emphasis on structured academics and testing, out-of-control schedules, absence of parents, poverty, fear of crime, substitution of organized sports, and high-tech play including video games, computer play, and pay-for-play places. All these are having detrimental effects on children's health, physical fitness, and emotional adjustment.

Play may be both constructive and destructive, rational and irrational. The emerging and rapidly growing alternatives to traditional spontaneous play have both positive and negative consequences. High-stakes testing and obesity and related diseases are among the obstacles to healthy development and learning that must be reconsidered and managed by parents and teachers and by policymakers and sponsors. Recess, built and natural playgrounds that are adapted to the wide range of children's developmental play needs, and indoor and outdoor learning through play and physical activity, are counters to the effects of play deprivation.

Thanks to highly sophisticated brain-imaging equipment, neuroscientists are making unprecedented inroads into understanding the role of experience in brain development. Brain science carries profound implications for a range of professions from medicine to criminology, and promises to become the new frontier in understanding child development and education. Among the emerging results of neuroscience are deeper insights into nature and nurture, infant plasticity, effects of play and play deprivation, consequences of neglect, emotionality, socialization, language and cognitive development, and motor functions. The implications for practitioners are growing stronger each year, and increasingly giving direction for growing healthy, competent children through child development and education.

 ## KEY TERMS

Axon
Brain structures (Schemata)
Cerebellum
Computerized axial tomography (CT)
Constructive play
Dendrites
Destructive play
Executive function
Fine-motor skills
Flow
Gross-motor skills
Infant plasticity
Irrational play
Language magnets
Magnetic resonance imaging (MRI)
Make-believe play
Motor neurons
Multiple intelligences

Myelination
Neurons
Neuroscience
Neurotheology
Neurotransmitters
Peak experiences
Play deprivation
Play therapy
Positron emission tomography (PET)
Pruning
Pseudoplay
Rational play
Rough-and-tumble play
Spirit of play
Spontaneous play
Sport culture
Symbolic inversion
Synapses
Transcendental play

 ## STUDY QUESTIONS

1. How has neuroscience contributed to the understanding of child development? What are the linkages between neural development and physical development, cognitive development, language development, and social development?
2. Explain the basic functions of the brain that lead to neural development. What is the role of early experience on brain development?
3. What are the effects of early sensory deprivation on child development? Give examples.
4. What are the connections between neuroscience and play? Prepare a defense of the role of play in neural development.

5. What recommendations would you offer to parents on child rearing and to teachers on teaching, based on contemporary knowledge of neuroscience?
6. What is play deprivation? What are the principal contributing factors? How can policymakers and educators help remedy play deprivation?
7. Play has been dichotomized as rational versus irrational, constructive versus destructive, normal versus abnormal, good versus bad. Should children be allowed to engage in irrational, abnormal play? Why or why not?
8. Distinguish among spontaneous play, organized sports, leisure, entertainment, and work. What are the advantages and disadvantages of each for promoting spontaneous play?
9. What are the major impediments to spontaneous play? How can parents and teachers help ensure opportunities for children to engage in spontaneous play?
10. What advantages and problems for child rearing do you anticipate for immersive reality play?
11. What are the pros and cons of high-stakes testing? What are the alternatives for ensuring quality and accountability?
12. Consider the role(s) you play with children. How would you modify your interactions to help ensure healthy brain development?

 ## REFERENCES

ABC News. (1996). Romania: What happened to the children? [Television series episode]. In *Turning Point*. New York: American Broadcasting Company.

Amen, D. G. (2010). *Change your brain, change your body*. New York: Harmony Books.

Amrein, A. L., & Berliner, D. C. (2002). *The impact of high-stakes tests on student academic performance*. Research Report. Tempe: Arizona State University Education Policy Studies Laboratory. Retrieved March 29, 2004, from http://www.asu.edu//educ/epsl/EPRU/epru_2002_Research_Writing.htm

Angier, N. (1992, October 22). The purpose of playful frolics: Training for adulthood. *New York Times*, pp. B5–B6.

Association for Childhood Education International (ACEI). (1991). ACEI position paper on standardized testing. Olney, MD: The Association.

Babcock, B. (Ed.). (1978). *The reversible world: Symbolic inversion in art and history*. Ithaca, NY: Cornell University Press.

Baker, D. (1937). *The kindergarten centennial 1837–1937.* Washington, DC: Association for Childhood Education International.

Barker, S. (1996). Brain science benefits from budget plan. *Nature, 382,* 105.

Beal, B. (1998). Symbolic inversion in the subculture of skateboarding. In S. Reifel (Ed.), *Play and culture studies: Vol. I. Diversions and divergences in fields of play.* Stamford, CT: Ablex.

Begley, S. (1996, February 29). Your child's brain. *Newsweek,* pp. 55–58.

Begley, S. (1997, Spring-Summer). How to build a baby's brain. *Newsweek Special Edition,* pp. 28–32.

Begley, S. (2000, February 22). Getting inside the brain. *Newsweek,* pp. 58–59.

Begley, S. (2001, May 6). Religion and the brain. *Newsweek,* pp. 50–57.

Begley, S. (2007). How the brain rewires itself. *Time, 169,* 5, pp. 72–79.

Begley, S. (2008). *Train your mind, change your brain.* New York: Ballantine Books.

Bekoff, M. (2001). Social play behavior: Cooperation, fairness, trust, and the evolution of morality. *Journal of Consciousness Studies, 8,* 8–81.

Bergen, D., & Coscia, J. (2001). *Brain research and childhood education: Implications for educators.* Olney, MD: Association for Childhood Education International.

Blakeslee, S. (1997, April 17). Studies show talking with infants shape basis of ability to think. *New York Times,* p. A-14.

Bloom, F. E., Coyle, J. T., & Georgopoulos, A. P. (Eds.) *The Dana Alliance's 2010 Progress Report on Brain Research.* New York: Dana Press.

Brandon, K. (2002). Pressure, stress and evaluations—all at age 5. *Austin American-Statesman,* p. A1.

Bransford, J. D., Brown, A. L., & Cocking, R. R. (Eds.). (1999). *How people learn: Brain, mind, experience, and school.* Washington, DC: National Academy Press.

Brown, S. (with Christopher Vaughan). (2009*). Play: How it shapes the brain, opens the imagination, and invigorates the soul.* New York: Avery.

Brown, S. L. (1994, December). Animals at play. *National Geographic,* pp. 2–35.

Brownlee, S. (1997, February 3). The case for frivolity. *U.S. News and World Report,* pp. 45–49.

Brownlee, S. (1999, August 9). Inside the teen brain. *U.S. News and World Report,* pp. 44–54.

Brownlee, S., & Miller, M. (1997, May 12). Lies parents tell themselves about why they work. *U.S. News and World Report, 122,* 58–73.

Bruer, J. T. (1997). Education and the brain: A bridge too far. *Educational Researcher, 26,* 4–16.

Bruer, J. T. (1999, May). In search of brain-based education. *Phi Delta Kappan,* pp. 649–657.

Caillois, R. (1961). *Man, play, and games.* New York: Free Press.

Carr, N. (2010). *The shallows: What the Internet is doing to our brains.* New York: W. W. Norton.

Center for the Future of Children. (1996). *The future of children.* Los Altos, CA: Author.

Children's Defense Fund. (1996). *The state of America's children: Yearbook.* Washington, DC: Children's Defense Fund.

Chugani, H. T. (1994). Development of regional brain glucose metabolism in relation to behavior and plasticity. In G. Dawson & K. W. Fischer (Eds.), *Human behavior and the developing brain* (pp. 153–175). New York: Guilford.

Crenson, M. (2001, January 6). Research into brain growth explains some of teens' troubles. Associated Press and *Austin American-Statesman,* p. A20.

Csikszentmihalyi, M. (1975). *Beyond boredom and anxiety.* San Francisco: Jossey-Bass.

Csikszentmihalyi, M. (1990). *Flow: The psychology of optimal experience.* New York: Harper & Row.

Deitz, W. H., & Gortmaker, S. L. (1985). Do we fatten our children at the television set? Obesity and television viewing in children and adolescents. *Pediatrics, 75,* 807–812.

Dennis, W. (1960). Causes of retardation among institutionalized children. *Journal of Genetic Psychology, 99,* 47–59.

Dennison, B., Strans, J. H., Mellits, E. D., & Charney, E. (1988). Childhood physical fitness tests: Predictor of adult physical levels? *Pediatrics, 82,* 3.

Devereux, E. (1976). Backyard versus Little League baseball: The impoverishment of children's games. In D. Landers (Ed.), *Social problems in athletics.* Urbana: University of Illinois Press.

Dewey, J. (1916). *Democracy and education.* New York: Free Press.

Donovan, M. S., Bransford, J. D., & Pellegrino, J. W. (Eds.). (1999). *How people learn: Bridging research and practice.* Washington, DC: National Academy Press.

Education Commission of the States and the Charles A. Dana Foundation. (1996). *Bridging the gap between neuroscience and education.* Denver, CO: Education Commission of the States.

Edwards, S. (2010). Neuroprotection: Guarding against injury and degeneration. In F. E. Bloom, J. T. Coyle, & A. P. Georgopoyelus. *The 2010 Progress Report on Brain Research.* The Dana Alliance for Brain Initiatives.

Eifermann, R. (1971). Social play in childhood. In R. Herron & B. Sutton-Smith (Eds.), *Child's play* (pp. 270–297). New York: Wiley.

Elias, M. (1995, February 27). Teens themselves say TV is a bad influence. *USA Today.*

Eliot, L. (2009). *Pink brain: Blue brain. How small differences grow into troublesome gaps—and what we can do about it.* Boston: Houghton-Mifflin.

Evans, G. W., & Schamberg, M. A. (2009). Childhood poverty, chronic stress, and adult working memory. *Proceedings of the National Academy of Science,* Early Edition (daily online), April 7, 106(14).

Evans, J. (1992). Children's leisure patterns: The shift to organized recreation. *Recreation Australia, 3*(4), 19–26.

Factor, J. (1988). *Captain Cook chased a crook*. Australia: Penguin.

Factor, J. (1993). Enriching the play environment: Creativity, culture and tradition. In *Proceedings* (Vol. 5), World Play Summit, Melbourne, Australia.

Frank, D. A., Klass, P. E., Earls, F., & Eisenberg, L. (1996). Infants and young children in orphanages: One view from pediatrics and child psychiatry. *Pediatrics, 97,* 573–580.

Frost, J. L. (1968). *Early childhood education rediscovered*. New York: Holt, Rinehart & Winston.

Frost, J. L. (1975). At risk! *Childhood Education, 51,* 298–304.

Frost, J. L. (1986). Children in a changing society. *Childhood Education, 62,* 242–249.

Frost, J. L. (1987). Conference reflections. In P. J. Heseltine (Ed.), *Creativity through play: Report from the IPA 10th World Conference*. Stockholm: International Association for the Child's Right to Play.

Frost, J. L. (1992). *Play and playscapes*. Albany, NY: Delmar.

Frost, J. L. (1999). The changing face of play. *Play, Policy, and Practice Connections, 4,* 6-7, 11. (Newsletter of the play, policy, and practice caucus of the National Association for the Education of Young Children.)

Frost, J. L. (2003). Bridging the gaps: Children in a changing society. *Childhood Education, 80,* 29–34. Olney, MD: Association for Childhood Education International.

Frost, J. L. (2004b). Introduction. In K. G. Burriss (Ed.), *Outdoor learning and play for elementary school*. Olney, MD: Association for Childhood Education International.

Frost, J. L. (2005a). Lessons from disasters: Play, work and the creative arts. *Childhood Education, 82,* 2–8.

Frost, J. L. (2006a). *The dissolution of outdoor play: Causes and consequences*. Retrieved from http://www.ipema.org/news/default.aspx.

Frost, J. L. (2010). *A history of children's play and play environments: Toward a contemporary child saving movement*. New York & London: Routledge Publishers.

Frost, J. L. & Brown, S. (2008). The consequences of play deprivation. *Playground Magazine, 8,* 3, 27–30.

Frost, J. F., Brown, P. S., Sutterby, J. A., & Thornton, C. D. (2004). *The developmental benefits of playgrounds*. Olney, MD: Association for Childhood Education International.

Frost, J. F., & Jacobs, P. (1995, Spring). Play deprivation and juvenile violence. *Dimensions, 23,* 14–20, 39.

Gardner, H. (1993). *Multiple intelligences: The theory in practice*. New York: Basic.

Gardner, H. (1999). *Intelligence reframed: Multiple intelligences for the 21st century*. New York: Basic.

Garza, M., Briley, S., & Reifel, S. (1985). Children's view of play. In J. L. Frost & S. Sunderlin (Eds.), *When children play* (pp. 31–37). Wheaton, MD: Association for Childhood Education International.

Geake, J. (2004). How children's brains think: Not left or right but both together. *Education 3-13, 32*(3), 65–72.

Gitlin-Weiner, K. (1998). Clinical perspectives on play. In D. P. Fromberg & D. Bergen (Eds.), *Play from birth to twelve and beyond: Contexts, perspectives, and meanings* (pp. 77–92). New York: Garland.

Goldfarb, W. (1953). The effects of early institutional care on adolescent personality. *Journal of Experimental Education, 12,* 106–129.

Goleman, D. (1995). *Emotional intelligence*. New York: Bantam.

Goleman, D. (2007). In S. Begley, *Train your mind, train your brain*. New York: Ballantine Books.

Hartup, W. W. (1992). *Having friends, making friends, and keeping friends: Relationships as educational contexts*. ED 345 854. Urbana, IL: ERIC Clearinghouse on Elementary and Early Childhood Education.

Head Start resists efforts to give pupils a real boost. (2003, February 10). *USA Today*, p. 14A.

Healy, J. H. (1997, August–September). Current brain research. *Scholastic Early Childhood Today*, pp. 42–43.

Hess, R. D., & Bear, R. M. (Eds.). (1968). *Early education*. Chicago: Aldine.

Hirsh-Pasek, K., & Golinkoff, R. M. (2003). *Einstein never used flash cards*. New York: Rodale.

Hirsh-Pasek, L., Golinkoff, R. M., Berk, L. E., & Singer, D. G. (2009). *A mandate for playful learning in the preschool*. New York: Oxford University Press.

Hohmann, C., & Weikart, D. (1995). *Educating young children: Active learning processes for preschool and child care programs*. Ypsilanti, MI: High/Scope Educational Research Foundation.

Hughes, B. (1998). Playwork in extremis: One of many applications of playwork's values, methods, and worth. In *Proceedings*, International World of Play Conference. San Antonio, TX: University of the Incarnate Word.

Huizinga, J. (1950). *Homo ludens: A study of the play-element in culture*. Boston: Beacon. (Original work published 1938)

Hunt, J. M. (1961). *Intelligence and experience*. New York: Ronald.

Isaacson, R. L. (1954). *Recovery "?" from early brain damage*. Paper presented at the National Conference on Early Intervention with High Risk Infants and Young Children, University of North Carolina at Chapel Hill.

James, W. (1890). *The principles of psychology*. Cambridge, MA: Harvard University Press, 110.

Johnson, S. (2004). *Mind wide open: Your brain and the neuroscience of everyday life*. New York: Scribner.

Katz, L. G. (1994). What can we learn from Reggio Emilia? In C. Edwards, L. Gandini, & G. Forman (Eds.), *The hundred languages of children: The Reggio Emilia approach to early childhood education* (pp. 19–37). Norwood, NJ: Ablex.

Kelly, J. (1976). Work and leisure: A simplified paradigm. *Journal of Leisure Research, 4,* 50–62.

Kleiber, D., & Barnett, L. A. (1980). Leisure in childhood. *Young Children, 35*(5), 47–53.

Landreth, G. (1991). *Play therapy: The art of the relationship.* Bristol, PA: Accelerated Development.

Lesley, N. (2010). The emerging science of gene expression and mental illness. In F. E. Bloom, J. T. Coyle, & A. P. Georgopovelus, *The 2010 Progress Report on Brain Research.* New York: The Dana Alliance for Brain Initiatives.

Lincoln, B. (1989). *Discourse and the construction of society: Comparative studies of myth, ritual, and classification.* New York: Oxford University Press.

Lipton, M. A. (1974). *Early experience and plasticity of the central nervous system.* Paper presented at the National Conference on Early Intervention with High Risk Infants and Young Children, University of North Carolina at Chapel Hill.

Long, K. (1997, June 4). Baby's brain begins distinguishing life experiences very early. *Austin American-Statesman,* p. E-4, E-6.

Louv, R. (2005). *Last child in the woods: Saving our children from nature-deficit disorder.* Chapel Hill, NC: Algonquin.

Marano, H. E. (2004). *A nation of wimps.* Retrieved April 25, 2006, from http://psychologytoday.com/articles/pto-20041112-000010.html

Medrich, E., Roizen, J., Ruben, V., & Buckley, S. (1982). *The serious business of growing up.* Los Angeles: University of California Press.

Meltzer, L. (Ed.) (2007). *Executive function in education.* New York: The Guilford Press.

Melzack, R., & Scott, T. H. (1957). The effects of early experience on the response to pain. *Journal of Comparative and Physiological Psychology, 50,* 155–161.

Melzack, R., & Thompson, W. R. (1956). Effects of early experience on social behavior. *Canadian Journal of Psychology, 10,* 82–90.

Nabhan, G. P., & Trimble, S. (1994). *The geography of childhood: Why children need wild places.* Boston: Beacon Press.

Nash. J. M. (1997, February 3). Fertile minds. *Time: Special Report*, pp. 48–56.

National Association for the Education of Young Children (NAEYC). (1988). *Testing of young children: Concerns and cautions.* Washington, DC: The Association.

Neville, H. (2007). In S. Begley, *Change your mind, change your brain.* New York: Ballantine Books.

*Newsweek.* (1997, Spring–Summer). [Special issue on children].

Nichols, S. L., & Berliner, D. C. (2007). *Collateral damage: How high stakes testing corrupts American schools.* Cambridge, MA: Harvard University Press.

Nichols, S. L., & Berliner, D. C. (2008, March). Taking the joy out of learning. *Educational Leadership, 65,* 6.

Nichols, S. L., Glass, G. V., & Berliner, D. C. (2005). *High stakes testing and student achievement: Problems for the No Child Left Behind Act.* Tempe: Arizona State University, Education Policy Studies Laboratory.

Ounce of Prevention Fund. (1996). *Starting smart: How early experiences affect brain development.* Chicago: Author.

Palmer, P. (1986). *The lively audience.* Sydney: Allen & Unwin.

Panksepp, J. (2010). Science of the brain as a gateway to understanding play. *American Journal of Play, 2, 3,* 245–277.

Pellegrini, A. D. (1998). Rough-and-tumble play from childhood through adolescence. In D. P. Fromberg & D. Bergen (Eds.), *Play from birth to twelve and beyond: Contexts, perspectives, and meanings* (pp. 401–408). New York: Garland.

Pellis, S., & Pellis, V. (2009). *The playful brain: Venturing to the limits of neuroscience.* Oxford: Oneworld Publications.

Perry, B. D. (1996). Incubated in terror. Neurodevelopmental factors in the "cycle of violence." In J. D. Osofsky (Ed.), *Children, youth and violence: Searching for solutions* (pp. 101–122). New York: Guilford.

Piaget, J. (1951). *Play, dreams and imitation in childhood* (C. Gattegno & F. M. Hodgson, Trans.). New York: International Universities Press. (Original work published 1945)

Piaget, J. (1952). *The origins of intelligence in children* (M. Cook, Trans.). New York: International Universities Press. (Original work published 1936)

Pinker, S. (2007). The mystery of consciousness. *Time, 169, 5,* 58–70.

Popham, W. J. (2002, February). Today's standardized tests are not the best way to evaluate schools or students: Right task—wrong tool. *American School Board Journal,* p. 21.

Postman, N. (1982). *The disappearance of childhood.* New York: Delacorte.

Ramey, C. T., & Ramey, S. L. (1996). *Prevention of intellectual disabilities: Early interventions to improve cognitive development.* Birmingham: University of Alabama Civitan International Research Center.

Ratey, J. J., with Hagerman, E. (2008). *Spark: The revolutionary new science of exercise and the brain.* New York: Little, Brown & Co.

Ravitz, D. (2010). *The death and life of the great American school system.* New York: Basic Books.

Renken, B., Egeland, B., Marvinney, S., Mangelsdorf, S., & Stroufe, L. A. (1989). Early childhood antecedents of aggression and passive-withdrawal in early elementary school. *Journal of Personality, 57,* 257–281.

Restak, R. (2009). *Think smart: A neuroscientist's prescription for improving your brain's performance.* New York: Penguin.

Roberts, A. (1980). *Out to play: The middle years of childhood.* Aberdeen: Aberdeen University Press.

Ross, J., & Gilbert, G. (1985). The national children and youth fitness study: A summary of the findings. *Journal of Health, Physical Education, Recreation and Dance, 56,* 45–60.

Ruiz, J. R., and the Helena Study Group. (2010). Attenuation of the effect of the FTO rs9939609 polymorphism on total and central body fat by physical activity of teenagers. *Archives of Pediatrics and Adolescent Medicine, 164*(4), 4.

Sabbagh, L. (2006). The teen brain, hard at work. *Scientific American Mind, 17,* 21–25.

Scheur, L. J., & Mitchell, D. (2003). Does physical activity influence academic performance? *Sportapolis.* Retrieved June 29, 2006, from http://www.sports-media.org/sportapolisnewsletter19.htm

Schlegel, A., & Barry, H. (1991). *Adolescence: An anthropological inquiry.* New York: Free Press.

Shapiro, L. (1997, May 12). The myth of quality time. *Newsweek.*

Shaw, P., Greenstein, D., Lerch, J., Clasen, R., Lenroot, N., Gogtay, A., Evans, J., Rappaport, J., & Giedd, J. (2006). Intellectual ability and cortical development in children and adolescents. *Nature, 440,* 676–679.

Shore, R. (1997). *Rethinking the brain: New insights into early development.* New York: Families and Work Institute.

Smith, A. (2005). *The brain's behind it: New knowledge about the brain and learning.* Norwalk, CT: Crown House.

Society for Neuroscience. (2003). Retrieved June 28, 2006, from *nimhpress@nimhgov.*

Society for Neuroscience. (2009). *2009 Annual Report: Evolving for the Future.* Washington, DC: Society for Neuroscience.

Sutterby, J. A., & Frost, J. L. (2002). Making playgrounds fit for children and children fit on playgrounds. *Young Children, 57*(3), 36–42.

Sutton-Smith, B. (Ed.). (1979). *Play and learning.* New York: Gardner.

Sutton-Smith, B. (1981). *A history of children's play: The New Zealand playground 1840–1950.* Philadelphia: University of Pennsylvania Press.

Sutton-Smith, B. (1985). Play research: State of the art. In J. Frost & S. Sunderlin (Eds.), *When children play.* Washington, DC: Association for Childhood Education International.

Sutton-Smith, B. (1997). *The ambiguity of play.* Cambridge, MA: Harvard University Press.

Sylwester, R. (1995). *A celebration of neurons: An educator's guide to the human brain.* Alexandria, VA: Association for Supervision and Curriculum Development.

Szala-Meneok, K. (1994). Christmas janneying and Easter drinking: Symbolic inversion, contingency, and ritual time in coastal Labrador. *Arctic Anthropology, 31*(1), 103–116.

Texas Education Agency. (2008). *Texas tests fitness of 2.6 million students; Finds elementary students are in best shape.* Retrieved July 8, 2008, from http://www.tea.state.us/comm/page1.html.

Thatcher, R. W., Lyon, G. R., Rumsey, J., & Krasnegor, N. (Eds.). (1996). *Developmental neuroimaging: Mapping the development of brain and behavior.* New York: Academic.

Thompson, R. A. (1997). *Early brain development and early intervention.* Lincoln: University of Nebraska.

Thompson, W. R., & Heron, W. (1954). The effects of restricting early experience on the problem-solving capacity of dogs. *Canadian Journal of Psychology, 8,* 17–31.

Tjossem, T. D. (Ed.). (1976). *Intervention strategies for high risk infants and young children.* Baltimore: University Park Press.

Tuan, Y. (1998). *Escapism.* Baltimore: Johns Hopkins University Press.

Underwood, A., & Plagens, P. (1997, Spring-Summer). Little artists and athletes. *Newsweek* [Special issue], pp. 14–15.

Valenzuela, A. (Ed.). (2005). *Leaving children behind: "Texas-style" accountability fails Latino youth.* Albany: State University of New York Press.

Vobejda, B. (1998, November 9). Study: Children watch less TV, spend more time on homework. *Austin American-Statesman,* p. A-4.

Vygotsky, L. S. (1976). Play and its role in the mental development of the child. In J. S. Bruner, A. Jolly, & K. Sylva (Eds.), *Play: Its role in development and evolution* (pp. 536–552). New York: Basic Books. (Original work published 1966)

Wing, L. A. (1995). Play is not the work of the child. *Early Childhood Research Quarterly, 10,* 2, 223–247.

Witte, A.V., Fobker, M., Gellner, R., Knecht, S., & Floel, A. (2009). Caloric restriction improves memory in elderly humans. *Proceedings of the National Academy of Sciences, 2009, 106*(4): 1255–1260.

Wolfe, P., & Brandt, R. (2000). What do we know from brain research? In E. N. Nunn & C. J. Boyatzis (Eds.), *Child growth and development* (7th ed., pp. 25–28). Guilford, CT: Dushkin/McGraw-Hill.

Zigler, E. (2009). In K. Hirsh-Pasek, R. M. Golinkoff, L. E. Berk, & D. G. Singer, *A mandate for playful learning in preschool.* New York: Oxford University Press.

# Play

## INFANTS AND TODDLERS

*AT 0, (10) J. put her nose close to her mother's and then pressed against it, which forced her to breathe much more loudly. This phenomenon at once interested her, but instead of merely repeating it or varying it so as to investigate it, she quickly screwed up her nose, sniffed and breathed out very hard (as if she were blowing her nose), then again thrust her nose against her mother's cheek, laughing heartily. These actions were repeated at least once a day for more than a month as a ritual.*

(Piaget, 1951, p. 94)

# INTRODUCTION: THE INTERACTIVE NATURE OF DEVELOPMENT AND PLAY

The first 3 years of life are unique in the span of early childhood development. The newborn infant is totally dependent upon a parent or caregiver for every need. As the infant develops and is able to move about, the close relationship between adult and child continues as experiences in a bigger environment become possible. Every domain of development depends on the interaction between the baby and the adults in her life. This very close relationship is the key for successful development. The infant responds to the adult, and the adult, in turn, responds to the infant.

One approach to describing this interactive relationship is a dance between the adult and child. Continuing relationships as the infant develops result in more advances in dancing in a larger context (Raikes & Edwards, 2009). A similar perspective is the notion of relationship-based caregiving. It is the dual nature of the relationship that guides the caregiving process. The parent or caregiver is responding to the child. The child has a major role in the intimate relationships. There are interactions when the child takes the lead and the parent or caregiver responds (Wittmer & Petersen, 2006). The interactive relationship is a partnership with alternating leading roles that affect all early development and play. In a responsive-reciprocal relationship, the adults sees the child as

- someone who is competent—an active, motivated learner;
- someone who looks to the adult for nurturance and guidance; and
- someone who is capable of cooperating in a relationship with an adult and who thrives when given the opportunity to do so (Mangione, 2006, p. 29).

Play begins very early in life as the adult guides the infant into playful interactions or responds to playful signals from the child. The adult makes toys and objects available for the new infant to explore, first visually and then physically when motor skills are more developed. There are two players, and their play is the dance. Throughout this chapter, development is discussed in terms of what infants and toddlers can do. However, the adult caregiver is a partner in that development.

In Chapter 2, we discussed that Jean Piaget's theory of play included his position that infants engage in activities that have the character of play. In the quotation cited at the beginning of the chapter, Piaget observed an early form of play in his daughter Jacqueline at 10 months. In this chapter, we describe the relationship between development and play in infants and toddlers. The nature and evolution of motor, cognitive, language, and social development are discussed, as well as examples of variations in development. The relationship between development and play in each developmental domain is explained with relevant examples of infant and toddler play.

After presenting information on development and play, we discuss the characteristics of infant and toddler play. It is important to understand the integrated nature of play; that is, developmental advances in each separate domain affect the characteristics of play in the other domains.

Although infants and toddlers initiate their own play activities, their ability to play benefits from play experiences with others. Adults, especially parents, facilitate play development in very young children. Adults provide toys, materials, and interactions that foster play in infants and toddlers. These interactions change as the child develops. As a result, play interactions with infants are different from those with toddlers.

Peers and siblings also have a role in infant and toddler play. Older siblings include younger brothers and sisters in their play activities. They, too, are able to promote play in siblings who are infants and toddlers.

The final part of the chapter addresses how adults facilitate play with infants and toddlers. Toys and materials that are appropriate for play are included.

## PHYSICAL AND MOTOR DEVELOPMENT

### Characteristics of Physical Development

The first 2 years are the most rapid period of development in children. In their first 2 years, infants and toddlers achieve more physical growth and development than in any other period of their childhood. By the end of the first year, the infant has tripled its weight and increased its length by 50%. Growth occurs in spurts, with periods of no development followed by a period of rapid change (Berk, 2007). Growth proceeds at a slower rate in the second year. Body proportions change. At birth, infants' heads are a fourth of their length. Gradually, growth in the trunk and legs pick up speed. Physical development is termed **cephalocaudal** because development emerges from the top of the body down to the legs. Another growth pattern moves from the center of the body outward, known as **proximodistal development.** The head, chest, and trunk grow first, followed by the arms and legs, and finally the hands and feet (Berger, 2009; McDevitt & Ormrod, 2004; Santrock, 2007).

An important characteristic of physical development is the growth of the brain. At birth, the brain has achieved a fourth of its adult weight and will develop to three-fourths of its adult weight by age 2. Skill growth is also rapid as a result of the increase in brain size (Nash, 1997). The appearance of teeth is another physical characteristic. The average age of appearance of first teeth is 6 months.

### Characteristics of Motor Development

Perhaps the most significant changes in the first 2 years are in the area of motor development. The newborn infant's motor abilities are described as **reflexes.** By the age of 2 years, the toddler has achieved full mobility and is able to climb stairs and run outdoors. Cephalocaudal and proximodistal development have resulted in development of gross- and fine-motor skills.

**Gross-Motor Skills**   Gross-motor skills involve large body movements that begin to emerge early. Motor development can be described as a system because separate abilities in motor skills work together to produce more advanced abilities. Motor skills that are developed separately later combine into a new skill. Control of the upper chest and head permits sitting with support. Kicking, reaching, and rocking on all fours lead to crawling, and then crawling, standing, and stepping lead to walking. When the child is able to walk without assistance, at about 12 months, the period of infancy is completed and toddlerhood begins. In the second year of life, mobility expands rapidly as the toddler tries new motor actions.

**Fine-Motor Skills**   Control of the arms and hands result in the development of fine-motor skills. Because fine-motor skills require coordination of emerging abilities, they also require a system approach to development (Berk, 2007). The first skill developed is the ability to grasp an object, which requires coordination of the eyes and hands. This skill is mastered at about 6 months, followed by exploration and practice in grasping objects in the environment. Other fine-motor skills developed during the first 2 years include transferring an object from one hand to the other, holding an object in each hand, clapping hands, and scribbling (McDevitt & Ormrod, 2004). The U.S. National Library of Medicine and National Institutes of Health (NIH) (2010) have provided developmental milestones for early development in different developmental domains. Figure 4.1 shows these milestones in physical development in the first and second years.

### Variations in Physical and Motor Development

Although physical and motor development occurs in the same sequence in infants and toddlers, much variation can be related to normal

**FIGURE 4.1**    Development Milestones in Physical and Motor Development at 12 Months and 24 Months

Physical and Motor Skills-12 months
The 12-month child is expected to:

- Triple the birth weight
- Grow to a height of 50% over birth length
- Have a head circumference equal to that of the chest
- Have one to eight teeth
- Pull to stand
- Walk with help or alone
- Sit down without help
- Bang two blocks together
- Turn through the pages of a book by flipping many at a time
- Have a precise pincer grasp
- Sleep 8–10 hours at night and take one to two naps

Physical and Motor Skills-24 months
The 24-months child:

- Able to turn a door knob
- Can browse through a book one page at a time
- Can build a tower of 6 to 7 cubes
- Can kick a ball without losing balance
- Can pick up objects wile standing, without losing balance (often occurs by 15 months, and would be cause for concern if you don't see it by 2 years)
- Can run with better coordination, although the stance may still be wide
- May be ready for toilet training
- Should have the first 16 teeth (the actual number of teeth can vary widely)
- At 24 months, they are about half their final adult height

*Source:* From Developmental milestones record-12 months and 2 years. U.S. National Library of Medicine & NIH National Institutes of Health. Retrieved July 23, 2010 from http://www.nim.nih.gov/medlineplus/ency/article/002012.htm

ranges in acquisition of skills. Some differences in physical development are the result of gender, ethnicity, and nutrition. Girls are slightly shorter than boys in infancy. African American infants tend to be larger and more advanced physically; Japanese infants tend to be smaller than U.S. norms (Brown et al., 1986; Super, 1981; Tanner, 1990).

Physical development is affected by inappropriate nutrition. Children who experience prenatal malnutrition and malnutrition after birth grow to be smaller in physical dimensions. Brain development is also affected. Mental delay can result from institutionalization during infancy or living in harsh, unresponsive environments (Kagan, Kearsley, & Zelazo, 1978; see Chapter 3). Deprivation and malnutrition can also result in delays in acquisition of physical abilities. Dennis (1960) found that infants raised in very deprived institutions in Iran did not move about on their own until after they were 2 years of age.

Cultural differences affect motor development. In Uganda and Jamaica, it is believed that infants in the Baganda community and West Indian populations are advanced in motor development because their mothers train them to sit up early. They experience a formal handling routine according to the traditions of their cultures and the belief that the babies will grow up to be strong and healthy. It is believed that infant care practices among the Kipsigis of Kenya and other African groups give them an advantage over Western infants. Unlike Western infants, who spend large amounts of time in a crib, African babies are held next to the adult's body all day as the adult works. Thus the baby is able to practice movement while in an upright position and experience the adult's physical movements, which promote early motor development (Berger, 2009). The Zinacanteco Indians of southern Mexico, in contrast, discourage progress in motor development. Because their environment is dangerous, mothers discourage the infants from acquiring crawling and walking skills (Berk, 2007; Hopkins & Westra, 1988).

Protecting infants and toddlers from dangerous environment may involve carrying them on the mother's or older sibling's back (Trawick-Smith, 2009). In African countries such as Burkina Faso and Senegal, cooking is done over outdoor fires. Family animals such as chickens, goats, and pigs might roam freely outside the home. To prevent the babies becoming soiled or injured, they are carried throughout the day in a shawl on the mother's back whether the mother is walking down the road, working in a field, washing clothes in a stream or community well, or preparing meals. The same practice of carrying very young children in a shawl on the mother's back is the predominant practice, particularly in rural areas in Guatemala.

## Play and Motor Development

Infants are able to engage in physical play shortly after birth. Very young infants use their senses for play. During the first months of life, infants use visual observation and other senses to engage in practice play.

As soon as young infants are able to grasp objects, their emerging physical abilities support their efforts at play. During the first year, much of the infants' first play is with their bodies. Infants play with their own fingers and toes and then use kicking and grasping to initiate play with objects. This first stage of physical play is **manipulative play.**

Between 1 and 4 months of age, play involves watching and practicing body actions (Garner, 1998). Infants watch their own body movements and enjoy bright colors and interesting sounds (McCall, 1979). By 4 months of age, infants learn to grasp and play with objects. Infants first explore the objects and then play with them. A first step in exploration is to bring the object to the mouth to explore it actively with the teeth and tongue. Exploration can also involve looking at the object. Banging the object might be the next step in exploratory behavior (McCune, 1986). Later, the infant can hold two objects and bang them together.

With the ability to sit, infants use visual assistance to grasp and explore objects. Between 4 and 12 months, they can bring their hands to midline to explore objects; and between 7 and 12 months, they can use both hands independently. Between 9 and 16 months, they are capable of making inferences about toys after very short periods of exploration (Garner, 1998; Wittmer & Petersen, 2006).

As the infant develops motor skills, the world of play enlarges. Each new physical skill, such as crawling, standing, and walking, is practiced until mastered. Garner (1998) reports that with lessened use of playpens, the age of onset of walking has decreased. After mastery has been completed, the baby is able to play using the new skill. As explained by Piaget (1976, p. 167), "In a word, he repeats his behavior not in any further effort to learn or to investigate, but for the mere joy of mastering it and showing off to himself his own power of subduing reality."

Next, infants and toddlers try out physical actions with toys. They learn to push, pull, and punch toys. They enjoy toys that have buttons to push and knobs to twirl. Emerging fine- and gross-motor skills are complemented as they fill and dump objects out of containers and experiment with new ways to play with common household objects (Copple & Bredekamp, 2009). They enjoy poking their fingers in holes and become interested in materials that make marks.

## Exploration or Play?

So far in this chapter, exploratory behaviors of infants and toddlers have been included within descriptions of play. Some play scholars differentiate between exploration and play, stating that not until the infant has completed exploration of an object or toy does play begin. Much of this separation between the two can be traced back to the work of Hutt. She explains the difference:

> Consideration has primarily been given to specific exploration of a novel object and its habituation as well as those responses, which might be termed play. By restricting myself to these responses directed towards the same stimulus object, I have tried to draw some distinction between exploration and play. These behaviors can be differentiated on a number of grounds. Investigative, inquisitive or specific exploration is directional, i.e. it is elicited by or oriented towards

certain environmental changes.... The goal is "getting to know the properties," and the particular responses of investigation are determined by the nature of the object.

Play, on the other hand, only occurs in a known environment, and when the animal or child feels he knows the properties of the object in that environment; this is apparent in the gradual relaxation of mood, evidenced not only by changes in facial expression, but in a greater diversity and variability of activities. In play the emphasis changes from the question of "what does this *object* do?" to "what can *I* do with this object?" (Hutt, 1976, p. 211)

Other scholars have extended and refined Hutt's definition. Athey (1984, p. 11) describes exploratory behavior as including "looking, touching, grasping, experimenting with parts of the body, vocalizing, and so forth." For Athey, the repetition of movements leads to playful repetition of the skill and establishes the neural pathways that make the movement readily accessible.

Wohlwill (1984, p. 143) cites Weisler and McCall's (1976) definition of exploration. "Exploratory behavior consists of a relatively stereotyped perceptual-motor examination of an object, situation, or event the function of which is to reduce subjective uncertainty (i.e., acquire information)." Wohlwill (1984) then defines play

as spontaneous activity, not directed at some externally imposed goal or serving some ulterior purpose, which involves manipulation of or other actions directed at an object or set of objects, resulting in some transformation of their location, arrangement, shape, etc., or of their meaning for the child (pretend play). (p. 144)

Wohlwill describes a sequence from exploration to play. It is when the child can transform the object and use pretense that exploration transitions into play. Exploration and play serve different purposes. Furthermore, the child's affect is different for the two behaviors. During exploration, the affect is neutral or mildly negative, whereas during play, the affect is marked by smiling, laughter, and other expressions of pleasure.

Infants and toddlers use motor skills in outdoor play.

Whether or not researchers distinguish between exploration and play, it is clear that one leads to the other. The child explores the object prior to playing with it. If Wohlwill's definition is correct, play with objects begins when cognitive development permits pretend play and transformation of objects. In the third edition of *Developmentally Appropriate Practice in Early Childhood Programs* (Copple & Bredekamp, 2009), the authors of the chapter on developmentally appropriate practice in the infant and toddler years combine exploration and play as one category. No distinction is made between the two terms in the descriptors of appropriate and contrasting indicators.

## Adult Roles in Motor Play

The topic of reciprocal interactions between adults and babies was introduced at the beginning of the chapter. This responsive and guiding role that parents and caregivers have in motor development means that they are aware and involved in many opportunities to provide play experiences as they observe infants' exploration and play. They are sensitive to individual children in caregiving situations and responsive to individual interests and abilities in motor play (Copple & Bredekamp, 2009). Parents and caregivers can encourage motor development by arranging the environment to provide support for emerging gross- and fine-motor skills. They

---

### WHAT PARENTS AND CAREGIVERS CAN DO TO PROMOTE MOTOR PLAY

1. Provide objects in the crib for looking at, reaching, and kicking.

2. Provide rattles and other objects to hold, bang together, and mouth.

3. Include a variety of toys for the child to experience.

4. Be certain that all toys and manipulatives are safe and childproof.

5. Encourage new physical actions such as rolling over, sitting up, and crawling.

6. Provide chairs and other sturdy objects to practice pulling up, standing, and walking.

7. Provide small finger foods such as cereal pieces or cracker for older babies to practice fine-motor skills and self-feeding.

---

can also interact with children to encourage play and assist them to play just beyond their current abilities.

Play with toys is enhanced by interaction and encouragement from adults. The adult can talk about what the baby is doing and provide assistance when needed. The dance between adult and child is initiated with play objects. The dance begins when the adult and baby are seated together with a few play objects. The baby shows an interest in the toy and initiates the play, or the adult offers a toy to the child. In the next step the infant explores the toy and the adult observes the infants actions. Next, the adult responds to the infant's play and talks about it, or shows some possibility that can extend play with the toy. In the last step, the child continues playing with the toy until he is finished. The child and adult have alternated in leading the play and responding to the play partner.

Motor development alone does not totally account for the child's ability to play. Cognitive development facilitates play activities, as demonstrated in the next section.

## COGNITIVE DEVELOPMENT

### Characteristics of Cognitive Development

Cognitive development, like physical development, proceeds at a rapid pace in infants and toddlers. Piaget (1951) proposed that infant thinking is quite different than that of older children and adults. He believed that intelligence in infancy depends on the senses and physical abilities or, in his terms, a **sensorimotor period.**

Infants are able to see, hear, taste, and smell from birth. They can use their senses to perceive the environment around them. Infant perception supports cognitive development. For example, Bower's (1989) research demonstrates that infants perceive the graspability of objects before they are able to grasp successfully. Infants also understand very early which objects can be sucked, can be made to move, or will make a noise. For example, the infant perceives differences in sucking the breast, a nipple on a bottle, and a pacifier. Later, as more mobility and cognitive development are accomplished, the infant acquires perception of depth and constancy of objects. The individual infant's perception depends on past experiences, cognitive awareness, and current use of the senses (Berger, 2009). Infants do not merely absorb the sensory information they encounter; in addition, they interpret and integrate it with their existing experiences.

Sensorimotor intelligence, then, results from infants behaving as active learners. The infant uses emerging physical abilities to grasp, bang, taste, shake, and otherwise interact with people and objects to extend sensory abilities and to aid cognitive growth. Piaget (1951) believed that infants actively use their senses and motor abilities to comprehend their world. The sensorimotor period of development is described in six substages. Intelligence becomes more advanced in each substage. Figure 4.2 describes each of these stages.

## Variations in Cognitive Development

Piaget's observations of infant development have been found to be quite accurate by researchers who have tested his theories. Multicultural scholars have confirmed that Piaget's view of cognitive development is culturally neutral (Hale-Benson, 1986). Infants follow Piaget's views of mental functioning that focus on universal thought processes. Kagan (1977) found that infants in Guatemala followed the same sequence in achieving object permanence as middle-class Euro-American children, although the Guatemalan children were slightly delayed in learning some skills. These kinds of research findings support Piaget's theory that cognitive development proceeds in predictable, invariant steps.

Nevertheless, some researchers have found that infants have greater cognitive capacity than Piaget described. Habituation-dishabituation studies have supported evidence of earlier understanding of object permanence as early as 3.5 months of age (Ballargeon & DeVos, 1991; Berk, 2007).

Recent brain research has found remarkable evidence that environmental conditions early in life affect the course of cognitive development. Nourishment, care, stimulation, and environment all affect brain development ( Siegel, 1999). During the first 3 years of life, the vast majority of synapses and cells in the child's brain are produced. The number of synapses increases with astonishing rapidity during the first 3 years, and the number remains for the first decade of life. After the first decade, the synapses that are not used are eliminated (Blakeslee, 1997; Greenspan & Wieder, 2005; Shore, 1997).

There is great variation in brain development during the first 3 years depending on the types of experiences available to the young child. How the child develops and learns during the first 3 years depends on the interplay between the child's genetic endowment and the experiences or nurture in the child's life; moreover, availability of playful activities affects not only the course of development but also the size of the brain (Begley, 1997; Brazelton & Greenspan, 2000; Nash, 1997). Availability of verbal language is also significant. Children under the age of 2 who hear rich adult language achieve more gains in cognitive development (Blakeslee, 1997).

The brain has the capacity to change; moreover, there are optimal periods when the brain is primed for specific types of learning (Begley, 1997; Shore, 1997). Appropriate stimulation, nutrition, and support can enhance brain development and learning (Poussaint & Linn, 1997), whereas negative factors in the environment can have adverse effects on cognitive development. Infants and toddlers of depressed mothers can have cognitive delay because of lack of appropriate stimulation. Neglect by parents, stressful living conditions, social deprivation, and other factors, including living in poverty, can result in a dramatic reduction in a child's capacity for later learning. Stress can be related to extended time in child care (Gunnar, 2006; Frost, 1998; Lott, 1998; Shonkoff & Phillips, 2000; Wittner, & Petersen, 2006).

The role of experience on brain development has been discussed. Many factors have outcomes in the types of experiences infants and toddlers affect their brain development. Shonkoff and Phillips (2000) proposed four major themes for addressing experience and brain development (pp. 183–184):

1. Developmental research says a great deal about the conditions that pose dangers to the developing brain and from which young children need to be protected. (See Chapter 3.)

2. The developing brain is open to influential experiences across broad periods of development.

3. The kinds of early experiences on which healthy brain development depends are ubiquitous in typical early human

**FIGURE 4.2** Cognitive Development and Play: Piaget's Substages

| Substages of the Sensorimotor Period | Examples of adult roles and Strategies | Materials |
|---|---|---|
| Stage 1: Simples reflexes (birth to 1 month) Infant uses sucking, looking, listening and grasping. | Dresses infant in clothes that encourage movement. Responds to infant's periods of alertness Sings and talks to infant. | Crib and nearby walls are decorated attractively. Objects are placed visually near the crib. Music is played at appropriate times. |
| Stage 2: Primary circular reactions (1 to 4 months) Infant begins to adapt reflexes to the environment (reflexes are adapted to specific objects; sucking is used with nipples and pacifiers; Repeats actions that please the adult Gazes at hand. | Provides change in the infant's environment. Carries and holds infant in different positions. Places toys in the infant's hand or within reach. Turns on musical toys. Initiates movement in crib toys. | Mobiles, rattles, musical toys. Objects that are safe to go in the infant's mouth and can be grasped and lifted. |
| Stage 3: Secondary circular reactions (4 to 8 months) Repeats actions that involve objects, toys, clothing, or people. Repeats an action over and over to experience the result. Repeats an action that elicits a positive reaction from an adult. | Responds to infant actions on crib toys and provides materials that encourage repetitive actions. Initiates actions with toys and waits for the infant to respond. Reacts with smiles and other facial expressions in response to the child. | Blocks, dolls, ball, and other toys. Use objects with contrasting colors, different sounds, and a variety of textures. |
| Stage 4: Coordination of secondary Circular reactions (8 to 12 months) The infant coordinates behaviors. Behaviors are goal directed. Emerging motor skills enable the child to involve more of the environment. The infant might try to reach a forbidden object, retrieve a hidden object, or use different vocalizations to hear the sounds. | Plays hide-the-object, puts objects under a blanket or behind the back. Verbalizes what is being done. | Toys, visually attractive objects. |

(continued)

**FIGURE 4.2** *Continued*

| Substages of the Sensorimotor Period | Examples of adult roles and Strategies | Materials |
|---|---|---|
| Stage 5: Tertiary circular reactions (12 to 18 months). Toddlers become creative and experiment with new behaviors. Tries different ways to vary a behavior. Experiments in how to use 2 objects (example: filling and emptying a bucket with different objects, throwing stones in the ocean). | Plays more complex forms of hide-the-object. Asks questions like, "Where is it?" or "Can you find it? Watches the toddler's responses and praises actions. Provides experiences in creative play with water toys. Encourages toddler to pretend sleeping, eating, talking on a cell phone. | Blanket, toys, play dishes, water toys, water basin, container with toys of different shapes and sizes. |
| Stage 6: Mental combinations (18–24 months). The toddler can engage in true problem solving. The toddler can anticipate what might happen if certain actions are taken. More advance understanding of object permanence. Can use pretense such as pretending to be eating. | Observes toddler's actions with toys with respect to how the toy was used. Identifies and responds to toddler's interests. Provides clothes, materials, and toys that promote pretend play. | Toys that require actions on the part of the child. Pegboards and pegs, matching and sorting games, nesting, stacking, and ordering materials. |

experience—just as nature intended. There should be concern for children with various types of deficits that preclude them from obtaining the experiences.

4. Abusive or neglectful care, growing up in a dangerous or toxic environment, and related conditions are manifest risks for healthy brain development.

The brain is extremely plastic during the infant and toddler period of development. Infants and toddlers who have strong attachments and a secure, supportive environment have optimal opportunity for brain development and learning. Infants and toddlers who experience serious stress, neglect, and trauma can recover if they are given sustained help. These young children need quick and intense intervention if they are to overcome developmental problems that can decrease their ability to learn (Lott, 1998; McDevett & Ormrod, 2004; Shonkoff & Phillips, 2000; Shore, 1997). (See Chapter 3.)

## Play and Cognitive Development

The section on motor play discussed how the infant's first play activities are limited to the senses and controlled by the ability to grasp an object. Once grasping skills have been developed and some mobility has been achieved, the infant's domain for play expands. Play is at first described in terms of the infant's sensory and motor modalities, but during the second half of the first and second year of development, cognitive development adds new dimensions to the young child's play activities.

Between the ages of 8 to 12 months, the infant is in Piaget's stage called *coordination of secondary circular reactions.* The infant is achieving the ability to walk and can coordinate several behaviors, such as playing with two objects and using true verbalizations. But, most important, memory has developed as demonstrated by the emergence of **object permanence,** meaning the child remembers an object when it is no longer visible. With the development of memory,

symbolic play or pretend play begins. Early pretend play is a solitary activity. Later, social pretend play emerges after 12 months of age (Howes & Matheson, 1992). The complexity of symbolic play has its own sequence of development. When the child is between 18 and 24 months and able to represent objects mentally and engage in pretend actions in the stage of mental combinations, symbolic play reflects planning on the toddler's part.

Piaget described the development of cognitive play in three stages—practice play, symbolic play, and games with rules—that parallel his stages of cognitive development. Practice or **functional play** appears during the sensorimotor period and continues in later periods of development. This first level of play involves the practice of some behavior that is repetitive. The action is pleasurable, and the child repeats actions that have been mastered (Buhler, 1937; Gottlieb, 1983). Practice play can be mental, such as repeatedly asking questions or making vocalizations such as babbling or singing for pleasure. (Berk, 2007).

**Symbolic play** also appears in the later months of the sensorimotor period and continues through the preoperational period. It is also described as pretend play and emerges when an absent object is represented by another object. There are stages in symbolic play with levels of play within each stage that develop between 10 and 24 months. In the first stage, the sensorimotor period, the infant engages in presymbolic play that lacks the characteristics of true pretend play. Presymbolic play is considered to be pre-representational because the child is primarily exploring and interacting with objects rather than using one object or gesture to represent another. The presymbolic levels of play are sensorimotor play (ages 2 to 12 months), nonfunctional play (ages 9 to 12 months), and functional play (10 to 18 months).

The second stage, symbolic stage I, has three levels of sophistication in pretend play. Within the three levels, the child moves beyond her own actions to including other people or objects. These efforts at symbolic play combine more elements until the most advanced stage of 2 years, when the toddler can use language to describe the pretend action and demonstrate that the pretending has been planned (McCune, 1986; Watson, 2008).

An important element of symbolic play is its relationship to early literacy. The child using symbolic play is able to use representational thought; the child is able to use symbolism to represent objects and events. As children practice representing objects and events, play becomes more abstract and more social. Thus, symbolic play serves as a foundation for literacy development. Children use a similar representational process in early literacy. Children move to symbolic representation where words are used to demonstrate the representation of an event or object. The toddler can use language to describe the pretend action and demonstrate that the pretending has been planned. Language is an important element in the abstraction of symbolic play. Understanding that oral words can be written down occurs after the infant and toddler year, but the first steps occur between 18 and 24 months (Stone, 2007; Stone & Stone, n.d.). Figure 4.3 charts the stages of development in symbolic play.

**Nature and infant/toddler play**    Infant and toddler curriculum has always included experiences in or from the natural environment. Teachers and caregivers have featured pictures of elements of nature, and introduced animals, insects, and flowers and other interesting and beautiful examples of nature in the classroom. In recent literature on play at all ages, infant/toddler educators and caregivers are encouraged to be even more intentional in allowing their children to explore nature, especially in the outdoor environment. Instead of the adult introducing an element in the classroom, children are taken outdoors and encouraged to follow their own interests in the environment. Infants would require the most adult guidance and supervision in this type of play, but toddlers can engage in more independent exploration. Current writers of information promoting nature play use terms such as exploring, investigating, and encounters. (Honig, 2004; McHenry & Buerk 2008; Williams, 2008).

Advocates of including nature in infant and toddler play recognize the difficulties

**FIGURE 4.3**    Levels of Symbolic Play in Infant and Toddler Development

| Level of Symbolic Play | Examples of Play |
|---|---|
| Presymbolic Play | The child explores toys |
|    Sensorimotor Play: 2–12 months | The child picks up and object and sets it down |
|    Nonfunctional Play: 9–12 months | The child mouths a spoon or puts a cell phone to its ear |
|    Properties of the object attract the child | The child pretends to be asleep |
|    The child understands how to use an object | The child pretends to eat or drink |
| Symbolic Play Stage 1: 13–19 months | The child pretends to sweep the floor |
|    The child plays with toys purposefully | The child pretends to feed a doll |
|    The child pretends at activities of other people or objects | The child discovers operations of a toy |
| Symbolic Play Stage 2: 19–24 months | The child combines two 2 toys in pretend |
|    The child extends symbolism beyond his or her own body | The child performs pretend activities with several objects (plate, spoon, cup) |
|    The child includes other receivers of action | The child plays with a toy with appropriate sounds (car, airplane). The child holds cell phone to ear and |
|    The child pretends at activities of others such animals, vehicles, etc. | presses keys |

encountered in taking babies outside and the efforts that must be taken to prevent injuries and possible problems with sensory exploration with bugs, mud, and water. Teachers often prefer to bring things into the classroom rather than take very young children explore outdoors. Preparing children for outdoor experiences can be very time consuming, especially when weather requires putting on outdoor clothing. Nevertheless, nothing can substitute for taking infants and toddlers outdoors and selecting play possibilities that will provide experiences with nature (Shaffer, Hall, & Lynch, 2009; Williams, 2008).

## Adult Roles in Cognitive Play

Knowledge of emerging cognitive development can also provide guidelines for supporting infant and toddler play. Adults have important roles in cognitive play. The environment and experiences provided to a child are significant in terms of the child's acquisition of knowledge about the immediate world. Adults also have a role in encouraging pretend play. Even when adults do not actively engage in pretend play, they can perform an indirect role. They can encourage pretend play when the infant has achieved object permanence and begins to use symbolism. Parents who provide opportunities for play and who engage in discussion and storytelling provide an environment and structure for pretend play. They can nurture pretend play by providing toys and materials that facilitate pretending (Wittner & Petersen, 2003). The mother/child dance in pretend play extends and broadens as the play experience becomes more complex, as demonstrated in Figure 4.3.

Earlier in the discussion of symbolic play it was noted that symbolic play serves as the foundation for early literacy. Symbolism in play leads to symbolism in language. The child also comes to understand that there are written symbols for spoken words. This does not occur in infancy, but the foundation is established. There are play activities that parents can introduce that set the stage for early literacy.

Infant attachment to significant adults indirectly affects pretend play. Infants and toddlers who are securely attached are more likely to engage in peer interactions and engage in more complex and sustained symbolic play (Pepler & Ross, 1981). Sibling play encourages pretend play. In an investigation of pretend play with a mother and with an older sibling, more pretend

---

**NATURE EXPERIENCES: EXPLORATION OR PLAY?**

Earlier in the chapter there was a section that discussed when infant/toddler activities constitute exploration, and when are they considered to be play. One definition said exploration occurs when the very young child is learning about the physical qualities of an object. Play occurs when the child moves from exploration to what can be done with the object. In nature play, advocates seem to merge exploration and play; indeed, they use scientific terms such as *scientific explorations*). The most important position taken in increased emphasis on nature experiences that involve child-initiated explorations is that nature should have a more prominent role in infant/toddler cognitive development. Whether exploration in nature should be qualified as play can be questioned. However, when one writer describes these natural activities as "messing about," it seems to come closer to being categorized as play (Shaffer, Hall, & Lynch, 2009).

---

**WHAT PARENTS AND CAREGIVERS CAN DO TO PROMOTE SYMBOLIC PLAY**

**Birth to 1 year**

- Talking and singing to babies invites reciprocal communications. The adult responds to the infant's vocalizations and encourages the baby to continue communicating.
- The adult uses the sounds of music and lullabies with the child.
- The adult makes the child aware of noises in the environment such as animal, vehicle, and other outdoor sounds.
- During the second half of the first year, the adult reads simple books and discusses pictures to help the child become familiar with books. The child engages in looking at the pictures and beginning to identify the sounds of words.

**Age 1 to Age 2**

- The adult initiates pretend games such as peekaboo and patty-cake. The games are repeated very frequently, thus facilitating the child's efforts to used receptive language. When the child attempts to say the words, expressive language emerges.
- The adult sings to the child and expands the singing to include alphabet songs and nursery rhymes.
- The adult provides multicolored toys of different shapes and sizes to encourage the use of perceptual skills.
- The adult talks to the child about events that are happening, things seen on a walk, or people known to the child.

**Age 2 to Age 3**

- The adult provides opportunities for role playing. Children act out the sequence of topics such as planting a garden, store, or visiting a friend. Through sequencing in make-believe play, the child grows toward story comprehension.
- The adult introduces puppet play and acting out stories that provide opportunities for children to use their imaginations (Zigler, 2006).

---

relationships were found between the infant and a sibling than with the infant and the mother. The infants also engaged in more role play with the older sibling than with the mother (Youngblade & Dunn, 1995).

At the end of the second year, the toddler is combining play with objects, symbolic play, and emerging language skills to enrich play episodes. Language development and how play with language emerges are addressed in the next section.

## Cultural Differences in Parent–Child Pretend Play

Parents from different parts of the world engage in pretend play differently (see Chapter 7). Haight, Parke, and Black (1997) describe these variations:

Available cross-cultural research suggests a relation between variation in parental beliefs about play, and their support of play. Turkish and Chinese parents generally view themselves as appropriate play partners for their children. In contrast, Mexican, Italian, Mayan, and Indonesian parents typically do not view play as particularly significant to children's development, and/or adult participation as appropriate. Consistent with these beliefs, naturalistic observations reveal that Turkish and Chinese parents typically participate in pretend play with their young children, whereas Mayan, Mexican, Italian, and Indonesian parents engage in relatively little or no parent–child pretending. (p. 271)

##  LANGUAGE DEVELOPMENT

### Characteristics of Language Development

How early does language development begin? It begins in the womb when the fetus hears her mother's voice and language in the environment. Babies who are 4 days old can distinguish between languages. Newborns show their preference for the language that is familiar by sucking more vigorously on a nipple when they hear it as compared to an unfamiliar language (Cowley, 1997).

Like cognitive development, acquisition of language during the first 2 years is an impressive achievement. Between birth and 2 years, infants and toddlers learn enough about their language to speak and develop a vocabulary ranging from 50 to 200 words (Berk, 2007). Children of every culture and country learn the language of their community. Italian babies, for example, understand names of different kinds of pasta quite early in life (Trawick-Smith, 2009). Children from bilingual families learn words from both languages before 18 months.

**Theories of Language Development** How do theorists explain language development? Three major theories have informed our understanding of how language develops. B. F. Skinner

(1957) initiated the **behaviorist theory** of language development. Skinner proposed that language is acquired through operant conditioning; that is, parents reinforce the baby's efforts at language. Subsequently, they reinforce the most correct forms of efforts to say words. Behaviorists also propose that the child learns language through imitation. The adult conditions the child to use correct language forms by rewarding efforts to imitate adult language.

Noam Chomsky (1957) understood that even very young children take charge of learning language. His theory was labeled as **nativist** because he believed that children have an innate ability to acquire language. He proposed that all children have a biologically based innate system for learning language that he called a **language acquisition device (LAD)**. Chomsky believed that the LAD contains a set of rules common to all languages that children use to understand the rules of their language.

A more recent theoretical approach, termed **interactionist,** is based on the fact that language is not acquired without socialization. Language cannot be acquired without a social context. Infants and toddlers have an innate capability to learn language facilitated by adult caregivers (Berger, 2009; Berk, 2007). Vygotsky (1984) proposed that language is learned in a social context. Language is centered in the sociocultural history of a population. The child as a member of the group learns the language to communicate in his community.

**Sequence of Language Development** All children learn language in the same sequence. Although the timing may vary for different languages, the developmental sequence is the same. From the moment of birth, the neonate uses cries and facial expressions to express his needs. He can distinguish his mother's voice from other voices and can discriminate among many different speech sounds (Berger, 2009). Thereafter, steps toward speech and the use of language develop at regular intervals.

**FIGURE 4.4** Sequence of Language Development: Birth to 2 Years

- **2 months:** The infant is developing a range of meaningful noises that can be discriminated by the mother. Cooing, fussing, and crying as well as laughing are used.
- **3–6 months:** New sounds such as squeals, croons, and vowel sounds are added. Parents direct their attention to what the baby is looking at and often verbally label what is seen.
- **6–10 months:** Utterances begin to include repetition of syllables known as babbling. Gestures such as pointing are also used to communicate. Babbling begins to incorporate the sounds of the infants language community. Deaf babies babble with their hands. (Berk, 2002)
- **10–12 months:** The infant comprehends simple words. Utterances sound more like adult words in intonation. Deaf babies communicate by expressing a sign.
- **13 months:** First words are spoken. Vocabulary increases steadily. Holophrastic speech is used. The infant uses a single word to express a complete thought. The child has a larger receptive than expressive vocabulary, meaning that the child understands more than she can express or verbalize.
- **13–18 months:** Continued growth of vocabulary using one-word utterances.
- **18 months:** Spurt in vocabulary development.
- **21 months:** Begins to combine two words in an utterance. Described as telegraphic speech because the child focuses on high-content words as in a telegram. Vocabulary expands rapidly. The toddler is beginning to understand rules of grammar.
- **24 months:** The toddler has a vocabulary of up to 200 words.

Figure 4.4 traces these steps between birth and 24 months.

## Variations in Language Development

There are wide variations in how rapidly language development occurs. Some variation can be very normal and based on differences in language style. Other variations can be a cause for concern, indicating a delay that warrants intervention.

A normal type of variation in language development and usage is language style. Berk (2007) describes these differences as referential style and expressive style. Toddlers who use a **referential style** use words to refer to objects; those who use an **expressive style** use more pronouns and social words. The vocabulary of toddlers who use a referential function for language grows more rapidly than those who use an expressive style because languages have more objects than social expressions.

Language differences are related to cultural and ethnic diversity. In addition, young children may be bilingual or speakers of another dialect or language. Any of these cultural differences can result in standard English language acquisition that appears to be at a different rate than native English speakers; however, Trawick-Smith (2009) cautions that these children should not be labeled as language delayed because they have a culturally derived communicative style or language difference. For example, U.S. mothers label objects more often than Japanese mothers; Japanese mothers engage their toddlers in social routines such as greeting family members more often than U.S. mothers. The nature of language development is different in children from these cultures (Fernald & Morikawa, 1993; Genishi & Dyson, 2009).

Infants and toddlers who are experiencing more than one language are often in a caregiving setting during the day. Often the caregivers look after babies who represent several different languages. If the caregiver speaks the child's home language, that language can be spoken with the child. If the caregiver does not speak the child's language or there are babies who represent several languages, the caregiver will use the local language. Different settings will

This child develops language and communication skills through play.

address the language variations differently depending on the languages represented among the caregivers. Regardless of the languages used with infants and toddlers, the most important factors are consistent routines, careful attention to nurturing the child, and provision of a secure environment. It is helpful to have caregivers who share a child's home language, but nurturing care makes the difference no matter what language is used (Pearson, 2006).

If a child is still having great difficulty in understanding and speaking language at age 2, she may have a serious language disorder (Kalb & Namuth, 1997). A hearing impairment, Down syndrome, or a general language delay can cause language delay. A child with general language delay might have minor damage in the brain or other factors such as poor health, poverty, or family stress. Language delay has multiple causes, and interventions must be planned for individual children (Trawick-Smith, 2009).

## The Role of Adults in Language Development

Adults have a major role in infant and toddler language development, as demonstrated in how parents of different cultures use language with their very young children. Although children have an innate ability to acquire language, their social interaction with adults is also a major factor in language acquisition.

Adults begin speaking to their babies during the first days of life. Moreover, they adjust their style of talking to fit the infant's stage of development. This type of baby talk is termed **parentese.** Parentese is higher in pitch, simpler in vocabulary, and shorter in sentence length. It uses more questions and commands and fewer complex sentences than adult talk.

People of all ages use parentese. Siblings are natural users of baby talk. At first the parent or other person does all of the talking. The infant is the interested recipient. The parent might engage in both sides of a conversation. The infant signals its responsiveness with smiling, gestures, and physical actions. Once the child begins to use **holophrastic speech,** or single words that can have more than one meaning, the parent interprets and clarifies the child's speech and meaning in the conversation. The toddler is trying to communicate in all efforts and speaking. The adults use labeling, expansion of the child's speech, and nonverbal smiling to support the child's development of language (Berger, 2009).

The language interaction between adults and infants has been described as a dance. The individual characteristics of the parent and child affect the nature of the dance. Parents who talk extensively to the child have more of an influence in the child's development of language than parents who use restricted language in their communications with the child.

The nature of the child's interaction also affects the interactive relationship. The child can affect the responsiveness of the parent. The infant's temperament or intelligence might affect how responsive the infant is to the mother. This in turn can affect the level of the mother's responsiveness to the child (Stevenson, 1989). In sum, in the interactive relationship or dance between mother and child, both partners affect the richness and extent of language that takes place. Both partners affect the other. The mother initiates the language relationship, but the child's responses can affect how much the mother continues the language conversations.

## Play and Language Development

Infants and toddlers play with language at a very early age. Before talking begins, the infant plays with babbling sounds. Garvey (1977b) documented infants producing a variety of such sounds between 6 and 10 months. At 1 year of age, the child engages in long periods of vocalizations of single vowels. Weir (1976) described these episodes of sound play as the child's monologues.

During the second year, the toddler uses sounds to enhance pretend play. Frost (1992, p. 41) describes this private speech as allowing the child "to identify events and actions of self, others, and objects such as the telephone, dog, and automobile horn." The child is using play with sounds to accompany pretend play with objects.

The toddler uses play with language after words appear and combinations of words begin. Weir (1976) described language play using **telegraphic speech** with a grammatical pattern and substitution of nouns as follows:

What color
What color blanket
What color mop
What color glass (p. 611)

## Adult Roles in Language Play

Language play is also a social activity in the infant and toddler years. The role of the parent, sibling, or other caregiver in using parentese with the child teaches the child the game of taking turns in speech. At first the mother takes the turn for both, but soon the infant engages in the play with cooing, babbling, and attempting vocalization. Play with language is extended with the first mother–infant games involving motor activities, such as peekaboo and patty-cake. The infant imitates the physical movements and gestures used by the mother and enjoys the

---

### WHAT PARENTS AND CAREGIVERS CAN DO TO PROMOTE LANGUAGE PLAY

1. Understand the need to be an active conversational partner. Initiate conversational episodes with the infant frequently during the day. Use caregiving episodes to talk to the baby.

2. Talk to the infant as if she understands. Use parentese strategies such as raising the pitch of your voice and speaking in an enthusiastic tone when engaging the infant in conversations.

3. Be sure to respond to the infant's efforts to communicate. React as if the infant did speak to you, and reward with a smile and other physical forms of encouragement.

4. Continue to initiate conversations with toddlers. Listen to them carefully; give them time to express themselves.

5. Do not be concerned with the inaccuracy of the toddler's use of language. Expand, repeat, and respond positively to the toddler's attempts to use language forms.

6. Make your toddler feel that she is understood when she has difficulty pronouncing words. Support all efforts.

---

**WHAT PARENTS AND CAREGIVERS CAN DO TO PROMOTE LITERACY**

1. Read often to infants and toddlers.

2. Show enthusiasm as you share books with the child.

3. Make the experience pleasurable.

4. Talk to the child about the book by pointing to pictures and talking about what is happening.

5. Name objects in picture books. (Armbruster, Lehr, & Osborn, 2002)

---

physical actions that accompany the games. Object permanence in cognitive development permits the child to enjoy the disappearance and reappearance of the play partner in peekaboo.

Parents and caregivers also follow the lead of the child in communicative language play. When the infant initiates the play with babbling, the adult responds by imitating the infant's vocalizations. The game continues with the infant and adult taking turns making new vocalizations.

Toddlers use emerging vocabulary to engage in symbolic play. McCune (1986) describes a child using a play screwdriver for a toothbrush by first labeling it in the example of planned symbolic games in Figure 4.3. This anticipates the more advanced play with language that emerges in the early childhood years when social development makes it possible for young children to interact in play activities.

##  BEGINNING STEPS IN LITERACY DEVELOPMENT

All of the language experiences in which infants and toddlers engage are essential for language development. Further, these experiences are also building foundations for literacy. Familiar songs and rhymes and mother–infant games are first steps in acquiring literacy.

Toddlers also learn that pictures can stand for real things and symbolize things in the world. Symbols in the environment give clues about things and places. For example, an 18-month-old toddler traveling with her mother and grandmother recognized signs along the highway—the McDonald's golden arches—and pointed to them as they passed, exclaiming, "McDonos!" Toddlers recognize packaging of favorite foods in the grocery store and can name some familiar food items. Often they are able to make these first connections through sibling and adult encouragement (Durkin, 1966; International Reading Association & National Association for the Education of Young Children, 1999).

The single most important activity that establishes foundations for literacy is reading aloud to infants and toddlers. The best opportunities for these experiences are when youngest children feel emotionally secure and are active participants in the activity.

## SOCIAL DEVELOPMENT

### Characteristics of Social Development

Infants have a need to be social. There is evidence of all the basic emotions very early in life. Infants vary greatly in temperament, which is influenced by both heredity and environment (Kagan, 1994). During the first 2 years, infants and toddlers develop an attachment to their caregivers that is affected by the circumstances in their environment. An important achievement during the first 2 years is the development of a sense of self that includes self-recognition and self-control.

**Theories of Social and Emotional Development**    Several theories inform our understanding of social development (see Chapter 2). Erik Erikson's (1963) psychosocial theory is based on Freud's psychoanalytic theory; Mahler's separation-individuation theory focuses on the development of self that occurs during the second year of life.

Erikson believed that emotional development occurs throughout the life span as the individual resolves life stages positively or negatively. During the first 2 years, the infant and toddler experiences the stages of **trust versus mistrust** and **autonomy versus shame and doubt.**

In the first stage of social development, trust versus mistrust, the infant learns whether the world is a secure place. The infant develops a sense of trust if her basic needs are met with consistency and continuity. But if the mother lacks sensitivity to the infant's needs and cannot be depended on to respond when the infant is hungry or uncomfortable, the infant develops a sense of mistrust.

During the second year, the toddler encounters the conflict of autonomy versus shame and doubt. Toddlers seek to become autonomous and independent. If the toddler encounters support and firmness as he seeks to control his own actions and body, autonomy will be the result. If, however, the adult is very restrictive and overcontrolling, the toddler will develop a sense of shame and will doubt his ability to act competently.

Margaret Mahler (Mahler, Pine, & Bergman, 1976) perceived social development to be based on an awareness of self that develops during the second year. This awareness develops in two phases: **symbiosis** and **separation-individuation.**

According to Mahler, symbiosis begins during the second month, when the infant is more alert and aware of events around her. The infant is fused with the mother and does not realize that people and events exist outside of herself. The infant's symbiotic relationship to the mother affects social development. If the infant experiences prompt and positive responses from the mother, development can proceed to the next phase. If the infant is handled harshly and inconsistently, she will have difficulty in moving away from the mother in the next phase.

In the separation-individuation phase, self-awareness is triggered. This phase begins at about 4 to 5 months, when the infant begins to separate from the mother. As toddlers become more mobile, they increasingly develop the capacity to initiate their movement away from the mother. Between 2 and 3 years of age, toddlers emerge with a positive sense of self if their experiences with adults have been supportive and gratifying. Toddlers who remain insecure have more difficulty in accepting themselves as separate people and in enjoying independence (Berk, 2007).

**Sequence of Emotional Development**    The first emotion expressed by newborn infants is distress. Brief smiles also emerge during the first days of life. A social smile that responds to a human voice or face occurs at about 6 weeks. Other emotions that can be identified in very young infants are joy, surprise, fear, anger, disgust, sadness, and interest (Izard, 1991).

During the second half of the first year, infants experience new emotions labeled stranger anxiety and separation anxiety. **Stranger anxiety** is expressed through fear of strangers that can emerge as early as 6 months. Response to a stranger also depends on temperament and the proximity of the stranger and the mother (Berger, 2009; Puckett & Black, 2005). **Separation anxiety** is fear of being left by the mother or other adult. A factor in separation anxiety is the development of memory, and it is expressed with anger.

## Variations in Social and Emotional Development

Infants and toddlers are beginning to form the personality that they will have as adults during the first 2 years of development. Individual differences in emotional reactions are known as **temperament** and can be identified in young infants. Thomas and Chess (1977) have described differences in temperament. Three basic temperaments as developed by Thomas and Chess are the easy child, the difficult child, and the slow-to-warm-up child. The **easy child** is generally cheerful, establishes regular routines as an infant, and adapts to new experiences easily. The **difficult child,** to the contrary, finds it difficult to establish routines and also has difficulty with new experiences. The **slow-to-warm-up child** reacts slowly to new experiences. This type of child exhibits lower reactions to stimuli from the environment and is generally inactive and negative in mood. Some children do not fit any of the patterns; rather, they are a blend of temperament characteristics. In addition, temperament can change over developmental periods. Although there are genetic influences in temperament, environment makes a contribution.

Sex and ethnic variations are also apparent in temperament and emotional development. For example, Chinese and Japanese babies are more easily soothed when they are upset, but they tend to be less active and more irritable. Male babies tend to be more active, which persists into childhood. Female children tend to be more anxious and timid (Berk, 2007).

## The Role of Adults in Social and Emotional Development

Parenting styles affect the development of temperament in their infants and toddlers. As we discussed in the previous section, there are ethnic differences in how parents approach child rearing. American mothers work for their babies to become autonomous, whereas Japanese mothers

teach their babies to become dependent on them. Parents perceive male infants to be better coordinated and strong, encouraging them to be physically active. Female infants are regarded as weaker and more delicate. They are encouraged to be dependent and close to the parents.

An important element of the parental role in emotional development is the development of **attachment,** the emotional connection between the infant and adult caregiver. It is hoped that the infant will achieve a **secure attachment** in which he will become close to the caregiver and develop confidence in exploring the environment. Unfortunately, some infants experience an **insecure attachment** that is troubled. The infant exhibits fear and anger toward the caregiver and has less confidence. These children were not readily comforted by the parents as infants and can exhibit lack of interest in the parent or overdependence (Berger, 2009; Lott, 1998; Waters & Cummings, 2000).

The relationship between parents and infants and toddlers can be described as a partnership. Temperament, attachment, and parenting styles interact in the developing relationship. The social partnership develops during the first months of infancy. By the age of 2 months, the infant is able to respond to the parent. Smiling and cooing in response to the parents deepen the attachment process. As face-to-face interactions proceed, the mother and infant are able to synchronize the relationship, thus deepening the social partnership. Both partners initiate and respond to the social behaviors of the other. They also adapt to repairing the synchrony when social interactions are not successful (Honig, 2002; Tronick, 1989). The evolving social interactions between caregiver and infant become play episodes that are discussed in the next section.

## Play and Social Development

Social play begins when the newborn infant is able to use a social smile in response to a caregiver's presence. Smiling at another expands

---

**DOES TOUCH MATTER?**

Is it important for infants and toddlers (and older young children) to experience human touch. Does touch affect the baby's ability to have a secure attachment with parents and other adults?

Carlson (2006) proposes that touch is essential for social and emotional development. Contrary to early childhood educators who are concerned about inappropriate touching, Carlson suggests that "touch is absolutely required for proper physical and cognitive development, it offers, powerful therapeutic benefits, the brain craves it, it is critical to forming secure attachments, and it fosters social and emotional development." Carlson concludes, "Touch is both a physiological and a psychological need. As educators we don't provide nearly enough of it, and without it horrible consequences await children."

*Source:* Carlson, F.M. (2006). Essential touch. Meeting the needs of young children (p. 28). Washington, DC: National Association for the Education of Young Children).

---

into babbling and cooing as the communicative repertoire expands. The first and most important play partner for infants and toddlers is the caregiver, whether it be a parent, sibling, or other adult. As discussed previously, the adult takes the initiative in engaging the infant in early social interactions. The infant in turn uses physical movement, facial expressions, and vocalizations to engage in socialization.

Infants and toddlers learn and practice social rules through early social games. They learn turn taking, role repetition, and mutual involvement through adult–infant play (Bruner & Sherwood, 1976; Power, 1985). The adult-infant games of peekaboo and patty-cake incorporate these rules.

**The Effects of Adult–Child Attachment and Play**   The strength of adult–child attachment in infant and toddler years can be seen in the later social competence and play of preschool children. Attachment studies have indicated that secure attachment in infancy predicts more positive affect and greater peer acceptance in play in the preschool years. Secure attachment is also predictive of more positive social engagement and more elaborate play styles (Waters, Wippman, & Sroufe, 1979).

## Peer Play

Infants are aware of their peers at an early age. In fact, they have unique reactions to another infant's presence, including looking intently, leaning forward, and making excited movements with their arms and legs (Fogel, 1979). Investigations of peer interaction during the first year have shown that more interaction occurs less than 1 year when there are no objects in the environment (Garner, 1998). In the second year, they can exchange smiles and vocalizing while playing together (Howes, Unger, & Seidner, 1989).

Toddlers are able to engage in limited forms of play with other children. Objects become more important for peer interactions and are used in early play encounters (Garner, 1998). Toddlers approach another child or adult to engage them in play. Toys serve as the mediators for play (Johnson, Christie, & Yawkey, 1999). The emergence of pretend play provides a vehicle for toddlers to engage in play together. They engage in identical pretend activities, such as pushing doll carriages and smiling at each other (Howes et al., 1989). They also participate in run-and-chase activities (Howes, 1987b).

## THE GAME

The Game is *not* important to the infant because people play it, but rather people become important to the infant because they play "The Game."

*Source:* J. Watson (1976), Smiling, cooing, and "The Game." In J. S. Bruner, A. Jolly, and K. Sylva (Eds.), *Play: Its role in development and evolution* (p. 275). New York: Basic.

Peekaboo surely must rank as one of the most universal forms of play between adults and infants. It is rich indeed in the mechanisms it exhibits. For, in point of fact, the game depends upon the infant's capacity to integrate a surprisingly wide range of phenomena. For one, the very playing of the game depends upon the child having some degree of mastery of object permanence, the capacity to recognize the continued existence of an object when it is out of sight . . . . The successful playing of the game is dependent in some measure on the child being able to keep track of the location in which a face has disappeared, the child showing more persistent effects when the reappearance of a face varies unexpectedly with respect to its prior position.

*Source:* J. S. Bruner & V. Sherwood (1976), Peekaboo and the learning of rule structures. In J. S. Bruner, A. Jolly, & K. Sylva (Eds.), *Play: Its role in development and evolution* (p. 278). New York: Basic.

**Temperament Differences and Peer Play**

Temperament variations in young children have been studied in terms of inhibited and uninhibited children (Kagan, Reznick, & Snidman, 1988). Inhibited 2-year-olds are more likely to be reticent in play with peers at age 4. Likewise, preschool children who have poor self-regulation of emotions seem to have anxiety during peer play when compared with children who have developed appropriate self-regulation (Rubin, Coplan, Fox, & Calkins, 1995).

Adults support infant play.

## Adult and Sibling Roles in Social Play

Adults serve in a support role in infant and toddler social play. Parents and caregivers encourage pretend play by providing materials and setting the stage for pretending. They might model pretend play using toys and objects. These supporting activities are called **scaffolding,** in that parents are eliciting play skills rather than directing them (Bruner & Sherwood, 1976; Power, 1985).

Adults are able to sustain the child's interest in play activities. The scaffolding that they do in structuring play events results in more complex play on the child's part. Mothers adapt play activities for the developmental needs of their child and vary their own behaviors and new materials in response to the child's changing interests or emotional reaction (Escalona, 1968). Other studies have supported that infant and toddler play are more sophisticated in children who have access to adult partners (Ross & Kay, 1980). Parents select games and enable the infant to play the game. They model the steps in the game and position the infant so he will focus on the game. Clues are given as to the

---

**HOW PARENTS AND CAREGIVERS CAN PROMOTE SOCIAL PLAY**

1. Engage in frequent face-to-face interactions to include comforting, talking, and responding to infant smiling and cooing.

2. Respond to infants when they show distress and seek comfort and attention.

3. Engage the baby in moderately stimulating experiences such as shaking rattles, tickling, moving mobiles, and arm movements.

4. Play interactive games such as peekaboo and patty-cake.

5. Provide consistency and affection in managing disciplinary problems.

6. Respond with help and guidance with toys, play with peers, and games when requested.

---

infant's role in the game, and the game changes as the infant matures and understands how to play the game (Beckwith, 1986).

Siblings tend to have a different role than parents in infant-toddler social play. Parents serve as social partners who support advances in social play, whereas siblings help the infants use the play skills that they have developed. They do not participate as social partners but play alongside the younger child (Dunn, 1983).

Each child is as unique in social development as she is in language development. Adults want to establish a secure and trusting environment for infants and toddlers. In addition, they can support or scaffold social play.

## CHARACTERISTICS OF INFANT AND TODDLER PLAY

Four basic characteristics in infant-toddler play were introduced in this chapter: motor play, object play, social play, and symbolic play. Each of these types of play is reviewed here, followed by information on how domains of development are integrated in play. In addition, gender differences in play emerge in toddlers. These differences are also discussed.

### Motor Play

Infants first engage in motor play as they gain control of their bodies. Initially, they play by themselves with body parts. One of the first manifestations of motor play is playing with fingers and toes. As they are able to sit, stand, and walk, they are able to use new motor skills to include objects and the environment in their play. Fine-motor development enables them to grasp and explore toys; gross-motor development permits them to reach new places and explore new things. Toddlers who use furniture or climbing equipment in their motor play repertoire accomplish climbing and running. Push-and-pull toys and riding toys now become important (Garner, 1998; Johnson et al., 1999).

### Object Play

Interest in objects first emerges at about 4 months. First activities with objects include mouthing, shaking, and banging of all objects. Later, infants differentiate which behaviors are appropriate for individual objects. For example, rattles are shaken and food and bottles are mouthed (Uzgiris & Hunt, 1975). At between 7 and 12 months, infants develop the ability to use both hands independently in object play. One hand can stabilize a toy while the other manipulates the object (Kimmerle, Mick, & Michel, 1995).

During the second year, mouthing decreases as the toddler moves from exploration to play. Toddlers enjoy action toys such as a jack-in-the-box or toys that respond with music or words when a string is pulled or a button pushed. By

Toys facilitate social play between peers.

the end of the second year, object play has expanded to include books, dolls, stuffed animals, and toys for water play (Garner, 1998).

## Social Play

Adults, particularly mothers and fathers, are the first play partners of infants and toddlers in many cultures (see Chapter 7). Social play begins in the first months as adults initiate play with simple exchanges of vocalizations. Tickle games become popular, but by 8 months begin to decrease as patty-cake and peekaboo games increase. By the end of the first year, give-and-take games and point-and-name games have emerged (Lockman & McHale, 1989).

Social play includes the unexpected. The infant responds to the playfulness of the parent with positive expressions that include gleeful vocalizations. The parent who varies the game of peekaboo elicits laughing responses. The element of surprise in rolling a ball differently intensifies the child's positive reaction (Johnson et al., 1999).

Play with objects is a major factor in social play. Toys facilitate social interactions between peers at play as toys are offered and accepted. Objects mediate interactions when they are used to move children from parallel play to interactive play (Johnson et al., 1999). At about 14 months, objects contribute in lengthening the time in interactive play (Jacobson, 1981). By the end of the second year, children in group settings begin to show a preference for certain play partners, and first friendships are formed (Howes, 1987a; Howes & Matheson, 1992).

## Symbolic Play

Symbolic play emerges at approximately 1 year of age. First examples of symbolic play include actions by the infant on herself. The infant pretends to drink from a bottle or eat. These activities are at first solitary, which later broaden to include eye contact with a peer. By age 2, toddlers engage in the same type of symbolic play alongside each other and then later exchange vocalizations and smiles as they play (Garner, 1998).

Combinations of symbolic actions begin to be used when the child pretends to feed the doll and then washes its face. Pretense with objects and inclusion of peers in pretend play are expanded as toddlers begin to play roles such as pretending to cook while a peer holds a doll or rocks it. In these examples, social play and object play support symbolic play. Finally, language play also facilitates other categories of play. Emerging abilities in language enable toddlers to engage in social and symbolic play activities with their peers. Objects, real or imagined, support their play.

## Gender Differences in Play

A child's gender identity emerges early in life, and when gender identity is established, the nature of play changes. Children's identification of whether they are boys or are girls will result in playing more with other children of their gender (Fagot, 1994; Fagot & Leve, 1998). Once children engage in gender-specific play, they tend to play more with same-gender peers and play less with opposite-gender peers. This tendency increases as the children grow older in the preschool years (Maccoby, 1988).

One source of gender segregation is culture. In some cultures, boys are separated from girls at a very early age. In others, there is little concern for sex segregation, particularly in Western Europe. When these children attend nursery schools, however, they play in same-sex groups (Fagot, 1994).

Family and parenting are a factor in gender differences in play. It has been proposed that parents interact differently with sons than daughters. Moreover, these differences extend to differences in how mothers or fathers interact with sons and daughters. Research on this topic has resulted in disparate results partly because differing research methods have affected findings, studies have resulted in conflicting results, and differences in children's personalities and behaviors affect parent interactions (Lindsey, Mize, & Pettit, 1997).

Sex-typed play choices can be seen at about 2 years. Boys spend more time playing with blocks, transportation toys, guns, and manipulative objects; girls spend more time playing with dolls, stuffed animals, and art materials (Fagot & Leve, 1998; also see Chapter 7).

## Creativity and Play

What is the role of creativity in toddler play? How do toddlers express creativity in their play?

For toddlers, creative activities are a part of exploratory play. When they engage in pretend play, they are using their imaginations to create or replicate a role. When they explore in the mud or make marks on a piece of paper, they are becoming aware they can make something that is theirs alone. Toddlers can engage in art, music, dramatic play, and aesthetic appreciation in their expressions of creativity.

**Creativity and Art**    Toddlers begin to become artists as they learn to explore with pencils, crayons, markers, and finger paint. They can explore with play dough and shaving cream, and they enjoy using glue and scrap materials to construct their art.

**Creativity and Music**    Infants begin to appreciate music before they are born. In infancy they respond to music using the physical and verbal abilities that are available to them. Quiet music induces sleep; bouncy music can encourage them to engage in creative movement. They can follow the leader to marching music and enjoy classical music during meals. They can learn simple songs and songs with finger plays.

**Creativity and Dramatic Play**    Once a toddler has engaged in symbolic play, experiences with dramatic play expand possibilities for pretending. In a group setting, dramatic play areas can facilitate the opportunities for dramatic play and permit children to express their feelings in a familiar housekeeping, store, or other thematic dramatic setup.

**Aesthetic Appreciation**    Whenever infants and toddlers are able to experience expressive arts, they are developing aesthetic appreciation. Sensory activities, experiences with books, engaging in listening to music and singing songs, and experiencing natural elements in the environment all foster a sense of beauty in the world. Fish, colorful plants, flowers, and interesting smells and sounds both indoors and outdoors help toddlers appreciate their surroundings.

## The Integrated Nature of Play

As just described, the emergence of play in infants and toddlers depends on development in social-emotional, physical, and cognitive domains. Higher, more complex levels of play result from advances in development that are mutually supportive. Advances in a domain of development result in changes in play in that domain. Garner (1998) describes these advances as follows:

> Changes in physical development, for example, result in changes in coordinated motor play. As children acquire gross motor skills that allow mobility, they can expand their exploration of the environment, and advanced fine motor skill promotes exploration through greater manipulation of objects. (p. 137)

**GEORGE AND WATER PLAY**

When he reaches the deck, George sets the bottle on the deck and then uses both hands to pull himself up. Standing, he holds the bottle in his right hand and goes up the stairs, one foot leading, stepping up so that both feet are together. He turns toward the right-hand deck and also climbs those two steps carefully. At times he stumbles and puts out his hand to correct his balance. Jacinta and Clarrisa are in the wooden tunnel, and George bends forward slightly to peek in and smile. He then turns to the vertical ladder, stands on top and tips the water down and watches the waterfall. When he sees me watching him from below, he gives me a huge grin.

*Source:* Adapted from Stephenson, A. (2002). What George taught me about toddlers and water. *Young Children, 57,* 11.

Categories of play are integrated or overlap. Again, Garner (1998) explains the process:

> Children engaged in exploratory play, for example, may be practicing newly acquired motor skills in the presence of familiar peers. Similarly, when children imitate each other's motor behaviors, the activity may be either practice play or social play, and when infants are practicing emerging motor skills; the activity may be play, exploration, or work. Because infants are not able to label their play, it may be especially difficult to identify pretense when observing certain motor actions. (p. 137)

A garden developed for infants and toddlers in an Early Head Start Program provided an excellent example of how play can support integrated development. A purpose of the garden was to expose the children to nature because of the concern that children are having fewer experiences with the natural world. In addition, a goal was to provide daily access to plants, insects, and soil. Science and physical development were integrated as children planted seeds, nurtured plants, and picked vegetables as well as explored natural elements in the garden. Integrated play and learning tied the garden with the classroom through creative activities, dramatic play, and storybooks related to the outdoor experiences (Torquati & Barber, 2005). Table 4.1 shows examples of integrated exploratory play.

##  ADULT ROLES IN INFANT AND TODDLER PLAY

Throughout this chapter, we have described how parents, other adults, and siblings contribute to infant and toddler play and development. In the examples of developmental play provided in terms of infants and toddlers of different ages in the previous section, play interactions of different types were discussed. Play interactions vary depending on the child's temperament, family environment, and play styles of both children and adults. Because a high percentage of infants and toddlers are placed in caregiving settings during the day, caregivers play a major role in adult–child play. We have already noted how cultural differences affect how parents play with their babies. In this section, we consider how mothers and fathers play differently with their very young children. Next we discuss caregiver roles in infant-toddler play in child-care settings.

Parenting styles are changing. Until recent decades, research on parent–infant interactions were almost exclusively focused on the mother as the play partner. However, with the advent of working mothers and the evolution of different roles for both parents, fathers are taking increasingly important roles in the care and nurture of their children. Research into this phenomenon has revealed that mothers and fathers play differently with infant and toddlers.

**TABLE 4.1**    Examples of Integrated Exploratory Play

| What Children Might Do | How the Behavior Relates to Mathematics | What Teachers Can Do |
|---|---|---|
| Dump blocks out of a bucket and put all of the blue ones in a pile. | Infants and toddlers look for exact matches because that is the level of classifying they can handle. They cannot understand that things can be the same and different at the same time (e.g., round and blue vs. square and blue). | Provide plenty of blocks and other toys and items of different shapes, colors, and sizes. |
| | | Play with children; notice what they do, and record observations. |
| | Classification skills will one day be used for the math content areas of measurement, patterning/algebra, and geometry/spatial. | Use words that describe attributes such as size, shape, and color: "You made a big pile of blue blocks." |
| Beat on a drum, shake a tambourine, or play another musical instrument. | Infants and toddlers are slowly constructing number sense (e.g., realizing that numbers have meaning), concepts of quantity, and other ideas through their interaction with the environment. | Provide plenty of sound makers (e.g., wrist bells, pots and wooden spoons, rhythm instruments), so children can experiment and experience rhythm and beat. |
| | These beginning number concepts will eventually lead to understanding one-to-one correspondence and quantification. | Encourage children to play and move along with recorded music. |
| | | Talk with children and describe what they are doing: "Shake, shake—shake, shake, shake. You made your own music." |

In spite of the fact that more mothers are working, they still tend to take the major responsibility for caregiving. Although fathers help in the evenings and on weekends, mothers still have the major responsibility for caring for the child (Thompson & Walker, 1989).

Fathers might provide less of the care of babies, but they do play with infants. In the first months of life, fathers might move the infant's arms and legs, zoom her through the air, or tickle her stomach. From the very beginning, fathers play more physically and more noisily with their infant. This physical play between parent and child later evolves into rough-and-tumble play, discussed in Chapter five (Carlson, 2006).

Mothers, in contrast, are more likely to blend play activities with caregiving routines. They talk or sing to the infant in a soothing manner (Parke & Tinsley, 1981). Their play is more verbal and instructive.

When parents play with toddlers, differences in play activities persist. Mothers help their toddlers play with toys, read to them, or play traditional games such as patty-cake and peek-aboo. Fathers engage in increasing amounts of physical play. They play chase and crawling games or wrestle with them. As a result, some researchers have found that toddlers are more responsive to their fathers than to their mothers (Clarke-Stewart, 1978).

Caregivers in child-care settings have a different type of support role for infant-toddler play. Because they are responsible for the care of a group of infants or toddlers, their play

## CONTRASTING ADULT ROLES IN GROUP SETTINGS

There can be contrasts in adult roles in infant and toddler programs. A mother experienced two contrasting approaches to how caregivers prepare and conduct play activities in play-groups for very young children.

At a playgroup sponsored by a community, activities were relaxed and unstructured with parents and the group leader sometimes playing with the children. On other occasions, they allowed the children to explore on their own with different types of toys.

In contrast, the second playgroup was conducted at a franchised child-care center. The teacher was well trained and planned around themes and acquisition of developmental skills. Activities were planned for children's play under the teacher's guidance.

The mother left these contrasting adult roles in playgroups with questions. Was one preferable to the other? The community playgroup was less structured, but the child-care center reflected strong preparation in developmentally appropriate play activities. Is there a best way for adults to play with infants and toddlers (A. Ford, 2006).

interactions are more likely to be brief. They interact with infants while other babies in their care are asleep. They might engage in talking with infants while they are changing them or while alternately feeding two or more infants.

Caregivers also have a more structured environment for infants and toddlers. They provide cognitive stimulation by providing toys that are appropriate for developmental levels. Like parents, they talk to the children about their play and encourage them to try new toys. Toddlers spend 50% of their time interacting with a caregiver in a child-care setting, 23% in social play, and 23% in object play (Howes, et al., 1989).

Social play is enhanced in group care. Toddlers have a group of potential playmates and an environment that encourages play both indoors and outdoors. Caregivers can assist toddlers in playing in the group setting and introduce opportunities for social interactions as they engage in a variety of play activities. Peer interactions can also take negative forms such as aggressive encounters or running that is out of control (Howes et al., 1989).

Recent research supports the benefits of quality child care for very young children that lasted into middle childhood. Quality of early

care was a factor in positive results socially and academically. Students in middle school who had attended child care that was responsive, stimulating, and structured had fewer behavior problems as teenagers (Vandell, et al., 2010; Votrube-Drzal, et al., 2010). Studies of children who had been in quality child care before age six did better academically (Vandell, et al., 2010). One study reported that students who had been in early child care had better math and reading scores in middle school (Dearing, et al., 2009). These and other studies affirm that quality child care between the ages of 2 and 5 have long lasting effects on social behavior and academic achievement, regardless of the families' income level. However, children from poverty homes benefited the most, supporting the need for access to quality early childhood care for very young children at risk for later achievement.

## TOYS AND MATERIALS FOR INFANT AND TODDLER PLAY

Parents and caregivers benefit from knowing about appropriate toys for infants and toddlers. Toys appropriate for infants who are not yet able to grasp might become dangerous once the infant can put them in her mouth. Parents should consider the following guidelines when selecting toys for their infants and toddlers:

- *Toys should be appropriate for the child's development.* Parents should select toys that are interesting and with which the child can play with successfully. They should be bright and colorful.
- *Toys should be safe and durable.* Toys should be able to withstand being mouthed, banged, and thrown. They should be free of small parts that can come off and be swallowed or cause the infant to choke.
- *Toys should complement the child's ability to grasp and manipulate.* Parents should consider the size, weight, and stability of the toy.
- *Toys should appeal to the child's senses.* Soft toys are desirable, as are toys that make a noise and/or can be acted on (poke, turn knobs, pull strings to initiate noises, etc.) (Bronson, 1995; Deiner, 1997).

Caregivers who serve infants and toddlers in group settings should provide toys of different categories that provide variety for very young children. Selection of toys should include a balance of the following categories (Deiner, 1997, p. 377):

- Materials that encourage awareness of self and others: toys with mirrors, dolls, and puppets
- Materials with varied textures: textured rattles and blocks and fuzzy puppets
- Materials that make noise: musical toys, rattles, and squeaky toys
- Materials that reflect ethnic diversity
- Materials for cuddling: soft stuffed dolls, animals, toys, and other huggables

Toys should be open ended and promote creative play. In the current high-tech world,

Puppet play facilitates social and language development.

many toys are run by computer chips and are programmed for specific actions. Moreover, the abundance of toys can be overwhelming. Children who are surrounded by too many playthings may be too distracted by the choices to use imagination, fantasy, and creativity in their play (Elkind, 2005).

The Consumer Product Safety Commission has developed lists of toys that are specific for different ages and developmental levels of infants and toddlers. Figure 4.5 lists toys for infants from birth to 6 months and from 7 to 12 months; Figure 4.6 lists toys and materials for toddlers 1 to 2 years old.

**FIGURE 4.5** Toys and Materials for Infants–0–6 Months

| Active Play | Manipulative Play | Make-Believe Play | Creative Play | Learning Play |
|---|---|---|---|---|
| <u>Outdoor or Gym Equipment</u><br>Infant swings with supervision<br><br><u>Sports Equipment</u> *from about six weeks*<br>• clutch balls<br>• texture balls.<br>• Soft squeeze balls | <u>Construction Toys</u><br>*from about 4 months*<br>• soft blocks<br><br><u>Manipulative Toys</u><br>*from about 6–8 weeks*<br>• simple rattles<br>• teethers<br>• light, sturdy, cloth toys<br>• squeeze toys<br>• toys suspended or to the side of infant for batting and grasping<br><br>*from about 4 months*<br>• disks, keys on ring<br>• interlocking plastic rings<br>• small hand-held manipulables<br>• toys on suction cups<br>• crib gyms (remove when child can up on hands and knees) | <u>Dolls</u><br>• soft baby dolls, soft-bodied dolls or rag dolls (all with molded hair)<br><br><u>Stuffed Toys</u><br>• small plush animals<br>• music box animals (operated by adult)<br>• grab-on soft toys<br><br><u>Puppets</u><br>• soft hand puppets (held and moved by adults)<br><br><u>Role Play Materials</u><br>• mirrors (large, unbreakable) fastened to crib, playpen or wall | <u>Audio-Visual Equipment</u><br>(Adult Operated)<br>• records, tapes or CDs (gentle regular rhythms, lullabies.<br>• music boxes | <u>Books</u><br>may enjoy listening to a story being read |

*(continued)*

121

**FIGURE 4.5** Continued

Toys and Materials for Older Infants–7–12 Months

| Active Play | Manipulative Play | Make-Believe Play | Creative Play | Learning Play |
|---|---|---|---|---|
| Push and Pull Toys<br>• push toys without rods (simple cars, animals on wheels or rollers) | Construction Toys<br>• soft blocks<br>• rubber blocks<br>• rounded wood blocks | Dolls<br>• soft baby dolls, soft-bodied dolls, or rag dolls—all with molded hair | Musical Instruments<br>• rubber or wood blocks that rattle or tinkle | Books<br>• cloth books<br>• plastic books<br>• small cardboard books |
| Outdoor or Gym Equipment<br>• infant swings (with adult supervision).<br>• soft low climbing platform for crawlers | Puzzles *from about 10 months*<br>• brightly colored, lightweight crib and playpen puzzles (2–3 pieces) | Stuffed Toys<br>• small plush animals music box animals (operated by adult)<br>• grab or soft toys<br>• big soft toys for hugging and roughhousing. | Art and Craft Materials *from about 12 months*<br>• large paper<br>• large crayons for scribbling | |
| Sports Equipment<br>• transparent balls<br>• chime balls<br>• flutter balls<br>• action balls | Manipulative Toys<br>• teethers<br>• light sturdy cloth toys<br>• toys on suction cups<br>• small, hand-held manipulables<br>• disks/keys on rings<br>• squeeze-squeak toys<br>• roly-poly toys<br>• activity boxes and cubes<br>• pop-up boxes (easy operation)<br>• containers with objects to empty and fill<br>• large rubber or plastic pop beads<br>• simple nesting cups<br>• stacking ring cones (few rings and safe sticks)<br>• graspable (unbreakable) mirror toys which can be held and played with | Puppets<br>• soft hand puppets–child may handle but must be operated by adult | Audio-Visual Equipment (adult operated)<br>• records, tapes, or CDs (simple songs, lullabies, music with simple rhythms)<br>• music boxes | |
| | Sand and Water Play Toys<br>• activity boxes for bath<br>• simple floating toys | Role Play Materials<br>• low wall-mounted mirrors to see self sit, creep, crawl, etc.<br><br>Transportation Toys<br>• simple push cars (one piece) | | |

*Source:* Adapted from *Which Toy for Which Child. A Consumer's Guide for Selecting Suitable Toys Ages Six Through Twelve.* Washington, DC: *U. S. Consumer Product Safety Commission, Pub. No. 285.*

**FIGURE 4.6** Toys and Materials for Toddlers

| Active Play | Manipulative Play | Make-Believe Play | Creative Play | Learning Play |
|---|---|---|---|---|
| Push and Pull Toys<br>• pull toys with strings<br>• doll carriages<br>• wagons<br>• small, light wheelbarrow<br>• push toys such as lawnmower, vacuum, shopping cart | Construction Play<br>• solid, wooden unit blocks<br>• large, hollow, building blocks<br>• plastic interlocking rings, large plastic nuts and bolts | Dolls<br>• soft-bodied dolls and rubber dolls<br>• dolls to fit in child's arms, also small, realistic dolls<br>• talking dolls operated by pulling string<br>• doll accessories-simple and sturdy | Musical Instruments<br>• all rhythm instruments—bells, rattles, cymbals, drums, triangle, rhythm sticks, sand blocks, xylophones | Games<br>• lotto matching games based on color pictures<br>• dominoes, especially giant dominoes<br>• board games based on chance with few pieces or pairs |
| Ride-On Toys<br>• realistic-looking ride-ons, tractors, motorcycles<br>• ride-ons with storage trays<br>• older toddlers, small tricycle | Puzzles<br>• 1–2 years, 2–3 pieces<br>• 2 to 2 1/2 years, 4–5 pieces<br>• 2 1/2 to 3 years, 6–12 pieces | • doll caretaking accessories<br>• simple removable garments<br><br>Stuffed Toys<br>• soft, plastic animals<br>• mother and baby combinations | Arts and Crafts Materials<br>• large crayons<br>• non-toxic paints and short-handled brushes with blunt ends<br>• blunt-end scissors<br>• sturdy markers | Specific Skill Development Toys<br>simple teaching toys for<br>• matching/sorting, shapes, colors, letters/sounds, numbers, concepts |
| Outdoor and Gym Equipment<br>• tunnels<br>• climbing structures and slides<br>• stationary outdoor equipment<br>• swings with curved, soft seats and restraining straps | Pattern-Making Toys<br>• peg boards with large pegs<br>• color cubes<br>• magnetic boards with shapes, animals, people<br>• older toddlers-color forms | • preference for realistic animals<br>• toys with music box inside<br><br>Puppets<br>• small hand puppets<br>• lightweight, sized to fit child's hand<br>• puppets doubling as stuffed toys | | |

*(continued)*

**FIGURE 4.6** *Continued*

| Active Play | Manipulative Play | Make-Believe Play | Creative Play | Learning Play |
|---|---|---|---|---|
| Sports Equipment<br>• sleds sized to child<br>• spinning seat<br>• pool toys–tubes and mats<br>• balls of all sizes | Manipulative Toys<br>• fit-together toys of 5–10 pieces<br>• nesting toys with multiple pieces including barrel toys that require screwing motion<br>• number/counting boards with large pegs<br>• shape sorters with common shapes<br>• pounding/hammering toys<br>• smelling jars (older toddlers)<br>• feel bag or box<br>• color/picture dominoes<br>• simple lotto matching games based on color, pictures<br><br>Dressing, Lacing Stringing Toys<br>• large colored beads<br>• lacing card or wooden shoe for lacing<br>• dressing books and dolls<br>• frames, cubes for lacing, buttoning, snapping<br><br>Sand and Water Play Toys<br>• bathtub activity centers<br>• nesting tub toys<br>• linking tub toys<br>• small boats<br>• small and large sandbox tools | Role Play Materials<br>• dress-ups and costumes<br>• child-sized stove, cooking board, refrigerator, microwave, dishwasher<br>• full-length mirror<br><br>Transportation Toys<br>• small, realistic cars<br>• vehicles with moving parts<br>• large plastic trucks with moving parts<br>• cars, trucks with removable figures, accessories<br>• small trains with simple coupling mechanism | | |

*Source:* Adapted from *Which Toy for Which Child: A Consumer's Guide for Selecting Suitable Toys, Ages Six Through Twelve.* Washington, DC, U. S. Consumer Product Safety Commission Pub. No. 285.

## ⬛ SUMMARY

The first 2 years of life are important for development and play. Neonates use emerging senses to engage in playlike activity. This engagement in pleasurable activities increases as new abilities in physical, cognitive, and social development widen possibilities for play.

Gross- and fine-motor skills development enables the infant and toddler to achieve mobility and to grasp and explore objects. Play using available sensory and motor abilities becomes more sophisticated as gross- and fine-motor skills are mastered. Play with body parts expands to play with toys as the infant can move about and manipulate objects. Adults facilitate in motor play by providing toys that complement the baby's development and encourage the infant to engage in play activities.

Cognitive development proceeds at a rapid pace. Cognitive development in stages and substages as described by Piaget help explain how infant and toddler intellectual development promote cognitive play. The substages in the sensorimotor stage of development explain how emerging physical and intellectual skills work together to extend infant and toddler play. Whereas early stages of play are limited to sensory and physical play, toddlers in the second year are able to engage in pretend play in increasingly sophisticated ways.

Language development follows a predictable sequence in all children. During the first 2 years, language development is impressive: Very young children are able to communicate with a rapidly growing vocabulary. Adults play a major role in language development, initiating language encounters with infants and clarifying and extending toddler language through the use of parentese. Infants and toddlers also engage in play with language following their own initiatives. Infants play with babbling sounds, and toddlers use developing grammatical patterns to engage in language play.

Social and emotional development depend on the parenting styles and emotional environment of the family. Cognitive development in the early months affects the expression of emotions and first experiences with fear and anxiety. The temperament of the infant and toddler affect their interactions with the adults in their lives and vice versa. The security experienced by the infant affects development of attachment with parents and caregivers.

Social play requires interactions with adults. Parents engage infants in social games and conversations that nurture attachment and confidence to explore and play. Although infants are aware and interested in their peers, social peer play emerges gradually in the second year as toddlers exchange toys, smile at playmates, and play alongside peers in the same activity.

Emerging development in social, physical, language, and cognitive domains interact in infant and toddler play. Developmental advances in individual domains support development in other domains that support advances and sophistication in abilities to play.

## ⬛ KEY TERMS

| | |
|---|---|
| Attachment | Parentese |
| Autonomy versus shame and doubt | Proximodistal development |
| Behaviorist theory | Referential style |
| Cephalocaudal development | Reflexes |
| Difficult child | Scaffolding |
| Easy child | Secure attachment |
| Expressive style | Sensorimotor period |
| Functional play | Separation anxiety |
| Holophrastic speech | Separation-individuation |
| Insecure attachment | Slow-to-warm-up child |
| Interactionist theory | Stranger anxiety |
| Language acquisition device (LAD) | Symbiosis |
| Manipulative play | Symbolic play |
| Nativist theory | Telegraphic speech |
| Object permanence | Temperament |
| | Trust versus mistrust |

## ⬛ STUDY QUESTIONS

1. How do cephalocaudal and proximodistal development explain the nature of growth in motor skills? Explain these patterns of development.
2. Describe three causes of differences in physical development.
3. Trace how emerging physical development affects how infants and toddlers play. Show the steps in the development of motor skills and play activities that can result from the new skills.

4. Explain cognitive development in terms of the sensorimotor period. How do children from different cultures vary in sensorimotor development?

5. Define symbolic or pretend play. How do toddlers engage in more sophisticated forms of symbolic play?

6. How do adults facilitate symbolic play?

7. Explain three theories of language development. How do they support an eclectic theory of language development?

8. How can cultural and ethnic differences affect language development?

9. How do adults support language through parentese? Explain how parentese facilitates language play.

10. How do the home environment and parenting practices affect social development?

11. What do theories of emotional development imply are needed for optimal emotional development?

12. How do temperament and attachment affect emotional development?

13. Explain how social games teach infants and toddlers how to play with others. Give examples.

14. What roles can adults play in supporting peer play? Why are peer play activities important for toddlers?

## REFERENCES

Armbruster, B. B., Lehr, R., & Osborn, J. (2002). *A child becomes a reader. Birth to preschool.* Jessup, MD: National Institute for Literacy.

Athey, I. (1984). Contributions of play to development. In T.D. Yawkey & A. D. Pellegrini (Eds.), *Child's play: Developmental and applied* (pp. 9–28). Hillsdale, NH: Erlbaum.

Ballargeon, R., & DeVos, J. (1991). Object permanence in young infants: Further evidence. *Child Development, 62,* 1227–1246.

Beckwith, L. (1986). Parent-infant interaction and infants' social-emotional development. In A. W. Gottfried & C. C. Brown (Eds.), *Play interactions* (pp. 279–292). Lexington, MA: Lexington.

Begley, S. (1996, February, 29). Your child's brain. *Newsweek,* pp. 55–58.

Berger, K. S. (2009). *The developing person through childhood* (5th ed.). New York: Worth.

Berk, L. E. (2007). *Infants, children, and adolescents* (4th ed.). Boston: Allyn & Bacon.

Blakeslee, S. (1997), April 17). Studies show talking with infants shapes basis of ability to think. *New York Times,* p. A-14.

Bower, T. G. R. (1989). *The rational infant: Learning in infancy.* New York: Freeman.

Brazelton, T. B., & Greenspan, S. I. (2000). *The irreducible needs of children: What every child must have to grow and learn.* New York: Perseus.

Bronson, M. B. (1995). *The right stuff for children birth to 8.* Washington, DC: National Association for the Education of Young Children.

Brown, J. E., Serdula, M., Cairns, K., Godes, J. R., Jacobs, D. R., Elmer, P., & Trowbridge, F. L. (1986). Ethnic group difference in nutritional status of young children from low-income areas of an urban county. *American Journal of Clinical Nutrition, 44,* 938–944.

Bruner, J. S., Jolly, A., & Sylva, K. (Eds.). (1976). *Play: Its role in development and evolution.* New York: Basic.

Bruner, J. S., & Sherwood, V. (1976). Peekaboo and the learning of rule structures. In J. S. Bruner, A. Jolly, & K. Sylva (Eds.), *Play: Its role in development and evolution* (pp. 277–285). New York: Basic.

Buhler, K. (1937). *The mental development of the child.* London: Routledge & Kegan Paul.

Carlson, F. M. (2006). *Essential touch. Meeting the needs of young children.* Washington, DC: National Association for the Education of Young Children.

Chomsky, N. (1957). *Syntactic structures.* The Hague: Mouton.

Clark-Stewart, A. (1978). And daddy makes three: The father's impact on mother and young child. *Child Development, 49,* 466–478.

Copple, C., & Bredekamp, S. (Eds.). (2009). *Developmentally appropriate practices in early childhood programs serving children from birth to age 8. (3rd ed.).* Washington, DC: National Association for the Education of Young Children.

Cowley, G. (1997, Spring-Summer). The language explosion. *Newsweek Special Edition,* pp. 16–21.

Dearing, E., McCartney, K., & Taylor, B. (2009). Does higher-quality early child care promote low-income children's math and reading achievement in Middle Childhood? *Child Development, 80,* 1329–1349.

Deiner, P. L. (1997). *Infants and toddlers: Development and program planning.* Fort Worth, TX: Harcourt Brace.

Dennis. W. (1960). Causes of retardation among institutionalized children. *Journal of Genetic Psychology, 99,* 47–59.

Dunn, J. (1983). Sibling relationships in early childhood. *Child Development, 54,* 787–811.

Durkin, D. (1966). *Children who read early.* New York: Teachers College Press.

Elkind, D. (2005, November/December). The changing world of toys and toy play. *Ex Exchange, 1661,* 11–13.

Erikson, E. H. (1963). *Child and society* (Rev. ed.). New York: Norton.

Escalona, S. (1968). *The roots of individuality.* Chicago: Aldine.

Fagot, B. I. (1994). Peer relations and the development of competence in boys and girls. *New Directions for Child Development, 65,* 53–65.

Fagot, B. I., & Leve, L. (1998). Gender identity and play. In D. P. Fromberg & D. Bergen (Eds.), *Play from birth to twelve and beyond: Contexts, perspectives, and meanings* (pp. 187–192).

Fernald, A., & Morikawa, H. (1993). Common themes and cultural variations in Japanese and American Mothers' speech to infants. *Child Development, 64,* 637–656.

Fogel, A. (1979). Peer vs. mother-directed behavior in 1- to 3-month-old infants. *Infant Behavior and Development, 2,* 215–216.

Ford, A. (2006). *The case of dueling playgroups.* Retrieved March 30, 2006 from *Suite101.com*

Frost, J. L. (1992). *Play and playscapes.* Albany, NY: Delmar.

Frost, J. L. (1998). *Neuroscience, play and child development.* Paper presented at the American Association for the Child's Right to Play Conference, Longmont, CO.

Garner, B. P. (1998). Play development from birth to age four. In D. P. Fromberg & D. Bergen (Eds.), *Play from birth to twelve and beyond: Contexts, perspectives, and meanings* (pp. 137–145). New York: Garland.

Garvey, C. (1977b). Play with language and speech In S. Ervin-Tripp & C. Mitchell-Kernan (Eds.), *Child discourses.* New York: Academic Press.

Genishi, C., & Dyson, A. H. (2009). *Children language and literacy: Diverse learners in diverse times.* New York: Teachers College Press & Washington, DC: National Association for the Education of Young Children.

Gottlieb, G. (1983). The psychobiological approach to developmental issues. In M. M. Haith & J. J. Campos (Eds.), P. G, Mussen (Series Ed.), *Handbook of child psychology:* Vol. 2. *Infancy and developmental psychobiology* (pp. 1–26). New York: Wiley.

Greenspan, S. I., & Wieder, S. (2005). *Infant and early childhood mental health: A comprehensive developmental approach to assessment and interaction.* Arlington, VA: American Psychiatric Publishing.

Gunnar, M. (2006). Stress, nurture and the young brain. In J. R. Lally, P. L. Mangione, & D. Greenwald (Eds.), *Concepts for care: 20 essays on infant/toddler development and learning* (pp. 41–42).

Haight. W. L., Parke, R. D., & Black, J. E. (1997). Mothers' and fathers' beliefs about and spontaneous participation in their toddlers' pretend play. *Merrill-Palmer Quarterly, 43,* 271–290.

Hale-Benson, J. E. (1986). *Black children: Their roots, culture, and learning styles.* Baltimore: Johns Hopkins University Press.

Honig, A. (2002). *Secure relationships: Nurturing infant-toddler attachment in early care settings.* Washington, DC: National Association for the Education of Young Children.

Hopkins, B., & Westra, T. (1968). Maternal handling and motor development: An intracultural study. *Genetic, Social and General Psychology Monographs, 14,* 377–420.

Howes, C. (1987a). Peer interaction of young children. *Monograph of the Society for Research in Child Development, 53*(1) serial No. 217.

Howes, C. (1987b). Social competence with peers in young children: Developmental sequences. *Developmental Review, 7,* 252–272.

Howes, C., & Matheson, C. C. (1992). Sequences in the development of competent play with peers: Social and social pretend play. *Developmental Psychology, 28,* 961–974.

Howes, C., Unger, O., & Seidner, L. B. (1989). Social pretend play in toddlers: Parallels with social play and with solitary pretend. *Child Development, 60,* 77–84.

Hutt, C. (1976). Exploration and play in children. In J. S. Bruner, A. Jolly, & K. Sylva (Eds.), *Play: Its role in development and evolution* (pp. 202–213). New York: Basic.

International Reading Association and National Association for the Education of Young Children. (1999). Learning to read and write: Developmentally appropriate practices for young children. A joint position statement of the International Reading Association (IRA) and the National Association for the Education of Young Children (NAEYC). In S. B. Newman, C. Copple, & S. Bredekamp (Eds.), *Learning to read and write: Developmentally appropriate practices for young children* (pp. 3–26). Washington, DC: National Association for the Education of Young Children.

Izard, C. E. (1991). *The psychology of emotions.* New York: Plenum.

Jacobson, J. L. (1981). The role of inanimate objects in early peer interaction. *Child Development, 52,* 618–626.

Johnson, J. E., Christie, J. F., & Yawkey, T. D. (1999). *Play, development, and early education.* Boston: Allyn & Bacon.

Kagan, J. (1977). The uses of cross-cultural research in dearly development. In P. H. Leiderman, S. R. Tulkin, & A. Rosenfield (Eds.), *Culture and infancy: Variations in the human experience* (pp. 271–286). New York: Academic Press.

Kagan, J. (1994, October 5). The realistic view of biology and behavior. *Chronicle of Higher Education,* p. A64.

Kagan, J., Kearsley, R. B., & Zelazo, P. R. (1978). *Infancy: Its place in human development.* Cambridge, MA: Harvard University Press.

Kagan, J., Reznick, J. S., & Sidman, N. (1988). Biological basis of childhood shyness. *Science, 240,* 167–171.

Kalb, C., & Namuth, T. (1977, Spring-Summer). When a child's science isn't golden. *Newsweek* [special edition], p. 23.

Kimmerle, M., Mick, L. A., & Michel, G. E. (1995). Bimanual role-differentiated toy play during infancy. *Infant Behavior and Development, 18,* 299–307.

Lindsey, E. W., Mize, J., & Petit, G. S. (1997). Differential play patterns of mothers and fathers of sons and daughters: Implication for children's gender role development. *Sex Roles, 37*, 643–661.

Lockman, J. J., & McHale, J. P. (1989). Object manipulation in infancy: Developmental and contextual determinants. In J. J. Lockman & N. L. Hazen (Eds.), *Action in social context: Perspectives on early development* (pp. 129–167). New York: Plenum.

Lott, D. H. (1998). Brain development, attachment, and impact of psychic vulnerability. *Psychiatric Times, xv.* Retrieved June 20, 1999, from *http://babyparenting.about .com*

Maccoby, E. E. (1988). Gender as a social category. *Developmental Psychology, 24*, 755–765.

Mahler, M. S., Pine, F., & Bergman, A. (1976). *The psychological birth of the human infant: Symbiosis and individuation.* New York: Basic.

Mangione, P. L. (2006). Creating responsive, reciprocal relationships with infants and toddlers. In J. R. Lally, P. L. Mangione, & D. Greenwald (Eds.), *Concepts for care: 20 essays on infant/toddler development and learning* (pp. 25–30). San Francisco: WestEd.

McCall, R. (1979). *Infants.* Cambridge, MA: Harvard University Press.

McCune, L. (1986). Symbolic development in normal and atypical infants. In G. Fein & M. Rivkin (Eds), *The young child at play. Review of research* (Vol. 4, pp. 45–62). Washington, DC: National Association for the Education of Young Children.

McDevitt, T. M., & Ormrod, J. E. (2004). *Child development. Educating and working with children and adolescents* (2nd ed.). Upper Saddle River, NJ: Pearson Education.

McHenry, J. D., & Buerk, K. J. (2008, January). Infants and toddlers meet the natural world. *Young Children, 63*, 22–25.

Nash, J. M. (1997). *Global paradox.* New York: Avon.

Parke, R. D., & Tinsley, B. R. (1981). The father's role in infancy: Determinants of involvement in caregiving and play. In M. E. Lamb (Ed.), *The role of the father in child development* (2nd ed., pp. 429–458). New York: Wiley.

Pearson, B. Z. (2006). Nurturing very young children who experience more than one language. In J. R. Lally, P. L. Mangione, & D. Greenwald (Eds.), *Concepts for care: 20 essays on infant/toddler development and learning.* San Francisco: WestEd.

Pepler, D. J., & Ross, H. S. (1981). The effects of play on convergent and divergent problem-Solving. *Child Development, 52*, 1202–1210.

Piaget, J. (1951). *Play, dreams, and imitation in childhood* (C. Gattegno & F. M. Hodgson, Trans). New York: International Universities Press. (Original work published 1945.)

Piaget, J. (1976). Mastery Play. In J. S. Bruner, A. Jolly, & K. Sylva (Eds.), *Play: Its role in development and evolution* (pp. 12–17). New York: Basic.

Poussaint, S. F., & Linn, S. (1997, Spring-Summer). Fragile: Handle with care. *Newsweek*, [Newsweek Special Issue], p. 33.

Power, T. G. (1985). Mother- and father-infant play: A developmental analysis. *Child Development, 56*, 1514–1524.

Puckett, B. B., & Black, J. K. (2005). *The young child. Development from prebirth through age eight* (4th ed.). Upper Saddle River, NJ: Pearson Education.

Raikes, H. H., & Edwards, C. P. (2009). *Extending the dance in caregiving. Enhancing attachment and relationships.* Baltimore: Brookes, & Washington, DC: National Association for the Education of Young Children.

Ross, H. S., & Kay, D. A. (1980). The origins of social games. In K. H. Rubin (Ed.), *Children's play.* (pp. 17–31). San Francisco: Jossey-Bass.

Rubin, K. H., Coplan, R. J., Fox, N. A., & Calkins, S. D. (1995). Emotionality, emotion regulation, and preschoolers social adaptation. *Development and Psychopathology, 7*, 49–62.

Santrock, J. W. (2007). *Children.* Dubuque: IA: Wm. C. Brown.

Shaffer, L. F., Hall, E., & Lynch, M. (2009, November). Toddler's scientific explorations: Encounters with insects. *Young Children, 64*, 18–23.

Shonkoff, J. P., & Phillips, D. A. (Eds.), *From neurons to neighborhoods: The science of early childhood development.* Committee on Integrating the Science of Early Childhood Development, National Research Council and Institute of Medicine. Washington, DC: National Academy Press.

Shore, R. (1997). *Rethinking the brain: New insights into early development.* New York: Families and Work Institute.

Siegel., D. J. (1999). *The developing mind. Toward a neurology of interpersonal experience.* New York: The Guilford Press.

Skinner, B. F. (1957). *Verbal behavior.* New York: Appleton-Century Crofts.

Stephenson, A. (2002). What George taught me about toddlers and water. *Young Children, 57*, 11–13.

Stevenson, M. B. (1989). The influences on the play of infants and toddlers. In M. N. Bloch & A. D. Pellegrini (Eds.), *The ecological context of children's play* (pp. 84–103). Norwood, NJ: Ablex.

Stone, S. J. (2007). *An analysis of mixed-age children's scaffolding during symbolic play trans formations.* Paper presented at AERA. Chicago, IL.

Stone, S. J., & Stone, W. (n.d.). *Symbolic play and emergent literacy.* Retrieved July 27, 2010 From www.iecp.play.org/ documents/brno/stonel.pdf

Super, C. M. (1981). Cross-cultural research on infancy. In H. Trianis & A. Heron (Eds.), *Handbook of cross-cultural psychology* (Vol. 4, pp. 11–53). Boston: Allyn & Bacon.

Tanner, J. M. (1990). *Foetus into man* (2nd ed.). Cambridge, MA: Harvard University Press.

Thomas, A., & Chess, S. (1977). *Temperament and development.* New York: Brunner/Mazel.

Thompson, I., & Walker, A. J. (1989). Gender in families: Women and men in marriage, work, and parenthood. *Journal of Marriage and the Family, 5*, 845–871.

Torquati, J., & Barber, J. (2005, May). Dancing with trees. Infants and toddlers in the garden. *Young Children, 60*, 40–41.

Trawick-Smith, J. (2006). *Early childhood development: A multicultural perspective*. (5th ed.). Upper Saddle River, NJ: Pearson Education.

Tronick, E. Z. (1989). Emotions and emotional communication in infants. *American Psychologist, 44*, 112–119.

U.S. Library of Medicine & National Institutes of Health. (Updated January, 26, 2010). Developmental milestones record-2 years. Retrieved July 23, 2010 from http://www.nim.nih.gov/medlineplus/ency/article/002012.htm.

Uzgiris, I., & Hunt, J. M. (1975). *Assessment in infancy*. Urbana: University of Illinois Press.

Vandell, D. L., Belsky, J., Burchinal, M., Steinberg, L., & Vandergrift, N. Do effects of early child care extend to age 15 years? Results from the NHICD study of early child care and youth development. *Child Development, 81*, 737–756.

Vortruba-Drzal, Coley, R. L., Maldonado-Carreno, Li-Grining, C. P., & Chase-Lansdale, P. L. (2010). Child care and the development of behavior problems among economically disadvantaged children in middle childhood. *Child Development, 81*, 1460–1467.

Vygotsky, L. S. (1984). *Thought and language*. Cambridge, MA: Harvard University Press.

Waters, E., & Cummings, E. M. (2000). A secure base from which to explore close relationships. *Child Development, 71*, 164–172.

Waters, E., Wippman, J., & Sroufe, L. (1979). Attachment, positive affect, and competence in the peer group: Two studies in construct validation. *Child Development, 50*, 821–829.

Watson, M. (2008). Stages and components of presymbolic and symbolic play. Retrieved July 27, 2010 from http://www.speechpathology.com/articles/article_detail.asp?

Weir, R. (1976). Playing with language. In J. S. Bruner, A. Jolly, & K. Sylva (Eds.), *Play: Its Role in development and evolution* (pp. 609–618).

Weisler, A., & McCall, R. B. (1976). Exploration and play: Resume and redirection. *American Psychologist, 31*, 492–498.

Williams, A. E. (2008, January). Exploring the natural world with infants and toddlers in an urban setting. *Young Children, 63*, 22–25.

Wittmer, D. S., & Petersen (2006). *Infant and toddler development and responsive program Planning*. Upper Saddle River, NJ: Pearson.

Wohlwill, J. F. (1984). Relationships between exploration and play. In T. D. Yawkey & A. D. Pellegrini (Eds.), *Child's play: Developmental and applied* (pp. 143–170).

Youngblade, L. M., & Dunn, J. (1995). Individual differences in young children's pretend play with mother and sibling: Links to relationships and understanding of other people's feelings and beliefs. *Child Development, 66*, 1472–1492.

Zigler, E. (2006). Play and its relationship to literacy. In J. R. Lally, P. L. Mangione, & D. Greenwald. *Concepts for care. 20 essays on infant/toddler development and learning* (pp. 53–58). San Francisco: WestEd.

# 5 Play in the Preschool Years

IN SPEAKING of play and its role in the preschooler's development, we are concerned with two fundamental questions; first, how play itself arises in development—its origin and genesis;

*second, the role of this developmental activity that we call play, as a form of development in the child of preschool age. Is play the leading form of activity for a child of this age, or is it simply the predominant form?*

*It seems to me that from the point of view of development, play is not the predominant form of activity, but it is in a sense, the leading source of development in the pre-school years.*

(Vygotsky, 1976, p. 53)

Play is the leading source of development in the ages between 2 and 6 according to Vygotsky. They are also the years when children play the most. When possible, they spend their days at play. They develop their bodies and minds through play while they are inventing games and dramatizing fantasies. Free play helps develop well-being by enabling children to pay attention and teaching them to affiliate with other children. Most of all, play makes kids happy (Burdette & Whitaker, 2005).

This chapter continues the relationship between development and play as described within motor, cognitive, language, and social domains of development. Milestones in development are noted as well as how play affects and reflects development in each domain.

Characteristics of preschool play and gender differences in play are described, followed by the role of adults in nurturing and facilitating play. This includes the nature of play in group settings. Types of play affected by gender differences will be discussed. Rough-and-tumble play, chase games, and superhero play are some of the types of play that will be included. The topics will be introduced in this chapter and discussed with regard to the preschool child. In Chapter 6, the topics will again be discussed regarding the school-age child at a more advanced level. Finally, the last section of the chapter discusses influences on children's play and how developmentally appropriate toys and materials are selected.

## PHYSICAL DEVELOPMENT

The preschool years are the period when young children acquire basic motor skills. The skills fall into two categories described in Chapter 4: fine motor and gross motor. Recall that fine-motor skills involve use of the hands and fingers, whereas gross-motor skills are the movements that allow the individual to become mobile and engage in skills requiring body movement. Perceptual-motor development is also discussed in terms of the relationship between movement and the environment.

Gallahue (1993) proposes that children move through a developmental progression in the acquisition of motor skills. This progression includes the reflexive movement phase, the rudimentary movement phase, the fundamental movement phase, and the specialized movement phase. The sequence of the appearance of these phases is universal, although the rate of acquisition of motor skills varies from child to child.

The **reflexive movement phase** ranges from birth to about 1 year. In this phase, the infant engages in reflexive movements, as described in Chapter 4.

The **rudimentary movement phase** includes the basic motor skills acquired in infancy: reaching, grasping and releasing objects, sitting, standing, and walking. The skills of the rudimentary movement phase acquired during the first 2 years form the foundation for the fundamental phase.

The **fundamental movement phase** occurs during the preschool years ranging from ages 2 to 3 to ages 6 to 7. During this phase, children gain increased control over their gross- and fine-motor movements. They are involved in developing and refining motor skills such as running, jumping, throwing, and catching. Control of each skill progresses through initial and elementary stages before reaching a mature stage. Children in this phase first learn skills in isolation from one another and then are able to combine them with other skills as coordinated movement.

The **specialized movement phase** begins at about 7 years and continues through the teen years and into adulthood.

Gallahue cautions that maturity and physical activity alone do not ensure that children will acquire fundamental movement skills in the preschool years. Children who do not master these skills are frustrated and experience failure later in recreational and sports activities. Knowledge of the process of fundamental motor skills can help early childhood educators to design appropriate curriculum and activities for children.

## Characteristics of Motor Development

**Gross-Motor Skills**  Whereas toddlers are gaining control over basic movement skills and mobility, preschoolers refine mobility skills through a range of motor activities involving the entire body. **Gross-motor development** includes (1) locomotor dexterity, which requires balance and movement, and (2) upper-body and arm skills (Berk, 2007; Santrock, 2007).

 **Locomotor skills** are those movements that permit the child to move about in some manner, such as jumping, hopping, running, and climbing. Jambor (1990) extended this basic list to include the following types of locomotion: rolling, creeping, crawling, climbing, stepping up and down, jumping, bouncing, hurdling, hopping, pumping a swing, and pushing or pulling a wagon. Marked-time climbing, or climbing up one step at a time, is mastered by

toddlers, but preschoolers can use alternating feet to climb stairs. At the latter stages of locomotor development during the preschool years, children are able to include galloping and skipping to running and jumping. They advance from riding a tricycle to a bicycle, and some older preschoolers are able to roller-skate and kick a soccer ball (J. E. Johnson, 1998; McDevitt & Ormrod, 2004; Mullen, 1984). Two basic upper-body and arm skills practiced during the preschool years are throwing and catching a ball.

**Fine-Motor Skills**  Preschool children gain more precision in **fine-motor development,** or the use of the hands and fingers, between the ages of 3 and 5. They acquire more control of finger movement, which allows them to become proficient in using small materials that require grasping and control. In preschool classrooms, children learn to work with puzzles; cut with scissors; use brushes, pencils, pens, and markers; and manipulate small blocks, counters, and modeling clay. They refine self-help skills used in dressing themselves by learning to button, use zippers and snaps, and tie shoelaces (J. E. Johnson, 1998; McDevitt & Ormrod, 2004; Wortham, 2010).

**Perceptual-Motor   Skills**  Perceptual-Motor **Development** refers to the child's developing ability to interact with the environment, combining use of the senses and motor skills. The developmental process consisting of using perceptual or sensory skills and motor skills is viewed as a combined process. Perceptual-motor development results from the interaction between sensory perception and motor actions in increasingly complex and skillful behaviors (Jambor, 1990; Mullen, 1984; Puckett & Black, 2005). More specifically, visual, auditory, and tactile sensory abilities are combined with emerging motor skills to develop perceptual-motor abilities.

Perceptual-motor skills include body awareness, spatial awareness, directional awareness, and temporal awareness. **Body awareness** means the child's developing capacity to understand body parts, what the body parts

**FIGURE 5.1**    Milestones in Physical Development: Ages 3 through 5

**Age 3**

| Gross Motor Development | Fine Motor Development |
|---|---|
| Climbs by alternating feet | Builds a tower with 9 or 10 blocks |
| Rides a tricycle | Manipulates small objects |
| Runs freely with little stumbling or falling | Turns book pages, one at a time |
| | Places small pegs in pegboard |

**Age 4**

| | |
|---|---|
| Stands on one foot and balances briefly | Uses scissors |
| Throws a ball overhand | Dresses and undresses |
| Kicks a ball | Strings beads |
| Hops on both feet | Eats with a spoon |
| | Uses crayons and markers |

**Age 5**

| | |
|---|---|
| Stands on one foot for at least 10 seconds | Brushes own teeth and cares for own needs |
| Can gallop, skip, hop, and do somersaults | Completes simple puzzles |
| Can propel a swing | Builds with small construction toys |
| May ride a bike | Uses a pencil |
| May learn to swim | Manipulates small blocks and modeling clay |

*Source:* Information from Child Development Chart: Preschool Milestones by Mayo Clinic. Retrieved August 4, 2010, from http://www.Mayoclinic.com/health/child-development/MY0016 and Frost-Wortham Developmental Checklist by Sue C. Wortham (2010). *Early childhood curriculum. Developmental bases for learning and teaching (5th ed.).* Pearson.

can do, and how to make the body more efficient. **Spatial awareness** refers to knowledge of how much space the body occupies and how to use the body in space. **Directional awareness** includes understanding of location and direction of the body in space, which extends to understanding directionality and objects in space. **Temporal awareness** is the development of awareness of the relationship between movement and time. Skills involving temporal awareness include rhythm and sequence. The sequence of events using a form of rhythm or pattern reflects temporal awareness (Gallahue, 1989; Jambor, 1990; McDevitt & Ormrod, 2004).

## Play and Physical Development

Play, especially outdoor play, is most commonly associated with physical exercise. Parents and teachers appreciate the child's need for opportunities for active physical activities. They may not, however, distinguish among free play, teacher-directed motor skills activities, and adult-directed sports. Each type of activity provides opportunities for physical exercise, but play is different in that it is initiated by the child.

Children today are more sedentary than they were 20 years ago (Helm & Boos, 1996). Inappropriate nutrition has resulted in an increase in obesity and poor physical condition and elevated blood pressure and cholesterol in young children (Berger, 2009; Mullen, 1984; Santrock, 2007). The increased number of both parents and single parents working outside the home has resulted in large numbers of latchkey children and children in after-school care (Frost, 1992; Helm & Boos, 1996). If today's children are to develop motor skills in the preschool years, they must be engaged in physical exercise

Dress-up clothes enhance sociodramatic play.

through both directed physical education programs and opportunities for free play in preschool and other group settings (Mullen, 1984).

**Directed Physical Play** Organized sports for preschool children are gaining in popularity. Four- and 5-year-old boys and girls often have the choice of participating on a soccer or T-ball team. Six-year-olds can join a football team. Gymnastic lessons are frequently offered for children as young as 3 years. Children enjoy these group activities and sports, are proud of their uniforms, and look forward to the games and performances. If handled correctly by adults, sports can have a positive effect, including the social experiences of being a part of a group. Nevertheless, sports activities are structured and adult led, and physical activities are limited to those related to the sport.

Motor skills activities likewise are directed by an adult. They play an important role in gross-motor development because the teacher can work with children in a variety of activities that ensure the child will develop the desired physical movements. Children's physical

development can be evaluated and attention given to correct inappropriate movements that can be an impediment to the child in later years when participating in sports and recreational physical activities (Gallahue, 1993; Mullen, 1984; Pica, 1997).

Because increasing numbers of preschool children spend much of their day in group settings, either child care or preschool classrooms in public schools, there is a growing awareness of the need for directed motor skills programs (Gabbard, 1995; Helm & Boos, 1996). Programs need to be developmental in that they reflect activities that are appropriate for the developmental needs of preschool children (Sanders, 2002). Evidence indicates that quality programs can have positive results for motor development (Bohren & Vlahov, 1989). These developmental motor skills programs should not be confused with perceptual skills programs originally designed to help students with academic difficulties. Perceptual-motor programs have been used widely in preschool programs despite research that indicates they are not effective in remediation of learning disabilities or appropriate for preschool classrooms (Campbell, 1997; Frost, 1992; Gallahue, 1993). A comprehensive preschool program should include locomotor skills to include walking, running, hopping, throwing, catching, and other motor skills described earlier in this chapter (Gallahue, 1993; Sanders, 2002). Fine-motor activities such as block construction, sand play, and art activities should be included in the overall program (Berk, 2007; Pica, 1997).

**Free Play** Motor skills can also be developed in free play on a playground that is equipped appropriately. Play environments with play apparatus that includes opportunities for upper-body exercise contribute to increased muscular endurance (Frost, 1992; Gabbard, 1979). Myers (1985) compared motor behaviors of kindergarten children who participated in a physical education class with children who participated on a well-developed playground during free play. She found that the children in free play engaged in significantly more motor behaviors in free play than in the structured physical education classes. Nevertheless, Frost (1992) suggests that the most effective teacher might be the one who provides a balance between directed and free-play activities. Children need time to mess around and do nothing. (See Chapter 11.)

Although a full range of motor skills can be nurtured through adult-directed activities, the opportunity for children to engage in physical movements related to spontaneous, natural play is needed as well. Young children particularly need to be outdoors where there is space for all kinds of physical movement as they engage in play activities alone or with their friends. Moreover, they need time and opportunity to participate in the social, sociodramatic, and cognitive elements possible in physical play. Because many parents feel a need to restrict children's play related to the dangers in contemporary urban and suburban environments and because sports activities may limit

time for outdoor play in a neighborhood setting, schools and other preschool centers should be aware of their responsibility in maintaining time for play both indoors and outdoors for the child's physical development (Wortham, 2010).

## Adult Roles in Physical Play

In an era when children spend large amounts of time watching television or video games rather than engaging in physical play, adults have a major responsibility in being diligent in including outdoor playtime for preschool children. Parents need to understand the need for free play at home or in a nearby public park. Teachers need to become knowledgeable about motor skill development and how they can develop structured activities that will include modeling of motor skills (Campbell, 1997; Sanders, 2002). They also need to include outdoor free play or similar play in an indoor physical play space. Teachers in public schools where recess has been eliminated or limited to structured activities need advocate for time for free physical play.

 ## COGNITIVE DEVELOPMENT

Children make major strides in cognitive development in the preschool years. These are years when children have more opportunities to explore the environment and learn new information. In this part of the chapter, we discuss how changes in thinking skills broaden children's knowledge about their world.

## Characteristics of Cognitive Development

Preschool children are characterized by preoperational thought. They have moved from the limitations of a sensorimotor approach to understanding their world to one of symbolism and intuitive thinking, as described in the next subsection.

## WHAT PARENTS, CAREGIVERS, AND TEACHERS CAN DO TO PROMOTE PHYSICAL PLAY

1. Adults can ensure that preschool children are given daily opportunities to engage in motor play.

2. Adults can make sure that the outdoor play environment contains play equipment that include opportunities to exercise all types of motor skills.

3. Adults can become advocates for outdoor play. Parents should find out the status of free-play opportunities in their child's preschool center and insist it be a part of the daily schedule (see Chapter 11).

4. Caregivers and teachers of preschool children should learn how to lead activities for the development of motor skills.

5. Caregivers in after-school programs for preschool programs should include opportunities for free physical play and limit television viewing when children are in their care.

6. Caregivers and preschool teachers can develop their schedule to alternate between quiet and more active play experiences.

7. Parents can be intentional in taking children to areas for physical play if there are no spaces at home.

8. Parents can limit television viewing and encourage children to engage in physical play instead.

9. Parents and caregivers can accept gender differences in play and support play behaviors of both boys and girls. (See the discussion of gender differences in play discussed later in this chapter and in Chapter 7.)

**Cognitive-Developmental Theory: Preoperational Thought**   Children between the ages of 2 and 7 are in Piaget's (1952) **preoperational stage** of development, in which children are able to represent objects and events mentally, thus permitting more complex symbolism. However, they are controlled by their perception; that is, they understand concepts in terms of what they can see.

Preoperational children are described as **egocentric,** concerned with their own thoughts and ideas and unable to consider the point of view of others. These characteristics of the preoperational period develop within two substages, the symbolic function substage and the intuitive thought substage.

The **symbolic function substage** occurs between the ages of 2 and 4. Symbolic thought allows the child to picture things mentally that are not present. Young children who have achieved symbolic function can use art experiences, especially scribbling, to represent things in their environment, such as houses, trees, flowers, and people. Symbolism also allows them to engage in pretend play.

Egocentrism in this substage results in the child's inability to distinguish between her own perspective and the perspective of another child or adult. In play, the child assumes that other children share her feelings and thoughts. She believes that other children share her feelings and may have difficulty relating to another child's ideas or emotions that are different from her own.

Piaget also characterized preoperational thinking as animistic in young children who may believe that inanimate objects are alive and can take action on their own. For example, he asked children about the movement of clouds and found that they believed clouds propel themselves through the sky.

Between the ages of 4 and 7, the preoperational child enters the **intuitive thought substage,** when primitive reasoning begins. The child's thought process is changing from one of symbolic thinking to intuitive, or inner, thinking. The child can organize objects into primitive collections but is unable to group objects in a consistent manner. This primitive system of organization is caused by centration. The child tends to center, or focus, on one characteristic or attribute. Two attributes cannot be considered at one time. As a result, the child may change from attribute to another when trying to organize a group of objects. If the child is asked to put a collection of shapes of different color into groups with the same characteristic, he can organize them by shape or by color, or he might change from one to the other during the activity. Once the child is able to move beyond centering, developmental characteristics of the concrete operational stage can emerge, which include classification and conservation (Piaget, 1952).

**Conservation** is the ability to understand that the physical attributes of material remain consistent, even altered or rearranged. For example, a child who can conserve understands that a ball of clay has the same amount when the shape is changed or the number of coins in a row is the same whether spaced close together or farther apart.

The ability to **classify** permits the child to consider the characteristics of objects (color, size, shape, texture, etc.) and to organize them into groups using a scheme for establishing the groups. Now the child can take the group of shapes used in the preceding example and decide to group them by color while ignoring their shape, or organize them by shape while ignoring their different colors.

**Recent Research and Preoperational Thought**

Many studies have reexamined Piaget's perception of thought in the preoperational stage of development. Do young children have animistic beliefs, and are they egocentric? An example of animistic beliefs is when young children believe that clouds can make themselves move across the sky or that animals have the same characteristics as people. Familiarity with the environment seems to be a factor in the nature of how preoperational children think. Another factor can be modification or alteration of the tasks. For example, if a puppet was used for conservation tasks rather than an adult, more 4-year-olds were able to solve the problem (Trawick-Smith, 2009). Gelman (1972) found that children can conserve number when the task includes three or four items instead of six or seven. Likewise, children can form global categories of familiar objects denoting that the capacity to classify hierarchically is present in the preschool years (Mandler, Bauer, & McDonough, 1991; Mervis & Crisafi, 1982; Ricco, 1989). Children's ability to adapt their conversations to fit the listener, such as a younger child, contradicts the notion that they are egocentric (Gelman & Shatz, 1978).

Research studies have revealed that familiarity with objects affects animistic thinking. Researchers in this characteristic believe that Piaget asked children about objects with which they had little experience. When questioned about more familiar objects, such as crayons, children know they are not alive. They make errors about vehicles because they appear to move on their own, but they err because of incomplete knowledge rather than the belief that inanimate objects are alive (Dolgin & Behrend, 1984).

Magical thinking (when children believe something magical or supernatural makes something happen) is also related to familiarity. Children believe that fairies and witches have supernatural powers but people and objects related to their everyday experiences don't. They think magic is related to events they cannot explain, but as they gain more experience, their beliefs in magic decline (Phelps & Woolley, 1994; Subbotsky, 1994).

Flavell and his colleagues (Flavell, Green, & Flavell, 1987) studied whether children are bound by perception. They found that young children were easily tricked by appearance versus reality. It was not until they were 6 or 7 years old that they could do well on appearance versus reality tasks. Make-believe play helps children master this concept. Children can differentiate between pretend and real experiences. Pretending helps children identify what is real versus what is unreal (Woolley & Wellman, 1990).

## Play and Cognitive Development

### Benefits of Play on Cognitive Development
Play is considered necessary for cognitive development and learning (Ellis, 1973; Piaget, 1962). Researchers have found that preschoolers who spend more time engaged in sociodramatic play are advanced in intellectual development. In addition, children who enjoy pretending score higher on tests of imagination and creativity. Novel play with objects may enhance children's ability to think inventively (Freyberg, 1973; Pepler & Ross, 1981).

Two essential ingredients of play are the involvement of the thinking processes and repetition of social interactions. Play is the foundation of academic learning. Pretend play fosters young children's ability to reason and assists children in separating meanings from objects. A child who is pretending that a block is a fire engine has applied the characteristics of a fire engine to a block. The meaning has been separated from the fire engine and applied to the block. The child has manipulated the meaning of a fire engine in the play experience (Berk & Winsler, 1995; Vygotsky, 1976; Yawkey & Diantoniis, 1984).

### Theoretical Views of Play and Cognitive Development
There are various viewpoints on how cognitive play develops in the young child. Piaget described levels of cognitive play that built on the work of Karl Buhler (1937). Smilansky (Smilansky & Shefatya, 1990) gave a different interpretation to levels of play in cognitive development. Vygotsky (1976) perceived that play permitted the child to function at a cognitive level higher than exhibited in other types of activities. Each of these theoretical approaches to developing hierarchical categories in cognitive play is described, followed by more recent perceptions of developmental characteristics of cognitive play.

*Piaget's Levels of Cognitive Play*   Piaget's two levels of play, practice play and symbolic play, were discussed in Chapter 4. Practice or functional play appears during the sensorimotor period, whereas symbolic play first appears in the sensorimotor period and develops into dramatic play in the preoperational period. Games with rules (when the child understands and follows the rules in a game) characterize the concrete operations period and continue in the formal operations period (Piaget, 1962; Rubin, 2001).

During the years from 4 through 7, dramatic or symbolic play is characterized as imitation of reality. Piaget described preschool dramatic play as including the features of orderliness, exact imitation of reality, and collective symbolism of play roles (Piaget, 1962). In dramatic play, children develop play themes and carry them out by playing different roles. Dramatic play enables children to use pretend or fantasy in their play in a more organized fashion as they engage in pretend play in more complex forms.

Piaget's highest category of play is games with rules, which emerges between the ages of 7 and 12. During these years, symbolic play declines and becomes rule governed. Children play games such as marbles with set rules. They are interested in competitive games. Children are becoming socialized as reflected in the ability to engage in activities in which rules must be followed.

*Smilansky's Levels of Cognitive Play.* Although Piaget did not describe collective dramatic play in terms of sociodramatic play, Smilansky (1968) included this category in stages of play development. She also included construction play as a category. She did not organize categories by levels of cognitive development but proposed that children from age 3 to school age alternate between the different types of play at different levels of complexity. For example, the child might engage in practice play in one play experience and dramatic play in a later play experience (Smilansky & Shefatya, 1990).

Smilansky described functional play as the first form to appear and points out that it continues into the early childhood years. It is based on the child's need for physical activity. The child uses repetition in physical actions, language, and manipulation of toys. This means that the child repeats various play activities over and over.

Constructive play first appears in early childhood and continues into adulthood. Sensorimotor activity is combined with a preconceived plan and creativity. The child has moved from handling objects and materials to constructing or building something.

Although Piaget described games with rules as the most complex form of play that emerges in the concrete operations period, Smilansky described this type of play as more elaborate. The child must be able to accept and adjust to prearranged rules. Social interactions are required, including the ability to control behavior and actions within rules. Games with rules also continue into adult life.

Dramatic play or pretend play first emerges during the second year in the form of pretend behavior. Dramatic play, for Smilansky, permits the child to imitate human relationships through symbolic representations. However, the symbolic representations are person oriented rather than object related, as found in symbolic play of younger children. When children can engage in person-oriented play with other children in various roles, dramatic play has achieved its most complex form, sociodramatic play (Smilansky & Shefatya, 1990), which is further described under "Social Development."

*Vygotsky's Perceptions of the Functions of Play*
Vygotsky (1976) focused on representational play and fantasy play rather than on stages of play. He described representational or make-believe play that emerges at the end of toddlerhood, develops in the early childhood years, and evolves into games with rules.

Representational play has specific functions. First, it permits the child to deal with unrealizable desires (Berk & Winsler, 1995). A young child pretending to use a cell phone is fantasizing that he is able to use the phone. Fantasy play appears when toddlers must learn to follow approved behaviors and delay gratification. As the child matures, more rules and routines are expected, and fantasy play expands. The child engages in imaginary play that is governed by rules.

Representational play, as described in Chapter 2, also allows children to separate objects and meaning. When the child substitutes one object for another, the representation helps the child separate an object's real meaning to a pretend meaning. Pretend play, then, represented in separating meaning from objects, serves as preparation for later abstract thinking and use of symbols, such as letters, for reading and writing (Berk & Winsler, 1995; Vygotsky, 1976).

For Vygotsky, the essential feature of play is self-restraint. In play, the child subordinates momentary desires to play roles. Moreover, the child willingly follows set rules for imaginary play, which enable her to follow rules in real life. Vygotsky (1976) believed that young children are able to follow such games with rules much younger than the age characterized in Piaget's stage of games with rules. He felt that observance of rules in fantasy play in the early childhood years leads to game play in the middle childhood years.

## Characteristics of Cognitive Play

**Current Views of Categories of Cognitive Play**    The work of Piaget, Vygotsky, and Smilansky provide a sound framework for understanding the role of play in cognitive play and vice versa. When the views of these theorists are combined, a more comprehensive picture emerges. Categories still guide our understanding of cognitive development and play:

Functional play (Piaget, Smilansky)

Constructive play (Smilansky, Vygotsky)

Symbolic/representational/dramatic play (Piaget, Smilansky, Vygotsky)

Games with rules (Piaget, Smilansky, Vygotsky)

Recent researchers caution against viewing play in terms of levels of performance or hierarchies (J. E. Johnson, 1998; Takhvar & Smith, 1990; Tegano & Burdette, 1991). Some researchers propose that children's play is complex and exceeds classification into categories. Children can be engaged in several categories of play simultaneously (Takhvar & Smith, 1990). Moreover, not only do play episodes include multiple categories that go beyond cognitive categories of play, but, "there is a need for additional modifiers to capture something about play tempo, intensity, style, and other important qualifiers. There is also the need to note information about the play setting and context" (J. E. Johnson, 1998, p. 146). The work of current researchers thus characterizes cognitive play as overlapping in both developmental levels and categories of play.

Functional play begins with practice play and play with objects in infancy. In early childhood, object play becomes more complex and goal oriented and incorporates construction play. Preschoolers use increasingly complex constructions that are elaborated by 5- and 6-year-olds through social interactions. As a child engages in repeated play with small blocks, the constructions become more complex.

When several children engage in constructing something with blocks, they exchange ideas and strategies for building the construction (J. E. Johnson, 1998; Rubin, Fein, & Vandenberg, 1983).

Representational or symbolic play also emerges prior to the early childhood years. Symbolic play begins with substitution or representation of one object for another (Piaget, 1952; Vygotsky, 1976) and becomes more complex in dramatic play that includes imitating, imagining, dramatizing, and role play in the early childhood years. Again, social interactions impact dramatic play, as do language and motor development. The interaction of domains of development on play is addressed later in the chapter.

Finally, games with rules begin early in life, particularly in the early childhood years, for Vygotsky (Berk & Winsler, 1995; Vygotsky, 1976). Piaget and Smilansky placed games with rules in the school-age years. J. E. Johnson (1998) clarifies this process by reporting that preschool children can observe the rules in simple games such as lotto, matching games, and games with spinners and dice. More sophisticated games with rules become possible when children achieve concrete operations.

As researchers continue to investigate cognitive play, they reinforce the understanding that the role of play in cognitive development is complex. Definitions of categories and levels of play are affected by many variables. For example, Tegano and Burdette (1991) found that how long children played made the transformation of functional play to constructive play easier; Takhvar and Smith (1990) found that Smilansky's categories of play are parallel rather than hierarchical.

## Adult Roles in Cognitive Play

If children are to benefit from cognitive play, adults have a role in providing play activities that will lead to thinking and problem solving. Vygotsky (1978) proposed that more competent

---

### COGNITIVE PLAY USING GROUP GAMES

Group games in the classroom can encourage cognitive development. Children who participate in games not only have an enjoyable play experience, but they also learn skills such as listening and learning to avoid auditory distractions, focussing and paying attention, and playing cooperatively with children in the group. Group games thus enhance cognitive learning in language, early literacy, and math.

Teachers should select or design games that are fun, involve cooperation, and are successful in promoting learning. Math games, games that require reading to follow instructions, and games that require players to work in teams fulfill the criteria for games and promote learning. Following are some criteria to follow when choosing group games:

- Games should have multiple developmental levels to accommodate differences in children.
- Games should have progressive challenges so children can demonstrate improvement.
- Games should be challenging so children need to apply themselves to solve game problems.
- Games should provide opportunities to learn from each other. (Torbert, 2005)

---

cognitive activities occur when the environment includes rich and varied materials. The child uses more advanced thinking when toys and materials are available to promote thinking and problem solving. However, it is the adults who enhance the activities through social interactions. In addition, if adults provide emotional security, children have a secure base for exploration of the environment (Howes & Smith, 1995).

Teachers and caregivers can further encourage cognitive and problem solving by teaching children to pay attention to how they use their senses. By modeling playful behaviors and problem solving through guided imagery using intervention lessons with senses, teachers can help young children to be more playful in their free-play interactions with their peers (Boyer, 1997a, 1997b).

Adults must distinguish between play as manipulation and play that is active education if they are to facilitate cognition through play. When children are merely manipulating materials without thinking actively, they are not constructing understanding. An example of play as

manipulation can be found on many preschool playgrounds. Many climbing structures designed within the last 15 years contain tic-tac-toe games in the form of cubes that can be rotated. Because most preschool children have little or no knowledge of the game, they turn the cubes to see the Xs and Os rotate rather than manipulate them to play the game. However, what initially appears as manipulative play can, in fact, be rich cognitive play. Teachers in a preschool classroom were concerned that children only used new flexible wheel blocks for constructing wheels that could be rolled. Extended observation, however, revealed that the construction and play with the wheels actually included the use of various types of mathematical and other concepts (Seo, 2003).

When children are engaged in active education, they bring interest, play, experimentation, and cooperation to the activity. For example, when children challenge themselves in practice play with jump ropes by trying to jump longer or to jump with two ropes, they exhibit some intent to learn. Likewise, experimentation is used when children construct props for

## WHAT PARENTS, CAREGIVERS, AND TEACHERS CAN DO TO PROMOTE COGNITIVE PLAY

1. Ensure that toys and materials provided to children are open ended and promote problem solving.

2. Provide opportunities for children to engage in dramatic play that encourages cooperation and negotiation.

3. Make available materials that encourage representation through construction.

4. Provide art materials that encourage expression of ideas through art experiences.

5. Offer simple games that include rules preschool children can follow.

6. Provide learning activities that accentuate the senses and playfulness that can be incorporated into play.

7. Engage children in simple games and cognitive activities that can later be played independently.

8. Make sure that construction and art materials are available in both the indoor and outdoor play environments.

9. Ensure dramatic play materials are available in both the indoor and outdoor play environments.

dramatic play or use cooperative negotiation when planning a dramatic play event (Chaille & Silvern, 1996). Again, the types of materials and play opportunities teachers provide make a difference in cognitive development through play (Gmitrova & Gmitrov, 2002).

## LANGUAGE AND LITERACY DEVELOPMENT

### Characteristics of Language Development

The preschool years are significant for language development in young children. Between the years of 2 and 6, children learn about 10,000 words. Language development is related to advances in cognitive development, follows rules of language, and is characterized by development in vocabulary, grammar, and pragmatics (Berk, 2007).

**Rule Systems**  Concurrent with acquisition of a remarkable number of words, children in the preschool years learn the rules of their language; that is, they learn morphology rules, syntax rules, and semantic rules. **Morphology** and **syntax rules** relate to understanding of the sounds and grammar of language; **semantic rules** explain vocabulary and meaning development.

*Grammatical Development*  By the age of 2, toddlers typically speak in two-word phrases, mostly composed of nouns and verbs with some adjectives and adverbs. As they develop longer statements, typical sentences contain four and five words by age 5. As children are able to express themselves using longer sentences, they demonstrate that they know rules of morphology, or the use of plurals, possession, and tense in nouns and verbs. For example, they are able to use the word *cats* when they are talking about more than one cat and can use prepositions to denote location such as *in* and *on*.

Complexity and length of verbal strings or utterances also reveal that the children are learning the syntactical rules or how words should be ordered in a sentence. They learn to ask questions and to make negative statements (Santrock, 2007).

The third system of rules in language development is semantic rules or the knowledge of meanings of words. Understanding of semantic rules is demonstrated through the children's use of an expanding vocabulary in the preschool years.

*Vocabulary Development* Young preschool children acquire vocabulary at an astonishing rate of an average of five words per day (Berk, 2007). Words are added daily in groups and make some basic assumptions about a word's meaning. Thereafter, children refine understanding of the meaning of the word as it is heard again and used in different contexts. Children also develop understanding of the meaning of words by contrasting them with words they already know (Berk, 2007).

*Pragmatic Development* Preschool children also learn the rules of conversation. The **pragmatics of language** are the rules of carrying on a conversation. Children must be able to learn to communicate with others in their language community. They must be able to listen to the statements made by others, ask questions, and interpret language functions required in conversations.

The ability to participate in a conversation develops at a very early age and is extended and refined as the child expands language abilities and has experiences in conversations. By age 4, preschool children have some understanding of the culturally accepted ways to carry on a conversation in their culture. They develop communicative competence when they are able to adapt their language to different situations (Berk, 2007; Puckett & Black, 2005).

## Characteristics of Literacy Development

Literacy development is directly related to language development. *Literacy* is defined as the ability to read and write. Although much communication is accomplished through oral language, the ability to read and write extends possibilities for transmitting and receiving information. As researchers learn more about how children become literate, it is clear that literacy, like oral language, begins in infancy; nevertheless, rapid advances are made in the development of literacy in the preschool years.

Although very young children are unable to interpret words in print and to write using adult forms of the alphabet and standard spelling, they become aware of books and written language at a very young age. Like acquisition of oral language, literacy occurs through interaction within the child and the literacy community. The uses of literacy experienced by the child through day-to-day living are the forces that influence the child's enculturation into reading and writing. The literacy activities within the child's language and cultural community will affect that child's understanding of the purposes and functions of literacy (Dyson & Genishi, 1993; Wortham, 2010).

Building on oral language development with books and environmental print, preschool children develop strategies for becoming literate. As a result of their experiences, children gradually come to understand that print, not just pictures, gives meaning to books. They come to recognize print, as well as the spacing between words, and learn that individual letters are used to form words (Fields, Groth, & Spangler, 2004; Roskos & Christie, 2004; Roskos, Christie, & Richgels, 2003).

Young children also develop literacy through writing efforts. They use scribbles, mock letters, letter reversals, and other print efforts as part of their natural growth toward literacy. Preschool children use trial and error and hypothesis testing in their efforts to understand reading and writing, just as they do in acquiring oral language (Morrow, 2004; Roskos & Christie, 2004; Roskos et al., 2003).

## Variations in Language and Literacy Development

Although virtually all children learn the language of their culture and achieve major milestones in language development by the age of 6, differences occur in language achievement. When children enter kindergarten, language differences can be great.

There are differences in families and cultures as to how much and what type of language is used. As a result, differences in language acquisition can be documented. First, girls tend to be more proficient than boys, and middle-class children are more advanced in language than lower-income children. Single-born children are more proficient than twins, and triplets are less proficient than twins (Berk, 2007).

Researchers who have studied familial and cultural differences in the language children hear have found that mothers talk more to daughters than to sons. Middle-class parents use more elaborated language with their children; parents in all groups talk more to first-born children than to later-born children and multiple-birth children. Some adults use strategies that foster language development, such as encouraging the child to talk and providing specific responses to the child's comments. Using Vygotsky's ideas on scaffolding, some parents provide new topics for discussion through experiences such as looking at and conversing about picture books and by taking children on excursions to new places in the community (Genishi & Dyson, 1984).

Diversity in children is another factor in language differences. Young children today represent many cultures and languages. The preschool child learning language is affected by language and cultural practices in the home language community. Although the rules of language remain the same, each child learns language in a unique environment (Genishi & Dyson, 2009). The new norm is diversity rather

---

**WHAT PARENTS, CAREGIVERS, AND TEACHERS CAN DO TO PROMOTE LANGUAGE AND LITERACY PLAY**

Adults have a major role in supporting language development in young children. But how they talk to children is an important factor. Adults can engage in intentional activities in their interactions with young children to nurture language. One strategy is to make sure that the child or children are talking at least half of the time instead of the teacher. The following will ensure that the child has an equal turn to talk when the adult listens.

1. The adult makes sure that taking turns is incorporated into conversations. The adult builds on the child's statements, questions, and responses to further the conversation.

2. The adult in a group setting engages in talking one-on-one with each child. The adult extends and revises what a child says so that the child has an opportunity to hear their own ideas restated.

3. The adult describes what children are doing when they are engaged in activities. This narration permits the teacher to introduce new vocabulary and sentence structures.

4. The adult uses words to help children understand new concepts. The teacher asks questions about science or other activities, and the children's responses lead to new questions and new conversations about the concept.

(National Institute for Literacy, 2009)

than all children learning language in a similar manner. For Genishi and Dyson, early education should make sense to children and teachers rather than working toward learning English as the major goal in language development. We discuss English Language Learners (ELLs) and develop programs for them. We discuss African American Speakers (AALs) less frequently, but their language differences are equally important.

## Play and Language and Literacy Development

When the relationship between language development and play is described, we can discuss play in two categories: how children play with language and how language is used in play. In the following sections, children's play with language is explained, followed by the role of play in language development and in literacy development .

**Play with Language**    In Chapter 4, very young children's play with language was described as sound play by infants and play with speech within a grammatical pattern by toddlers. This process continues in the preschool child as part of a system of play with language. Pellegrini (1984, p. 46) describes speech play as "[a] mode whereby young children explore and manipulate the many aspects of their language system." The play process includes play with the phonological, semantic, and pragmatic aspects of language in which the process of the play is more important than communication. Cazden (1974) proposes that children explore the elements of language and develop a metalinguistic awareness, or understanding of the rule system, through play with language.

Cazden also explains that there is a hierarchy in how children play with language. Play with phonological sounds occurs first in the infant, followed by syntactical play when toddlers are able to use two-word utterances in telegraphic speech. Semantic play involves play with word

meanings that later advances to the use of narratives and rhymes (Opie & Opie, 1959). Cazden warns that the categories do not develop independently, nor do they imply that one precedes the other. For example, Pellegrini (1984) cites Bruner's (1974, 1975) research in which infants conveyed meaning to caregivers through gestures rather than sounds. Likewise, McCune (1985) considers the use of an object in pretend play to be the equivalent of using a word to label the imagined object.

Davidson (1998) provides many examples of children's play with language. She describes the phonological play of a toddler who had completed building with blocks as follows:

> Now it's don un un
> Done un un un un.
>    (Garvey, 1993, p. 62, cited in Davidson, 1998)

Examples of more purposeful play are children's use of jokes such as knock-knock jokes or inappropriate use of words. Thus, a 2-year-old says "meow" as the sound for a dog in a farmyard picture, and a 4-year-old calls her doll "Poopy-head" (Davidson, 1998).

**Play and Language Development**    Beginning efforts to play with language are solitary activities as infants babble and play with language sounds. Older children collaborate in play with language by telling jokes and using chants and parodies of rhymes. When language is used in play, it is necessarily a social event. It is used as a tool in their play, especially pretend or dramatic play. Language is used to plan play episodes, carry out roles, and talk about play events.

When planning for play, children must use persuasive language if they are to take charge during the play event that follows. During dramatic play, the child must use tone of voice and expressions that are representative of the role or character being played. The language children use when playing pretend is similar to the language they have heard from books. This language is like the language in a story when they play a character or narrate their play with small figures (Davidson, 1998).

Children demonstrate metalinguistic awareness when they talk about the language they will use in pretend play. They might give instructions to each other as to what should be said and how the children should express their part of the dialogue or conversation in play. An example is when one child tells another, "You need to yell at me to clean, "cause you're the mean stepsister" (Davidson, 1998, p. 181).

**Play and Literacy Development** Pretend play also has a role in the development of literacy in preschool children. The ability to use pretend talk and symbolism is related to literacy. The storylike language used by children in role play described earlier, and the explicit and elaborated language used in dramatic play episodes, can be related to later literacy (Roskos, 1990). Symbolic transformations used by 3-year-olds in play predicts their writing status at age 5, and their use of oral language in dramatic play predicts later reading achievement (Roskos & Neuman, 1998).

Dramatic play that involves role play and make-believe supports the development of literate oral language because children are motivated to generate explicit and elaborated language in their play. Engaging in sociodramatic play leads to the later ability to encode information in words (Pellegrini, 1984).

Children who experience opportunities for dramatic play that include information about literacy are more directly informed about components of literacy. Teachers in preschool settings and parents can provide literacy experiences that promote literacy development through play (Neuman & Roskos, 1991; Roskos & Neuman, 1993, 1998a; Roskos & Christie, 2004).

### Adult Roles in Language and Literacy Play

Adults make a difference in the development of language and literacy through play. It has already been established that the use of expanded language with children results in a higher level of language development than the use of restricted language (Wilcox-Herzog & Kontos, 1998).

Adult support and participation in children's play also can promote the development of language and literacy. Children play at higher levels, stay on task, and solve more problems when teachers make suggestions, ask open-ended questions, and use elaborated language (Klenk, 2001; Pellegrini, 1984; Roskos & Christie, 2004).

Literacy can also be promoted through adult support and participation in play. Through play, children engage in social routines and skills that are related to reading and writing (Roskos & Neuman, 1993). Adults can facilitate literacy development by providing materials such as writing pads and pencils for center play (Christie, 1994; Vukelich, 1989). Theme centers such as an office, store, or another topic that entails reading and writing can enhance children's interest in using developmental literacy skills (Klenk, 2001).

Teachers and caregivers can engage in children's literacy play by observing and encouraging the use of literacy activities in play, by joining play that includes the use of books and writing materials, or by providing literacy objects as children participate in a play event (Roskos & Neuman, 1993). The teacher can take a leadership role by introducing specific literacy props and modeling how children can incorporate literacy activities into their play (Roskos & Christie, 2004; Roskos & Neuman, 1993; Vukelich, 1989).

## SOCIAL DEVELOPMENT

### Characteristics of Social-Emotional Development

During the preschool years, children increasingly understand themselves as individuals; in addition, they understand themselves as part of a social world. They are becoming more autonomous, and their cognitive abilities permit them to understand how they fit into their

---

**WHAT PARENTS, CAREGIVERS, AND TEACHERS CAN DO
TO PROMOTE LANGUAGE AND LITERACY PLAY**

1. Promote language play by engaging in play experiences with children and by modeling expanded language, using language in dramatic play roles, and giving suggestions for how language can be used in play events.

2. Promote literacy play by providing props and materials for dramatic play that encourages the incorporation of literacy behaviors.

3. Encourage literacy play by showing approval when children incorporate literacy materials in play.

4. Facilitate literacy play by joining in play and modeling the use of literacy materials.

5. Promote literacy by planning theme centers that focus on literacy activities.

---

family and a group of friends. Important characterizations of social and emotional development are self-concept, self-esteem, and self-regulation of emotions. Relationships with others are exhibited through the development of empathy and social competence. The nature and direction of social-emotional development are affected by their relationships with their parents, siblings, and peers. They are in Erikson's stage of initiative versus guilt, described in Chapter 4. If they can feel secure after separating from their parents and feel competent in their abilities, they can develop autonomy and eagerly participate in new tasks and experiences.

**Self-Concept**  A major social accomplishment between the ages of 3 and 6 is the development of self-concept. Young children develop a firm awareness that they are separate from others and have individual characteristics. Their **self-concept** is partially defined by physical characteristics, but it is defined even more significantly by their mastery of skills and competencies (Berger, 2009; Berk, 2007).

**Self-Esteem**  Preschoolers begin the task of making judgments about their own worth and competencies, their **self-esteem.** They tend to overestimate their mastery of new skills and underestimate how hard new tasks are. They

feel that they are liked or disliked depending on how well they can do things and are easily influenced by parental approval or disapproval. They are rapidly acquiring new skills and translating these accomplishments into positive or negative feelings about themselves (Harter, 1990).

**Self-Regulation of Emotions**  Children develop an awareness and understanding of their feelings in the preschool years, and this promotes the **self-regulation of emotions.** As a result of their greater understanding of the causes of emotions in themselves and others, they are able to initiate behaviors that permit them to cope. Children pick up strategies for coping with emotions from their parents. Those whose parents have difficulty controlling anger and hostility have similar problems (Gottman & Katz, 1989). Children who have difficulties in controlling negative emotions also tend to get along poorly with peers (Berk, 2007; Eisenberg et al., 1993).

**Empathy**  A significant characteristic of the preschool years is the development of **empathy,** the ability to understand and respond to the feelings of others. Preschoolers can provide comfort and support for a peer, sibling, or parent. Expanding language development enables them to use words as well as gestures to console others. They can explain another child's emotions, as well as the causes of those emotions. Children who exhibit empathy are more likely to be able to use positive social behavior (Berger, 2009; Eisenberg & Miller, 1987).

**Parent–Child Relationships**    Social-emotional development is affected by the relationships children have with their parents and other adults as well as with other children. Perhaps the most significant relationship is the one with parents and caregivers because of their influence in guiding the child's development. Factors that affect the parent–child relationship include parenting style, the child's temperament, and the type of discipline that parents use. The dynamic nature of the interaction of these three factors is complex, and social development occurs within the tension among them. Parents can have authoritarian, authoritative, and permissive parenting styles, with many variations. The child's temperament in turn influences the parenting style the parent adopts. A child who is compliant makes it easy for a parent to be authoritative, whereas a difficult child's behaviors make it more likely that authoritarian parenting strategies will be deemed necessary (Dix, 1991). A positive fit between the parenting style and the child's personality have more positive results on the child's social and emotional development than a poor fit between the two (Kochanska, 1993).

**Sibling Relationships**    A preschool child's social-emotional development is also impacted by the relationship with siblings in the family. Siblings have a strong but different relationship than parents and children. There is a wide variation in sibling relationships, which is affected by the personalities of the children, birth order, and parent–child relationships. In addition, parent–child relationships are different for each child. The influence that siblings have on a preschool child's social and emotional development can be nurturing and supporting or full of conflict (Berger, 2009).

**Peer Relationships**    Peer relationships also affect the social-emotional development of preschool children. Social development is affected by the opportunities the child has to engage in activities with other children. Preschool children who attend day care or a preschool program have more opportunity to interact socially; however, the quality of the program can affect whether the child becomes more socially competent or, instead, more assertive and aggressive (Hayes, Palmer, & Zaslow, 1990; Zigler & Lang, 1990).

**Social Competence**    Progress in the characteristics of social development in the preschool years leads to **social competence.** Indeed, it is the overarching characteristic of positive social development.

A definition of social competence is difficult to describe because researchers understand it differently. Creasey, Jarvis, and Berk (1998, p. 118) have synthesized diverse descriptors and definitions: "socially competent children exhibit a positive demeanor around or toward others, have accurate social information processing abilities, and display social behaviors that lead them to be well liked by others."

Various factors can affect the child's development of social competence. Infants with insecure attachment can be predicted to be more dependent and less curious and have less positive effect during social interactions, leading to less-optimal relationships with peers during the preschool years (Creasey et al., 1998). Later interactions with parents and siblings affect social competence. The child's social network of parents and siblings provides opportunities to observe and practice social skills that can be introduced into emerging peer relationships (MacDonald & Parke, 1984). Parents and caregivers also influence social competence by arranging social interactions and coaching young children on how to interact appropriately in social interactions.

Quality of attachment to preschool teachers and quality of caregiving settings have an impact on social competence. Children who are enrolled in poor-quality day care have more problems with social competence than children enrolled in high-quality day care (Howes & Matheson, 1992; Howes & Stewart, 1987). As a result, factors external to family influences can "support, compensate for, or even undermine the influence of the family context" (Creasey et al., 1998, p. 120).

**Prosocial Development and Behaviors**  The development of prosocial behaviors is related to the topic of social competence. Preschool children's ability to develop prosocial behaviors will affect them socially. Preschool children who have difficulties with prosocial behaviors may not be accepted later in school. Prosocial development between the ages of 2 and 6 can be described as these abilities evolve.

Ages 2 to 3:

- Children gain an understanding of the perspectives of others
- Children try to comfort others
- Children become aware of social behaviors and standards of behaviors

Ages 3 to 4:

- Children can make lasting friendships
- Children can resolve small conflicts by themselves
- Children have a sense of self and know that they have their own ideas

Ages 4 to 6

- Children can play more cooperatively
- Children expand social relationships outside the family
- Children reflect their developing personalities in their social relationships (Landry, 2002)

A child's relationship with parents affects her prosocial development. A parenting style that is authoritative yet warm and responsive helps a child develop positive social behavior. Such parents expect their children to live up to their standards and values. They use mild power assertion, explain desired behaviors, and model social behaviors. Prosocial behavior is encouraged when parents model altruism and have nurturant relationships with their children.

Negative parenting results in negative social behaviors in children. Parents who are demanding and authoritarian without warmth may interfere with prosocial development. Extremes of negative parenting, including child abuse, tend to result in a lack of prosocial response to others' distress as well as more aggression (Broderick & Blewitt, 2006).

The child's personality affects the development of prosocial behavior. A child's sociability is fostered when he tends to participate in preschool activities and is low in shyness. Sociable children are more likely to help other children. In contrast, children who are inhibited, especially with strangers, likely will have lower empathy with others. Children who have positive prosocial behaviors are viewed by adults as socially skilled and have effective coping skills. Their social, problem-solving skills are high, and they are likely to have more friends than inhibited children. Also they are less aggressive.

Prosocial skills are related to assertiveness and dominance. Those who issue commands and defend their possessions are high in sympathy rather than displaying personal distress. Children who are not simply assertive, but want to dominate others, may have fewer prosocial behaviors (Eisenberg, Fabes, & Spinrad, 2005).

How can parents, teachers, and caregivers promote prosocial development in the preschool years? Landry (2002) provides some tips.

1. Model and encourage caring behaviors.
2. Help children understand how their behavior affects others.
3. Encourage responsibility by assigning tasks.
4. Teach children social skills in contacts with their peers.
5. Teach children how to resolve conflicts and develop interpersonal negotiation skills.

## CHILDREN, ELECTRONIC MEDIA, AND PROSOCIAL SKILLS

Can viewing television teach young children prosocial skills? It depends on the type of programming. Repeated exposure to prosocial television can affect social behavior. *Sesame Street* and *Mr. Rogers's Neighborhood* increased children's positive attention to others. Children who viewed *Sesame Street* extensively, over time, developed more positive attitudes toward people of different groups. The prosocial effects of television viewing increase sharply between the ages of three and seven. (Wilson, 2008)

## Play and Social-Emotional Development

Earlier in the chapter, we characterized the preschool years as the play years. This description is particularly apt for social development because much of the progress occurs through play. In this part of the chapter, we review the relationship of theory to social play, as well as current perspectives on the developmental progression of social play. With this theoretical foundation in place, characteristics of social play are discussed to include play and social competence, sociodramatic play, and variations in the development of social play.

**Theoretical Views of Play and Social Development**    Piaget's cognitive-developmental theory, Erickson's psychosocial theory, and Vygotsky's sociocultural theory have significant contributions toward understanding the relationship between play and social development. In addition, Sutton-Smith has advocated that play can also be viewed from an evolutionary perspective.

Although Piaget (1962) felt that play has a primary role in the child's development, he placed little emphasis on play as a factor in the child's responses to the social environment. Nevertheless, he saw a role for peer interactions within play for social-cognitive development. More specifically, play interactions helped children understand that other players have perspectives different from their own. Play, for Piaget, provides children with opportunities to

develop social competence through ongoing interactions.

Erikson (1963) maintained there is a relationship between make-believe play and wider society. Make-believe play permits children to learn about their social world and to try out new social skills. Moreover, play facilitates the understanding of cultural roles and to integrate accepted social norms into their own personalities. For Erikson, as for Piaget, play promotes a child who is socially competent.

Vygotsky's sociocultural theory has a significant role for play in that he proposed that make-believe play in the preschool years is vital for the acquisition of social and cognitive competence. Vygotsky suggested that make-believe play required children to initiate an imaginary situation and follow a set of rules to play out the situation; the child is able to act separately from reality. This type of planned pretend play helps children choose between courses of action (Creasey et al., 1998). Make-believe play also forces young children to control their impulses and subject themselves to the rules of play; moreover, Vygotsky believed that all imaginary situations devised by young children follow social rules. Through make-believe play, children develop an understanding of social norms and try to uphold those social expectations (Berk, 1994).

Sutton-Smith (1976) and others maintain that there is a relationship between play and evolution. Much of children's social play resembles that of primates and is necessary for survival. For example, rough-and-tumble play, in which both children and primates engage, offers a survival benefit in that it provides experiences in being dominant that later promote self-confidence in social interactions. It must be noted that more recently Sutton-Smith (1997) has embraced a wider understanding of play. He suggests that the usual psychological theories of play present a sanitized, middle-class perspective of play (Vandenberg, 1985). The negative social attributes of play, such as violence and aggression, are given less importance. In addition, he believes that too much stress has been placed on the function of play to promote development and progress and to describe what is done as a comparison with animal play (Sutton-Smith, 1997).

## Characteristics of Social Play

Social development in the preschool years permits young children to include others in their pretend and dramatic play. Whereas infants and toddlers use their ability to symbolize in solitary play, preschoolers use their expanded cognitive and social abilities to play with their peers (Bretherton, 1985). In this section, some aspects of social play that contribute to social development and vice versa are discussed. The characteristics include understanding the developmental levels of social play, play and social competence, the expression of emotions or feelings through play, and sociodramatic play.

**Developmental Levels of Social Play** We are indebted to the work of Parten (1932) in observing and describing how social play develops in preschool children. In her studies of young children, Parten observed that social play increases with age. As introduced in Chapter 2, she described development of social play into six categories: unoccupied behavior, onlooker behavior, solitary play, parallel play, associative play, and cooperative play. Rubin (2001) has revised the categories into non-play behaviors, social play and cognitive play. Non-play behaviors and play behaviors are discussed next.

### Non-Play Behaviors

**Unoccupied Behavior.** The child is not playing but occupies herself with watching anything that happens to be of momentary interest. When there is nothing exciting taking place, she plays with her own body, gets on and off chairs, just stands around, follows the teacher, or sits in one spot glancing around the room (or playground).

**Onlooker Behavior.** The child spends most of her time watching the other children play. She often talks to the children being observed, asks questions or give suggestions, but does not overtly enter into the play. This type differs from unoccupied in that the onlooker is definitely observing particular groups of children. The child stands or sits within speaking distance from other children.

**Transition.** The child is moving from one activity to another. The child might be setting up an activity, watching another activity, or searching for an object.

**Active Conversation.** The child is being spoken to by another child and listens and responds to the child. Shared laughter would fit into this category.

**Aggression.** The child is engaged in negative behaviors with another child. The child might be kicking, hitting, or grabbing.

**Rough-and-Tumble Play.** The child is engaged in playful fighting, running about, and other playful physical contact.

### Social Play

**Solitary Play.** The child plays alone and independently with toys that are different from those used by the children within speaking distance and makes no effort to get close to other children. He pursues his own activity without reference to what others are doing.

**Parallel Play.** The child plays independently, but the activity chosen naturally brings her among other children. She plays with toys that are similar to those the children around her are using, but she plays with the toys as she sees fit and does not try to influence or modify the activity of the children near her. She plays beside—rather than with—the other children.

**Group Play.** Goals of the play are group centered. The child plays with other children in making some product, playing games, or dramatizing a life situation.

Parten's categories of developmental levels of social play provided the first guidelines for understanding how young children progress from playing by themselves to becoming social players. Researchers have continued to refine and redefine Parten's categories in light of their own observations of social play. Two areas of research have focused on the definition of solitary play and frequency of play in the six categories.

In Parten's classification, the child's movement from solitary play to more social categories of play is a positive developmental step. Although Parten believed solitary play was the least mature form of play, subsequent research defined other, more mature, roles for solitary play. Kenneth H. Rubin and others have found different indicators for the role of solitary play. In what he defines as nonsocial play, Rubin (1982) found that socially competent 4-year-olds who were popular with their peers engaged in solitary or parallel play activities such as artwork and block construction. From their own work, Moore, Evertson, and Brophy (1974) found that almost half of the solitary play they observed consisted of goal-directed activities and educational play. The findings from these and other similar studies indicate that solitary play might not be the result of social immaturity, but rather a desirable form of play (Moore et al., 1974; Rubin, 1982; Rubin, Maioni, & Hornung, 1976).

Studies of solitary play reveal various reasons why children prefer solitary play. The choice may be simply because some tasks are best accomplished alone or because a child wishes to have some time alone for self-reflection (Burger, 1995; Katz & Buchholtz, 1999). Time alone may result in constructive behaviors. Children might experience peace of mind, self-regulation, and control over their environment (Luckey & Fabes, 2005). Although solitary play may indicate shyness or peer rejection for some, solitary constructive play can be related to happier moods and increased alertness (Katz & Buchholtz, 1999).

Another area of research has been the percentages of children who engage in the six categories of social play. Researchers have differed in their findings as to what percentages of children engage in parallel, associative, and cooperative play (Bakeman & Brownlee, 1980; Barnes, 1971; Rubin et al., 1976) when compared to Parten's findings in 1932. Two conclusions have surfaced from these studies and others: Today's preschoolers are less skilled in the higher levels of social play (Frost, 1992), and social class can have a bearing on levels of social play (Rubin et al., 1976; Smilansky, 1968). In addition, the context of the child's play has a bearing on the maturity demonstrated in solitary play.

Rubin and his colleagues and others have continued to develop their understanding of the progression of social play (Coplan, Rubin, Fox, Calkins, & Stewart, 1994; Rubin & Coplan, 1998; Rubin et al., 1983). Rubin and Coplan (1998) report that Piaget's structural components of play and Smilansky's stages of play can be used to better understand progress in social play. To understand children's social participation, observers need to view play content within the context of the play (Rubin et al., 1976). The Play Observation Scale (see Figure 5-2), developed to achieve this purpose, shows how a broader exploration of social play indicators was achieved (Rubin, 1986; Rubin & Coplan, 1998). The Play Observation Scale was revised in 2001 (Rubin, 2001).

In their continued work, researchers have made the following conclusions about levels of social play:

**FIGURE 5.2**   Play Observation Scale

Play Observation Scale Coding Sheet (2001)

Name of Child_____   ID_____   Cohort_____   Age_____

Free Play Session _____

| | **Time Sample** | | | | | |
|---|---|---|---|---|---|---|
| | :10 | :20 | :30 | :40 | :50 | :60 |
| uncodable | | | | | | |
| out of room | | | | | | |
| transitional | | | | | | |
| unoccupied | | | | | | |
| onlooker | | | | | | |
| *Solitary Behaviors:* | | | | | | |
| Occupied | | | | | | |
| Constructive | | | | | | |
| Exploratory | | | | | | |
| Functional | | | | | | |
| Dramatic | | | | | | |
| Games | | | | | | |
| *Parallel Behaviors:* | | | | | | |
| Occupied | | | | | | |
| Constructive | | | | | | |
| Exploratory | | | | | | |
| Functional | | | | | | |
| Dramatic | | | | | | |
| Games | | | | | | |
| *Group Behaviors:* | | | | | | |
| Occupied | | | | | | |
| Constructive | | | | | | |
| Exploratory | | | | | | |
| Functional | | | | | | |
| Dramatic | | | | | | |
| Games | | | | | | |
| *Peer Conversation* | | | | | | |
| *Double Coded Behaviors:* | | | | | | |
| Anxious Behaviors | | | | | | |
| Hovering | | | | | | |
| Aggression | | | | | | |
| Rough-and-Tumble | | | | | | |

*Conversation/Interacting With:* 1_____ 2_____ 3_____ 4_____ 5_____ 6_____

1. Social play becomes more prominent during the preschool years to include an increase in the frequency of social contacts, longer social episodes, and more varied social episodes (Jones, 1972; Holmberg, 1980; Rubin, 2001; Rubin, Watson, & Jambor, 1978).

2. Although preschoolers tend to spend more time playing alone or near others, they play with a wider range of peers (Howes, 1983).

3. The major developmental change in preschool play is related to cognitive-developmental maturity within the categories rather than change in the amount of play in the categories. The frequency of play in the categories remains the same during the preschool years; the significant changes come in sociodramatic play and games with rules (Rubin, 2001; Rubin et al., 1978).

*Sociodramatic Play*    **Sociodramatic play** is the most advanced form of social and symbolic play. In sociodramatic play, children carry out imitation and drama and fantasy play together. Sociodramatic play involves role playing in which children imitate real-life people and experiences that they have had themselves. Make-believe is also a component because it serves as an aid to imitation. It allows the children to represent real-life events and include their imaginations in carrying out their roles. The child's abilities in sociodramatic play improve with experience and, as she plays with different children, her play becomes more varied to include new interpretations and ideas (Smilansky & Shefatya, 1990).

Smilansky (1968) characterizes six criteria of dramatic play that evolve into sociodramatic play. She defines the first four criteria as dramatic play and the last two as sociodramatic play as follows (Smilansky & Shefatya, 1990):

- *Imitative role play.*   The child undertakes a make-believe role and expresses it in imitative action and/or verbalization.

- *Make-believe with regard to objects.*   Movements or verbal declarations and/or materials or toys that are not replicas of the object itself are substituted for real objects.

- *Verbal make-believe with regard to actions and situations.*   Verbal descriptions or declarations are substituted for actions and situations.

- *Persistence in role play.*   The child continues within a role or play theme for at least 10 minutes.

- *Interaction.*   At least two players interact within the context of a play episode.

- *Verbal communication.*   There is some verbal interaction related to the play episode. (p. 24)

Smilansky and Shefatya prefer the terms *make-believe* and *pretend play* to *symbolic play* and feel that role play is too narrow a description of what children are doing when they are engaged in sociodramatic play. They prefer the term *sociodramatic play* because "[i]t involves not only representation and pretense, but also reality orientation, organizational skills, reasoning and argumentation, social skills, etc." (Smilansky & Shefatya, 1990, p. 27).

Sociodramatic play is the vehicle whereby young children use all of their developmental attributes. Children combine physical, cognitive, language, and social play in carrying out a play theme or event. Observation of sociodramatic play provides snapshots of a child's development.

**Play as Expression of Feelings.**   Unlike adults, preschool children are not able to verbalize how they feel. They experience feelings similar to those of adults, but they express them through play. Because they feel safe in play, and because play is a primary activity in the preschool years, young children exhibit the full range of their feelings in play activities (Landreth & Hohmeyer, 1998).

Freud (1935) proposed that play can be cathartic. Children use play to reduce anxiety and understand traumatic experiences. They may recreate an unpleasant experience such as an automobile accident over and over to assimilate it and diminish the intensity of feelings (Frost, 1992; Schaefer, 1993).

Children also use play to express their positive feelings, such as joy and contentment, as well as their aggressive feelings. As they externalize these feelings through play, they develop a sense of mastery and control. After they express negative feelings, such as fear and aggression, they can move on to express more positive feelings. When negative feelings have been resolved, children can move to other types of expression in their play (Landreth & Hohmeyer, 1998).

Although expression of emotions can be exhibited in solitary play, sociodramatic play has a major function in emotional development. As they take roles in dramatic play, young children can act out relationships and experience the feelings of the person in the role they are playing. For example a child role playing a sick child might express sympathy in the play activity. By engaging in different roles, they can express emotional responses to the roles, which lead them to understand differences in feelings and develop problem-solving skills (Cohen & Stern, 1983). Sociodramatic play promotes emotional development and feelings that results in a greater feeling of power, sense of happiness, and positive self-regard (Piers & Landau, 1980; Singer & Singer, 1977).

## Variations in Social Competence and Play

Developmental changes in social development lead to progress in social play in preschool children; however, there are individual differences in social play just as there are differences in social development. These differences in sociability are generally consistent or stable over time. Children who are less competent in peer interactions in early childhood might be at risk for later problems that can include school dropout, depression, and aggression. Some of the factors that can affect individual differences have been widely researched. These include genetic differences, parenting style and effectiveness in child rearing, and effective peer relations (Rubin & Coplan, 1998).

**Genetic Differences**  Genetic factors manifest in ways such as differences in twins and gifted preschool children. Identical twins are more similar in sociability than fraternal twins.

Shyness that can be identified in younger fraternal twins can be seen later in school-age children (Plomin & Daniels, 1986; Scarr, 1968). Gifted children, to the contrary, can find play to be a valuable activity. Although children studied by Wright (1990) engaged extensively in solitary and nonplay activities, they were highly social and deliberately used strategies that would bring them in contact with their peers.

**Parenting Style and Effectiveness in Child Rearing**  Evidence indicates that parenting style affects sociability in children. Parents who are authoritative have children who tend to be socially responsible and are friendly and cooperative in peer interactions. Children of authoritative parents have been found to have positive self-esteem and be prosocial. In contrast, parents who are authoritarian or permissive tend to have children who are socially withdrawn, incompetent, or aggressive (Baumrind, 1991; Roopnarine, 1987).

Parents who are effective in child rearing have children who are competent in social play. Effective parents show their infants and young children how to engage in more sophisticated symbolic play and make-believe themes, model play, support social-linguistic skills, and encourage pretend play. They arrange play activities for their young children; as a result, their children tend to be able to initiate peer contacts and display prosocial behaviors with their playmates. Caregivers in child-care settings can also affect socially competent play (Creasey et al., 1998; Howes & Stewart, 1987; Ladd & Hart, 1992; Rubin, Maioni, & Hornung, 1976).

There is a lack of complex social play interactions in low-quality child-care centers, however. Families who do not provide mentoring and social play opportunities for their preschool children have children who do not have the background for advanced social play (Howes & Stewart, 1987; Rubin et al., 1976; Smilansky, 1968). Family social class was found to be a factor in competent social play by these researchers.

**Effective Peer Relations**   Children who are socially competent are able to engage in successful peer play. They are able to use proactive methods to join a group and use advanced social skills to recruit play partners. During the preschool years, socially competent children become more skilled in understanding the play cues exhibited by peers and improve in negotiating play themes (Goncu, 1993; Howes, 1987a). Moreover, children who are skilled in peer interactions are more likely to engage in high levels of fantasy play (Creasey et al., 1998).

## Variations in Sociodramatic Play

Preschool children's differences in social play have been documented in the previous sections. These differences provide a logical sequence into understanding differences in sociodramatic play. Again, Smilansky's work (1968; Smilansky & Shefatya, 1990) provides the leadership in understanding these differences.

Smilansky conducted extensive research on sociodramatic play that resulted in three conclusions: Lower-class children engage in less and poorer quality sociodramatic play than middle-class children; children who have deficits in sociodramatic play are the result of parents' child-rearing attitudes and practices regarding their child's sociodramatic play; and training in sociodramatic play can ameliorate the deficits described (McLoyd, 1986).

Smilansky's early work led to much research on differences in sociodramatic play. The findings of these studies did not always agree. Most researchers confirmed Smilansky's findings that middle-class preschoolers participate in sociodramatic play more often than lower-class preschoolers (Fein & Stork, 1981; Rosen, 1974). Some studies, however, found no difference (Rubin et al., 1976), and one study (Eifermann, 1971) noted differences that favored lower-class children.

Research on individual differences in sociodramatic play continues. In addition to socioeconomic differences, researchers also study such factors as the effects of the environment (Frost, 1992) and the sociodramatic play of mixed-age groups (Stone & Christie, 1996). Socioeconomic differences are discussed in detail later in this chapter.

## Adult Roles in Social Play

If adults are to support social play in preschool children, they need to understand and value both social and sociodramatic play. First and foremost, adults need to believe in the importance of social play for preschool children. Both parents and teachers must be advocates for daily social play opportunities, and their roles are different.

Parents are significant role models for social play. Parenting styles affect how socially competent their children will be. In addition, parents can coach their children on prosocial behaviors and model how their children can develop friendships. They can provide play partners for their children by arranging play dates with peers. They can also widen friendships by inviting a variety of children to play.

Parents, teachers, and caregivers can encourage both social and sociodramatic play. Daily opportunities for free play are important in preschool classrooms. In addition, the props and materials that teachers provide can stimulate sociodramatic play. Teachers can model role playing by entering into children's sociodramatic play episodes or by making suggestions for dramatic play themes. Frequent changes of toys and materials enrich sociodramatic play. A variety of props can support specific play themes.

Adults would do well to appreciate the positive characteristics of rough-and-tumble play, superhero play, and chase games. Although caregivers and teachers express concern about violent themes and possible injuries in superhero and rough-and-tumble play, they can take a broader view and try to see the benefits of these types of sociodramatic play for young children.

**WHAT PARENTS, CAREGIVERS, AND TEACHERS CAN DO TO PROMOTE SOCIAL AND SOCIODRAMATIC PLAY**

1. Make provisions for preschool children to engage in social play both at home and in group settings.

2. Facilitate play with a wide group of peers to encourage child-initiated relationships.

3. Guide children in developing prosocial skills that will help them be successful members in play groups.

4. Engage in children's play to model social skills and appropriate play behaviors.

5. Provide props and materials for sociodramatic play.

6. Supply props that are specific for play themes, for example, a magnifying glass for playing detective.

7. Suggest or model roles in sociodramatic play.

8. Offer intervention and redirecting strategies for children who express aggression in play to help them use more positive social behaviors.

Teachers and caregivers also support social competence through play. They can support positive social interactions and provide support and intervention for children who are not socially successful by suggesting appropriate play behaviors or how to engage in a play activity in a more positive manner.

## CHARACTERISTICS OF PRESCHOOL PLAY

### The Integrated Nature of Play

In earlier sections, characteristics of play were discussed within each domain of development. The relationships between development and play in the preschool years were drawn for motor, cognitive, language, and social-emotional development. In this section, we discuss play in terms of overall development.

All domains of development are engaged in preschool children's play. Moreover, the level of development in each domain affects a child's ability to use other developmental domains in play. Children who are socially mature are able to bring their social skills into leadership roles in sociodramatic play. Ability in expressive language affects a child's social interactions and level of participation in sociodramatic play. Motor skills impact how preschool children use physical movement in fantasy or thematic play.

The next section describes factors that impact individual differences in play. This is followed by a discussion of the types of play that characterize the play years in preschool children. These include games that involve gender differences, rough-and-tumble play, superhero play, and chase games.

### Variations in Development and Play

Individual children vary in their development and play. In the discussion of social development and play, we discussed individual variations in terms of parenting practices and of differences in temperament, social competence, and effectiveness in peer relations. Now looking at differences in play as an integrated process, individual variations are discussed in terms of cultural and socioeconomic status and of gender differences.

**Socioeconomic Status and Cultural Differences in Play**   In the earlier section on sociodramatic play, we discussed the work of Smilansky (1968), which investigated socioeconomic differences in play with children from different cultures. Because much of the research that has been conducted has included both socioeconomic and cultural factors, these two are discussed together to explain play differences in preschool children.

Low income or poverty can have negative effects on child play. Children from homes with limited income may not have access to high-quality play environments, expensive toys and equipment, and enriching experiences outside their immediate home environment (J. E. Johnson, 1998). When quality of play is affected as a consequence, children engage in lower forms of play such as exploration and functional play instead of higher forms of play such as constructive and sociodramatic play (Pellegrini & Boyd, 1993; Smilansky, 1990).

When cultural factors interact with socioeconomic factors, variations in play are more complex. Although some elements of play such as sociality of play and imagination are similar across cultures, expressive or recreational play, especially play themes, are more likely to reflect specific cultures (J. E. Johnson, 1998).

Differences in the amount and types of play have been observed in different cultures. In some cultures, children are observed engaging in complex and elaborate games. Particular games are simpler in some cultures and nonexistent in others (Frost, 1992; Hughes, 1999; see Chapter 7). In addition, some researchers have proposed that children from cultures where work comes early in childhood engage in limited forms of play. However, research has demonstrated that children who engage in adult work or are from poverty-level homes do engage in dramatic play with other children. Their play does not depend on having toys or materials for pretense play, nor are same-age

peers a crucial element (Johnson et al., 1999; Schwartzman, 1978).

Cultural differences among U.S. children can affect sociodramatic play. For example, Korean American children engage in less pretend play and can become uncomfortable in pretend play activities. At the same time, Korean American children engage in more exploratory play (Farver, Kim, & Lee-Shen, 2000; Klein & Chen, 2002; Trawick-Smith, 2009).

**Gender Differences in Play**   The ability to label gender affects the emergence of gender-segregated play, as introduced at the beginning of this section. Children who can label gender are more likely to play with same-gender children and more likely to select gender-identified toys; and girls who label gender early are less likely to engage in aggressive play than other children (Fagot & Leve, 1998).

Smilansky's (1968) play categories can be used to identify gender difference in play. There is little difference in functional play; however, boys are more likely to engage in constructive play (Rubin, Watson, & Jambor, 1978). In dramatic play, boys and girls take on different roles. Girls are more likely to engage in social roles, whereas boys engage in mock battles (Johnson & Roopnarine, 1983). Girls engage in feminine or housekeeping roles in fantasy play; boys engage in superhero and adventure themes (Johnson et al., 1999; Sutton-Smith, 1979).

In addition to the differences just cited, many characteristics of preschool play are gender specific. Girls use verbal interactions and suggestions while playing creatively with toys. In physical play, boys engage in more rough-and-tumble play than girls. In social play, girls play in small groups; boys play in larger, more organized groups (Ausch, 1994; Fagot & Leve, 1998; Neppl & Murray, 1997).

There are differences in how boys and girls play games. Girls play games that involve taking turns and avoid addressing conflicts. Boys, in contrast, engage in games that do not have

Children of all cultures play.

specific rules. They enjoy negotiation and disagreements because it makes the game more interesting (Ausch, 1994). In other types of social interactions, girls seek help from others in the environment, whereas boys tend to play independently.

Boys engage in more aggressive play than girls, which increases between infancy and school age. Although there are cultural differences in aggression in play, the predominance of aggression in boy's play rather than girl's play persists. It is significant to note that in the United States, a list of sex-role, stereotyped toys for boys includes guns, knives, and other fighting tools (Fagot & Leve, 1998).

The information provided about differences in play related to gender are but a fraction of the research that has been conducted on the topic; several other characteristics of preschool play can also be explored. In the sections that follow, rough-and-tumble play, superhero play, and chase games are discussed. Although they are described as separate kinds of play, in reality they are frequently combined as children engage in dramatic play.

**Rough-and-Tumble Play**  Rough-and-tumble play has been characterized as friendly fighting or play fighting. It also may entail hitting and wrestling, but it is significantly different from real fighting. Although rough-and-tumble play is more prevalent in the primary grades (Pellegrini & Boyd, 1993), Jones (1976) first witnessed this type of play when observing nursery school children. He describes seven movement patterns that tended to occur in this type of play: "These are running, chasing, and fleeing; wrestling; jumping up and down with both feet together . . .; beating at each other with an object but not hitting; laughing" (p. 355). A major difference between real fighting and rough-and-tumble play is the fact that children are laughing and smiling as they play. Carlson (2009) characterizes the differences in play behaviors between the two. When children are play fighting or using rough-and-tumble play, they laugh, run, jump, open beat (tag), wrestle, chase, and flee. Whey they are being aggressive, they fixate, frown, hit, push, or take and grab.

What is the nature of rough-and-tumble play in the preschool years? It is typified by reciprocal role-taking. Several children are engaged in the activity and take turns in roles such as "bad guys" and "good guys" (Johnson et al., 1999; Pellegrini & Boyd, 1993). The children might be engaged in a play theme that also includes running and chasing and play fighting. They might change roles during the play episode and replay the scenario. Jones (1976) gives the examples of tag and "cowboys and Indians." Today, play themes might include reenactment of favorite television shows, movies, or cartoons.

Recent writers on preschool rough-and-tumble play have discussed specific developmental benefits. When children use this whole-body type of play, the physical exertion promotes cardiovascular health. It also fills the need for human touch (Carlson, 2006, 2009). Moreover, children become skilled at giving and detecting signals about the play episode, including when it is coming to an end (Carlson, 2009). As children change roles in the play, they are setting foundations for future social relationships.

There are gender differences in preschool rough-and-tumble play. In a study of girls-only play, themes of "putting the baby to bed" and a magic rabbit were part of the physical play. In boys-only play, the play themes were from recent media and included a "robot war" and karate fighting (Jarvis, 2006).

There are continuing concerns as to whether children should be allowed to engage in rough-and-tumble play in the preschool. Parents and teachers fear the play will turn into real fighting or that children might be hurt. Many adults seem not to recognize the differences between rough-and-tumble play and real fighting (Carlson, 2009; Tannock, 2009, 2010). In reality, rough-and-tumble play evolves into fighting only 1% of the time (Scott & Panksepp, 2003).

Although preschool children engage in rough-and-tumble play 5% of the time in free play, this type of play increases to 10% to 17% of play in primary grade years (J. E. Johnson, 1998). Rough-and-tumble play is discussed in more detail in Chapter 6.

**Superhero Play**  Rough-and-tumble play and superhero play are closely related. Indeed, teachers often fail to notice any difference between the two because superhero play is often a part of rough-and-tumble play. There is a difference, however, in that rough-and-tumble play can occur without superhero play.

**Superhero play** is a result of television programming for young children. As children reflect their favorite programs in their dramatic play, superhero play results. Boyd (1997, p. 23) defines superhero play as follows: "Superhero play refers to the active, physical play of children pretending to be media characters imbued with extraordinary abilities, including superhuman strength or the ability to transform themselves into superhuman entities."

Superhero play appeals particularly to boys for several reasons. First, it permits young boys to engage in running, wrestling, jumping, and shouting that are characteristic of rough-and-tumble play. Second, superheroes possess powers children wish they had; they can feel as though they are strong and powerful when they engage in superhero roles. Third, preschool boys are attracted to superhero play because they can pit good against evil and play roles that are always good (Bauer & Dettore, 1997).

As is the case with rough-and-tumble play, teachers commonly ban superhero play in their classrooms and on the playground. They might be concerned about the violent content, viewing it as aggressive and frightening as well as bizarre (Carlsson-Paige & Levin, 1995). As in the case of rough-and-tumble play, they are concerned that children can get hurt when the play gets out of control and because it can escalate into noisy and chaotic play (Bauer & Dettore, 1997; Church, 2004).

Part of the concern about superhero play is the perception that it is escalating. Little concrete evidence, however, indicates this is so. Boyd (1997) asserts that much of the data used to support the increase is based on anecdotal reports and may include a lack of objectivity on the part of teachers. Furthermore, teachers characterize superhero play as characterized by fighting, martial arts moves, and kicking. These play behaviors are reportedly the main source of teachers' concerns (Bergen, 1994; Carlsson-Paige & Levin, 1991, 1995). Teachers also make a connection between preschool play and later membership in adolescent gangs (Boyd, 1997).

Superhero play actually offers benefits, again similar to benefits of rough-and-tumble play. First, superhero play is engaged in by friends, thus promoting friendships between children. Second, children can use superhero play to elevate their status within the group. They select players similar in strength or choose a slightly stronger partner (Smith & Boulton, 1990). Because preschoolers are not in control of many aspects of their lives, superhero play helps them establish their own identity. When they imitate heros who are able to overcome challenges, they not only experience power, but they begin to understand the difference between good and evil.

Banning superhero play can have negative results. Undesirable behaviors that can result when teachers ban superhero play include children feeling guilty about engaging in superhero play or learning to be deceptive when engaging in superhero play. They can fear talking to adults about their interests in superhero play (Carlsson-Paige & Levin, 1990). Teachers send the message that such play is wrong for them, as is being interested in some of the values such as good and evil that are part of superhero themes (Boyd, 1997). Teachers also lose opportunities to incorporate superhero characters as a positive influence in children's development and learning (Bauer & Dettore, 1997). Carlsson-Paige and Levin (1995) suggest to teachers that superheroes can be used to instill positive behaviors in children if they are used as a motivational tool.

Some writers on superhero play offer suggestions for managing such play. One suggestion is for the teacher to discuss real heroes. Another is to play along with the children and guide the play. However, long lists of ways to manage children's superhero play can lead to the loss of spontaneity in children's play (Kid Source online, 2010). In the opinion of this author, overmanaging or setting up scenarios for superhero play can defeat some of the benefits children experience in free-play activities. (See Adult Roles in Preschool Play later in this chapter.)

**Block Play**   Blocks have been a part of preschool classrooms for over a century. The first small blocks were introduced by Frederick Froebel (1902), the father of the kindergarten movement. With the understanding of development of motor skills during the child study movement early in the 20th century came larger blocks designed to complement the emerging motor skills of young children.

The reality that boys play with blocks more frequently than girls is not discussed in some sources; nevertheless, Stitzel (2009) suggests that all children be invited to play in the block center. Boys and girls benefit from opportunities to play together and work together on a real project, and girls will enjoy becoming skilled at building with blocks. Other suggestions for encouraging the inclusion of girls in the block center is to locate the blocks next to the dramatic play area, have a girls-only time for block play, or establishing a separate block play area for girls (Tokarz, 2008). Perhaps the most effective way to increase girls' participation is to communicate frequently that the block center is for all children to use (Stitzel, 2009).

Blocks provide avenues for cognitive learning, creative expression, and social interaction. They can be used to demonstrate elements of stories, thematic curriculum, or to promote language. They can also be used as a focus for a preschool science curriculum (Chalufour & Worth, 2004). Blocks are enjoyed by toddlers under 3 and continue into the primary grade years, but the peak interest in block building is during the preschool years. A developmental sequence in building with blocks becomes more complex as motor and cognitive development advance. Toddlers clap blocks together and make simple constructions. Preschoolers use emerging understanding of space to construct more complex structures (Kamii, Miyakawa, & Kato, 2004; Reifel, 1983). The element of representation and symbolism becomes a part of block play as they are used to construct buildings, walls, ramps, and roads (Reifel, 1984; Reifel & Yeatman, 1991).

Children enjoy carrying out their own ideas for block play; nevertheless, adults can encourage block play. Blocks can be combined with other play items to broaden children's motivation for block constructions. The addition of small vehicles can promote the construction of garages and roads. Storybooks and writing materials can provide suggestions to link block play with literacy (Wellhausen & Giles, 2005/ 2006).

Teachers have a more direct role when they engage in block play to guide or direct block play. The teacher might suggest block construction based on a classroom theme of study (Reifel & Yeatman, 1991). Comments such as "Can you build a house for the three bears?" can be a motivator for block play. Suggestions to add to children's constructions can enhance the complexity of structures. Blocks can also be the focus of a preschool science curriculum. Beginning with exploration, the curriculum evolves into experiences with scientific topics (Chalufour & Worth, 2004).

Language becomes a natural extension of block play as children working with blocks engage in conversations with each other or the teacher. In addition, levels of social play can be observed as children engage in solitary, parallel, and cooperative play. Sociodramatic play occurs as children play out the creation of their structures (Reifel & Yeatman, 1991; Wellhausen & Giles, 2005/2006).

**Chase Games**    Running and chasing are a part of rough-and-tumble play, as described earlier. Here we discuss chase games as a separate type of play that emerges in the preschool years and continues to expand and develop after children enter school. Although many writers on the subject prefer to discuss chasing as a subelement of rough-and-tumble play (Humphreys & Smith, 1984; Pellegrini, 1995), we support the premise that chase games are worthy of discussion as a separate category.

How are chase games defined as a separate category? **Chase games** involve physical skill, strategy and, possibly also, tagging and hiding (Clarke, 1999). Chasing can include cross-gender play as well as same-gender play (Thorne, 1995). There can be a sequence in the chasing game: initiation with a provocation such as a taunt or poke; the chasing; and the end when the chaser is outdistanced, the chased is caught and perhaps wrestled to the ground, or the chased reaches a safety zone (Thorne, 1995).

Both boys and girls engage in chase games, although boys participate more frequently than girls (Pellegrini, 1995). Chase games are found in many cultures, with cultural differences. Four common types of cultural differences are variations on individual and group chases: An individual chases a group, a group chases an individual, an individual chases an individual, and a group chases a group (Clarke, 1999; Opie & Opie, 1969; Sutton-Smith, 1972).

Gender differences in chase games are apparent as well. When same-gender chasing occurs, the chasing between boys frequently ends in wrestling or play fighting (supporting the connection with rough-and-tumble play). Girls, however, are less physical. They might flee for a safety zone where they can stop and then reenter the game.

Cross-gender chasing is frequently labeled, such as "girls chase the boys" or "catch and kiss" (Thorne, 1995; Jarvis, 2006). However, Jarvis reported that she has never seen a boy kiss a girl in her extensive research observing chasing games; the boy touches or tags the girl. Cross-gender chasing is also characterized by discussions and retellings of the chase episode. Individuals may call for help or offer to assist one of the groups involved in the chase.

## Creativity and Play

Preschoolers engage in all types of creativity in their play. Their emerging abilities in cognition, language, fine-motor skills, and social development make it possible to weave creativity into their everyday play activities. They are creative with speech, sociodramatic play themes, classroom materials that include art and music materials, and the constructions they make with large blocks and small manipulative materials. Their world can be rich with opportunities for creative expression.

Young children's creativity features three unique characteristics. First, creative children can be sensitive to internal and external stimuli. Second, they demonstrate a lack of inhibition, becoming completely absorbed in the creative activity. Third, they have a unique ability to use imagination and fantasy in their play (Isenberg & Jalongo, 2006).

The relationship between play and creativity has generated great interest. Lieberman (1965) studied the relationship between playfulness traits and divergent thinking. She found that children who were the most playful were also the most creative. Smilansky (1968) observed a relationship between creativity and sociodramatic play. She found that children with higher levels of pretend play or sociodramatic play had more successful achievement later in school. She also described how children with lower levels of sociodramatic play could be guided to use more creative thinking and extension of play themes.

Johnson (1976) also found a relationship between fantasy play styles and creativity. He was able to describe a relationship between social fantasy play and divergent thinking tasks. He suggested that this relationship leads to the ability to generate a variety of ideas. Pepler and Ross (1981) also found that children who had divergent play experiences used more imagination in responding to divergent thinking tasks. Their study also indicated that play with unstructured materials rather than structured materials leads to creativity. Likewise, social play is more beneficial for creativity than

Children enjoy creating together.

nonsocial dramatic play (Johnson, 1976). Finally, the availability of an enriched and flexible play environment with less-intrusive adult intervention facilitates creativity in play (Pepler, 1979).

## ADULT ROLES IN PRESCHOOL PLAY

Parents, caregivers, and teachers have important roles in preschool children's play. They serve as facilitators, models, supervisors, and participants in children's play. In this section, we take a look at adult roles in sex-typed behavior, aggressive play, and involvement in play activities.

Earlier in the chapter, we discussed how preschool children begin to engage in gender play and how this process is refined as children get older. The trend in recent decades has been away from gender differences in play. With the advent of higher percentages of working mothers, fathers taking responsibility for tasks in the home, and fathers spending more time playing with their children, preschool children exhibit less gender-based play. As a couple of examples, girls now engage in more sports that were once thought to be a male form of play, and preschool boys are more likely to role-play fathers in nurturing roles in dramatic play.

At one time there was an effort on the part of teachers to advocate cross-gender play and to focus on eliminating stereotypical gender play. However, we are cautioned to be aware of ethnic and cultural groups who oppose moving away from traditional gender roles in children's play (Johnson et al., 1999). In some circumstances, however, parents and teachers can foster play that is gender neutral. Parents can treat their children's play in an equitable manner. Equal time should be spent with children of either gender and equal emphasis placed on toys and activities. Fathers and mothers should include girls in traditional male games and engage their sons in cooking and other household activities that were once thought to be females' territory.

Parents have an important role in preschool play.

Another adult role in preschool play is as supervisor. Caregivers and teachers working in group settings supervise larger numbers of children at play. They must decide whether play activities are appropriate and safe. Children who play aggressively are a concern. Supervisors can limit aggression and redirect children who are aggressive or violent (Kuykendall, 1996). This type of play behavior is distinct from rough-and-tumble and superhero play, which can pose no threat when play episodes are carried out in a positive manner. Teachers also are concerned about playground safety (see Chapter 13).

Teachers can provide opportunities for children to broaden their play by arranging the indoor and outdoor environments with activities for both genders. Many kindergarten teachers have had a majority of "female"-type activities because of their concern for noise and safety. Large wooden blocks, work benches, and dramatic play themes that focus on male roles rather than female roles can provide opportunities for children to engage in these roles.

How much should adults become involved in children's play? Throughout the chapter, we have made suggestions as to how parents, caregivers, and teachers can promote play in individual developmental domains. But the question of too much adult involvement in children's play is valid. For example, when parents or teachers get too involved in children's play, they tend to take over the play episode or become too directive. When this happens, children play at a lower level or lose interest in the activity. Research study results have shown that adult involvement is most effective when the adult becomes a coplayer or provides suggestions and materials to enrich play. Adults are least effective when they are uninvolved or merely observe play. At the other extreme, they are equally ineffective when they become instructors or directors of play (Johnson et al., 1999; Roskos & Neuman, 1993). Almon (2009, p. 42) defines the problem: "Real—play that is initiated and directed by children and that bubbles up from within the child rather than being imposed by adults—has largely disappeared from the landscape of childhood in the United States." Parents and teachers should remind themselves frequently of the importance of free play in children's lives.

 ## TOYS AND MATERIALS FOR PRESCHOOL PLAY

Young children are strongly influenced by toys that are marketed on television. Many of these toys are related to cartoon shows, current children's movies, or children's television programs that feature violence and action figures. Unfortunately, these toys have little play value and can be related to aggressive play (Frost, 1992). They do not stimulate imagination, dramatic play, or creativity. Over the past 50 years, the transformation of toys has included more technology, and they are mass produced with unlimited variety. These toys contribute to a decline in the imaginative activities of young children (Elkind, 2005). More specifically, preschool children are increasingly spending their time with handheld electronic games and video players. Parents use these toys to keep children entertained in many settings, including restaurants and when traveling (Almon, 2009). Almon believes we are training our children to turn to the screen rather than conceive their own ideas and express their own creativity.

More appropriate choices are toys that are unstructured, diverse in playability, and simple in design. Parents, teachers, and caregivers can also consider play in developmental domains in their choices of toys and materials for preschool children. They will want to include a balance of toys for different types of play. The Consumer Product Safety Commission (n.d.) has developed lists of toys for children ages 3 to 5. Suggestions are described by the following categories: Active Play, Manipulative Play, Creative Play, Make-Believe Play, and Learning Play (Figure 5-3).

**FIGURE 5.3** Toys for Preschoolers—3, 4, and 5 Years

| Active Play | Manipulative Play | Make-Believe Play |
|---|---|---|
| **Push and Pull Toys** | *from age 4* | **Dolls** |
| • small wagons | • design materials, mosaic blocks, felt boards | • realistic dolls with detail and accessories |
| • small wheelbarrow | | • dolls with hair, moving eyes, movable limbs, special features |
| • push toys resembling adult tools. | *from age 5* | |
| • doll carriages and strollers from age 5 | • simple weaving | *from age 5* |
| • full size wagons, scooters | • small beads to string | • child-proportioned dolls with clothes |
| | | • paper dolls to be punched out |
| *Ride-on Toys* | **Manipulative Toys** | |
| • tricycles sized to child | • matching toys by color, shape, or picture | **Stuffed Toys** |
| • 3-and 4-wheel pedal toys | • sorting toys, number rods | • stuffed toys with accessories |
| • vehicles with steering mechanisms | • number boards with smaller pegs | • realistic-looking toys |
| | • simple counting toys, lock boxes | • music box toys |
| *from age 4* | • nesting toys with multiple pieces and screw closing | |
| • low-slung tricycles | | *from age 5* |
| • battery-operated ride-ons | *from age 4* | • collecting toys in sets |
| | • geometrical concept toys | |
| *from age 5* | | **Puppets** |
| • small bicycle with training devices wheels and footbrakes | *from age 5* | • simple sock or mitten puppets |
| • bicycle helmet | • simple models of mechanical devices or natural objects, more complex lotto matching toys | • finger puppets |
| | | • simple puppet theater |
| **Outdoor and Gym Equipment** | | • hand and arm puppets, puppets with limbs |
| • stationary outdoor climbing equipment | **Dressing. Lacing, Stringing Toys** | |
| • slides with slide rails and ladders | • frames/cards to button, hook, tie | **Role Play Materials** |
| • swings with curved, soft seats | | • dress-ups costumes of all types |
| • balance board | *from age 5* | • realistic detailed equipment |
| | • simple sewing kits with thick cloth and blunt needle | • housekeeping and cooking equipment |
| *from age 4* | | • toy telephones, cell phones, camera |
| • equipment with movable parts, seesaws, hanging rings | **Sand and Water Play Toys** | • toys for thematic play (store, doctor) |
| • swings with flat seats (plastic or rubber belts | • large and small sandbox tools | |
| • rope ladders and ropes | • wind-up bath toys, bath activity centers | **Play Scenes** |
| • gym sets with enclosures for pretend house or fort | | • scenes with a variety of realistic accessories and working parts |
| | *from age 4* | • favorite themes-garage, farm, airport, space, fort |
| **Sports Equipment** | • sand molds, water pumps | • action/adventure sets, action figures |
| • balls of all sizes | • realistic working models or boats | • simple dollhouse |
| • double-blade ice skates | | |
| • sleds size graded | | |

from age 4
- lightweight soft baseball and bat
- junior-sized soccer ball
- speed-graded roller skates with plastic wheels, no ball bearings
- kites
- wading pool

from age 5
- jump ropes
- skis (sized to child)
- flying disks
- flat-nosed magnetic or Velcro darts

## Construction Toys
- solid wood unit blocks
- large hollow blocks
- interlocking building systems

## Puzzles
- fit-in or framed puzzles
  age 3, up to 20 pieces
  age 4, 20–30 pieces
  age 5, up to 50 pieces
- simple jigsaw puzzles
- number or letter puzzles, puzzle clocks

## Pattern-Making Toys
- bead stringing
- peg board with small pegs
- color cubes/color forms
- magnetic boards with shapes

## Transportation Toys
- toy cars of all sizes with realistic details
- large-scale trucks, road machinery that really work
- action/adventure vehicle sets
- small, realistic trains

from age 5
- small trains with tracks, wind-up cars, train coupling systems

---

## Creative Play

### Musical Instruments
- all rhythm instruments
- xylophones
- instruments that require blowing
- wind-up music boxes
- piano-one finger tunes

### Arts and Craft Materials
- large crayons with many colors
- magic markers
- finger and tempura paint
- adjustable easel
- brushes of various sizes
- clay, including tools
- chalkboards and chalk of various sizes
- scissors with rounded ends

## Learning Play

### Games
- dominoes (color or number)
- simple matching and lotto games based on color, pictures
- simple card games
- bingo (picture)

from age 4
- first simple board games with few rules
- games requiring simple fine-motor coordination picking up or balancing objects)

### Specific Skills Development Toys
simple electronic and other teaching toys for
- matching/sorting
- shapes, colors
- numbers, letters

(continued)

**FIGURE 5.3** *Continued*

- paste and glue
- simple sewing kits

*from age 4*
- workbench with hammer, nails, saw

*from age 5*
- smaller crayons, water color paints

**Audio-Visual Equipment**

- adult-operated tape and CD player

*from age 4*
- simple video games

*from age 5*
- radio

*from age 4*
- simple computer programs for teaching color matching, letters, classification, numbers, sounds
- simple science models

*from age 5*
- science materials-magnets, flashlight, shells and rocks, magnifying glass, stethoscope, prism, aquarium, terrarium
- clock
- printing set
- computer
- simple calculator
- computer programs to teach simple programming

**Books**

- picture books, simple stories, rhymes
- complex pop-up books

*age 3 interests*
- here-and-now stories
- animal stories
- alphabet books
- words and rhymes

*age 4 interests*
- wild stories, silly humor
- information books
- familiar places, people

*age 5 interests*
- realistic stories
- poetry
- primers
- animals that behave like people

*Source:* Information from *Which Toy for Which Child. A Consumer's Guide for Selecting Suitable Toys Ages Birth Through Five. Washington, DC: U. S. Consumer Product Safety Commission, Pub. No. 285.*

## SUMMARY

Children make major progress in development during the preschool years, which is reflected in their play. In motor development, their gross-motor skills include acquisition of fundamental movement skills and perceptual-motor development. Progress in fine-motor skills results in the ability to use art and writing materials and work puzzles and small construction toys. Play occurs both at home and in preschool group settings. Although preschool children engage in free play, they also enjoy teacher-directed activities in group settings. Although physical development specialists suggest that motor development programs should be a part of preschool curriculum, few early childhood educators are trained to provide a quality program.

Children are in the preoperational stage in cognitive development when primitive reasoning begins. Play promotes cognitive development. For example, sociodramatic play promotes intellectual development to include imagination and creativity. Children move through stages of play that have been described in various ways by various theorists, including Piaget, Vygotsky, and Smilansky. The stages reflect the child's cognitive progress and ability to use cognitive advances in play.

Development in language and literacy permit preschool children to communicate with others. During the years between 3 and 6, children acquire the major components of their language to include morphology rules, syntax rules, and semantic rules. Their vocabulary increases dramatically. They also learn rules of conversation and the nature of literacy. Through experiences with books, stories, and writing activities, young children learn about written language and take initial steps in acquiring literacy. These emerging interests in language and literacy are reflected in their play, particularly sociodramatic play.

Social development provides young children with the ability to understand themselves and others. They continue to develop social relationships with adults and peers and establish friendships through play. Social competence is a factor in successful play relationships.

Social development is reflected in social and sociodramatic play. Children reflect their social development in stages of social play that begin with individual play and move to collaboration in group play. Sociodramatic play includes pretend play and role play. Children make-believe in carrying out play themes within a group of children. Sociodramatic play incorporates all domains of development and facilitates the expression of feelings. The types and levels of sociodramatic play engaged in by young children reflects differences in gender, temperament, and parenting styles and effectiveness. Although there are cultural and socioeconomic differences in sociodramatic play, all children engage in such play, even in cultures where children participate in work early in their lives.

Unique forms of play in the preschool years include rough-and-tumble play, superhero play, and chase games. Although some teachers are wary of these types of play activities, they are particularly a part of boys' sociodramatic play. Girls also engage in rough-and-tumble play and chase games but differently than boys.

Adults assume a major role in children's play. The time and type of play engaged in by parents and other adults affect the quality of preschool play. They provide materials, ideas, and serve as coplayers with children. However, extremes of adult involvement are not conducive to enriched play. When adults are disinterested or merely watch play, their lack of involvement has a negative effect. Likewise, when they are overinvolved or too directive, the child's interest and play level are diminished.

## KEY TERMS

Body awareness
Chase games
Classification
Conservation
Directional awareness
Egocentric
Empathy
Fine-motor development
Fundamental movement
  phase
Gross-motor development
Intuitive thought substage
Locomotor skills
Morphology rules
Perceptual-motor
  development
Pragmatics of language
Preoperational stage

Reflexive movement
  phase
Rough-and-tumble play
Rudimentary movement
  phase
Self-concept
Self-esteem
Self-regulation of emotions
Semantic rules
Social competence
Sociodramatic play
Spatial awareness
Specialized movement
  phase
Superhero play
Symbolic function substage
Syntax rules
Temporal awareness

## STUDY QUESTIONS

1. How does play support motor development in the preschool years?
2. Why do some educators advocate that motor development programs are needed in preschool settings?
3. Why is it important for parents to provide time for preschool children's play?
4. How does cognitive development in the preschool years affect how children play?
5. How can cognitive play in the preschool years predict later academic success?
6. Define and describe current thinking on hierarchical categories in cognitive development and play.
7. Why do some theorists question that there is a hierarchy in cognitive categories in play?
8. Describe how adults can promote cognition through play in an appropriate manner.
9. How can play promote literacy development? Give examples.
10. Why are there variations in language development? What are some factors that affect language development?
11. Explain how children play with language in the preschool language.
12. How do preschool children use language to support their play?
13. How do parents affect language and literacy development?
14. How does social competence predict success in sociodramatic play?
15. Describe some of the relationships in the preschool child's life that affect social competence.
16. How does pretend play help preschool children develop social skills?
17. Why do some children develop positive social skills and others do not?
18. Explain how social play proceeds through stages and why some researchers question those stages.
19. Explain factors that can result in variations in social competence and play.
20. Why is Smilansky's work on sociodramatic play significant in understanding variations in levels of sociodramatic play?
21. What evidence do we have that boys and girls play differently in the preschool years? Give examples of differences.
22. Explain rough-and-tumble play, superhero play, and chase games. How are these types of play related?
23. What do preschool children need from their parents to maximize their play?
24. Explain different adult roles that can promote and broaden preschool play.

## REFERENCES

Almon, J. (2009, March/April). The fear of play. *Exchange*, 42–44.

Ausch, L. (1994). Gender comparisons of young children's social interaction in cooperative play Activity. *Sex roles, 31*, 225–239.

Bakeman, R., & Brownlee, J. (1980). The strategic use of parallel play: A sequential analysis. *Child Development, 51*, 873–878.

Barnes, K. E. (1971). Preschool play norms: A replication. *Developmental Psychology, 5*, 99–103.

Bauer, K. L., & Dettore, E. (1997). Superhero play: What's a teacher to do? *Early Childhood Education Journal, 25*, 17–21.

Baumrind, D. (1991). To nurture nature. *Behavioral and Brain Sciences, 14*, 386.

Berk, L. E. (1994). Vygotsky's theory: The importance of make-believe play. *Young Children, 50*, 30–39.

Berk, L. E., & Winsler, A. (1995). *Scaffolding children's learning: Vygotsky and early childhood education.* Washington, DC: National Association for the Education of Young Children.

Bohren, J. M., & Vlahov, E. (1989, July). *Comparison of motor development in preschool children.* (ERIC Document Reproduction Service No. 312053)

Boyd, B. J. (1997). Teacher response to superhero play: To ban or not to ban. *Childhood Education, 74*, 23–28.

Boyer, W. A. R. (1997a). Enhancing playfulness with sensorial stimulation. *Journal of Research in Childhood Education, 12*, 78–87.

Boyer, W. A. R. (1997b). Playfulness enhancement through classroom intervention for the 21st Century. *Childhood Education, 74*, 90–96.

Bretherton, I. (1985). Attachment theory: Retrospect and prospect. In I. Bretherton & E. Water (Eds.), Growing points of attachment theory and research. *Monographs of the Society for Research and Development, 50* (1–2, Serial No. 209).

Broderick, P. C., & Blewitt, P. (2006). *The life span: Human development for helping professionals* (2nd ed.). Upper Saddle River, NJ: Pearson.

Bruner, J. (1974). The ontogenesis of speech acts. *Journal of Child Language, 2*, 1–19.

Bruner, J. (1975). From communication to language—a psychological perspective. *Cognition, 3*, 255–287.

Burdette, H. L., & Whitaker, R. C. (2005). *Focusing on free play benefits in children's development.* Nemours Foundation Children's Health News. Retrieved September 30, 2006, from *http:/kidshealth.org/research/freeplay.html*

Burger, J. (1995). Individual differences in preference for solitude. *Journal on Research for Personality, 29,* 85–108.

Campbell, L. (1997). Perceptual-motor programs, movement, and young children's needs: Some challenges for teachers. *Australian Journal of Early Childhood, 22,* 37–42.

Carlson, F. (2006). *Essential touch: Meeting the needs of young children.* Washington, DC: National Association for the Education of Young Children.

Carlson, F. (2009, July/August). Rough and tumble play 101. *Exchange, 70–73.*

Carlsson-Paige, N., & Levin, D. E. (1990). *Who's calling the shots? How to respond effectively to children's fascination with war play and war toys.* Philadelphia: New Society Publishers.

Carlsson-Paige, N., & Levin, D. E. (1991). The subversion of healthy development and play: Teachers' reactions to the Teenage Mutant Ninja Turtles. *Day Care and Early Education, 19,* 14–20.

Carlsson-Paige, N., & Levin, D. E. (1995). Can teachers resolve the war-play dilemma? *Young Children, 50,* 62–63.

Caster, T. J. (1984). The young child's play and social and emotional development. In T. E. Yawkey & A. D. Pellegrini (Eds.), *Child's play and child therapy* (pp. 17–30). Lancaster, PA: Technomic.

Cazden, C. (1974). Play with language and metalinguistic awareness: One dimension of language experience. *Urban Review, 7,* 23–39.

Chaille, C., & Silvern, S. (1996). Understanding through play. *Childhood Education, 72,* 274–279.

Chalufour, I., & Worth, K. (2004). *Building structures with young children.* St. Paul, MN: Redleaf.

Christie, J. (1994). Literacy play interventions: A review of empirical research. In S. Reifel (Ed.), *Advances in early education and day care* (Vol. 6, pp. 3–24). Greenwich, CT: JAI.

Church, B. (2004). *Exploring early childhood.* Victoria, Australia: Pearson Australia.

Clarke, L. J. (1999). Development reflected in chase games. In S. Reifel (Ed.), *Play and culture studies* (Vol. 2, pp. 73–82). Sanford, CT: Ablex.

Cohen, D., & Stern, V. (1983). *Observing and recording the behavior of young children* (2nd ed.). New York: Teachers College Press.

Consumer Product Safety Commission (n.d.). *Which toy for which child: A consumer's guide for selecting suitable toys.* Washington, DC: Author.

Coplan, R. J., Rubin, K. H., Fox, N. A., Calkins, S. D., & Stewart, S. L. (1994). Being alone, playing alone, and acting alone: Distinguishing among reticence, and passive- and active-solitude in young children. *Child Development, 65,* 129–178.

Creasey, G. L., Jarvis, P. A., & Berk, L. E. (1998). Play and social competence. In O. N. Saracho & B. Spodek (Eds.), *Multiple perspectives on play in early childhood education* (pp. 116–143). Albany: State University of New York Press.

Dix, T. (1991). The affective organization of parenting: Adaptive and maladaptive processes. *Psychological Bulletin, 110,* 3–25.

Dolgin, K. G., & Behrend, D. A. (1984). Children's knowledge about animates and inanimates. *Child Development, 55,* 1646–1650.

Dunn, J. (1983). Sibling relationships in early childhood. *Child Development, 54,* 787–811.

Dyson, A. H., & Genishi, C. (1993). Visions of children as language users: Language and language education in early childhood. In B. Spodek (Ed.), *Handbook of research On the education of young children* (pp. 122–136). New York: Macmillan.

Eifermann, R. (1971). Social play in childhood. In R. Herron & B. Sutton-Smith (Eds.), *Child's play* (pp. 270–297). New York: Wiley.

Eisenberg, N., Fabes, R. A., Bernzweig, J., Karbon, J., Poulin, R., & Hanish, L. (1993). The relations of emotionality and regulation to preschoolers' social skills and sociometric status. *Child Development, 64,* 1418–1438.

Eisenberg, N., Fabes, R. A., & Spinrad, T. L. (2005). Prosocial development. In *Handbook Of child psychology* (5th ed., Vol. 3, pp. 701–778). New York: Wiley and Sons.

Eisenberg, N., & Miller, P. A. (1987). The relations of empathy to prosocial behaviors. *Psychological Bulletin, 101,* 91–119.

Ellis, J. J. (1973). *Why people play.* Upper Saddle River, NJ: Prentice Hall.

Farver, J., Kim, Y., & Lee-Shen. (2000). Within central differences in Korean American and European American preschoolers social pretend play. *Journal of Cross-Cultural Psychology, 31,* 583–602.

Fields, M. V., Groth, L., & Spangler, I. L. (2004). *Let's begin reading right* (5th ed.). Upper Saddle River, NJ: Prentice Hall.

Flavell, J. H., Green, F. L., & Flavell, E. R. (1987). Development of knowledge about the appearance-reality distinction. *Monographs of the Society for Research in Child Development, 51*(1, Serial No. 212).

Freud, S. (1935). *A general introduction to psychoanalysis* (Joan Riviare, Trans.). New York: Modern Library.

Freyburg, J. T. (1973). Increasing the imaginative play of urban disadvantaged kindergarten children through systematic training. In J. L. Singer (Ed.), *The child's world of make-believe* (pp. 129–154). New York: Academic Press.

Froebel, F. (1902). *Education of man* (W. N. Hailmann, Trans.). New York: Appleton. (Original work published 1844)

Gabbard, C. (1979). *Playground apparatus experience and muscular endurance among children 4–6.* (ERIC Document Reproduction Service, SP 022; ED228190)

Gabbard, C. (1995). P. E. For preschoolers: The right way. *Principal, 74,* 21–24.

Gallahue, D. L. (1989). *Understanding motor development: Infants, children, adolescents.* Dubuque, IA: Brown and Benchmark.

Gallahue, D. L. (1993). Motor development and movement skill acquisition in early childhood education. In B. Spodek (Ed.), *Handbook of research on the education of young children* (pp. 24–41). New York: Macmillan.

Garvey, C. (1993). *Play* (Enlarged ed.). Cambridge, MA: Harvard University Press.

Gelman, R. (1972). Logical capacity of very young children: Number invariance rules. *Child Development, 43,* 75–90.

Gelman, R., & Shatz, M. (1978). Appropriate speech adjustments: The operation of conversational constraints on talk to two-year-olds. In M. Lewis & L. A. Rosenblum (Eds.), *Interaction, conversation, and the development of language* (pp. 27–61). New York: Wiley.

Genishi, C., & Dyson, A. H. (1984). *Language assessment in the early years.* Norwood, NJ: Ablex.

Genishi, C., & Dyson, A. H. (2009). *Children language and literacy: Diverse learners in diverse times.* New York: Teachers College Press, & Washington, DC: National Association for the Education of Young Children.

Gmitrova, V., & Gmitrov, J. (2002). The impact of teacher-directed and child-directed play pretend play on cognitive competence in kindergarten. *Early Childhood Education Journal, 30,* 241–246.

Goncu, A. (1993). Development of intersubjectivity in the dyadic play of preschoolers. *Early Childhood Research Quarterly, 8,* 99–116.

Gottlieb, G. (1983). The psychobiological approach to developmental issues. In M. M. Haith & J. J. Campos (Eds.), P. H. Mussen (series Ed.), *Handbook of child psychology: Vol. 2: In fancy and developmental psychobiology* (pp. 1–26). New York: Wiley.

Gottman, J. M., & Katz, L. F. (1989). Effects of marital discord on young children's peer interaction and health. *Developmental Psychology, 25,* 373–381.

Harter, S. (1990). Issues in the assessment of the self-concept of children and adolescents. In A. LaCreca (Ed.), *Through the eyes of a child* (pp. 292–325). Boston: Allyn & Bacon.

Hayes, C. D., Palmer, J. L., & Zaslow, M. J. (Eds.). (1990). *Child care choices.* Washington, DC: National Association for the Education of Children.

Helm, J. H., & Boos, S. (1996). Increasing the physical educator's impact: Consulting, collaborating, and teacher training in early childhood programs. *Journal of Physical Education, Recreation & Dance, 67,* 26–31.

Holmberg, M. C. (1980). The development of social exchange patterns from 12 to 42 months. *Child Development, 51,* 618–626.

Howes, C. (1983). Patterns of friendship. *Child Development, 54,* 1041–1052.

Howes, C., & Smith, E. (1995). Relations among child care quality, teacher behavior, children's play activities, emotional security, and cognitive activity in child care. *Early Childhood Research Quarterly, 10,* 381–404.

Hughes, F. P. (1999). *Children, play, and development.* Boston: Allyn & Bacon.

Humphreys, A. P., & Smith, P. K. (1984). Rough-and-tumble play in preschool and playground. In P. K. Smith (Ed.), *Play in animals and humans* (pp. 241–270). Oxford: Blackwell.

Isenberg, J. P., & Jalongo, M. R. (2006). *Creative thinking and arts-based learning: Preschool through fourth grade* (4th ed.). Upper Saddle River, NJ: Pearson Merrill.

Jambor, T. (1990). Promoting perceptual-motor development in young children's play. In S. C. Wortham & J. L. Frost (Eds.), *Playgrounds for young children: National survey and perspectives* (pp. 147–166). Reston, VA: American Alliance for Health, Physical Education, Recreation, and Dance.

Jarvis, P. (2006). Rough and tumble play: Lessons in life. *Evolutionary Psychology, 4,* 330–346. Retrieved August 12, 2010, from http://www.epjournal.net/filestore/ep043303462.pdf

Johnson, J., & Roopnarine, J. (1983). The preschool classroom and sex differences in children's play. In M. Liss (Ed.), *Social and cognitive skills* (pp. 193–218). New York: Academic.

Johnson, J. E. (1976). Relations of divergent thinking and intelligence test scores with social and nonsocial make-believe play of preschool children. *Child Development, 47,* 1200–1203.

Johnson, J. E., Christie, J. F., & Yawkey, T. D. (1999). *Play and early childhood development* (2nd ed.). New York: Longman.

Jones, N. B. (1972). Categories of child-child interaction. In N. Blurton Jones (Ed.), *Ethological studies of child behaviour* (pp. 97–127). Cambridge, MA: Cambridge University Press.

Jones, N. B. (1976). Rough-and-tumble-play among nursery school children. In J. S. Bruner, A. Jolly, & K. Sylva (Eds.), *Play: Its role in development and evolution* (pp. 352–363). New York: Basic.

Kamii, C., Myakawa, Y., & Kato, Y. (2004). The development of logico-mathematical knowledge in a block-building activity at ages 1-4. *Journal of Research in Childhood Education, 19,* 44–57.

Katz, J., & Buchholtz, E. (1999). "I did it myself": The necessity of solo play for preschoolers. *Early Childhood Development and Care, 155,* 39–50.

Kid Source Online. (2010). *When children imitate superheroes.* Retrieved August 18, 2010, from http://www.kidsource.com/parenting/imitate.hero.html

Kimmerle, M., Mick, L. A., & Michel, G. E. (1995). Bimanual role-differentiated toy play during infancy. *Infant Behavior and Development, 18,* 299–307.

Klein, M. D., & Chen, D. (2002). *Working with children from diverse backgrounds.* Albany, NY: Delmar.

Klenk, L. (2001). Playing literacy in preschool classroom. *Childhood Education, 77,* 150–157.

Kochanska, G. (1993). Toward a synthesis of parental socializations and child temperament in early development of conscience. *Child Development, 64,* 325–347.

Kuykendall, J. (1966, January). Is gun play OK for kids? *Education Digest,* pp. 12–15.

Ladd, G. W., & Hart, C. H. (1992). Creating informal play opportunities: Are parents' and pre-schoolers' initiation related to children's competence with peers? *Developmental Psychology, 28,* 1179–1187.

Landreth, G., & Hohmeyer, L. (1998). Play as the language of children's feelings. In D. P. Fromberg & D. Bergen (Eds.), *Birth from birth to twelve and beyond: Contexts, perspectives, and meanings* (pp. 193–198). New York: Garland.

Landry, S. H. (2002). *Pathways to competence: Encouraging healthy social and emotional development in young children* (3rd ed.). Baltimore, MD: Brookes Publishing.

Lieberman, J. (1965). Playfulness and divergent thinking: An investigation of their relationship at the kindergarten level. *Journal of Creative Behavior, 1,* 391–397.

Linn, S. (2009, March/April). Too much and too many: How commercialism and screen technology combine to rob children of creative play. *Exchange,* 44–52.

Luckey, A. J., & Fabes, R. A. (2005, October). Understanding nonsocial play in early childhood. *Early Childhood Education Journal, 33,* 67–72.

MacDonald, K., & Parke, R. (1984). Bridging the gap: Parent-child play interaction and peer interactive competence. *Child Development, 55,* 1265–1277.

Mandler, J. M., Bauer, P. J., & McDonough, L. (1991). Separating the sheep from the goats: Differentiating global categories. *Cognitive Psychology, 23,* 263–298.

Mayo Clinic.com. *Child development chart: Preschool milestones.* Retrieved August 4, 2010, from http://www.mayoclinc.com/health/child-development/my00136

McCune, L. (1983). Play-language relationships and symbolic development. In C. C. Brown & A. W. Gottfried (Eds.), *Play interactions: The role of toys and parental involvement in children's development* (pp. 28–45). Skillman, NJ: Johnson & Johnson Baby Products.

McLoyd, V. C. (1986). Social class and pretend play. In A. W. Gottfried & C. C. Brown (Eds.), *Play interactions: The contributions of play materials and parental involvement to children's development* (pp. 175–193). Lexington, MA: Heath.

Mervis, C. B., & Crisafi, M. A. (1982). Order of acquisition of subordinate-, basic-, and super-ordinate-level categories. *Child Development, 53,* 258–266.

Moore, N. V., Evertson, C. D., & Brophy, J. E. (1974). Solitary Play: Some functional reconsiderations. *Developmental Psychology, 10,* 830–835.

Morrow, L. M. (2004). *Literacy development in the early years* (5th ed.). Boston: Allyn & Bacon.

Mullen, M. R. (1984). Motor development and child's play. In T. D. Yawkey & A. D. Pellegrini (Eds.), *Child's play and play therapy* (pp. 7–16). Lancaster, PA: Technomic.

Myers, G. D. (1985). Motor behavior of kindergartners during physical education and free play. In J. L. Frost & S. Sunderlin (Eds.), *When children play* (pp. 151–156). Olney, MD: Association for Childhood Education International.

National Institute for Literacy. (2009). *Learning to talk and listen.* Washington, DC: Author.

Neppl, T. K., & Murray, A. D. (1997). Social dominance and play patterns among preschoolers: Gender comparisons. *Sex Roles, 36,* 381–393.

Neuman, S., & Roskos, K. (1991). Peers as literacy informants: A description of young children's literature: A description of young children's literacy conversations in play. *Early Childhood Research Quarterly, 6,* 233–248.

Opie, I., & Opie, P. (1959). *The lore and language of school children.* New York: Oxford University Press.

Opie, I., & Opie, P. (1969). *Children's games with things.* New York: Oxford University Press.

Parten, M. (1932). Social participation among preschool children. *Journal of Abnormal and Social Psychology, 27,* 243–262.

Pellegrini, A. D. (1984). Children's play and language: Infancy through early childhood. In T. D. Yawkey & A. D. Pellegrini (Eds.), *Child's play and play therapy* (pp. 45–58). Lancaster, PA: Technomic.

Pellegrini, A. D. (1995). *School recess and playground behavior: Educational and developmental roles.* Albany: State University of New York Press.

Pellegrini, A. D., & Boyd, B. (1993). The role of play in early childhood development and education: Issues in definition and function. In B. Spodek (Ed.), *Handbook of research on the education of young children* (pp. 105–121). New York: Macmillan.

Pellis, S. M., & Pellis, V. C. (2007). Rough and tumble play and the development of the social brain. *Association of Psychological Science, 16,* 95–98.

Pepler, D. (1979). *Effects of convergent and divergent play experience on preschoolers' problem solving.* Unpublished doctoral dissertation, University of Waterloo, Ontario, Canada.

Pepler, D. J., & Ross, H. S. (1981). The effects of play on convergent and divergent problem-solving. *Child Development, 52,* 1202–1210.

Phelps, K. E., & Woolley, J. D. (1994). The form and function of young children's magical beliefs. *Developmental Psychology, 30,* 385–394.

Piaget, J. (1962). *Play, drama, and imitation in childhood.* New York: Norton.

Pica, R. (1997). Beyond physical development: Why young children need to move. *Young Children, 52,* 4–11.

Piers, M. W., & Landau, G. M. (1980). *The gift of play.* New York: Walker.

Plomin, R., & Daniels, D. (1986). Genetics and shyness. In W. H. Jones, J. M. Cheek, & S. R. Briggs (Eds.), *Shyness:*

*Perspectives on research and treatment* (pp. 63–80). New York: Plenum.

Reifel, S. (1983). Part-whole relations: Some structural features on children's representational block play. *Child Care Quarterly, 12,* 144–151.

Reifel, S. (1984). Block construction: children's developmental landmarks in representation of space. *Young Children, 40,* 61–67.

Reifel, S., & Yeatman, J. (1991). Action, talk, and though in block play. In B. Scales, M. Almy, A. Nicolopoulou, & S. Ervin-Tripp (Eds.), *Play and the social context of development* (pp. 156–172). New York: Teachers College Press.

Ricco, R. B. (1989). Operational thought and the acquisition of taxonomic relations involving figurative dissimilarity. *Developmental Psychology, 25,* 996–1003.

Roopnarine, J. L. (1987). Social interaction in the peer group: Relationships to perceptions of parenting and to children's interpersonal awareness and problem solving ability. *Journal of Applied Developmental Psychology, 8,* 351–362.

Rosen, C. E. (1974). The effects of sociodramatic play on problem-solving behavior among culturally disadvantaged preschool children. *Child Development, 45,* 920–927.

Roskos, K. (1990). A taxonomic view of pretend play among four- and five-year-old children. *Early childhood Research Quarterly, 5,* 495–572.

Roskos, K., & Christie, J. (2004). Examining the play-literacy interface: A critical review and future directions. In E. Zigler, D. Sinder, & S. Boship-Josef (Eds.), *Children's play: The roots of reading* (pp. 95–103).

Roskos, K., Christie, J. F., & Richgels, D. I. (2003). The essentials of early literacy instruction. *Young children, 58,* 52–60.

Roskos, K., & Neuman, S. (1998). Descriptive observations of adults' facilitation of literacy in young children's play. *Early Childhood Research Quarterly, 8,* 77–98.

Rubin, K. H. (1982). Nonsocial play in pre-schoolers: - Necessary evil? *Child Development, 53,* 651–657.

Rubin, K. H. (1986). Play, peer reactions, and social development. In A. W. Gottfried & C. C. Brown (Eds.), *Play interactions* (pp. 163–173). Lexington, MA: Heath.

Rubin, K. H. (2001). *The Play Observation Scale (POS)* Revised. Silver Spring, MD: Center for Children, Relationships, and Culture, University of Maryland.

Rubin, K. H., & Coplan, R. J. (1998). Social and nonsocial play in childhood: An individual differences perspective. In O. N. Saracho & B. Spodek (Eds.), *Multiple perspectives on play in early childhood education* (pp. 144–170). Albany: State University of New York Press.

Rubin, K. H., Fein, G. G., & Vandenberg, B. (1983). Play. In E. M. Hetherington (Ed.), P. H. Mussen (Series Ed.), *Handbook of child psychology: Vol. 4: Socialization, personality, and social development* (pp. 693–774). New York: Wiley.

Rubin, K. H., Maioni, T. L., & Homung, M. (1976). Free play behaviors in middle and lower class preschoolers: Parten and Piaget revisited. *Child Development, 47,* 414–419.

Rubin, K. H., Watson, K. S., & Jambor, T. W. (1976). Free play behaviors in preschool and kindergarten children. *Child Development, 49,* 534–536.

Sanders, S. W. (2002). *Active for life.* Washington, DC: National Association for the Education of Young Children.

Scarr, S. (1968). Environment bias in twin studies. *Eugenics Quarterly, 15,* 34–40.

Schaefer, C. E. (Ed.). (1993). *The therapeutic powers of play.* Northvale, NJ: Aronson.

Schwartzman, H. (1978). *Transformations: The anthropology of children's play.* New York: Plenum.

Scott, E., & Panksepp, J. (2003). Rough and tumble play in human children. *Aggressive Behavior, 29,* 539–551.

Seo, K. H. (2003). What children's play tells us about teaching mathematics. *Young Children, 58,* 28–35.

Shore, R. (1997). *Rethinking the brain: New insights into early development.* New York: Families and Work Institute.

Singer, D. G., & Singer, J. L. (1977). *Partners in play.* New York: Random House.

Singer, D. G., & Singer, J. L. (2005). *Imagination and play in the electronic age.* Cambridge, MA: Harvard University Press.

Skinner, B. F. (1957). *Verbal behavior.* New York: Appleton-Century Crofts.

Smilansky, S. (1968). *The effects of sociodramatic play on disadvantaged preschool children.* New York: Wiley.

Smilansky, S. (1990). Sociodramatic play: Its relevance to behavior and achievement in school. In E. Klugman & S. Smilansky (Eds.), *Children's play and learning: Perspectives and policy implications* (pp. 18–42). New York: Teachers College Press.

Smilansky, S., & Shefatya, L. (1990). *Facilitating play: A medium for promoting cognitive, socioemotional and academic development in young children.* Gaithersburg, MD: Psychosocial and Educational Publications.

Smith, P. K., & Boulton, M. (1990). Rough-and-tumble play, aggression, and dominance: Perceptions and behavior in children's encounters. *Human Development, 33,* 271–282.

Stephenson, A. (2002). What George taught me about toddlers and water. *Young Children, 57,* 11–13.

Stevenson, M. B. (1989). The influences on the play of infants and toddlers. In M. N. Bloch & D. Pellegrini (Eds.), *The ecological content of children's play* (pp. 84–103). Norwood, NJ: Ablex.

Stitzel, K. (2009). Block play for all. *Exchange Every Day.* Retrieved July 20, 2009, from www.exchangeeveryday@ccie.com

Stone, S. J., & Christie, J. F. (1996). Collaborative literacy learning during sociodramatic play in a multi-age (K-2) primary classroom. *Journal of Research in Childhood Education, 10,* 123–133.

Subbotsky, E. V. (1994). Early rationality and magical thinking in preschoolers" space and time. *British Journal of Developmental Psychology, 12*, 97–108.

Sutton-Smith, B. (1972). *The folkgames of children.* Austin: University of Texas Press.

Sutton-Smith, B. (1976). Current research and theory on play, games, and sports. In T. Craig (Ed.), *The humanistic and mental health aspects of sports, exercise, and recreation.* Chicago, American Medical Association.

Sutton-Smith, B. (1979). *Play and learning.* New York: Gardner.

Sutton-Smith, B. (1997). *The ambiguity of play.* Cambridge, MA: Harvard University Press.

Takhvar, M., & Smith, P. K. (1990). A review and critique of Smilansky's classification scheme And the "nested hierarchy" of play categories. *Journal of Research in Childhood Education, 4*, 112–122.

Tanner, J. M. (1990). *Foetus into man* (2nd ed.). Cambridge, MA: Harvard University Press.

Tannock, M. T. (2009). Rough and tumble play: An investigation of the perceptions of educators and young children. *Early Childhood Education Journal, 35*, 351–361.

Tannock, M. T. (2010). Young children's rough and tumble play. Retrieved August 16, 2010, from www.museumofplay.org/tasp.files/ppts/tannockroughandtumblepaper.ppt

Tegano, D. W., & Burdette, M. P. (1991). Length of activity periods and play behavior of preschool children. *Journal of Research in Childhood Education, 5*, 93–99.

Thorne, B. (1995). *Gender play: Girls and boys.* New Brunswick, NJ: Rutgers University Press.

Tokarz, B. (2008). Block play: It's not just for boys anymore: Strategies for encouraging girls" block play. *Exchange,* 68–71.

Torbert, M. (2005). Using active group games to develop basic life skills. *Young Children, 60*, 72–78.

U.S. Consumer Product Safety Commission. (n.d.). *Which toy for which child: A consumer's guide for selecting suitable toys. Ages birth through five* (Pub. No. 285). Washington, DC: Author.

Vandenberg, B. (1985). Beyond the ethology of play. In C. C. Brown & A. W. Gottfried (Eds.), *Play interactions* (pp. 3–10). Lexington, MA: Heath.

Vukelich, C. (1989, December). *A description of young children's writing in two play settings with and without adult support.* Paper presented at the 39th National Reading Conference, Austin, TX.

Vygotsky, L. S. (1976). Play and its role in the mental development of the child. In J. S. Bruner, A. Jolly, & K. Sylva (Eds.), *Play: Its role in development and evolution* (pp. 536–552). New York: Basic Books. (Original work published 1966)

Vygotsky, L. S. (1984). *Thought and language.* Cambridge, MA: MIT Press.

Wellhausen, K., & Giles, R. M. (2005/2006). Building literacy opportunities into children's block play: What every teacher should know. *Childhood Education, 82*, 74–78.

Wilcox-Herzog, A., & Kontos, S. (1998). The nature of teacher talk in early childhood classrooms and its relationship to children's play with objects and peers. *Journal of Genetic Psychology, 159*, 301–325.

Wilson, B. J. (2008, Spring). Media and children's aggression, fear, and altruism. *Children and Electronic Media, 18.* Retrieved August 10, 2010, from http://www.princeton.edu/futureofchildren/publications/journals

Woolley, J. D., & Wellman, H. M. (1990). Young children's understanding of realities, nonrealities, and appearances. *Child Development, 61*, 946–961.

Wortham, S. C. (2010). *Early childhood curriculum: Developmental bases for learning and teaching* (5th ed.). Upper Saddle River, NJ: Pearson.

Wright, L. (1990). The social and nonsocial behavior of precocious preschoolers during free play. *Roeper Review, 12*, 268–273.

Yawkey, T. D., & Diantoniis, J. M. (1984). Relationship between child's play and cognitive development and learning in infancy birth through age 8. In T. D. Yawkey & A. D. Pellegrino (Eds.), *Child's play and play therapy* (pp. 31–43). Lancaster, PA: Technomic.

Zigler, E., & Lang, M. E. (1990). *Child care choices.* New York: Free Press.

# 6 Play and the School-Age Child

*IT WAS on the afternoon of the day of Christmas Eve, and I was in Mrs. Prothero's garden waiting for cats, with her son Jim. It was snowing. It was always snowing at Christmas. December, in my memory, is white as Lapland, though there were no reindeers. But there were cats. Patient, cold, and callous, our hands wrapped in socks, we waited to snowball the cats. Sleek and long as jaguars*

*and horrible-whiskered, spitting and snarling, they would slink and sidle over the white back-garden walls, and the lynx-eyed hunters, Jim and I, fur-capped and moccasined trappers from Hudson Bay, off Mumbles Road, would hurl our deadly snowballs at the green of their eyes. The wise cats never appeared. We were so still, Eskimo-footed arctic marksmen in the muffling silence of the eternal snows—eternal, ever since Wednesday—that we never heard Mrs. Prothero's first cry from her igloo at the bottom of the garden. Or, if we heard it at all, it was to us, like the far-off challenge of our enemy and prey, the neighbor's polar cat. But soon the voice grew louder. "Fire!" cried Mrs. Prothero, and she beat the dinner-gong.*

(Thomas, 1954, n.p.)

## PLAY IN THE 21ST CENTURY: INHIBITING FACTORS

Changes in contemporary culture, lifestyles, and legislation to raise school achievement have affected children's opportunities for play in the school-age years. Elementary play, particularly free outdoor play, has diminished in the United States for various reasons. As one writer puts it, "There is a modern mindset that does not value play and even fears it" (Almon, 2009, p. 42). There is fear of injury on playgrounds, fear of strangers, and other dangers that can be called "the fear of play" (Almon, 2009, p. 42). This fear leads parents to want to create a life for their child that is as safe and risk-free as possible. We seek to amuse ourselves via entertainment centers with flat-screen televisions, smart phones, and iPods. The focus on social networks and other computer communications by adults is translated into children's interests in computer and video games, and an addiction to texting on cell phones. "We train them from infancy onward to turn to the screen rather than to their own creativity" (Almon, 2009, 43).

Factors such as fear of physical injuries and violent play behaviors have caused teachers to put less value on play. The era of accountability and new standards for learning and assessment have forced teachers to put more focus on academic learning. An emphasis on testing and teaching to the test resulting from the passage of the No Child Left Behind Act (NCLB) (U.S. Department of Education, 2001) has almost eliminated outdoor and indoor play activities related to the elementary-grade curriculum.

As Dylan Thomas recalled about his own childhood, children in elementary school have not lost their interest in play. Dramatic play continues, as do other types of play first observed in preschool children such as rough-and-tumble play and chase games. Accomplishments in cognitive, physical, and social development add new dimensions to how children play.

There is, however, a definite difference in opportunities for play and social expectations for sports activities that can preclude opportunities for school-age children to hang out and engage in free play. One of the issues discussed in this chapter is the lack of play opportunities at schools, especially the elimination of recess in the interest of improvement of student achievement. While the preschool years were described as play years in Chapter 5, once children enter elementary school, parents and teachers seem to place little value on free play and fail to understand its benefits (Manning, 1993, 1998). Some forms of play are available to school-age children, as described under sections on physical, cognitive, language, and social development. We also discuss general characteristics of play as well as adult roles in providing play both within and outside the school environment.

Throughout the chapter, current restraints on play will be noted and discussed. However, there is a renewed interest in play and concern that children are missing out on the kinds of play experiences Dylan Thomas described. This chapter also advocates play for school-age children and presents information and ideas on how play can be valued for them.

## PHYSICAL DEVELOPMENT

During the school years, children's physical development in more refined gross- and fine-motor skills are manifested in the emergence of new forms of play. School-age children are more skilled in skipping, hopping, climbing, and chasing. They learn to ride bicycles and improve their ability to draw, color, and use a computer keyboard. Later, they are able to construct model planes and other more complex constructions (J. E. Johnson, 1998).

Gallahue (1993) describes the elementary school years as the specialized movement phase introduced in Chapter 4. During this period, children continue in the development of mature movement skills that will carry on until adulthood. Differences in fundamental movement abilities also become more varied. Although children may have the potential to develop fundamental movements to their most mature stage, differences in opportunities and the effectiveness of development in the early childhood years have influenced their skill levels. Children vary widely in their abilities, and

problems have become evident in many children that affect their successful participation in group play and sports. As is true for younger children, a quality motor and movement development program is needed to correct problems and maximize opportunity for children to develop mature levels of skills.

Various factors affect physical development during the elementary years. At one extreme, many children lack a balanced diet and suffer from malnutrition that affects motor development and later learning. At the other extreme, obesity has become a problem in affluent nations such as the United States. Obese children develop high blood pressure and problematic cholesterol levels that used to be limited to adult health issues (Unger, Kruger, & Christoffel, 1990; U.S. Department of Health and Human Services, 2004; Zeisel, 1986). School-age children experience higher rates of illness during the first 2 years of elementary school. Many children, particularly those from low-income homes, tend to develop chronic health problems. Asthma, cystic fibrosis, cancer, and acquired immune deficiency syndrome (AIDS) are illnesses that affect school-age children's development and learning (Berk, 2007).

Injuries are another cause of differences in physical development. Although the incidence of injuries begins to rise in early childhood, the frequency increases steadily during the years of middle childhood and into adolescence. Boys have a higher injury rate than girls, and auto and bicycle collisions account for a majority of the injuries (Brooks & Roberts, 1990).

### Characteristics of Motor Development

Growth is slower and more regular during elementary school years. Between the ages of 6 to 8, boys are taller and heavier. This trend changes by the age of 10, when girls experience more dramatic physical growth. Large motor development focuses on the legs, which lengthen more than the upper body. There is more diversity in individual growth that can be attributed to genetics, nutrition, and other environmental factors (Berk, 2007).

**Gross-Motor Skills**  Improved motor skills in school-age children is reflected in flexibility, balance, and agility. There is more flexibility in swinging a bat or engaging in tumbling. Improved balance supports participation in sports, and agility can be seen when children jump rope, play tag, soccer, and hopscotch. Six- and 7-year-old children are still inaccurate in batting and more successful at T-ball. Older school-age children can also throw and kick a ball with greater force. They are also able to participate in handball, tennis, basketball, and football (Berk, 2007; Cratty, 1986; Thomas, 1984).

**Fine-Motor Skills**  Refinement in fine-motor skills is exhibited in many of the activities of school-age children. Children's writing and drawing skills continue to develop throughout elementary school. A first-grade child, age 6, can generally write his name, the letters of the alphabet, and numbers. His writing is large until he can move from using the entire arm to using the wrist and fingers. Older school-age children form letters more accurately and use letters of uniform height and spacing. By third grade, refinements in writing skills prepare children to move into cursive writing.

Children's drawings also reflect their progress in fine-motor skills. They are able to use more detail and organization in their drawings. Older school-age children can represent depth in their drawings as they master linear perspective. This skill begins to emerge at about age 9 or 10 (Berk, 2007; Trawick-Smith, 2009).

Fine-motor development is reflected in the types of activities school-age children select. In addition to building model airplanes or engaging in computer activities, working with puzzles and practicing yo-yo skills are popular activities.

**Variations in Motor Skill Development**
Variations in motor skills during elementary school years can be attributed to social class

and sex differences. Students who come from affluent families are more likely to have gymnastic, tennis, skating, swimming, and dancing lessons than children from less-affluent homes. These children also have more opportunities to engage in team sports.

Significant differences in skills development are gender based. Girls continue to be more advanced in fine-motor skills; boys gain an advantage in gross-motor skills. Girls are better at handwriting and drawing; boys outperform girls in throwing and kicking (Cratty, 1986).

These differences seem to be environmental rather than derived from variations in physical development. Parents have higher expectations in physical abilities for boys than for girls. In addition, children view sports as more important for boys. Girls perceive that they have less talent in sports than their male peers (Coakly, 1990; Eccles & Harold, 1991). In recent years, this trend has begun to change. More girls are participating in organized sports in the elementary grades, and parental expectations for girls to excel in sports have increased accordingly. Note, however, that there is a concern for the role of organized sports for both genders in the primary grades because developmental limitations make it difficult for children to master the skills needed for these sports (Berger, 2009).

## Play and Physical Development

**Outdoor Play**  Physical play in the elementary school years is increasingly influenced by peers. Children, particularly boys, engage in outdoor play with their peers on playgrounds, ball fields, and recreation centers where there are facilities and equipment that can be accessed for games and sports. Not only does such play provide vigorous physical activity for school-age children, but socialization is also a benefit (J. E. Johnson, 1998). Although children of this age seek to be away from direct adult supervision in their play, this type of opportunity is not always readily available because some working parents require that their children remain at home after school for safety reasons, and also because school schedules have decreased opportunities for outdoor play in the interest of academic achievement and concern for inappropriate out-door play behaviors (Blatchford, 1996; Manning, 1998; Pellegrini & Bjorklund, 1996). Elementary school teachers vary in the value they place on play. Teachers in rural schools are more likely to provide more time for play than urban teachers. Moreover, teachers' attitudes affect play time. Teachers who have a positive attitude toward play are more likely to provide play opportunities than those with less positive attitudes toward play (Newman, Brody, & Beauchamp, 1996).

There is also a concern for the safety of outdoor play. The urbanization of the United States has made it difficult for elementary school children to play outdoors. Public play spaces are invaded by drug traffickers, homeless transients, and vagrants. The gun epidemic has increased incidents of violence on the streets where children might play (Edelman, 1994). Concern over lawsuits has resulted in inaccessibility of vacant property and schoolyards where children might gather to play. Although many urban children have found ways to continue outdoor play by being creative in using their environment (Dargan & Zeitlin, 1998), a majority of children living in cities and smaller urban communities find themselves transported from one location to another by public or private transportation and engage in physical play in basement playrooms, rooftop play areas, and within their family home or apartment (Rivkin, 1998).

**Risk Taking in Play** One characteristic of school-age play is the desire for physical challenge and risk taking. Children seek to test their physical skills in their play to find out what they can and cannot do. They challenge themselves by trying new skills and learn through trial and error what their capabilities and limitations are (Jambor, 1998). An example is the game of tag. Individual players take physical risks in running, jumping, and performing other motor skills to avoid being caught. In more structured playground environments they challenge themselves in mazes, physical exercise equipment, and complex climbing structures.

A concern for adults is whether to permit risk-taking activities because of the danger of injury. Another concern is when more capable players lead children who are less physically developed to challenges they cannot handle. The availability of appropriate equipment that provides challenges for school-age children is a primary factor in whether children will be exposed to excess danger. Inappropriate equipment that does not include levels of challenge will lead to dangerous risk-taking behaviors as children seek to make the play equipment more interesting. Examples include children climbing to the top of swinging equipment or climbing structures and young children playing on equipment designed for older children.

The need for challenge is a natural part of motor development for school-age children. They learn to understand their developing capabilities and extend their challenges. Because adults are rightfully concerned about dangerous risk taking, they need to provide environments where challenges are provided but within reasonably safe limits. Playgrounds that eliminate all challenges are sterile and uninteresting to children. But play environments that have dangerous risk factors can provide too high a level of challenge that can encourage children into inappropriate risk-taking activities (Jambor, 1998; Wallach, 1992).

**Directed Play** When children enter elementary school, their daily or weekly schedules include periods for physical education. The physical education teacher engages the children in activities for motor skill development that include games and sports. Can these activities be described as play?

Hopper (1996) promotes the idea of the physical education lesson as play. He believes that games and playful aspects of physical education activities are similar to the criteria given for free play. He urges physical education teachers to reinterpret the meaning and importance of play and to incorporate it into directed play activities in the physical education program. Others believe that because students enjoy directed game activities and engage in behaviors such as running, chasing, and fleeing found in free-play chase games, such behaviors in directed tag games qualify them as play (Belka, 1998). Furthermore, attempts to teach children how to be inclusive in selection of play partners in directed game activities also can be described as a form of play. A program to teach fairness in play during recess, labeled "Play Fair," may be used to teach students to eliminate bullying on the playground and to include all students as players in games. Although the activities are teacher directed during a recess period, the intent is for students to become fair in their free play (Chuoke & Eyman, 1997).

School-age children engage in vigorous outdoor play and organized games.

Participation in organized sports also becomes more important during the school-age years. Although there is justifiable concern about the adult dominance of sports and adult-imposed rules rather than child-initiated and child-dominated play, increasing numbers of school-age children participate in one or more sports. Supporters of sports as a form of play suggest that sports also contain many of the elements used to describe play. They compare the purposes for involvement in informal games such as the opportunity to be with friends a similar purpose for involvement in sports. Although children engaged in sports are concerned for winning as an important goal, they also engage in playful pranks, verbal banter, and trading insults. Another side effect of participation is enjoying playful behavior in addition to playing baseball, basketball, or football (Hilliard, 1998).

**Free Play**   Earlier in this section on physical development and play, the description of the play of school-age children included outdoor play as an important element. The need for outdoor play was discussed as well as factors that limit outdoor play in the larger community where children live. Recess is another source for free play; however, at the beginning of the chapter limitations or elimination of recess as a current trend in elementary schools was introduced as an important variable in the opportunities school-age children have to play. The issue of whether recess—or "break time," as it is labeled in Great Britain—is needed by school-age children and should be a relevant part of the curriculum in elementary schools is a controversial topic (Elkind, 2006).

One subtopic of the issue is whether school-age children need time for recess and unstructured play. Indeed, research on play at school has shown that physical development is not a priority among many educators (Trawick-Smith, 2009). Many schools that have eliminated recess employ educators who believe physical education periods are sufficient for the physical needs of elementary school children. Opponents of recess voice concerns about aggressive play, playground bullies, and the loss of time from academic activities (O'Brien, 2003; J. E. Smith, 1984; Robert Wood Johnson Foundation, 2007).

Proponents of recess express concern that many children do not have opportunities for free outdoor play outside school hours either because they are in scheduled activities or organized sports most school days. If they live in an urban area, safe areas may not be available for outdoor play. Furthermore, working parents might forbid outdoor play when they are away from home (Elkind, 2006).

Proponents of recess periods also propose that social as well as physical benefits can result during recess; moreover, as a respite from attention to classroom tasks, outdoor play can help bring about academic benefits (Harris, 2010; Jambor, 1999; Taras, 2005). Social skills such as learning to work in groups, resolve conflicts, and use negotiation are benefited by outdoor play (Ginsburg, 2007). Although the long-term benefits of recess are not currently available, evidence indicates that children's attention wanes when they are expected to work for sustained periods. Recess provides the break that allows them to give maximum attention to their work once again (O'Brien, 2003; Pellegrini & Bjorklund, 1996; Zygmunt-Fillwalk & Bilello, 2005). Researchers caution, however, that little research supports the role of play for academic success in the elementary grades (Glickman, 1984). Recess is also an opportunity for aggression, as many teachers point out, and without proper supervision, it can be a negative factor in the school experience (Pellegrini & Smith, 1993).

Although proponents of recess suggest that vigorous physical play occurs when children are provided with regular outdoor play periods, many children in fact select quiet, passive play activities, and some children prefer to use their play period in indoor activities. A study of recess activities of school-age children at different ages revealed that the type of activities engaged in changed over time (Blatchford, 1996). Seven-year-olds reported spending their time running around and playing games. Ball games and chasing games were most popular. By 11 years, girls preferred pretending and skipping games; football dominated the boys' play.

The issue of whether recess should be retained in the elementary school continues. In fact, the U.S. Department of Education's National Center for Educational Statistics reported that 83% to 88% of elementary schools provide recess for their students (Viadero, 2006). Glickman (1984) proposes that definitive research is needed linking achievement with outdoor play before elementary schools will see recess as a priority. The implication seems to be that elementary educators do not perceive the value of physical play as a reason for scheduling recess. Only overwhelming evidence that there is a positive connection between free play periods in the school day and increased achievement will change the trends to reduce or eliminate recess periods.

## Adult Roles in Physical Play

The discussion in Chapter 5 indicated that directed play might be found in preschool settings, but structured motor development programs are not commonly found in programs for children younger than age 6. Once children enter elementary schools, however, physical education classes are the rule rather than the exception. Trained physical educators work with students regularly and seek to refine motor skills and teach the basics of sports and games. Although motor development is the primary purpose for physical education programs, a playful and enjoyable experience is also advocated for directed programs (Hilliard, 1998; Hopper, 1996).

Classroom teachers should also have a role in providing physical play. Although teachers might believe they have no responsibility because the physical education teacher conducts the program for physical development, they, too,

**TWENTY-FIRST CENTURY FAMILY PLAY**

On a summer weekend on the Texas coast, families created their own solutions to the problems of outdoor play in urban areas. On Friday afternoon, a large recreational vehicle (RV) resort began to fill with families who had come to play. Some were individual families, and others were part of a group of families arriving and setting up their campers. Out came tricycles, small and large bicycles, skateboards, strollers, cooking grills, and lawn chairs. By late afternoon, the groups were in full action, children riding their wheel toys, a father skateboarding with his son, and much socializing around the RVs. Some groups were multi-generations who sat together much of the day when they were not engaged in physical activities. The small groups that walked back and forth to the large swimming pool extended the play possibilities. Many of these families had ventured from nearby cities where apartment dwelling and streets with high traffic prohibited outdoor activities. On Saturday, many families went to the beach or fishing on a nearby causeway. Water sports were possible on the large water area inside a bay area. Kayaks and small boats pulling water skiers shared the bay with a variety of ocean birds.

On Sunday afternoon, the process was reversed. Adults started packing up all the gear they had unloaded on Friday while children made the last rounds of the long streets in the resort. Balls and other game toys were put in the camper or the back of a pickup for the return home. At dusk on Sunday night, the RV resort was quiet and peaceful for the permanent residents who waited to enjoy the groups that would populate their small, transient community the next weekend.

should become advocates for opportunities for physical play beyond directed activities. This advocacy would include time for free play and maintenance of quality outdoor play environments that provide challenge as well as a safe place to play (Trawick-Smith, 2009). Both physical education and regular classroom teachers can work together to achieve this goal on behalf of the physical development of school-age children.

Parents definitely have a role in the physical play of their children. Because research shows that parental influence and expectation affect the physical play and participation in sports of their children (Coakly, 1990; Eccles & Harold, 1991), parents should be sensitive to how they can affect participation in physical play. Parents also can be sensitive to providing opportunities for school-age children to engage in free play. Understanding the limitations of environment, safety issues, and time for free play, they can encourage their children to have a balance of activities during after-school hours and weekends. A balance is particularly needed between sports and free play and sedentary activities, such as watching television and engaging in video and computer games.

## COGNITIVE DEVELOPMENT

School-age children think differently than preschool children. Cognitive changes make it possible for them to plan using cognitive resources, remember important information using thinking strategies, and solve problems using thinking and reasoning skills. Children become aware of their intellectual abilities and can recognize their strengths and weaknesses. They understand how to think and are aware when they are using "good thinking" (Berger, 2009).

Unlike preschool children, school-age children can focus on the task at hand. They are

---

**WHAT PARENTS, CAREGIVERS, AND TEACHERS CAN DO
TO PROMOTE PHYSICAL PLAY**

1. Adults can work to ensure that school-age children have time and opportunities for free play both at school and outside school hours.

2. Adults can ensure that quality outdoor play environments are available for school-age children both at school and in the larger community.

3. Parents can work to influence their children to enjoy a balance between physical activities and sedentary activities when they are at home.

4. Parents can encourage their children to be selective in sports participation so that they also have opportunities for child-initiated play in addition to adult-directed physical play.

5. Parents can encourage children of both genders to participate in sports and physical play while accepting gender differences in play selections.

6. Parents can encourage and support their children's interests for play.

7. Parents can plan and engage in family activities together. The whole family can engage in bicycle riding, hiking, swimming, and outdoor games.

---

able to screen out distractions and concentrate on their work. Moreover, they know when they need to use selective thinking and where they should focus their attention.

The cognitive competencies of school-age children develop rapidly during the school-age years. Whereas preschool children are intuitive thinkers who center on one characteristic at a time, school-age children use deliberate thinking strategies and mental planning to accomplish tasks in learning. In Piaget's (1952) cognitive developmental theory, school-age children use mental abilities that are within the **concrete operational stage.** New thinking abilities can also be attributed to the information-processing approach to mental development. These new abilities characterize their cognitive development.

## Characteristics of Cognitive Development

**Concrete Operational Thought**  Children's thinking in the concrete operational stage is more logical and organized than in the preoperational period. The word *operations* is relevant

because children use mental actions or mental operations in a logical manner. This mental ability is evidenced when a child **decenters,** or focuses, on more than one aspect of a task or uses **reversibility,** or mentally works through a series of mental actions and then reverses the process. School-age children can learn subtraction, multiplication, and division because they are able to understand that subtraction is the reverse process of addition and that division reverses multiplication (McDevitt & Ormrod, 2004).

Children who have achieved concrete operations can use classes and subclasses to classify objects. School-age children enjoy collecting objects and can classify them by more than one characteristic. Berk (2007) provides the example of a child who sorts his collection of baseball cards first by one attribute, such as team membership, and then by another attribute, such as playing position.

Other characteristics of concrete operational thinking are **seriation,** or the ability to order items by some dimension such as length or diameter, and **spatial reasoning,** an understanding of space that permits children to give directions on how to get from one point to another. They can combine distance with speed and understand that the faster the speed, the shorter the time to reach a distant point or location (Acredolo, Adams, & Schmid, 1984).

A limitation of concrete operational thinking is that it depends on the child's concrete experiences. Children can use logical thinking when it deals with concrete information they can perceive (Berk, 2007). This ability cannot yet be applied in abstract contexts. In addition, the ability to use concrete operational thinking is a gradual process. School-age children cannot readily use logical thinking in a familiar context and transfer it in a more general application to less familiar concepts. For example, the child who can classify baseball cards might not be able to classify trees by some given category without experiences to become familiar with the trees and categories.

**Thinking Strategies**   Cognitive changes in the school-age child can also be explained by looking at how information is processed. Some characteristics of mental strategies that can be attributed to this approach are selective attention, the use of memory strategies, and knowledge growth.

School-age children are able to focus on a task, or use **selective attention,** in their learning. Whereas preschool children are easily distracted when working on a learning activity, school-age children are able to screen out distractions and focus on information relevant to their task. They use selective attention for both memorizing and problem solving. In problem solving, the child can focus on the information that pertains to finding a solution. To remember important information, the child focuses on relevant strategies that will assist in retaining the material (Flavell, Miller, & Miller, 1993; Miller, 1993).

Children can use specific strategies to memorize information. They use *organization* strategies to place the material into a logical order, *rehearsal* strategies to repeat the information to be remembered, and *retrieval* strategies to be able to recall the information when needed. These strategies for remembering information

are called **mnemonics,** or memory aids (Berger, 2009).

The more advanced thinking skills developed during the school-age years lead to significant cognitive growth. The more information the child is able to acquire, the more substantial the growth. In other words, the more connections made in the brain from input and storage of new information, the more competent the child becomes. As the amount of information increases, the child is able to also increase the rapidity of thinking and to develop metacognition, an awareness of the cognitive processes being used (Flavell et al., 1993).

## Variations in Cognitive Development

All children do not achieve concrete operational thinking uniformly. There appear to be cultural and environmental differences. Children who have extensive interest and exposure to a type of information will achieve concrete operational thinking in that topic. For example, the child with extensive experience in computers can apply concrete operational thinking and information-processing skills to challenges encountered in using the computer. Likewise, Mexican children whose parents make pottery for a living acquire conservation skills sooner than the Piagetian descriptions (McDevitt & Ormrod, 2004). But children in cultures where there is no formal schooling are delayed in understanding conservation tasks compared to children who attend school from the age of 6 or 7. Some researchers thus believe that acquisition of concrete operational thinking is not spontaneous but socially generated. The practical activities in specific cultures lead to the logic required in Piagetian tasks (Berk, 2007; Flavell et al., 1993).

Another cognitive variation is in intelligence. Variations in intelligence become more obvious in school-age children. One approach to comparing intelligence is to use intelligence quotient (IQ). Children range in IQ as measured on standardized intelligence tests.

Howard Gardner (1993) has described a different approach to understanding variations in intelligence. Gardner believes there are seven types of intelligence: linguistic, logico-mathematical, musical, spatial, kinesthetic, interpersonal, and intrapersonal skills. Each type of intelligence involves cognitive skills, and variations occur in children in each type of intelligence. Children will be stronger in some types of intelligence and weaker in others.

Regardless of individual and cultural differences, children in all cultures gain in their ability to use thought in learning. Whether one looks at information processing as the source for advancement in thinking, the cognitive developmental theory, or Gardner's intelligences, school-age children use logic and mental strategies in their learning. The ability to develop memory strategies and to organize information within more than one characteristic is applied to their cognitive play.

## Play and Cognitive Development

In Chapter 5, we discussed levels of cognitive play based on the theories of Piaget and Smilansky. Although they disagreed on the developmental level needed to engage in the highest form of play, both agreed that games with rules follow lower levels of play such as practice play and symbolic play. Games with rules require concrete operational thinking, motor skills, and social competence. In the following section, games with rules are discussed as well as advances in pretend play and technological play.

## Characteristics of Cognitive Play

**Games with Rules**    J. E. Johnson (1998) describes how preschool children can engage in simple games such as lotto and board games with spinners. It is not until children have achieved concrete operations that they can engage in a wide array of different types of games with rules. When they are capable of designing and implementing a plan or strategy and playing in both competition and cooperation with other players, they are able to participate in all types of games with consistent and complex rules.

Between the ages of 8 and 12, games are very popular with school-age children. Some of the games are constant, such as tag; others are cyclical or seasonal, such as marbles or hopscotch (Manning, 1998). These games require cooperation among players as well as the ability to remain engaged in play activities for a longer period of time. But, most important, players must be able to submit to the rules and to exercise self-control as a game player.

Games with rules that are child initiated evolve from practice and symbolic play. Like the ability to use concrete operational thinking, the transformation into games with rules can be gradual and specific to familiar play activities. Practice play, where children engage in practicing a motor skill such as jumping, can evolve into a game with rules when children agree on rules for jumping that can result in a winner (DeVries, 1998).

The ability to devise games with rules can evolve in stages. DeVries and Fernie (1990) were able to trace the stages in developing rules for the game tic-tac-toe by watching children move from putting pieces in squares without waiting turns to taking turns and using blocking strategies to defeat another player.

When children invent games, they understand they have to develop rules to play the game as well as rules for social functioning. Opportunities to design games within the classroom help children learn to work cooperatively and have autonomy as part of the group of classmates. By creating rules, students feel ownership and responsibility for how they participate in games (Castle, 1998; DeVries & Zan, 1994).

Piaget (1965) was able to observe stages in playing marbles from exploring the ability to shoot a marble in preschool children to the development of complex and consistent rules in older children. Teachers also teach and use games with rules in the classroom. Once children have acquired the ability to participate in rule-governed activities, teachers can use games as instructional tools and to introduce a playful atmosphere into the classroom. Games have been incorporated into science, mathematics, and reading as well as physical education (Barta & Schaelling, 1998; DeVries & Kohlberg, 1990; Hewitt, 1997; Jarrett, 1997; Kamii & DeVries, 1980; Owens & Sanders, 1998).

**Pretend Play**　School-age children do not engage in pretend play as much once they have entered the elementary grades. However, they continue this type of play away from school, building forts and tree houses and also using miniature figures in fantasy play. Older children engage in performing plays (Manning, 1998). Many girls enjoy using Barbie dolls in pretend play; boys frequently spend many hours playing with miniature vehicles of various types.

## Adult Roles in Cognitive Play

Throughout this chapter we have discussed the difficulties teachers have in integrating play into the school-age classroom. In a time of testing and accountability teachers may not have the freedom to include play into learning activities.

However, there are strategies teachers can use because play is so very important in the elementary years.

One strategy is to provide a more relaxed classroom environment by including opportunities for children to make choices in their learning activities (Riley & Jones, 2010). Games are a major playful activity. There are computer games available, but a games center can be established where there are collections of games that have a learning component. Reading games are most common as will be discussed later in the chapter, but games can be designed that apply to mathematics and other content areas. Some games can be adapted board games that feature questions related to learning objectives in the curriculum. The problems or questions posed can be changed as the curriculum changes. Math games in particular can permit children to practice math skills with the game (Kamii, 2000). Games are chosen rather than assigned to maintain the spirit of play. Classroom teachers have become adept at documenting how these activities relate to specific state standards.

---

### WHAT PARENTS, CAREGIVERS, AND TEACHERS CAN DO TO PROMOTE COGNITIVE PLAY

1. Adults can provide children with games that permit experience with games with rules to develop.

2. Adults can provide free play periods that will give children opportunities to develop their own games with rules.

3. Teachers can incorporate a playful environment in the classroom that will foster cognitive play.

4. Teachers can incorporate games into classroom learning experiences that will help students develop a playful approach to learning.

5. Teachers can use learning activities that will promote concrete operational thinking and information-processing skills in classroom games.

6. Adults can play games with children that will foster the use of planning and mental strategies.

7. Teachers can set up interest centers where children can use their imagination and ideas with the materials without any assignment.

Children's choices and learning through play activities can be accommodated within thematic or project learning (Wortham 2010). Possible activities to learn concepts in a theme can include choices, self-initiated activities, and play opportunities. For example, in a study of transportation, children learned about vehicles, roads, and bridges. Children used blocks, clay, paper and crayons, rulers, and markers to demonstrate the structure of a bridge. Children drew on their knowledge of mathematics, science, reading, social studies, art, and technology to explore and demonstrate their understanding of bridges (Fu, 2000).

The National Association for the Education of Young Children described an appropriate environment for school-age children (Copple & Bredekamp, 2009):

> Teachers foster a learning environment that encourages exploration, initiative, peer interactions, and cognitive growth. They choose materials that comfortably challenge children's skills. A variety of spaces are provided in the classroom, including comfortable work areas where children can interact and work together als also places for silent or shared reading, working on construction projects, writing, playing math or language, games, and exploring science.

## LANGUAGE AND LITERACY DEVELOPMENT

If language development is characterized as an explosion during the preschool years, school-age language development can be described as more subtle but equally important. Changes in language development are consistent during school-age years, although they are less dramatic than in preschool years. Vocabulary, grammar, and pragmatics continue to be expanded and refined. In addition, school-age children develop an awareness of language. Their emerging thinking skills permit them to think about language and plan how they will express themselves. The interrelationship between cognitive development and language development is reflected in literacy development as the child develops new skills in writing and reading.

## Characteristics of Language Development

**Vocabulary Development**   On average, school-age children learn about 20 new words a day. Many words are picked up in the context of reading. In addition, they are able to analyze words to derive their meaning. The ability to think about words enhances vocabulary development in addition to understanding that some words have multiple meanings. The grasp of multiple meanings enables children to engage in humor as they tell riddles and jokes (Berk, 2007; Waggoner & Palermo, 1989).

**Grammatical Development**   Preschool children have essentially mastered the grammar of their language; however, school-age children improve in more complex grammatical constructions. Cognitive development enables children to learn more subtle elements of grammar, such as the use of passive voice and infinitive phrases (Chomsky, 1969; Romaine, 1984).

**Pragmatic Development**   Although preschoolers begin to understand the use of pragmatics, school-age children steadily improve in their communication skills. Through their ability to listen carefully, understand what others will think is funny, and remember how to tell a joke, school-age children use their growing ability to use pragmatics in conversations involving humor. They also learn the functions of polite speech and are able to use them—for example, when making a request (Berger, 2009).

**Code Switching**   School-age children understand different language codes and can move from one to another. They know they can use swearing with their friends but not with their parents or teachers. They are aware of a formal language code used in the classroom as compared with a more restricted or colloquial code (slang) with friends in the lunchroom or on the playground (Romaine, 1984; Trawick-Smith, 2009).

**Bilingualism and Nonstandard English**
School-age children become aware of the use of nonstandard English or dialects. All language cultures have an informal language that can be dialectical. Children from different regions of the United States speak in different dialects, as do children from unique cultures within a region (Berger, 2009).

Many children speak more than one language. As they enter elementary school, children who speak a language other than English will learn English as a second language. Children who continue to use a language other than English are **bilingual,** or capable of speaking two languages (Diaz, 1985).

Children who are bilingual and children who speak a dialect benefit from daily interaction with speakers of standard English. This is true whether the interaction is with peers or adults. At the same time, teachers accept the child's language while guiding expansion and refinement using standard English. There is currently controversy as to how bilingual school-age children should be taught. For decades, there have been bilingual programs in which children are taught or supported in their home language while learning English. More recently, English only, or an immersion process in English, is preferred in some states.

The school environment that has children who speak several different languages affords opportunities for children and challenges for teachers. The children can learn appreciation for other languages. At the same time, teachers can use language differences to enrich the understanding of the role of language. Assisting children who speak other languages is complex when the teacher seeks to meet individual language development and needs (Quiocho & Ulanoff, 2009). For example, Trawick-Smith (2009) gives the example of a Korean child trying to get the attention of another child using Korean words. The teacher noticed the confusion occurring on the part of both children. She explained to the English-speaking child that the Korean child wanted to show him something. At the same time she helped the Korean child to address the other in English. Understanding of different languages and appreciation of recognizing efforts to communicate were taught to both children.

## Characteristics of Literacy Development

School-age children continue the journey into literacy begun in the preschool years. For many children, entry into first grade is anticipated as the time they will learn to read and write. In emergent literacy-based primary classrooms, children use emergent writing and reading skills as they individually acquire more advanced levels of literacy. Children are taught phonics and word identification skills as they are encountered in their writing efforts and reading activities. Some classrooms focus on instruction in reading and writing skills; others are a blend of various approaches to literacy (Bradley & Pottle, 2001). Moreover, children can benefit from frequent experiences with varied forms of literacy, including informational texts (Walker, Kragler, Martin, & Arnett, 2003).

The beginning stages of reading are followed by refinement in reading and writing in each subsequent grade. By the end of elementary school, children have moved from learning to read and write to using reading and writing to learn. Play with literacy enhances the process, as does using literacy in play activities. Playful literacy, or using playful activities in literacy instruction, can be a valuable experiences in literacy development (Scully & Roberts, 2002).

## Language and Literacy Development and Play

Infants begin play with language by playing with the sounds of language. Preschoolers begin to use language in their sociodramatic play, both within the play and in a metalinguistic capacity as they talk about their play. School-age children also use language in a supportive role as an element of their play but are subtler in incorporating language into their play activities.

**Play with Language**   Although younger children are able to tell simple jokes, such as knock-knock jokes, older children use jokes and riddles in a broader perspective. School-age children were described earlier as understanding that words can have more than one meaning. This double meaning of words is used in jokes and riddles, which are collected and used as social rituals with friends and new acquaintances.

Jokes can be used to try out off-color language and humorous insults. Older elementary school children try out playful insults on each other, and the ensuing dialogue can become a contest as they try to outdo each other in trading insults (Davidson, 1998).

**Language and Pretend Play**   We have mentioned that school-age children tend to use pretend play outside of the school environment. Another characteristic of pretend play is that language is now substituted for the more physical enactments of play in preschool children. Pretend play takes on the character of a story and is planned carefully before its enactment. It can focus on toys, such as Barbie dolls, with the creation of a story line for the toys, or be more abstract, with only a dialogue to support the pretend story. Boys might play out a sports event such as football or reenact a movie with language to support the plot. Davidson suggests that the difference between pretend play and storytelling becomes blurred in school-age children because they are simultaneously creating a story and using language to support pretend play.

**Language and Social Play**   In the discussion about motor development and play, jump rope was described as a favorite game for school-age girls. They now combine their enjoyment of jump rope with that of rhymes, so these games then become a socialization activity in play. Children learn traditional jump rope rhymes and invent new ones.

Language is also used for social rituals. School-age children organize clubs with secret passwords and special phrases that outsiders cannot understand. Pig Latin is an example of the special language that can accompany membership in a social club. This and other language variations invented by children require an understanding of how words are composed and the development of new rules for the invented language (Davidson, 1998).

## Adult Roles in Language and Literacy Play

In much of the play that occurs in preschool settings, teachers play a facilitative role in encouraging play. They might engage in play with the children to encourage higher forms of play, but the children tend to initiate most of the play activities.

As children enter elementary school, play becomes more teacher directed. As seen earlier in motor play and cognitive play, the teacher either directs the activity, as in the case of the physical education teacher, or designs the activity, such as cognitive games in different subject areas.

In the case of language and literacy play, especially literacy play, there is some discussion in the literature as to what the teacher's role should be. Emergent literacy is seen as developing within the child with reading and writing evolving through opportunities to engage in literacy activities through sociodramatic play. As children enter a more teacher-directed learning environment in first grade, there is some concern that these opportunities can become lost (Scully & Roberts, 2002).

Some researchers regard symbolic play as essential for literacy. They propose that language and literacy learning occur naturally in symbolic play contexts. The teacher serves as a facilitator in setting up play environments that incorporate literacy activities. Likewise, the

## WHAT PARENTS, CAREGIVERS, AND TEACHERS CAN DO TO PROMOTE LANGUAGE AND LITERACY PLAY

1. Teachers can incorporate literacy and sociodramatic centers into primary-grade classrooms to support student-initiated activities with literacy.

2. Adults can provide opportunities for children to have time for play where conversation can be incorporated into play.

3. Adults can encourage children in learning rhymes and chants as well as developing their own.

4. Adults can engage children in games such as Scrabble where literacy skills can be practiced in a playful mode.

5. Teachers can design and encourage students to design board games that incorporate literacy skills.

teacher scaffolds, or supports, language and literacy development by modeling literacy during play activities (Chang & Yawkey, 1998; Morrow & Rand, 1991a; Pickett, 1998; Vygotsky, 1977).

Primary-grade teachers, especially first-grade teachers, might not perceive the use of play centers as important for the acquisition of literacy skills. Even if they would like to use play centers for literacy, they might not include them because of pressures for children to read and write using more formal approaches (Patton & Mercer, 1996). In an effort to help primary-grade teachers continue a more facilitative role using play to promote literacy, suggestions have been offered as to how centers can be incorporated into the classroom that can accomplish the desired literacy objectives. Block play (Pickett, 1998), symbolic play (Chang & Yawkey, 1998), and sociodramatic play (Patton & Mercer, 1996; Stone & Christie, 1996) are proposed as avenues for primary-grade teachers to use to facilitate and model literacy skills. Although such teaching approaches might seem inappropriate to some primary-grade teachers, evidence indicates that literacy and symbolic and sociodramatic play are natural partners in a continuum of literacy development that begins in

## SERIOUS PLAYERS IN THE PRIMARY CLASSROOM

Selma Wasserman (2000) refers to students in the primary grades as serious players. She advocates active learning experiences where children are empowered to make their own choices for literacy play activities. She refers to the child in such a classroom as a can-do child doing serious play in a can-do classroom. Her suggestions for creative play in language arts include:

1. Choosing a word and acting it out in a pantomime, to see if the other children can guess the word.

2. Playing word games, for example seeing how many words can be made using a set of letters.

3. Writing as many words as the children can think of that begin or end with the letters *st*.

4. Inventing words that rhyme with hard-to-rhyme words like *spaghetti* or *octopus* (p. 159).

preschool and continues into school-age class-rooms (Chang & Yawkey, 1998; Pellegrini & Galda, 1990).

# SOCIAL AND EMOTIONAL DEVELOPMENT

As children move through the elementary school grades, they undergo major personality changes and experience many factors that affect their social and emotional development. Although their family remains an important influence, peer relationships and success in school are also significant to the success of their development. They continue in the progress of development in self-concept and self-esteem, but emerging cognitive skills permit taking perspective and developing morals. Erikson (1963) labeled this period of social development **industry versus inferiority.**

The emotional tasks faced by school-age children, according to Erikson, is whether they will develop confidence and competence in useful skills and tasks or whether they will feel inferior and unable to be successful. If children are able to meet the challenges of this period of development, they become industrious and seek mastery over their learning. If they are unable to meet the challenges, they become sad and pessimistic, feeling they are unable to succeed and be good at anything (Berk, 2007). As they work alongside their peers in school, children become aware of their own abilities as well as those of their peers. They are able to evaluate their strengths and weaknesses and compare themselves with their classmates. Their social development permits them to have lasting relationships with peers and friends. Social and emotional development interact with characteristics of social development.

## Characteristics of Social-Emotional Development

**Self-Concept**    Children continue in their development of self-concept in the school-age years. In comparing themselves with others, they are able to make social comparisons. They compare their appearance, abilities, and accomplishments with those of their classmates. Their interactions with others include the emerging ability to use perspective taking in their social relationships, which enables them to understand what others are thinking or to take the other person's viewpoint into account. They interpret what others think about them into their concept about themselves (Rosenberg, 1979).

**Self-Esteem**    Because school-age children are more aware of their own successes and failures, they have much more information about their performance than they did as preschoolers. They use feedback from their own evaluation of performance plus feedback from others to assess their self-esteem in terms of their physical, academic, and social abilities. They are able to describe their overall feeling of self-worth by combining their achievements in these three categories. Although they are able to be fairly realistic in appraising their own characteristics, they tend to give themselves lower ratings than they did as overly optimistic preschoolers.

Students who see themselves as successful in social development, or have a **positive self-esteem,** believe their successes are related to their ability—they become success oriented. On the negative side, children who see themselves as failures and unable to succeed develop **learned helplessness.** They feel their failures are related to bad luck and cannot be changed by hard work. They give up on trying to succeed in school and social tasks and depend on others to help them (Dweck & Leggett, 1988).

**Perspective Taking**    When children are able to imagine what others are thinking and feeling, they are affected in how they react in social situations. **Perspective taking** helps them get along with others. Children go through stages of perspective taking (Selman, 1976) and develop individual abilities. Children who are good perspective takers are more likely to express empathy and compassion. They are better at social problem solving in that they are able to find solutions to difficult social situations. Children with very poor social skills lack an awareness of others' thoughts and points of view. They exhibit angry and aggressive behaviors and are likely to mistreat their peers (Berk, 2007).

**Moral Development**   A parallel characteristic of perspective taking is **moral development,** which advances in the school-age years through children's increasing understanding of others' perspectives. They are developing ideas of fairness and merit. They also can recognize that special consideration should be given to their peers who are at a disadvantage. Their developing ideas of fairness are supported by social interactions and adult encouragement and advice (Damon, 1990).

**Peer Relationships**   Elementary school children are able to organize into peer groups that consist of leaders and followers. These peer groups become a **peer culture** that is expressed in uniform dress and ritual activities. Children who are accepted into a group or club acquire a sense of group identity. Through their experiences in the peer group, children learn about participation in social organizations and acquire social skills.

In addition to their own social groups, school-age children enjoy more structured organizational groups such as 4-H groups and scouting. With adult guidance, children grow in moral and social understanding through community service and group projects.

Some children make friends and are accepted into social groups more easily than others. Children who are accepted by their peers are more likely to have later positive social adjustment. Children who are rejected, in contrast, develop a low sense of self-esteem and are likely to have emotional and social problems as well as poor school performance (Ollendick, Weist, Borden, & Greene, 1992).

**Parent–Child Relationships**   Parent–child relationships change in school-age years; however, the quality of parent–child interactions plays a major role in the child's social development.

School-age children's parents spend less time with them than they did when they were preschoolers, and they find that their children are easier to manage. A major task for parents is to promote responsible behavior in their children and how to deal with school problems. Some parents are uncertain about how to relate to the school and how much they should become involved in the child's homework. Effective parents are able to include the child in some of the decisions that must be made. They can develop a cooperative relationship with their child and appeal to the child's ability to think logically in problem-solving situations.

There are also negative influences on parent–child relationships. Many U.S. children experience divorce in their family, and new family relationships can cause disturbed relationships over a period of at least 2 years. Divorce and remarriage can result in children having to adapt to new stepparents and blended families (Lutz, 1983).

**Sibling Relationships**   Siblings can provide support and companionship during school-age years. However, they also experience rivalry and conflict. Children who receive less parental support and attention are more likely to express resentment toward a sibling that they perceive as getting more approval and attention. Siblings who are close in age are more likely to engage in quarreling and antagonism. Birth order has an effect as well because older children receive more pressure to behave maturely and succeed in school. Younger siblings tend to be more popular with age-mates, perhaps as a result of learning to get along with the older sibling (Berk, 2007).

Social understanding and moral development in the school-age years can be summarized as follows:

- Children are increasingly aware of the psychological characteristics of others.
- Children recognize that other children interpret experiences.

Siblings provide support and companionship.

- Children have an increasing empathy for others who are suffering or needy.
- Children are knowledgeable of social conventions for appropriate behavior.
- Children recognize that they should meet others' needs as well as their own.
- Children experience feelings of shame for moral wrongdoings (McDevitt & Ormrod, 2004, p. 444).

## Play and Social-Emotional Development

Chapter 5 presented an extended discussion of how young children develop social competence reflected in their play. The role of parenting in children's social competence was described, as well as how children engage in social play and sociodramatic play. In this chapter, the direction of social competence developed in the preschool years is described as predictive of successful social interactions in school-age years. Characteristics of social play in school-age children are similar to those in preschool years; however, peer relationships are more important to successful social play than parenting roles.

**Theoretical Views of Social Play**    The theories of Piaget (1962), Vygotsky (Creasey et al., 1998), Parten (1932), and Smilansky (1968) helped define development in social play in the preschool years.

In school-age children, two approaches now describe social play. Earlier in the chapter, we characterized children's play as dominated by games with rules. Piaget and Smilansky both believed that games with rules comprise the highest level of social play. Games with rules bring together social, physical, and cognitive development in children as they engage in games and sports in elementary school.

Social play of school-age children also fits Parten's (1932) highest category of play, cooperative play. Children's cognitive development permits them to understand the ideas and thoughts of others; social development makes it possible for children to interact with children in social play by appreciating the needs of others and using problem-solving skills to work through difficulties in social play. Keeping in mind that games with rules, cooperative play, social competence, and peer influence and relationships are the primary factors in school-age play, we next look at the characteristics of social play in school-age children.

## Characteristics of Social Play

Rubin and his colleagues have conducted longitudinal studies of social play (Coplan & Rubin, 1998) and have found that social play is relatively stable when preschool play is compared with school-age play. In their observations of social play, they found that peer-rated social competence at age 7 could predict either higher self-regard or self-reported loneliness in later childhood (Rubin, Chen, McDougall, Bowker, & McKinnon, 1995). Social play competence in preschool years could be traced to peer-rated social competence or peer rejection in school-age children. However, these researchers cautioned that frequent social play in itself was not predictive of later social competence and that not all preschoolers who engaged in a high frequency of social play grew up to be well-adjusted teenagers (Coplan & Rubin, 1998).

Manning (1998) summarizes the characteristics of social play in school-age children when their physical, cognitive, language, and social skills support each other, as follows:

> Ten- to 12-year-old children, in particular, develop the social skills necessary to participate in complex, cooperative forms of play. The complexity and flexibility of their verbal as well as nonverbal communication contribute to this cooperative potential. They are also able to make friends, interact competently and confidently in social situations, and build on their increasing social skills (Manning, 1993). These enhanced social skills allow children to see others' perspectives and allow them to realize the benefits of playing socially and cooperatively. Actual play, which requires social skills, might consist of games, team sports, and organized activities. (p. 157)

Manning's description includes how the ability to cooperate enhances social play because such play encourages cooperation and fosters the development of social skills. The trend at the current time, however, is away from cooperation and toward more competition. Educators seem not to understand that child-initiated social play is important for the development of social skills. Some encourage competition in physical education classes and sports activities, which removes opportunities for social development through play (Manning, 1998).

## Variations in Social Competence and Play

**Effective Peer Relations**   We can see from the discussion about characteristics of social play in school-age children that social competence is not uniform in children, especially after they enter elementary grades. Children vary in how they are accepted by their peers, and acceptance or rejection affects how successful children are in engaging in all types of play activities. Children who develop social competence in the preschool years are more likely to be accepted into peer group play. Rejected children are likely to be left out of group play activities, ending up feeling lonely and unworthy.

School personnel are attempting to address the problems of rejected children on public school playgrounds. One cause of rejection is children's play behaviors. Some children have problems in understanding how to enter a play group (Dodge, Coie, Pettit, & Price, 1990), and teachers can help them learn these skills so they can enjoy playing with peers.

Educators in school settings are also trying to ameliorate the plight of children who are excluded from play or teased. Researchers developed a project that initiated a policy of play inclusion in which the rule is "You can't say you can't play" (Sapon-Shevin, Dobbelaere, Corrigan, Goodman, & Mastin, 1998). In the project classroom, teachers used the rule with their children and followed through with guidance to see that all children were included in classroom and outdoor play. Teachers experimented with different ways to use the rule with their classes. Many issues were raised by older elementary school students, who questioned whether students should be made to include all children into their play groups. They also questioned whether there were situations when group size was limited, thus forcing some children to be left out.

Although teachers try to provide strategies for individual children to be accepted into play groups, there is also the element of peer culture in how children choose playmates. Children are learning how to manage their social interactions and friendships when they are engaged in group play. Children could be restricted from a play group because there was no role in themed play. However, the play group might also be extended when a child would offer ideas to the group on role or plot ideas for themed play. Thus the size of the social group changed as children learned the dynamics of play group affiliations (Wohlwend, 2004/2005). Moreover, this type of experience with dynamic social relationships through group play promotes social competence (Stegelin, 2005).

**Aggression and Bullying in Play**   Two negative behaviors related to social play are **aggression** in play and **bullying** (Shantz, 1986). Although boys are responsible for the majority of incidents of aggression, girls, too, can be described as aggressive. However, the type of aggression exhibited is different for the two genders. Boys tend to be physically aggressive, whereas girls are verbally aggressive and bully through rumor and body language. Older girls sexual harassment through e-mail messages (Cole, Cornell, & Sheras, 2006; McNamee & Mercurio, 2008; Scarpaci, 2006).

Incidents of bullying are increasing. Half of all children in the United States are bullied at some point in their lives. One in two victims is bullied on a regular basis (McNamee & Mercurio, 2008). The public has become more aware of bullying and school violence because of media coverage (Lawrence & Adams, 2006; Stover, 2006).

Researchers have looked at both the causes and the outcomes of aggression. The assumption has been that peers reject aggressive children, but studies have found mixed results. On the one hand, Cairns, Cairns, Neckerman, Gest, and Gairepy (1988) found that aggressive children had their own social networks that included children who were also aggressive. They were picked as best friends as frequently as non-aggressive peers. Moreover, bullies often feel powerful, superior, and justified in their aggressive behaviors (Bullock, 2002).

A different type of information was found in a study of 8- and 9-year-old boys. Aggressive boys were found to spend more time alone without being involved in play activities. They changed the peers they played with more often and showed and received more negative behaviors than a control group. This study determined that aggressive boys misinterpret play invitations, which leads them to fights rather than play. They are more self-centered and not as interested in the reactions of peers in play. They have poor social skills and have had negative experiences in play relationships with others, which has become a spiraling problem leading to more aggression (Willner, 1991).

Bullying is a form of aggressive play. Olweus (1993b) defines bullying as "exposure, repeatedly and over time, to negative actions (words, physical contact, making faces, gesturing), or intentional exclusion from a group on the part of one or more other students" (p. 9). Boys are more likely to be bullies, but girls and boys are equally likely to become recipients of bullying (Froschl & Sprung, 1999). Although bullying begins in the early childhood years, it is most significant in later grades. Children who learn patterns of bullying in the early years may develop a pattern of violence in later life (Baumeister, 2001).

The role of teachers in reacting to bullying affects the frequency of the behavior. Researchers have found that teachers do relatively little to stop bullying, either because they are unaware it

## CYBERNET BULLIES

With the advent of the age of technology and the Internet, school-age children have found a new avenue of communication and interests. Computer use is now almost as common as viewing television in many American homes. Chat rooms, or sites where computer users can chat continuously, are very popular with elementary school children as well as older teenagers. This ability to communicate continuously through chat sites has led to cyberbullies where children are taunted, teased, and experience inappropriate language and embarrassing comments.

The effect of cyberbullying can be just as damaging as face-to-face encounters. The British Broadcasting Company (April 28, 2006) reported instances of children committing suicide or demonstrating traumatic effects of being bullied on the Internet. This type of bullying is much more difficult to identify and control. As cyber communication expands through text messaging and other forms of wireless communication, the practice will surely spread.

---

**BULLYING PREVENTION PROGRAMS**

Some bullying prevention programs that work are listed below. Contact information is included.

- The Olweus Bullying Prevention Program (www.clemson.edu/olweus/)
- *BullysafeUSA* (www.bullysafeusa.com)
- The Don't Laugh at Me Program (DLAM) (www.operationrespect.org)
- Peaceful Schools Project/Menninger Clinic (www.backoffbully.com)
- Promoting Alternative Thinking Strategies (PATHS) (www.colorado.edu.cspv/blueprints/model/programs/PATHS.html)
- Steps to Respect Program (www.cfchildren.org)

---

is occurring or because they want the children to work out their own problems. When teachers do not intervene, children believe they condone the behavior (Bullock, 2002). Children may also perceive that boys are being given permission to tease and bully (Olweus, 1993b, 1994).

There seem to be behavioral characteristics of children who are the victims of aggression and bullying. Aggressive children did not expect their victims to fight back. In addition, the victims were quick to show their pain and stress to the aggressors. The victimized children were likely to be rejected, and students expected that no punishment would result from attacking them (Perry, Williard, & Perry, 1990). Children who were bullied were younger and weaker, and they appeared anxious and insecure. They often reacted by crying and withdrawing (Bullock, 2002).

In spite of the common belief that nothing can be done to stop bullying, efforts can be made to prevent this type of aggressive behavior. One approach is to address the issue of bullying with younger children before it becomes serious during school-age years. Preschool teachers can use intervention and teaching strategies to help children understand more positive play behaviors. Parents, too, must be part of the solution by keeping apprised of bullying behavior and involving themselves in helping their own children avoid bullying of their peers (Froschl & Sprung, 1999).

School intervention policies can address the problem of bullying. The school, including teachers and children, can develop policies and strategies for appropriate behavior and sanctions against bullies (Lickona, 2000; Olweus, 1997, 2003; Piotrowski & Hoot, 2008). Such projects have been developed to reduce bullying by children on the playground and inside the school. Sessions conducted by a counselor and school resource officer raised sensitivity to the problem, and student–teacher partnerships fostered positive interactions and provided protection from possible bullies on the playground. Parents were advised when their child was a bully or was being bullied and given suggestions on how to help their child (Moravcik, 2005; Youngerman, 1998).

There are now many programs available to help parents, teachers, and school groups to decrease and help prevent bullying. The names of some of these programs can be seen in the box, Bullying Prevention Programs (McNamee & Mecurio, 2008).

## From Sociodramatic Play to Structured Dramatics

Sociodramatic play permeates the social play of preschool children. In Chapter 5, we considered the importance and evolution of sociodramatic play, especially as it related to the work of Smilansky (Smilansky & Shefatya, 1990). This emphasis on children's sociodramatic play drops substantially in the school-age years. It is not necessarily that children's interest in sociodramatic play has declined but that opportunities for and approval of sociodramatic play are lost in school during the primary grades. Instead, older children can engage in this type of play only in the home environment (Dunn, 1998).

Creative dramatics becomes the accepted form of dramatic play in school in the primary years and can extend through all elementary school grades. Definitions of creative drama include "improvised drama [that] exists primarily for the enjoyment and benefit of the players" (Mellou, 1994, p. 126). This type of play is characterized as appropriate for children from the age of 5 or 6 and older, and the teacher has a role in guiding and facilitating dramatic enactment. A theatrical presentation is not the goal of creative dramatics; moreover, improvisation is part of the process. The dramatization can change and expand as the children use their imagination and play in pretending (J. E. Johnson, 1998).

Teachers also see creative dramatics as preparation for a dramatic performance. Although the children are engaged in inventing or developing the dramatic play, the teacher has more of a directive role in structuring the performance and guiding the children in perfecting the production (Schooley, 1995). In addition, the creative drama presentation may include making costumes and other props (Soefje, 1998).

It may be asked at what point does creative dramatics eliminate the child's dramatic play? Is there a need to understand a difference between creative dramatics and dramatic productions? Do children need to continue in sociodramatic play within the school setting in the school-age years? It is clear that the pattern is toward more structure and teacher direction and less emphasis on children's natural creations in dramatic play. Is there room for both in elementary classrooms? Are there benefits in sociodramatic play as described in the preschool years that continue to be important for school-age children? There are definite differences in untutored dramatic play and tutored creative drama (Mellou, 1994). Teachers need to understand the differences as well as the benefits of both types of dramatic play and creative drama.

## WHAT PARENTS, CAREGIVERS, AND TEACHERS CAN DO TO PROMOTE SOCIAL AND SOCIODRAMATIC PLAY

1. Adults can observe social behaviors and intervene to encourage positive social behaviors.
2. Adults can work with individual children who are rejected socially or use inappropriate bullying or aggressive play behaviors.
3. Adults can facilitate opportunities for rejected children to be included in peer play groups.
4. Adults can help popular children be accepting of children who have difficulty being accepted socially.
5. Adults can facilitate sociodramatic play in school-age children. Teachers can accomplish this goal by including theme-related dramatic play centers that include appropriate props related to the classroom curriculum.
6. Teachers can include opportunities for creative dramatics and dramatic productions within the classroom curriculum.

## Adult Roles in Social and Sociodramatic Play

It is during the elementary school years that social competence and acceptance in play groups become most apparent. Positive play behaviors include development of friendships and acceptance into peer groups. Negative play behaviors are obvious in children who become playground bullies and those who are isolated and lonely because they are rejected.

Parents and teachers can play significant roles in intervening in helping children use positive social skills in their group interactions and play. Efforts to reduce exclusion from play were described earlier; however, evidence indicates that teachers do not necessarily see it as their responsibility to intervene when bullies prevail or when children are isolated from social groups on the playground. Parents need to be aware whether their child is aggressive or a bully so they can work with the teacher in eliminating inappropriate behaviors. Likewise, parents and teachers need to work together in assisting children who are socially rejected and excluded from opportunities to play with their peers.

Adults also need to understand the role of sociodramatic play in school-age children. Parents can support and encourage sociodramatic play when children are playing together in the home environment. Teachers need to provide for sociodramatic play as well as creative dramatics in the curriculum.

## ◪ CHARACTERISTICS OF SCHOOL-AGE PLAY

### The Integrated Nature of Play

School-age children use all of their capabilities in their play. The types of play engaged in reflect their abilities and interests as well as how well developed they are in a particular domain. Children who are physically competent are more likely to enjoy participating in physical games and sports; students who are more adept socially are more likely to use their social skills in play. Although language, cognitive, motor, and social skills are all required for play, definite differences in ability and motivation have appeared by the time children enter school. Opportunity for participation also affects how skilled children become in sports and other activities such as ballet and music.

## Gender Differences in Play

Earlier in the chapter, gender differences in play were partially attributed to parental expectations, particularly in the case of physical play. These differences are also affected by social expectations; however, currently there is more of an emphasis on gender-equitable play with more equal opportunities provided for boys and girls. Gender differences persist, though, in school-age children in all types of play, as discussed in the following sections.

**Gender Differences in Physical Play**   In the school-age years, boys tend to play outdoors more than girls. Boys play in larger groups than girls and tend to play more in same-age groups (Vaughter, Sadh, & Vozzola, 1994). Both boys and girls tend to play at or near their homes. Boys spend more of their time in ball games; girls spend their play time in conversations, apparatus play, and games that require taking turns (Tracy, 1987).

In mixed-school settings, girls tend to stay closer to an adult than boys; however, when in an all-girl group, girls are willing to venture farther away from an adult (Maccoby, 1990). Both boys and girls prefer to play with same-gender peers rather than in mixed groups (Maccoby, 1998).

**Gender Differences in Social Play**   School-age children demonstrate gender differences in their social play. Boys engage in play that is less mature than girls' play. They are occupied more often in solitary-functional play and rough-and-tumble play. Girls, in contrast, spend more time in quiet activities such as peer conversations and parallel and constructive play (Rubin, Fein, & Vandenberg, 1983).

Gender differences can be noted by grade level. One study found that boys in fourth grade engage in more group play than girls. Boys reflect this in a high frequency of rough-and-tumble play. Contrasted with this boisterous play is the predominance of conversational activities on the part of fourth-grade girls (Moller, Hymel, & Rubin, 1992).

### Gender Differences in Electronic Game Play

Boys spend more time playing electronic games than girls do; moreover, the most popular games present stereotyped characterizations of men and women: Men are pictured as aggressors; women are portrayed as victims. It is possible that girls are not attracted to electronic games because women have secondary, negative roles in the games (Provenzo, 1991). A study of preferences showed that both boys and girls preferred games that were violent. However, boys preferred realistic violence and girls preferred fantasy violence (Buchman & Funk, 1996).

Boys seem to enjoy playing electronic games more than girls, which thus explains the more extensive time they engage in these games. Evidence indicates that some children are at risk from playing these games when preexisting adjustment problems are affected or new problems are precipitated (Funk & Buchman, 1996).

### Gender Differences in Rough-and-Tumble Play

We discuss gender differences in rough-and-tumble play more comprehensively in the next section; for now, we point out a few of them. First, boys engage in rough-and-tumble play more than girls. However, girls who have a brother, father, or other male family member who play with them are more likely to engage in rough-and-tumble play. For boys, rough-and-tumble play is part of growing up. They are more physically active, and their abilities are part of belonging to the male gender (Reed, 2005; Reed & Brown, 2005). Boys' physically active play includes issues of dominance and status. Girls prefer more sedentary play, and

they explore cooperative relationships. They are concerned with being nice and developing friendship groups. On the other hand, boys are interested in adventure, risk taking, and flouting authority (Jarvis, 2006; Maccoby, 1998; Pellegrini, 2005). Cultural differences affect this type of play. For example, according to Garvey (1990), boys engage in more rowdy play than girls among the Mixtecans of Mexico and Taira of Okinawa. However, among the Pilaga Indians, girls also participate in rough play (Manning, 1998). Finally, boys are most likely to select boys for rough-and-tumble play. To the contrary, when girls engage in this sort of play, they select both boys and girls (Pellegrini, 1998).

## Rough-and-Tumble Play

Rough-and-tumble play reaches a peak during the elementary school years. It accounts for about 5% of the play of preschool children but up to 17% of school-age play. It declines again in middle school.

Because aggression and aggressive play are important factors in school-age children's play, it would follow that the comparison of play fighting and aggression would be a part of the understanding of rough-and-tumble play among elementary school children. In discussing the topic in the preschool years in Chapter 5, we made a comparison between the behaviors in play fighting and real fighting. Also discussed was the reality that teachers do not recognize the differences between play fighting and real fighting. This type of comparison continues when discussing school-age children. Teachers in primary grades also reported difficulty in differentiating between the two in a primary school study (Schafer & Smith, 1996). Nevertheless, there are other significant differences in play fighting or rough-and-tumble play related to the play of rejected children and bullies and the play of children who are socially skilled and accepted by their peers.

Running, chasing, fleeing, and wrestling behaviors characterize rough-and-tumble play.

Rough-and-tumble play reaches a peak during the elementary school years.

When engaged in this play, children often remain together when the episode has ended and move on to other activities (Pellegrini, 1988). In rough-and-tumble play, children often exchange roles or discuss roles (Burns & Brainerd, 1979). In aggressive play, to the contrary, children do not play together after an incidence of fighting with aggression, nor do they exchange roles. The perpetrator of the aggression does not trade roles with the victim (Pellegrini, 1998). Moreover, in a review of studies of aggression, researchers found that boys were more aggressive than girls in 67% of the studies (Maccoby & Jacklin, 1974).

## Chase Games

Rough-and-tumble play includes chasing; however, in Chapter 4, we discussed chasing as a type of play in itself. Chase games involve physical skill, strategy, and tagging and hiding (Clarke, 1999). Although chase games begin in the preschool years, they extend into the school-age years.

> The last stage of chase games occurs from ages 7 to 11. Chasing occurs primarily within the context of organized games. There are predetermined rules for the game and social consequences for those who break a rule. Thus chase games complement other cognitive and social categories of development in each stage and complement advances in development in other domains.

School-age children play chase games differently than preschool children. One theme of chase games is the threat of kissing, particularly in the primary grades. This type of cross-gender chasing is accepted in primary-grade children but stops in intermediate-grade children, especially if wrestling or other types of rough-and-tumble play is involved (Thorne, 1995). Other chase games involve giving and getting cooties or some other type of contamination. Called "pollution games," chase games in this context might involve rejected children or children who are considered unequal, such as children of different ethnic groups. This included girls by the boys in a playground study who considered girls to be inferior (Thorne, 1995).

## War Toys

Play with war toys has been associated with aggression by teachers. Although preschool children like to engage in fantasy play with guns and other weapons, this type of play persists into elementary schools, where it is generally banned. Play with war toys is primarily of interest to boys, who use guns and weapons to carry out fantasy play. It seems that boys label the play as play fighting or part of rough-and-tumble play, whereas adults characterize it as violent play causing aggression. Prohibition of war toys themselves does not discourage war play. Children use other substitutes for weapons (Wegener-Spohring, 1989).

It is not clear that the war toys themselves cause aggressive play. In a study of research on the relationship between war toys and aggressive play, Sutton-Smith (1988) found unclear results. Play fighting supported with war toys is generally sociodramatic play in which children carry out movie or television roles. Thus the toys may not be the only or most significant influence toward aggression.

War toys can be used for many purposes. One possibility is when they are transformed in pretend play into something else (Bagley & Chaille, 1996). Goldstein (1995) cites 25 possible reasons that children play with war toys from his study of the literature on this topic. Although some of the reasons are directly or indirectly related to aggression and violence, some purposes can lead to nonviolent play.

Adult views of war toy play are at odds with the perception of the players and researchers. Adults view play fighting in this context as violent and aggressive (Conner, 1989; Kuykendall, 1996). Furthermore, although research does not support the premise that war toys cause aggressive play (Conner, 1989), parents and teachers believe that war-toy play will lead to more serious forms of aggression and should be eliminated from the home and school environment (Kuykendall, 1996 Meyerhoff, 2008; Strom & Strom, 2005).

Parents may also believe the play with guns will lead to criminal activity later in life. Meyerhoff (2008) points out the both criminals and law-abiding citizens probably played with toy guns as children. He suggests that parents substitute action figures and toys that have rescue themes to replace war-toy play.

## Creativity and Play

When young children enter the school years, their capabilities to be creative are full of possibility. They can use painting, photography, musical performance, drama composition and performance, computer programming, and dance as some of the venues for creativity and expression. School-age children are eager inventors and artists who demonstrate confidence and competence in their creative endeavors.

However, the same negative attitudes toward time for play that limit recess in elementary grades are also reflected in lack of time for creative activities (Manning, 1998). Unfortunately, the push for increased academic achievement has taken a toll on opportunities for creativity. Moreover, the school environment is accused of suppressing creativity in the elementary grades through a lack of understanding of the nature of creativity or a focus on convergent rather than divergent thinking. The enthusiasm for being creators in the preschool years is replaced with being passive spectators. Elementary school children often become more cautious and less innovative (Isenberg & Jalongo, 2006). Some of the characteristics of schools that discourage creativity are strict time limits for activities, an emphasis on memorization and convergent tasks, and an overemphasis on valuing conformity and following directions. Schools that nurture creativity, to the contrary, have the following practices (Isenberg & Jalongo, 2006, p. 26):

1. Positive emotional climate
2. Process valued as well as product
3. Flexible schedules
4. Support for creative thought and artistic expression
5. Mechanisms for peer support
6. Minimized competition and external rewards
7. Adults who value children's creative thought and artistic expression

Contemporary school cultures commonly mitigate against creativity; nevertheless, many teachers naturally incorporate creativity into classroom activities without impinging on the stress on academic achievement. Teachers who understand creativity know the difference between predesigned art activities and opportunities for individual expression. They understand the difference between teacher-designed games and student efforts to create games to play with their peers. They understand the difference between developing ideas for classroom projects and nurturing students' ability to plan and implement curriculum activities. Creativity will emerge in the classroom where innovative thinking is valued and encouraged. If the classroom is truly supportive of student ideas and efforts to use creative expression, students will use their individual interests and talents to participate in classroom activities.

## ADULT ROLES IN SCHOOL-AGE PLAY

Adults have different roles in children's play when they enter the elementary school. Partly because of a different perspective on the value of play and partly because the classroom environment is more teacher directed than in the preschool years, adult roles are more directed in play. Teachers who use play for learning experiences in the classroom engage children in games, perhaps in designing games. Children might participate in creative dramatics, but this, too, is more likely to have quite a bit of teacher direction. Opportunities to facilitate child-initiated play and to encourage exploratory play are not as common as in the preschool classroom.

Physical education teachers also engage in adult-directed activities with students. They teach games and sports during structured class times. Students have opportunities to engage in play, but they have been planned by the teacher and are supervised by the teacher.

If there is a time for free play outdoors, teachers play a supervisory role for the most part. They do not engage in play activities with the children, and sometimes offer little supervision, as noted in the section on rough-and-tumble play.

Parents also teach their children how to play sports. Fathers, particularly, work with their sons and daughters to learn baseball, basketball, soccer, and other sports. Fathers, and occasionally mothers, serve as coaches for Little League teams or other recreational clubs such as Boy Scouts, Girl Scouts, and church youth groups.

A major role of parents is to provide transportation to organized play activities. It might be of an informal nature, as when parents take their

child to play with a friend at the friend's house. More time is spent taking children to practice for a team. Parents with several children spend many hours after school and on Saturdays transporting their children to practice and games. A parallel role in these activities is to attend the games and support the child's team.

Parents also engage in quieter forms of play in the home as the family plays card and board games. This practice has declined with the advent of video games and computer games, which are more likely to be solitary forms of play. Some parents do participate in video games that have more than one player, however.

Overall, parents spend less time in participating in children's play in the school-age years. This is offset by the increased amount of time spent in the car transporting children to organized sports lessons and activities.

### Issues in School-Age Play

In various sections of this chapter, we discussed the benefits of play for different domains of development in the school-age years. Although much of the information is about outdoor play, play in the classroom is equally important. Yet reality tells us that there is a conflict between advocates of play and supporters of the emphasis on academics. In the face of declining opportunities for outdoor play at school as well as disappearing playgrounds, less has been said about the elimination of play in the classroom. The stress of preparing children for achievement tests and the evolving importance of rating schools according to levels of student achievement scores has had a profound influence on classroom strategies. Now an emerging trend tying teacher pay to student performance has increased the level of teacher concern and anxiety.

Although there is a strong emphasis on academics and mastery of skills rather than integration of play into the indoor learning environment, there are also voices speaking out to develop advocacy for play (Holmes, 2005; Stegelin, 2005). In the meantime, teachers can use certain strategies to integrate play behaviors into classroom curriculum. Mathematics, literacy, and science are two areas where skills can be taught through concrete materials, games, and natural artifacts (see Figure 6.1). Teachers and children can make games that are tied to specific skills that appear on standardized tests. Mental play, word play, and problem-solving games promote thinking within curriculum and instruction. Teachers can justify playlike behaviors in the classroom in the effort to help all children learn.

**FIGURE 6.1**    Toys for Primary School Ages 6, 7, and 8 Years

| Active Play | Manipulative Play | Make-Believe Play |
|---|---|---|
| **Ride-On Toys**<br>two-wheeled bike (sized to child)<br>push scooters<br>battery-powered ride-ons | **Construction Toys**<br>large sets of blocks or bricks (80–100 pieces)<br>construction sets (wood, plastic, metal)<br>complex, can manipulate tiny nuts and screws<br>sets with motorized parts<br>complex gear systems<br>can copy or build models following instructions-prefer sets that have realistic models | **Dolls**<br>lots of accessories, clothes, and special equipment<br>big bay dolls or dolls of own age, fashion dolls,<br>teenage dolls, collector dolls, paper dolls, fantasy<br>character dolls/action figures, doll house dolls |
| **Outdoor and Gym Equipment**<br>complex gym sets with rings, bars, swings, ropes, rope ladders slides<br>complex climbing structures<br>jump ropes | | **Stuffed Toys**<br>small, collectible toys<br>large, floppy stuffed toys<br>very realistic toys<br>replicas of famous animals<br>unusual stuffed toys |
| **Sports Equipment**<br>regular baseball bat and ball<br>basketball (junior size)<br>soccer<br>regular flying disks<br>adult-sized football<br>roller and ice skates<br>ski equipment<br>hockey equipment<br>badminton equipment<br>ping pong<br>office,<br>horseshoes<br>croquet<br>sleds<br>toboggans | **Puzzles**<br>jigsaws (50–100 pieces)<br>three-dimensional puzzles<br>map puzzles<br>more complex tangrams<br><br>**Pattern Making Toys**<br>design/pattern toys various types of materials to produce products<br>• wood<br>• plastic<br>• paper<br>• cardboard<br>• beads<br>• ceramic tiles<br>• cloth<br>• block printing<br>• design kits<br><br>**Manipulative Toys**<br>complex lock boxes<br>balance scales<br>small number rods and blocks<br>math models—illustrating fractions and arithmetic, etc.<br>Mechanical models-levers, pulleys, Pendulums, etc. | **Puppets**<br>puppet theater with curtains and scenery<br>soft hand puppets, rod puppets, puppets with arms,<br>jointed puppets<br><br>**Role-Play Materials**<br>wall and hand mirrors<br>realistic accessories for role play that really work<br>adult role dress-ups and elaborate make-up<br>magic and disguise kits<br>props for dramatic play (store, school, library,<br>robots, space, etc.<br>cooking and sewing equipment that really works<br><br>**Play Scenes**<br>doll houses (number of rooms, stories, special furniture and dolls<br>models with more grown-up themes (space, military-toy soldiers |

| Active Play | Manipulative Play | Make-Believe Play |
|---|---|---|
| | **Dressing, Lacing, and Stringing Toys**<br>stringing beads of any size, simple sewing, weaving, braiding making simple clothes for doll jewelry kits, spool knitting, sewing kits, handloom, braiding materials | **Transportation Toys**<br>little vehicles, collectible vehicles large-scale realistic trucks, planes, with working parts elaborate wood or metal train sets simple remote control vehicles electric racing cars |

| Creative Play | Learning Play |
|---|---|

**Creative Play**

### Musical Instruments

rhythm instruments
learning to play real instruments
and reading music
formal music lessons
formal dancing lessons
acrobatics

### Arts and Crafts Materials

crayons, paint markers, pencils,
pastels, and art chalks
variety of papers
sletch pads
construction paper and cardboards
all glues
regular scissors
clay-oil based and self-hardening
plaster of paris
stencils
papier mache
looms (Heddle and looper)
knitting spool
leatherwork kits
jewelry-making kits
bead/braiding kits
sewing kits with needles
mosaic tile kits
woodworking tools
beginning photography-real camera
model airplane, other kits

### Audio Visual Equipment

record or tape player to run by
self radio
blank tapes to make own recordings
more complex stories and books on
records or tape

**Learning Play**

### Games

simple strategy and rule games such as
dominoes, marbles, race games, card games,
strategy games, bingo, arithmetic games, etc.

### Specific Skill Development Toys

conceptual models-human body, physical
world, stars, space, moon
science kits, chemistry set, science models,
weather kit
calculator
clocks and watches
balance and other scales
protractor
microscope
telescope/binoculars
real typewriter or computer
more complex printing sets
more complex video and computer games
electronic/computer teaching games
- arithmetic
- drawing/graphics
- story writing
- word processing
- simple programming concepts
- music writing

### Books

developing individual interests
common interests
- childhood classics
- myths and legends
- biographies
- poetry
- fairy tales
- dictionaries
- books about children, animals, nature, space, planes, etc.

*Source*: Adapted from *Which Toy for Which Child: A Consumer's Guide for Selecting Suitable Toys Ages Six Through Twelve, Pub. No. 286*, Washington, DC, U.S. Consumer Product Safety Commission.

## TOYS AND MATERIALS FOR SCHOOL-AGE PLAY

The nature of toys and materials shifts in the elementary grades to complement children's abilities and interests in play. The Consumer Product Safety Commission (n.d.) has outlined play materials that are appropriate for school-age children. Although they are described as appropriate for primary-grade children, most are also appropriate for older children in elementary grades. Table 6.1 shows the variety of materials that can be used.

**TABLE 6.1** Toys and Materials for School-Age Children

| Overview of Play Materials for Primary-School Children—6 through 8 Years | |
|---|---|
| **Social and Fantasy Play Materials** | **Exploration and Mastery Play Materials** |
| **Mirrors**<br>Same as for adult use<br><br>**Dolls**<br>Washable, rubber/vinyl baby dolls (with culturally relevant features and skin tones) (for younger children—age 6)<br>Accessories (culturally relevant) for caretaking—feeding, diapering, and sleeping (for younger children—age 6)<br>Smaller people figures for use with blocks or construction materials (for fantasy scenes and models)<br><br>**Role-play materials**<br>Materials for creating and practicing real-life activities—play money with correct denominations, book- and letter-creating materials<br><br>**Puppets**<br>Puppets that represent familiar and fantasy figures for acting out stories (children can create their own)<br>Simple puppet theater—children can construct own (children can create props and scenery)<br><br>**Stuffed toys/play animals**<br>Realistic rubber, wood, or vinyl animals to incorporate into scenes and models or that show characteristics of animals being studied (such as reptiles and dinosaurs)<br><br>**Play scenes**<br>Small people/animal figures and supporting materials with which to construct fantasy scenes or models related to curriculum themes<br><br>**Transportation toys**<br>Small, exact (metal) replicas preferred by children of this age range are not usually used in school settings, but more generic small models are useful<br>Construction or workbench materials for children to use to make models of forms of transportation | **Construction materials**<br>Large number of varied materials for detailed construction and for creating models (can use metal parts and tiny nuts and bolts)<br><br>**Puzzles**<br>Three-dimensional puzzles<br>Jigsaw puzzles (50 to 100 pieces)<br><br>**Pattern-making materials**<br>Mosaic tiles, geometric puzzles<br>Materials for creating permanent designs (art and craft materials)<br><br>**Dressing, lacing, stringing, materials**<br>Bead-stringing, braiding, weaving, spool-knitting, and sewing materials now used in arts and crafts<br><br>**Specific skill-development materials**<br>Printing materials, typewriters, materials for making books<br>Math manipulatives, fraction and geometrical materials<br>Measuring materials—balance scales, rulers, graded cups for liquids, etc.<br>Science materials—prism, magnifying materials, stethoscope<br>Natural materials to examine and classify<br>Plants and animals to study and care for<br>Computer programs for language arts, number, and concept development and for problem-solving activities<br><br>**Games**<br>Simple card and board games<br>Word games, reading and spelling games<br>Guessing games<br>Memory games (Concentration)<br>Number and counting games (dominoes, Parcheesi)<br>Beginning strategy games (checkers, Chinese checkers)<br><br>**Books**<br>Books at a variety of difficulty levels for children to read<br>Storybooks for reading aloud<br>Poetry, rhymes, humorous books, adventure books, myths<br>Books made by children |

| Music, Art, and Movement Play Materials | Gross-Motor Play Materials |
|---|---|
| **Art and craft materials**<br>Large variety of crayons, markers, colored pencils, art chalks, and pastels (many colors)<br>Paintbrushes of various sizes<br>A variety of paints, including watercolors<br>A variety of art papers for drawing, tracing, painting<br>Regular scissors<br>Pastes and glues (nontoxic)<br>Collage materials<br>Clay that hardens<br>Tools (including pottery wheel)<br>More complex printing equipment<br>Craft materials, such as simple looms, leather for sewing and braiding, papier-mâché, plaster of paris, small beads for jewelry making, etc.<br>Workbench with more tools and wood for projects (with careful supervision)<br><br>**Musical instruments**<br>Real instruments, such as recorders (sometimes used for group lessons in school settings)<br>A wider range of instruments for children to explore (borrowed or brought in by parents or special guests)<br><br>**Audiovisual materials**<br>Music for singing<br>Music for movement, including dancing (folk dancing by age 8)<br>Music, singing, rhymes, and stories for listening<br>Audiovisual materials that children can use independently | **Balls and sports equipment**<br>Youth- or standard-size balls and equipment for beginning team play (kickball, baseball, etc.)<br>Materials for target activities (to practice skills)<br><br>**Ride-on equipment**<br>(Children may be interested in riding bicycles, but this is no longer included as a school activity)<br><br>**Outdoor and gym equipment**<br>Complex climbing structures, such as those appropriate for age 5 (including ropes, ladders, hanging bars, rings) |

*Note:* Although the four categories provide a useful classification, play materials can typically be used in more than one way and could be listed under more than one of the categories.

*Source:* From *The Right Stuff for Children Birth to 8* (pp. 120–121) by M. B. Bronson, 1995, Washington, DC: National Association for the Education of Young Children. Reprinted with permission.

## SUMMARY

Play takes on different dimensions in the school-age child. Peer play becomes very important, as do games and sports. Advances in physical, cognitive, and social development combine to enable children to enjoy play activities with their peers.

Physical development enters a period when gross- and fine-motor abilities are refined and strengthened. Through practice, children are able to engage in many more activities; however, there are variations in the opportunities available to children to engage in physical activities. Poor nutrition, illness, and injuries can affect motor development, as can the lack of opportunities to participate in group sports and instruction in sports such as tennis and swimming.

Gender differences in physical development can be related to parental and societal expectations that are different for boys and girls. The interests of boys and girls are also a factor in their selection of activities.

School-age children have fewer opportunities for free play partly because schools are placing more emphasis on academic instruction and partly because fears persist that students will injure themselves on the school playground. Parents who are unavailable after school also might expect children to remain indoors until they return from work. Although there are many proponents of making free play available at school through recess periods, current trends are for less free play rather than more.

Children enter the concrete operational period in cognitive development, which enables them to use logical and organized thinking. These advances in cognition help explain children's interests in games and sports because they are able to participate in games with rules. Children can follow rules for a game as well as develop rules for their own games. Thus, games with rules become more popular and pretend play declines.

Developments in language and literacy also extend possibilities for participation in play. Children play with language as they tell jokes and engage in social rituals. They trade playful insults with their friends and use special language with peers in their social groups.

Social development also enters a significant period as children face challenges in becoming competent learners and members of social groups. They become aware of their abilities and weaknesses and are able to evaluate themselves in comparison with their peers. Self-concept and self-esteem are part of their social development. If they see themselves as successful in school and with their peers, they become success oriented. Unfortunately, many see themselves as failures or realize they are rejected in social and play situations.

Success in social development is reflected in success or rejection in social play. Although school personnel may attempt to help rejected children, many children find themselves in a lonely situation or victimized by others.

Aggression and bullying are common factors in children's play. Although teachers are aware of these aspects of school-age play, they might not see it as their responsibility to intervene. Fortunately, a few structured programs are available to help all children be included in play.

School-age play is characterized by an interest in sports and games and play with a group of peers. There are gender differences in play. Boys are most likely to engage in rough play and play outdoors, whereas girls are more likely to engage in conversations and engage in play that requires taking turns. Boys play electronic games more than girls, and both genders participate in chase games.

Adults have a more directive role in school-age play. Both in the classroom and on the playground, adults engage in directed play opportunities to the limitation or exclusion of child-initiated or free play. Physical education teachers conduct structured classes rather than encourage free play. Classroom teachers place less emphasis on exploration through play and more on classroom games and teacher-directed activities such as creative dramatics. Parents spend less time with their children in play activities, but they support their children's participation in sports and lessons for individual sports and games. Parents do teach their children games with rules and spend time transporting their children to organized activities.

## KEY TERMS

| | |
|---|---|
| Aggression | Moral development |
| Bilingual | Peer culture |
| Bullying | Perspective taking |
| Concrete operational stage | Positive self-esteem |
| Decenter | Reversibility |
| Industry versus inferiority | Selective attention |
| Learned helplessness | Seriation |
| Mnemonics | Spatial reasoning |

## STUDY QUESTIONS

1. Why is free play less of a priority for adults than to school-age children?
2. How does physical development facilitate more sophisticated forms of play in school-age children?
3. Why do some children gain more in motor skills than others? Describe several factors that can affect physical development.
4. Describe some reasons that outdoor play environments might be less available to elementary school children today.
5. Why do school-age children like to take risks in play? How can this interest be helpful for development, and how can it be dangerous?

6. Some people are proponents of recess; some are opposed to recess. Discuss both sides of the issue.

7. What roles should classroom teachers have in physical play? How can they advocate for children's development through play?

8. How does cognitive development in school-age children facilitate participation in games with rules? Describe cognitive characteristics that enable participation in games and sports.

9. How does information processing help explain cognitive development?

10. How does the ability to play games with rules evolve? Explain how cognitive advances help children play games more effectively.

11. How do code switching and other language differences become important in school-age children? Give examples of how children use more than one code in language.

12. Describe how language development advances socialization in school-age children.

13. How do teachers interpret their role in social play in the classroom? How is social play reflected in the elementary school curriculum?

14. How does social development determine social acceptance in school-age children? Describe some factors that affect acceptance or rejection into peer social groups.

15. How do self-concept and self-esteem help explain social development in school-age children?

16. Are peer relationships the most important element of school-age social development? Explain why or why not.

17. Cooperative play is seen as most important for social development, whereas our society emphasizes competition. How do these factors conflict in promoting children's play?

18. How does aggression characterize social play? Explain the differences between play fighting and aggression.

19. What should be the teacher's role regarding aggression and bullying? What can teachers do to reduce bullying?

20. Distinguish among sociodramatic play, creative dramatics, and dramatic productions. Are all essential for elementary school classrooms?

21. How do boys and girls play differently in the school-age years? Give examples.

22. How do accepted and rejected children engage in play fighting differently in elementary school? Why do rejected children engage in play fighting longer than their more popular peers?

23. How is school-age play in chase games different than preschool play? Describe how school-age children expand in how they participate in chase games.

24. Are war toys good or bad for children? Give arguments for both positions.

25. What role should parents have in organized sports? How can they determine how much their children should participate in sports?

## REFERENCES

Acredelo, C., Adams, A., & Schmid, J. (1984). On the understanding of the relationships between speed, duration, and distance. *Child Development, 55*, 2151–2159.

Bagley, D. M., & Chaille, C. (1996). Transforming play: An analysis of first-, third-, and fifth- graders' play. *Journal of Research in Childhood Education, 10*, 134–142.

Barta, J., & Schaelling, D. (1998). Games we play: Connecting mathematics and culture in the Classroom. *Teaching Children Mathematics, 4*, 388–393.

Baumeister, R (2001). Violent pride: Do people turn violent because of self-hate or self-love? *Scientific American, 284*, 96–101.

Belka, D. E. (1998). Strategies for teaching tag games. *Journal of Physical Education, 69*, 40–43.

Blatchford, P. (1996). We did more then: Changes in pupils' perceptions for breaktime (recess) From 7 to 16. *Journal of Research in Childhood Education, 11*, 14–24.

Bradley, D. H., & Pottle, P. R. (2001). Supporting emergent writers through on-the-spot conferencing and publishing. *Young Children, 56*, 20–27.

British Broadcasting Company. (2006, April 28). BBC World News, radio newscast.

Brooks, P. H., & Roberts, M. C. (1990). Social science and the prevention of children's injuries. *Social Policy Report of the Society for Research in Child Development, 4.*

Buchman, D. D., & Funk, J.B. (1996). Video and computer games in the 90s: Children's time commitment and games preference. *Children Today, 24*, 12–16.

Bullock, J. R. (2002). Bullying among children. *Young Children, 78*, 130–133.

Burns, S., & Brainerd, C. (1979). Effects of constructive and dramatic play on perspective taking in young children. *Developmental Psychology, 15*, 512–521.

Cairns, R. B. Cairns, B. D., Neckermann, H. J., Gets, S. D., & Gairepy, J. (1988). Social networks and aggressive behavior: Peer support or peer rejection? *Developmental Psychology, 24*, 815–82.

Castle, K. (1998). Children's rule knowledge in invented games. *Journal of Research in Childhood Education, 12*, 197–209.

Chang, P.-Y., & Yawkey, T. D. (1998). Symbolic play and literacy learning: Classroom materials and teacher's roles. *Reading Improvement 35*, 172–177.

Chomsky, C. (1969). *The acquisition of syntax in children from five to ten.* Cambridge, MA: MIT Press.

Chuoke, M., & Eyman, B. (1997). Play fair—and not just at recess. *Educational Leadership, 54*, 53–55.

Coakly, J. (1990). *Sport and society: Issues and controversy* (4th ed.). St. Louis: Mosby.

Cole, J., Cornell, D., & Sheras, P. (2006). Identification of school bullies by survey methods. *Professional School Counseling 9*, 305–313.

Conner, K. (1980). Aggression: Is it in the eye of the beholder? *Play and Culture, 2*, 213–217.

Coplan, R. J., & Rubin, K. H. (1988). Social play. In D.P. Fromberg and D. Bergen (Eds.), *Play from firth to twelve and beyond: contexts, perspectives, and meanings* (pp. 368–377). New York: Garland.

Copple, C., & Bredekamp, S. (Eds.). (2009). *Developmentally appropriate practice in early childhood programs serving children from birth through age 8* (3rd ed.). Washington, DC: NAEYC.

Cratty, B. J. (1986). *Perceptual and motor development in infants and children* (3rd ed.). Upper Saddle River, NJ: Prentice-Hall.

Damon, W. (1990). Self-concept, adolescent. In R. M. Lerner, A. C. Petersen, & J. Brooks-Gunn Eds.), *The encyclopedia of adolescence* (Vol. 2, pp. 87–91). New York: Garland.

Dargan, A., & Zeitlin, S. (1998). City play. In D.P. Fromberg and D. Bergen (Eds.), *Play from birth to twelve and beyond: Contexts, perspectives, and meanings* (pp. 219–224). New York: Garland.

Davidson, J. E. F. (1998). Language and play: Natural partners. In D. P. Fromberg & D. Bergen (Eds.), *Play from birth to twelve and beyond: Contexts, perspectives, and meanings* (pp. 174–184). New York: Garland.

DeVries, R. (1998). Games with rules. In D. P. Fromberg & D. Bergen (Eds.), *Play from birth to twelve and beyond: Contexts, perspectives, and meanings* (pp. 409–415). New York: Garland.

DeVries, R., & Fernie, D. (1990). Stages in children's play of tic tac toe. *Journal of Research in Childhood Education, 4*, 98–111.

DeVries, R., & Kohlberg, L. (1990). *Constructivist early education: Overview and comparison with with other programs.* Washington, DC: National Association for the Education of Young Children.

DeVries, R., & Zan, B. (1994). *Moral classrooms, moral children.* New York: Teachers College Press.

Diaz, R.M. (1985). Bilingual cognitive development: Addressing three gaps in current research. *Child Development, 56*, 1376–1388.

Dodge, K. A., Coie, J. D., Pettit, G. S., & Price, J. M. (1990). Peer Status and aggression in boys' Groups: Developmental and contextual analyses. *Child Development, 61*, 1289–1309.

Dunn, J. (1998). "This time I'll be the golden bird": A call for more child-structured dramatic Play. *Research in Drama Education, 3*, 55–66.

Dweck, C. S., & Leggett, E. L. (1988). A social-cognitive approach to motivation and personality. *Psychological Review, 95*, 256–273.

Eccles, J. S., & Harold, R. D. (1991). Gender differences to sport involvement: Applying the Eccles' expectancy-value model. *Journal of Applied Sport Psychology, 3*, 7–35.

Edelman, M. W. (1994, Autumn). Cease fire! Stopping the war against children. *Harvard Medical Bulletin, 68*, 18–23.

Elkind, D. (2006). The values of outdoor play. *Exchange, 171*, 6–11.

Flavell, J. H., Miller, P. H., & Miller, S.A. (1993). *Cognitive development.* (3rd ed.). Upper Saddle River, NJ: Prentice Hall.

Fromberg, D. P. (1998). Play issues in early childhood education. In C. Seefeldt (Ed.), *Continuing issues in early childhood education* (3rd ed., pp. 190–212). Upper Saddle River, NJ: Merrill/Prentice Hall.

Froschl, M., & Sprung, B. (1999). On purpose: Addressing teaching and bullying in early childhood. *Young Children, 54*, 70–72.

Fu, V. (2000). The primary classroom. Retrieved August 23, 2010 from *http://www.eduplace.com/science/frofdev/articles/fu/html*

Funk, J. B., & Buchman, D. D. (1996). Children's perceptions of gender differences in social approval for playing electronic games. *Sex Roles, 35*, 219–231.

Gardner, H. (1993). *Multiple intelligences: The theory in practice.* New York: Basic.

Garvey, C. (1990). *Play.* Cambridge, MA: Oxford University Press.

Ginsberg, K. R. (2007). The importance of play in promoting healthy child development and maintaining strong parent-child bonds. Retrieved August 11, from *www.wrif.org/goto/sports4kids*

Glickman, C. D. (1984). Play in public school settings: A philosophical question. In T. D. Yawkey & A. D. Pellegrini (Eds.), *Child's Play: Developmental and applied* (pp 255–271). Hillsdale, NJ: Erlbaum.

Goldstein, J. (1995). Aggressive toy play. In A. D. Pellegrini (Ed.), *The future of play therapy* (pp. 127–147). Albany: State University of New York Press.

Harris, J. (2010, Spring). The real magic work: Recess. *Focus on Elementary, 22*, 1, 2–7.

Hewitt, P. (1997). Games in instruction that lead to environmentally responsible behavior. *Journal of Environmental Education, 28*, 35–37.

Hilliard, D. C. (1998). Sport as play (and work). In D. P. Fromberg & D. Bergen, (Eds.), *Play from birth to* twelve and beyond: Contexts, perspectives, and meanings (pp. 416–423). New York: Garland.

Hopper, T. F. (1996, October). Play is what we desire in physical education. *A phenomenological analysis.* (EDRS ED398805).

Jambor, T. (1998). Challenge and risk-taking in play: In D.P. Fromberg & D. Bergen (Eds.), *Play from birth to twelve and beyond: Contexts, perspectives, and meanings.* (pp. 319– 323). New York: Garland.

Jambor, T. (1999). Recess and social development. Retrieved April 27, 2006 from *www.Earlychildhood.com/articles/ index.*

Jarrett, O. S. (1997). Science and math through role-play centers in the elementary school classroom. *Science Activities, 34,* 13–19.

Jarvis, P. (2006). "Rough and tumble play: Lessons in life. *Evolutionary Psychology, 4,* 330–346.

Kamii, C. (2000). *First graders dividing 62 by 5: A teacher uses Piaget's theory.* New York: Teachers College Press.

Kamii, C. (2003). *Young children reinvent arithmetic* (2nd ed.). New York: Teachers College Press.

Kami, C., & DeVries, R. (1980). *Group games in early education: Implications of Piaget's theory.* Washington, DC: National Association for the Education of Young Children.

Lawrence, G., & Adams, F. (2006). For every bully there is a victim. *American Secondary Education, 35,* 66–71.

Lickona, T. (2000). Sticks and stones may break my bones AND names will hurt me. Thirteen ways to prevent peer cruelty. *Our Children, 26,* 12–14.

Lin, S.-H., & Reifel, S. (1999). Context and meanings in Taiwanese kindergarten play. In S. Reifel (Ed.), *Play and culture studies* (Vol. 2, pp. 151–176).

Lutz, P. (1983). The stepfamily: An adolescent perspective. *Family relations, 32,* 367–375.

Maccoby, E. E. (1990). Gender and relationships: A developmental account. *American Psychologist, 45,* 513–520.

Maccoby, E. E. (1998). Gender as a social category. *Developmental Psychology, 24,* 755–765.

Maccoby, E. E., & Jacklin, C. N. (1974). *The psychology of sex differences.* Stanford, CA: Stanford University Press.

Manning, M. L. (1993). *Developmentally appropriate middle level schools.* Olney, MD: Association for Childhood Education International.

Manning, M. L. (1998). *Play development from ages eight to twelve and beyond: Contexts, Perspectives, and meanings.* (pp. 154–162). New York: Garland.

McNamee, A., & Mercurio, M. (2008). School-wide intervention in the childhood bullying triangle. *Childhood Education, 84,* 370–378.

Mellou, E. (1994). Tutored-untutored dramatic play: Similarities and differences. *Early Childhood Development and Care, 100,* 119–130.

Meyerhoff, M. K. (2008, September) Making peace with war toys. Pediatrics for Parents. Retrieved August, 17, 2010

from http://findarticles.com/p/articles/mi_9_24ai_ N30952165/

Miller, P. H. (1993). *Theories of developmental psychology* (3rd ed.). New York: Freeman. Moller, L. C., Hymel, S., & Rubin, K. H. (1992). Sex typing in play and popularity in middle- Childhood. *Sex Roles, 26,* 331–353.

Moravcik, M. E. (2005, October 23). What parents and kids need to know about bullies. *The Arizona Republic,* p. B3.

Morrow, L. M., & Rand, M. K. (1991a). Preparing the classroom environment to promote Literacy through play. In J. Christie (Ed.), *Play and early literacy development* (pp. 141–165). Albany: State University of New York Press.

Morrow, L. M., & Rand, M. K.(1991b). Promoting literacy through play through physical design changes. *Reading Teacher, 44,* 396–402.

Newman, J. Brody, P. J., & Beauchamp, H. M. (1996). Teacher's attitudes and policies regarding Play in elementary schools. *Psychology in the Schools 33,* 61–69.

O'Brien, L. M. (2003). The reward and restrictions of recess: Reflections on being a playground Volunteer. *Childhood Education, 79,* 161–168.

Ollendick, T. H., Weist, M. D., Borden, M. C., & Greene, R. W. (1992). Sociometric staus and academic, behavioral and psychological adjustment: A five-year longitudinal study. *Journal of Counseling and Clinical Psychology, 60,* 80–87.

Olweus, D. (1993a). Bullies on the playground: The role of victimization. In C. Hart (Ed.), *Children on playgrounds* (pp. 85–128). Albany: State University of New York Press.

Olweus, D. (1993b). *Bullying at school: What we know and what we can do.* Oxford, England: Blackwell.

Olweus, D.(1994). Annotation: Bullying at school: Basic facts and effects of a school-based Intervention program. *Journal of Child Psychology and Psychiatry, 35,* 1171–1190.

Owens, K. D., & Sanders, R. L. (1998). Severe weather game. *Science Activities, 35,* 9–12.

Parten, M. (1932). Social participation among preschool children. *Journal of Abnormal and Social Psychology, 28,* 243–262.

Parten, M. (1933). Social play among preschool children. *Journal of Abnormal & Social Psychology, 28,* 136–147.

Patton, M. M., & Mercer, J. (1996). "Hey! Where's the toys?" Play and literacy in first grade. *Childhood Education, 73,* 10–13.

Pellegrini, A. D. (1988). Elementary school children's rough-and-tumble play and social Competence. *Developmental Psychology, 24,* 802–806.

Pellegrini, A. D. (1998). Rough-and-tumble play from childhood through adolescence. In D. P. Fromberg & D. Bergen (Eds.), *Play from birth to twelve and beyond: Contexts, perspectives, and meanings* (pp. 401–408). New York: Garland.

Pellegrini, A. D. (2005). *Recess: Its role in education and development.* Mahwah, NJ: Erlbaum.

Pellegrini, A. D., & Galda, L. (1990). Ten years after: A reexamination of symbolic play and Literacy research. *Reading Research Quarterly, 28*, 162–177.

Pellegrini, A. D., & Smith, P. K. (1993). School recess: Implications for education and Development. *Review of Educational Research, 63*, 51–67.

Perry, D. G., Williard, J. D., & Perry, L. C. (1990). Peers' perceptions of the consequences that victimized children provide aggressors. *Child Development, 61*, 1310–1325.

Piaget, J. (1965). *The moral judgment of the child.* New York: Free Press (Original work published 1932).

Pickett, L. (1998). Literacy learning during block play. *Journal of Research in Children's Education, 12*, 225–230.

Piotroski, D., & Hoot, J. (2008). Bullying and violence in schools. What teachers should know and do. *Childhood Education, 84*, 357–363.

Provenzo, E. F. (1991). *Video kids: Making sense of Nintendo.* Cambridge, MA: Harvard University Press.

Quiocho, A. L., & Ulanoff, S. H. (2009). *Differentiated literacy instruction for English language Learners.* Boston: Allyn & Bacon an imprint of Pearson.

Reed, T. (2005). A qualitative approach to boys rough and tumble play: There is more than meets the eye. In F. McMahon, D. Lytle, & B. Sutton-Smith (Eds.), *Play as an interdisciplinary synthesis. Vol. 6. Play and culture studies* (pp. 53–72).

Reed, T., & Brown, M. (2005). Rough and tumble play: An integral part of growing up. In K.Burris & B. Boyd (Eds.), *Outdoor learning and play.* Olney, MD: Association of Childhood Educational International.

Riley, J. G., & Jones, R. B. (2010, Spring). Acknowledging learning through pla in the primary Grades. *Childhood Education, 86*, 146–149.

Rivkin, M. (1998). Children's outdoor play. In D. P. Fromberg & D. Bergen (Eds.), *Play from birth to twelve and beyond: Contexts, perspectives, and meanings* (pp. 225–231). New York: Garland.

Robert Wood Johnson Foundation (2007). *Why the undervalued playtime may be America's best intervention for healthy kids and healthy schools.* Retrieved August 11, 2010 from *www.rwif.org/goto/sports4kids*

Romaine, S. (1984). *The language of children and adolescents: the acquisition of Communication competence.* Oxford, UK: Blackwell.

Rosenberg, M. (1970). *Conceiving the self.* New York: Basic.

Rubin, K. H., Chen, X., McDougall, P., Bowker, A., & McKinnon, J. (1995). The Waterloo Longitudinal Project: Predicting, internalizing and externalizing problems in adolescence. *Development and Psychotherapy, 7*, 751–764.

Sapon-Shevin, M. Dobblelaere A., Corrigan, C., Goodman, K., & Mastin, M.(1998). Everyone here can play. *Educational Leadership, 56*, 42–45.

Scarpaci, R. T. (2006). Bullying: Effective strategies for its prevention. *Kappa Delta Pi Record, 42*, 170–174.

Schaefer, M., & Smith, P. K. (1996). Teachers' perceptions of play fighting and real fighting in primary school. *Educational Research, 38*, 173–181.

Schooley, M. (1995). Students in wonderland. *Teaching PreK-8, 25*, 43.

Scully, P., & Roberts, H. (2002). Phonics, expository writing, and reading aloud: Playful literacy In the primary grades. *Early Childhood Education Journal, 30*, 93–99.

Selman, R. L. (1976). Social-cognitive understanding: A guide to educational and clinical practice. In T. Lickona, (Ed.), *Moral development and behavior: Theory, research and social issues* (pp. 299–316). New York: Holt, Rinehart & Winston.

Shantz, D. W. (1986). Conflict, aggression, and peer status: An observational study. *Child Development, 57*, 1322–1332.

Smith, J. E. (1984). Non-accidental injury to children: A review of behavioral interventions. *Behavior Research and Therapy, 22*, 331–337.

Soefje, A. (1998). Way off Broadway. *Teaching PreK-8, 28*, 44–46.

Stegelin, D. A. (2005). Making the case for play policy: research-based reasons for supporting play-based environments. *Young Children, 60*, 76–85.

Stover, D. (2006). Treating cyberbullying as a school violence issue. *The Education Digest 72, 4*, 40–42.

Strom, R., & Strom, P. R. (2005). Teaching through play and respecting the motivation of preschoolers. In D. M. McInerney, & S. W. Van Etten (Eds.), *Sociocultural influences on motivation and learning.* Greenwich, CT: Information Age Publishing, Inc.

Sutton-Smith, B. (1988). War toys and childhood aggression. *Play and Culture, 1*, 2–5.

Taras, H. (2005). Physical activity and student performance at school. *Journal of School Health, 75*, 214–218.

Thomas, D. (1954). Waiting for cats. *A child's Christmas in Wales.* Norfolk, CT: New Directions.

Thomas, J. R. (1984). Children's motor skill development. In J. R. Thomas (Ed.), *Motor development during childhood and adolescence* (pp. 91–104). Minneapolis: Burgess.

Tracy, D. M. (1987). Toys, spatial ability, and science and mathematics achievement: Are they related? *Sex Roles, 17*, 115–138.

Unger, R., Kruger, L., & Christoffel, K. K. (1990). Childhood obesity: Medical and family correlates and age of onset, *Clinical Pediatrics, 29*, 368–372.

U.S. Department of Education. (2001). *Elementary and Secondary Education Part C— Homeless Education.* Washington, DC: Author.

U.S. Department of Health and Human Services, (2004). Citing "dangerous increase in deaths," HHS launches new strategies against overweight epidemic. Retrieved April 27, 2006 From *www.hhs.gov/news/press/2004pres*

Vaughter, R. M., Sadh, D., & Vozzola, E. (1994). Sex similarities and differences in types of play in games and sports. *Psychology of Women Quarterly, 18,* 86–103.

Viadero, D. (2006, May 24). Survey finds majority of elementary schools still offer recess time. *Education Week.* Retrieved June 5, 2006 from *www.edweek.org*

Vygotsky, L. S. (1977). Play and its role in the mental development of the child. In M. Cole (Ed), *Soviet developmental psychology* (pp. 76–99). White Plains, NY: Sharpe.

Waggoner, J. E., & Palermo, D. S. (1989). Betty is a bouncing bubble: Children's Comprehension of emotion-descriptive metaphors. *Developmental Psychology, 25,* 152–163.

Walker, C., Kragler, S., Martin, I., & Arnett, A. (2003). Facilitating the use of informational texts in a first-grade classroom. *Childhood Education, 79,* 152–159.

Wallach, E. (1992, April). What did we do wrong? *Parks and Recreation, 26,* 53–57, 83.

Wasserman, S. (2000). *Serious players in the primary classroom. Empowering children through active learning experiences.* New York: Teachers College Press.

Wegener-Spohring, G. (1989). War toys and aggressive games. *Play and Culture, 2,* 35–47.

Willner, A. H. (1991). Behavioral deficiencies of aggressive 8-9 year old boys. An observational study. *Aggressive Behavior, 17,* 135–154.

Wohlwend, K. E. (2004/2005). Chasing friendship. Acceptance, rejection, and recess play. *Childhood Education, 81,* 77–82.

Wortham, S. C. (2010). *Early childhood curriculum. Developmental bases for learning and teaching.* (5th ed.). Upper Saddle River, NJ: Pearson.

Youngerman, S. (1998). The power of cross-level partnerships. *Educational Leadership, 56,* 58–60.

Zeisel, S. H. (1986). Dietary influences on neurotransmission. *Advances in Pediatrics, 33,* 23–48.

Zygmunt-Filwalk, E., & Bilello, T. E. (2005). Parent's victory in reclaiming recess for their children. *Childhood Education,* 19–23.

# 7 Culture and Gender in Play

*We played robber now and then about a month. . . . We hadn't robbed nobody, hadn't killed any people, but only just pretended. We used to hop out of the woods and go charging down on hog-drivers and women in carts taking garden stuff to market, but we*

*never hived any of them. . . . and then he said he had got secret news by his spies that next day a whole parcel of Spanish merchants and rich A'Rabs was going to camp in Cave Hollow with two hundred elephants, and six hundred camels, . . . all loaded down with di'monds . . . It warn't anything but a Sunday-school picnic, and only a primer class at that. We busted it up, and chased the children up the hollow; but we never got anything but some doughnuts and jam . . .*

(Twain, 1884/2003, pp. 12–13)

Girls and boys all around the world play, some in ways that we recognize and others in ways that are not so familiar to us. When Mark Twain's Huckleberry Finn describes his pretend play with other boys, we can recognize the very boyish attack games that they played with innocent bystanders. Not so familiar to us are the play opponents that the boys imagine; we do not have the same point of reference that they had for "Spanish merchants and rich A'Rabs" who might be camping in their woods. The play is at once familiar and unfamiliar. We might also see the significance of the frisky boys taking on the Sunday-school picnic; we are getting a sense of how those players are challenging authority. But what does a "primer class" mean to us now? And would we ever expect to hear about such play associated with girls? Play exists worldwide as a human activity, but research has informed us only to varying degrees about what play is and what that play means to children in different parts of the world (or at different times in history). What we know about play is shaped by the differing research agendas of scholars, including anthropologists, ethnographers, developmentalists, and other cross-cultural social scientists. Those scholars, cumulatively, provide a fractured picture of play in children's lives. One reason for the fractures in our picture is a difference in research agendas; scholars do not share common definitions of play, interests in children, or conceptions of the play's role in human life.

Some researchers might be interested in how Huck's play reflects social structure; what are the boys rebelling against? Others might be interested in how children understand world politics; what made the "Spanish merchants and rich A'Rabs" appropriate foes for the boys' pretend? Others might be interested in knowing how boys of that era had so much time and freedom to play as they did. Play may appear as either a central or a marginal topic for scholars, allowing them to see more or less play in their investigations. Neither are scholars of one mind when they study culture or ethnicity. Scholars who study peoples from different parts of the world, from different language groups, or with unique customs and beliefs may have diverse understandings of what culture may mean. Play may or may not be central to their work.

Despite the lack of a concentrated effort to understand play in different cultures, we have amassed many findings about children's play around the world. These findings point to play as a common feature of children's lives; children everywhere play. Research also tells us that the conditions of children's play vary a great deal, depending on the values, beliefs, practices, institutions, and tools that surround them; culture does contribute to children's play. To understand more fully the play that we see and support in our culture, whether it be pretend games, jumping rope, or computer games, we would do well to understand children's play in other cultures. As our already diverse culture becomes increasingly multicultural, we will need the lenses of cross-cultural studies to understand the confluence of meanings about play that are forming in American play settings. (See Roopnarine, Johnson, & Hooper, 1994, for a collection of studies on children's play in various parts of the world; a number of those studies are reviewed in this chapter.)

Cultures vary in the degree to which children's play is supported or constrained. We have evidence that in different cultures, children are limited by safety in where and how they can play; girls may play less because they may have more chores; gender-appropriate play may be imposed; appropriate scripts for play may be imposed; cooperation, rather than competition, may be supported; community size may create play options; and lack of a "benign environment" may inhibit play. Other cultures may not share the things we take for granted when we play or think about play as we do. (Lancy, 2002)

As mentioned earlier, the social sciences are not of one voice when researchers study the diverse manifestations of human behavior, including play. Scholars have created concepts of culture, ethnicity, geography, race, linguistics, and custom to explain why people in one area act the same way or differently than people in another area. Many of these concepts were first articulated by E. B. Tyler (1871), who saw culture as including humans' habits or capabilities that are acquired through our social interactions, including customs, beliefs, morals, law, art, and knowledge; Tyler was an early student of games. More current views of culture vary from Tyler's, to include tools, practices, values, beliefs, and institutions. For this chapter, we do not appropriate a particular view or definition of culture. We assume there are unique features (like those listed earlier) associated with any self-identified group of people, and those features can be called play in different cultures (Edwards, 2000; Schwartzman, 1978; Whiting,

1980; Whiting & Edwards, 1988; Whiting & Whiting, 1975).

These features may be associated with play within a culture. For example, in a comparative study of Japanese and American preschool pretend play, boys pretended in the school playhouse. "Tetsu and other boys left home for work (as police officers), and Toshi stayed home to do household duties. While he waited alone, he cooked a meal. When the boys came home, they performed the Banshaku ritual (alcohol drinking ritual before supper) common among Japanese men, and Toshi served them a meal" (p. 37). The way the Banshaku ritual appears in Japanese preschool boys' pretend play (and not in the play of Japanese girls or in the play of children in any other culture) is something we can begin to understand only with knowledge of Japanese customs and gender roles. We will see in this chapter that tools (i.e., toys), customs (e.g., rituals), beliefs (about how play contributes to a culture), and institutions (informal or organized settings for play) all contribute to cultural variations in play, including gender differences (Suito & Reifel, 1993).

A unique contribution of cultural or anthropological research is its methodology, which emphasizes but is not limited to ethnography. **Ethnography** is the description of a group, based on intensive observation and interviews of people as they engage in their habitual activities. This method allows anthropologists to describe customs that are meaningful for participants. Students of culture look at what people ordinarily do, not at how they behave in laboratory or contrived situations. Such an approach allows people to express those patterns of behavior that give meaning to their lives over the course of their lives. The ethnographer's challenge is to describe those patterns, discern what they mean to participants, and then relate the patterns and meanings to larger conceptions of human development.

Finding play can be a challenge for researchers. Schwartzman (1978) offers the following account: "The *masansa* or children's villages have been infrequently described in the ethnographic literature for this area [Zaire]. Masansa are built during the dry season, when the weather is good and food is not in short supply and children have few economic duties to perform. Younger and older children participate in this activity, each with a role to play as they set about to re-create elaborately the life of the village" (p. 170). How is African *masansa* role play like or unlike Japanese Banshaku role play, as a pattern of role play, as a meaningful activity for the players, as a meaningful activity for their respective cultures, and as a contributor to children's socialization to their societies? Ethnography requires a detailed description and interpretation of play in its context; it is not enough for ethnographers to say that children in each of these settings are demonstrating a type of play that we all call role play. The methods of cultural study demand a rich, sometimes called "thick," narrative description and analysis that reflects actions and meanings in their context. Such description frequently requires extensive narrative presentation of play events.

In Chapter 1 on the history of play, we introduced the work of Johan Huizinga (1938/1950). In his argument that play forms culture and civilization, Huizinga drew on documented evidence of play practices from many sources and many cultures. Some of those sources are presented here. However, many of the pieces of evidence that he presented were fragmented observations, anecdotes taken from reports of practices from different cultures. Huizinga's work drew on anthropological and other forms of inquiry and related to issues of culture and civilization, but it was historical work, not ethnographic. As this chapter illustrates, Huizinga's historical argument touches on cultural issues related to play, but scholars of culture have attended to matters that go well beyond his work.

This chapter describes research on play and culture, including thinking about the relationship between children's play and gender. Traditional anthropological research on children and

play is reviewed, including contemporary work that points to the importance of migration, diversity, and play in multicultural contexts. Family and peer contributions to play are at the core of this discussion and lead to questions about how play can be best understood. The play literature on gender differences builds on the cultural literature, pointing to and detailing the differences in boys' and girls' play relationships, their preferences and activities, and the kinds of play texts they enact. Although this chapter may not explain the meaning of boys' and girls' play in all cultures, we hope it will direct you to questions you can ask about play that may not be culturally familiar to you.

##  THE ROOTS OF CULTURAL PLAY RESEARCH

Masses of existing research on culture, gender, and play have accumulated over decades. Two earlier publications provide thorough reviews of cultural research. Schwartzman (1978) extensively treats cross-cultural research that focuses on or addresses some aspect of play. Slaughter and Dombrowski (1989) update Schwartzman's review, raising critical questions about current trends in play research. Both of those publications are reviewed and made current in this chapter, followed by a presentation of cross-cultural and gender play research that has appeared more recently. We encourage you to read Schwartzman and Slaughter and Dombrowski for comprehensive, detailed presentations of the research that serves as background for what follows in this chapter.

### The Work of Helen Schwartzman

Helen Schwartzman was one of the first scholars to integrate research on children's play from an anthropological perspective. Her 1978 book, *Transformations: The Anthropology of Children's Play,* serves as a landmark for researchers on children's play. It provides an extensive review of research and thinking that shaped scholarship to that date. Schwartzman does a number of things in this book. First, she situates play in the context of culture. Second, she distinguishes between the study of play in general and the study of children's play in particular. Third, she explores the ideologies and metaphors that have shaped cultural perspectives on play. Fourth, she identifies predominant theoretical views that give researchers the questions they attempt to answer with their research. Finally, she presents an argument and data for considering children's play as a significant text that relates to its cultural context; play is a culturally meaningful activity that can be read (described and interpreted) by group members. Given the pivotal importance of *Transformations* for our understanding of connections between children's play and culture, we look at a number of Schwartzman's points and elaborate on them with more current material (Reifel, 2007).

From an anthropological perspective, with its concern for the customs, beliefs, institutions, and values of a culture, children's play can serve any number of purposes. Children's play, like adult recreation, may express a culture's values, or it may create the cohesive bonds that allow culture to maintain itself. Although considerable variation is evident in the amount and kind of play that children and adults display in different cultures, some consensus indicates that children's play differs from adult play in the sense that it provides children with some form of socialization into their cultures. Part of this socialization can be understood in terms of child development, but students of culture show us that efforts to develop children can be understood only in terms of the culture in which they are growing. Children's play serves to bind children to their societies in ways that are uniquely meaningful to each society.

How have anthropologists described this socialization process? Schwartzman identifies a number of metaphors that anthropologists have used in their interpretations of children's play. These metaphors typify children in their play activity as being primitive, copycat, personality trainee, monkey, or critic. Some of these metaphors (e.g., copycat, monkey) suggest an imitative view of play; play allows children to practice those things they see adults doing and they will be doing themselves when they grow up. Interpretations like these echo theories like Groos's (1901) on practice play (see Chapter 1). Other metaphors (e.g., personality trainee) suggest that children are acquiring a sense of how to act and who they are as actors in their culture, building on theories such as Freud's psychodynamics (see Chapter 2). All of the metaphors address some aspect of the nature–nurture debate, with its questions about how much of human behavior is biologically determined and how much is shaped by environment; much of the anthropological agenda has tended to favor environmental (i.e., cultural) explanations.

The bulk of *Transformations* is Schwartzman's impressive integration of the anthropological play literature. In a series of chapters, she shows how play can be further understood in terms of data on game diffusion, **play functions,** projecting personality, communication, and subjectively meaningful events. Her review of these topics leads her to raise questions about definitions of play, which she does in her final chapters. Some of these topics have only historical interest for us; others tell us a great deal about development. In either case, patterns of data show us the commonalities of play, its diversity, and a variety of ways we can make sense of play.

**Game Diffusion**    The notion of cultural diffusion is not as prevalent as it was a century, or even a half century, ago, although it continues to echo in the form of debates about the relative statuses and values of different cultures, diversity, and multiculturalism. If one begins with the assumption that some cultures are superior to others and that more advanced customs transfer from "superior" to "lesser" cultures, then it should be possible to follow the trail as

Western players are not as familiar with card games such as Hwatu or Hanafuda.

customs (e.g., games) from "civilized" cultures begin to appear in so-called primitive societies. Some anthropologists set out to demonstrate this spread, or diffusion, of higher culture to primitive groups by looking at the emergence of any number of (typically, but not always European) customs, including children's games, toys, songs, and rhymes, in (typically) underdeveloped countries. For example, Tyler (1879/ 1971) argued that the similarities between the Mexican *patolli* game and Hindu *pachisi* (both games are precursors of backgammon) could not be related to chance; the game, like all of the other high achievements of ancient Mexican cultures, must have migrated to Mexico from Asia. Other anthropologists, who opposed the notion of any culture being superior or lesser, set out to show that every culture had indigenous children's play customs that were every bit as sophisticated as the customs that were coming from other lands. For example, Roth (1902) catalogued hundreds of Australian aboriginal games, including more than 70 string games that reflected animal and human symbolism.

Today we tend to see questions such as these as representative of ethnocentric or racist thinking. Beyond these concerns, we still have from this group of studies a grand collection of observations of different forms of play from diverse cultures around the world. Some of the observations are fragmentary; others are systematic and extensive. We can see the universality of certain forms of play (e.g., chase games, ball games, imitative games), as well as how they appear within their cultures (e.g., among boys or girls, when chores are done, with or without adults). What we cannot see is those instances or forms of play that the ethnographers overlooked or missed as they attempted to answer their questions about diffusion. And, because those earlier researchers were working without the benefit of contemporary play theories, we are left with a stunningly wide range of play types (e.g., games of dexterity, games of pursuit, "little girl" game—summer) that may not make sense to us now.

The tradition of creating typologies of games and play, begun during the earliest years of diffusion studies, continues today.

Contemporary studies on games continue to organize analysis according to types, such as chucking and fetching, marbles, and skipping. Others emulate some of the diffusion methodology by looking at the game of hopscotch as it transforms as a gender-linked activity over time and geography (Opie & Opie, 1997; Van Rheenan, 2000).

**Play Functions** A second anthropological approach to the study of play, as described by Schwartzman, deals with questions of function. This approach is more familiar to child development students in that it assumes that play has a developmental influence on children. The ways children play are associated with socialization into their societies, including the acquisition of gender roles, values, and understandings about social institutions. Children during play may also begin to acquire a sense of power relations and acceptable roles in their society. Again, play patterns are documented by ethnographic description over time.

For example, Schwartzman uses Salter's (1974) study to illustrate how Australian aboriginal children's play prepares them for political, economic, "worldview" (i.e., spiritual), and "normative" customs in their culture. Salter describes how games like hide-and-seek and mud-ball fights prepare children for political relationships. Economic preparation comes through tree climbing and playing with miniature canoes, both of which are key to economic survival. Children acquire the group's worldview by means of playing string games and singing. Pretend families and doll play are a foundation for normative participation in the culture. Play is described as a functional set of activities that take the children from childhood and prepare them for what they will do later.

Much of the cultural research on the functions of play shares the developmental assumption, or rhetoric, about how play serves human development (Sutton-Smith, 1997). This cultural approach to children's play differs from noncultural views in a number of ways. First, it links particular descriptions of play to the culture in which they take place. Play activity is described in a manner that makes it unique to the setting in which it occurs. Related to this point is the assumption that the same play activity, seen in a different culture, might have a very different function. A behavioral pattern in one culture may not have the same meaning as the same behavior in another culture. (We return to this point in our summary comments on Schwartzman.)

Functional approaches to ethnographic children's play research continue to inform us about children and play. In a study of a Kpelle town in the African country of Liberia, play is central to children's daily life and socialization. Although children must participate in the work of the town, as an economic necessity, there are rich opportunities for play of many sorts. Make-believe role-play activities (called *nee'-pele* in that culture) allow children to acquire skills in farming, weaving, providing for the family, and harvesting palm nuts. Make-believe of this form is an opportunity to practice adult roles and for adults to teach children about those roles. As they get older, children will participate in games such as *sua-kpe'* and *kpasa* (hunting and fighting games for boys), hiding games (*loo-pele* for both girls and boys, including *sua-iseler,* a wild-animal game), drawing play (*pelin-pele* for both girls and boys), stone-tossing games, and many others. These games require that children learn how to play (rules, as described by Piaget [1965]), as well as "showing sense." Having sense is highly valued by the Kpelle, for whom a sensible response to their environment is necessary for survival. Children's play including songs, dance, stories, and other activities promotes the acquisition of values. Play, as observed and described by adult informants, prepares children functionally for roles, customs, beliefs, and values they will practice as adult Kpelle. (Lancy, 1996)

**Projecting Personality** Schwartzman gives credit to Sigmund Freud and his contributions to anthropological studies of children's play in her discussion of play as projecting. The unique function of play as a reflection of personality or character is demonstrated in a number of ways. Children's play is credited as the setting where nature and nurture create a socialized community member, where psychological imperatives meet each culture's socializing influences. Play reflects, or projects, those imperatives in ways that are unique for each culture.

A case in point is a study of six field sites around the world, consisting of communities in India, the Philippines, Okinawa, Kenya, Mexico, and the United States. Long-term, detailed descriptions of growing up in these communities create a model of personality development that revealed itself in each community in terms of child-rearing practices, the community's ecology, and resulting adult behavior, cultural products, and child behavior. Play, in the form of games, fantasy, and other forms of recreation, was seen as the outcome of this model, reflecting the influences of the other factors. Instead of functioning to define who the child is within a culture, play functions to express who the child is as an individual (Whiting & Child, 1953; Whiting & Whiting, 1975).

This projective approach to play studies continues with an ethnography of home play sessions with the 6- to 7-year-old daughter of a dual-career American family. The analysis deals with one girl's patterns of play (her imaginary play themes about self, good and evil, relationships, female power, intellect, parenting, and gender, as well as the stages she went through during the course of play). It also addresses her play relationship with the researcher (recognizing the child's needs, adult power, and how their relationship changes over time). The author shows how play is an expression of the child's ways of dealing with her experiences growing up in her family and society, as well as how play allows her to grow. The study offers evidence and insight into the unique opportunities of social play, as well as the complex challenges for adults as they try to enter child's play. (Kelly-Byrne, 1989)

**Communication** The issue of communication as part of play is of particular interest to Schwartzman because it served as a framework for her own empirical study of preschoolers' play. A necessary and unique feature of pretend play is the communication that must occur for it to happen. As Bateson (1955/2000) argues, play is a "framed" activity whereby we begin to act "as if" something else were real. When we play space monsters, we are not really space monsters, but we act and communicate as if we were. Bateson calls attention to the layers of meaning in actions and to the communications we must use to make those layers apparent to playmates. Part of that communication is about the frame (when we stop being children and begin being space monsters, and when we return), which takes the form of signals, indicating "This is play." We are supposed to know the actions that follow are not intended to be interpreted as real. The communications of pretend play are seen as an important developmental foundation for later social and cognitive functioning. We need these decontextualizing experiences (taking actions out of a real context and putting them into play) so we can better take roles, think about experience while not in that experience (i.e., speculate, theorize), and correctly interpret others' signals (e.g., do words and actions signal romance or something else?). Culture operates with webs of social agreement about shared experience, shared beliefs, and our abilities to communicate about them (see Chapter 2).

Schwartzman (1978) describes in a range of studies the complexity of communications during play and the meanings that communications can signal . She recounts Geertz's classic 1972 study of cockfighting in Bali, where the very real interpersonal hostilities of the Balinese are shown in the violent contest of their fighting birds; the play frame (it is only a fighting game) sets the players apart from reality, where they are not allowed to express their antipathies, into a play setting where their emotions can be given expression. She also details the child play communication strategies identified by Garvey (1977), as described in Chapter 2.

The communicative aspects of play have been explored in more current studies in English-speaking and other countries. One study documents a range of communications and framed meanings in Taiwanese kindergarten play. In their analysis of the influences of physical and social context on children's use of play materials, space, time, incorporation of experiences from outside school into play, classroom culture, social relations, and social custom, these authors identify culturally characteristic pretense, such as making sugar cane out of clay and peeling it before pretending to sell it; negation of pretense after the teacher signaled the end of play time (". . . then we got married and the end"; p. 163); and explicit instructions to a playmate about how to accept an object respectfully (within this culture) while pretending to play doctor's office ("Use both hands to receive it"; p. 172). The frames about which children communicate when they play reflect unique cultural meanings. Unique meanings in cultural context appear-irrespective of school program structure (Chang & Reifel, 2003; Trawick-Smith, 2010; Lin & Reifel, 1999).

**Subjectively Meaningful Events**    Schwartzman also acknowledges that children's play has an element of cognitive meaning for players, which she calls "minding play." Children think when they play, and they learn. Anthropologists and others have studied constructing meaning in a number of ways, including explorations of the thinking of players and their use of language in play. Schwartzman reviews the work of Piaget, Vygotsky, and Bruner to demonstrate the ways that play engages the mind (see Chapter 2). She also looks at research

on language use to see how children's play is the setting for the development of a narrative. Kirshenblatt-Gimlett's (1976) review of *Speech Play* provides ample evidence for ways that children's minds are engaged by playing with sounds, rhymes, other sound patterns, and ultimately, jokes. From the ethnographer's point of view, these examples of children's speech play are important samplings of what children do in the everyday context of their lives. Relevant examples are humor, secret languages, verbal contests and games. Humor studies demonstrate the diverse use of "thoughtful" language around the world (Abrahams, 1962; Brewster, 1939; Dundes, Leach & Ozkok, 1970; Goldstein, 1971; Gossen, 1976; Opie & Opie, 1959; Wolfenstein, 1954).

More recent studies have looked at the stories children tell when they are playing. Building on Paley's (1981) approach to documenting children's classroom play narratives, researchers analyzed 582 stories told by 28 preschool children over the course of a school year. Their analysis of these spontaneously generated stories revealed that girls' stories reflected an orderly, domestic world of family relationships, whereas boys' stories were active, violent, and fragmented. Girls' narratives were far more likely to center on idealized characters (princesses and princes); boys' narratives more often created stories about monsters and bad guys. These stories "provided vivid evidence of the social significance of gender distinctions in the lives of young children" (Nicolopoulou, Scales, & Weintraub, 1994; Scales and Cook-Gumperz, 1993, p. 182).

**Definitions of Play**    In her final chapters, Schwartzman (1978) analyzes the nonethnographic play literature to understand how other social scientists make use of children's play. She reviews classic ecological, ethological, and experimental studies to see how play is treated in these studies. Although the ecological and ethological studies conform to the naturalistic principles of ethnography, they fail to relate observed behaviors to any cultural meaning system. Experimental studies seldom pretend to reflect naturalistic circumstances that the participants might experience in ordinary play. These differing approaches lead to lack of definition about what play is and what it means to participants in their cultures (Barker & Wright, 1966; Blurton Jones, 1972; Hutt, 1970).

As a solution to this problem, Schwartzman suggests that play cannot be defined simply in terms of the environments where it takes place (after all, those environments vary a great deal from culture to culture) or of specific behaviors (which may mean something entirely different in another culture). The ethnographic point of view requires that play be seen as a "text in context," a described set of naturally occurring actions that are connected with the larger society in which they occur. We cannot read the text of play without knowing about the society in which it takes place, in general and in particular. Schwartzman (1986) later modified this view, by arguing that the play needed to be seen as "text in context, and context in text." It is not enough to relate what we see of play to the larger culture, but we must also see how that culture and the players' individual experiences bring culture to their play text. Play does not only reflect experience; play also shapes experience.

In *Transformations,* Schwartzman addresses any number of topics that are of interest to students of child development, including the cognitive, social, and emotional functions of play for development. She also deals with subjects that are of less interest to traditional developmentalists, such as game diffusion that looks at how games transfer from one region to another, not at the players themselves. Much of the evidence that she presents tends to support the idea that play is an adaptive activity for all humans but an activity nurtured in many different ways by the unique aspects of cultures. That perspective is echoed by more recent scholars who are interested in the cultural and economic diversity of the United States and its children.

## The Work of Slaughter and Dombrowski

Diversity in American culture, as well as a general trend toward migration in many parts of the world, has increased interest in the likely role of culture in human development. Play scholars are among the forefront of social scientists who are taking diversity to heart in their attempts to understand more about children as they grow. Slaughter and Dombrowski, in their 1989 review and research agenda, build on Schwartzman's arguments by using her view of "play in context" to call attention to issues of ethnic and socioeconomic diversity in development. Their interests are primarily psychological, but they recognize that psychological processes are very much shaped by the contexts in which they operate. (Greenfield & Cocking, 1994)

A unique and useful contribution of this argument is the authors' recognition that "culture should be expanded to include a focus on intergenerational transmission of behavior in both culturally continuous and discontinuous contexts" (p. 285). Aspects of culture are important within their original settings, but they also have weight when people migrate to a new setting, as when people move to a setting where different aspects of culture exist. Families carry beliefs and traditions with them when they move, but in new settings they may have different meanings. Slaughter and Dombrowski argue that children should be studied both in continuous contexts, where their cultures have remained in place for generations, and in "discontinuous" contexts, where because of migration they may be encountering multiple cultural influences. This argument also applies to studies of groups that may have subgroups that exist at different socioeconomic levels, where the culture of poverty or affluence may contribute to developmental processes such as play. The research agenda suggested by their writing will require much work, for example, looking at different migrant groups in the United States (or any country with immigrants) to see how their cultures and play have meaning in relationship to new contexts.

Slaughter and Dombrowski challenge views of beneficial play development, citing a number of debates and other evidence to question the cross-cultural and cross-social class generality of classic, normative descriptions. For example, are there cultural and economic differences associated with differences in play that may predict later deficits in social and cognitive functioning? If we subscribe to classic descriptions of play based on Western cultural norms, then any differences we see in the play of non-Western children could mistakenly be associated with other developmental deficits (e.g., school achievement) (Sutton-Smith, 1983) unless we situate differences in play within their larger cultural and social ecology (McLoyd, 1980, 1983). Traditional descriptions of play and its correlates may be perfectly valid within the societies where it has been studied, but expressions of play will vary. As Slaughter and Dombrowski (1989, p. 290) state, "Children's social and pretend play appear to be biologically based, sustained as an evolutionary contribution to human psychological growth and development," but "cultural transmission regulates the expression (i.e., the amount, content, breadth or range, mood, meaning) of this play. Further, over time it is probable that the play itself reciprocally impacts culture" (p. 304).

These authors give full weight to nature and to nurture as sources for human play; they grant both biological and cultural influences on play. The challenging aspect of their argument is to begin to identify those expressions of play that are different from those that appear in the traditional literature and from our own culturally limited experiences. Slaughter and Dombrowski assist with their review of play in socially continuous, discontinuous, and subcultural contexts. Those studies are summarized in Table 7.1.

Based on a review of these studies, Slaughter and Dombrowski argue that few studies have accounted adequately both for play and its

Families play in a variety of ways.

development and for cultural influences. Children's play must be understood in the "cultural ecology" (p. 304), or social context, in which it is meaningful. This is true for children who are growing up in a social setting that has remained constant for generations, in a social setting to which their parents have migrated, or in social settings that represent multiple cultures. Socioeconomic status is a dimension of culture that should always be considered. Understanding the perspectives of participants, including their customs, beliefs, and values, is necessary for understanding children's play. Slaughter and Dombrowski's view seems to be consistent with some of the basic tenets of ethnography.

**TABLE 7.1** Culturally Significant Play Findings from Slaughter and Dombrowski (1989)

| Study | Culture | Findings |
|---|---|---|
| ***Continuous Contexts*** | | |
| Bloch (1984, 1989) | Senegal and America | Time spent crafting toys; play with those toys; infant–age 6 gross-motor, rough-and-tumble, constructive, music and art play; boys (ages 5–6) decrease pretend play; younger children more functional play; Americans did more play of all types, mostly gross-motor and television viewing. |
| Udwin and Shmukler (1981) | Israel and South Africa | Similar amounts of pretend with lower-SES preschoolers in both cultures; relatively less pretend time for South African middle SES, compared to Israeli middle SES. |
| Al-Shatti and Johnson (1984) | Kuwait and America | No statistical differences between cultures or genders; descriptive differences: Kuwaiti girls more sociodramatic play than Kuwaiti boys; American girls less sociodramatic play than American boys; American girls more functional play than American boys. |
| Yawkey and Alverez-Dominques (1984) | Puerto Rico and America | Hispanic girls more reality-oriented play than Anglo girls; Hispanic boys more functional play than American boys; Anglo boys more fantasy play than Hispanic boys; American girls more functional play than American boys; American boys and girls more functional and fantasy than reality oriented; Hispanic girls more reality than functional, and vice versa for Hispanic boys. |
| Bower, Ilgaz-Carden, and Noori (1982) | Turkey and Iran | No SES differences in Turkey in play space used; Iranian middle SES more toys and space for play. |
| Hrncir, Speller, and West (1983) | Bermuda and America | Bermudans at 12 months at play level behind Americans. |
| ***Discontinuous Contexts*** | | |
| Christman (1979) | Mexican American | Sociodramatic play lower for boys than girls at age 3, but equal at age 4. |
| Robinson (1978) | Vietnamese refugees (America) | Boys (ages 9–12) more competitive and aggressive; girls more accommodating and passive; differ from American in relation strengthening and rule clarifying. |
| Young (1985) | Canada (various origins) | Non-Anglos gained social status from skilled soccer play. |
| Child (1983) | East Asian (England) | Less pretend than English children (preschool); Muslim and Sikhs less play, less often, less playfulness; English initiated more play; Asians more likely to play alone. |
| Ariel and Sever (1980) | Arab and Israeli | Rural Arabs (ages 5–6) less pretend, interaction, fewer modes; less talk. |

*(continued)*

**TABLE 7.1**    *Continued*

| Study | Culture | Findings |
|---|---|---|
| ***Subcultures*** | | |
| Nevius (1982; Nevius, Filgo, Soldier, and Simmons-Rains, 1983) | Multicultural (African American, Mexican American, Anglo) | Incidence of play too low to compare groups. |
| McLoyd (1980) | African American | African American preschool pretend utterances were like Anglo pretend, but girls did more transformations of social roles. |
| Lefever (1981) | African American | Relates ritualized language play to self-protection in low-SES groups. |
| Montare and Boone (1980) | Puerto Rican, Anglo | Puerto Rican boys (ages 9–13) showed more aggression in team play sessions, as did Anglos with absent fathers. |

## Context: Expanding on Developmental Views

The scholarship reviewed thus far, presented within frameworks articulated by Schwartzman (1978) and Slaughter and Dombrowski (1989), provides a challenge to traditional developmental views of play, without dismissing them. There can be no doubt that some sort of common strand of children's play cuts across cultures; play is in our nature. These cultural studies of play raise serious questions about what aspects of play are shared and how we can communicate about similarities and differences. Slaughter and Dombrowski and others raise questions about the norms of play development, but that does not mean play development does not exist. Cultural studies of play provide us with a larger repertoire of children's play to consider, as well as more understanding of what play means to them and their families. By putting play in cultural context, we begin to ask additional questions about what we might look for as children play (e.g., novel forms of language play, expression of customs that are foreign to us), as well as how we talk about play with people from cultures other than our own (e.g., if we call activities "play," will others dismiss our words as meaningless?). It is also fair to consider historical context for play activities; what may be culturally sanctioned play for boys in one era may become sanctioned for girls during another era. We return to these questions after reviewing three current strands of research that are informing us about the diversity of play.

##  CULTURAL INFLUENCES ON CHILDREN'S PLAY

What does culture contribute to children's play? What features of culture create opportunities for play in some contexts but apparently not in others? What are universal commonalities to play, and what are play's subtle variations across cultures? Although we do not yet have answers to these questions for every group of people around the world, we do know partial answers to each. In the following sections, we explore these topics and others, based on research carried on since 1989. Patterns of findings are presented according to these themes that reflect different aspects of culture and play: family influences on play and differences in group play. Issues and findings related to gender and play are presented, then discussed in a section of their own.

The complexity of issues related to culture, gender, and play are reflected in current research. One experiment conducted in Taiwan, where children's dolls are typically White in appearance (blue eyes, blond, fair skin), reflects the power of Western toy markets on toy availability. Urban and rural boys and girls were given either a White or an Asian doll for home play, and then assessed in terms of racial attitudes and self-concept. Girls, more than boys, preferred the White doll and were biased toward Whites, more so for urban children who are exposed to more Western media and culture. Positive attitudes toward the White dolls were the norm. Few studies look at the relationships of toy markets to culture, gender, and developmental factors. (Chang & Reifel, 2003)

## Family Influences on Play

Play is often described in terms of its socialization functions. By means of play, society shapes children to become participants in the larger group. These perspectives on play, heavily influenced by developmental theories, reflect beliefs that play, at least in certain forms, contributes to meaningful social interactions that become adaptive for individuals in their social groups (see Chapter 2). We can see such views expressed in many ways, including assertions about play: Children learn to get along with one another; they learn to become team members; they learn their place; they learn to take different roles; they learn social rules, or morality; they learn to communicate; they learn to think out loud; and so on. As the fictional troublemaker Huck Finn illustrates, there can also be questions about how much freedom children are allowed as they play. Many of these assertions are made about peers playing with one another, but they also apply to play within the social group we call the family. Over the past two decades, we have seen growth in the number of studies done of play in family settings here and abroad.

Parental influences on play have been of particular interest to a number of scholars. In the United States, observational studies of mother–child play in the home, as well as interview studies with mothers and fathers about their play with their children, show how American mothers (typically) facilitate play through direct and indirect means. Direct means include, for example, teaching children to pretend by introducing the play frame to infants, prompting pretend, and elaborating children's expressions. American parents might use indirect means of promoting play by arranging the home environment, especially with replica toys, and inspiring play by expressing positive affect. Although there is clearly a range of things that middle-class American parents might do to promote children's play, it seems that play for children is generally valued in American culture (Haight, 1998; Haight, Masiello, Dickson, Huckeby, & Black, 1994; Haight & Miller, 1992, 1993; Haight, Parke, & Black, 1997; Haight & Sachs, 1995; Haight, Wang, Fung, Williams, & Mintz, et al., 1999).

What about play within families in other cultures? We know that children play in different ways, but how do parents and other family members participate in the play lives of children? A number of studies from various places around the world reveal diversity in terms of play participation and apparent attitudes toward play. For example, the study of Kpelle play in Africa indicates that parents believe that play does contribute to children's future roles and common sense but play (especially pretend) is viewed with "mild tolerance" by adults (Lancy, 1996, p. 91). Most adults are so engaged with work that they do not have time to play with their children, which is a common pattern in subsistence cultures. In other, nonsubsistence cultures, adults may pay attention to play in different ways (Bloch, 1989; Bloch & Adler, 1994; Schwartzman, 1978).

Although play was not the primary focus of monograph on learning and development, research provided cross-cultural description of mother–child interactions that support cognition. American mothers described themselves as, and acted like, playmates more often than did Guatemalan mothers; tribal Indian mothers facilitate, more than participate, in play. Turkish mothers appear to play with their children as much as American mothers do. Attitudes about play, as well as engagement in labor, appear to contribute to maternal participation in play. These analyses were limited to mother–child observations, so there is no evidence whether other adults or relatives play with those children (Rogoff, Mistry, Goncu, & Mosier, 1993; Goncu & Mosier, 1991).

Observational and interview studies comparing the play of American and Mexican families found that Mexican mothers do not believe play to be important for children's development; in fact, they do not play with their children. Children within this culture do have older play partners, in siblings and other family members. A similar set of findings is reported for Italian families. Mothers of young children do not see their role to include play, leaving that activity to older siblings and neighbors. Italian mothers appear to believe that whatever play is appropriate for children will be provided by others. These apparent low levels of parental involvement in child play are in contrast to American parental involvement, but these studies suggest that other family members and neighbors engage young children in play, probably providing the same developmental benefits that American children obtain. And, as we will see in the discussion of differences in group play that follows, there are also cultural differences in peer relationships in preschool peer play (Farver, 1993; Farver & Howes, 1993; New, 1994; Xu, Farver, Schwartz & Chang, 2003).

Research done in Asian countries reveals different, sometimes conflicting, patterns of mother–child play. Chinese parents view play as beneficial for children and see themselves as play partners, much as American mothers do. Taiwanese mothers tend to be highly engaged in their preschoolers' play, although the specificity of their involvement was a good deal more differentiated than the pattern provided by Haight and her colleagues. In a laboratory-like setting in an urban Taipei neighborhood, researchers found that mothers provided developmentally nuanced support for pretend play. Contingent statements clarified 2-year-olds' pretend actions and attributed meanings to them; they added details to the play of 3-year-olds and elaborated roles for 4-year-olds. As children grew older, mothers provided increasing challenges during pretend, requiring more events in play scripts, demonstrating toy use to enhance pretend, and progressing from factual questions to reasoning questions about enacted events. Mothers verbally connected pretend actions for 3-year-olds and converted playful accidents into pretend themes for 4-year-olds. Older children got more coaching from their mothers about toy use and how to elaborate events. Mothers of children at all ages verbally interpreted what they saw, showed compliance to children's play themes, and challenged children to include additional elements in their play. Mothers taught what their children needed to know to make pretense meaningful, whether how to use a stethoscope to act like a doctor or where to store toy vegetables when they are not being cooked. The nuanced scaffolding that these mothers provided reflects a complex, intuitive sense of components of play (action related to object, then related to meaning; meanings related to roles; roles as part of scripts). These findings were confirmed in Korean mother–child play, in pretend, puzzle solving, and storytelling contexts. The value of play for children's learning and development is apparent (Chin & Reifel, 2000; Haight, 1998; Haight & Miller, 1992, 1993; Haight, Wang, Fung, Williams, & Mintz, 1995; Jwa & Frost, 2003).

Parents may have indirect influence on their children's play by means of the settings they arrange for play. Some evidence exists on cultural variation on these influences. Play observed in American and South Korean middle- and working-class homes revealed the value of play, apparent in the high incidence of play at home, as opposed to school work, other work, or conversation. Pretend and academic play (i.e., with academic objects and information) were common forms of play in both cultures, but Korean middle-class children showed significantly more academic play. Middle-class girls in both cultures were more apt to engage in academic play. Children in both cultures were more likely to play alone or with peers than with parents, but when parents did play with children, it was far more likely to be the mother (significantly so in Korea). Home settings in these cultures had different effects on play. How parents stereotype play will also influence children's play choices (Haight, 1998; Karnik & Tudge, 2010; Tudge, Lee, & Putman, 1998; Zosuls, et al., 2009).

The level of parental involvement in Korean and Korean American children's play is echoed in work showing the value that Korean culture places on academic goals for children, and play at home is not believed to contribute to that goal. Parents and teachers with Korean backgrounds were less likely to play with their children, and as a result the children engaged in more parallel and less pretend play than did Anglo-American children. (Farver, Kim, & Lee, 1995)

Parents from different cultures may or may not play with their children, and if they do play with their children, they may do so to varying degrees. If parents do not play with children, suggestive findings tell us that others in that culture will engage children in play. In some cases, parents may not become playmates for their children for clear reasons. For example, if parents must work at a subsistence level, then there is no time or energy for play. It may be that attitudes and beliefs follow such subsistence needs, so parents who are working hard just to get by will value play less and downplay

the importance of play for their children. Or beliefs about play may not relate to socioeconomic status. Parents who believe in play may simply decide to play more with their children, as Indonesian mothers and fathers do with their toddlers. Likewise, parents with more resources may have more time and energy to play, and they may have attitudes and beliefs that reflect their practices. Or, as the Italian data suggest, parents may assume that children will naturally get whatever play they need (Farver & Wimbarti, 1995; New, 1994).

Irrespective of the links between adult participation in children's play and prevailing values, the patterns of diversity that exist among cultures provide challenges to practitioners. If adults value play and think that children should be playing, then supporting play in schools and neighborhoods is not a problem. If adults, for cultural or personal reasons, do not value play, it is more difficult to describe its benefits and argue that children should be engaging in it. This may be especially true if the forms of play that adults see are alien to their cultural or gender-linked experiences; those adults may not have a way of relating to the play or of valuing it. These challenges become especially problematic in diverse communities, where teachers, parents, and other community members may come from differing backgrounds. (Holmes, 1999)

Current studies are attempting to understand more about the interesting mixture of views about play in diverse classrooms. Parents, teachers, and children have varying understandings of play and its functions. Teachers and parents can communicate to understand more about those understandings and use that knowledge for the benefit of children who do not come from similar backgrounds. Such efforts can enhance children's play and development (Buchanan, Benedict, et al., 2010; Moon & Reifel, 2008; Moore & Gilliard, 2010; Riojas-Cortez, 2001; Riojas-Cortez & Flores, 2004; Schellhaas, Burts & Aghayan, 2010; Ugaste, 2007).

Cultural differences in adult–child relationships during play may add to confusion for children in diverse play settings. If children come from a culture where adults are not part of child play, they may have difficulty understanding why a teacher or play leader would be trying to engage them in play; adults would not be expected to do such a thing. Children who are familiar with adults as playmates may have different expectations for adult support during play. Diverse classrooms may bring together these practices and require sensitive responses to the needs of children.

## Differences in Group Play

Adults can have significant roles in contributing to children's play, depending on the culture where we look. Likewise, the role of peers in play can vary a great deal, depending on culture. Peer interactions, whether within families, neighborhoods, or classrooms, should have a distinctive caste by virtue of the culture associated with that play. The examples reported earlier speak to this point; culturally unique customs appear in children's dramatic play, as do desired social roles. Sometimes the aspects of culture that appear in play are fleeting but significant. One ethnographic study that supports an analysis of continuities and discontinuities between Mexican American Head Start children's home and school experiences, notes many instances of play. One telling example is an older brother who interrupted his play with a friend to correct his sister, who was not playing as he thought she should be. Even though his sister was younger, the boy made use of the formal pronoun used to address his sister, reflecting the respect associated with family relationships in this culture. The subtleties of culture can appear in many ways in children's play (Lin & Reifel, 1999; Suito & Reifel, 1993; Trawick-Smith, 2010; Woods, 1997).

One dimension of play for which there are demonstrable cultural differences is playfulness. Playfulness is an aspect of play having to do with the humor, joy, and spontaneity of activities. In a series of studies, teachers rated children with a 31-item instrument that reflects six traditional dispositions of play (from Rubin, Fein, & Vandenberg, 1983). American children were found by their teachers to be significantly more playful than were Japanese children. Factor analysis revealed that dimensions of playfulness were different in these cultures. Japanese playfulness is associated with 17 of 28 items, with "Finds unusual things to do" and "Uses toys/objects in unusual ways" appearing high in the factor loadings, and "Active involvement" ("Gets very involved/forgets what is going on") appearing as a significant factor. American playfulness is associated with 21 of the 28 items, with "Invents new games" and "Is imaginative" having high load factors, and "Externality" ("Looks to others to tell him/her what to do") as a significant factor. Playfulness characterizes peer school play in both cultures but in very different ways (Lieberman, 1965; Rogers et al., 1998; Taylor, Rogers, & Kaiser, 1999).

Some of the reasons for the cultural differences in classroom play in Japan and the United States may be explained by a survey of Japanese play. The forms of play are similar in Japan as in other Western and Asian countries. Leisure time for children in Japan is filled with television, comics, games, sports, and video games. Play for young children is integrated into the school curriculum, where it is assumed that play influences development. Teachers are taught to consider play in terms of health, human relations, environment, language, and creative expressions, but these dimensions are interpreted in terms of inclusiveness (playing with others) rather than emphasizing individual expressiveness. Playing to be part of the group, learning a group ethos, is emphasized more than developing individuality and uniqueness, as is done in American schools (Lewis, 1994; Takeuchi, 1994; Tobin, Hsueh & Karasawa, 2009; Trawick-Smith, 2010).

Beliefs about play and playfulness vary, as does how Japanese and American preschoolers structure their classroom role play. Communications about play were described and analyzed, in terms of deciding about roles to play, actually playing those roles, and gender differences. Girls in both cultures were more likely to identify play roles, especially family kinship roles. Japanese girls were much more likely to argue about who will take what role, valuing the role of mother most of all; mother was seen as an authority role in both cultures. Japanese boys were more likely to play house unaffiliated with other players, and American boys were the only ones seen to take the baby role. Gender stereotypes appeared in both cultures, with mothers doing housekeeping and fathers leaving for work outside the home. Boys in both groups, when playing in single-sex groups, would enact meal preparation and serving, but their roles were never identified. American children were far more likely to play nonfamily roles (e.g., pilot, cashier, Superman) in the housekeeping play area than were the Japanese; the range of legitimate play roles for Japanese children, especially boys, was far more restricted. This study suggests that culture may contribute to play by providing a set of roles (particularly gender-linked roles) that can be played during pretend. An implication is that children from different cultures who play together in diverse settings may not share a common repertoire of acceptable roles (Garvey, 1977; Suito & Reifel, 1993).

Another thing that children from diverse cultural backgrounds may not share is the facility to communicate about playing with one another. One study reported the difficulties of a troubled African American boy who appeared unhappy and secluded during play time in a preschool. This boy's efforts to play with others were rejected consistently. Systematic observation of his play efforts, making use of Corsaro's framework for understanding ritualized patterns to access play (1979, 1985), showed that his typical entry efforts were with African American speech style, which was not familiar to potential playmates. Teachers did note that this child had, on one occasion, used an entry ritual in the style of a television superhero and had been successful. Teachers encouraged his use of this style, which was very familiar to other children in the classroom. The African American boy used this approach to enter play and found common ground for continuing peer play (Scales, 1996; Van Hoorn et al., 2007).

An analysis of multicultural toys in diverse classrooms found that it is not easy for teachers to include multicultural materials into the curriculum. Images of children, as reflected by multicultural toys, raise complex interwoven layers of meanings about how we use toys and their relationships to real life. Play may reduce or essentialize meanings, controlling and dominating children rather than helping them make sense of the world. What does it mean if every set of multicultural doll families has the same number of family members, when family size might have particular meanings for some? How do standard playhouses suggest an image of "home" that may be biased? Postmodern theories allow us to look at the layers of meanings related to the toys that children are provided at school. (Johnson, 2005)

Other cross-cultural studies of preschool play provide additional differences to consider when observing social play. Corsaro documents a range of social play actions, some of which have their parallels in American and other cultures. Italian children make do when they are not provided play materials that suit their pretend interests, such as when they convert sticks to guns and swords to play fight; we see similar strategies in American settings. Italian children are more often left to their own devices for resolving conflicts, but when teachers do intervene, they help children think of social rules; this pattern also does not seem foreign to children in the United States. What may seem more strange is the lack of emphasis on the individual in Italian play settings. Children are expected to play in groups, discuss in groups, and consider the welfare of the entire group rather than individual interests. Play is not a matter of personal expression; players must recognize the interests of everyone in the community (Corsaro, 2003; Corsaro & Rizzo, 1988; Corsaro & Schwarz, 1991).

Cultures adapt to their physical settings, and play activities reflect those cultures and settings. A comparison of the games of rural Nigeria, the Igbo people, with those of the rural United States (Indiana), the Hoosiers, found that children in both cultures were engaged in spontaneous neighborhood play, not organized events. Children in both groups averaged age 8, although the Igbo included significantly younger children in their play groups (age 5, as opposed to age 6 for the Americans). Games lasted varying lengths of time for both groups. Environment played a key role in play, with the Igbo playing far more outdoors in the morning when it was cooler, and the Hoosiers playing more in the afternoon; about 25% of games were played in the evening in both cultures. A higher proportion of Igbo games were mixed gender. The objects that children used as they played were typically manufactured for the Hoosiers (paper bags, string, pen tops) and natural materials for the Igbo (banana leaves, water, seeds). Games were rule bound in both cultures, but the Igbo adhered to the rules, whereas the Hoosiers argued about and changed rules. There was more gross-motor physical movement in Igbo games, although some high-level activity occurred in both groups. Traditional games were evident in both cultures—for example, checkers, tag, and Red Rover for the Hoosiers; hopscotch (*swehi*), throw seeds (*itu okwe*), and leopard and sheep (*agu na aturu*) for the Igbo. The Igbo had more penalties, both mild and harsh, for infractions of rules than did the Hoosiers. (Nwokah & Ikekeonwu, 1998)

Peer groups and social relationships among them may influence aggression in different ways in China, with play victims not taking the roles we might expect. Environment and culture—in these cases, the play objects and customs of these groups—were reflected in documented games. Both help socialize children to cultural concerns (Xu, Farver, Schwartz, & Chang, 2003, 2004).

With an increase in diversity within American schools, we are more aware of the blending of groups of children within classrooms. Study of the play of diverse children in primary grades found that kindergarten children were less likely to play with children from other ethnic groups, whereas third graders engaged in much more cross-ethnic play. We have no indication that any efforts were made to facilitate this grade-linked increase in cultural mixing. Younger children may not have had appropriate communication skills to establish and maintain play with peers; older children had learned those adaptive play skills. Studies of preschool children indicate that language differences tend to segregate players, at least initially in their school experiences. In diverse settings where multiple languages are present, children gravitate toward those with whom they can communicate while they play (Clawson, 2002; Howes & Wu, 1990; Sutterby, 2001).

Current research has affirmed the existence of unique play activities in a range of cultures. Eskimo girls make "storyknives" on which they carve symbols relevant to their culture. Chinese and Taiwanese children have holiday festivals, when they celebrate with fireworks, lanterns, or kites. Maori children in New Zealand walk on stilts that they make. Polynesians have *keu tictoc*, a chase game where children hold hands to form a swinging line. South African children enduring apartheid constructed toys that gave them a sense of power. The consensus is that these unique forms of play reflect particular cultural values and are given differing meaning within their cultures. Case studies of play in different cultures introduce us to play practices we may not be familiar with because they situate play in its context. Case studies can allow us to look for broader patterns that explain the role of play in children's lives. There may be more or less time for play, more or fewer resources given to play, more or less adult support for play, but the universality of play is apparent (Best, 1925; Cooney & Sha, 1999; deMarrais, Nelson, & Baker, 1994; Martini, 1994; Pan, 1994; Peffer, 2009; Trawick-Smith, 2010).

What children play with, their approach to play, the roles they take, and how they communicate about their play all vary with cultural influences. Each culture may have its own unique play forms, but each form makes sense within the culture for its own reasons. Japanese children do not like to pretend to be a baby in the family because babies have low status in their culture. Italian mothers do not play much with their children because they believe that others in the family will. Mexican mothers do not play with their children because the mothers must work; older siblings do play with children. Peer play is valued in Nigeria for developing common sense; in the United States it is the basis for social skill, moral reasoning, and social cognition; in Korea peer play is less valued. American child developmentalists and Japanese educators agree that play supports learning and development in the early childhood classroom, but they differ about what play is; Korean adults see no value in non-academic play. These findings, as well as the others presented here, require that we take customs, values, and beliefs into account when we observe children from diverse backgrounds as they play.

## Gender and Play

*Thereafter the summer passed in routine contentment. Routine contentment was: improving our treehouse that rested between giant twin chinaberry trees in the back yard, fussing, running through our list of dramas based on the works of Oliver Optic, Victor Appleton, and Edgar Rice Burroughs. In this matter we were lucky to have Dill. He played the character parts formerly thrust upon me—the ape in* Tarzan*, Mr. Crabtree in* The Rover Boys*, Mr. Damon in* Tom Swift*.* (Lee, 1960, p. 8)

The differences between the play of boys and girls are noted in research findings around the world. Scholars who look at play and gender are well aware of pronounced differences between boys and girls in the roles that children play, the tendency of boys and girls to segregate themselves into same-gender play groups, patterns of play and toy preferences, how parents respond to the play of girls and boys, and many other issues. We know the differences in boy and girl play well enough, so that authors such as Harper Lee can use play as a way to indicate the tomboy character of her heroine Scout in *To Kill a Mockingbird*; Scout climbed trees and dominated the neighbor boy Dill. We are to see that she is strong and not girly. An author can signal us about Scout's character, but different theoretical and rhetorical perspectives complicate findings from studies. Some researchers are interested in seeing how play functions in children's gender socialization; others may look at issues of identity formation or cultural replication. The underlying issue—the interplay of nature (a biological basis for gender) and nurture (how contexts participate in gender formation)—suggests research must be evaluated along a number of dimensions that authors do not always address (e.g., Fagot & Kronsberg, 1982; Fagot & Leve, 1998; Geary, 1998; Maccoby, 1990; Ruble & Martin, 1998; Schwartzman, 1977; Sutton-Smith, 1997).

Those who point to male/female differences in primate play note the nature of play and gender. A long history of research documents male/female differences in nonhuman primate infants and juveniles. Monkeys, chimpanzees, baboons, and other primates tend to play in gender-segregated groups. Research documents the onset of this gender socialization from infancy in rhesus monkeys, and how males and females grow up playing with age-cohort, same-gender mates. This early socialization contributes to troop social structure, including social hierarchy and gender roles. Easily recognizable patterns of play for males and females across species suggest there may be a genetic and adaptive basis connecting gender and play. (Biben, 1989; Cheney, 1978; O'Neill-Wagner, Bolig, & Price, 2001).

Differences between boys' and girls' play have been explained by a number of theories. It may be that both boys and girls prefer certain toys and gravitate to others who share those interests, or it may be that as children acquire a beginning conceptual understanding of sex differences, they find playmates like themselves. Others have argued that gender segregation may be related to preferences for compatible play interactions; one finds playmates who act like oneself. From a social constructionist perspective, one may argue that play is a setting for expressing aspects of gender roles being explored by the players; boys and girls explore and express different perceptions of who they are in the world. All of these theories recognize the nature of play; children are biologically gendered and bring that fact with them. Distinctions among these theories seem to lie in the degree of nurture that occurs during play. We know boys like boy toys, but what makes adults give boys those toys? We know that boys are more active than girls and girls are more verbal, but do we as a culture provide play opportunities to enhance or diminish those differences? Do we direct children to forms of expression that highlight rather than reduce differences in play? (Kohlberg, 1966; Maccoby, 1990; Moller & Serbin, 1996; Scales & Cook-Gumperz, 1993; Zosuls, et al., 2009).

Play as an avenue for nurturing children toward their expected gender roles is noted.

Boys and girls are treated differently from their birth, if not before. As soon as pregnancy and gender are medically confirmed in U.S. society, for many families the first question asked is, "Is it a boy or a girl?" Toy selection for newborns, room decoration, and interactive play are different for girls and boys. The context of play as a socializing influence on gender development is pronounced, and it surely varies from culture to culture. Families, media, and peer relations (as a vector for culture) all contribute to how we see gender differences in play (Lindsey & Mize, 2001).

**Social Relationship Differences**   A number of the studies reported so far include findings about differences in girls' and boys' play. Nigerian rural children play more mixed-gender games than do American children. Kuwaiti preschool girls engage in pretend play more than boys. Vietnamese immigrant school-age boys are more competitive and aggressive; girls are more accommodating and passive. Hispanic preschool girls play more reality-based pretend than functional games, and the reverse is true for boys. Japanese preschool girls have a wider range of possible pretend

Girls' clapping games are familiar in most parts of the United States.

roles than do boys, but neither has as many as American preschoolers. Preschool boys create more fragmented play narratives about monsters and superheroes, whereas girls create cohesive play texts about domestic relationships. These and many other findings point to the importance of gender when we talk about play and development (Al-Shatti & Johnson, 1984; Nwokah & Ikekeonwu, 1998; Robinson, 1978; Scales & Cook-Gumperz, 1993; Suito & Reifel, 1993; Yawkey & Alverez-Dominques, 1984).

The range of findings about play and gender in Western societies has been well reviewed by a number of scholars who specialize in this field of research. Gender segregation during play early in life is a common Western observation, as are different styles of play for boys and girls. Boys' play is typified by competition, aggression, rules, and relatively low levels of talk; girls' play is relational, inclusive, and highly verbal. As some of the studies reported indicate, these generalizations are far from universal; in some cultures play-linked gender segregation may appear much later or simply be less prevalent. In this section, we briefly review a number of theories and related data dealing with issues of gender, culture, and play (Bloch, 1989; Fagot & Leve, 1998; Nwokah & Ikekeonwu, 1998; Ramsey, 1998; Sutton-Smith, 1997).

Although there are many studies of play and gender in other cultures, much of the discourse about the topic is dominated by studies done in Western settings and using Western developmental norms for play. Differences in boys' and girls' play are described in terms of gender identity, in which children's knowledge of their gender predicts how they play in group settings or at home. Such knowledge may lead to greater cooperation in segregated play groups. Preferences for gender segregation may also relate to the type of play as well as the sex of the playmate, with younger children (aged 2 years and 6 months) of both sexes opting for same-sex partners, and older girls (aged 4–5) opting for cooperative play with boys choosing

boy playmates. In most of these studies, the roles of cultural and parental expectations are not considered. Neither do we learn about the contexts or texts of the play that children create in these studies (Fagot, 1994; Fagot & Leinbach, 1989; Fagot, Leinbach, & Hagan, 1986; Fagot & Leve, 1999; Jarrett, Farokhi, Young, & Davies, 2001; Leaper, 1994; Moller & Serbin, 1996; Ruble & Martin, 1998; Schwartzman, 1986; Serbin & Sprafkin, 1986; Tietz & Shine, 2000).

**Differences in Play Preferences and Activities**
A long-standing tradition in child development describes the different play preferences and activities of girls and boys. Some of the earliest developmental research pointed to gender differences in play. Using interviews and observations of children in laboratories, those researchers describe familiar patterns of play. Girls prefer to paint, draw, model with clay, look at books, and play with dolls; girls' play tends to be more sedentary. Boys like to build with blocks, play with cars and trucks, ride toy vehicles, and overall tend to be more active. (Bott, 1928; Farwell, 1930; Van Alstyne, 1932).

Such differences in preferences continue to the present day, with gender-typed play activities noted in a broad review of research. Boys are still observed to be more physical, including physical contact (e.g., chasing, rough-and-tumble,) during play, with girls being more social-skills oriented and precise in their physical activities (e.g., clapping games, jacks). A number of studies describing the play preferences of ethnically diverse elementary students (up to grade 5) found activity-level differences between boys and girls, with boys involved in more ball games and girls tending to play synchronized or traditional games (e.g., Red Rover) (Fishbein, Malone, & Stegelin, 2009; Jarrett et al., 2001; Ramsey, 1998; Ruble & Martin, 1998).

**Differences in Play Texts**   A number of recent efforts have explored the gendered construction of play in childhood, looking in particular at our assumptions about what toys and play mean to us culturally, and how our gender understandings may bias us toward replication of stereotypical gender expectations. Girls construct gender in their early childhood classroom, using gender discourses in play that appears to contribute to how girls construct their senses of who they are as girls. A number of analyses have looked at girls' play, in particular, as it relates to play materials provided for girls. Barbie doll play as well as girl pretense show how play might construct identity. The pronounced influence of commercial culture on play creates discourses that have particular meanings for children. Hughes and MacNaughton (2001) conclude there is a balance between "children's active creation of identities within the discourses that they have acquired as a result of their specific social and material circumstances" and "the increasing ability of major corporations to influence the availability of particular discourses of identity" (p. 127). Toys, markets, media, families, and peers all provide specific, particular contributions to gendered play (Blaise, 2005; Hughes & MacNaughton, 2001; Lamb & Brown, 2006; MacNaughton, 1997, 1999; Reifel, 2009).

As already noted, boys' play tends to be more active: Boys tend to move more quickly, use louder voices, and move about the play space (perhaps on vehicles) with little regard to ongoing activities. There has been some note of the active, if not violent, role-play characters that boys choose, as opposed to the quieter, more domestic doll play of girls. There has been growing interest in the characteristically male form of play called rough-and-tumble. Rough-and-tumble is often seen as play fighting, although many teachers have difficulty distinguishing play fighting from real fighting, thereby missing the play element in rough-and-tumble. It is difficult for many adults to identify the text of rough-and-tumble because it does not often fit into a recognizable narrative of pretend. But many boys participate freely and happily in rough-and-tumble, laughing as they roll around together on the ground or shove

one another in order to establish dominance and maintain social status. Boys use a number of signals to indicate that their rough-and-tumble actions are play: positive affect, minimal physical contact, reciprocity, and continued affiliation. Although pleasurable for the players, this male play text evokes ambivalence in many, and it needs further study (Carlsson-Paige & Levin, 1990, 1995, 2006; Pellegrini, 1988, 1995, 2002; Pellegrini & Smith, 1998; Smith, Smees, Pellegrini & Menesini, 2002).

Play is often the setting for negative activity, such as bullying. A number of studies conducted in natural and laboratory settings are showing a complicated set of relationships among bullying, aggression, and gender. Both boys and girls can bully, but boys are more likely to bully and to be physically aggressive, whereas girl bullies use more indirect, relational aggression. Girl's relational aggression appears to be more language linked, suggesting that boys and girls have different ways of negotiating dominance among playmates. How to deal with aggression and dominance in play groups is complicated by gender and type of aggressive behavior (Bonica, Arnold, Fisher, & Zeljo, 2003; Bullock, 2002; Crick, Casas, & Mosher, 1997; Ostrov & Keating, 2004; Ostrov et al., 2004).

More of the texts and context of gender-linked play appear in the writings of Vivian Paley. She recounts her teaching efforts in a kindergarten classroom where children's relations become subject matter for research and practice. The stories that children create while they play become part of the curriculum and reflect differences between the texts of boys and girls. The rules that boys and girls make about their play (e.g., "No superheroes in the doll corner") reveal much about the text of gender relationships during play. The ownership of play by children is affirmed when Paley attempted to impose her rules on what children chose to do when they play. These accounts reveal how children come to make sense of issues such as gender in the course of their play. (Paley, 1981, 1984, 1992, 2004).

Studies of gender and play conducted in Western settings, like those reported here, point to dimensions of play that may vary for boys and girls. They provide particulars about play that make sense in terms of theories of gender identity. What they do not do is relate those particulars to the cultural context in which these children are developing. Play provides one avenue for children to explore and express gender, but, as Slaughter and Dombrowski (1989) point out, at some point play may contribute to culture. The children's play we support is nurturing gender development as much as it is allowing for exploration. The range of expressions of gender and play revealed from cross-cultural research suggest different ways that play is associated with culturally sanctioned gender development. The fictional heroine Scout is allowed to be a tomboy in her culture; girls in other cultures may not be given that option.

## SUMMARY

The vast body of literature on culture and play that has been sampled and reported here tends to support the universality of children's play as a natural human activity nurtured quite differently in various cultures. Depending on a culture's environment and economic conditions, play may take certain forms. Beliefs about play and the value it is given by members of a culture influence the degree to which adults engage and support children. How they play, and what meaning that play has for them, depends on their culture. These conditions affect the amount of play, customs reflected in play, gender roles associated with play, and objects considered appropriate for play. Irrespective of any of these conditions, children play.

As cultures come together, by means of migration and a global economy, we are seeing more settings where children from diverse backgrounds are meeting. Play is typically part of these settings, but there might not be universal agreement about what play is. Games known in one part of the world are unfamiliar in another. Rituals for initiating play might not be shared. Participation by adults with children

in their play might be a source of confusion. The subtleties of play might interrupt its performance, when something as simple as playing house becomes an event where legitimate and valued gender roles are ambiguous and where scripts for household rituals are not shared. This chapter points to the importance of knowing diverse cultures, to better understand the particular features of children's play. We have described some of the features of play that may be relevant. A number of recent publications have provided sensitive guidance for professionals (Dockett & Fleer, 1999; Johnson, 2005; MacNaughton, 1997; Moon & Reifel, 2008; Paley, 2004; Ramsey, 1998; Roopnarine, Johnson, & Hooper, 1994; Van Hoorn, Scales, Nourot, & Alward, 2011; Trawick-Smith, 2010; Wood, 2009).

Different groups of people nurture play to support the maintenance of the group. The customs, beliefs, values, and institutions of a culture are tied to play, whether in the form of play activities that socialize children into the group, adult efforts to engage in or support play, or activities that reflect the environment of the culture. Anthropology has provided much of this work, and ethnography, the primary methodology of anthropology, offers detailed description of play in the settings where it is meaningful. The classic works of Schwartzman (1978) and Slaughter and Dombrowski (1989) discuss culturally relevant aspects of play that frame our review of the literature: game diffusion, play functions, projecting personality, communication, subjectively meaningful events, continuous and discontinuous culture, and subcultures (including migration and socioeconomic status). Review of this literature reveals that children's play is a multifaceted human activity that is difficult to understand from any one perspective. Much of children's play around the world can be understood in terms of how play contributes to child socialization within a culture, as well as how culture shapes play.

Recent research continues these themes, pointing to the particular meanings of play within different cultures. The diversity of play activities is demonstrated through reviews on family influences on play and differences in group play in various cultures around the world. Parental values and beliefs about play vary a great deal, as does the degree to which parents play with their children. Cultural support for play may be pronounced or not. Peer play is equally diverse in different cultures, with unique forms of play still appearing in local cultures. Subtle but significant influences of culture appear in peer play, in the form of variations in games, roles taken (or not taken), play communications, and size and range of play groups. Gender differences in play are also a source of variation in a number of senses. Boys and girls play differently all around the world, but the ways they play differently appear to be influenced to some degree by values and beliefs. Differences between the play of boys and girls in different cultural settings reveal that play is to a great degree nurtured. It is important to note the particular cultural, material, and social contexts for play that girls and boys experience. The fictional characters Huck and Scout were allowed to play as they did, even if it led to trouble. Different contexts might not have been so supportive.

Issues of understanding and working with diversity are raised by these reviews. As children from different cultural backgrounds come together, related to migration and the world economy, opportunities for peer relationships must be filtered through an understanding of play as a part of culture. Knowing that play reflects particular customs, values, and beliefs that may be different than our own should be a first step toward engaging diverse children in meaningful play.

## KEY TERMS

Ethnography  
Game diffusion  
Play functions  
Text in context  
Continuous contexts  

Discontinuous  
   contexts  
Nature/gender  
Nurture/gender  
Play texts  

## STUDY QUESTIONS

1. Identify your own cultural heritage. Ask your parents and grandparents (or other older relatives) how they played as children. What did they pretend, and what games did they play? What did it mean for them to play? How is their play characteristic of your cultural heritage?
2. Ask your family members how they played with you when you were an infant and toddler. What games did they play with you? What were their reasons for playing with you? What do you think you gained from such play?

3. With a group of friends, discuss the play and games you remember from childhood. Try to include friends who come from a different region of the country or from a different country. What play is the same, and what differences are there? How does your immediate environment (setting, objects, playmates) shape childhood play, and what aspects of play seem common to all?
4. Select one play activity (e.g., pretend house play, a chase game) and find a description of that activity in two different cultures. How are those activities alike in both cultures, and how are they different? How does each play activity have particular meaning for its culture?
5. With a group of men and women, discuss the play and games you remember from childhood. What play is the same, and what differences are there? What do group members think they gained from childhood play? Why was play fun?
6. You are a teacher of a kindergarten class that includes immigrant children from Mexico, Taiwan, and Italy. What might you ask parents of these children about their past experiences? What aspects of play might you observe as these children play in your classroom?
7. Select a game familiar to you. What functions might this game be promoting? How might the game shape or reflect personality? How are players being socialized by this game?
8. Interview boys and girls about pretend play. What roles do they take when they play? What roles will they not take? Ask them why or why not.
9. Children communicate with each other as they play. List the ways that they communicate, and identify similarities and differences between cultural groups.

## REFERENCES

Abrahams, R. D. (1962). Playing the dozens. *Journal of American Folklore, 75*, 209–220.

Al-Shatti, A., & Johnson, J. (1984). *Free play behaviors of middle class Kuwaitis and American children.* Paper presented at the annual meeting of the American Educational Research Association, New Orleans.

Ariel, S., & Sever, I. (1980). Play in the desert and play in the town: On play activities of Bedouin Arab children. In H. Schwartzman (Ed.), *Play and culture* (pp. 164–174). West Point, NY: Leisure Press.

Barker, R., & Wright, H. F. (1966). *One boy's day*. Hamden, CT: Archon.

Bateson, G. (2000). *Steps to an ecology of mind*. Chicago: University of Chicago Press. (Original work published 1955)

Best, E. (1925). *Games and pastimes of the Maori. Dominion Museum Bulletin*, No. 8.

Biben, M. (1989). Effects of social environment on play in squirrel monkeys: Resolving Harlequin's dilemma. *Ethology, 81*, 72–82.

Blaise, M. (2005). *Playing it straight: Uncovering gender discourses in the early childhood classroom*. New York: Routledge.

Bloch, M. N. (1984). Play materials. *Childhood Education, 60*, 345–348.

Bloch, M. N. (1989). Young boys' and girls' play at home and in the community: A cultural-ecological framework. In M. N. Bloch & A. D. Pellegrini (Eds.), *The ecological context of children's play* (pp. 120–154). Norwood, NJ: Ablex.

Bloch, M. N., & Adler, S. (1994). African children's play and the emergence of the sexual division of labor. In J. L. Roopnarine, J. E. Johnson, & F. H. Hooper (Eds.), *Children's play in diverse cultures* (pp. 148–178). Albany: State University of New York Press.

Blurton Jones, N. (Ed.). (1972). *Ethological studies of child behaviour*. Cambridge, MA: Cambridge University Press.

Bonica, C., Arnold, D. H., Fisher, P. H., & Zeljo, K. (2003). Relational aggression, relational victimization, and language development in preschoolers. *Social Development, 12*(4), 551–562.

Bott, H. (1928). Observations of play activities in a nursery school. *Genetic Psychology Monographs, 4*, 44–88.

Bower, E., Ilgaz-Carden, A., & Noori, K. (1982). Measurement of play structures: Cross-cultural considerations. *Journal of Cross-Cultural Psychology, 13*, 315–329.

Buchanan, T.K., Benedict, J., et al. (2010). Early childhood education students' reflections: Volunteering after hurricanes Katrina and Rita. *Journal of Early Childhood Teacher Education, 28*, 83–88.

Bullock, J. R. (2002). Bullying among children. *Young Children, 78*, 130–133.

Carlsson-Paige, N., & Levin, D. E. (1990). *Who's calling the shots? How to respond effectively to children's fascination with war play and war toys*. Philadelphia: New Society Publishers.

Carlsson-Paige, N., & Levin, D. E. (1995). Can teachers resolve the war-play dilemma? *Young Children, 50*, 62–63.

Carlsson-Paige, N., & Levin, D. E. (2006). *The war play dilemma* (2nd Ed.). New York: Teachers College Press.

Chang, L.-C., & Reifel, S. (2003). Play, racial attitudes, and self-concept in Taiwan. In D. Lytle (Ed.), *Play and educational theory and practice (Play and Culture Studies*, Vol. 5) (pp. 257–275). Westport, CT: Praeger.

Cheney, D. (1978). The play partners of immature baboons. *Animal Behavior, 26*, 1038–1050.

Child, E. (1983). Play and culture: A study of English and Asian children. *Leisure Studies, 2*, 169–186.

Chin, J. H., & Reifel, S. (2000). Maternal scaffolding of Taiwanese play: Qualitative patterns. In S. Reifel (Ed.), *Play and culture studies: Vol. 3. Play in and out of context*. Stamford, CT: Ablex.

Christman, M. (1979). A look at sociodramatic play among Mexican-American children. *Childhood Education, 55*, 106–110.

Clawson, M. A. (2002). Play of language-minority children in early childhood settings. In J. L. Roopnarine (Ed.), *Play and culture studies: Vol. 4. Social-cognitive, and contextual issues in the fields of play* (pp. 93–110). Westport, CT: Ablex.

Cooney, M. H., & Sha, J. (1999). Play in the day of Qiaoqiao: A Chinese perspective. *Child Study Journal, 29*(2), 97–111.

Corsaro, W. (1979). We're friends, right? Children's use of access rituals in a nursery school. *Language in Society, 8*, 315–336.

Corsaro, W. (1985). *Friendship and peer culture in the early years*. Norwood, NJ: Ablex.

Corsaro, W. A. (2003). *"We're friends, right?" Inside kids' culture*. Washington, DC: Joseph Henry Press.

Corsaro, W., & Rizzo, T. (1988). *Discussione* and friendship: Socialization processes in the peer culture of Italian nursery school children. *American Sociological Review, 53*, 879–894.

Corsaro, W. A., & Schwarz, K. (1991). Peer play and socialization in two cultures: Implications for research and practice. In B. Scales, M. Almy, A. Nicolopoulou, & S. Ervin-Tripp (Eds.), *Play and the social context of development in early care and education* (pp. 234–254). New York: Teachers College Press.

Crick, N. R., Casas, J. F., & Mosher, M. (1997). Relational and overt aggression in preschool. *Developmental Psychology, 33*(4), 579–588.

deMarrais, K. B., Nelson, P. A., & Baker, J. H. (1994). Meaning in mud: Yup'ik Eskimo girls at play. In J. L. Roopnarine, J. E. Johnson, & F. H. Hooper (Eds.), *Children's play in diverse cultures* (pp. 179–209). Albany: State University of New York Press.

Dockett, S., & Fleer, M. (1999). *Play and pedagogy in early childhood: Bending the rules*. Orlando, FL: Harcourt Brace.

Dundes, A., Leach, J. W., & Ozkok, B. (1970). Strategy of Turkish boys' verbal dueling rhymes. *Journal of American Folklore, 83*, 325–349.

Edwards, C. P. (2000). Children's play in cross-cultural perspective: A new look at the six cultures study. *Cross-Cultural Research, 34*(4), 318–339.

Fagot, B. I. (1994). Peer relations and the development of competence in boys and girls. *New Directions for Child Development, 65,* 53–65.

Fagot, B. I., & Kronsberg, S. J. (1982). Sex differences: Biological and social factors influencing the behavior of young boys and girls. In S. G. Moore & C. R. Cooper (Eds.), *The young child: Reviews of research* (Vol. 3, pp. 193–210). Washington, DC: National Association for the Education of Young Children.

Fagot, B. I., & Leinbach, M. D. (1989). The young child's gender schema: Environmental input, internal organization. *Child Development, 60,* 663–672.

Fagot, B. I., Leinbach, M. D., & Hagan, R. (1986). Gender labeling and the adoption of sex-typed behaviors. *Developmental Psychology, 22,* 440–443.

Fagot, B. I., & Leve, L. (1998). Gender identity and play. In D. P. Fromberg & D. Bergen (Eds.), *Play from birth to twelve and beyond: Contexts, perspectives, and meanings* (pp. 187–192). New York: Garland.

Farver, J. (1993). Cultural differences in scaffolding pretend play: A comparison of American and Mexican American mother-child and sibling-child pairs. In K. MacDonald (Ed.), *Parent-child play: Descriptions and implications* (pp. 349–366). Albany: State University of New York Press.

Farver, J., & Howes, C. (1993). Cultural differences in American and Mexican mother-child pretend play. *Merrill-Palmer Quarterly, 39,* 344–358.

Farver, J., Kim, Y. K, & Lee, Y. (1995). Cultural differences in Korean- and Anglo-American preschoolers' social interaction and play behaviors. *Child Development, 66,* 1088–1099.

Farver, J., Kim, Y., & Lee-Shen, Y. (2000). Within cultural differences in Korean American and European American preschoolers social pretend play. *Journal of Cross-Cultural Psychology, 31,* 583–602.

Farver, J., & Wimbarti, S. (1995). Indonesian toddlers' social play with their mothers and older siblings. *Child Development, 66,* 1493–1503.

Farwell, L. (1930). Reactions of kindergarten, first, and second grade children to constructive play materials. *Genetic Psychology Monographs, 8,* 431–562.

Fishbein, H., Malone, D.M., & Stegelin, D.A. (2009). Playmate preferences of preschool children based on race, sex, and perceived physical attractiveness. In D. Kuschner (Ed.), *From children to red hatters: Diverse images and issues of play* (Play & Culture Studies, V. 9, pp. 74–92). Lanham, MD: University Press of American.

Garvey, C. (1977). *Play.* Cambridge, MA: Harvard University Press.

Geary, D.C. (1998). *Male, female: The evolution of human sex differences.* Washington, DC: American Psychological Association.

Geertz, C. (1972). Deep play: Notes on the Balinese cockfight. *Daedalus, 101,* 1–37.

Goldstein, K. S. (1971). Strategy in counting out: An ethnographic folklore field study. In E. Avedon & B. Sutton-Smith (Eds.), *The study of games* (pp. 167–178). New York: Wiley.

Goncu, A., & Mosier, C. (1991). *Cultural variations in the play of toddlers.* Paper presented at the biannual meeting of the Society for Research in Child Development, Seattle, WA.

Gossen, G. H. (1976). Verbal dueling in Chamula. In B. Kirshenblatt-Gimblett (Ed.), *Speech play* (pp. 121–146). Philadelphia: University of Pennsylvania Press.

Greenfield, P. M., & Cocking, R. (1994). *Cross-cultural roots of minority child development.* Mahwah, NJ: Erlbaum.

Groos, K. (1901). *The play of man.* New York: Appleton.

Haight, W. (1998). Adult direct and indirect influences on play. In D. P. Fromberg & D. Bergen (Eds.), *Play from birth to twelve and beyond: Contexts, perspective, and meanings* (pp. 259–265). New York: Garland.

Haight, W., Masiello, T., Dickson, L., Huckeby E., & Black, J. (1994). The everyday contexts and social functions of spontaneous mother-child play in the home. *Merrill-Palmer Quarterly, 40,* 509–533.

Haight, W. L., & Miller, P. J. (1992). The development of everyday pretend play: A longitudinal study of mothers' participation. *Merrill-Palmer Quarterly, 38,* 331–349.

Haight, W. L., & Miller, P. J. (1993). *Pretending at home: Early development in a sociocultural context.* Albany: State University of New York Press.

Haight, W. L., Parke, R. D., & Black, J. E. (1997). Mothers' and fathers' beliefs about and spontaneous participation in their toddlers' pretend play. *Merrill-Palmer Quarterly, 43,* 271–290.

Haight, W., & Sachs, K. (1995). A longitudinal study of the enactment of negative emotion during mother-child pretend play from 1–4 years. In L. Sperry & P. Smiley (Eds.), *New directions in child development: Developmental dimensions of self and other* (pp. 33–46). San Francisco: Jossey-Bass.

Haight, W., Wang, X., Fung, H., Williams, K., & Mintz, J. (1995). *The ecology of everyday pretending in three cultural communities.* Paper presented at the biannual meeting of the Society for Research in Child Development, Indianapolis, IN.

Haight, W. L., Wang, X., Fung, H. H., Williams, K., & Mintz, J. (1999). Universal, developmental, and variable aspects of young children's play: A cross cultural comparison of pretending at home. *Child Development, 70*(6), 1477–1488.

Holmes, R. (1999). Kindergarten and college students' view of play and work at home and at school. In S. Reifel (Ed.), *Play and culture studies* (Vol. 2, pp. 59–72). Stamford, CT: Ablex.

Howes, C., & Wu, F. (1990). Peer interactions and friendships in an ethnically diverse school setting. *Child Development, 61,* 537–541.

Hrncir, E., Speller, G., & West, M. (1983). *What are we testing? A cross-cultural comparison of infant competence.* (ERIC Document Reproduction Service No. ED230309)

Hughes, P., & MacNaughton, G. (2001). Fractured or manufactured: Gendered identities and culture in the early years. In S. Grieshaber & G. Cannella (Eds.), *Embracing identities in early childhood education: Diversity and possibilities* (pp. 114–130). New York: Teachers College Press.

Huizinga, J. (1950). *Homo ludens: A study of the play-element in culture.* Boston: Beacon. (Original work published 1938).

Hutt, C. (1970). Specific and diverse exploration. In H. W. Reese & L. P. Lipsett (Eds.), *Advances in child development and behavior* (Vol. 5). New York: Academic Press.

Jarrett, O. S., Farokhi, B., Young, C., & Davies, G. (2001). Boys and girls at play: Recess at a southern urban elementary school. In S. Reifel (Ed.), *Play and culture studies: Vol. 3. Play in and out of context* (pp. 147–170). Stamford, CT: Ablex.

Johnson, R. (2005). The amorphous pretend play curriculum: Theorizing embodied synthetic multicultural props. In S. Ryan & S. Grieshaber (Eds.), *Practical transformations and transformational practices: Globalization, postmodernism, and early childhood education: Vol. 14. Advances in early education and day care* (pp. 93–108). New York: Elsevier/JAI.

Jwa, S., & Frost, J. L. (2003). Contextual differences in Korean mother-child interactions: A study of scaffolding behaviors. In D. Lytle (Ed.), *Play and educational theory and practice: Vol. 5. Play and Culture Studies* (pp. 299–322). Westport, CT: Praeger.

Karnik, R., & Tudge, J. (2010). The reality of pretend play: Ethnic, socioeconomic, and gender variations in young children's involvement. In E. E. Nwokah (Ed.), *Play as engagement and communication* (*Play & Culture Studies*, V. 10, pp. 63-81). Lanham, MD: University Press of American.

Kelly-Byrne, D. (1989). *A child's play life: An ethnographic study.* New York: Teachers College Press.

Kohlberg, L. (1966). A cognitive-developmental analysis of children's sex role concepts and attitudes. In E. E. Maccoby (Ed.),*The development of sex differences* (pp. 82–172). Stanford, CA: Stanford University Press.

Lamb, S., & Brown, L.M. (2006). *Packaging girlhood: Rescuing our daughters from marketers' schemes.* New York: St. Martin's Press.

Lancy, D. F. (1996). *Playing on the mother-ground: Cultural routines for children's development.* New York: Guilford.

Leaper, C. (1994). Exploring the consequence of gender segregation on social relationships. In C. Leaper (Ed.), W. Damon (Series Ed.), *New directions for child development: Vol. 65. Childhood gender segregation: Causes and consequences* (pp. 67–86). San Francisco: Jossey-Bass.

Lee, H. (1960). *To kill a mockingbird.* New York: Warner.

Lefever, H. (1981). "Playing the dozens": A mechanism for social control. *Phylon, 42,* 73–85.

Lewis, C. C. (1994). The roots of discipline in Japanese preschools: Meeting children's needs for friendship and contribution. In S. Reifel (Ed.), *Advances in early education and day care: Vol. 6. Topics in early literacy, teacher preparation, and international perspectives on early care* (pp. 259–278). Greenwich, CT: JAI.

Lieberman, J. (1965). Playfulness and divergent thinking: An investigation of their relationship at the kindergarten level. *Journal of Creative Behavior, 1,* 391–397.

Lin, S.-H., & Reifel, S. (1999). Context and meanings in Taiwanese kindergarten play. In S. Reifel (Ed.), *Play and culture studies* (Vol. 2, pp. 151–176). Stamford, CT: Ablex.

Lindsey, E. W., & Mize, J. (2001). Contextual differences in parent-child play: Implications for children's gender role development. *Sex Roles: A Journal of Research, 44* (3–4), 55–76.

Maccoby, E. E. (1990). Gender and relationships: A developmental account. *American Psychologist, 45,* 513–520.

MacNaughton, G. (1997). Who's got the power? Rethinking equity strategies in early childhood. *International Journal of Early Years Education, 5,* 57–66.

MacNaughton, G. (1999). Even pink tents have glass ceilings: Crossing the gender boundaries in pretend play. In E. Dau & E. Jones (Eds.), *Child's play: Revisiting play in early childhood settings.* Australia New South Wales. (ERIC Document Reproduction Services No. ED433969).

Martini, M. (1994). Peer interactions in Polynesia: A view from the Marquesas. In J. L. Roopnarine, J. E. Johnson, & F. H. Hooper (Eds.), *Children's play in diverse cultures* (pp. 73–103). Albany: State University of New York Press.

McLoyd, V. (1980). Verbally expressed modes of transformation in the fantasy play of black preschool children. *Child Development, 51,* 1133–1139.

McLoyd, V. (1983). Class, culture, and pretend play: A reply to Sutton-Smith and Smith. *Developmental Review, 3,* 11–17.

Moller, L. C., & Serbin, L. A. (1996). Antecedents of toddler gender segregation: Cognitive consonance, gender-typed toy preferences and behavioral compatibility. *Sex Roles, 28,* 136–147.

Montare, A., & Boone, S. (1980). Aggression and paternal absence: Racial-ethnic differences among inner-city boys. *Journal of Genetic Psychology, 137,* 223–232.

Moon, K., & Reifel, S. (2008). Play and literacy learning in a diverse language prekindergarten classroom. *Contemporary Issues in Early Childhood, 8*(4), 49–65.

Moore, R., & Gilliard, J. L. (2010). Preservice teachers' perceptions of culture in early care and education programs on a Native American Indian reservation. *Journal of Early Childhood Teacher Education, 28,* 17–30.

Nevius, J. (1982). Social participation and culture in play groups of young children. *Journal of Social Psychology, 116,* 291–292.

Nevius, J., Filgo, D., Soldier, L., & Simmons-Rains, B. (1983). Relation of social participation to activity in young children's free choice play. *Educational & Psychological Research, 3,* 95–102.

New, R. S. (1994). Child's play—*una cosanaturale:* An Italian perspective. In J. L. Roopnarine, J. E. Johnson, & F. H. Hooper (Eds.), *Children's play in diverse cultures* (pp. 123–147). Albany: State University of New York Press.

Nicolopoulou, A., Scales, G., & Weintraub, J. (1994). Gender differences in the symbolic imagination in stories of four-year-olds. In A. Dyson & C. Genishi (Eds.), *The need for story: Cultural diversity in classroom and community* (pp. 102–123). Urbana, IL: National Council of Teachers of English.

Nwokah, E. E., & Ikekeonwu, C. (1998). A sociocultural comparison of Nigerian and American children's games. In M. Duncan, G. Chick, & A. Aycock (Eds.), S. Reifel (Series Ed.), *Play and culture studies: Vol. 1. Diversions and divergences in fields of play* (pp. 59–76). Greenwich, CT: Ablex.

O'Neill-Wagner, P., Bolig, R., & Price, C. S. (2001). Developmental aspects of play-partner selection in young rhesus monkeys. In J. L. Roopnarine (Ed.), *Play and culture studies: Vol. 4. Conceptual, social-cognitive, and contextual issues in the fields of play* (pp. 111–126). Westport, CT: Ablex.

Opie, I., & Opie, P. (1959). *The lore and language of schoolchildren.* New York: Oxford University Press.

Opie, I., & Opie, P. (1997). *Children's games with things.* New York: Oxford University Press.

Ostrov, J. M., & Keating, C. F. (2004). Gender differences in preschool aggression during free play and structured interactions: An observational study. *Social Development, 13(2),* 255–277.

Ostrov, J. M., Woods, K. E., Jansen, E. A., Casas, J. F., & Crick, N. R. (2004). An observational study of delivered and received aggression, gender, and social-psychological adjustment in preschool: "This white crayon doesn't work . . ." *Early Childhood Research Quarterly, 19,* 355–371.

Paley, V. G. (1981). *Wally's stories.* Cambridge, MA: Harvard University Press.

Paley, V. G. (1984). *Boys and girls: Superheroes in the doll corner.* Chicago: University of Chicago Press.

Paley, V. G. (1992). *You can't say you can't play.* Cambridge, MA: Harvard University Press.

Paley, V.G. (2000). *White teacher* (2nd Ed.). Cambridge, MA: Harvard University Press.

Paley, V. G. (2004). *A child's work: The importance of fantasy play.* Chicago: University of Chicago Press.

Pan, H.-L. W. (1994). Children's play in Taiwan. In J. L. Roopnarine, J. E. Johnson, & F. H. Hooper (Eds.), *Children's play in diverse cultures* (pp. 31–50). Albany: State University of New York Press.

Peffer, J. (2009). *Art and the end of apartheid.* Minneapolis: University of Minnesota Press.

Pellegrini, A. D. (1988). Elementary school children's rough-and-tumble play and social competence. *Developmental Psychology, 24,* 802–806.

Pellegrini, A. D. (1995). *School recess and playground behavior: Educational and developmental roles.* Albany: State University of New York Press.

Pellegrini, A. D. (2002). Perceptions of play fighting and real fighting: Effects of sex and participant status. In J. L. Roopnarine (Ed.), *Play and culture studies: Vol. 4. Social-cognitive, and contextual issues in the fields of play* (pp. 223–233). Westport, CT: Ablex.

Pellegrini, A. D., & Smith, P. K. (1998). Physical activity play: The nature and function of a neglected aspect of play. *Child Development, 69,* 577–598.

Piaget, J. (1965). *The moral judgment of the child.* New York: Free Press. (Original work published 1932.)

Ramsey, P. G. (1998). Diversity and play: Influences of race, culture, class, and gender. In D. P. Fromberg & D. Bergen (Eds.),*Play from birth to twelve and beyond: Contexts, perspectives, and meanings* (pp. 23–33). New York: Garland.

Reifel, S. (2007). Hermeneutic text analysis of play: Exploring meaningful early childhood classroom events. In J. A. Hatch (Ed.), *Early childhood qualitative research* (pp. 25–42). New York: Routledge.

Reifel, S. (2009). Girls' doll play in educational, virtual, ideological, and market contexts: A case analysis of controversy. *Contemporary Issues in Early Childhood, 10(4),* 343–352.

Riojas-Cortez, M. (2001). Preschoolers' funds of knowledge displayed through sociodramatic play episodes in a bilingual classroom. *Early Childhood Education Journal, 29(1),* 35–40.

Riojas-Cortez, M., & Flores, B.B. (2004). *Los padres y los maestros:* Perspectives of play among bilingual stakeholders in public schools. In S. Reifel & M. Brown (Eds.), *Social Contexts of Early Education, and Reconceptualizing Play (II)* (*Advances in Early Education and Day Care,* V. 13, pp. 267–288). New York: Elsevier.

Robinson, C. (1978). *The uses of order and disorder in play: An analysis of Vietnamese refugee children's play.* (ERIC Document Reproduction Service No. ED153944).

Rogers, C. S., Impara, J. C., Frary, R. B., Harris, T., Meeks, A., Semanic-Lauth, S., & Reynolds, M. R. (1998). Measuring playfulness: Development of the Child Behaviors Inventory of Playfulness. In M. Duncan, G. Chick, & A. Aycock (Eds.), S. Reifel (Series Ed.), *Play and culture studies: Vol. 1. Diversions and divergences in fields of play* (pp. 151–168). Greenwich, CT: Ablex.

Rogoff, B., Mistry, A., Goncu, A., & Mosier, C. (1993). Guided participation in cultural activity by toddlers and caregivers.*Monographs of the Society for Research in Child Development, 58,* Serial No. 236.

Roopnarine, J. L., Johnson, J. E., & Hooper, F. H. (Eds.). (1994). *Children's play in diverse cultures.* Albany: State University of New York Press.

Roth, W. E. (1902). Games, sports, and amusements. *North Queensland Ethnography,* Bulletin No. 4.

Rubin, K. H., Fein, G. G., & Vandenberg, B. (1983). Play. In E. M. Hetherington (Ed.), P. H. Mussen (Series Ed.), *Handbook of child psychology: Vol. 4. Socialization, personality, and social development* (pp. 693–774). New York: Wiley.

Ruble, D. N., & Martin, C. L. (1998). Gender development. In N. Eisenberg (Ed.), *Handbook of child psychology: Social, emotional, and personality development.* (Vol. 3, 5th ed., pp. 933–1016). New York: Wiley.

Salter, M.A. (1974). *Play: A medium of cultural stability.* Paper presented at the International Seminar on the History of Physical Education and Sport, Vienna.

Scales, B. (1996). Researching the hidden curriculum. In J. Chafel & S. Reifel (Ed.), S. Reifel (Series Ed.) *Advances in early education and day care: Vol. 8. Theory and practice in early childhood teaching* (pp. 237–259). Greenwich, CT: JAI.

Scales, B., & Cook-Gumperz, J. (1993). Gender in narrative and play: A view from the frontier. In S. Reifel (Ed.), *Advances in early education and day care: Vol. 5. Perspectives on developmentally appropriate practice* (pp. 167–195). Greenwich, CT: JAI.

Schellhaas, A., Burts, D.C., & Aghayan, C. (2010). Reflecting on "Project Katrina" and developmentally appropriate practices: A graduate student's perspective. *Journal of Early Childhood Teacher Education, 28,* 77–81.

Schwartzman, H. (1978). *Transformations: The anthropology of children's play.* New York: Plenum.

Schwartzman, H. G. (1986). A cross-cultural perspective on child-structured play activities and materials. In A. W. Gottfried & C. C. Brown (Eds.), *Play interactions: The contribution of play materials and parental involvement to children's development* (pp. 13–30). Lexington, MA: Lexington.

Serbin, L. A., & Sprafkin, C. (1986). The salience of gender and the process of sex typing in three- to seven-year-old children. *Child Development, 57,* 1188–1199.

Slaughter, D. T., & Dombrowski, J. (1989). Cultural continuities and discontinuities: Impact on social and pretend play. In M. N. Bloch & A. D. Pellegrini (Eds.), *The ecological context of children's play* (pp. 282–310). Norwood, NJ: Ablex.

Smith, P. K., Smees, R., Pellegrini, A.D., & Menesini, E. (2002). Comparing pupil and teacher perceptions for playful fighting, serious fighting, and positive peer interaction. In J. L. Roopnarine (Ed.), *Play and culture studies: Vol. 4. Social-cognitive, and contextual issues in the fields of play* (pp. 235–245). Westport, CT: Ablex.

Suito, N., & Reifel, S. (1993). Aspects of gender role in American and Japanese play. *Journal of Play Theory & Research, 1,* 26–54.

Sutterby, J. A. (2001). *Todos somos amigas: Cross-cultural and cross-linguistic play interactions in a two-way immersion prekindergarten classroom.* Unpublished doctoral dissertation. University of Texas, Austin.

Sutton-Smith, B. (1983). Commentary on social class differences in socio-dramatic play in historical context: A reply to McLoyd. *Developmental Review, 3,* 1–5.

Sutton-Smith, B. (1997). *The ambiguity of play.* Cambridge, MA: Harvard University Press.

Takeuchi, M. (1994). Children's play in Japan. In J. L. Roopnarine, J. E. Johnson, & F. H. Hooper (Eds.), *Children's play in diverse cultures* (pp. 51–72). Albany: State University of New York Press.

Taylor, S. I., Rogers, C. S., & Kaiser, J. (1999). A comparison of playfulness among American and Japanese preschoolers. In S. Reifel (Ed.), *Play and Culture Studies* (Vol. 2. pp. 143–150). Stamford, CT: Ablex.

Tietz, J., & Shine, S. (2000). The interaction of gender and play style in the development of gender segregation. In S. Reifel (Ed.), *Play and culture studies: Vol. 3. Play in and out of context* (pp. 131–146). Stamford, CT: Ablex.

Tobin, J., Hsueh, Y., & Karasawa, M. (2009). *Preschool in three cultures revisited: China, Japan, and the United States.* Chicago: University of Chicago Press.

Trawick-Smith, J. (2010). Drawing back the lens on play: A frame analysis of young children's play in Puerto Rico. *Early Education and Development, 21(4),* 536–567.

Tudge, J., Lee, S., & Putnam, S. (1998). Young children's play in socio-cultural context: South Korea and the United States. In M. C. Duncan, G. Chick, & A. Aycock (Eds.), S. Reifel (Series Ed.), *Play and culture studies: Vol. 1. Diversions and divergences in fields of play* (pp. 77–90). Greenwich, CT: Ablex.

Twain, M. (2003). *The adventures of Huckleberry Finn.* New York: Bantam. (Original work published 1884.)

Tyler, E. B. (1871). *Primitive culture: Researches into the development of mythology, philosophy, language, art and custom.* London: Murray.

Tyler, E. B. (1971). The history of games. In E. M. Avedon & B. Sutton-Smith (Eds.), *The study of games* (pp. 63–76). New York: Wiley. (Original work published 1879.)

Udwin, O., & Shmukler, D. (1981). The influence of socio-cultural, economic and home background factors on children's ability to engage in imaginative play. *Developmental Psychology, 17,* 66–72.

Ugaste, A. (2007). The cultural-historical approach to play in the kindergarten context. In T. Jambor & J. Gils (Eds.), *Several perspectives on children's play: Scientific reflections for practitioners* (pp. 105-118). Philadelphia: Garant.

Van Alstyne, D. (1932). *Play behavior and choice of play materials of preschool children.* Chicago: University of Chicago Press.

Van Hoorn, J., Scales, B., Nourot, P. M., & Alward, K. R. (2007). *Play at the center of the curriculum* (3rd ed.). Upper Saddle River, NJ: Merrill/Prentice Hall.

Van Rheenan, D. (2000). Boys who play hopscotch: The historical divide of a gendered space. In S. Reifel (Ed.), *Play and culture studies: Vol. 3. Play in and out of context* (pp. 111–130). Stamford, CT: Ablex.

Whiting, B. B. (1980). Culture and social behavior. *Ethos, 2,* 95–116.

Whiting, B. B., & Edwards, C. P. (1988). *Children of different worlds: The formation of social behavior.* Cambridge, MA: Harvard University Press.

Whiting, B. B., & Whiting, J. (1975). *Children of six cultures.* Cambridge, MA: Harvard University Press.

Whiting, J.W., & Child, I.L. (1953). *Child training and personality: A cross-cultural study.* New Haven, CT: Yale University Press.

Wolfenstein, M. (1954). *Children's humor: A psychological analysis.* Glencoe, IL: Free Press.

Wood, E. (2009). Conceptualizing a pedagogy of play: International perspectives from theory, policy and practice. In D. Kuschner (Ed.), *From children to red hatters: Diverse images and issues of play* (*Play & Culture Studies*, V. 9, pp. 166-189). Lanham, MD: University Press of American.

Woods, I. C. (1997). *Rethinking Froebel's kindergarten metaphor: Culture and development in multiple settings.* Unpublished doctoral dissertation, University of Texas, Austin.

Xu, Y., Farver, J. M., Schwartz, D., & Chang, L. (2003). Identifying aggressive victims in Chinese children's peer groups. *International Journal of Behavioral Development, 27,* 243–252.

Yawkey, T., & Alverez-Dominques, J. (1984). *Comparisons of free play behaviors of Hispanic and Anglo middle-class SES five-year-olds.* Paper presented at the annual meeting of the American Educational Research Association, New Orleans.

Young, J. (1985). The cultural significance of (male) children's playground activities. *Alberta Journal of Educational Research, 31,* 125–138.

Zosuls, K., et al. (2009). The acquisition of gender labels in infancy: Implications for gender-typed play. *Developmental Psychology, 79,* 284–302.

# 8 Play and the Curriculum

**Jeffrey Trawick-Smith**
*Eastern Connecticut State University*

*A play-centered curriculum is not a laissez-faire curriculum in which anything goes. It is a curriculum that uses the power of play to foster children's development. It is an emergent curriculum in which teachers take an active role in balancing spontaneous play, guided play, directed play, and teacher-directed activities.*

(Van Hoorn, Nourot, Scales, & Alward, 2007)

*While play can be educational in the school sense, we should never forget that its much more vital role in learning has to do with child culture, not with adult culture; and furthermore, it has a festive role to perform that is often the very antithesis of our own educational concerns.*

(Sutton-Smith, 1998, p. 34)

*Uh-oh, here comes Mrs. R. Now she's going to ask us, "What are you playing?" and then you have to answer, and then she just talks and talks and talks, and we can never finish the castle for Queen Wonder.*

(A 4–year-old child in a dramatic play center, warning a peer about an approaching teacher)

Most educators advocate a play-based curriculum, especially for young children (Copple, 2009; Van Hoorn et al., 2007). But what does that mean? There is much disagreement in the field about why and how play should be integrated and enhanced in classrooms. This chapter explores the similarities and differences among the various approaches to play found in schools and centers. We examine the purposes for including play, the types of activities and classroom arrangements included, and the outcomes of these approaches.

 ## COMMON ELEMENTS OF PLAY-BASED CURRICULUM MODELS

**Play-based classrooms** often appear to be quite similar. Their play spaces may be organized in a similar fashion; they include like materials. Daily schedules often resemble one another, each offering extended periods of time for free play. Usually, such programs include methods for observing and facilitating children's play. These common elements of play-based classrooms are examined first.

## Classroom Centers and Their Arrangement

Most play-oriented programs are arranged into clearly defined **play centers** (or *learning centers*). Table 8.1 presents types of centers typically found in play-based classrooms. These centers are often constructed and organized in special ways to enhance play. Research on classroom space has shown that three play center design features promote play development and learning (Clayton, Forton, & Doolittle, 2001; Curtis & Carter, 2003; Trawick-Smith, 1992): (a) logical arrangement of space and materials, (b) a modified open-plan design, and (c) stimulus shelters.

**Arrangement of Space and Materials** A logical arrangement of centers has been found to increase play frequency and quality and to promote learning. Such an arrangement is one in which compatible materials are positioned near one another and far away from incompatible ones. In most play-based classrooms, for example, blocks, dramatic play, or motor play centers are placed together and far away from quieter centers, such as the book, computer, and science areas. In logically organized classrooms, messy

**TABLE 8.1** Common Classroom Play Centers

| Play Center | Sample Materials |
| --- | --- |
| Dramatic play center | Dress-up clothes<br>Dòlls<br>Housekeeping props (dishes, mirror, plastic tools, etc.)<br>Thematic props (post office props, grocery store props, etc.)<br>Literacy props (checkbooks, grocery lists, envelopes, etc.) |
| Block area | Set of hardwood blocks<br>Set of large hollow blocks<br>Set of smaller table blocks<br>Replica play sets (farm sets, parking garage sets, train sets)<br>Replica play toys (plastic people, toy cars, dinosaurs, etc.) |
| Art center | Paint (tempera, watercolor sets, block printing paints, etc.)<br>Paper (construction, butcher, posterboard, cardboard, etc.)<br>Drawing implements (markers, crayons, chalk, pens, etc.)<br>Collage media (buttons, seeds, beans, cut-and-paste materials)<br>Sculpting materials (clay, sand, plaster, wire, papier-mâché) |
| Music center | Recorded music and tape recorders with headphones<br>Stringed instruments (autoharp, child-made guitars, etc.)<br>Percussion instruments (drums, rhythm sticks and blocks)<br>Shakers (maracas, child-made rain sticks, etc.)<br>Materials for reading and composing music (song charts, music writing<br>   materials, sheet music, etc.) |
| Book center | Collection of high-quality children's literature<br>Big books<br>Child-made books<br>Puppets of characters from children's books<br>Comfortable sites for reading (bean bags, carpet squares, couches, etc.) |
| Writing center | Writing implements (pens, computer, movable alphabet)<br>Child journals<br>Blank books<br>Clipboards<br>Stationery and envelopes |
| Manipulatives center | Legos<br>Puzzles<br>Bristle blocks<br>Lacing boards<br>Peg boards |
| Math/science/cognitive center | Geoboards<br>Ordering and categorization games<br>Card and dice games<br>Scientific tools (magnifying glasses, balances, thermometers, etc.)<br>Live animals for observation and care |

(*continued*)

**TABLE 8.1** *Continued*

| Play Center | Sample Materials |
| --- | --- |
| Water/textural center | Water table with measuring and floating materials<br>Toy ships, fish, and people for water play<br>Sand<br>Beans, rice, and other textural materials<br>Funnels, tubes, and other tools for pouring experiments |
| Motor play (indoors) | Riding toys<br>Small climber/play house<br>Balls<br>Obstacle courses<br>Jump ropes |
| Motor play (outdoors) | Riding toys<br>Large playscape with slides, swinging tires, lofts, and climbing nets<br>Sand boxes<br>Hills for climbing and rolling<br>Large parachutes and balls |

areas, such as art or water play, are situated over washable floor surfaces and near a source of water. Less active, more intimate activities are provided far away from louder ones and are situated on softer surfaces, such as carpeting. Comfortable cushions or couches may be provided for these quieter play experiences.

Logical arrangement of materials *within* centers is also important. Both research and anecdotal evidence have shown that children will acquire greater cognitive skills if they are enrolled in classrooms where the materials themselves are ordered in clear and logical ways within each play area (Curtis & Carter, 2003; Golbeck, Rand, & Soundy, 1986; Isbel & Excelby, 2001; Olds, 2000). For example, materials of like function might be stored in the same place in the dramatic play area (e.g., cooking and eating materials on one shelf, dolls and doll clothes on another, and plastic tools, work boots, and hard hats on another). In the block center, blocks might be stored on shelves based on shape. Within shelves, smaller blocks might be placed on upper shelves, larger blocks on lower ones. Cleanup time then becomes an elaborate categorization task.

**Modified Open-Plan Design** One effective way that play centers can be defined is through the use of visual partitions—bookshelves, bulletin boards, and other dividers that separate one area from another. In his classic research on play space, Moore and his colleagues (2000, 2002; Moore, Sugyama, & O'Donnell, 2003) discovered that a **modified open-plan design**—one in which centers are divided on two or three sides, but left open on at least one side for easy access—was superior to other arrangements in promoting play persistence and quality. In another study, visual partitioning was found to double the rate of children's engagement in play tasks in child care settings (Trawick-Smith & Landry-Fitzsimmons, 1992).

The preschool classroom floor plan shown in Figure 8.1 reflects a modified open-plan design and a logical arrangement of learning centers. Figure 8.2 shows these same design features for a third-grade classroom.

**Stimulus Shelters** A final design concept that has been found to contribute to development is the provision of a **stimulus shelter,** a space for children to be alone and to enjoy a brief

In a modified open plan design, visual partitions separate one area from another.

respite from active classroom life. Cozy spaces for just one or two children that are separated from the rest of the classroom have been found to contribute to feelings of comfort and security in school (Evans, 2005; Maxwell, 2007; Moore, 2002). A small loft filled with pillows, dolls, and puppets is an example.

**Balance of Play Materials** Most play-based programs include similar kinds of materials; Table 8.1 presents examples of these. A **balance of play materials** has been found to be most critical to the quality of children's play. Prescott (1987, 2008) has found that a good balance between complex versus simple materials and

---

### WHAT TEACHERS AND CAREGIVERS CAN DO: CREATING PLAY CENTERS THAT SUPPORT PLAY

1. Include a variety of different learning centers that encourage children to create, investigate, pretend, and solve problems, including blocks, dramatic play, art, science, math, literacy and books, and motor play activities.

2. Arrange centers so quieter areas are away from louder, messy activities are near water, and complementary centers, such as blocks and dramatic play or writing and books, are together.

3. Organize materials within centers, using labels and pictures, so children (and teachers) know where things can be found or put away during clean up time.

4. Partition centers on two or three sides, using dividers or bookshelves to shelter play activities and create a cozy feel.

5. Add a soft, inviting getaway space, in which one or two children can spend time, when they want a break from active classroom life.

**FIGURE 8.1** Preschool Classroom Floor Plan Reflecting Design Principles

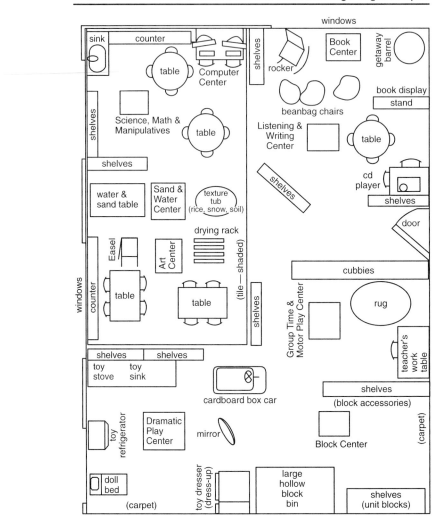

open-ended versus closed ones was associated with greater play involvement and a smoother day in child-care centers. She defines *complex materials* as those with many uses (e.g., sculpting clay), whereas *simple materials* have only one or a few (e.g., a book). She describes *open-ended materials* as those with which children are able to express themselves freely and creatively (e.g., hardwood blocks) and *closed materials* as those with only a single use (e.g., an ordering game in which objects are arranged by size).

Prescott's research suggests that children benefit from an optimal mix of these various types of toys, games, and art media.

Prescott notes that balance among activities can be achieved within a single play center. To create more open-ended opportunities within a science area, for example, blank scientific journals and art materials can be added for sketching and writing. To add closed, convergent experiences to the block center, photos of buildings in the neighborhood can be posted for

**FIGURE 8.2** Primary Grade Floor Plan Reflecting Design Principles

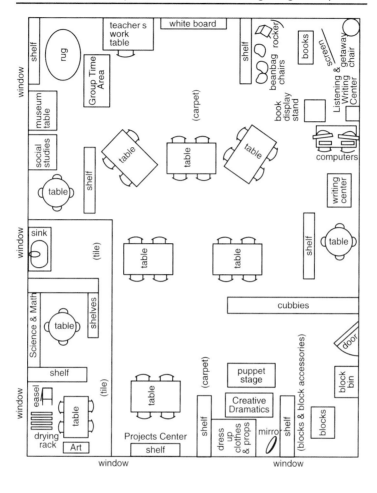

children to replicate. "Copy play cards" can be included, cards with sketches of block structures of varying degrees of complexity that children may choose to build.

Other researchers have discovered that nonrealistic materials—nondescript objects, such as boxes, cardboard pieces, or rubber shapes—contribute to play quality, particularly in the dramatic play center (Doctoroff, 2001; McLoyd, 1986a). In one study of play materials, it was discovered that the optimal balance between nonrealistic and realistic play objects was related to age (Trawick-Smith, 1993). For 2-and 3-year-olds, a center with only realistic props—toy kitchen

equipment or dolls, for example—elicited more language and symbolic play. For 4-year-olds, a center with a blend of realistic and nonrealistic props was most effective. Five- and 6-year-olds engaged in more language and make-believe in a center with only nonrealistic props.

A new kind of balance among play materials is now being considered in classroom planning: the balance between virtual and physical materials (Wang & Hoot, 2006). A growing body of research has found that physical play objects and computer-based materials provide distinctly different challenges and play opportunities for children. For example, in physical block building, children engage in more social interaction and collaboration and acquire physical knowledge through concrete experiences with balance and spatial relationships (Reifel & Yeatman, 1991; Trawick-Smith, Russell, & Swaminathan, 2010). In contrast, an electronic block building program at the computer enables them to perform unique, complex operations on shapes—rotating, flipping, enlarging, shrinking, and even cutting them in half (Clements & Samara, 2007). In the dramatic play area, children use physical props to enact pretend roles and events and create make-believe worlds. With painting and drawing programs, they engage in "graphic-narrative play," in which they narrate and even enact stories as they draw, using make believe voices, sound effects, and pretend actions (Takeuchi, 1994; Wright, 2007; Wright & Samaras, 1986). Prescott's guideline of balancing of play materials still applies, even with this new technology. Computer software should be balanced between creative, open-ended software and problem solving programs. More important, great care should be taken not to allow play to fall out of balance with too much computer play. With a barrage of sights and sounds from electronic media bombarding children in some American living rooms, the classroom may be the one place where children can engage in significant physical play with peers.

**Divergent Activities and Creative Expression**
Most play-based curricula focus on creative *process*—the imaginative expression of ideas and open-ended experimentation—rather than on end *products.* Activities that require divergent thinking are most common. For example, a play-oriented program is more likely to include a wide range of open-ended art materials (e.g., paint, markers, and sculpting clay) than an art project with a single intended outcome (e.g., making clown faces that all turn out the same). In a typical play-based curriculum, mathematics problems are more likely to have multiple solutions and multiple answers (e.g., constructing triangles in different ways with geo boards). Right answer–oriented math worksheets are less prevalent. This emphasis on creative process is based on several important research findings on play and divergent thinking:

## BLOCKS: "A SUPER TOY?"

This chapter suggests that parents, teachers, and caregivers provide a balance of materials that encourage open-ended expression and also convergent problem-solving. Toys that promote social interaction and verbalization are also important to include. Is there a single toy that can do all of these things? In a study of preschool children's free play with 64 different classroom materials, only one toy scored highest on all measures of play value: blocks (Trawick-Smith, Russell, & Swaminathan, 2010). Blocks scored extremely high on their ability to promote creative self-expression. More than other toys, blocks led children to invent and pretend in highly imaginative ways. Blocks also scored highest in this study on their effect on problem-solving and convergent thinking. When children were not creating with blocks, they were found to solve interesting problems of space, number, and balance. Finally, blocks had the highest ratings in their impact on social interaction and language use. Children were found to frequently build together, discussing and planning their structures.

These findings led the authors to conclude that blocks are a "super toy"—a material that does almost everything for children in terms of development—thinking, learning, problem-solving, creating, and interacting socially.

1. Open-ended play activities have been found to be related to **ideational fluency,** an ability to generate many and varied ideas in writing, language interactions, and art (Fisher, 1992; Lloyd & Howe, 2003).

2. Play has been found to lead to more effective problem solving because play experiences enable children to generate more solutions to challenging problems (Curran, 1999; Wyver & Spence, 1999).

## Safety

Play can be active and even rough. Common to all play programs is an overriding concern about safety. Not only does a safe space protect children—which is paramount—but it also allows for greater independence (National Association for the Education of Young Children, 2005). Children can explore and express themselves more freely when adults do not need to intervene constantly for safety reasons. Table 8.2 presents several major safety concerns and how materials and space can be planned to address them.

Regardless of how well play spaces are planned, however, there is no substitute for vigilant supervision. Adequate numbers of adults are needed in a classroom to keep children safe. NAEYC (2005) recommends an adult to child ratio of from 1:3 to 1:5 for infants and toddlers, with at least two adults always present. For preschool children, a ratio of from 1:4 to 1:10 is recommended, with no fewer than two adults supervising. A 1:10 ratio is encouraged for children who are older.

The mere presence of adults is not adequate to ensure that play will be safe (Schwebel, 2006). In a survey conducted by Peterson, Ewigman, and Kivlahan (1993), consensus was found among child development specialists and parents about how much supervision is needed: For children under 5, *constant* supervision is required. That is, very young children should never be out of sight of an adult. According to the survey, children of age 6 and older should not play on their own for more

than 5 minutes without an adult checking on them. These recommendations are based on the assumption that children are playing in safe spaces. Nearly all of those interviewed agreed that when children are playing in high-risk areas—where there are unsafe surfaces and materials or nearby traffic, for example—constant supervision is required at any age.

## Schedule of the Day

Most teachers in play-based programs follow a daily schedule that allows adequate time for play and a balance between active and quiet experiences. At least an hour of uninterrupted free play time is recommended for younger children (Bredekamp & Copple, 2009; Johnson et al., 2005). Even this time period may not be adequate. Several authors have reported that some children spend 45 minutes to an hour planning their play—designing play sets, negotiating roles, and discussing themes (Enz & Christie, 1997; Trawick-Smith, 1994b). At the end of an hour, some children may just be beginning actual play!

A **quiet-active-quiet schedule** is illustrated most clearly in the well-known High/Scope program, examined in a later section (Schweinhart, Montie, Xiang, Barnett, Belfield, & M. Nores, 2005). In this model, children follow a **plan-do-review structure.** They begin each day with a reflective teacher-directed group time in which they plan their play activities. Next comes a period of active playing. Another quiet period follows this play time, in which children review and evaluate their accomplishments. In this model, child-directed free play and teacher-guided, small-group activities are also alternated. Even the most ardent play enthusiasts believe that active periods should be occasionally broken up by short rest times.

## Observation and Assessment of Play

Most play-based programs include frequent observation and assessment of children's play. A fundamental role of teachers and caregivers is to

**TABLE 8.2**   Safety Concerns and Ways to Address Them

| Safety Concern | Protecting Children in the Classroom |
|---|---|
| Falling | Lofts, climbers, and other climbing equipment should have protective, 38-inch railings and should not be higher than several inches above children's reach. Impact-absorbing surfaces should extend at least four feet beyond the "fall zone" under climbing equipment (National Program for Playground Safety, 1999). |
| | Surfacing material should be 6 inches deep under moderately high climbers (5 feet or less) and up to 12 inches deep for higher equipment (NAEYC, 1998a). |
| | Unsafe equipment, such as slides without platform railings, trampolines, and unstable or imbalanced riding toys, should be avoided and children should wear impact- absorbing helmets when riding on tricycles, wagons, or bicycles (Sayre & Gallagher, 2001). |
| | For infants, cribs should have railings that are at least three quarters of a child's height (Kendrick, Kaufmann, & Messenger, 1991), and walkers should be avoided (Sayre & Gallagher, 2001). |
| | Indoor play surfaces should be made of a nonslip material and should be free of water or unmarked obstacles. |
| Traffic Accidents | All play spaces should be fenced and active play should take place far away from vehicular traffic. |
| Cuts, Scrapes, Pinches, and Splinters | All toys and equipment should be free of sharp or protruding areas, wood splinters, rough areas, chipping paint, and rust. Areas that can pinch or crush fingers, such as the bottoms of seesaws or merry-go-rounds, should be completely enclosed (Sayre & Gallagher, 2001). Play surfaces should be kept free of glass and other sharp objects. |
| Entrapment and Suffocation | Any opening in play equipment must be smaller than the width and length of a child's head—between 3.5 and 9 inches (Sayre & Gallagher, 2001). The distance between crib slats should be no more than 2.75 inches (Kendrick et al., 1991). Shades, drapes, and blinds should be tied out of reach and children's clothing should be free of strings, hooks, or buttons that might get caught in the equipment (Sayre & Gallagher, 2001). |
| | Toys and materials smaller than 1.25 inches in diameter should be avoided; plastic foam plates and cups and plastic utensils should not be used (Sayre & Gallagher, 2001). |
| Poisoning | Medications should be dated, appropriately administered, and stored out of reach. Only safe, nontoxic houseplants—such as jade plants, coleus, hen-and-chickens, rubber plants, and dracaena—should be displayed (Kendrick et al., 1991). |
| | Art supplies should be avoided that may contain toxic materials or are easily inhaled, such as powdered clay or tempera paint, lead-based glazes and paints, paints that require solvents to clean, commercial dyes, permanent markers, instant papier-mâché, instant or solvent-based glues, and aerosol sprays (Kendrick et al., 1991). |

step back from classroom interactions to study and record what children are doing. A recent study of a high quality child development center found that teachers spend more than 50% of their time during free play intently observing children's play interactions (Trawick-Smith, 2010). Observation is important, not just to determine if children are playing in useful ways, but to learn about their overall development. Are children highly engaged in their play, or do they wander, stare off, or flit from one activity to another? Are they interacting with peers in positive ways or exhibiting aggression or social isolation? Do they use language to express play ideas or have difficulty communicating with peers? Do they demonstrate important advancements in thinking and learning or struggle to solve problems or learn new things? Play can become a window through which teachers can observe these aspects of children's development.

There are many methods of observing and assessing play. The two most common in play-oriented programs are **anecdotal records** and **observation checklists**.

**Anecdotal Records.** Anecdotal records are brief, rich descriptions of children's behavior that are written by the teacher during daily classroom interactions. Skilled teachers learn to jot notes on what a particular child is doing during free play time, while also attending to the needs of other children. Usually, the teacher quickly writes an observation in a small notebook, then, soon after, expands what is written into a descriptive account. The following is an example of an anecdotal record that was written in a preschool classroom:

> B. tries to play with three other children in the sand box. One of the children, a girl, says, "No, you can't play." B. responds, "I can play." He steps very close to the girl. He clenches his fists. "I can play!" he shouts. The girl frowns and leaves the sand box. Other children follow her. "We're leaving," one of the boys says quietly, walking away. Only B. is now left in the sandbox. He picks up a scoop, shovels some sand, pours it out, then quickly leaves the sand box.

Notice several things about this anecdotal record:

1. The teacher selects a particularly interesting play interaction to record—one that reveals something about the child's overall development and peer relationships.

2. The teacher describes behaviors, but doesn't interpret. So, the teacher does not write, "B. is angry," but rather, "he steps very close" and "he clenches his fists."

3. The teacher writes a very rich and detailed description of children at play. The anecdotal record includes facial expressions, body language, dialogue, physical movement, and other descriptors. It includes a description of the whole play setting, including what all the children are doing.

4. The teacher has written many anecdotal records—not just this one—about the child, B., in various play contexts. Why? If B. performs this behavior only once, it might be concluded that he is just in a bad mood. If he behaves in this way over three or four observation periods, it can be inferred that he is having difficulty interacting with peers.

## Observation Checklists

An observation checklist is a listing of behaviors that teachers can watch for in children's play. When teachers see one of these behaviors, they make a mark on the checklist to indicate that it was performed. Over an observation period, they can get a quick picture of how frequently these behaviors were performed by an individual child. There are many different observation checklists related to children's play. An example of an elaborate checklist used by researchers, the Play Observation Scale, was presented in Chapter 5. Teachers usually use a simpler tool in the classroom. An easy-to-use play checklist is presented in Table 8.3, based on the work of several pioneers in play research (Frost, 1992; Parten, 1932; Piaget, 1962; Rubin, 2001). As shown in the table, the left-hand column lists a variety of different types of play that children might engage in within a classroom. The top

**TABLE 8.3**    Observation Checklist Type of Play and Level of Social Participation.

| Type of Play \ Social Participation | Unoccupied Behavior | Onlooking | Solitary Play | Parallel Play | Cooperative (Group) Play |
|---|---|---|---|---|---|
| Motor Play | | | | | |
| Pretend Play | | | | / | |
| Construction Play | | | | | /// |
| Games | | | | | |
| Art/Music Play | | | | | |
| Exploration/Problem-solving | | | | | |

/ = one observation

row lists the levels of social participation that children show in their play; each of these levels is defined in Chapter 5. Teachers observe both the type and social level of a child's play and, every 15 seconds or so, put a check mark in the space that best indicates what the child is doing at that moment. For example, a teacher may observe that a child is engaged in pretend play and that she is playing parallel to another child. So, the teacher makes a mark in the corresponding box as shown in the table. On three other observation periods, the child is engaged in highly cooperative play with peers in the block area, so the teacher places marks in the appropriate space, as shown. Over time, many marks will be made on the checklist. At a glance the teacher can see the kind of play the child engages in and how social that play is. More important, the teacher can identify the type of play in which the child is most likely to engage with peers. So, the block area may be the ideal place for a teacher to facilitate peers interactions for this particular child.

## Adult Interactions in Children's Play

Most play-oriented curriculum models encourage some adult-child interaction during play. In some programs, these interactions are very brief—with a teacher simply providing new materials, asking a question, or simply observing, then moving on to another area of the classroom, so children can play undisturbed. In other models, teachers have specific learning goals to meet when they interact with children in play. They may guide children's use of literacy in their pretend play, for example, or prompt mathematical thinking when children are solving a problem. The ways adults interact with children on the playground are examined in later chapters.

Regardless of approach, there are several guidelines that most teachers and caregivers adhere to when playing with children (Trawick-Smith & Dzuirgot, 2010; Winsler, 2003). First and foremost, they strive never to interrupt a play activity in progress. The point of interacting with children at play is to support what they are currently doing, not to take over, redirect, or in other ways control play. Related to this, teachers carefully observe children's play, prior to joining them, so that they can learn what children are playing, note any needs for play support, and plan what interventions, if any, will be useful. Often, after observation, teachers will choose not to enter children's play at all.

Once a decision has been made to interact with students in play, teachers in most play-based curriculum models give just the amount of guidance children need to continue playing independently—no more, no less. A teacher may notice a child is having trouble joining peers in a pretend grocery store theme. He may briefly guide the child in purchasing some groceries, then withdraw, once the child is playing with others. Another teacher might see a child struggling with a puzzle and ask one or two questions that help the child solve the problem on her own. In one study, only "good-fit" teacher-child play interactions—those in which the teacher gave just the amount of help a child needed—were found to lead to ongoing autonomous play (Trawick-Smith & Dzuirgot, 2010).

In play-oriented classrooms, teachers rarely interact with children for long periods in play. An important step in playing with children is to exit. Exiting play can be a tricky matter. Sometimes when an adult leaves a play setting the activity falls apart. Children may follow the teacher out of the center or beg her or him to remain. There are several common exiting behaviors that solve these problems. Teachers can simply wait for children to become so absorbed in play that they don't notice their exit. For some types of play, an exit can be built in to the play theme, itself. For example, a teacher pretending to eat with children at a make-believe restaurant might say, "Oh, my. Look at the time! I need to get back to work. Can I pay for my meal now?" Teachers can phase out of play. A teacher might say, "You keep building; I'm going to check to see if there's enough paint in the art center. I'll be right back." Upon return, the teacher remains standing and merely watches children.

In a final step in interacting with children at play, teachers observe the effects of their involvement. Are children playing on their own in more complex, symbolic, or social ways? If so, the interaction has been a success.

 ## VARIATIONS IN PLAY-BASED CURRICULUM MODELS

Although most play-based classrooms share these common elements, they also have fundamental differences. To demonstrate this, the classroom interactions of three different teachers

---

### WHAT PARENTS, TEACHERS, AND CAREGIVERS CAN DO:

Guidelines for Interacting with Children at Play

1. Observe first before joining children at play. Determine what children are playing, what help they need, and whether your assistance is necessary at all.

2. Plan the purpose of your interaction. Is it to promote social interaction and language? To enrich children's pretend? If you can't think of a purpose, this may not be a good time to enter children's play.

3. Tailor your interactions to what children are currently doing and what they need. Do not give too much support; assist children in playing on their own.

4. Avoid taking over or directing children's play. Follow the child's lead and never interrupt a play theme in progress.

5. Exit children's play quickly. As enjoyable as play with children can be, your role is to facilitate autonomous play, not to become a continuous play partner.

6. Observe the results of your interactions. Did your involvement enrich play? Interrupt it? Reflect on which types of interactions with children worked best and refine and add to these.

are presented in this section. Each teacher represents a unique approach to play found in schools and centers.

## The Trust-in-Play Approach

A kindergarten classroom is arranged into seven distinct learning centers. Two children have now chosen to play in one of these: the dramatic play area, which has been arranged into an elaborate make-believe hospital. As the children discuss their play theme, select imaginary roles, and then enact these, their teacher observes from a distance. He takes note of their language and social behavior and studies their emotional responses to the hospital play theme. Do the children show concern or distress over medical props or play enactments? Are both able to play out anxieties about medical encounters and gain mastery over them?

Recognizing that the two children are engaged in rich and meaningful play, he chooses not to intervene in any way and allows the two to continue with their pretend theme for over an hour, even postponing snack time so they are able to reach a satisfying conclusion.

This teacher provides many opportunities for open-ended play during much of the school day. To him, play *is* the curriculum. He adheres to a **trust-in-play** approach that holds that unrestricted, self-directed activity is essential for positive development. He believes that children should be allowed to pursue their own play interests; he shows great faith that children, in free play, will naturally select those experiences that are most meaningful and useful to them. He also views play as a way for children to bring anxieties to the surface and to overcome them. A primary purpose of play, from his perspective, is to assist children in gaining mastery over negative experiences and to resolve emotional conflicts in a healthy manner.

This teacher interacts with children in play very rarely. He believes that adult interference might interrupt the process of resolving inner conflicts or pursuing self-felt needs. He views play as having an important, although indirect, influence on learning in academic areas.

Children cannot achieve important academic standards, he believes, if they are anxious, depressed, or doubt their self-worth or abilities. Through play, children gain the emotional well-being to learn effectively.

His approach is shared by many teachers in the field. In studies of preschool play interactions, teachers were found to spend only 15% to 20% of class time interacting with children in play (File, 1994; Trawick-Smith & Dziurgot, 2010; Wilcox-Herzog & Kontos, 1998). Some prominent play theorists also hold the view that adults should not interfere in children's activities (Brown & Freeman, 2001). Sutton-Smith (1990) has argued that adults cannot be trusted to intervene in childhood pursuits, because they too quickly lapse into "didactic play bumblings" (p. 5).

Many questions arise about this approach to play: What happens if some children do not engage in useful forms of play? What if some are unable to play at all because of social or cognitive limitations or other special needs? How can a teacher be certain that playing will help students learn to read or to do math or to meet other state and national academic standards? Is a trust-in-play approach really just an example of laissez-faire teaching?

## The Facilitate-Play Approach

A kindergarten classroom is arranged into learning centers. The teacher provides materials and activities and encourages children to play independently. Occasionally, he enters the dramatic play area to intervene. Two 5–year-olds are now sitting rather passively in this center. One child rocks in a small rocking chair, holding a doll; the other repetitively stirs a spoon in a small pan on top of a pretend stove. Neither child speaks to the other. After observing for a few minutes, the teacher moves over to them. "Mmm," he murmurs, sitting down at a small table. "Something smells so good. I'm hungry. Is it almost dinnertime?"

"What?" the child at the stove asks.

"Will dinner be ready soon?" the teacher repeats.

"Oh, yes," the child says and begins to set dishes on the table in front of him. "We have spaghetti today."

"Spaghetti. Yum," the teacher comments, then, turning to the child in the rocker, he asks, "I'll bet your baby is hungry, too. Is she old enough to eat spaghetti?"

This child quickly joins the child and teacher at the table. "Yes. Babies can eat spaghetti. I can feed her."

"Great," the teacher answers. "Why don't we all eat now? Let's say we're a family."

"Yeah, and I'll be the mother," one child responds.

"And I'll be the other mother," her peer adds.

The interactions of this teacher exemplify a **facilitate-play approach.** He is striving to enhance specific play abilities—make-believe actions, role playing, and social interactions, for example. His assumption is that enhancing these aspects of children's play leads to higher-quality play interactions over time. These interactions will, in turn, contribute to positive development in the long run (Bennett et al., 1997; Hanline, Milton, & Phelps, 2009a, 2009b; Marcon, 2002).

A distinct feature of this teacher's approach is his focus on certain types of play that are known to support children's development. In this example, he is striving to enhance sociodramatic play—a type of play that has been found to be related to cognitive and social development. In other interactions, he may promote other forms of play—block building, games, and motor play—which have also been linked to positive development (Thorp, Stahmer, & Schreibman, 1995; Smilansky & Shefatya, 1990).

This teacher believes that play influences academic learning indirectly. As children play, they acquire specific play abilities that, in turn, contribute to reading or math skill. Children who engage in high-quality dramatic play, for example, learn how to invent and structure stories. Eventually, they will become more competent writers (Trawick-Smith, 2001). Children who play board games acquire specific game-playing skills, such as counting the number of spaces one moves or reading numerals on a spinner. In time, these children will excel in

math abilities (Cutler, Gilkerson, Parrott, & Bowne, 2002; Ramani & Siegler, 2008).

Concerns have been raised about such an approach to play. One worry is that adult involvement will inhibit creative expression and imagination (Trawick-Smith, 1994a). Are children really playing when they are being guided in pretense by an adult (Sutton-Smith, 1998)? Multicultural scholars have posed other questions: Are these specific play forms—say, sociodramatic play—important and equally valued in all cultures? When we enhance make-believe, are we really teaching all children to play in ways that are most common and appreciated in Western societies (Trawick-Smith, 1998a; 2006; 2010)?

## The Learn-and-Teach-through-Play Approach

In a preschool classroom, children spend most of their morning playing in centers. One 4-year-old is building with blocks. A teacher watches as he constructs a farm, which includes a block enclosure—a corral—into which he has placed plastic farm animals. At a certain point, the teacher approaches and says, "Tell me about what you're building."

"A farm," the child answers. "See? The animals are in the farm."

"Yes, I see," responds the teacher enthusiastically. She pauses, then asks, "Are these pigs inside or outside the fence?"

"Um." The child studies his structure and animals a moment. "Inside."

"Inside the fence. I see," the teacher reiterates. She moves away for a time and allows the child to play independently.

She now approaches two other children who are painting. She studies their work a moment and then asks, "Tell me about what you're doing."

"This is the castle where the queen lives," one child answers, pointing to her painting.

"Me, too," the other child says.

"You're making two castles," the teacher comments.

"Right. One, two," one child counts.

"How are your castles different?" the teacher asks.

"Oh, well, mine's really big," a child responds. "See? It's big."

"Your castle is bigger than Sara's? How else are your castles different?"

"I know," the other child says. "There's more green. More green in mine."

"You have more green in yours, I see. And Sara has more blue," the teacher summarizes. She watches the children a minute more and then quietly leaves the art center.

This teacher has adopted a **learn-and-teach-through-play** approach. Like the first two teachers, she provides many play opportunities in her classroom. However, she intervenes regularly to promote certain non-play concepts and skills. As shown in the preceding description, such interventions are often responsive and spontaneous. The teacher usually makes a decision, on the spot, about which abilities—cognitive, social, or physical—to enhance. Play, from this teacher's view, is an enjoyable medium through which she can enhance certain areas of development and learning.

This teacher uses play to address state and national academic standards. She teaches reading by including books or writing materials within play centers and guiding children in using these. Prompting children to write signs for their block city is an example. She asks questions about size, amount, or spatial relationships to enhance math skills as children play with blocks.

Questions can be raised about this approach as well. Play enthusiasts might ask, Do these interventions—queries about shapes, for example—interrupt creative expression and make-believe? Can a child's activity even be considered play once a teacher has interceded? Advocates of more teacher-directed programs might ask a different set of questions: Is play intervention the most efficient way to promote cognitive or social growth? Wouldn't learning be somewhat haphazard using this approach? Would a child be distracted from learning by other stimuli in an active play environment? Wouldn't a quiet teacher-directed lesson on size or color be more effective?

All three of the teachers described here would claim that they are using play to achieve positive outcomes in the classroom. In fact, they would likely argue their own approach to play is most effective in meeting critical state and national standards in literacy, mathematics, and other academic areas that are receiving emphasis in schools. Yet their strategies are quite different. These three approaches are contrasted in Table 8.4. In the following sections, several curriculum models that reflect these three teaching approaches are described.

 ## CURRICULUM MODELS OF THE TRUST-IN-PLAY APPROACH

Many teachers adopt a trust-in-play approach, as the first teacher, above, has done. They provide rich materials and ample space and encourage children to play completely independently. Usually long periods of free play—indoors and outdoors—are included. Perhaps the best example of this approach may be found in descriptions of the early nursery schools that opened in the 1920s in the United States—the Teachers College Nursery School of Columbia University and the University of Iowa Child Welfare Research Station, for example. These were the first and perhaps the purest of the play-based programs; their influence on later classroom practice in early childhood education has been long lasting.

Although these programs did not comprise a curriculum model per se (they varied markedly in a variety of ways), they were uniform in an adherence to a psychoanalytic theory. Their overall goals were to promote social development and mental health. Based on Freud's (1961) view of play, classrooms were designed so that children could spend the majority of their time expressing themselves in open-ended ways with toys and art media. Children engaged in make-believe, built with blocks, sculpted, and painted. The role of the teacher was primarily to serve as an attachment figure who would respond with warmth and interest when children needed

**TABLE 8.4** Approaches to Play

| Approach to Play | Key Theorists | Underlying Assumptions | Examples |
|---|---|---|---|
| Trust-in-play Approach | Axline (1947b); Freud (1961) | Children benefit most from self-guided play with open-ended play materials. Play leads naturally to learning and developmental outcomes; adult involvement might actually interfere with this process. | A kindergarten teacher provides a traditional "housekeeping corner," equipped with home-related play props. He observes children playing themes or issues of concern or interest but does not intervene. Only as children ask for special props or other materials does he provide these. He believes that children are drawn to learning in literacy, math and all other areas, as these come up naturally in play. |
| Facilitate-play Approach | Bodrova & Leong (2003); DeVries et al. (2002a); Smilansky (1968); Trawick-Smith (1994, 2010) | Adults can facilitate play by creating special classroom environments and interacting in children's activities in purposeful ways. Certain kinds of play—pretend, construction play, and games, for example—are particularly useful and should be emphasized. | A preschool teacher sets up a dramatic play center as a pretend restaurant. As children play there, she intervenes to encourage more make-believe, verbalization, social interaction, and persistence. She guides children toward more complex, symbolic, and social play in her interactions. |
| Learn-and-teach-through-play Approach | Biber (1977); Gandini (1997); Hohmann & Weikart (1995); Isenberg & Jalongo (2006a); Neuman & Roskos (1997) | Play is an ideal context for learning specific academic and social skills. Teachers can enter play activities and intentionally promote one or more areas of learning without interrupting children's play themes. The focus is on helping children learn a concept or skill through play, rather than enhancing the play, itself. | A second-grade teacher wishes to meet state standards in math and social competence. He moves over to a group of children who are arguing about the outcome of a card game. In order to help settle the dispute, he asks questions that guide children in both quantifying ("So, how do you know you won more cards?") and conflict resolution ("What do we do to solve the problem?"). |

attention, reassurance, or assistance. Teachers also were informal therapists, who helped children talk out or play out conflicts and anxieties (Katz, 1970). Teachers of these early nursery schools were keen observers and recorders of behavior; they carefully documented the healthy social and emotional growth of their students.

Certainly, teachers in these free-play programs were concerned with intellectual development and academic learning. However, their belief was that if children, through play, became socially competent and emotionally healthy, they would be in the best position to succeed later in school.

Research on the outcomes of these early programs is scant; those studies that have been conducted are inconclusive. In an early review of investigations of "free-play nursery programs," Sears and Dowley (1963) conclude that these classrooms did not, "radically alter personalities of children, but certain social participation skills are enhanced and can be observed several years later" (p. 850). Traditional free-play nursery school classrooms were included in a well-known longitudinal comparison study of program models (Schweinhart & Weikart, 1996). In investigations over more than 20 years, children who attended these programs did not differ significantly in intellectual or achievement measures from those who attended either a direct instructional preschool (Distar) or one with adult play intervention (High/Scope). Subjects in this free-play preschool group did fare better than the Distar group on social development measures, but slightly less well than those attending High/Scope preschools (Schweinhart & Weikart, 1996).

Newer child care–quality research has given pause to proponents of a purely trust-in-play approach, however. The frequency and quality of adult engagement in children's play has been found to be related to attachment to caregivers, the intellectual quality of children's activities, and long-term academic and social outcomes (Howes, Phillips, & Whitebrook, 1992; Howes, Ritchie, & Bowman, 2002; Howes & Smith, 1995;

Mashburn et al., 2008). Studies on inclusive classrooms have, likewise, shown that adult intervention can significantly increase the frequency and complexity of play for children with special needs (Kok, Kong, & Bernard-Opitz, 2002; Lantz, Nelson, & Loftin, 2004). So, trusting purely in play, with little or no adult facilitation, is not fully supported by current research.

## CURRICULUM MODELS OF THE FACILITATE-PLAY APPROACH

A number of classroom models have been designed not only to encourage but also to actively facilitate play. The second teacher in the examples above has adopted such an approach. In most cases, these models are administered in classrooms not unlike those described under the trust-in-play approach. A full complement of play activities and centers are usually included. What sets these programs apart is that they emphasize teacher guidance to promote specific play abilities. Adult interactions with children are planned to support such activities as make-believe or games with rules.

### Smilansky's Sociodramatic Play Intervention

Smilansky (1968) developed a model designed to facilitate **sociodramatic play**—that is, make-believe role playing with peers. Developed for use with low-income immigrant children in Israel, Smilansky's model is based on four key assumptions:

1. High quality sociodramatic play is related to social and cognitive development and school success.

2. Not all children engage in sociodramatic play; some who do perform play enactments that are less social, imaginative, verbal, or organized.

3. Absence of sociodramatic play abilities among children of low socioeconomic

Adult play interactions should enrich what children are currently doing.

status may explain their academic difficulties in later childhood.

4. Adult intervention can increase the quantity and quality of sociodramatic play, which will, over time, enhance overall cognitive development.

Smilansky's strategy includes four steps, described in Table 8.5. Children are first provided with rich experiences (e.g., field trips, stories) on which they may later base play in the sociodramatic play center. This is an important step, Smilansky (1968) argues, because

**TABLE 8.5**　Steps in Smilansky's (Smilansky & Shefatya, 1990) Sociodramatic Play Intervention Program

| Steps | Examples |
|---|---|
| **Step 1:** Provide unique experiences for children to recreate in play. | A kindergarten teacher takes his class on a field trip to a pediatrician's office. |
| **Step 2:** Create a special play center with thematic props that relate to these unique experiences. | A make-believe doctor's office, including medical props, a cot to resemble an examining table, and a waiting area, is created in the dramatic play center of the kindergarten. |
| **Step 3:** Observe children's play, and note play strengths and deficits. Identify children who need special support in play. | A teacher notices that one child only watches others play in the pediatrician's office and rarely engages in make-believe. |
| **Step 4:** Intervene in children's sociodramatic play, either from within or outside the play theme, to address play deficits. | A teacher pretends to be a patient who has a cough and asks a child who only watches if she would listen to his lungs with a stethoscope. When another child shows interest, he facilitates play between this withdrawn child and her peer. |

children who lack such experience may not be able to pretend at all (Smilansky & Shefatya, 1990). Next, a special play area, equipped with props related to these field trips or experiences, is created within the sociodramatic play center of the classroom. After a trip to the grocery store, for example, a make-believe store with empty cans and boxes, plastic produce, and a cash register might be provided.

A third step in the program involves observation of children's play and the identification of individuals who show play deficits. A full description of the criteria Smilansky suggested for assessing play ability was provided in Chapter 5. Some children do not interact with peers; others rarely assume the roles of make-believe characters. Some are unable to use objects to pretend or quickly switch from one role to another without developing elaborate themes or enactments. Such children are targeted for intervention.

In the final step, teachers play along with children to address these observed play deficits, following specific guidelines: They observe first before entering a play setting, so they fully understand children's play in progress. They intervene in sociodramatic play only if it is determined that children need support. Teachers can enter play from inside the role-playing theme, by taking a role themselves. For example, a teacher might enter children's restaurant play by pretending to be a customer who is ordering lunch. At other times, the teacher might intervene from outside the role playing, merely asking interesting questions or offering new props. A teacher might ask a group of children who are playing filling station, "What will you use for a hose to pump the gas?" Teachers must not force themselves on children as they play, Smilansky urges, and should honor their students' wishes to be left alone. In the following classroom example, a teacher uses an inside-of-play intervention to enhance several important elements of play—make-believe, verbal communication, and social interaction:

Child A sits alone in the dramatic play center dressing and undressing a doll. She doesn't look at or interact with the other children who play near her. A teacher observes her for a few minutes, then intervenes.

| | |
|---|---|
| *Teacher:* | Is your baby hungry? We could make her some dinner. |
| *Child A:* | (Says nothing, continues dressing the doll) |
| *Teacher:* | If she's hungry let me know. We could make her a big meal in the kitchen. (Moves over to the kitchen and begins to pull out pans and dishes, playing along parallel to Child A.) |
| *Child A:* | (Moves over to the teacher) My baby's hungry. |
| *Teacher:* | Okay. Let's see. What should we make her? |
| *Child A:* | Baby food. |
| *Child B:* | (Moving over to the teacher) Here, I'll make the food. |
| *Teacher:* | Why don't you and Celeste work together? I'll rock the baby. (Rocks the doll.) |
| *Child C:* | Can I play? |
| *Child B:* | No. We're making the supper, right, Celeste? |
| *Child A:* | (Nods, says nothing.) |
| *Teacher:* | Why don't you cut vegetables, Sara? |
| *Child C:* | Okay. Celeste, can I have a knife? |
| *Child A:* | I'm using it. (Hands Child C another plastic knife.) Here. |
| *Child B:* | What's your baby named, Celeste? |
| *Child A:* | Lawanda. |
| *Child B:* | Okay, Lawanda, your supper's ready. |

All three children and the teacher sit down to eat. Children B and C direct questions and conversation to both the teacher and Child A. Child A nods or gives single-word responses. After a few minutes the teacher leaves the table. Child A plays with her peers for many minutes until cleanup time. (Trawick-Smith, 1994a, p. 61)

Smilansky's (1968) own research has demonstrated that her approach enhances the frequency and complexity of play. Others have

In games, children think about and adhere to rules and take the perspective of others.

found that her interventions (or those similar to hers) can promote intellectual development (Bondioli, 2001; Christie, 1983; Saltz, Dixon, & Johnson, 1977; Trawick-Smith, 1998b); language (Levy, Wolfgang, & Koorland, 1992); school achievement (Smilansky & Shefatya, 1990); and social abilities (Smith, Dalgleish, & Herzmark, 1981; Udwin, 1983).

## Kamii and DeVries' Group Games

A very different approach to facilitating play has been developed by Kamii and DeVries (DeVries, Zan, Hildebrandt, Edmiaston, & Sales, 2002; Kamii, 1999, 2000, 2003; Kamii & DeVries, 1980). A major focus of their model is to enhance children's game playing. Influenced by Piaget's theory of play and development, Kamii and DeVries advocate initiating traditional childhood games in the curriculum. They argue that such games are especially challenging—cognitively and socially—because children must think about and adhere to rules and take the perspectives of peers as they play. Games are also an enjoyable setting for children to make moral decisions. In board games, for example, children must set aside their own personal needs—a desire to win—and conform to agreed-on rules (e.g., moving only the number of spaces shown on the dice). Failing to abide by rules interferes with game playing and may disrupt the game altogether.

Children think about the feelings and motives of their peers and anticipate what actions they will take next as they play games (DeVries, 2002; Kamii, 2000, 2003). In a game of checkers, for example, a child makes a move based on predictions about an opponent's thoughts and intentions. A child who wants to avoid going back to "start" after landing on a certain space in a board game might try to convince opponents to suspend the rules. To persuade other players, she must consider what they are thinking or feeling. Additionally, many games encourage children to acquire specific concepts of number (e.g., scorekeeping or board games with dice), space (e.g., checkers), literacy (e.g., a game with written rules), and decentration (e.g., an "I'm thinking of something" game) (Ramani & Siegler, 2008).

Some teachers raise concerns about competition. Do children suffer stress in game playing? Do games nurture competitive, noncooperative interactions? Kamii and DeVries (DeVries et al., 2001; Kamii & DeVries, 1980) argue that games are actually quite cooperative, since children must all adopt a single set of rules to play. They must take turns, communicate, and collaborate when setting up a game or putting materials away. In most cases, games are relaxed and nonliteral, so children find it easier to suspend their own desires and to follow rules.

## BOARD GAMES: A KEY TO MATHEMATICAL THINKING?

Kamii and DeVries (1980) have proposed that playing games with rules can promote many different areas of development. In a series of recent studies, Ramani and Siegler (2008) discovered that board games have an impact on at least one very important cognitive process—mathematical thinking. In one study, a group of preschoolers living in poverty were asked to play a board game which included spaces that had numbers on them. A spinner was used to determine how many spaces to travel on each turn. These children were shown how to play, then were asked to play the game with peers in four different 20 minutes sessions. Another group of preschoolers played a game that was identical in every respect except that there were colors on the spaces, instead of numbers. A spinner with colors was used to determine a player's movement on the board. At the end of four game-playing sessions, children who played the game with numbers showed significant increases on four measures of counting and number understanding. The group playing with the color game did not. In a second study, preschoolers' game playing at home was compared to their mathematical abilities. Consistent with findings of the first study, children who played more board games with their families scored higher on mathematical assessments.

Television watching and computer play are replacing family games in American homes. These authors contend that this trend threatens children's early mathematical development. They recommend that board games be included in all early educational programs.

Kamii and DeVries (1980) provide guidelines for teaching interactions during group games. The role of an adult is to ask interesting questions, guide children's problem solving, or facilitate the clashes of opinion that inevitably arise. The teacher can prompt children to set up the game and negotiate rules. In a game of musical chairs, a teacher might ask, "Can you get enough chairs so that we all have one?" A teacher might settle a dispute about rules by asking, "Do you want to say that you don't have to go all the way back to the start when you land on that space?" Playing along with children, a teacher might ask questions that guide their thinking (e.g., "Who has won the most cards so far? How do you know?"). All interactions are designed to facilitate the game playing itself. DeVries and Kohlberg (1990) emphasize that teachers should build on what children are doing rather than interrupt them. The following narrative illustrates this approach:

Three 5-year-olds have just completed a traditional game of Memory. "I won!" one young player announces.

A teacher approaches and asks, "How did you figure out that you won the most cards?"

"Well, because," exclaims the child, holding a mass of cards in one hand and then placing them next to a classmate's pile in comparison. "See? I've got more!"

"Does everyone agree?" the teacher asks.

"Wait a minute!" another child protests. "Let me look at something." He spreads his cards end to end in a line on the floor. This line contains so many cards that it extends from the math area out into the center of the classroom. He makes similar lines, next to his own, with each of his playmate's cards.

The teacher, observing this, asks, "Well, what do you think?"

"Look. See?" he answers. "*My* line is longer. *I* won."

"Does everyone agree with that?" the teacher asks the group. "Are there any other ways to figure out who won?"

With the teacher's encouragement, the group continues to try solutions to the problem until snack time.

Kamii and DeVries (Kamii, 1999, 2000, 2003; Kamii & DeVries, 1980) present an elaborate theoretical justification for game playing, generally, and for many traditional childhood games, specifically. They have conducted qualitative investigations of game playing in which spatial reasoning, quantification, perspective taking, and other social-cognitive processes have been described (DeVries, Zan, Hildebrand, Edmiaston, & Sales, 2001; Kamii, 1999, 2000, 2003).

## Tools of the Mind Curriculum

Bodrova and Leong (2006) have developed a preschool and kindergarten curriculum, called **Tools of the Mind**, that focuses primarily on supporting pretend play. Based on the work of Russian psychologyist Lev Vygotsky (1977), this model provides a variety of experiences aimed at enhancing mental tools that aid learning, such as memory, self-regulation, and attention. Two things that are critical for acquiring these tools, according to Vygotsky, are interactions with more competent adults and peers and environments that support thinking. To Vygotsky one of the most important environments for learning is pretend play. Accordingly, Bodrova and Leong have included extensive opportunities for both interactions and play in the daily schedule of their model.

A variety of activities, some teacher-directed, are planned in a Tools of the Mind classroom. A significant portion of a preschool or kindergarten day is devoted to child-centered pretend play. Vygotsky believed that such play is an ideal context for children to acquire self-regulation, because, when children step into the roles of adults in make believe, they behave as if they were, "a head taller," (Vygotsky, 1977, p. 102). They exhibit more control over their actions, engage in more mature thinking, and speak in longer, more complex sentences. However, Bodrova and Leong believe that children in modern life often need support in learning how to engage in more mature pretend play. In some families, television watching and computer use inhibit the learning of play skills. Some

children with special needs are unable to play at all. So, the Tools of the Mind curriculum involves steps to prepare children for play.

Children are encouraged, first, to plan for play. After a group-time discussion about a particular play center that has been created in the classroom, and perhaps a teacher demonstration of role playing, children discuss, draw, or write about the various roles and actions they plan to enact in the center. For example, if a pretend school has been created, one child might draw and talk about how she plans to be a school bus driver, who will drive the bus, open the door so children can come in, scold children who are being too loud, honk the horn, and say goodbye when children get off at school. Ideas for roles to play are also posted, with pictures and print in the various parts of the play center to prompt children when they run out of ideas.

As children play, Bodrova and Leong recommend that adults interact with them in unobtrusive ways—that is, *scaffold* children's activities. Borrowing again from Vygotsky, they suggest that teachers match their interactions to the needs of individuals. If a child is playing in a mature, complex way, no adult involvement is needed. If they are in great need of support—wandering, misusing materials, or staring off—slightly more guidance is warranted. However, Bodrova and Leong suggest that the place where an adult interaction is most useful is when children are in the **zone of proximal development**. According to Vygotsky, this is a situation in which a child can master a particular task or learn a certain concept with just a small amount of support from someone else. This could involve a hint, question, suggestion, or the modeling of particular play behaviors by an adult. Bodrova and Leong urge caution in adult play interactions. Adults must never interrupt children's play or overly direct their activities. The goal is to enrich what children are currently doing and to bring pretend play to a more mature level, not to promote other, extraneous thinking and learning. Adults' involvement in play should be brief too. Once teachers have offered some support, they should withdraw and observe the impact of their interactions.

The following vignette illustrates how a teacher in a Tools of the Mind classroom might scaffold children's pretend play in a make-believe ice cream stand:

Four-year-old Katie stands in the dramatic play center of her preschool classroom, which has been transformed into an ice cream shop. She watches two peers, Michelle and Dani, pretend to serve ice cream. Other children crowd up to a cardboard box counter to order, but Katie holds back. She smiles briefly at the activities of her peers, showing she is very interested in their play. But she does not join them. A teacher enters the center and observes Katie carefully, noting her desire to play but inability to do so. After several minutes she intervenes.

| | |
|---|---|
| *Teacher:* | (Standing next to Katie, speaking to the two girls serving ice cream) I love ice cream. But, let's see, what flavor should I order? Hmm. I think maybe strawberry. Michelle, can I have a strawberry cone please? |
| *Katie:* | (Watches intently, says nothing.) |
| *Michelle:* | (Using a gesture to hand over an ice cream cone.) Here you go, it's strawberry. It's very fresh today! |
| *Teacher:* | (Pretending to lick ice cream.) Mmm. Sure is! (Turning to Katie) This is the best ice cream I've eaten. |
| *Katie:* | (Smiles and nods) |
| *Teacher:* | (Speaking to Dani, who is serving ice cream) Dani, you might check and see if Katie wants ice cream. She looks pretty hungry. |
| *Katie:* | (Smiles, shyly steps behind the teacher) |
| *Michelle:* | Oh here, Katie. Ice cream coming right up. Get her ice cream, Dani. |
| *Dani:* | She needs to pay the money first. |
| *Michelle:* | What flavor, Katie? |
| *Katie:* | (Steps out from behind the teacher and smiles) |
| *Teacher:* | I chose strawberry, Katie. But you could also have chocolate, vanilla, and even some sprinkles. |
| *Katie:* | (Very quietly) Chocolate. |

| | |
|---|---|
| *Dani:* | Pay first. |
| *Teacher:* | Can you pretend to pay some money, Katie? Then they'll serve you some chocolate. (Gestures to show how you pretend to pay money for ice cream) |
| *Katie:* | (Imitates the teacher's gesture) Chocolate. |
| *Michelle:* | (With enthusiasm, holding out an imaginary ice cream cone.) Here, Katie. Here. |
| *Dani:* | No, I give Katie the ice cream. (Makes a gesture to show he is serving Katie.) |
| *Katie:* | (Makes a fist to stand for the ice cream cone she has purchased and begins to lick it.) It's chocolate. |
| *Michelle:* | Yeah, but we have some bubblegum ice cream, too. (Offers Katie yet another make believe ice cream cone.) |
| *Katie:* | (Pretends to accept the ice cream and begins eating.) |

The teacher takes several steps back and watches as Katie stands near the two girls, her fist clenched around her pretend cone. The girls continue to serve both Katie and other children. Noting that Katie is pretending and making a slight connection with her peers, the teacher chooses to withdraw from the play area.

The teacher in this vignette is providing the level of guidance that Katie needs to begin pretending. She focuses her interactions on helping Katie learn specific pretend actions—paying money, licking ice cream—the kind of make-believe enactments that are characteristic of more mature players. Once Katie begins to pretend, the teacher withdraws. The vignette shows one other important feature of the Tools of the Mind curriculum, as well—the role of "expert" peers in play. Based on Vygotsky's work, Bodrova and Leong place great emphasis in their model on peer interactions—particularly those in which more mature players scaffold the make believe of those less competent. From their view, an expert player can scaffold a younger child's play as successfully (if not more so) than an adult can.

The Tools of the Mind curriculum also includes literacy and mathematical experiences, cooperative learning activities, and self-regulation games and activities. However, the focus remains on play and the important mental tools that are sharpened through make believe.

There is a good deal of research to support the Tools of the Mind curriculum. The use of scaffolding strategies by parents and teachers to support children's development has been studied extensively. Scaffolding play has been found to enhance play competencies and social skills (Kohler, Anthony, Steighner, & Hoyson, 2001; Kok, Kong, & Bernard-Opitz, 2002; Lantz et al., 2004; Skellinger & Hill, 1994), autonomous play (Trawick-Smith, 2010), verbal communication (Young, 1997), and problem solving in classrooms (Rogoff, 1994) and at home (Freund, 1989; Roach, Barrat, Miller, & Leavitt, 1998; Rogoff, Mistry, Goncu, & Mosler, 1993).

The Tools of the Mind curriculum, itself, has been found to be effective in promoting important developmental outcomes. Children enrolled in Tools of the Mind preschools have been found to score higher on measures of self-regulation than those in traditional high-quality programs (Barnett, Jung, Yarosz, Thomas, Hornbeck, Stechuk, & Burns, 2008; Diamond, Barnett, Thomas, & Munroe, 2007). In a case study conducted by the authors of the model, children who attended a Tools of the Mind preschool showed gains in a number of oral language and literacy measures (Bodrova & Leong, 2001).

## THE LEARN-AND-TEACH-THROUGH-PLAY APPROACH

The third teacher in the above examples has adopted an approach to play that focuses on meeting specific learning outcomes, rather than facilitating play, itself. In modern classrooms, such an approach is often inspired by the standards movement—the national trend toward identifying and assessing mastery of specific academic standards in public schools. Teachers in these programs provide materials and intervene in children's play to enhance a wide range of concepts and skills—most particularly literacy, math, and language. They also see play as a context for promoting social skills and more

Music play enhances creativity, language, and cognitive processes.

general cognitive abilities, such as problem solving and scientific experimentation.

## The Bank Street Model

The **Bank Street** program—designed for children from preschool through the primary grades—is one of the most well-known and fully elaborated play-based approaches in early childhood education (Goffin & Wilson, 2001). It was developed by luminaries in the field: Harriet Johnson (1928), Lucy Sprague Mitchell (1950), Caroline Pratt (1948), and Barbara Biber (1977). In its earliest design, this model resembled a trust-in-play program. Its main goals were to nurture social development and mental health (Biber, 1977).

During the 1960s and 1970s, as a greater focus was placed on early cognitive development, the program evolved to address intellectual goals more fully. A modern Bank Street classroom includes goals for learning in all major academic subjects, with a special emphasis on language and literacy. Play has become a vehicle for enhancing important cognitive skills, in the Bank Street model, rather than an end goal, in and of itself.

Play activities found in most preschool and child-care programs today—pretend play, sand and water play, blocks, puzzles, clay, painting, swings, and riding toys—have their origins in the Bank Street approach. These activities are arranged into well-defined "interest centers" that are logically organized yet flexible. Spatial arrangement is regularly modified to meet the specific needs of children (e.g., a new animal care center might be added in response to children's interests, or the dramatic play center may be expanded to accommodate a more active group). The schedule of the day in the Bank Street classroom—which is also flexible—includes individual, small-group, and large-group play and learning. Passive teacher-directed lessons are deemphasized. The academic goals of the program are achieved primarily in the interest centers—math and science areas, for example,

are designed to promote independent experimentation and problem solving. All play centers are embellished with much print—written labels, teacher messages, and job charts.

Over the past few decades, Bank Street authors have more clearly defined the role for teachers in children's play. A greater emphasis has been placed on guiding the development of "cognitive proficiency" (Biber, Shapiro, & Wickens, 1971, p. 4). In a Bank Street classroom, teachers engage in four teaching strategies, as they interact with children in play: (1) observe and assess levels of thinking; (2) "verbally respond, amplify, rephrase, and correct children's comments, confusions, and actions" (Biber et al., 1971, p. 4); (3) foster higher levels of thinking; and (4) pose challenging problems for children to solve. Verbal elaboration on children's activities is particularly emphasized; it is through conversation with children in play that higher levels of thinking are stimulated (Biber et al., 1971).

The following is an example of a typical Bank Street teacher–child play interaction in a classroom art center:

> A child is painting at an easel; a teacher studies her activities a moment and then asks, "Tell me about what you're painting."
>
> "Red flower," the child mutters.
>
> "I see. You're painting red flowers—one, two, three of them."
>
> "Yeah," the child answers proudly.
>
> "Are you going to paint a whole garden?" the teacher asks.
>
> "What?"
>
> "Will you paint a whole garden, with lots of flowers?"
>
> "Oh. Yes," the child responds.
>
> "Will your flowers be of all different colors?" the teacher asks.
>
> "Yes. I'm going to use yellow, I think," the child says.
>
> "And blue and green?" the teacher asks.

"Yeah, and brown. A whole garden," the child says, selecting a new color and resuming her painting.

Although this interaction is not highly intrusive, its focus is obviously on elaborating on the child's thinking in a purposeful way. Note that the aim is not to enhance the play itself—in this case, painting—but to promote broader cognitive and verbal abilities.

There is little research on outcomes of the Bank Street approach. Most empirical evaluations of the program have been aimed at describing classroom interactions or verifying that the model has been properly implemented (Zimiles, 1986). In one investigation, children in Bank Street classrooms were found to interact more often with peers, to express more high-order cognitive statements and questions, and to show more autonomy in thought and action than those attending more traditional kindergarten to grade 3 classrooms (Ross & Zimiles, 1976). In a program comparison study, subjects who attended Bank Street programs were found to perform less well on traditional achievement tests but more competently on problem-solving tasks than those from typical elementary schools (Minuchin, Biber, Shapiro, & Zimiles, 1969).

## The Creative Curriculum

Another common play-oriented model is the **Creative Curriculum**, which is used widely in Head Start centers, community-based preschools, and public schools. Developed by Dodge and her colleagues (Dodge, Colker, & Heroman, 2002), the curriculum is designed for infants, toddlers, preschool-aged children, and for family child care homes. The program prescribes 10 permanent play centers; the same 10 are to be included in every Creative Curriculum classroom. Teachers are guided in how these centers are to be arranged. A daily schedule that includes a balance of child-centered play and teacher-guided group activities is also specified.

Play materials and activities in centers are developed to address a set of 50 specific academic and developmental outcomes that are aligned to the national standards of professional organizations and the expectations for learning of typical elementary schools. A block center might be equipped with patterns to copy in order to address a particular math standard, for example. The sensory table might have a set of measuring cups to address another. Play spaces and materials also reflect themes that have been selected for study on a particular week. For example, if a beach theme is selected, the discovery center might include photos of various beaches to categorize or match; the dramatic play center might be arranged into a pretend beach with towels, swimming gear, sunglasses, and a lifeguard station. From these descriptions of the Creative Curriculum, it is easy to see that play is used primarily as a medium for learning and teaching specific content and skills.

Teachers conduct small and large group lessons, but also have an important role during play periods. First, they interact with children at centers to extend their understandings of the theme being explored and to promote the acquisition of one or more of the 50 learning outcomes. For example, a teacher might ask children to count dots on a die during a board game in the discovery center, and in the dramatic play center encourage children to write a shopping list during make-believe grocery store play. Some of these interactions are preplanned, guided by the teacher's knowledge of a child's need to master a particular skill. Other interactions come within teachable moments, when a spontaneous question or hint will enhance a child's learning.

A second role of adults during play periods is to observe and assess learning. Creative Curriculum teachers write anecdotal records, photograph children's accomplishments, and collect samples of children's work as children interact in play centers. These artifacts are collected to show children's progress on one or more learning outcomes. They are assembled into portfolios for each child and analyzed; data from these analyses are recorded in an elaborate electronic data base available through the program's developers. An important feature of the Creative Curriculum is the use of assessment data to plan future play activities and lessons. For example, based on an anecdotal record revealing a child's need for more support in scientific inquiry, a teacher might plan to intervene in that child's play at the science center.

Developers of the Creative Curriculum describe this model as "scientifically based," citing a variety of studies on early learning and development upon which the program is designed (Dodge, Colker, & Heroman, 2002). However, the few well-designed studies that have been conducted on the model, itself, have yielded mixed findings. Three studies funded by the U.S. Department of Education report that the curriculum had no significant effect on children's language, literacy, or mathematics (Henry, Ponder, Rickman, Mashburn, & Gordon, 2004; Preschool Curriculum Evaluation Research Consortium, 2008a, 2008b). Further research is needed to determine the program's impact on other cognitive or social and emotional measures.

## High/Scope

**High/Scope** is an early childhood curriculum that has been adopted widely in both public and private preschool and kindergarten programs. Its prevalence around the country is due, in part, to the astounding and headline-grabbing results of a longitudinal study on its outcomes (Schweinhart & Weikart, 1996). Positive social benefits for children who have attended the program (for just 1 year at age 4) have been found to persist through age 27. The stated goal of the program is to promote the cognitive development of preschool children, based on Piaget's (1952) work. The High/Scope classroom includes extended periods of free play in carefully designed centers. However, as with other learn-and-teach-through-play approaches, play is viewed as primarily an enjoyable context in which children can learn.

The earliest High/Scope programs contained four major play areas: dramatic play, blocks, quiet activities (e.g., puzzles, lotto games, books), and art. In later years, more literacy activities and a computer have been added to the model. Centers contain high-interest and concrete play materials that children may use in a variety of ways. These are carefully organized. Blocks may be ordered by shape and size; plastic tools in the dramatic play center may be arranged from longest to shortest. A well-known feature of High/Scope is its plan-do-review schedule, described earlier. In an initial planning session, children decide which play activities they will pursue during an upcoming free-choice period. Their plans are often presented verbally in a group discussion; teachers comment on and guide this planning process. In some kindergartens, children are encouraged to record their plans in writing by making marks next to pictures of centers they plan to visit or actually writing out their planned activities on a special planning form.

The "do" portion of the schedule involves actual play in centers. Some children follow their plans exactly; others deviate from these during the course of the day. In a "review" session—another group time—children recall the activities they have completed. They revisit their plans and compare intended activities with actual accomplishments. After this plan-do-review routine, small-group teacher-guided projects are conducted. A final circle time experience completes the schedule.

The model includes very specific guidelines for adult intervention in these play activities (Schweinhart & Weikart, 1996). Adults interact with children to teach very specific concepts and skills that are identified as goals of the program. Unlike Bank Street or the Creative Curriculum, which prescribe somewhat general and open-ended outcomes to enhance in play, the High/Scope model targets very specific cognitive skills. Through questions and conversations teachers facilitate mental processes like classification, ordering, spatial relations, time, and number—all drawn directly from Piaget's work.

The description of teacher 4 earlier in this chapter serves as a good illustration of the High/Scope method of play intervention. The following is another example:

A 5-year-old is constructing two buildings with blocks. As he works on his structures, the teacher moves into the area and says, "You're making two buildings! Great! How are these two buildings different?"

"Different?" the child responds. "This one's bigger."

"Bigger?" the teacher repeats.

"Yeah, see?" the child touches the top of one of his block structures.

"Right, it's taller. This building's taller than that building," the teacher replies, pointing to each structure.

"Yeah."

"How else are they different?" the teacher continues to query.

"Well, this one has more," the child answers.

"More blocks?" the teacher asks.

"Of course, silly," the child answers. "I used more."

This teacher interacts in children's play to teach about comparisons, not to enhance the block play itself. In fact, he has approached the play setting with a very specific skill already in mind—one of a finite set of cognitive abilities taught during such interactions.

Although research shows long-term benefits of the High/Scope model, criticisms are prevalent in the literature, particularly from those who oppose heavy-handed interventions in play. DeVries and Kohlberg (1990) argue that High/Scope teachers' questions are often delivered completely outside the child's intended play goals or interests and can disrupt what the child is doing and thinking.

## Roskos and Neuman's Literacy Play Model

A play-based model that focuses specifically on literacy has been proposed by Roskos and Neuman (1998b, 2003). This approach is based on the assumption that in sociodramatic play,

children regularly engage in **literacy routines**, reading and writing actions they have observed adults perform in real life. A child in a make-believe grocery store may write a grocery list, just as she has seen her father do. Another child, in a library play theme, may read and check out books as he has observed at his local library. Thus sociodramatic play is an ideal context for children to practice **functional uses of print** (Neuman & Roskos, 1998a, 2003).

In this approach, teachers create special sociodramatic play centers that include an extensive collection of literacy props—pens and markers, pads of paper, stationery and envelopes, books, and signs. Often these props are related to specific play themes. If the sociodramatic play area is organized as a grocery store, for example, shopping lists, coupons, sale advertisements, checkbook stubs, and product labels are provided. Merely offering such props may not be sufficient to promote literacy play, these authors contend. Interactions with other children are often necessary. A child with more print experience can support the reading and writing of a less competent peer (Neuman & Roskos, 1991; Stone & Christie, 1996). Play experiences within mixed-ability peer groups are an important feature of this model.

Teachers can enhance literacy play, as well, through thoughtful play interventions. Adult modeling of functional uses of print is especially emphasized (Enz & Christie, 1997; Roskos & Neuman, 1998a). A child who does not play with literacy props in a pretend restaurant center may be prompted to do so through a unobtrusive teacher demonstration: "I think I'll look at the menu and see what I can order."

The following is another example of a teacher facilitating literacy play:

Two 4-year-olds are playing in a pretend post office that has been created in the dramatic play area. They mail envelopes in a mailbox that has been provided. A teacher moves into the center.

*Teacher:*    (Speaks to no one in particular.) I haven't written to my mother in so long. I think I'll jot her a note. (Places stationery, envelopes, and markers on the table; begins to write.) Let's see. I think I'll write, "Dear Mom."

*Child A:* (Approaches the teacher.) Can I write one?

*Teacher:* Sure. Who will you write to?

*Child A:* (In a pretend, adult-like voice) Well, I need to write to my daughter. She has moved away, and I need to write her. Come on, Maria. Let's write to our daughters, okay?

*Teacher:* You have daughters? How old are they?

*Child A:* Let's say they're teenagers.

*Child B:* Okay. We can write 'em and mail 'em. (Points to the make-believe post office.)

The two children write and discuss their letters. The teacher continues to write with them. Finally, the children place their letters in envelopes, address these in scribble writing, and mail them at the post office.

*Child A:* Let's say I'm the daughter now and I get your letter, okay? (Takes an envelope from the mailbox and now assumes a different voice) Oh. A letter! What does this say? (Shows the letter to the teacher)

*Teacher:* You should ask Maria. (Points to child B)

*Child B:* (Takes the letter from child A; runs her fingers along the scribbles) "Dear Daughter. Please come home now. Aren't you scared by yourself? Love, Mommy."

The children continue to play mother and daughter, writing more letters and mailing them. The teacher eventually leaves the play area. (Trawick-Smith, p. 73)

The teacher in this example facilitates literacy by providing props and modeling their use. When one child has trouble reading another's letter, the teacher encourages peer interaction. Research has shown that this approach can increase the frequency of literacy activity and

---

### LITERACY PLAY: IS IT REALLY PLAY ANYMORE?

The Roskos and Neuman model, presented in this chapter, is based on the assumption that play is an ideal context for helping young children learn to read and write (Neuman & Roskos, 1991; Roskos & Neuman, 2003). However, concerns have been raised about using play to enhance literacy. A question some researchers are now asking is whether literacy play is still really play (Kuschner, 2010; Trawick-Smith, 1994a; Trawick-Smith & Picard, 2003). When a child playing in a pretend bakery pauses to read the book, *The Little Red Hen,* has she suspended her make-believe in order to read this story? Can she still be playing the role of baker as she does this? (Real bakers usually don't stop in their work to read!) When a child in a pretend post office discontinues his sorting and delivery of mail to write a letter to his mother, is he still pretending? When he asks a teacher how to write "I miss you, Mommy" is he really carrying out the role of a postal worker? In each case, some argue, literacy is disrupting ongoing play? Play is being turned into something else.

Does this mean literacy materials should not be included in a dramatic play center? Trawick-Smith and Picard (2003) suggest that books and writing implements can be included in play, so long as they can be used to enhance, rather than detract from, role playing. A pad of paper and markers can be provided so that make-believe shoppers can write out a shopping list if they choose. A book about going to the doctor can be read to a pretend patient (a doll) by a make believe parent who is trying to comfort her in the waiting room of a doctor's office. According to these authors, only when literacy can enhance play should it be included in a dramatic play center.

foster print awareness (Morrow & Rand, 1991b; Neuman & Roskos, 1991; Roskos & Neuman, 2003; Vukelich, 1991).

## Reggio Emilia-Inspired Programs

A final play-oriented model to be considered in this section is the Reggio Emilia approach, which has been implemented for decades in infant, toddler, and preschool classrooms in a region in northern Italy. Many preschools in the United States, called **Reggio Emilia-inspired programs,** borrow heavily from the philosophy and approaches of the original Reggio Emilia model. These American programs also incorporate elements that reflect American research and thinking, so they vary in some ways from the Italian preschools. Reggio Emilia-inspired programs incorporate traditional play experiences—dramatic play, blocks, games, and outdoor activities. At the center of the Reggio Emilia-inspired curriculum, however, are in-depth investigations of topics of interest to children. These investigations almost always include artistic expression with a wide variety of media. There is some debate about whether such projects and art experiences are true play. Since children in Reggio Emilia-inspired programs can choose whether or not to engage in these experiences, along with pretend and construction play activities, and since these projects are based on children's questions and curiosities, the model is included here as a play-based program.

Reggio Emilia-inspired programs do support and extend children's play, itself, as facilitate-play models do. In particular, teachers in these programs enhance child-centered artistic expression. For example, through informal interactions during play periods, teachers strive to enhance the accuracy, complexity, and media variation in their students' art. Children are afforded as much time as they need to complete play tasks or artistic efforts. As one researcher notes, "Time is not set by a clock. Children's own sense of time and their personal rhythm are considered in planning and carrying out activities and projects" (Gandini, 1997, p. 17). These practices clearly enhance children's artistic and play abilities. However, the primary goal of classroom activities in this model is not to promote play, but to enhance "intellectual adaptation" through artistic expression and other playful experiences (Edwards, Gandini, & Forman, 1998; Gandini, Hill, Cadwell, & Schwall, 2005). Art and other play activities are designed to provide new understandings about the world, not just opportunities to express existing ideas or feeling. For example, children may be guided in an in-depth study of clouds, based on their expressed interest. They are then encouraged to engage in artistic or play activities related to clouds and weather that help them to understand more deeply what they have learned from their observations and learning experiences (Gandini, 1997). Teachers in Reggio Emilia-inspired programs sometimes avoid using words like *art* or *play*, but prefer the phrase *symbolic representation* to indicate that these expressive activities are used to represent, consolidate, and extend learning.

Reggio Emilia-inspired programs include several unique features that are borrowed from the original Italian approach. Collaboration is emphasized; children are encouraged to plan and work with peers in all play activities, especially as they engage in artistic representation. During a Reggio Emilia-inspired free play period, one might observe a group of children building a complete city from blocks, another group creating a papier-mâché sculpture of a lion, and yet another using markers, paint, and photographs to represent the findings of a scientific experiment they have just conducted. Assessment of learning also tends to emphasize collaboration. After children engage in learning experiences and represent these artistically, teachers will often organize their work onto elaborate panels, displayed throughout the classroom. Called **documentation panels**, these displays show artistically what the group has learned over the course of a particular investigation. These may be examined by children, teachers, and parents to determine what children have learned from a particular project. The collective work of the group is documented, not individual achievement.

Another unique feature of the Reggio Emilia-inspired approach is an emphasis on children's on-going work on projects over several days or weeks. The following example, based on a story told by a Reggio Emilia-inspired first grade teacher (Tarini, 1997, pp. 56–59), illustrates this.

During free-choice time, a child approaches a teacher and says, "Know what? I'm going to make a butterfly."

"You're going to draw it?" the teacher responds.

"Yeah. With crayons and markers, maybe," the child replies.

"You know, there's a beautiful book with photographs of many different types of butterflies in our book center. Did you ever look at it?" the teacher asks. "You could bring it over to the art table, if you want. It might give you some ideas."

"Okay," the child answers enthusiastically. She studies the book and draws a sketch of a butterfly in the art center. Her work has captured the attention of two other children who join her. They study the book, as well, and create drawings.

On the next day, during free choice time, the children return to the center and look over their drawings and the butterfly book. The teacher sits down with them. "Your drawings show a lot of things you learned about butterflies from the book," she says.

"Yeah, but we're not done," one child says. "We just made first drafts." She uses a term children in Reggio Emilia-inspired classrooms are very familiar with. Children are encouraged to make multiple drafts of their work, each draft showing something new they have learned.

"Great. Let me point out something before you do your next draft," the teacher says, pointing to a page in the butterfly book. "Did you notice that real butterflies don't have faces and smiles like people do? See? No faces. Also, look at this. See how the wings go out like this?"

The children study the photo intently for several seconds. "Oh," responds one child. "No faces. We can't have faces on butterflies!" All three laugh, then begin to draw more accurate drafts of butterflies.

On a third day the children still show interest in butterflies, so the teacher uses paint to add color to their one of their previous drawings. The three children immediately begin painting one of their previous sketches, based on what they see in the butterfly book. A remarkably realistic-looking butterfly is the result. The children now ask the teacher if they can make another butterfly, "just like this one, but really big." The teacher guides them by setting up a document projector that shows the image of their butterfly painting on a large sheet of paper taped onto a wall. The children use paint to recreate their very small butterfly into a large one. As they do this, they add still more detail to the butterfly, based on their study of the book. The teacher reports that this is the most sophisticated artistic representation she has ever seen by children of this age.

Because the Reggio Emilia approach was conceived of and first implemented by practitioners, evidence of its outcomes has been in the form of rich narratives about children's classroom activities. The remarkably artistic and intellectual achievements of children from Reggio Emilia, Italy, have been described and analyzed by teachers and researchers (Edwards, Gandini, & Forman, 1998; Malaguzzi, 1993; New, 2003). A number of American educators have implemented aspects of the approach in their classrooms and have described positive experiences and outcomes for students (Breig-Allen & Dillon, 1997; Haigh, 1997; Saltz, 1997).

Questions have been raised about whether a Reggio-Emilia inspired curriculum can achieve the academic outcomes of the standards-based American school system. Will activities and interventions in this model lead to significant gains on traditional measures of achievement? Play advocates raise different a different concern. Does adult intervention in artistic expression to promote learning interfere with children's self-expression? Can adult-guided symbolic representation of this model even be considered true play? Anecdotal evidence indicates that an adaptation of the model can be successfully implemented in U.S. schools in ways that ensure child-directed play and the achievement of learning outcomes (Wurm, 2005).

## Borrowing the Best from Each Approach

Which approach to play is most effective? Which strategy or strategies reviewed in this chapter should be adopted in classrooms? A teacher might wish to borrow key concepts from *each* approach, particularly those ideas that have been supported by research. Based on the perspectives of trust-in-play advocates, teachers might increase time for purely child-directed free play that includes no adult involvement. Teachers can use these periods for observing and assessing play and the social-emotional development of their students. They might provide more open-ended play materials during these time periods that allow the expression of and mastery over anxieties or social problems. Teachers borrowing from this approach might also extend play time on the playground, so that children can enjoy the emotional exhilaration of a beautiful day and engage in movement activities that contribute to physical health.

The facilitate-play approach might also be implemented during parts of the day. In some play periods, teachers might interact with children to enhance specific types of play that support development—sociodramatic play, construction play, motor play, and games, for example. In these interactions, teachers would strive to promote play, itself, without ulterior motives for academic learning. They might enhance make believe by modeling the role of a pretend character. They might ask children in an open-ended way about what they're building with blocks. They might facilitate a discussion of who goes first in a board game that is just underway. Such interventions promote play abilities that, in turn, will enhance other areas of development over time.

Play might also be used, in some situations, to promote specific academic learning, as teaching-and-learning-through-play advocates would propose. Teachers might identify just the right moments to ask questions, pose problems, or present new information in play. Such interactions can address national academic and local academic standards. A child might be asked to make predictions when playing in the science center. Another might be asked to count which player won the most cards in a game of Memory. So long as such interactions are not too obtrusive or too frequent, they can enhance students' learning, while still allowing children to maintain control over their own play.

 **SUMMARY**

Based on research showing that play promotes learning and development, many teachers incorporate play activities within their curriculum. Most play-based classrooms share common features. The classroom environment is usually arranged into play centers, spaces where children can play and learn independently. These are organized in logical ways, visually partitioned with shelves or dividers to minimize distraction, and equipped with a balance of complex and simple, open and closed, and realistic and nonrealistic materials. Because play can be very active, play centers include important safety features, such as protective railings and cushioned undersurfaces for lofts and climbing equipment and an absence of sharp corners, splinters, toxic materials, and rust. The daily schedule for a play-based curriculum usually reflects an even balance of quiet and active experiences. This includes an uninterrupted time block of at least an hour for play activities.

In play-based programs, teachers observe and assess development as children are playing. The most common method of recording play development is writing anecdotal records—brief descriptions of children's activities that can later be expanded and analyzed. Some teachers also use observation checklists that indicate the frequency of certain types of play and the levels of social participation for each student. Teachers often interact with children in play in play-oriented classrooms to promote development.

Although play-based classrooms usually include these common elements, there is much variation in

how play is included in the curriculum. Three different approaches to classroom play can be identified.
In a trust-in-play model, teachers encourage children
to play on their own, with little restriction. Teacher
involvement in play is minimal. Research reveals
that such an approach may lead to some positive
outcomes for children, but that appropriate adult
involvement in children's play is more effective in
promoting learning and development.

In contrast, the facilitate-play model, emphasizes
adult–child play interactions to facilitate specific
types of play—sociodramatic play or games with
rules, for example. Research suggests that this
approach not only enhances the type of play being
addressed but also can lead to broader developmental outcomes over time, such as language acquisition
or mathematical reasoning. In a third approach,
learn-and-teach-through-play, the curriculum is
designed to achieve specific academic goals through
play. Research suggests that this approach can
enhance learning, so long as play is not interrupted
by heavy-handed adult intrusion or materials that
distract from play itself.

Given the research on these various approaches,
teachers should consider borrowing the best elements of each approach. Sometimes children should
be left to play on their own; other times adult interactions focused on promoting specific types of play
should be implemented. Occasionally, teachers
should take advantage of teachable moments in play
to achieve a particular learning goal.

##  KEY TERMS

Anecdotal records
Balance of play materials
Bank Street
Constructivist
    perspective
Creative Curriculum
Documentation panels
Facilitate-play
    approach
High/Scope program
Learn-and-teach-through-
    play approach
Literacy routines
Modified open plan
    design
Observation checklists

Plan-do-review
    structure
Play centers
Play-based classrooms
Quiet-active-quiet
    schedule
Reggio Emilia-inspired
    programs
Scaffolding
Sociodramatic play
Stimulus shelter
Tools of the Mind
    curriculum
Trust-in-play approach
Zone of proximal
    development

## STUDY QUESTIONS

1. What are three fundamental ideas for arranging
   play centers that are applied in most play-based
   classrooms?
2. What is a modified open plan design, and how
   does it contribute to children's development?
3. Research has suggested that a balance of play
   materials promotes play development. Which
   types of play materials should be balanced?
4. What is a common pattern of classroom scheduling in most play-based programs, and why is it
   important?
5. What are three major approaches to including play
   in the classroom? How do they differ in regard to
   assumptions about play and development?
6. What fundamental beliefs about play are
   expressed by trust-in-play advocates?
7. What do proponents of a facilitate-play
   approach believe?
8. What does research suggest about this facilitate-
   play model?
9. What are the major features of the games with
   rules model of Kamii and DeVries? What do
   research findings indicate about the benefits of
   games?
10. What are the beliefs about play reflected in the
    Tools of the Mind curriculum? What do prelimi-
    nary studies of this model show?
11. Why is the modern Bank Street model considered
    a learn-and-teach-through-play model? How is it
    different from facilitate-play approaches?
12. What are the primary features of the Creative
    Curriculum? Why is this program considered a
    learn-and-teach-through-play model?
13. What are some of the unique characteristics of
    the High/Scope model? What does research
    indicate about its long-term benefits for
    children?
14. What are the approaches to facilitating literacy
    play in the Roskos & Neuman model? What
    does research show about teaching reading and
    writing through play?
15. How is play used in a Reggio Emilia-inspired
    classroom? Why is the Reggio Emilia model con-
    sidered a learn-and-teach-through-play approach?
16. What ideas from *each* approach to play do you
    believe are useful to teachers?
17. Which approach to play best reflects your own
    beliefs about play and child development?

# REFERENCES

Axline, V. (1947). *Play therapy.* New York: Ballantine.

Barnett, W. S., Jung, K., Yarosz, D. J., Thomas, J., Hornbeck, A., Stechuk, R., & Burns, S. (2008). Educational effects of the Tools of the Mind curriculum: A randomized trial. *Early Childhood Research Quarterly, 23,* 299–313.

Bennet, N., Wood, L., & Rogers, S. (1997). *Teaching through play: Teacher's thinking in classroom practice.* Buckingham, UK: Open University Press.

Berk, L., & Winsler, A. (1995). *Scaffolding children's learning: Vygotsky and early childhood education.* Washington, DC: National Association for the Education of Young Children.

Bereiter, C., & Engelmann, S. (1966). *Teaching the culturally disadvantaged child in the preschool.* Upper Saddle River, NJ: Prentice Hall.

Betancourt, F., & Zeiler, M. (1971). The choices and preferences of nursery school children. *Journal of Applied Behavior Analysis, 4,* 299–304.

Biber, B. (1977). A developmental-interaction approach: Bank Street College of Education. In M. Day & R. Parker (Eds.), *The preschool in action* (pp. 421–460). Boston: Allyn & Bacon.

Biber, B., Shapiro, E., & Wickens, D. (1971). *Promoting cognitive growth from a developmental interaction point of view.* Washington, DC: National Association for the Education of Young Children.

Bloch, M. N., & Adler, S. M. (1994). African children's play and the emergence of the sexual division of labor. In J. L. Roopnarine, J. E. Johnson, & F. R. Hooper (Eds.), *Children's play in diverse cultures* (pp. 148–178). Albany: State University of New York Press.

Bodrova, E., & Leong, D. J. (1998). Adult influences on play: The Vygotskian approach. In D. Fromberg & D. Bergen (Eds.), *Play from birth to twelve and beyond: Contexts, perspectives, and meanings* (pp. 277–282). New York: Garland.

Bodrova, E., & Leong, D. (2001). Tools of the Mind: A case study of implementing the Vygotskian approach in American early childhood and primary programs. International Bureau of Education, P.O. Box 199, 1211 Geneva 20, Switzerland

Bodrova, E., & Leong, D. (2003). Chopsticks and counting chips: Do play and foundational skills need to compete for the teacher's attention in an early childhood classroom? *Young Children, 58,* 10–17.

Bodrova, E., & Leong, D. (2006). *Tools of the mind: The Vygotskian approach to early childhood education.* Upper Saddle River, NJ: Merrill/Prentice Hall.

Bondioli, A. (2001). The adult as tutor in fostering children's symbolic play. In A. Goncu & E. Klein (Eds.), *Children in play, story, and school* (pp.107–131). New York: Guilford.

Bredekamp, S., & Copple, C. (1997). *Developmentally appropriate practice in early childhood programs.* Washington, DC: National Association for the Education of Young Children.

Breig-Allen, C., & Dillon, J. U. (1997). Implementing the process of change in a public school setting. In J. Hendrick (Ed.), *First steps toward teaching the Reggio way* (pp. 126–140). Upper Saddle River, NJ: Merrill/Prentice Hall.

Brown, M. & Freeman, N. (2001). "We don't play that way in school": The moral and ethical dimensions of controlling children's play. In S. Reifel & M. Brown (Eds.), *Advances in early education and day care, volume 11. Early education and care, and reconceptualizing play* (pp. 257–275). New York: JAI.

Burts, D., Hart, C., DeWolf, D., Ray, J., Manual, K., & Fleege, P. (1993). Developmental appropriateness of kindergarten programs and academic outcomes in first grade. *Journal of Research in Childhood Education, 8,* 23–31.

Christie, J. (1983). The effects of play tutoring on young children's cognitive performance. *Journal of Educational Research, 76,* 326–330.

Christie, J. (1994). Literacy play interventions: A review of empirical research. In S. Reifel (Ed.), *Advances in early education and day care* (Vol. 6, pp. 3–24). Greenwich, CT: JAI.

Christie, J., & Stone, S. (1999). Collaborative literacy in print-enriched play centers: Exploring the "zone" in same-age and multi-age groupings. *Journal of Literacy Research, 3,* 109–131.

Clayton, M., Forton, M., & Doolittle, L. (2001). *Classroom Spaces That Work.* Turners Falls, MA: Northeast Foundation for Children.

Clements, D. H., & Samara, J. (2007). Effects of a preschool mathematics curriculum: Summary research on the Building Blocks project. Journal for Research in Mathematics Education 38(2), 136–163.

Connecticut State Department of Education. (1999). *Connecticut's Preschool Curriculum Framework.* Hartford, CT: author.

Copple, C., & Bredekamp, S. (2006). *Basics of developmentally appropriate practice.* Washington, DC: NAEYC.

Copple, C., & Bredekamp, S. (2009). *Developmentally Appropriate Practice in Early Childhood Programs Serving Children from Birth through Age 8,* 3rd ed. Washington, DC: NAEYC.

Corsaro, W. A. (2003). *"We're friends, right?" Inside kids' culture.* Washington, DC: Joseph Henry Press.

Curran, J. (1999). Constraints of pretend play: Implicit and explicit rules. *Journal of Research in Childhood Education, 14,* 47–55.

Curtis, D., & Carter, M. (2003). *Designs for Living and Learning: Transforming Early Childhood Environments.* St. Paul: Redleaf Press.

Cutler, K. M., Gilkerson, D., Parrott, S., & Bowne, M. T. (2002). Developing math games based on children's literature. *Young Children, 58,* (1), 22–27.

Davidson, J. (1998). Language and play. In D. Fromberg & D. Bergen (Eds.) *Play from birth to twelve: Contexts, perspectives, and meanings* (pp. 175–183). New York: Garland.

DeVries, R., & Kohlberg, L. (1990). *Constructivist early education: Overview and comparison with other programs.*

Washington, DC: National Association for the Education of Young Children.

DeVries, R. (2002). *Developing constructivist early childhood curriculum: practical principals and activities.* New York: Teachers College Press.

DeVries, R., Zan, B. Hildebrandt, C., Edmiaston, R., & Sales, C. (2001). *Developing a constructivist early childhood curriculum.* New York: Teachers College Press.

Dewey, J. (1913). *Interest and effort in education.* Edwardsville: Southern Illinois Press.

Diamond, A., Barnett, W. S., Thomas, J., & Munroe, S. (2007). Preschool program improves cognitive control. *Science, 318,* 1387–1389.

Doctoroff, S. (2001). Adapting the physical environment to meet the needs of all young children for play. *Journal of Early Childhood Education, 29,* 105–109.

Edwards, C., Gandini, L., & Forman, G. (Eds). (1998). *The hundred languages of children: The Reggio Emilia approach to early childhood education.* Norwood, NJ: Ablex.

Enz, B., & Christie, J. (1997). Teacher play interaction styles: Effects on play behavior and relationships with teacher training and experience. *International Journal of Early Childhood Education, 2,* 55–75.

Evans, G. W. (2006). Child development and the physical environment. *Annual Review of Psychology, 57,* 423–451.

Fein, G., & Wiltz, N. (1998). Play as children see it. In D. Fromberg & D. Bergen (Eds.), *Play from birth to twelve and beyond* (pp. 37–49). New York: Garland.

File, N. (1994). Children's play, teacher-child interactions, and teacher beliefs in integrated early childhood programs. *Early Childhood Research Quarterly, 9,* 223–240.

Fisher, E. (1992). The impact of play on development: A meta-analysis. *Play & Culture, 5,* 159–181.

Freud, S. (1961). *Beyond the pleasure principle.* New York: Norton.

Freund, L. S. (1989). Maternal regulation of children's problem solving behavior and its impact on children's performance. *Child Development, 61,* 113–126.

Galda, L. (1982). Playing about a story: It's impact on comprehension. *The Reading Teacher, 55,* 52–55.

Galda, L. (2000). *Looking through the far away end: Creating a literature-based reading curriculum with second graders.* Newark, DE: International Reading Association.

Gandini, L. (1997). Foundations of the Reggio Emilia approach. In J. Hendrick (Ed.), *First steps toward teaching the Reggio way* (pp. 14–25). Upper Saddle River, NJ: Merrill/Prentice Hall.

Gandini, L., Hill, L., Cadwell, L., & Schwall, C. (2005). In the spirit of the studio: learning from the atelier of Reggio Emilia. New York: Teachers College Press.

Goffin, S. G., & Wilson, C. (2001). *Curriculum models and early childhood education: Appraising the relationship* (2nd ed.). Upper Saddle River, NJ: Merrill/Prentice Hall.

Golbeck, S., Rand, M., & Soundy, C. (1986). Constructing a model of large-scale space with the space in view:

Effects of guidance and cognitive re-structuring in preschoolers. *Merrill-Palmer Quarterly, 32,* 187–203.

Haigh, K. (1997). How the Reggio approach has influenced an inner city program: Exploring Reggio in Head Start and subsidized child care. In J. Hendrick (Ed.), *First steps toward teaching the Reggio way* (pp. 152–166). Upper Saddle River, NJ: Merrill/Prentice Hall.

Hart, C., Burts, D., Durland, M. A., Charlesworth, R., DeWolf, M., & Fleege, P. (1998). Stress behaviors and activity type participation of preschoolers in more or less developmentally appropriate classrooms: SES and sex differences. *Journal of Research in Childhood Education, 12,* 98–116.

Henry, G. T., Ponder, B. D., Rickman, D. K., Mashburn, A. J., Henderson, L. W., & Gordon, C. S. (2004). *An evaluation of the implementation of Georgia's pre-K program: Report of the findings from the Georgia early childhood study (2002–03).* Atlanta, GA: Georgia State University, Andrew Young School of Policy Studies.

Hohman, M., & Weikart, D. (1995). *Educating young children: Active learning processes for preschool and child care programs.* Ypsilanti, MI: High/Scope Educational Research Foundation.

Howes, C., Phillips, D., & Whitebrook, M. (1992). Thresholds of quality in child care centers and children's social and emotional development. *Child Development, 63,* 449–460.

Howes, C., Ritchie, S., & Bowman, B. (2002). *A matter of trust: Connecting teachers and learners in the early childhood classroom.* New York: Teachers College Press.

Howes, C., & Smith, E. (1995). Relations among child care quality, teacher behavior, children's play activities, emotional security, and cognitive activity in child care. *Early Childhood Research Quarterly, 10,* 381–404.

Hughes, F. P. (1998). *Children, play and development.* Boston: Allyn & Bacon.

Hustedt, J. T. (2002). Scaffolding and the transfer of problem-solving skills from low-income mothers to their preschoolers. *Dissertation Abstracts International, 62,* pp. 5997.

Isbell, C., Exelby, B., Exelby, G., & Isbell, R. (2001). *Early learning environments that work.* New York: Gryphon House.

Johnson, J. E., Christie, J. F., and Wardle, F. (2005). *Play, development, and early education.* Boston, MA: Pearson.

Kamii, C. (1999). *Young children reinvent arithmetic: Implications of Piaget's theory.* New York: Teachers College Press.

Kamii, C. (2000). *First graders dividing 62 by 5: A teacher uses Piaget's theory.* New York: Teachers College Press.

Kamii, C. (2003). *Young children continue to reinvent arithmetic: Implications of Piaget's theory.* New York: Teachers College Press.

Kamii, C., & DeVries, R. (1980). *Group games in early education: Implications of Piaget's theory.* Washington, DC: National Association for the Education of Young Children.

Katz, L. G. (1970). Teaching in preschools: Roles and goals. *Children, 17,* 43–48.

Katz, L. G. (1997). The challenges of the Reggio Emilia approach. In J. Hendrick (Ed.), *First steps toward teaching the Reggio way* (pp. 103–111). Upper Saddle River, NJ: Merrill/Prentice Hall.

Kendrick, A., Kaufmann, R., & Messenger, K. (1991). *Healthy young children.* Washington, DC: NAEYC.

Kim, S. (1999). The effects of storytelling and pretend play on cognitive processes and short and long term narrative recall. *Child Study Journal, 29,* 175–191.

Kohler, F., Anthony, L., Steighner, S., & Hoyson, M. (2001). Teaching social skills in the integrated preschool: An examination of naturalistic tactics. *Topics in Early Childhood Special Education, 21,* 1–16.

Kok, A., Kong, T., & Bernard-Opitz, V. (2002). A comparison of the effects of structured play and facilitated play approaches on children with autism. *Autism, 6,* 181–196.

Lantz, J. E., Nelson, J. M., & Loftin, R. L. (2004). Guiding children with autism in play applying the integrated play group model in school settings. *Teaching Exceptional Children, 37,* 8–14.

Levy, A., Wolfgang, C., & Koorland, M. (1992). Sociodramatic play as a method for enhancing language performance of kindergarten age students. *Early Childhood Research Quarterly, 7,* 245–262.

Lloyd, B., & Howe, N. (2003). Solitary play and divergent and convergent thinking skills in preschool children. *Early Childhood Research Quarterly, 18,* 22–41.

Lowenfeld, V. (1947). *Creative and mental growth.* New York: Macmillan.

Lowry, P. (1993). Privacy in the preschool environment. *Children's Environments, 10,* 46–61.

Malaguzzi, L. (1993). For an education based on relationships. *Young Children, 49,* 9–12.

Marcon, M. (2002). Moving up the grades: Relationship between preschool model and later school success. *Early Childhood Research and Practice, 4,* 1.

McCaslin, N. (1990). *Creative drama in the classroom.* White Plains, NY: Longman.

Maxwell, L. E. (2007). Competency in child care settings: The role of the physical environment. *Environment and Behavior, 39,* 229–245.

McLoyd, V. (1986a). Scaffolds or shackles? The role of toys in preschool children's pretend play. In G. Fein & M. Rivkin (Eds.), *The young child at play: Reviews of research* (Vol. 4, pp. 63–78). Washington, DC: National Association for the Education of Young Children.

McLoyd, V. C. (1986b). Social class and pretend play. In A. W. Gottfried & C. C. Brown (Eds.), *Play interactions: The contribution of play materials and parental involvement to children's development* (pp. 175–196). Lexington, MA: Heath.

Miller, L. B., & Bizzell, R. P. (1983). Long-term effects of four preschool programs: Sixth, seventh, and eighth grades. In J. Trawick-Smith (Ed.), *Preschool education* (pp. 41–56). Bloomington, IN: Phi Delta Kappa.

Minuchin, P., Biber, B., Shapiro, E., & Zimiles, H. (1969). *The psychological impact of school experience.* New York: Basic Books.

Mitchell, L. S. (1950). *Our children and our schools.* New York: Simon & Schuster.

Moore, G. T. (1995). Comprehensive Bibliography on Child Care & Preschool Design. Milwaukee: University of Wisconsin—Milwaukee.

Moore, G. T. (2000). *Resources in Environment-Behavior Studies.* Milwaukee: University of Wisconsin—Milwaukee.

Moore, G. T. (2002). Designed environments for young children: Empirical findings and implications for planning and design. In M. Gallop, & J. McCormick (Eds.). Children and Young People's Environments. Dunedin, New Zealand: University of Otago.

Moore, G. T. (2003, July). *Children's physical environments rating scale.* Paper presented at the Australian Early Childhood Education 2003 Conference, Hobart, Australia.

Moore, G.T., & Marans, R.W. (1997). *Advances in environment, behavior, and design.* New York: Plenum.

Morrow, L., & Rand, M. (1991). Preparing the classroom environment to promote literacy during play. In J. Christie (Ed.), *Play and early literacy development* (pp. 141–165). Albany: State University of New York Press.

National Association for the Education of Young Children. (1998). *Accreditation criteria and procedures of the National Association for the Education of Young Children.* Washington, DC: NAEYC.

National Association for the Education of Young Children. (2005). *NAEYC early childhood program standards and accreditation criteria: the mark of quality in early childhood education.* Washington, DC: NAEYC.

National Center for Education Research. (2008). *Creative Curriculum: Effects of preschool curriculum programs on school readiness* (pp. 55–64). Washington, DC: U.S. Department of Education.

National Council of Teachers of Mathematics (2000). *Principles and standards for school mathematics.* Reston, VA: author.

National Program for Playground Safety. (1999). *Playground Safety.* Cedar Rapids, IA: Author.

National Science Teachers Association. (2003). *National Science Education Standards.* Arlington, VA: Author.

Neuman, S., & Roskos, K. (1991). Peers as literacy informants: A description of young children's literacy conversations in play. *Early Childhood Research Quarterly, 6,* 233–248.

Neuman, S., & Roskos, K. (1997). Literacy knowledge in practice: Contexts of participation for young writers and readers. *Reading Research Quarterly, 32,* 10–32.

New, R. (2003). Reggio Emilia: New ways to think about schooling. *Educational Leadership, 60,* 34–38.

Anita Rui Olds (2000). *Child Care Design Guide.* New York: McGraw Hill.

Paley, V. (2004). *A child's work: The importance of fantasy play.* Chicago: University of Chicago Press.

Peterson, L., Ewigman, B., & Kivlahan, C. (1993). Judgments regarding appropriate child supervision to prevent injury: The role of environmental risk and child age. *Child Development, 64,* 934–950.

Piaget, J. (1962). *Play, dreams, and imitation in childhood.* New York: Norton.

Pratt, C. (1948). *I learn from children.* New York: Simon & Schuster.

Preschool Curriculum Evaluation Research (PCER) Consortium. (2008a). Creative curriculum: University of North Carolina study. In *Effects of preschool curriculum programs on school readiness* (pp. 55–64). Washington, DC: National Center for Education Research, Institute of Education Sciences, U.S. Department of Education.

Preschool Curriculum Evaluation Research (PCER) Consortium. (2008b). *Bright Beginnings* and *Creative Curriculum:* Vanderbilt University study. In *Effects of preschool curriculum programs on school readiness* (pp. 41–54). Washington, DC: National Center for Education Research, Institute of Education Sciences, U.S. Department of Education.

Prescott, E. (1987). The environment as organizer of intent in child care. In C. S. Weinstein & T. G. David (Eds.), *Spaces for children: The built environment and child development* (pp. 73–86). New York: Plenum.

Prescott, E. (2008). The physical environment: A powerful regulator of experience. *Exchange,* March/April, 14–19.

Roach, M., Barrat, M., Miller, J., & Leavitt, L. (1998). The structure of mother-child play: Young children with Down Syndrome and typically developing children. *Developmental Psychology, 34,* 77–87.

Reifel, S. (1984). Block construction: Children's developmental landmarks in representation of space. *Young Children, 40,* 61–67.

Reifel, S., & Yeatman, J. (1991). Action, talk, and thought in the block corner: Developmental trends. In B. Scales, M. Almy, A. Nicolopoulou, & S. Ervin-Tripp (Eds.), *Play and the social context of development in early care and education* (pp. 156–172). New York: Teachers College Press.

Reifel, S., & Yeatman, J. (1993). From category to context: Considering classroom play. *Early Childhood Research Quarterly, 8,* 347–367.

Rogoff, B. (1994). Observing sociocultural activity on three planes: Participatory appropriation, guided participation, apprenticeship. In A. Alvarez, P. del Rio, & J. V. Wertsch (Eds.), *Perspectives in sociocultural research.* Cambridge: Cambridge University Press.

Rogoff, B., Mistry, A., Goncu, A., & Mosler, C. (1993). Guided participation in cultural activity by toddlers and caregivers. *Monographs of the Society for Research in Child Development, 58,* Serial Number 236.

Roskos, K., & Neuman, S. (1998). Play as an opportunity for literacy. In O. Saracho & B. Spodek (Eds.), *Multiple perspectives on play in early childhood education* (pp. 100–115). Albany: State University of New York Press.

Roskos, K., & Neuman, S. (2003). Environment and its influences for early literacy teaching and learning. In S. Neuman, & D. Dickinson (Eds.), *Handbook of early literacy, Volume 1* (pp. 281–294). New York: Guilford Press.

Ross, S., & Zimiles, H. (1976). The differentiated child behavior observation system. *Instructional Science, 5,* 325–342.

Saltz, E., & Johnson, J. (1974). Training for thematic fantasy play in culturally disadvantaged children: Preliminary results. *Journal of Educational Psychology, 66,* 623–630.

Saltz, E., Dixon, D., & Johnson, J. (1977). Training disadvantaged preschoolers on various fantasy activities: Effects on cognitive functioning and impulse control. *Child Development, 48,* 367–380.

Saltz, R. (1997). The Reggio Emilia influence at the University of Michigan-Dearborn Child Development Center: Challenges and change. In J. Hendrick (Ed.), *First steps toward teaching the Reggio way* (pp. 167–180). Upper Saddle River, NJ: Merrill/Prentice Hall.

Sayre, N. E., & Gallagher, J. D. (2001). *The young child and the environment: Issues related to health, nutrition, safety, and physical activity.* Boston: Allyn & Bacon.

Scarlett, W. G., Naudeau, S., Salonius-Pasternak, G., & Ponte, I. (2005). *Children's play.* Thousand Oaks, CA: Sage.

Schwebel, D. C. (2006). Safety on the playground: Mechanisms through which adult supervision might prevent child playground injury. *Journal of Clinical Psychology in Medical Settings,13,* 135–143.

Schweinhart, L., & Weikart, D. (1996). Lasting differences: *The High/Scope preschool curriculum comparison study through age 23.* Monographs of the High/Scope Educational Research Foundation, No. 12. Ypsilanti, MI: High/Scope Press.

Schweinhart, L. J., Montie, J., Xiang, Z., Barnett, W. S., Belfield, C. R., & Nores, M. (2005). *Lifetime effects: The High/Scope Perry Preschool study through age 40.* Ypsilanti, MI: High Scope Foundation.

Sears, P., & Dowley, E. (1963). Research on teaching in the nursery school: In N. Gage (Ed.), *Handbook of research on teaching* (pp. 814–864). Skokie, IL: Rand McNally.

Skellinger, A., & Hill, E. (1994). Effects of a shared teacher-child play intervention on the play skills of three young children who are blind. *Journal of Visual Impairment and Blindness, 88,* 433–445.

Skinner, B. F. (1966). What is the experimental analysis of behavior? *Journal of the Experimental Analysis of Behavior, 9,* 1–2.

Smilansky, S. (1968). *The effects of sociodramatic play on disadvantaged preschool children.* New York: Wiley.

Smilansky, S., & Shefatya, L. (1990). *Facilitating play: A medium for promoting cognitive, socioemotional, and academic development in young children.* Gaithersburg, MD: Psychosocial & Educational Publications.

Smith, P. K., Dalgleish, & Herzmark, G. (1981). A comparison of the effects of fantasy play tutoring and skills tutoring in nursery classes. *International Journal of Behavioral Development, 4,* 421–444.

Snow, C. E. (2003). Ensuring reading success for African American children. In B. Bowman (Ed.) *Love to read:*

*Essays in developing and enhancing early literacy skills of African American children* (pp. 17–30). Washington, DC: National Black Child Institute.

Stipek, D., Feiler, R., Daniels, D. Milburn, S. (1995). Effects of different instructional approaches on young children's achievement and motivation. *Child Development*, *66*, 209–223.

Stone, S., & Christie, J. (1996). Collaborative literacy learning during sociodramatic play in a multiage (K-2) primary classroom. *Journal of Research in Childhood Education*, *10*, 123–133.

Sutton-Smith, B. (1990). Playfully yours. *TASP Newsletter*, *16*, 2–5.

Sutton-Smith, B. (1998a). *The ambiguity of play*. Cambridge, MA: Harvard University Press.

Sutton-Smith, B. (1998b). The struggle between sacred play and festive play. In D. Bergen (Ed.) *Play as a medium for learning and development* (pp. 32–34). Olney Maryland: ACEI.

Tarini, E. (1997). Reflections on a year in Reggio Emilia: Key concepts in rethinking and learning the Reggio way. In J. Hendrick (Ed.), *First steps toward teaching the Reggio way* (pp. 56–69). Upper Saddle River, NJ: Merrill/Prentice Hall.

Thorp, D., Stahmer, A., & Schreibman, L. (1995). Effects of sociodramatic play training on children with autism. *Journal of Autism and Developmental Disorders, 25,* 265–282.

Tompkins, G. E., & Hoskisson, K. (1995). *Language arts: Content and teaching strategies*. Upper Saddle River, NJ: Merrill/Prentice Hall.

Trawick-Smith, J. (1992). The physical classroom environment: How it affects learning and development. *Dimensions of Early Childhood, 20,* 34–42.

Trawick-Smith, J. (1993, April). *Effects of realistic, non-realistic, and mixed-realism play environments on young children symbolization, social interaction, and language.* Paper presented at the annual meeting of the American Educational Research Association, Atlanta.

Trawick-Smith, J. (1994a). *Interactions in the classroom: Facilitating play in the early years.* Upper Saddle River, NJ: Prentice Hall.

Trawick-Smith, J. (1994b, April). *A qualitative study of young children's metaplay.* Paper presented at the annual meeting of the American Educational Research Association, New Orleans.

Trawick-Smith, J. (1998a, April). *A socio-cultural perspective on children's play: Lessons from an ethnographic study in Puerto Rico.* Paper presented at the annual meeting of the American Educational Research Association, San Francisco.

Trawick-Smith, J. (1998b). Why play training works: An integrated model for play intervention. *Journal of Research in Childhood Education*, *12*, 117–129.

Trawick-Smith, J. (2001). The play frame and the "Fictional Dream": The bidirectional relationship between metaplay and story writing. In S. Reifel & M. Brown (Eds.), *Advances in early education and day care, volume 11. Early education and care, and reconceptualizing play* (pp. 322–338). New York: JAI.

Trawick-Smith, J. (2006). *Early childhood development: A multicultural perspective*, fourth edition. Upper Saddle River, NJ: Merrill/Prentice Hall.

Trawick-Smith, J., & Landry-Fitzsimmons, K. (1992). A descriptive study of spatial arrangement in a family child care home. *Child and Youth Care Quarterly, 21,* 97–114.

Trawick-Smith, J. & Picard, T. (2003). Literacy play: Is it really play anymore? *Childhood Education, 79,* (4), 229–231.

Trawick-Smith, J., Russell, H., & Swaminathan, S. (2010). Measuring the Effects of Toys on the Cognitive, Creative, and Social Play Behaviors of Preschool Children. *Early Child Development and Care.*

Udwin, O. (1983). Imaginative play as an intervention method with institutionalized preschool children. *British Journal of Educational Psychology*, *53*, 32–39.

U.S. Department of Health and Human Services. (2003). Path to positive child outcomes. Washington, DC: Author.

Van Hoorn, J., Scales, B., Nourot, P., & Alward, K. (2002). *Play at the center of the curriculum.* Upper Saddle River, NJ: Merrill/Prentice Hall.

Vukelich, C. (1991, December). *Learning about the functions of writing: The effects of three play interventions on children's development and knowledge about writing.* Paper presented at the annual meeting of the National Reading Conference, Palm Springs.

Vygotsky, L. (1977). Play and its role in the mental development of the child. In M. Cole (Ed.), *Soviet developmental psychology* (pp. 76–99). White Plains, NY: Sharpe.

Wachs, T. D. (1979). Proximal experience and early cognitive-intellectual development: The physical environment. *Merrill-Palmer Quarterly*, *25*, 3–41.

Wang, X. C. & Hoot, J. L. (Eds.). (2006). Information and communication technology in early childhood education. *Early Education and Development*, *17*, 317–322.

Wilcox-Herzog, A., & Kontos, S. (1998). The nature of teacher talk in early childhood classrooms and its relationship to children's play with objects and peers. *Journal of Genetic Psychology*, *159*, 301–325.

Wyver, S., & Spence, S. (1999). Play and Divergent Problem Solving: Evidence Supporting a Reciprocal Relationship. *Early Education and Development*, *10*, 419–444.

Young, S. K. (1997). The effects of teachers' scaffolding on children verbal communication in dramatic play. *Korean Journal of Child Studies*, **18**, 229–240.

Zimiles, H. (1986). The Bank Street approach. In J. L. Roopnarine & J. Johnson (Eds.), *Approaches to early childhood education* (pp. 163–178). Upper Saddle River, NJ: Merrill/Prentice Hall.

# 9

# Creating Play Environments

*THAT WAS the main thing about kids then: we spent an awful lot of time-doing nothing. . . . All of us, for a long time, spent a long time picking wild flowers. Catching tadpoles. Looking for arrowheads. Getting our feet wet. Playing with mud. And sand. And water. You understand, not doing anything. What there was*

*to do with sand was let it run through your fingers. What there was to do with mud was pat it, and thrust in it, lift it up and throw it down. . . . My world as a kid was full of things that grownups didn't care about.*

(Smith, 1957, pp. 92, 123)

*IN PLAY, rules and boundaries are defined by the players themselves. This step is first base—and so it is. This sidewalk square is jail, this broken antenna is a gun—and through the magic of play they are.*

(Dargan & Zeitlin, 2000, p. 74)

*The concept of playground . . . will eventually be replaced by a more vital and comprehensive concept of outdoor environments for people of all ages, combining elements of nature, a wide array of play activities, and involving all family members in specially designed environments within their own immediate neighborhoods.*

(Joe L. Frost & Barry L. Klein, 1979, p. 204)

Although some aspects of indoor play environments are discussed in this chapter, the major focus is on the creation of outdoor play environments for and/or with children of all ages. Chapter 8, "Play and the Curriculum," focuses on classroom play environments. The initial impulse was to title this chapter "*Designing* Play Environments." "Designing" was discarded in favor of "creating," for the former lacks the imagination and energy that children's play environments deserve and need. The current emphasis on designing for children is eroding the creativity and imagination that is characteristic of free, spontaneous play in natural environments, and, all too frequently, designers do not involve children in their work. Throughout the industrialized world, designers and engineers are increasingly standardizing children's play equipment and playgrounds and organizing them into tidy, uniform packages that differ little from place to place. As a result, the natural wonders of earlier childhoods of neighborhoods and wilderness are all but lost to a growing number of children, especially those living in the concrete and steel jungles of megacities such as New York, Seoul, London, and Hong Kong. We cannot take children to the countryside every day, but we can bring important elements of the countryside to them, and we can involve children in the ongoing development of their play environments. Indeed, adults can provide places and times for children's play and then stand back and let them work their own magic.

## THEN AND NOW

Children's playgrounds throughout history were the wilderness, fields, streams, and hills of the country and the roads, streets, and vacant places of villages, towns, and cities. The term *playground* refers to all those places where children gather to play their free, spontaneous games. Only during the past few decades have children vacated these natural playgrounds for their growing love affair with video games, texting, and social networking. Even in rural America few children are still roaming in a free-ranging manner, unaccompanied by adults. When out of school, they are not commonly found in neighborhoods digging in sand, building forts, playing traditional games, climbing, or playing ball games. They are rapidly disappearing from the natural terrain of creeks, hills, and fields, and like their urban counterparts, are turning to their indoor, sedentary cyber toys for entertainment.

In urban areas, natural play areas are disappearing because of building in common areas, shifting housing patterns, and loss of adult support for natural, creative play. The natural spaces—woods, streams, and so on—are fenced off from school play yards as farms are lost and urban development gains force. Urban adults are still involved in children's play lives but primarily in organized play, sports, and cyber play rather than in creative, outdoor play.

Paul Hogan (1995), a pioneer of children's play and play environments, wrote a delightful book, *Philadelphia Boyhood: Growing Up in the 1930's,* that reveals the joys of growing up in an extended family and a supporting neighborhood before our preoccupation with TV, computers, video games, theme parks, and designer playthings (see new Chapter 11 on technology) took over. Two of the present authors were growing up in rural areas at that same time, but despite the geographical distinctions, there were more common factors than differences in country and city work and play.

Like city kids, country kids worked from an early age. Paul earned his own money from age 7 or 8 and was taught to be very frugal to the point of embarrassment if caught spending too freely. Country kids helped with farm chores before they started to school and were frequently working alongside adults in the fields before completing elementary school. Work was to be done well; it was satisfying and contributed to the welfare of the entire family. When Paul was 10, he sold and delivered the *Saturday Evening Post.* At that age, country kids were selling and delivering a few copies of a weekly newspaper *Grit,* by horseback to neighbors scattered over several miles.

City kids were inventive, creating such items as diving helmets from cans, surfboards from old ironing boards, bicycles with wings, and what Paul called "skateos"—variations on modern-day scooters, made from old roller skates and scrap lumber. Having no paved surfaces to accommodate rolling devices, country kids carved stick horses from scrap cuttings from sawmills; made rubber guns from pieces of wood, clothes pins, and strips of old inner tubes; and rounded up calves on weekends for rodeos in the barnyard.

No matter where you lived, there always seemed to be a tree house nearby. Paul called his "the greatest tree house in the whole wide world." These could be situated in a shade tree in a backyard or in a huge oak tree on a hillside. Tree houses were places of great pride, to be shown to friends who came to play, to be clubhouses, or simply to serve as hideouts for getting away and reflection. They were also places to sharpen tool-using and building skills and for enjoying all sorts of make-believe play. Now, tree houses are prohibited by zoning laws in many urban areas.

City playgrounds were vacant lots, often with hills and valleys for digging, sledding in the winter, and sliding on cardboard boxes year round. Flat areas were used for the popular sport of the season. No one dumped trash on Paul's neighborhood playground. Early city playground developers bulldozed the trees, leveled the hills, installed playground equipment, paved the area with cinders or asphalt, and designated the site an official playground. Country playgrounds were the hills, streams, rivers, and barn lots. Kids swam and fished during the summer and played traditional games throughout the year. Pets were common companions in their play.

In the country, organized games in neighborhoods and at schools were taught by older peers and adults. These included games of chance using marbles and spinning tops. A wide range of running and chasing games were taught or invented and seemed to follow a season of high interest that could last for several days or weeks before attention was redirected. Groups of kids of all ages would choose up sides for war games and ball games, sometimes playing baseball with homemade balls and no gloves or a hockey-type game called shinny, using tree limbs and tin cans.

Early 20th-century childhoods in rural areas, especially on farms and ranches where cattle and growing plants was a way of life were filled with happy memories about work, play, friends, places, family, and community cohesiveness. Loneliness was not a familiar concept. The downsides included lack of modern prescription drugs and medical expertise. Childhood illnesses were usually long and fraught with risk. Dental care and hospital treatment were relatively primitive and painful.

Among the most compelling differences between childhoods then and now are the early work ethic; the close family ties; the warm, friendly, supportive, personal interactions with family, friends, and community residents; the freedom to roam at will and engage in creative, constructive play; the need to improvise; the pride in good work and the joy of creating with simple, natural, or scrap materials; the favorite places; the time for reflection; the competitive games and socialization with live people and animals rather than machines. Then and now, living poor in the slums of cities was vastly different than living poor on country farms. Obviously, we cannot go back in time, but adults can help children recapture compelling opportunities to play traditional street games, create from raw materials, and play in nature (Chapters 3 and 12).

 ## HISTORY OF PLAY ENVIRONMENTS IN AMERICA

The first formal (built) playgrounds in the United States were called outdoor gymnasia. They were influenced by the German emphasis on physical fitness and introduced to America in 1821 at the Salem, Massachusetts, Latin School (Mero, 1908). They were essentially sets of indoor-type gymnastic equipment adapted for outdoor use. The outdoor gymnasia had succumbed to lack of interest before the end of the 19th century. They were developed for older boys, but later, in 1886, Dr. Marie Zakerzewska, an American visitor to Berlin, wrote to the chairman of the Massachusetts Emergency and Hygiene Association about heaps of sand in Berlin parks where young children played and influenced the establishment of the first *sandgartens* in Boston in 1886 (Sapora & Mitchell, 1948). These rapidly became popular with children of all ages and were gradually integrated into playgrounds for older children.

Friedrich Froebel originated the first kindergarten in Germany in 1837. Despite this early date, he was a proponent of play and considered it very important in the educative process. Indeed, his first playgrounds were nature itself (Froebel, 1902, p. 111). His kindergarten children played much as early 20th-century American children played: channeling streams and building dams, bridges, and mills. They prepared and cared for gardens, observed small insects and animals, explored old walls and vaults, and cared for pets. They used open areas for traditional games such as wrestling, war games, ball games, and chase games. Froebel understood not only the educational benefits of play but also its therapeutic qualities:

> Play is the purest, most spiritual activity of man at this stage, and at the same time, typical of human life as a whole—of the inner hidden natural life in man and all things. It gives, therefore, joy, freedom, contentment, inner and outer rest, peace with the world. (Froebel, cited in Harris, 1906, p. 55)

The first organized playgrounds in the United States were called outdoor gymnasia.

He proposed that every town have its own "playground" to help ensure that children in urban areas were not deprived of the rich physical, mental, and moral advantages available in country children's play.

The early American kindergartens responded to Froebel's call for play and "self-activity" by adding swings, seesaws, various toys, and climbing apparatus to their playgrounds. Over time, such devices supplanted many of the rich natural environments that Froebel favored. Early American child-development leaders such as Susan Blow (1909, p.158) not only supported the creative, natural environments and the gifts and occupations (manipulative materials) proposed by Froebel, but also proposed that early childhood programs be focused around children's free, creative play in rich environments, both indoors and outdoors. Both the nursery school movement and the kindergarten movement of the early 1900s were focused much more heavily on play than were public schools and public parks. This was largely related to the influence of Froebel and John Dewey, the creation of child study centers at universities around the country,

and the formation of the Association for Childhood Education International and the National Association for the Education of Young Children. As early as the 1920s, playgrounds at the leading nursery schools were superior to practically all contemporary public schools and because of their emphasis on learning through play, many were called play schools (Frost, 1992, p. 118; Frost, 2010a). Unfortunately, making kindergartens a part of public schools has diminished the role of play and outdoor play environments in favor of meeting standards and academic activities.

Early 20th-century playgrounds featured manufactured equipment and stressed physical development. Manufactured playgrounds were established in Charlesbank, Massachusetts, in 1889 and in Boston in 1900. About this time, Massachusetts passed a law requiring all towns with 10,000 or more people to establish public playgrounds (Mero, 1908, p. 242; Playground and Recreation Association of America, 1909, p. 19). By 1913, leaders in the playground and recreation movement saw that the dismal state of public school playgrounds had begun to promote change. Curtis (1913) proposed that schools increase the size of their playgrounds, provide play equipment, keep the equipment and grounds in good condition, and put someone in charge of the playground.

Early 1900s school and park playgrounds featured primarily exercise equipment with heights well over 15 feet, with hard earth surfaces underneath (gradually replaced by asphalt and concrete), and were replete with hazardous elements—giant slides, poorly manufactured equipment, and rotating devices that could inflict serious injury to users. Curtis (1913) lamented these conditions, stating that he "knew of half a dozen broken arms resulting in a week from a new set of poorly made seesaws" (p. 26).

As early as 1905, supervised public park playgrounds had been established in 35 American cities. This number grew to 90 in 1907 and to 336 in 1909 (Knapp & Hartsoe, 1979, p. 28). Rapidly growing interest led to the establishment of the Playground Association of America (PAA) in 1907 and to the creation of its journal, *The Playground.* This journal is a rich source for early history of American playgrounds. By 1910, support had arisen for a broader conception of play and playgrounds, and the PAA was renamed the Playground and Recreation Association of America (PRAA) and the journal retitled *Recreation.* Consequently, the early focus on children's play and playgrounds was modified to include a wide array of social work, civic affairs, and recreation. In 1930, the focus on play and playgrounds was further diluted by changing the PRAA's name to the National Recreation Association (NRA) (Knapp & Hartsoe, 1979, p. 104). Play and playgrounds were by this time a relatively minor consideration in the association. In 1966, the NRA merged with several other associations to form the National Recreation and Park Association (NRPA). In recent years, the NRPA has expanded its interest and activities in play and both natural and built playgrounds, and, once again, these critical topics are receiving attention and support.

The evolution of public school and public park playgrounds followed a parallel path that can roughly be divided into three eras: manufactured appliance era, novelty era, and modern era (Frost & Wortham, 1988). Because of recent developments, we redesignate the modern era (1970s–1980s) as the modular design era and added a new designation—standardized era—for the far-reaching events shaping playgrounds beginning during the 1980s. Now, during the second decade of the 21st century, playground design has entered the postmodern era, focusing on integrating natural and built features to accommodate spaces of different sizes, locations, and landforms. The expanding vision is for integrated indoor–outdoor learning and play, integrated semi-structured and free, exploratory play and learning as during physical education and recess, and reintroducing children to regular outdoor physical activity and the benefits of both technology and nature. Children need balance (Frost, 2010a).

Manufactured swings, slides, jungle gyms, merry-go-rounds, giant slides, seesaws, and trapeze devices dominated the playground market throughout most of the 1900s. Following the diversion of steel to war equipment during World War II and its lack of availability for manufacturing play equipment, many manufacturers, designers, architects, engineers, and handymen created novel playground devices to stimulate the imagination and lend aesthetic qualities to playgrounds. This novelty era, roughly the 1950s and 1960s, emphasized fixed, lifeless, molded concrete forms with bizarre color schemes, theme villages, replicas of amusement park devices, and theme equipment patterned after animal figures and stagecoaches. After Sputnik, rockets and space devices gained popularity, and manufacturers continued to expand their offerings.

During the 1970s and 1980s, a few manufacturers began to seek expert assistance in designing playground equipment. The most influential result was the growing emphasis on modular wood equipment—that is, decks and play devices (play events) attached together to promote challenge, continuity, and linkage. Jay Beckwith (1985), a California designer who continues to influence play equipment design, was one of the most innovative and influential professionals in this movement.

Beginning in the late 1980s, after the publication of the United States Consumer Product Safety Commission's (USCPSC) *Handbook for Public Playground Safety: Volumes I and II* in 1981, followed in 1993 by the publication of the American Society for Testing and Materials (ASTM) *Standard Consumer Safety Performance Specification for Playground Equipment for Public Use,* a new playground era had emerged that we designated the standardized era. Concerns for safety led to the establishment of specific guidelines/standards for public playground equipment that limited the creativity of designers as standards were expanded. In part because of the threat of litigation resulting from injuries, playground sponsors applied safety guidelines/standards intended for manufactured equipment to other features of playgrounds. These included natural features, such as animal habitats, gardens, and plants, and portable materials, such as construction materials and tools. Consequently, playground equipment gained a degree of standardization never before seen and contributed to limitations on creativity, flexibility, challenge, and natural features of playgrounds. Fortunately, a growing number of public schools and public park professionals were learning to make playgrounds more child friendly and more attuned to nature and basic developmental needs.

During the last two decades of the 20th century, the historic benefits of outdoor play and challenging, creative playgrounds began to gain rapid attention, and a backlash against efforts to standardize play and play environments was underway (Frost & Sunderlin, 1985). By the first decade of the 21st century, major changes in play environments were emerging and the modern era had arrived (Frost, et al., 2004; Frost, 2010a, 2010b). New energy was evident as researchers, writers, and child development scholars set about to conduct and refine research and return outdoor free play to its fundamental place in children's health, fitness, learning, and development (e.g., Ohanian, 2002; Louv, 2006, 2008; Ratey, 2008; Miller & Almon, 2009; Brown, 2009; Hirsh-Pasek, 2009; Pellis & Pellis, 2009; Frost, 2010a).

Reaction to the decline of recess, loss of free play in neighborhoods, fear of predators and lawsuits, and high-stakes testing were depriving children of their historic legacy of free, spontaneous play. The negative consequences of play deprivation on children's health, development and welfare was resulting in an emerging child-saving movement involving professional organizations, charitable organizations, foundations, business, and government (Frost, 2010a). By 2010, the crisis of obesity and related health consequences and the failure of children to succeed in school had expanded around the globe. Growing international awareness of the need to rescue children from the ravages of poor diet, sedentary indoor activity, high stakes testing, and loss of outdoor play had reached the attention of the highest levels of government. First Lady Michelle Obama, with the support of President Barack Obama, federal agencies, and numerous national organizations, established the "Let's Move" campaign, aimed at eliminating childhood obesity within a generation.

The contemporary movement to save children from the ravages of play deprivation, obesity, and related effects on health and development is, in many respects, similar to the child-saving movement in the largest cities of America about a century ago. That early movement resulted in part from the rapid immigration of rural Americans and people from other countries to the largest American cities. City slums were teeming with orphans and abandoned children attempting to survive in the mean streets. Eventually, charitable people and organizations combined their resources to form the early movement that rescued tens of thousands of children from the harshest poverty and set them on paths to normal lifestyles of play, work, and vocation (see Frost, 2010 for detailed accounts).

## INTEGRATING INDOORS AND OUTDOORS

Both indoor and outdoor play environments are essential for children's health and development, especially for young children in preschools, child-care centers and early primary grades. The key is to prepare spaces, complementary and integrated, to ensure the most significant influence on children's play and development. For young children, learning through play and exploration in varied contexts is brain sensitive and essential for learning and general welfare.

Integrating indoor and outdoor environments for playful learning is further enhanced by integrating nature and built playgrounds. This is especially essential for the thousands of small child-development centers and school nationwide with limited space. Open spaces for organized games, construction activities, fantasy play, chase, and rough-and-tumble play are key as children develop greater skills and seek more space for their group games. In addition, children need natural and built props or equipment, for swinging, brachiating, climbing, jumping, and the like. During growing seasons, a wide variety of plants, butterfly gardens, vegetable gardens, and natural habitats add the mystique of nature and promote learning and a range of developmental benefits (Nabhan & Trimble, 1994; Moore & Wong, 1997; Greenman, 2005; Goodenough, 2007, 2008; Keeler, 2008; *PlayRights,* 2009: Moore, et al., 2009, Danks, 2010).

During sustained droughts and winters, some benefits are lost and the natural playground appears barren, but wise adults can assist children with learning from nature in all seasons. Benefits for learning through hands-on activity and opportunities for developing fitness in nature are complemented by outdoor open games areas and built apparatus for sustained aerobic activity. Given the scope and specificity

of national and state safety standards, school administrators are frequently unsure how to create standards-compliant playgrounds solely from natural materials. Consequently, a typical and growing pattern is to combine or integrate nature into existing public school playgrounds. Many preschools adopted nature-scapes almost a century ago and many natural elements— sand, water, scrap parts, gardens, and so on, have endured and remain integral components of play and learning (Frost, 2010a). Whatever the elements constituting the playground, they must enhance learning and promote fitness, creativity, and imagination.

Child development centers in industrialized countries, especially the United States, typically direct more time and resources to creating indoor play environments than to outdoor environments. This may result from limited space, slim resources, or merely misunderstanding the important roles of the outdoors for children's development. There are indeed advantages of the outdoors that cannot readily be provided indoors. Consequently, the best play and learning places for children flow between the two spaces. A partially or completely covered transition area—deck or porch—provides shaded space on sunny days and shelter from inclement weather. This covered space also allows extension of the classroom that is especially useful for messy play such as sand, water, and art activities.

The unique benefits of outdoor play are extensive. Because large equipment is available and a greater range of movement is possible, playgrounds enhance motor development (Myers, 1985), and promote motor skills (Poest, Williams, Witt, & Atwood, 1990), manipulative skills (Pepler & Ross, 1981), and social skills (Eisenberg & Harris, 1984) in ways that are not feasible in the confined space of indoor classrooms (Frost, et al., 2004). Playgrounds are superior to indoor settings for activities that are messy or loud (Greenman, 1985, 2005). Logistic problems of containing, transporting, and using sand, water, and other fluid materials are reduced. A wider variety of opportunities for sensory stimulation—sounds, smells, textures (Olds, 1987)—are available. Furthermore, friendly, non-violent, rough-and-tumble play and superhero or war play that cannot be allowed indoors can be accommodated outdoors. The loud voices and high activity levels on the playground complement the inside voices and controlled movement that must be moderated indoors.

Spending time outdoors is essential for good health. After being virtually eliminated decades ago, a new condition, childhood rickets has re-entered the scene. Rickets was treated successfully with vitamin D supplements in food and with exposure to sunlight, until food and drinks lacking supplement began to disappear from diets, recess began to be reduced and eliminated, and children stayed indoors at home. Children with light skins need 15 to 20 minutes of sunlight a day and those with dark skins need more (Rajakumar & Thomas, 2005; National Institutes of Health, 2008).

The playground appears to be more influential than the classroom in developing peer culture (Ladd & Price, 1993). This results from greater luxury of space and a more flexible environment (Hartup & Larsen, 1993; Olweus, 1993a). The relatively unconstrained context of the playground permits greater freedom of selectivity in interacting with peers (Boulton & Smith, 1993), which may lead to learning positive social behaviors if teachers are supportive (Pettit & Harrist, 1993). Consequently, play leaders may expect that a greater range of social behavior may result from the freedom and flexibility available in the outdoor environment.

An extensive observational study of preschool children (Shin & Frost, 1995), conducted in well-equipped indoor and outdoor play environments at the University of Texas, concluded that the outdoor environment is more influential on symbolic play than the indoor environment for both boys and girls. This outcome resulted from the relatively greater availability of low-realistic, low-structured natural materials, spaciousness, and teacher involvement in this particular outdoor environment. The nature and intensity of play on playgrounds is influenced by the availability of materials.

The playground can and should offer a much wider variety of natural materials than the indoors can readily accommodate—many textures, including grass, dirt, stone, brick, plastic, metal, bark, leaves, sand, and water, as well as a larger variety of plants, gardens, nature areas, and living things. Well-planned storage areas on the playground make a wide range of equipment available that cannot be used as efficiently in the classroom—tricycles, wagons, wheelbarrows, tools, construction materials, and organized game equipment. Together, the indoors and outdoors extend opportunities for complexity, challenge, variety, and novelty, all ingredients for supporting creativity, learning, and development (Frost & Strickland, 1985; Frost & Sunderlin, 1985).

Children play differently outdoors than they play indoors. Language on the playground is more complex than indoor language (Tizard, Philps, & Plewis, 1976). Boys engage in more dramatic play outdoors than indoors (Henniger, 1985). Girls play more assertively outdoors (Yerkes, 1982). Both boys and girls engage in more gross-motor play outdoors (Campbell & Frost, 1985). Active outdoor play enhances fitness (Poest et al., 1990) and general health and brain development (Ratey, 2008). Many extol the virtues of fresh air and the outdoors in reducing respiratory infections, inhibiting the spread of germs, and maintaining healthy immune systems. Some exposure to sunlight is beneficial to children, but too much can be damaging. Research on the broad developmental benefits of playgrounds is examined comprehensively in Frost et al. (2004). *See Appendix: Playground Checklist, for an extensive aid to planning the creation, use, and care of playgrounds.*

## PLAY ENVIRONMENTS AND CHILD DEVELOPMENT

Perhaps the most common error by adults who create environments is their failure to consider the natural play and development of children.

Few child development professionals are skillful in design, and few designers are skillful in child development. The aspiring designer must be an avid student, an observer of children, one who knows the nature of play across developmental stages. Chronological age, although an approximate indicator of children's cognitive, language, social, and motor abilities, does not reveal precise information about an individual child's play needs.

Children should not always be segregated by age on the playground for there is a playground culture (Sutton-Smith, 1990) that must be respected. Children learn from each other, and the culture of the playground, passed on from older to younger children, helps preserve traditional games, promote society's prevailing values and mores, and teach negotiation and cooperation. Younger children play differently than older children, but many possibilities still exist for cooperative play and interrelationships between children of various ages.

One of the most destructive decisions with which we must now contend is that of school boards and administrators who foolishly deprive children of time for free, creative play by abolishing recess or reducing recess to brief 10- to 15-minute periods, allowing little time for play after time spent in moving to and from the playground is deducted. This growing trend, aimed at providing more time for academics, robs children of time for play and, consequently, of the many cognitive, social, linguistic, motor, and therapeutic benefits of traditional recess play.

Traditional recess should not be reduced, set aside, or replaced by organized physical education or sports. Recess play, which should be essentially free, unstructured play, is different from organized games or sports in many respects. First, it should be free, allowing children to play almost any way they choose. Second, it should be supported by a wide range of materials—built and natural. Third, it should allow children to explore and learn according to their natural tendencies and needs. Finally, it should allow children to learn from one another.

Consequently, different age groups should have many opportunities to play together, and time-honored recess and free play must be preserved.

## Infant and Toddler Indoor and Outdoor Play Environments

Infant and toddler outdoor play spaces are separated from play spaces of older children to prevent accidental contact that could injure the very young child, but skillful play leaders plan for mutual play times where older children are playing with and assisting younger children in their play under the guidance of adults. Toddlers are beginning to engage in make-believe play, an activity initiated earlier in such games as peekaboo with parents, but their major play-related activities are exploration and motor or exercise play (Berk, 1994b; Vygotsky, 1966). The key to creating or designing play spaces for this and other age groups is to include materials and opportunities to engage in all the natural play activities that are characteristic of that age or developmental group (Frost, 1992, 1997; see also Figure 9.1).

The play of infants is relatively simple in appearance but powerful in developmental consequences. Their sensorimotor play is well named, for they are tasting, feeling, and hearing in a seemingly endless pattern of movement. Their indoor and outdoor play areas are relatively small but clean, with playthings selected for safety and sensory stimulation. As infants grow into toddlerhood, they become avid explorers, testing everything in their immediate surroundings. Their playground contains a wide array of grasping toys, blocks, push-pull toys, textures, and sounds. With adult assistance, they begin to use miniature swings, slides, and small wheeled vehicles.

## Preschool Play Environments

As children grow into the preschool years (age 2 to 5 years), they engage in make-believe play in earnest and are learning to use wheeled vehicles and large playground apparatus independently.

**FIGURE 9.1**    Ages, Dominant Types of Play, and Materials for Play

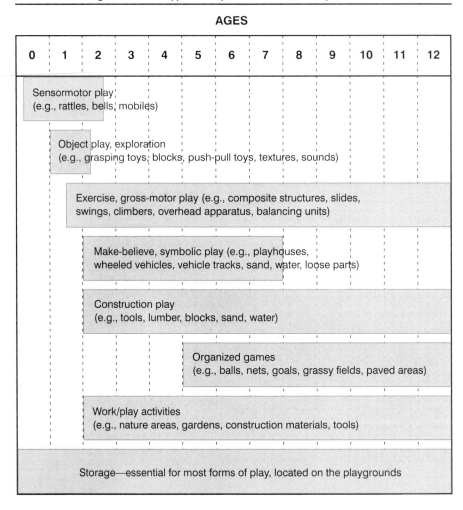

They are also engaging extensively in gross-motor or exercise play and construction play. Their playgrounds are larger and more complex, providing for a more extensive array of play than needed for toddlers. The materials and equipment needed for make-believe play include playhouses, wheeled vehicles, vehicle tracks, sand, water, and a wide range of loose parts or portable materials. For construction play, toddlers need tools, lumber, blocks, sand, and water. As they develop a serious interest in organized games, beginning at about age 4 to 5, the playground must be expanded to include flat grassy areas for ball games and chase games, and small paved areas with nets and other equipment for organized games.

The more formal playgrounds, typically seen at child-care centers and schools, are organized to accommodate gross-motor (exercise) play, make-believe (symbolic) play, and construction play. There should be storage for portable materials (loose parts), sand and water play equipment, large equipment for gross-motor play (sliding, swinging, climbing, balancing, etc.), materials and areas for make-believe play (cars, boats, sand, wheeled vehicles, playhouses, etc.), and materials for construction (sand, water, tools, building blocks and lumber, etc.). Preschooler's play is further enhanced by including nature areas, gardens, and pets in the playground. The social behavior of children closely parallels the quality and richness of their play environments. Barren, boring playgrounds and lack of supportive adults result in children abusing the environment and one another.

## School-Age Play Environments

The play of school-age children (age 5 to 12 years) gradually shifts from an emphasis on make-believe play to organized games (e.g., football, hopscotch, chase games, basketball, four square, rough-and-tumble play) and exercise equipment, including overhead equipment such as horizontal ladders and ring treks. Some organized games, such as basketball, require paved surfaces; others, such as baseball, require flat grassy areas. The shift in focus from make-believe play of the preschooler to the growing frequency of playing organized games of the school-age child should transition gradually, with continual attention to providing play materials and equipment for cognitive, social, and language development through the primary grades. The overall space requirements for playgrounds increase as older children are accommodated.

The school-age child's growing need for order, structure, and industry (Erikson, 1950) can be accommodated on the playground through work/play activities such as construction with tools and building materials, art, and gardens, as well as varied types of games, such as soccer, skateboarding, and ice- and in-line skating. Interest in construction play and work/play activities depends largely on whether storage is available to house the wide array of portable materials needed for such play and whether play leaders are available to encourage such activities. In sum, the playground should meet the developmental play needs of the children who will be playing there (see Figure 9.1).

Children are increasingly influenced by their peers as they approach adolescence. They are changing physically, developing logical thinking, and becoming increasingly interested in the opposite sex. Spaces and equipment for make-believe play are gradually replaced by spaces and equipment for socializing, hanging out, and practicing athletic skills. Adolescents need strong, supportive adults who help them sort out changing feelings and conceptions, engage in positive social interactions, and find their way into organized activities (e.g., sports, clubs) that allow them to engage in positive, constructive roles. Of course, contemporary adolescents, even younger children, are increasingly looking to video games, movies, and telephone and computer interaction with both friends and strangers for socialization and information gathering. Such activity should be monitored by adults and not be allowed to replace traditional creative play.

## Creating Play Environments

The traditional method of preparing a playground for schools, parks, and child-care centers is to install fixed equipment in a row, using whatever space is available. Such play places are neither developmentally sound nor economically astute. Contemporary playgrounds are frequently limited in space and must be carefully planned to accommodate large numbers of children and simultaneously provide for a range of play. The first step is to develop a master plan, an ultimate, ideal representation of the desired playground (Figure 9.2). The master plan is a sketch or overhead view of the site, showing the initial location of fences, adjacent buildings, sidewalks, fixed equipment, storage, water fountains, water sources, shelters, vegetation, gardens, natural features, and any other structures that occupy space.

The master plan should be the joint effort of representative groups: parents, teachers or caretakers, board officials, potential contributors, and people with special skills such as architects, child development specialists, and playground

**FIGURE 9.2**   Master Plan for a Preschool Playground

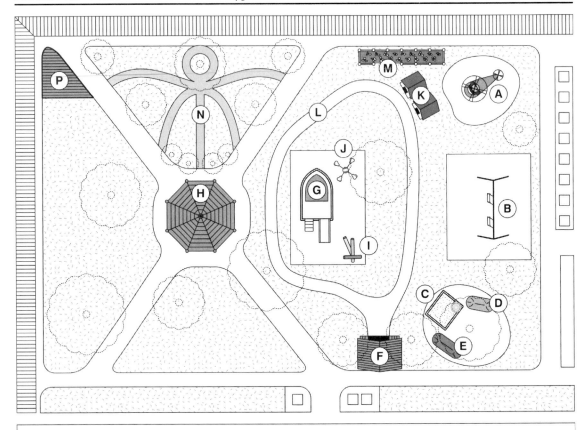

| | | |
|---|---|---|
| A. HELICOPTER | G. SHIP | L. VEHICLE TRACK |
| B. SWINGS | H. GAZEBO | M. GARDENS |
| C. SAND / WATER STRUCTURE | I. TALK TUBES | N. NATURE AREA |
| D. DIGGER | J. FOUR-SEAT TEETER | O. ORGANIZED GAMES (not shown) |
| E. EXPLORATION CENTER | K. PLAY HOUSES | P. DECK |
| F. TOY GARAGE. SITE BUILT | | |

specialists. Children should take active roles in playground planning and in the actual ongoing creation. Good playgrounds are never finished but should be constantly evolving to accommodate users' changing interests and abilities. Many sponsoring groups have limited resources and must prioritize or establish stages for purchasing materials and equipment.

The master plan helps ensure that the steps taken are contributing to a high-quality product. The master plan is merely a first step. The best playgrounds, like the best classrooms, are continually evolving and should be modified day to day and week to week to provide the challenge, novelty, and diversity that developing children need. They should reflect the creative contributions of children at all stages.

Basic factors need to be considered in the initial planning of playgrounds (see the Appendix titled "Playground Checklist"). These include the contents of playgrounds —space, play materials and equipment, natural features, storage, location of utilities, fences, numbers and ages of children, and types of disabilities among children.

A second consideration is safety of playgrounds, which now means compliance with national safety guidelines and standards. A third major factor is functions of playgrounds—to nurture, support, encourage, and integrate forms of play, interaction between children, interaction between children and nature, and between children and materials.

## Space

Density affects children's play and social behavior, but the results of research are mixed, suggesting that factors other than space affect children's play behavior in environments of varying densities (Frost, Shin, & Jacobs, 1998). Most of the studies of play space are conducted in indoor contexts. Children in crowded physical contexts engage in passive behaviors such as standing around and looking on, as well as random and deviant behaviors (Preiser, 1972). Children engage in more fights, involving more children, on high-density playgrounds than on low-density playgrounds (Ginsburg, 1975).

Campbell and Dil (1985) found no significant effect of crowding in space reduced from 46 square feet per child to 29 square feet. However, there was a notable exception. One child was profoundly and negatively affected by the crowded condition, suggesting that effects on individual children should be considered when assessing the impact of crowding. To further complicate the issue of density or crowding, Loo and Kennelly (1979) observed greater passivity (less aggression, less social contact, but more interruption of activities) among 4- and 5-year-old children in small rooms than among those in larger rooms. Social factors appear to play a role in effects of crowding.

Peck and Goldman (1978) found positive effects of increased social density on children's play behavior. Greater social density was related to increases in imaginative play and sharing play themes. There was no significant relationship between density and aggression. Exposure to many peers may contribute to sharing play themes.

Collectively, the research shows that a range of factors—including space, number of children, individual differences in children, and social and cultural factors—influence play behavior. The ingenuity of adults in planning the play environment and their skills in interacting with children can allow positive play opportunities in limited spaces.

There are clearly thresholds of reasonable density levels beyond which conditions would become intolerable for adults and children. The ideal space for preschool/primary playgrounds is more than 100 square feet per child playing there at a given time and a total area of about 10,000 square feet (100 x 100 feet). Given good design of the playground, this allows for the simultaneous play of about 100 children, including a limited open space for organized games, a feature that may not be available in many urban sites. This amount of space also allows for the inclusion of the various features described in Figure 9.2.

Reducing space significantly means that availability and size of materials and equipment must be reduced, wheeled vehicle tracks and organized games areas must be reduced or downsized, storage must be very carefully designed, special features such as gardens and nature areas must be reduced in size, and greater supervision must be provided. In addition, play schedules must be reworked to prevent overcrowding.

**Use of Space** Once the location of the proposed playground is determined, the use of that space must be planned. The first step is to secure utility plans of the site to determine where underground or aboveground utilities (septic systems, sewer lines, telephone cables, etc.) are located. Care must be taken to avoid damaging or conflicting with these, particularly when preparing to construct berms or hills for natural play or digging holes for supporting superstructures or large fixed equipment. The second step is to determine usage patterns for the site. How many children and what age groups will be involved? How will children be scheduled (schools or child-care centers) or anticipated (public parks)?

Special, exciting playgrounds can be created in limited spaces, using many natural and inexpensive materials.

The third step is to lay out in general fashion a preliminary pattern of arrangement for large permanent, fixed equipment. Safety guidelines or standards applicable to the geographic region or country must be consulted. Safety standards are applicable to manufactured equipment (e.g., swings, superstructures, slides, gross-motor equipment) and, unfortunately, also exert growing influence on the wide range of creative and natural materials that should be available on playgrounds. Landscape architects with children in schools may volunteer to assist in selecting natural features and creating natural wonderlands to complement built equipment.

Manufacturer's representatives offer free planning service for laying out space arrangements for the manufactured equipment they sell. Several are willing to collaborate with environmental professionals in projects that integrate natural features. Unfortunately, not many include children in their planning. They commonly provide computer drawings and specifications for equipment and layout on the site and assist with a range of factors: selecting equipment for various age groups, explaining the differences between materials used in manufacturing equipment (plastic, metal, wood), describing the play value of various equipment components, choosing safety surfaces, evaluating old equipment, and selecting installers. Bear firmly in mind that manufactured equipment is a minor dimension of highly creative and imaginative playgrounds, and turn to other resources for help in integrating manufactured and natural, creative elements into a playground.

The fourth step is to secure materials and equipment and install or develop permanent features such as storage, nature areas, organized games areas, and fences. Many communities, child-care centers, and schools plan with specialists and build their own playground equipment. The steps involved in one such community built project are detailed in Altmyer and Zeiger (1997). The American Community Built Playground Association (*www.communitybuilt.com*) offers help to those planning to organize the community and build their own playgrounds. Research and experience of long-term designers is useful in planning exciting natural and built play environments for children (see Nabhan & Trimble, 1994; Stine, 1997; Greenman, 2005; Tai et al., 2006; Spencer & Blades, 2006; Keeler, 2008; Moore et al., 2009; Danks, 2010; Frost et al., 2010).

## The University of Texas Play and Play Environments Research Project

Research at the University of Texas between 1975 and 2011 included numerous studies of children's play and play environments including PhD dissertations, articles, and books (Frost & Sunderlin, 1985; Frost et al., 2004; Frost, 2010). During the 1970s, the research playgrounds were developed by adults and children using scrap materials and built equipment complemented with gardens, sand and water play areas, loose parts or portable materials, and trees. Safety standards and growing litigation changed the focus from self-built to manufactured equipment during the 1980s, but gardens, loose parts, and natural habitats remained. Because no two playgrounds are identical, caution should be taken in

Loose parts are essential features of playground, especially for imaginative and constructive play.

generalizing from one play environment to another. However, over time and in several studies, useful generalizations for selecting and using play equipment have resulted from the research.

Typical methods used in the studies that follow included both quantitative and qualitative methods employing collection of anecdotal data, interviews of children and teachers, time sampling observations, participant observation, child/observer interaction journals, terrain mapping, videotaping, and use of wireless transmission systems. Equipment choices were only one of several variables included in the studies. Choices are clustered here. For example, climbers may refer to tire climbers, bar climbers, arch climbers, and traditional monkey bars. Overhead equipment refers to chinning bars, horizontal ladders, ring treks, and track rides. In 2010, loose

parts, popular in adventure playgrounds of Europe since World War II but little used in public school and park playgrounds, were gaining popularity. Note below the emphasis (underlines) pointing out children's strong preference for such flexible and creative play materials, especially for fantasy or make believe and constructive play.

**Toddler Play Choices**    A study of toddlers (24 to 35 months) focused on both stationary equipment and <u>loose parts (portable materials)</u>. The most frequently chosen or most popular fixed equipment in order of preference was the Volkswagen car, fort enclosure, slides, swings, climbers, playhouse, parallel bars and assorted bars, and clatter bridge. Least frequently chosen were picnic table, steering wheel, barrel, and bench. Most popular loose parts were sand, tricycles, assorted containers, cooking pots, funnels, and scoops. Least popular were cable spools, tire barrel, potato masher, and sifter. <u>Fixed equipment choices were 25% of total, and loose parts choices were 75% of total</u>. (Winter, 1983). Toddlers seek increasingly difficult motor challenges in addition to their seemingly innate propensities to engage in make-believe or pretend play.

Keesee's (1990) study of toddlers (ages 18 to 36 months) began with an analysis of children's play and equipment choices on a very sterile playground and followed with a study after refinement of the playground to make it developmentally appropriate. The most popular fixed equipment on the redesigned playground was the play cube with climbing elements and symbolic play components, followed in order of preference by the dirt hill, platform swing, slide, play deck, sound board, and steering wheel.

<u>Most frequently chosen loose parts in order of preference (most to least) were riding vehicles, sandbox and sand toys, dress-up items, brooms, and gardening tools.</u> Least chosen <u>loose parts</u> included steering wheels, ball, wheelbarrow, pea gravel, and bugs. Fixed equipment accounted for 29% of all choices and loose parts for 71%.

In sum, loose parts are much more popular on toddler playgrounds than is fixed equipment. However, superstructures featuring places to engage in symbolic play as well as exercise or motor play are very popular and valuable play elements as are sand, sand play materials, playhouses, dress-up materials, and wheeled vehicles and tracks. Water play, which is also very popular with toddlers, was not provided during the studies reported here. This is a very common fault that should be corrected.

**Preschool Equipment Choices**  A study of 4- and 5-year-olds at a university child-care center (Shin, 1994) examined play choices in both indoor and outdoor play environments. Children engaged in symbolic (make-believe or imaginative) play in every play area on the playground. However, the frequencies of using equipment varied from area to area. Children's most frequent choice of play area was sand, play areas followed in descending order by open space, model car, superstructure area, swings, and bushes. Water play and wheeled vehicle play were not available during the study. Boys most often chose open space and car for symbolic play; girls most often chose the sand play areas and the car.

A study of 4- and 5-year-old children's play compared equipment choices on a preschool playground (playground A) featuring well-equipped, expensive, state-of-the-art equipment versus a well-equipped playground (playground B) featuring inexpensive equipment built on site by volunteers (Park, 1998). Playground A contained 23 pieces of equipment, and playground B contained 28. Most frequent choices on playground A in order of preference (most to least), were open space, used primarily for rough-and-tumble and chase games, sand areas, swings, superstructure, tricycle play, and garden. Least popular were six instructive panels such as tic-tac-toe, fixed animal figures, and fixed world globe. Water play was very popular during the weekly scheduled activity.

Playground B, featuring equipment made on site by volunteers, did not have a superstructure.

Art table and art activity were the top choice, in part because of the interest of a teacher and the availability of many art materials on a deck adjacent to the classroom. Following in descending order were open space, five types of swings, horizontal ladder and climbers, play decks, slide, trampoline, ropes, playhouse, and sandbox. Playhouses are best used in conjunction with wheeled vehicle tracks and sand areas. This playground had no wheeled vehicle equipment, and the extensively stocked art area attracted much of the play away from the sandbox.

A study of 4-year-olds was conducted by Ihn (1998) at the playground designated by Park as playground A (described earlier). The top choice of boys was loose parts, followed in descending order by open space, swing, sand, wheeled vehicles, playhouse, and teeter-totter. Least chosen were the superstructure (containing only one major play event—a slide), fixed animal figures, instructive panels, and world globe. Leading choices for girls were loose parts, open space, swing, sand, wheeled vehicles, and teeter-totter. Least used were the instructive panels, fixed animals, and world globe.

In both Park's and Ihn's studies, gardening accounted for only 4% of play because gardening was supervised by an interested teacher on a periodic, planned basis. In other words, gardening is not usually considered as free play to be chosen at will by children but is planned and supervised to ensure skills in using tools and good planting and cultivation procedures. Similarly, art activity is rarely seen on playgrounds unless adults take a leadership role in planning, providing space and materials, and scheduling and assisting children. When adults take leadership roles, both gardening and art are rich developmentally beneficial activities for children.

Both fixed and portable equipment (loose parts) are important for children's play. Each type of equipment stimulates children to engage in different forms of play. Each complements the other in providing broader, richer play. In Chiang's (1985) study of 3-, 5-, and 7-year-old children, both age and gender were identified as important variables in selecting equipment. For example, as symbolic play gradually gives way to organized games and symbolic and constructive play become more elaborate, materials and space to support such play are needed.

Many playgrounds do not contain loose parts or storage facilities to house them. Riddell (1992) studied kindergarten children's play behaviors and equipment choices on two playgrounds. One, playground A, contained a wide range of fixed equipment and loose parts; the other, playground B, featured fixed pieces of equipment that were several decades old and designed for elementary school children. No loose parts were allowed because there was no place to store them.

Playground A choices (most to least) were playhouse, superstructure, swings, loose parts, open space, tire car, sand area (sand was depleted), and plastic train tunnels. Wheeled vehicles were not in service. Playground B choices in order (most to least) were superstructure, open space, swings, slides, horizontal bars, arch climber, S climber, seesaws, and chinning bars. The play on playground A included a range of symbolic, constructive, exercise, and open-space play (organized games, chase games, and rough-and-tumble play). Play on playground B was almost exclusively exercise (climbers, overhead apparatus, swings, and slides) and open-space play.

Children's play during the preschool years is heavily influenced by the materials and equipment provided for them. Collectively, the studies show that adults can support play that matches the developmental needs and stages of children by the choices of spaces and materials they provide. From developmental perspectives, playgrounds should be stocked with a rich array of portable and fixed materials for free play and gardens, art areas, nature areas, and animal habitats for directed play/work activities.

Superstructures featuring a mix of play events—slides, tunnels, clatter bridges, climbers, sliding poles, parallel bars, and overhead apparatus for exercise play, and contained space for symbolic play—should be available for typical children age 3 and older. Swings and spring-mounted teeter-totters stimulate motor development and a sense of balance and are just plain fun. Instructive panels attached to superstructures appear to be a waste of resources. Children use playground equipment for playing, not for engaging in classroom-type instructional activity. The environment should change as children develop to ensure challenge and novelty. Superstructures that feature limited play events—for example, a superstructure with several slides and no climbers or overhead apparatus—are clearly not wise choices for children's motor development. A wide mix of loose parts, including wheeled vehicles and tracks, with convenient storage on the playground, are needed to enrich children's symbolic and motor play and to support organized games.

**School-Age Equipment Choices**    Most first-grade children engage in every major form of play and need very extensively equipped playgrounds. Their most common choices of play equipment and areas include open spaces, superstructures, loose parts, swings, slides, climbers, overhead equipment, playhouses, sand and water (when provided), and cars or boats for dramatic play (Moore, 1992). Storage continues to be essential. Wheeled vehicles, tracks, and supporting parts, such as playhouses, gas pumps, street signs, sand diggers for loading wagons, and talk tubes for conversation, continue to be very popular and have high play value.

As children grow into the middle elementary grades, their play equipment needs change. A simple dirt mound continues to attract second graders, especially boys, playing superhero games and rough-and-tumble. Girls and boys continue to use loose parts in constructive and make-believe play (Myers, 1981). Linked overhead apparatus such as horizontal ladders, ring treks, and track rides are very popular with second- and third-grade children (Deacon, 1994;

Myers, 1981). By third grade, children (especially boys) are engaging extensively in organized games on open fields and courts; constructing with loose parts; playing in sand, dirt, and water; building forts, using overhead apparatus and climbers extensively; and seeking out special places for socialization (especially girls). These special places may be large open decks on superstructures, wheelchair decks, or bounded areas under trees. Interestingly, they still use tricycles when allowed (even though the tricycles are quite small for the children's size) and may use the tricycle paths for jogging.

**Recent and Continuing Research**  More recent studies in the University of Texas playground research project examined 4- to 12-year-olds' choices, developmental use patterns, and motivations in using overhead apparatus, climbing apparatus, nature areas, and swings. Yet another study examined the relevance of height for child development. These studies include comprehensive reviews of research on each major subject and original studies of children at play. They are valuable for making decisions about creating playgrounds, play leadership or play work, and revising national playground safety guidelines and standards. Space allows only a brief overview, but aspects of these studies were compiled into two books published by the Association for Childhood Education International (Frost et al, 2004; Frost et al, in Hoot & Szente, 2010), influenced a series of articles in *Playground Magazine* during 2008 and 2009, and a book (Frost, 2010).

In sum, playground equipment designed for climbing, upper body activity, and swinging is extremely valuable for the total development of boys and girls, preschool through elementary school, and such equipment should be carefully selected to provide a wide range of challenging motor and social activities (see Figure 9.3). Chronological age is a weak predictor of individual differences because with increased practice using challenging equipment, children develop perceptual motor skills at a rapid, sometimes remarkable rate. Most children at age 3 can successfully navigate properly designed overhead apparatus after only a few opportunities to freely use the equipment. The most notable exceptions are obese children, who frequently do not have the requisite strength and quickly lose motivation. Motor development on overhead apparatus, climbing equipment, and swings follows a predictable and observable developmental sequence from awkward, crude, primitive movements to rapidly refined, elaborate movements requiring considerable strength, coordination, and flexibility.

Extensive observations and interviews with children and teachers indicate that children's motivations for such motor activity are to some degree inborn or genetic (in other words, they climb because it's there). Yet modeling and encouragement (scaffolding) by other children and adults and apparent feelings of power and success lead children to continue the activity and to expand and elaborate the motor patterns employed.

Height is a key variable in provision of challenge and attraction and simultaneously a major variable in weighing hazards. The higher the child climbs, the faster she falls, and the more serious the consequences. Consequently, playground equipment should be limited in height while still presenting challenge and an acceptable level of risk. Resilient surfacing under and around equipment, selected to match the potential fall height from equipment, are key variables in playground safety. Attention to such safety variables as height cannot be overemphasized. Children must take reasonable risks in order to develop motor and cognitive skills (supported by brain development) to learn to protect themselves in challenging play.

Having considered the steps essential in creating conventional playgrounds featuring both natural and manufactured equipment, we now consider the magical qualities that transform play environments from merely good to very special.

In small or large spaces, built and natural materials and equipment can be selected to allow many forms of play and learning.

**Integration of Natural Features into Outdoor Play and Learning Environments** From the beginning, during the 1970's, small compact gardens were incorporated into the playgrounds where most of the research just described was conducted—Redeemer Lutheran School in Austin, Texas, enrolling 500 multiethnic children, toddlers through middle school. The preschool program has three applicants for every available space. In recent years, through the cooperation of school administrators, the work and skill of Danna Keyburn, teacher and naturalist, O. T. Greer, and John and Charles Saegert and many experienced volunteers, the three Redeemer School playgrounds were further transformed into a natural wonderland of opportunities for preschool through elementary school children to interact, study, and learn in extensive natural and built outdoor classrooms.

The special features include a covered outdoor classroom, butterfly gardens, herb gardens, vegetable gardens, facilities for pets, tools, water collection facilities, animal habitats, greenhouses, and an extensive wildflower, grass, and tree wetlands area named "The land down under" by a 5-year-old (see cover photo). Here, children have a miniature wilderness area with hills for sliding and rolling, water for

finding tadpoles, and hidden spaces in the grass for building shelters and dens. An indoor rainbow room with computer microscopes and water-quality testing equipment and the covered outdoor classroom support animal and plant study and help integrate indoor and outdoor activities and learning. The children participate in studies on tracking monarch butterfly migration and monarch caterpillar mortality and provide herbs for Meals on Wheels, a food program for homebound people. Boy Scouts earn Eagle Scout ranking through work in the natural environments. Compare the potential of such rich, imaginative spaces and opportunities with common science teaching/learning in schools, where curriculum is driven by standard high-stakes testing.

One of the Redeemer School butterfly gardens was certified as a Schoolyard Habitat by the National Wildlife Federation in 2004. The classroom gardens were awarded a 2004 Youth Garden Grant from the National Gardening Association and an Environmental Excellence prize from SeaWorld and Fujifilm. The director of the activity earned the Marva Beck Teacher of the Year Award by the Junior Master Gardener (JMG) program. JMG is an international youth gardening program established by the Texas Cooperative Extension Service and the Department of Horticulture at Texas A & M. Groups are active in all 50 states and 10 foreign countries (see *http://jmgkids.us/*). Funding sources for the Redeemer gardens include PlayCore, Dell, IBM, Community Hospital Foundation, Thrivent for Lutherans, and private donations.

The nature gardens program is being expanded into a school for children with disabilities and into a school enrolling predominantly minority, low-income children. The Redeemer program has already been expanded to study the results of integrating year-round recess play and outdoor nature study on children's behavior, learning, and development. Many Redeemer children broaden their wilderness experiences by attending Camp Lone Star, operated by the Lutheran Outdoor Ministries of Texas.

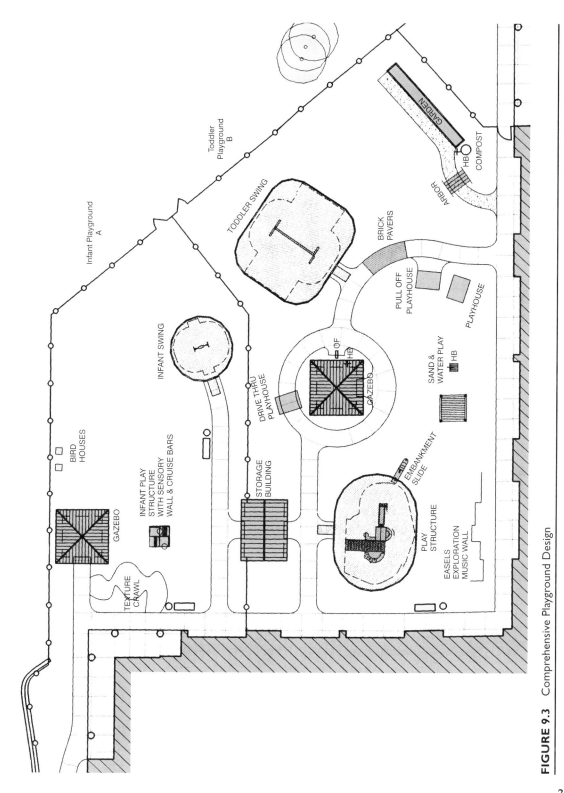

**FIGURE 9.3** Comprehensive Playground Design

*Source:* Printed by permission of the United States Services Automobile Association (USAA), Bright Horizons, and HKS Incorporated (Joe Frost, design consultant).

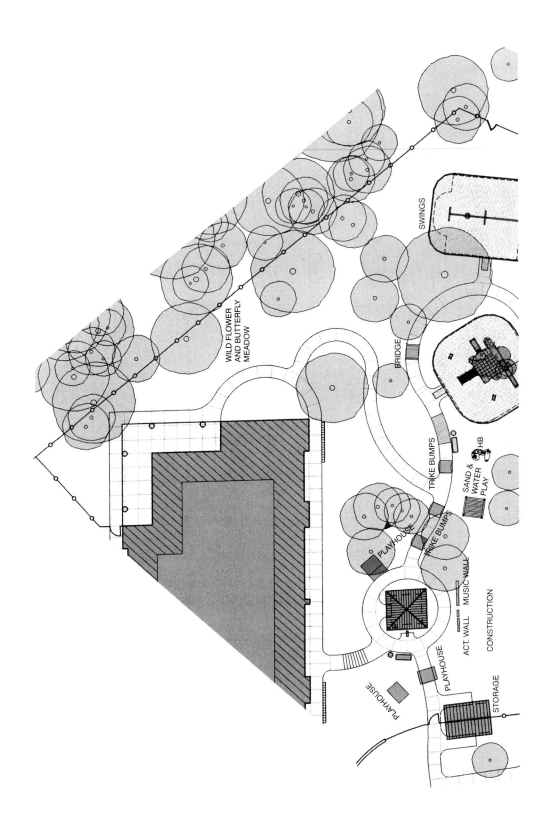

WILD FLOWER
AND BUTTERFLY
MEADOW

SWINGS

BRIDGE

TRIKE BUMPS

SAND &
WATER
PLAY

HB

TRIKE BUMPS

PLAYHOUSE

MUSIC WALL

ACT. WALL

CONSTRUCTION

PLAYHOUSE

PLAYHOUSE

STORAGE

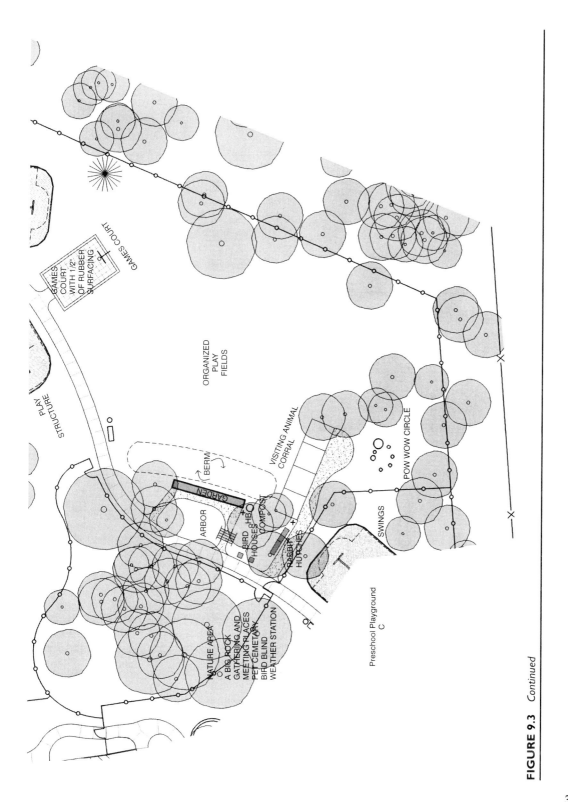

**FIGURE 9.3** Continued

307

The outdoor classroom allows close integration of hands-on and indoor science and language activities.

## CREATING SPECIAL PLAY PLACES: NATURE AND MAGICAL QUALITIES

The typical playground is far too tame (Shell, 1994). Children need wild places (Nabhan & Trimble, 1994). Current play practice mitigates against children making mud holes, cooking over open fires, building their own houses, resolving their own disputes, and creating their own special play places. The best natural play places may lack the glitz of arcades and theme parks, but they still catch and hold the attention of techno-savvy youth. Few piece of equipment designed by an adult can substitute for the child's own creation.

Unfortunately, few countries have extended thought and action about children's playgrounds beyond the traditional concept of swings, slides, monkey bars, and merry-go-rounds, all in a row around an open field. The best of the adventure playgrounds (Frost, 1992; Frost & Klein, 1979) of Scandinavian countries and Western Europe come closest among large-scale organized playgrounds to meeting criteria for "magical playscapes" (Talbot & Frost, 1989). Only a few adventure playgrounds exist in the United States, but many playgrounds developed in recent years do contain some adventure components, and gardens, animals, and natural

features for children's play and work are gaining popularity.

How do we transform playgrounds from the conventional to natural, magical, special places that preserve and enhance children's sense of wonder? We first extend and complement the concept of playground from structured, high-tech, manufactured, designed, standard, and age appropriate, to natural, creative, enchanted, vibrant, unique, mystical, rich, abundant, and developmentally appropriate.

Children and sensitive, skillful adults working together can provide natural elements and magical qualities in a continuing process. The needs are extensive—sand, water, storage, portable materials, tools, gardens, green houses, nature areas, hills, streams, trails, animal habitats, construction materials, spaces for group and solitary play, and transition areas (porches and decks) between classrooms and playgrounds.

**Favorite Places**    Francis (1995) interviewed gardeners in California and Norway to identify the different meanings that people attach to childhood gardens. Using childhood memories of gardens, he identified common qualities to illustrate design, planning, and management issues for children's gardens. The order of most to least frequently mentioned remembered element was vegetation and natural elements, such as trees, bushes, and flowers; structures, such as cabins, barns, tool sheds, and fire pits; specific gardens areas, such as flower beds, paths, sandboxes, tree swings, and sports areas; and shelter and privacy areas, such as those among the big trees and in naturally sheltered areas. In describing favorite places, most mentioned protected, sheltered, or hidden areas, mostly under trees or bushes. Other researchers (Bartlett, 1990; Hart, 1979; Hester, 1985) confirm Francis's conclusions that rough, natural places are remembered and sought out more frequently than manicured places.

Children's gardens and natural habitats should contain certain essential elements, including good soil, water, trees (some large), places for tending growing vegetables, fruit trees, habitats for birds and insects, pets, a playhouse, greenhouses, hiding places, places to dig in the earth, a compost area, an area for native plants, and a storage shed with tools and supplies. For help on getting started with a schoolyard habitat, see the National Wildlife Federation website at *www.nwf.org*.

## Making Play Environments Magical

We seek to help children recapture the enchanted moments of early childhood, the special memories of dewy mornings in the countryside, the secret hiding places in the forest, the captivating moments with sand castles on a beach, the special comfort and aromas of grandmother baking in her kitchen, the sense of accomplishment from creating with found and natural materials. What are these magical qualities that can be included in any playground? The following characteristics of magical play environments were adapted from Talbot and Frost (1989). See also Frost et al, 2010c; Frost, 2009).

**Big and Little**   The miniature worlds of storybooks capture most effectively the fairy-tale imaginations of young children. Children of all ages delight in the tiny, miniature, charming, or diminutive, which offer a sense of power and allow them to play out their deepest conflicts or desires. As they grow, their fascination with the miniature is extended to model building, dolls, figurines, toy trains, small trains in parks, and the miniature in nature—insects, tiny animals, snowflakes, cocoons, pebbles, veins in a leaf.

The giant, heroic, colossal scale reduces children and adults to equals and creates a new sense of grandeur. Children are in awe of dinosaurs, full-size trains, 18-wheelers, and airplanes. Where space allows, replicas or antiques enhance the wonder of the playground. In small playgrounds, elevated platforms can capture views of distant places, opening up a world of huge buildings and expansive, changing skies and clouds, and enabling children to gain a sense of distance and vastness of scale.

**Story Time**   The fairy-tale world of children's literature is peopled with brownies, pixies, elves, leprechauns, and animals that act and talk like people. Children love hearing stories of these creatures and delight in reliving their fantasies in make-believe play. The outdoor setting for story time and reliving time-honored fairy tales and favorite stories can be one and the same—a cozy enclosure, framed by trees and flowering shrubs.

**Real versus Sham**   Children often prefer the real thing over the sham. The real may be more durable, more valuable, more functional, or associated with past experience. The hammer Mom or Dad uses is more valuable than a plastic imitation. The real truck or fire engine, complete with horn, whistle, steering wheel, levers, and gauges, imparts attributes that a mere copy cannot have.

**Sensuality**   Infants and toddlers are essentially sensory beings, trying out and sharpening their senses with everything within visual, auditory, or tactile reach. Create with children a sensory path with textures, the sounds of animals and mobiles, the smells and colors of blooming plants, trickling water and shifting sand—all combining to engage children's senses and remain in their memories. People never outgrow their need for sensory stimulation and beauty. Play spaces should be beautiful as well as functional (Olds, 1989).

**Connection with the Past**   A centuries-old oak tree in Austin, Texas, drew worldwide attention when it was deliberately poisoned by a vandal. Money and letters of advice for saving the tree poured in from many places. The media covered the story for months. Similar scenarios are played out around the world as historical artifacts or elements of nature are threatened.

Age and history bestow a magical aura. Natural forests are more compelling than pine plantations; hoary old oaks are more magical than young saplings; old coal-fired locomotives are more awe inspiring than modern electrical engines.

The prevailing mentality is to bulldoze everything of value from a site before creating a playground. Thus everything of historical value—old ivy-covered stone fences, brick and stone walks, old buildings, rare plants, hills, streams—is damaged or destroyed. Somehow, the contrived replacements are never quite so imaginative, never have the tales to tell, never conjure up the images, and never quite have the lasting effects of the real thing.

**The Unique and Exotic**    Children are intrigued by novelty, incongruity, unpredictability, out-of-placeness—something not provided by the playground catalog and not seen except in special places. Giant musical instruments made durable for outdoor use and requiring whole bodies to manipulate, tire dinosaurs that stretch the scale of the usual, enclosures of winding vines—all lend uniqueness and a special state of pride, awe, and consciousness to surroundings.

Objects need not have obvious purpose. If they are foreign, strange, or rare, they lend a special quality that transcends utility beyond their static nature. "Within sameness there is difference" (Huxley, 1954, p. 61). A flower garden and an old fountain may yield nothing of concrete worth, yet they lend beauty and elicit reflection and awareness of a larger or higher order of things.

**Loose Parts (Portable Materials) and Simple Tools**    Children of industrialized countries are losing their ability to use tools (Ikeda, 1979) because fearful parents restrict their use and plastic imitations supplant the real things. The freedom to roam, explore, and create from scratch that children of previous generations enjoyed has all but disappeared for millions of children (Gill, 2007; Frost, 2010; Skenazy, 2009). Places children build for themselves are far more valuable than those built for them. Children in playgrounds and gardens need tools, a wide selection of building materials, and a play leader who knows when to help and when to step out. Tools and loose parts allow children to be their own designers. The best playgrounds and gardens are changed and transformed by children and are never finished.

**Special or Sacred Places**    For a place to be special and enchanting, it needs to have a certain atmosphere, a sense of enclosure about it, a feeling of serenity, an atmosphere of natural beauty. An amphitheater built for children, surrounded by plants and made special with a pool for fish, a bird bath, or wind chimes, creates a mood-setting focus. Light and shadowy features created by the sun filtering through an overhead trellis covered with flowering vines create a pattern of beauty and mystique.

In his study of children's special places in England and on the island of Carriacou in the West Indies, Sobel (1993) learned from children about their special places—forts, bases, houses, tree houses, tree forts, dens, playhouses, and bush houses—all referring to places that were special or important to the children. He found that shared places were important throughout middle childhood (ages 8 to 11), for both boys and girls, but that private places became more important around ages 10 and 11. Children 5 to 7 years old and 12 to 15 years old claimed that they did not build or use such places; the older children implied that this was "kid's stuff."

These places ranged from those constructed from found or scavenged materials to those merely found and claimed. At first, they were found close to home but tended to be located farther away as children grew older. Sobel surmised that basic to children's attraction to such special places is their need for privacy and self-sufficiency, and creating them is one of the ways that they prepare themselves physically and psychologically for puberty in adolescence.

Special places are places to retreat, places to look at the world from a place of one's own, places to transform the environment, to make a place for oneself and develop a sense of personal order, a sense of place (Hart, 1979). Sobel (1993) adds that forts are special places, that these often secret places are sacrosanct and defended, and outsiders are not welcome.

Small, manageable places in the world should be safe, calm, and reassuring. They are our own, whether for having doll parties or for a clubhouse. "To experience a place deeply is to bond with a place" (Sobel, 1993, p. 159). Taking one's

The "Land Down Under," named by a child, is a miniature wilderness created in a rainwater retention pond.

place in the larger community depends on children's bonding with natural places during childhood. "Sense of place describes the feeling that exists between people and the environments in which they live" (Moore & Wong, 1997, p. 65).

The responsibility of adults is to ensure that children have opportunities and access to special or sacred places (Singer & Singer, 1990), with unstructured time and a few props for cultivating games of pretend and developing their imagination—where they can find and create their own natural, private, special places, and, in so doing, develop a sense of place and bond with nature.

**Doing Nothing**   Smith (1957, p. 92), reflecting on his childhood play, says, "[W]e spent an awful lot of time doing nothing. There was an occupation called 'just running around.' It was no game. It had no rules. It didn't start and it didn't stop."

When Christopher Robin told Pooh, "What I like doing best is nothing" (Milne, 1928), he was living in a world that allowed reflecting, daydreaming, messing around, playing or not playing, working or not working. Today's children of industrialized nations live in a world of schedules, lessons, and practices that no longer values daydreaming, reflecting, relaxing, enjoying free play, or doing nothing. Adults unwittingly assume that television compensates for privacy, reflection, and reading, but in reality television structures time, distorts reality, and robs children of reading, playing, and reflecting. Children need time to mess around in enchanted places and time to be just kids. The favorite fishing or swimming hole or the fish pond, wild places, tree-shaded picnic grounds, vine-covered enclosures, fire pits for warming or cooking, and shaded nooks for reading books all invite children to stop and reflect, to slow down and experience the magical.

## ☐ DESTINATIONS FOR PLAY AND LEARNING

### Theme Parks, Children's Museums, Wilderness Camps, and Nature

Computer technology makes it possible to create entertainment devices that give the participant the illusion of reality, an illusion so virtually real that it is difficult for the human mind to perceive the difference between fake reality and real reality. The potential positive applications are remarkable, promising to bring worlds that most can never visit into every home and classroom.

Super rides closely simulate the sensations felt by jet fighter pilots and astronauts, manipulating inertia and g-forces to give the greatest possible thrill. Some exceed 100 miles per hour and exert g-forces rivaling that of the space shuttle. A growing number of reports show possible brain damage resulting from the extreme g-forces (Rosenberg, 2002, p. 49). The effects on children are yet to be thoroughly explored.

Theme parks are drawing over 324 million visitors each year and reaping revenues of $9.9 billion (International Association of Amusement Parks and Attractions, 2003). The mammoth Universal Studios Orlando theme park, near Orlando, Florida, features five huge islands with virtual reality experiences focused around popular superheroes or selected movies. The paying participants are part of the action and experience sensations similar or equivalent to the real thing. Not far away, in the Orlando area, Walt Disney World spreads over 7,000 acres and offers over 40 major adventures. The designers of immersive reality theme parks and video arcades work with several goals: to leave the participant with a satisfied feeling of having accomplished something, to feel alive, to control danger, to exhilarate, to terrify, and to experience fear and anxiety. Naturally, these emotions are accompanied by a rush of chemicals in the brain, especially adrenaline, that create profound physiological changes in the players. The pulse rate quickens, the hands sweat, the pupils dilate, breathing quickens, and the mouth becomes dry. This is especially true for the giant roller coasters that team with immersive reality entertainment to attract thrill seekers to theme parks.

Lest the reader be left to believe that all theme parks showcase violence, sex, and terror, we must consider those that emphasize wholesome entertainment, exploration, discovery, history, family interaction, challenge, and imaginative play. For example, Silver Dollar City in Branson, Missouri, has been named one of the top three theme parks in the world by the International Association of Amusement Parks and Attractions and was named the top theme park in America in 1998. The park is a friendly 1890s village surrounded by nature's beauty, featuring more than 100 traditional craftspeople, fast, fun (but not "suicidal") rides, 50 family-friendly shows daily, the world's largest tree house, interactive geographic adventures created by the Smithsonian Institution and the National Geographic Society, shows and games designed after Nickelodeon's television programs, special features for toddlers, and a hands-on Imagination Station featuring Lego bricks for creative construction. The emphasis is on interactive learning opportunities that are fun and exciting and combine education, entertainment, and play.

**Children's Museums**    Fortunately, there are other counters to the influences of poorly conceived and often abused play and entertainment venues. The best children's museums are exemplars for recreating natural and scientific wonders and transforming them into tools for creativity, exploration, discovery, and intrigue. Children's museums are the fastest growing type of cultural institution, with more than 100 of them opening between 1990 and 2003. During this period, attendance tripled, reaching 24 million in 2002 (Association of Children's Museums, 2003). By 2007, more than 30 million visitors were attending and there were 341 ACM member museums in 22 countries. Here, the child sees and feels the richness of raw materials for construction and art, bends and shapes her mind while exploring and discovering properties and functions, and sharpens reflexes and technical skills by manipulating simple tools and technology. A growing number of children's museums are expanding into the outdoors to complement indoor activities. These are further enriched by the growing availability of children's gardens sponsored by various urban agencies.

The Association of Children's Museums (ACM) describes children's museums as places where flash cards and rote memorization are set aside, and children engage in experiential learning. Researchers at the 2007 ACM conference reported that early imaginative play that fosters creativity, curiosity, empathy, and self-esteem may be a better predictor of academic success than passive tools and kiddie college courses. They maintained that "play equals learning" and confirmed that museums are places to play and therefore places to learn. Contemporary children's museums are places where adults and children can engage in interactive exploration, adventure, and learning together, quite unlike the staid activity of observing exhibits in traditional museums. The best exhibits are hands-on, participatory, and interesting, with certain common features (Forman, 1998). First, children in the age range for which the exhibit is designed can quickly discern its purpose, second, children can control the events within the exhibit. Third, these changes are within the difficulty levels of the age group designations. Fourth, the exhibit requires more than a single reaction to a simple act. Finally, the exhibit or activity leads children to solve interesting problems.

Children's museum exhibits are designed to send four messages: explore materials, engage in pretend play, explore concepts, and self-regulate (Shine & Acosta, 1999). Parents and children follow different paths. Children choose to explore the materials and engage in pretend play. Adults engage in attempts to explore materials and concepts with their children and to guide them toward self-regulation of social behaviors. Adult actions appropriate for very young children may not be congruent with older children's interests. Children tend to prize autonomy and approach pretend play with intensity, persistence,

and through interaction with co-players. Consequently, parent–child interactions may be brief and sporadic as children resist interference in their play.

The natural links between children's museums and play took on new dimensions in July 2006 when the Strong Museum in Rochester, New York, emerged from an extensive makeover to become the National Museum of Play and the second largest children's museum in the United States. Reopening with imaginative displays on children's literature and the significance of play, there are plans to emphasize fairy-tale landscapes, qualities of play, a huge toy collection, and a family center for integrating education and entertainment. In 2007, the International Play Association (IPA:USA) and the Association for the Study of Play (TASP) combined their annual conferences at the Strong Museum. In that same year, the Strong Museum became the headquarters of TASP and initiated a major research journal, the *American Journal of Play*.

## Organized Camps for Children

A century ago, reformers created special places for children intended to teach honesty, civic values, respect for public property, work skills, and love of nature. Special places included summer camps for children. The earliest such camp, the Gunnery Camp, was established in Washington, Connecticut, in 1861. This camp provided for fishing, trapping, swimming, games, campfires, and storytelling, and other activities such as council fires, dances, and other outdoor skills were borrowed from Native Americans. As such camps spread, they were seen as positive alternatives to children loafing on the streets during school vacations and were valued for the escape they provided from the regimentation of schools.

Some leaders, a century ago, extended their philanthropic work across a broad range of activities for children and appeared to understand the values of play and recreation in natural settings. Luther Gulick was a lecturer at New York University and director of Physical Education in the New York City Schools. His writing

The Toledo, Ohio, Children's Zoo occupies 1.5 acres designed to simulate nature. It features a rock climbing wall, tree house, spider web, water and sand, loose parts for construction, animals, gardens, and green spaces. Children's zoos, museums, summer camps, and other play and learning venues for children are expanding play environments nationwide.

promoted a philosophy of the benefits of play and work that embraced free-time activities—art, literature, mother-child play, flights of creativity and genius, and all of social life. Gulick played prominent roles in forming the American play and playgrounds movement, organized folk dancing, evening recreation centers, summer playgrounds, and vacation schools, and he worked with many organizations to improve play, hygiene, recreation, and education. All this, yet he is perhaps best known for his and his wife's establishment of the Luther Gulick camps for girls in 1910 and for founding the Camp Fire Girls in 1912.

The early 1900s were a period of unprecedented progress in establishing play destinations for children—the play and playgrounds movement, the school gardens movement, the children's museum movement, the nature study movement, and the organized camping movement. These efforts were reinforced by emerging concerns about the disappearance of wilderness areas. By 2007, there were 7,000 members of the American Camping Association and 2,400 accredited camps. Fortunately, such naturalists as Theodore Roosevelt and John Muir valued nature and played key roles in establishing and protecting wilderness land. Roosevelt also understood the value of play and recreation and served as honorary chairman of the Playground Association of America.

Children of all ages love water play.

Even during this early period a century ago, gardens, museums, camps, and parks were valued for provision of play. The dynamic leaders of that era valued such venues for engaging in multiple forms of play, developing physical skills, learning simple skills, use of tools, responsibility, cooperation, civic responsibility, observation, decision making, and hands-on learning in the outdoors in every branch of schoolwork. These play and learning environments were also valued for promoting general development, fitness, and health, providing beauty, sunlight, fresh air, and freedom from the vice and crime of the slums. How modern this sounds!

All these sub-movements of an early ecology of child-saving survived throughout the 20th century and exist today—enriched, expanded, and more relevant than ever for preserving play and nature for children. Organized summer camps, children's museums, children's zoos, nature study and school gardens, and park and school playgrounds form an **ecosystem for children's outdoor play, development, and learning.** Most children no longer have ready access to expansive natural areas or the wilderness. We can create with children little pieces of such spaces in backyards, schoolyards, and neighborhood parks. And we can expand school programs to ensure that all children have access—both through transportation and skilled adults—to integrate the indoor environments of home and school with the compelling, awe-inspiring, special places of nature and the built and natural wonders of the **destination venues** discussed here.

## SUMMARY

Where do we look for models that will support the creation of imaginative play environments? The countryside, of course, is nature's own unexcelled outdoor play environment. Here, children experience an infinite range of qualities that are both the concrete and the symbolic stuff of play—rarity, incongruity, unpredictability, mystery, abundance, color, texture, ambiance, scale, imagery, creation, shape, risk, and motion. Compact gardens and natural animal habitats are additional examples of the wisest adaptations of the countryside to confined spaces and limited resources. For adults, a small garden, even a square foot, offers food and aesthetic beauty. For children, the potential benefits extend well beyond these basic needs to support expanding knowledge of nature and incorporate an infinite range of creative activities.

Creating play environments in restricted spaces is not merely a matter of cost or of space, but of imagination and ingenuity. Just as there is good play (healthy play), or play with positive effects, and bad play (unhealthy play) (e.g., bullying, cruelty, sadism, extreme violence), with deleterious effects, there are also good play environments and bad play environments.

Good play environments have magical qualities that transcend the here and now, the humdrum, and the typical. They have flow qualities that take the child to other places and other times. They are permeated with awe and wonder, both in reality and in imaginative qualities. Bad play environments are stark and immutable, controlled by adults, lacking resiliency and enchantment. Few dreams can be spun there, and few instincts can be played out. The wonders of nature, the joys of imagery, the delights of creating are all but lost for children restricted to such play places. The best play places for child development centers and schools integrate the indoor and outdoor learning programs, and integrate built and natural materials to match the developmental play needs of children (Frost, 2009, 2010c). Those who create play environments for children have a choice, no matter what the context—small town, city, or megalopolis. The difference lies in how we value children's play, what we are willing to do, and how much energy we are willing to expend.

 **KEY TERMS**

Contents of playgrounds
Destination venues
Ecosystems for outdoor
    play, development, and
    learning.
Functions of playgrounds
Integrated playgrounds
Let's Move Campaign
Magical playgrounds
Master plan

Modular design era
Natural features
Outdoor gymnasia
Permanent features
Playground culture
Safety of playgrounds
*Sandgarten*
Social density
Standardized era
Usage patterns

 **STUDY QUESTIONS**

1. How did city and country play environments of the Depression era differ from today's play environments? How do these differences affect children's development?

2. Trace the development of formal playgrounds from their beginnings in the United States to the present time. Which era best represented developmentally appropriate play environments? Why?

3. Why is it necessary to provide different play opportunities indoors versus outdoors? Describe how indoor and outdoor play environments can be complementary.

4. Why is it important for creators/designers of play environments to have a working knowledge of child development?

5. Identify key differences in good playgrounds for different age groups: infants/toddlers, preschoolers, and school-age children. Locate playgrounds in your neighborhood or city that were prepared for these age groups. Using the Playground Rating System, assess their relative merits.

6. Why is a master plan needed when designing or creating playgrounds? What are the appropriate steps in creating a master plan? How can children be involved? Should there be deviations from the plan? Why?

7. How does social density on playgrounds affect play behaviors?

8. What are the major factors to consider in determining equipment layout and use patterns on playgrounds?

9. How does one transform conventional playgrounds into magical playgrounds? Why is this important?

10. Explain "sense of place." Observe at neighborhood homes, parks, schools, and woodlands for special places. Describe them. How do they contribute to healthy development?

11. Why is recess important for children? How is recess time used by teachers and children in your area schools? What changes would you propose?

12. How do structured and free play differ? What are their respective benefits? Disadvantages?

13. How do the benefits of playing in natural play environments differ from playing in built or manufactured environments? Are both needed?

 **REFERENCES**

Altmyer, D. J., & Zeigler, J. B. (1997). Project playgrounds: "We can do this together." *Parks and Recreation, 32*(4), 74–82.

American Society for Testing and Materials. (1988). *Standard consumer safety performance specification for playground equipment for public use*. West Conshohocken, PA: Author.

Association of Children's Museums. (2003). *ACM press room* [Electronic version]. Retrieved from *www.childrensmuseums.org*

Bartlett, S. (1990). A childhood remembered. *Children's Environments Quarterly, 7*(4), 2–4.

Beckwith, J. (1985). Equipment selection criteria for modern playgrounds. In J. L. Frost & S. Sunderlin (Eds.), *When children play* (pp. 209–214). Washington, DC: Association for Childhood Education International.

Berk, L. E. (1994b). Vygotsky's theory: The importance of make-believe play. *Young Children, 50,* 30–39.

Blow, S. E. (1909). *Symbolic education: A commentary on Froebel's "mother play."* New York: Appleton.

Boulton, M., & Smith, P. (1993). Ethnic, gender partner, and activity preferences in mixed-race schools in the U.K.: Playground observations. In C. Hart (Ed.), *Children on playgrounds* (pp. 210–238). Albany: State University of New York Press.

Brown, S., with Vaughan, C. (2009). *Play: How it shapes the brain, opens the imagination, and invigorates the soul.* New York: Avery.

Campbell, S. D., & Frost, J. L. (1985). Equipment choices of primar-age children on conventional and creative playgrounds. In J. L. Frost & S. Sunderlin (Eds.). *When children play (pp. 89–101).* Wheaton, MD: Association for Childhood Education International.

Campbell, S. D., & Dil, N. (1985). The impact of changes in spatial density on children's behaviors in a day care setting. In J. L. Frost & S. Sunderlin (Eds.), *When children play* (pp. 255–264). Wheaton, MD: Association for Childhood Education International.

Chiang, L. (1985). *Developmental differences in children's use of play materials.* Unpublished doctoral dissertation, University of Texas, Austin.

Curtis, H. S. (1913). *The reorganized school playground.* U.S. Bureau of Education, No. 40. Washington, DC: U.S. Government Printing Office.

Dargan, A., & Zeitlin, S. (2000). City play. In D. P. Fromberg & D. Bergen (Eds.). *Play from birth to twelve and beyond: Contexts, perspectives, and meanings. (pp. 219–224).* New York: Garland.

Deacon, S. R. (1994). *Analysis of children's equipment choices and play behaviors across three play environments.* Unpublished doctoral dissertation, University of Texas, Austin.

Eisenberg, N., & Harris, J. D. (1984). Social competence: A developmental perspective. *School Psychology Review, 13,* 267–277.

Erikson, E. H. (1950). *Childhood and society.* New York: Norton.

Forman, F. (1998). Constructive play. In D. Fromberg & D. Bergen (Eds.), *Play from birth to twelve and beyond: Contexts, perspectives, and meanings* (pp. 392–400). New York: Garland.

Francis, M. (1995). Childhood's garden: Memory and meaning of gardens. *Children's Environments, 12*(2), 183–191.

Froebel, F. (1902). *Education of man* (W. N. Hailmann, Trans.). New York: Appleton. (Original work published 1826)

Frost, J. L. (1992). *Play and playscapes.* Albany, NY: Delmar.

Frost, J. L. (1997). Child development and playgrounds. *Parks and Recreation, 32*(4), 54–60.

Frost, J. L. (2009). Back to nature and the emerging child saving movement: Restoring children's outdoor play. *C&NN Leadership Writing Series.* Vol. 1, No. 3. Children and Nature Network.

Frost, J. L (2010a). *A history of children's play and play environments: Toward a contemporary child-saving movement.* New York & London: Routledge.

Frost, J. L. (2010b). Back to nature and the emerging child saving movement. *Leadership Writing Series.* Retrieved March 31, 2011, from http://www.childrenandnature .org/downloads/CNN_LWS_Vol1_03.pdf http://www .childrenandnature.org/publications/Vol. 1, No. 3.

Frost, J. L., Brown, P. S., Sutterby, J. A., & Thornton, C. D. (2004). *The developmental benefits of playgrounds.* Olney, MD: Association for Childhood Education International.

Frost, J. L., Keyburn, D., & Sutterby, J. (2010c). Transforming a sterile urban schoolyard into a nature wonderland. In J. L. Hoot & J. Szente, *The earth is our home: Children caring for the environment.* Olney, MD: Association for Childhood Education International.

Frost, J. L., & Klein, B. J. (1979). *Children's play and playgrounds.* Boston: Allyn & Bacon.

Frost, J. L., Shin, D., & Jacobs, P. J. (1998). Physical environments and children's play. In O. N. Saracho & B. Spodek (Eds.), *Multiple perspectives on play in early childhood education.* Albany: State University of New York Press.

Frost, J. L., & Strickland, E. (1985). Equipment choices of young children during free play. In J. L. Frost & S. Sunderlin (Eds.), *When children play* (pp. 93–101). Wheaton, MD: Association for Childhood Education International.

Frost, J. L., & Sunderlin, S. (Eds.) (1985). *When children play: Proceedings of the International Conference on Play and Play Environments.* Wheaton, MD: Association for Childhood Education International.

Frost, J. L., & Wortham, S. C. (1988). The evolution of American playgrounds. *Young Children, 43*(5), 19–28.

Gill, T. (2007). *No fear: Growing up in a risk averse society.* London: Calouste Gulbenkian Foundation.

Ginsburg, H. J. (1975). *Variations of aggressive interaction among male elementary school children as a function of spatial density.* Paper presented at the meeting of the society for Research in Child Development, Denver, CO.

Goodenough. E. (Ed.). (2007). *Where do the children play? A study guide to the film.* Ann Arbor: Michigan Television.

Goodenough, E. (Ed.). (2008). *A place for play.* The National Institute for Play.

Greenman, J. (1985). Babies get out: Outdoor settings for infant-toddler play. *Beginnings, 2,* 7–10.

Greenman, J. (2005). *Caring spaces, learning places: Children's environments that work.* Redmond, WA: Exchange Press.

Harris, W. T. (Ed.). (1906). *The mottoes and commentaries of Friedrich Froebel's mother play.* New York: Appleton.

Hart, R. A. (1979). *Children's experience of place.* New York: Irvington.

Hartup, W., & Larsen, B. (1993). Conflict and context in peer relations. In C. Hart (Ed.), *Children on playgrounds* (pp. 44–84). Albany: State University of New York Press.

Henniger, M. L. (1985). Preschool children's play behaviors in an indoor and outdoor environment. In J. L. Frost &

S. Sunderlin (Eds.), *When children play* (pp. 145–149). Wheaton, MD: Association for Childhood Education International.

Hester, R. T. (1985). Subconscious landscapes in the heart. *Places, 2,* 10–22.

Hirsh-Pasek, K., Golinkoff, M., Berk, L. E., & Singer, D. G. (2009). *A mandate for playful learning in preschool.* New York: Oxford University Press.

Hogan, P. (1995). *Philadelphia boyhood.* Vienna, VA: Holbrook & Kellogg.

Huxley, A. (1954). *The doors of perception: Heaven and hell.* New York: Harper & Row.

Ihn, H. J. (1998). *Preschool children's play behaviors and equipment choices in an outdoor environment.* Unpublished research report, University of Texas, Austin.

Ikeda, D. (1979). *Glass children and other essays* (B. Watson, Trans.). Tokyo: Kodanska International.

*International Association of Amusement Parks and Attractions.* (2003). Retrieved June 2006, from *http://www.saferparks.org*

Keeler, R. (2008). *Natural playscapes: Creating outdoor play environments for the soul.* Redmond WA: Exchange Press.

Keesee, I. H. (1990). *A comparison of outdoor play environments for toddlers.* Unpublished doctoral dissertation, University of Texas, Austin.

Knapp, R. F., & Hartsoe, C. E. (1979). *Play for America: The National Recreation Association 1906–1965.* Arlington, VA: National Recreation and Park Association.

Ladd, G., & Price, J. (1993). Play styles of peer-accepted and peer-rejected children on the playground. In C. Hart (Ed.), *Children on playgrounds* (pp. 130–161). Albany: State University of New York Press.

Loo, C., & Kennelly, D. (1979). Social density: Its effects on behaviors and perceptions of preschoolers. *Environmental Psychology and Non-Verbal Behavior, 3,* 131–146.

Louv, R. (2006, rev. ed. 2008). *Last child in the woods: Saving our children from nature-deficit disorder.* Chapel Hill, NC: Algonquin Books.

Mero, E. B. (1908). *American playgrounds: Their construction, equipment, maintenance and utility.* Boston: American Gymnasia.

Miller, E., & Almon, J. (2009). *Crisis in the kindergarten: Why children need to play in school.* College Park, MD: Alliance for Childhood.

Milne, A. A. (1928). *House at Pooh corner.* New York: Dutton.

Moore, M. R. (1992). *An analysis of outdoor play environments and play behaviors.* Unpublished doctoral dissertation, University of Texas, Austin.

Moore, R., et al. (2009). *Creating and retrofitting play environments: Best practices guidelines.* NC State University: PlayCore and Natural Learning Initiative.

Moore, R. C., & Wong, H. H. (1997). *Natural learning: Creating environments for rediscovering nature's way of teaching.* Berkeley, CA: MIG Communications.

Myers, G. D. (1985). Motor behavior of kindergartners during physical education and free play. In J. L. Frost & S. Sunderlin (Eds.), *When children play* (pp. 151–156). Wheaton, MD: Association for Childhood Education International.

Myers, J. B. (1981). *Children's perceived vs. actual choices of playground equipment as viewed by themselves and their teachers.* Unpublished doctoral dissertation, University of Texas, Austin.

Nabhan, G. P., & Trimble, S. (1994). *The geography of childhood: Why children need wild places.* Boston: Beacon Press.

National Institutes of Health, Office of Dietary Supplements. (2008). *Dietary supplement fact sheet: Vitamin D.* http://ods.od.nih.gov/factsheets/vitamind.asp.

Ohanian, S. (2002). *What happened to recess and why are our children struggling in kindergarten?* New York: McGraw-Hill.

Olds, A. (1987). Designing spaces for infants and toddlers. In C. Weinstein & T. David (Eds.), *Spaces for children: The built environment and child development.* New York: Plenum.

Olds, A. R. (1989). Psychological and physiological harmony in child care centers. *Children's Environments Quarterly, 6,* 8–16.

Olweus, D. (1993a). Bullies on the playground: The role of victimization. In C. Hart (Ed.), *Children on playgrounds* (pp. 85–128). Albany: State University of New York Press.

Park, Y. S. (1998). *Preschool children's play behaviors and equipment choices on two playgrounds.* Unpublished master's thesis, University of Texas, Austin.

Peck, J., & Goldman, R. (1978). *The behaviors of kindergarten children under selected conditions of the physical and social environment.* Paper presented at the meeting of the American Educational Research Association, Toronto, Canada.

Pellis, S., & Pellis, V. (2009). *The playful brain: Venturing to the limits of neuroscience.* Oxford, England: Oneworld Publications.

Pepler, D. J., & Ross, H. S. (1981). The effects of play on convergent and divergent problem-solving. *Child Development, 52,* 1202–1210.

Pettit, G., & Harrist, A. (1993). Children's aggressive and socially unskilled playground behavior with peers: Origins in early family relations. In C. Hart (Ed.), *Children on playgrounds* (pp. 240–270). Albany: State University of New York Press.

Playground and Recreation Association of America. (1909). *Proceedings of the third annual conference of the Playground Association* (Vol. 3, pp. 2–24). N.p.: Author.

*PlayRights Magazine.* (2009, April). *Special issue: The importance of play in nature.* International Play Association Official Journal.

Poest, C. A., Williams, J. R., Witt, D. D., & Atwood, M. E. (1990). Challenge to move: Large muscle development in young children. *Young Children, 45,* 4–10.

Preiser, W. F. E. (1972). Work in progress: The behavior of nursery school children under different spatial densities. *Man Environment Systems, 2,* 247–250.

Rajakumar, K., & Thomas, S. (2005). Reemerging nutritional rickets: A historical perspective. *Archives of Pediatric and Adolescent Medicine, 159,* 335–41.

Ratey, J. J., with Hagerman, E. (2008). *Spark: The revolutionary new science of exercise and the brain.* New York: Little, Brown & Co.

Riddell, C. J. (1992). *The effects of contrasting playgrounds on the play behaviors of kindergarten children.* Unpublished master's thesis, University of Texas, Austin.

Rosenberg, D. (2002, June 10). Fighting g-forces. *Newsweek.*

Sapora, A. V., & Mitchell, E. D. (1948). *The theory of play and recreation.* New York: Ronald.

Shell, E. R. (1994). Kids don't need equipment, they need opportunity. *Smithsonian, 25*(4), 79–86.

Shin, D. (1994). *Preschool children's symbolic play indoors and outdoors.* Unpublished doctoral dissertation, University of Texas, Austin.

Shin, D., & Frost, J. L. (1995). Preschool children's symbolic play indoors and outdoors. *International Play Journal, 3*(2), 83–96.

Shine, S., & Acosta, T. Y. (1999). The effect of the physical and social environment on parent-child interactions: A qualitative analysis of pretend play in a children's museum. *Play and Culture Studies, 2,* 123–139.

Singer, D., & Singer, J. L. (1990). *The house of make-believe.* Cambridge, MA: Harvard University Press.

Skenazy, L. (2009). *Free-range kids: Giving our children the freedom we had without going nuts with worry.* New York: Wiley.

Smith, R. P. (1957). *"Where did you go?" "Out" "What did you do?" "Nothing."* New York: Norton.

Sobel, D. (1993). *Children's special places: Exploring the role of forts, dens, and bush houses in middle childhood.* Tucson, AZ: Zephyr.

Spencer, C., & Blades, M. (Eds.). (2006). *Children and their environments: Learning, using and designing Spaces.* Cambridge, UK: Cambridge University Press.

Stine, S. (1997). *Landscapes for learning: Creating outdoor environments for children and youth.* New York: John Wiley.

Sutton-Smith, B. (1990b). The school playground as festival. *Children's Environments Quarterly, 7,* 3–7.

Tai, L., Hague, M. T., McLellan, G. K., & Knight, E. J. (2006). *Designing outdoor environments for children.* New York: McGraw-Hill.

Talbot, J., & Frost, J. L. (1989). Magical playscapes. *Childhood Education, 66*(1), 11–19.

Tizard, B., Philps, J., & Plewis, I. (1976). Play in preschool centers: II. Effects on play of the child's social class and of the educational orientation of the center. *Journal of School Psychology and Psychiatry, 17,* 265–274.

U.S. Consumer Product Safety Commission. (1981). *Handbook for public playground safety* (Vols. I and II). Washington, DC: Author.

Winter, S. M. (1983). *Toddler play behaviors and equipment choices in an outdoor playground.* Unpublished doctoral dissertation. Austin: University of Texas.

Vygotsky, L. S. (1966). Play and its role in the mental development of the child. *Soviet Psychology, 12*(6), 62–76.

Yerkes, R. (1982). *Caring spaces, learning places: Children's environments that work.* Redmond, WA: Exchange.

# 10 Play and Children with Disabilities

ALTHOUGH ADULTS may permit non-disabled children to engage in play that does not lead directly to learning goals, they may not believe that the non-disabled child has time to "just play." If play is to be used appropriately in early intervention, it must be evaluated not only in terms of its effectiveness in meeting intervention goals but also in relation to its role in helping children

*to feel in control of their lives, use their preferred modes of interactions, and freely imagine a wide range of possibilities. While this may be more difficult for the handicapped child to do, it is also crucial to the development of their self-worth and their competence.*

(Bergen, 1991, p. 20)

All children play. Children with special needs may engage in play differently than their peers without disabilities; nonetheless, play is an important element in their overall development and learning.

The nature of play for children with special needs depends on the disability or combination of disabling factors, the opportunities for play, the accessibility of toys and a modified play environment, and the presence of peers and adults to facilitate and encourage play.

In this chapter, we explore how children with special needs play, why play is important, and how we can maximize their opportunities for play. First, we will review the types of special needs present in children, following with a discussion of how families and programs use early intervention through play to enhance children's developmental potential. Next, we discuss different types of disabling conditions and how they affect a child's play.

The variables that influence the play of children with special needs, including the play environment and assistive technology, are studied next. The role of adults in expanding children's play is described, as well as the influence of acceptance by peers in inclusion settings during preschool and school-age years.

The play of children with special needs is a significant factor in assessment and diagnosis of a child's disabilities. A discussion of play-based assessment explains how the child's play provides a window into developmental differences and clues as to how adults can use play with children with special needs to enhance development and higher levels of play behaviors.

 ## THE NATURE OF DISABILITIES AND IMPAIRMENTS

When determining how to discuss the different types of disabilities and impairments that children experience that can affect ability to play and benefit from play, different organizational patterns can be used. One earlier approach was to classify disabilities in terms of intellectual impairments, physical disabilities, and emotional disorders (Rubin et al., 1983). A more comprehensive approach is to discuss disabilities and impairments in developmental categories such as motor, cognitive, communications, social-emotional, and sensory and health impairments (Dunlap, 2009). The Individuals with Disabilities Education Act (IDEA) uses 11 terms that cut across developmental categories:

- Mental retardation
- Specific learning disability
- Emotional disturbance
- Autism
- Speech or language impairment
- Hearing impairment
- Visual impairment including blindness
- Orthopedic impairment
- Other health impairments
- Multiple disabilities
- Traumatic brain injury (Raver, 2009)

The level of impairment varies from child to child. Some are affected more seriously than others. Each child is considered as an individual rather than being grouped with all children with that particular special need.

Some conditions cause children to be at risk for developmental delay or disabilities. Some **biological risk factors** can include premature babies, prenatal difficulties during pregnancy, or complications during labor. Infants and toddlers who ingest toxic substances are also at risk. An example is the deaths and serious illnesses of infants in China in recent years when a commercial infant formula was found to have toxic additives to increase the volume of the milk.

Children can be at risk because of the environment in which they lived before and after birth. **Environmental risk factors** can result from the mother living in substandard or deprived environments. One risk factor is low income. Children of low-income families are less likely to have an appropriate play environment, books, developmental toys, and life experiences that foster language and conceptual development. Environmental risk factors can result from parents who take drugs, physical and mental abuse, poor nutrition, or mothers who drink heavily during pregnancy.

Refugee children can be at significant risk from escaping war in their homeland or having their home and community destroyed by famine, flood, or war (Waniganayake, 2001). Early identification and treatment can reduce the possibility of negative outcomes from physical and environmental factors that can affect development and learning.

In this chapter, disabilities and impairments are grouped by developmental categories. Disabilities, delays, impairment, and risk factors are grouped within each category. Some factors are more common than others. Indicators of delays are included. Figure 10.1 charts the different categories, indicators, or causes of disabilities or impairments, as well as the types of delay or impairments.

## Motor Disabilities and Impairments

Children with **motor impairments** have physical restrictions that affect use of the limbs, hands, and trunk, as well as control, mobility, and strength. Some indicators that can alert adults to motor delays include:

- The child tires easily
- The child falls or trips frequently
- The child has balance problems
- The child avoids gross motor activities (Dunlap, 2009).

Accidents, such as automobile accidents, can also cause motor impairment. Limb amputation caused by a disease results in motor impairment. Because mobility is affected, many children must use wheelchairs or other orthopedic appliances such as crutches and walkers. Mobility is affected by cerebral palsy, muscular dystrophy, multiple sclerosis and spina bifida.

**Spina bifida**   **Spina bifida** develops when the spinal cord is not fully developed and has an opening that affects protection of the cord. There are three types of spina bifida that determine how much physical impairment is involved. With significant impairment, loss of bowel and bladder control, bone deformities, motor impairment, paralysis, and hydrocephalus can result. **Hydrocephalus** is a collection of spinal fluid in the brain. If left untreated, it can result in retardation and seizures. Surgical implantation of a tube into the brain allows the fluid to drain and blood to circulate properly.

**Cerebral palsy**   One of the most common orthopedic impairments is caused by injury to the brain before or during birth, **cerebral palsy**, a neuromuscular disability, can cause mild to severe impairment of motor skills. Children with mild to moderate cases are able to walk and use other motor movements, although with some awkwardness. Children who have severe involvement often have other disabilities, such

**FIGURE 10.1**   Disabilities and Impairments

**Motor**
**Indicators of Gross Motor Delays**

Tires easily
Falls or trips frequently
Balance problems
Avoids gross motor activities
Frequently behind during
  transitions

**Types of Motor Disabilities**

Cerebral Palsy
Muscular Dystrophy
Multiple Sclerosis
Spina Bifida
Amputations
Rett Syndrome

**Social-Emotional**
**Causes**

Biological
Environmental

**Types of Social-Emotional**
**Disabilities**

ADD
Oppositional Defiant Disorder
Conduct Disorders
Pervasive Developmental
  Disorder
Autism
Asperger's Syndrome
Childhood Disintegrative
  Disorder
Rett Syndrome
Mood Disorders
  Reactive Attachment Disorder
  Depression
  Anxiety Disorders

**Cognitive Causes**
**Genetic Conditions**

Down Syndrome
Fragile X Syndrome
Rett Syndrome
Problems during pregnancy
Birth Complications
Prematurity
  Low birth weight
  Environmental conditions
  Social conditions

**Types of Cognitive Delay**

Mental Retardation
Down Syndrome
Learning Disabilities
Traumatic Brain Injury
Multiple Disabilities

**Sensory**
**Impairments**

Hearing
Vision
Touch, Smell and Taste

**Auditory Disabilities**
**Causes**

Alport's Syndrome
Pendred's Syndrome
Waardenburg's Syndrome
Family history
Complications during pregnancy
Birth complications
Obstruction in ear canal
Congenital malformation
Illness
Trauma

**Visual Disabilities Causes**
Eye damage
Incorrect eye shape
Brain abnormalities
Prenatal Factors
Head trauma
Cerebral Palsy

**Types of Visual Impairments**
Partial sighted
Legally blind
Lack of visual acuity

**Communications**
**Indicators of Speech and Language Delay**

Inability to pay attention
Inconsistent prelinguistic skills
Receptive language delay
Expressive language delay
Articulation Skills
  Voice
  Fluency
  Oral motor Skills

**Health Impairments**
**Prenatal Causes**

Methamphetamine
Alcohol
Cocaine
Pediatric HIV/AIDS

**Types of Health**
**Impairments**

Epilepsy
Cystic Fibrosis
Cancer
Heart Defects
Diabetes
Hemophilia
Asthma
Cytomegalovirus
Nephritis
Rheumatic Fever
Sickle Cell Anemia
Tuberculosis

as mental retardation, and they have little or no mobility.

**Muscular dystrophy**    A progressive disease that results in progressive degeneration of the voluntary muscles of the arms and legs, **muscular dystrophy** causes increasing muscular weakness and coordination problems as children grow older. It is genetic in origin, and symptoms can appear in children as young as 3 years. Symptoms can include an appearance of awkwardness, walking on tiptoes, severe curvature of the spine, and other postural abnormalities. There can be periods of remission; however, children gradually lose the ability to walk, and early death usually results during adolescence or the early 20s. (See Figure 10.1).

**Cognitive Disabilities and Impairments** Cognitive disabilities and impairments can be caused by genetic conditions, problems during pregnancy, and birth complications. Ingestion of lead paint or exposure to alcohol during prenatal development can lead to cognitive delay. Two genetic conditions leading to cognitive delays are *Down Syndrome* and *Fragile X Syndrome.* A child with Down syndrome experiences cognitive delay that results in mental retardation. Other types of cognitive delay are learning disabilities, traumatic brain injury, and multiple disabilities. A child with cognitive delay or mental retardation is unable to use thinking skills to the level that is characteristic of normal development. (See Figure 10.1).

**Communication Disabilities and Impairments**    There are several language behaviors that indicate language delay, including:

- The child is unable to pay attention.
- The child has inconsistent prelinguistic skills.
- The child has a delay in receptive or expressive language.
- The child has articulation difficulties.

Delay in language development can result from environmental or medical causes. A child can have a limited ability to communicate, characterized by immature use of language and vocabulary. A communication disorder might be characterized by difficulty in articulating or expressing things through language. There might be speech deficits that limit verbalization, such as stuttering or inability to utter sounds correctly. Regardless of the type of delay or disorder, the child experiences a delay in ability to communicate with others that can affect social interactions. (See Figure 10.1).

## Social-Emotional Disabilities or Disorders

Children with **emotional** or **behavioral disorders** have atypical social development. They exhibit deviations from age-appropriate behavior that can cause them to be very aggressive or very withdrawn. The behavior problems that result can include aggression, anxiety, academic disability, and depression (Luebke, Epstein, & Cullinan, 1987). Behavioral deviations can be caused by psychological, environmental, and physiological causes. Psychological causes can include bereavement related to the loss of a parent through divorce or death. Parenting methods of child management and teacher management strategies are environmental factors. Physiological factors can include genetic predispositions. Children with ADHD can also have behavior problems. Three types of behavior problems to be discussed here are children with autism spectrum disorder, children with ADHD, and behavior of abused and neglected children. Autism spectrum disorder has a physiological cause, whereas inappropriate parenting can lead to abused and neglected children.

**Autism Spectrum Disorder (ASD)**    Autism spectrum disorder is a group of disorders with similar features. It is also known as **pervasive developmental disorders. Asperger's syndrome** and **autism** are two disorders that are part of autism spectrum disorder. (National Institute of Health & Eunice Kennedy Shriver National Institute of Child Health & Human Development, 2010; National Institute of Mental Health (2010). ASD can cause severe and pervasive impairment in thinking, feeling, language, and in relating to others. The disorders are usually first diagnosed in the preschool years and can range from a mild form (Asperger's syndrome) to a more severe form (autism).

Children with autism disorder experience severe emotional disturbance. Autism is first noticeable at about 2 ½ years of age and is more common in boys than girls. Behaviors exhibited by children with autism disorder include head banging, echolalia speech (repetition of a word), extremely delayed expressive language, and stereotypical body movements. It is thought that autism is a biological problem that occurs during prenatal or perinatal stages of development. Children with autism disorder can seem to be insensitive to sounds and events around them and have difficulty in interacting with others socially. They apparently fail to recognize that the outside world is different from the self (Atlas & Lapidus, 1987). Children with autism disorder often experience mental retardation as well. Autism is more common in boys, siblings of children with autism, and people with other disorders, such as Fragile X Syndrome.

Children with Asperger's syndrome have difficulty with social situations. Symptoms can be mild to severe. Some symptoms include a dislike of changes in routines, avoidance of eye contact or staring, unusual facial expressions, have delayed motor development, and talking a lot. To be diagnosed with Asperger's syndrome, a child must have a combination of symptoms and severe trouble with social situations (WebMD, 2010).

**Attention Deficit Hyperactivity Disorder.** Children with **attention deficit hyperactivity disorder (ADHD)** experience a delay in their ability to lengthen attention span, resist distractions, and focus on learning tasks. They can be impulsive and hyperactive in their behavior but do not have a mental disorder. They may have difficulties with social interactions and adjusting to group settings. ADHD is difficult to categorize because different types of behaviors can be manifested in a child who is diagnosed as having ADHD.

**Abused and Neglected Children.** Children can be abused emotionally, physically, or sexually, or be neglected. Frequently, abused children experience more than one form of abuse. Although many abused children are aggressive and use inappropriate social behaviors, they are equally likely to be withdrawn and passive. Aggressive children can be disruptive and antisocial, whereas withdrawn children might make no attempts to interact with other children. Children who have been sexually abused might use inappropriate sexual behaviors in social interactions with their peers. Physically abused children might wear clothing that is seasonally inappropriate to cover physical signs of abuse. Neglected children might be dressed inappropriately or in dirty clothing because they have received minimal care and supervision.

## Sensory Impairments

**Hearing Impairments** Children with hearing impairments are not able to hear sounds normally because of a malfunction of the ear or associated nerves. The degree of impairment varies from mild to severe and can be temporary or permanent. Conductive hearing losses prevent sound waves from reaching the brain through nerve fibers. Sensory-neural losses result form damage to nerve fibers and are hereditary or result from medical causes. Although conductive hearing losses can be repaired through surgery, sensory-neural losses are irreversible.

**Visual Impairments** **Visual impairments** are caused by eye damage, incorrect eye shape, brain abnormalities, prenatal factors, head trauma, and cerebral palsy. A child with visual impairments can have low vision, be legally blind, or lack visual acuity. Mild visual impairments can be restored in children who are legally blind.

**Health Impairments**  A variety of health impairments can affect a child's ability to engage in normal activities. Some of the health conditions are genetic in origin; others have been caused by environmental factors. Each of the conditions impairs the child's ability to participate with other children because of limitations of strength and stamina. Health impairments that can limit children's activities include heart conditions, bronchial asthma, diabetes, rheumatic fever, hemophilia, lead poisoning, cystic fibrosis, sickle-cell anemia, and tuberculosis. Health impairments can be caused prenatally by the mother's use of methamphetamines, alcohol, cocaine, and pediatric HIV/AIDS.

## Children with Multiple Disabilities

Unfortunately, children with disabilities frequently have a combination of conditions. For example, children with visual impairments can also have hearing impairments. Mental retardation can accompany visual and hearing impairments. As mentioned earlier, children with cognitive delay or mental retardation can also have language delay and communication disorders. Children with behavior disorders can also experience language abnormalities or cognitive delay. Children with ADHD can experience cognitive difficulties, although they typically have normal intelligence.

It is important to understand the nature of disabilities if we are to understand how these conditions and variations from normal development affect how children play. It is easier to understand the limitations children with physical disabilities face and how their play is affected compared to children with behavioral or mental disabilities. When a combination of conditions is present, providing play opportunities is even more challenging.

## CHILDREN WITH EXCEPTIONAL ABILITIES

Gifted children have a high level of development for their chronological age. These children are characterized by high intelligence and/or high creativity. Some children have a specialized talent that may be expressed in sports, the arts, mathematics, or the sciences. Gifted and talented children are inquisitive, persistent, and highly motivated to pursue their interests.

### Gifted Children and Play

Gifted children are interested in play, although observations on the playground might seem to indicate that they are loners and only engage in solitary play. Several factors can contribute to this misperception.

The gifted child needs to have friendships and play with peers who have similar advanced ability levels. Moreover, they are more likely to have one or two friends rather than move among larger social groups. They have play interests that are more advanced than same-age playmates. Because of their advanced language and conceptual skills, they may be perceived to be bossy and thus poorly received by their classmates (Porter, 2001).

The policies for entrance and promotion in public schools in the United States further restrict play and friendship opportunities for gifted children. In many states, children are denied early entrance into elementary schools and are prevented from making significant acceleration in grade commensurate with their intellectual abilities and are advanced achievement. Current policies of inclusion of children with diverse abilities and disabilities do not address the learning needs of gifted children. The focus on inclusion has been on working with children with disabilities. Thus gifted children are not included relative to their advanced learning abilities. Opportunities to have friendships and play and learn with intellectual peers receive little consideration (Kearney, 1996; Osborn, 2006). For example, a 5-year-old who is 3 years advanced in intellectual development who can play chess and other games with complex rules and build complex structures will have difficulty finding a play partner who can engage in this type of play (Osborn, 2006).

Gifted children enjoy playing. They want to have friends. They play at their mental level rather than at their chronological levels. A significant requirement for them to be able to engage in their play interests is to have like-minded friends. They do not choose to be social isolates and engage only in solitary play. If they are fortunate enough to be schooled with other gifted children, they can engage in play that is appropriate for the level of development. If other gifted children are not available, playing with older playmates can also be enjoyable (Gross, 2002; Osborn, 2006).

## DISABILITIES AND PLAY

It is difficult to study the play of children with disabilities. First, because handicapping conditions can involve a wide range of disabilities, it can be difficult to determine the cause of differences in play. Moreover, many studies are flawed and fail to separate developmental differences from differences caused by a disabling condition (Quinn & Rubin, 1984). In addition, depending on the nature of the disability, research on the play of children with disabilities can be conducted by researchers from different professions. Thus researchers in medicine, mental health professionals, and educational psychologists might be studying play for different purposes and with different results. Some research studies are conducted with individual children and do not consider the effect of peer relationships or behaviors in a group setting (Hughes, 1998; Quinn & Rubin, 1984).

Regardless of these limitations, a growing body of information is available on the play of children with disabilities with implications for practice. In the following sections, we discuss how play is affected by different disabilities. The role of adults in the child's play is also described, particularly in regard to how adults can expand the play of children with disabilities.

## Children with Visual Impairments

**Characteristics of Play**   There are significant differences between the play of sighted children and that of blind children. Troster and Bambring (1994) have summarized the research based on these differences:

It has been found that, in comparison to sighted children, blind children do the following:

1. Explore their surroundings and the objects in their surroundings less often (Fraiberg, 1977; Olson, 1981; Sandler & Wills, 1965; Troster & Bambring, 1992, 1993; Wills, 1972).

2. As infants and preschoolers, they frequently engage in solitary play that is repetitive and stereotyped (Freeman et al., 1989; Parsons, 1986; Sandler, 1963; Warren, 1984; Wills, 1972).

3. Exhibit less spontaneous play; far more than sighted children, they have to be taught how to play (Burlingham, 1961, 1967, 1972, 1975; Rothschild, 1960; Sandler, 1963; Sandler & Wills, 1965; Tait, 1972c; Wills, 1965, 1968, 1970).

4. Do not or only rarely imitate the routine activities of the caregivers (Fraiberg, 1977; Sandler & Wills, 1965).

5. Play less frequently with stuffed animals and dolls and rarely engage in animism (Warren, 1984; Wills, 1979).

6. Play less frequently with peers and usually direct their play toward adults (Schneekloth, 1989; Tait, 1972a, 1972b; Wills, 1968, 1970).

7. Exhibit clear delays in the development of symbolic play and role play (Fraiberg & Adelson, 1973; Sandler & Wills, 1965; Tait, 1972a, 1972b; Wills, 1968, 1970).

8. Engage in play that contains fewer aggressive elements (Burlingham, 1961, 1965; Fraiberg, 1968; Wills, 1970, 1981) (pp. 421–422).

Blind children enjoy outdoor play.

These characteristics of the play of blind children as compared to sighted children can be explained further. Children with visual impairments often have developmental delays in other domains of development that could easily affect their play skills (Warren, 1984). Moreover, overprotection by adults or fear of dangers might result in limited attempts to engage in play (Rettig, 1994; Schneekloth, 1989). Although sighted children spend most of their playtime interacting with other children, children with visual impairments spend 56% of their time playing alone (Schneekloth, 1989).

Because visual impairment makes it difficult for these children to orient themselves to space and time and to separate reality from nonreality, they need more time to adapt themselves to a play environment (Frost, 1992; Frost & Klein, 1979; Hughes, 1998). Moreover, because of these limitations, the child who is blind or has limited vision is unable to respond to the quick and perhaps unpredictable movements of sighted children and responds less quickly to different activities. Changes in play activities thus may also be more difficult for children with visual impairment who also have difficulty in moving from the known to the unknown (Rettig, 1994).

Children with visual impairments may also experience language delay and have been found to use language differently from their sighted peers. Children with visual impairments are slower to develop a sense of self and there is a delay in using *I* as a pronoun. This is related to a delay in symbolic play (Fraiberg & Adelson, 1973). Blind children tend to ask more questions of adults in an effort to further their understanding of the environment, whereas sighted children use language to relate to objects or to refer to past experiences (Erin, 1990). An additional problem is that children with visual impairments experience obstacles to interpreting nonverbal communication that can impede interacting with sighted children.

There are differences in the cognitive play of children who are visually impaired and their peers with normal sight. In object play, sighted children use their eyes to explore objects, whereas children with visual impairments use eyes, hands, feet, and other parts of their body to explore objects (Hughes, Dote-Kwan, & Dolendo, 1998; Preisler & Palmer, 1989). Moreover, their lack of interest in exploring toys in the environment might be related to a lack of experiences and the tendency to be more interested in their bodies than the environment. Preisler and Palmer (1989) found them to be more interested in environmental elements that opened and closed, such as doors, than toys. Unsurprisingly, the materials and equipment provided in the environment also affect the amount of exploratory play as much as the visual capacity of young children (Skellenger, Rosenblum, & Jager, 1997).

**The Role of Adults**    When discussing the role of adults in the play of children with disabilities, a major purpose is to intervene and help the child develop play skills. Here are five intervention strategies that can be used to enhance the play skills of children with visual impairments (Rettig, 1994):

1. Specific instruction in play skills
2. Manipulating toys and playthings
3. Adapting the setting
4. The use of peers without disabilities
5. The role of adults (pp. 413–414)

The involvement of adults in play activities is crucial in the acquisition of play skills. Adults must not only be involved in play activities but also systematically incorporate play into the curriculum in group settings.

Children with visual impairments may need intervention in how to play with toys or peers. Adults should provide a variety of real objects for play and assist children in the symbolic use of the objects. Exploration can include household items and objects such as doorknobs, locks and keys, plastic bowls, wooden spoons, and pots and pans (Recchia, 1987; Schneekloth, 1989). Toys should be selected to encourage symbolic representation. Dolls are effective, and so are wooden trucks (Rettig, 1994). Adults can provide experiences with objects that sighted children acquire automatically, for example, learning to pour from a pitcher into a cup (Skellinger & Hill, 1994).

Adults can support play by providing opportunity to explore in a safe, familiar environment. Children with low vision need opportunities for motor play so they can develop the same abilities as their sighted peers (Schneekloth, 1989). Schneekloth suggests that visually impaired children need guided exploration experiences to understand their surroundings. The environment should also include a soft area where visually impaired children can move about freely without fear of injury.

Children should be assisted in becoming autonomous and independent in play. Adults should assist children in developing social interactions with other children. If they are using stereotyped behaviors, they can be guided in using more imagination and fantasy so their play with sighted peers can be enhanced. To encourage play interactions between sighted and visually impaired children, the adult should start with one sighted playmate and then gradually increase the number of sighted children in the group (Recchia, 1987). Sighted children need to understand the nature of a visual impairment. The teacher should help them acquire information about what it means to be blind or have low vision and encourage them to play with children who are visually impaired (Rettig, 1994).

## Children with Hearing Impairments

**Characteristics of Play**   Children with hearing impairments are less affected in their play than children with visual impairments. The most significant factor is delay in language, which results in less interest in make-believe play or fantasy play than their hearing peers have. They engage less often in sociodramatic play and use less symbolism of objects than children with normal hearing ability (Esposito & Koorland, 1989; Hughes, 1998).

Social interactions with hearing children can be facilitated if signing is used in a group setting or if hearing children are given information on how to communicate with children who are learning to lip-read. Children with hearing impairments who are placed in self-contained classes for children are likely to play in a less sophisticated manner than children who are placed in integrated settings with hearing children. Parten's (1932) level of parallel play was observed more often in the self-contained setting for hearing-impaired children; associative play was more common in the integrated setting in a study conducted by Esposito and Koorland (1989).

**The Role of Adults**   Because children with hearing impairments can engage in all forms of play, adults do not have to teach them how to play with objects or guide them in the use of materials and equipment. Acting as a facilitator of communication between children who have hearing impairments and children who hear normally is an important role. Modeling and engaging in pretend play is also helpful in expanding children's use of sociodramatic play and symbolic play.

One of the authors designed a playscape for a preschool for children with hearing impairments. The school was integrated in that children with normal hearing were also enrolled at the school. In discussing how children used the play environment, particularly the outdoor environment, the teachers saw their major responsibility was finding lost hearing aids. The children's favorite play activity was to roll down a long grassy hill under large shade trees. Children invariably lost their hearing aids on the way down the hill, and the teachers were constantly on the alert to locate the aids.

The playscape also had an outdoor center for sociodramatic play. The teachers strategically rotated the props and materials located in the center and encouraged children to engage in sociodramatic play by playing alongside them when necessary.

## Children with Motor Impairments

**Characteristics of Play**   Describing the play of children with motor impairments is challenging because there are so many kinds of motor impairments, and the severity of the impairment varies. The most significant limitation is in play that involves physical activity. Indoor play is the least affected because some of the activities do not require gross-motor skills. With modifications in classroom space to accommodate wheelchairs and other physical assistance devices, children with mobility problems can be included in games and other play activities with a minimum of adaptation. Unless the child has other disabling conditions, social interactions are affected only to the extent that children without disabilities are guided in accepting the child's limitations and can modify their play to include the child.

A factor in the ability to play of a child with severe physical limitations is the use of **positioning equipment**, which provides support and proper positioning to permit children to carry out daily self-care activities and engage in play (e.g., toilet seats, car seats, prone standers, strollers, and crawlers). This equipment not only permits a child with weak muscle support to be placed in a sitting position but can also provide mobility for some children. At a minimum, the positioning equipment makes it possible for children to use their hands to play with objects (O'Brien et al., 1998).

Outdoor play is more of a concern. Lack of mobility or limitations in mobility makes it difficult for the child to participate in physical play with peers who are not disabled. Access to play equipment on the playground is a major goal in making it possible for children with physical limitations to engage in play. Swings can be adapted to hold a wheel chair. Climbing structures can have ramps for crawling or ascending in a wheelchair. Raised sand tables and water play activities can be positioned to accommodate a wheelchair. Making the environment accessible to children with motor impairments is discussed later in the chapter.

Inclusion in sports is an important factor for older children. Virtually all children would like to be included in sports to the extent they are able to participate. The popularity of Special Olympics programs for citizens who are mentally retarded testifies to the need for availability of sports activities for children with all types of disabilities, but especially for children with motor impairments.

A challenge in school settings is including children with motor impairments in sports and other physical activities with their peers who are not disabled. Including students with motor impairments in physical education classes is possible. In a race, fellow classmate can act as legs for a child in a wheelchair by pushing him along. Likewise, a classmate can hold the hand of a child that has low-vision or blindness and guide her in participating in a physical activity

(Burkour, 1998; Kozub & Porretta, 1996; Moucha et al., 1997).

**The Role of Adults**   The Americans with Disabilities Act (ADA) ensures the rights of people with disabilities to have access to all aspects of community life, including participation in physical activities and integrated settings. For children with motor impairments, this means that settings and activities must be adapted to their individual needs. Teachers, physical education coaches, and sports leaders must find ways to adapt and accommodate to provide support on an individual basis. The goal is to remove barriers to participation in physical activities.

Burkour (1998) suggests the following to include children with disabilities in youth sports:

• *Skill assessments/task analysis:*   clearly identifying all of the physical, sensory, learning, communication, and socialization skills needed to be successful. Looking at the child's participation in an activity from beginning to end can do this.

• *Focus on maximizing abilities:*   using individual strengths. Not everyone has to do every aspect of every sport independently to be successful.

• *Ask everyone for accommodation ideas:*   the child, family, teachers, recreation therapists, physical therapists, and particularly other children. These children will come up with the most unobtrusive adaptations that will not get in the way of fun. (p. 73)

Burkour (1998) further believes that "adaptations can be made by making adjustments in leading/teaching/communication, placement in positions on the field/court, performance expectations, and rules of the game" (p. 73). For example, a child in a wheelchair can have a pusher to run her through the bases in baseball. Another example is the use of a brightly colored basketball for a child with a visual impairment.

## Children at Risk for Developmental Delay or a Disability

As discussed earlier, children can be diagnosed as being at risk for normal development because of biological factors or environmental factors. They might also have a condition that has been diagnosed as a disability. The main focus for at-risk children is to prevent delay or to minimize the effects of a disability. Early intervention programs are used to maximize potential of at-risk children; moreover, characteristics of play are used in diagnostic assessment to determine the child's status and needs. In the following sections on developmental delay, we develop more fully the characteristics of play for at-risk children, placing more emphasis on the role of adults in using play for intervention purposes.

**Characteristics of Play**   The play of at-risk children can be described in terms of sensorimotor/practice play, symbolic play, and social play. The sensorimotor play of at-risk children develops similarly to that of nonrisk children; however, if play indicates differences, it can give early indications of a possible delay or disabling conditions. For example, children who exhibit a narrower range of sensorimotor activities might be found to be visually impaired or autistic or to have a motor impairment.

The level of symbolic play with play objects is affected in children who have sensory-impairment, mentally retardation and autism who show less ability to use complex object transformations in their play. Children with Down syndrome and autism tend to use more repetitive play with objects, as do infants and toddlers exposed prenatally to PCP and/or cocaine (Bergen, 1991; Hughes, 1998). Preterm infants might also present delay and limitations in play with objects that might be more related to a shorter period of development than can be explained by the difference between chronological age and gestational age. Chronological age is the child's actual age, whereas gestational age is related to prenatal development and how long the fetus has been in the womb (Hughes, 1998; Ruff, Lawson, Parinello, & Weissberg, 1990). Children who have attention deficit disorder (ADD) may have difficulty in focusing their play. They may begin several activities without completing any of them (Gitlin-Weiner, 1998).

At-risk children are particularly vulnerable to delays in social play. Interactive adult–child social play routines can be impaired in children with visual, motor, cognitive, or emotional impairments. Social interactions between mothers and children are influenced by the responsiveness of the other. Children born to teenage mothers can have delays in social play because the mothers may have fewer social support systems, are less knowledgeable about parenting, and are especially sensitive to babies who seem to be unresponsive (Fewell & Wheeden, 1998; Helm, Comfort, Bailey, & Simeonsson, 1990). Children who develop poor social interactions with adults may also experience delay and distortions in social play interactions with peers (Bergen, 1991).

**The Role of Adults**   Infants, toddlers, and preschool children who are found to be at risk for development or a disability are generally served through interventions to enhance development and minimize the risk or handicapping condition. Services might be provided directly to the child, indirectly through parents and other adult caregivers, or both. Thus both the adults who interact with the child and specialists who provide assistance in the intervention are engaged in improving conditions for the at-risk child (Gitlin-Weiner, 1998).

Play has a significant role in development for at-risk children. Providers of intervention services in settings outside the home include play in the curriculum for children at risk for delay as well as for children with diagnosed disabilities. Parents and other caregivers at home need to know how to use play and how to enhance the child's ability to play. Bergen (1991) expresses concern that play be used appropriately for intervention purposes. Although the adult plays a major role in helping children learn to play, a child's need to play and purposes for play should be the major focus of play activities. It is very easy for adults to use play activities within intervention services to advance their own agenda rather than the child's play agenda. Because of their concern for helping the child, play activities can become work activities. Bergen cautions that play for at-risk children should have the same purposes as for children who are not at risk and do not have a disability. In addition, it is possible that under conditions of environmental risk, the parent may not have the desire or ability to provide appropriate social play interactions. In any case, a distinction should be made between appropriate play interactions and activities that are directive rather than playful.

Children whose normal development is at risk need assistance in using appropriate play behaviors. Play activities provide opportunities for adults to help children compensate for their risk status. Children with biological risk factors, environmental risk factors, and health impairments may have common or unique needs for play activities. It is important for adults to observe children's play to determine the successes and needs of each child.

A primary cause of delayed play behavior is serious emotional and social impairments. Adults should guide these children in self-selected play activities during a period of free play. They might demonstrate appropriate social behavior or redirect the child to use a different social behavior. This might be particularly evident in children who have lived with environmental risk factors. Children who experienced environments that are insecure, unsafe, or without adequate nurture need adult support that will help them develop emotionally. Improvement in social and emotional development will be observed in subsequent play behaviors.

Children with health impairments might have limitations in play because they lack the strength to engage in vigorous physical activities. Adults can provide quieter play alternatives that permit the child to engage in play that is less physically demanding, such as sand and water play. These activities can be embedded within other activities so that children might find them to be an attractive play choice.

Children who have difficulty in persisting or following through with play choices need help focusing and in completing play activities. Whether children have ADD or simply too few opportunities to play, they can be encouraged by adults to select a play activity that is highly motivating and praised for engaging in the activity and finishing it. Children can also be teamed with other children who can provide leadership and direction in play.

## Children with Cognitive Delay and Mental Retardation

**Characteristics of Play**   Literature describing the play of children with cognitive delay is limited when compared to the information available for other types of disabilities. There are multiple causes for this lack of data. First, much of the research has been done with individual children and is limited to the study of their play with objects. Second, a lot of the research has been medical in nature. Study of play has been for diagnostic purposes and to determine skill levels rather than to understand the child's ability to play (Gleason, 1990). Third, research results have been inaccurate in that the researchers seemed to be unaware of the nature of early development that includes individual differences in rate of development in children without developmental delays. Even more significant was the assumption for many decades of the 20th century that children with cognitive delay are not interested in play or have to be taught to play (Bergen, 1991; Hughes, 1998). The error of this assumption was documented in the play of two institutionalized males with severe developmental disabilities who were able to initiate play with toy lawnmowers (Gleason, 1990). When comparing the recorded abilities of the males in clinical training with the motor and social skills used in the play

episode, it was found that the abilities in play were much more advanced than the abilities used in structured play therapy sessions.

It is not surprising, given the limitations in research just cited, that information gained from research on cognitive delay and play is unclear; nevertheless, the conclusion seems to be that when equated for mental age, children with retardation do not differ from children with normal development in some characteristics of play. Nor do they differ in their preferences for unstructured activities versus structured activities. They prefer child-centered or child-initiated activities to adult-directed activities (Hupp, Boat, & Alpert, 1992; Quinn & Rubin, 1984).

**The Role of Adults**   Adults can use play as an assessment tool to identify specific delays that need intervention, as a skill that can be taught to parents of infants who are at risk for delay, and as a strategy that can be used in intervention programs (Bergen, 1991). This is a new direction from earlier methods of intervention that were based on behaviorist theory that focused on shaping behavior using adult reinforcement strategies. The new direction of using play with at-risk children for parent intervention is derived from the literature on early social play routines of normally developing infants and toddlers. The value of social play between adults and infants or toddlers is also valuable for children with cognitive delay or mental retardation.

However, techniques used for children with cognitive delay are adapted to use a range of directive to playful strategies. In directed play, the teacher or adult guides the child in how to engage in a play activity. An adult uses a playful strategy when they engage in a play activity with the child and play along with them. These strategies are taught to parents and used by caregivers in intervention programs. Parents and adults involved in intervention are taught to be playful and responsive to their children.

Intervention specialists also use play in their individual intervention goals for young children, especially to increase symbolic play. Modeling by adults is used to demonstrate symbolic play roles, with more structured coaching used for children who are severely impaired.

A balance between free play and guided play should prevail in play intervention programs for toddlers and preschool children. Nevertheless, it is natural for adults to be more directive in play with children who have cognitive delays than they are with nondelayed peers. Integration of skills teaching into play routines can improve play and development. Free play can also facilitate development, especially when adapted toys and play environments ease social interaction between children.

Some people question whether a balance between guided play and free play can be achieved in intervention programs. When adult educators become focused on achieving the goals of intervention, do the activities cease to be play? If the child loses the opportunity for internal motivation and control and is not given the opportunity to decide what to play and who to play with, the play activity becomes "nonplay" (Bergen, 1991).

The challenge for adult providers of intervention for children with cognitive delay or mental retardation is to affirm the child's ability and interest in engaging in play. They need to remind themselves constantly that these children also have the right to free play, and adult-directed play is different from child-initiated play. The child with cognitive delay needs both, as do children with other types of disabilities. Directed play will have a natural place in the intervention process; however, free play will have to be deliberately worked into the daily schedule. After a directed play activity, the teacher might help the child select a toy to play with independently. Another strategy is to introduce a play activity in a center, and then leave the child in the center to continue playing as she wishes. Perhaps the best strategy is for the teacher to lead the child near classmates who are playing and offer the child the opportunity to do the same activity. For example, if

children in a group are playing at the sand table, the teacher can lead the child near the sand table, discuss what the children are doing, and offer the child a sand toy. Any attempts to play should be encouraged.

## Children with Language Delay and Communication Disorders

**Characteristics of Play**   The focus of research on the play of children with language delay or a communication disorder has been in two primary areas: symbolic play and social relationships with peers. The interest in symbolic play stems from the relationship between the development of speech and the development of symbolic functioning. The two types of development have a parallel course, with major advances emerging in the second year (Fenson, 1986). The question has been, if a child is delayed in language development, will she also experience symbolic play deficits? Although a number of researchers have found a relationship between language delay and symbolic play deficits, the correlation does not necessarily indicate that children with delayed speech will have deficits in symbolic play (Lombardino, Stein, Kricos, & Wolf, 1986; Tamis-LeMonda & Bornstein, 1991). In many studies, children with speech impairments did engage in make-believe play, but it occurred less often and was of a less mature level than the play of children whose speech was not delayed (Quinn & Rubin, 1984; Rubin et al., 1983). Moreover, children with good expressive language are at an advantage in verbal-symbolic play (Rescorla & Goossens, 1992).

In the case of symbolic play with objects, children with language impairments are capable of engaging in object substitutions and object transformations. Again, they exhibit this form of play less frequently than their peers with typical language development (Casby, 1997). This difference is more significant in older children. At younger ages, language delay is not as important because language plays a more limited role in symbolic play. The difference seems to emerge at about age 4 or 5, when language-impaired children use less complexity in their play activities (Lovell, Hoyle, & Siddall, 1968; Terrell & Schwartz, 1988).

Less research has been conducted on peer relations among children with communication disorders (Guralnick, Conner, Hammond, Gottman, & Kinnish, 1996). Because much variation occurs in language development in normally developing children, the differences in play for children with language disorders can be very similar to those for children with normal language development. Nevertheless, some characteristics indicate the presence of peer interaction problems. In group settings, children with communication disorders interact more with adults than with peers, are less likely to respond to peer initiations for play, and tend to be ignored more often by peers (Guralnick et al., 1996; Hadley & Rice, 1991).

The social setting can make a difference in peer relationships. The comparative ages of the children as well as whether children with language delays play in settings with peers with typical language development is thought to affect the level of symbolic play. However, studies comparing mainstreamed children with children in self-contained classrooms have found no difference in the level of play for children with language disorders (Guralnick et al., 1996).

Although children with language impairments may lag behind their peers in object play and sociodramatic play, they benefit from playing in integrated settings (Hughes, 1998). Children who have normal language development do experience obstacles in communication when playing with children who have difficulty expressing themselves; however, children without communication difficulties adjust their verbal interactions to the developmental characteristics of children with communication disorders (Shatz & Gelman, 1973). Children in classrooms with children who have language delay or a communication disorder can learn how to communicate and interact with these children.

**The Role of Adults** Adults who work with children with language delays and language disorders need to be skilled in providing language intervention within play. Adults can serve as facilitators of communication between children at play without directing the play activity. They can encourage the child with language delay to use verbalizations and model appropriate language. Modeling of language in sociodramatic play can also guide the child with language delay in how to engage in more sophisticated language.

The teacher can encourage children who have typical language development to ask a child with language delay to play with them. The children with typical language can be taught to be a play leader and share higher language levels with children who are language impaired. Even preschool children are able to be a leader in playgroups and to be intentional in including children with language and other impairments.

## Children with Autism

**Characteristics of Play** Some children with developmental delay or disabilities also experience delay in some characteristics of play. Children with autism have a pattern of development that is distorted (Quinn & Rubin, 1984). Play patterns of autistic children are also different from children with other types of delay and disabilities.

Autistic children do not generally engage in symbolic play. This seems to be true regardless of the intelligence of the child. Children with severe mental retardation do engage in symbolic play; highly intelligent autistic children do not (Hill & McCune-Nicolich, 1981; Hughes, 1998; Sigman & Sena, 1993). One explanation for the lack of make-believe in their play is that autistic children lack basic representational skills (Baron-Cohen, Leslie, & Frith, 1985). That is, autistic children are unable to assign one object to represent another or to represent to themselves symbolic mental states, for example, for dolls or for roles that they might themselves play (Hughes, 1998).

A teacher works with an autistic child.

Other researchers believe that autistic children do have the ability to represent or symbolize. They believe that the lack of symbolic play is related to lack of motivation. Lewis and Boucher (1988), who were able to elicit make-believe play in autistic children through adult instructions about toys, supported this position. However, the children did not display this type of activity in spontaneous play. It is also projected that poor social contact and a poor level of receptive language skills might also hinder symbolic play (Rutter, 1983; Wing, Gould, Yeates, & Brierly, 1977). Because such children lack peer interactions in play, their play can be rigid and unimaginative (Wolfberg & Schuler, 1993). Even when autistic children have opportunities to play with peers, unless they receive support, they are likely to remain in isolation outside nearby group play.

Autistic children tend to engage in repetitive and stereotyped manipulation in toy and object play. They are less likely to use toys appropriately or to engage in complex toy play (Tilton & Ottinger, 1964). Nevertheless, not all autistic children display stereotyped play behaviors; many play similarly to children with mental retardation and children with normal play behaviors (Quinn & Rubin, 1984).

**The Role of Adults**   Historically, autistic children have been taught play skills through behaviorist methods that include rewards for using appropriate play behaviors. This approach is problematic: The play is highly structured and adult led; moreover, the desired play behaviors do not generalize in unstructured play situations (Rubin et al., 1983; Stahmer & Schreibman, 1992; Wolfberg & Schuler, 1993). Alternatives to adult-directed intervention strategies are more child initiated and focus on planned environments and opportunities to play with peers in groups. In the Integrated Play Group Model approach (Wolfberg & Schuler, 1993), play opportunities have eight components:

- *Natural integrated settings.* Children engage in play with other children. Play partners are socially competent, and peer-mediated approaches are used to encourage social interaction.

- *Well-designed play spaces.* The spaces include consideration of spatial density and size, organization of materials, spatial arrangements, and accessibility.

- *Selection of play materials.* Play materials are selected for their influence on the play and social behavior of children with autism. The toys include constructive and sociodramatic toys that can be used by children with different abilities.

- *A consistent schedule and routine.* Children with autism respond to predictability and consistency. The play environment includes a consistent play group schedule and ongoing routines.

- *Balanced play groups.* Play groups include familiar peers who are limited in number. They meet to play consistently and include peers of different ages and developmental statuses.

• *Focus on child competence.*   Children with autism are evaluated for their individual competencies in play. Play support is provided to match the child's "zone of proximal development" (Vygotsky, 1978; see Chapter 2).

• *Guided participation.*   The adult's interactive role is to guide the children in participating in increasing social and sophisticated levels of play. Adult-imposed structure is avoided, and adult support is gradually decreased and removed to encourage the child to demonstrate increasing competence.

• *Full immersion in play.*   Children engage in the whole play experience rather than having play taught as discrete tasks. Children are encouraged to take roles in play with more advanced children. Adults use support and collaboration to encourage more sophisticated object and sociodramatic play.

Wolfberg and Schuler (1993) report dramatic gains in a study they conducted using the model. However, as in many research studies conducted with children with autism and other disabling conditions, only three children were included. Limited play research with children with autism indicates that the strategies used in the model are a promising alternative to structured teaching of play skills. However, much more research is needed to confirm success in enhancing play skills.

Visual cues have also been used with young children with autism spectrum disorders to aid play with other children. Like the Wolfberg and Schuler report, a small group of three or four was used to include one child with autism. Children with autism who tended to keep to themselves were paired with one other child. Cues using pictures and written phrases were introduced to the children and tutored before play sessions. Play sessions were scheduled for a minimum of 15 minutes. The teacher at first monitored the play session and then moved away as the children become adept at using the cues (Ganz & Flores, 2010).

## Abused and Neglected Children

**Characteristics of Play**   There are some indicators that abused and neglected children play differently from their peers who have not experienced abuse. In addition, the type of abuse can affect play behaviors differently.

A study comparing abused children with a control group (Alessandri, 1994) found the following differences (Hughes, 1998):

> Abused children played in less mature ways, both socially and cognitively, than did the children in the control group, engaged in less play overall, involved themselves less often in group and parallel play, and used the play materials in less imaginative and more stereotyped ways. Their fantasy themes were more imitative and less creative. They repeatedly played out domestic scenes, for example, whereas the control group also played the roles of fantasy characters, such as monsters or superheroes. (p. 182)

**Sexually Abused Children**   The type of abuse affects the play behaviors of young children. Sexually abused children had an absence of fantasy play, suggesting a need to occupy the present. Play themes were essentially domestic, as Alessandri (1994) reported, as were repetition of play themes (Harper, 1991). Sexually abused children have been found to be more passive than children who have not been abused, but they are not necessarily antisocial or negative. They usually play quietly by themselves (Fagot, Hagan, Youngblade, & Potter, 1989). Some researchers have found sexually abused children to be more focused on the sexual features of anatomically correct dolls than children who have not been sexually abused (August & Forman, 1989; Jampole & Weber, 1987). However, Cohn (1991) found that children who have not experienced abuse are equally likely to engage in sexual types of play with dolls.

**Physically Abused Children**   Play themes of physically abused children were more action oriented, including fights, wars, and sudden disasters. Physically abused children tend to be disruptive and uncommunicative. Unlike sexually abused children, they are antisocial (Fagot et al., 1989). Harper (1991) characterized their play as fantasy, aggressive, and chaotic. There was more variety in their play themes in Harper's study, and one child continually played themes that ended in loss.

One must use caution in generalizing the behaviors, found in two studies, to describe abused children in general. Very little research has dealt with the play of abused children, and the samples in the studies cited was very small; nevertheless, they provide some indicators of how the play of abused children can reflect negative experiences in their lives.

**The Role of Adults**   The abused children discussed in the previous section were included in studies comparing the play of children who have been abused with children who have not been abused. Teachers in preschool and school-age settings will encounter both types of children. The play behaviors of abused children may not appear to be all that different from play behaviors of other children. Aggressive and antisocial play can have many causes. Repetitive theme play and passive play can characterize children other than children who have been sexually abused. Regardless, the teacher's role is to guide children in ways to play appropriately and expanding sociodramatic play to include many types of themes. All children who use aggression in play need to have alternatives introduced or avenues to express frustration and anger. However, the teacher would do well to be aware of the differences in play behaviors and be alert to the possibility that the child has been experiencing abuse.

## ▱ THE ROLE OF THE ENVIRONMENT

Thus far, research on the play of children with disabilities have focused on how their play compares with the play of children without

disabilities. Although many studies cited in earlier sections were conducted in laboratory classrooms where children were selected and grouped for the length of the study, many other studies were conducted with children in existing classrooms. The classrooms exemplified inclusion or integration, in keeping with the practice of placing children with disabilities in classrooms with children who have typical development.

In this section, we move from comparing children with disabilities with peers to looking at how effective inclusive classrooms have been in socially integrating children with disabilities with their peers. Because social interaction occurs primarily through play, it is interesting to take a look at how children with disabilities benefit from engaging in play in integrated settings. Part of the effectiveness of play in these settings depends on teacher behaviors and how teachers affect children's play. We also discuss available research on teacher interactions with children's play.

## Influences of Inclusion Classrooms on Children's Play

A major goal of intervention programs is to help children with disabilities develop social competence. A concern about inclusion has been whether children with disabilities are socially integrated with peers who do not have disabilities, or whether they are merely integrated in a physical sense (Guralnick, 1990). Therefore, studying peer play in integrated settings is one way to determine whether children with disabilities are benefiting from the chance to interact socially with peers of normal development. Social interaction can be a way for children with disabilities to overcome language delay and to acquire developmental skills. Social play is also perceived to benefit children who tend to stick to less complex forms of play as a result of a disability (Kontos, Moore, & Giorgetti, 1998).

Study of children's play in integrated programs shows that children with disabilities are not isolated; however, they are not as involved or accepted as children who are developing typically. Children with disabilities initiate and receive opportunities for social play less often and have fewer reciprocal friendships. They are less involved in higher levels of social play (associative, cooperative) than their peers with typical development, and they generally lag behind them in social development (File, 1994; Guralnick & Groom, 1987, 1988; Guralnick & Weinhouse, 1984; Kontos et al., 1998).

Nonetheless, children with typical development showed positive attitudes toward children with disabilities (Hess & Sexton, 2002). In programs where children were placed in play groups, social skills groups, and cooperative learning groups, children with normal development expressed personal interest in, and a desire to be friends with, children with disabilities (Kamps, Lopez, Kemmerer, Potucek, & Harrell, 1998). Peer-mediated activities in inclusion classrooms were found to increase peer interactions, and children with disabilities benefited both academically and socially. Nevertheless, a 2-year study of students served in an inclusion setting found that the sociometric status of students with disabilities was lower than that of typically developing peers. Students with disabilities received fewer nominations for "most liked" and more nominations for "least liked" than peers with typical development (Sale & Carey, 1995). In another study, first graders reported in interviews that children with disabilities did not really belong to the group (Schnorr, 1990).

Children with disabilities can benefit from inclusion in mixed-age classrooms. Children with disabilities placed in a classroom with children of different ages achieved sophistication in play with toys that was not achieved in a classroom with peers of the same age. The researchers proposed that the children with disabilities were influenced by the sophistication of play demonstrated by the older children who were developing normally in the play setting. Nevertheless, social mastery did not improve for children with disabilities. As in other studies, children without disabilities were more likely to engage in social mastery than children with disabilities (Blasco, Bailey, & Burchinal, 1993).

The teacher plays an important role in inclusion classrooms. The teacher's attitude toward inclusion can have an effect on successful social relationships. Teachers with a positive attitude toward inclusion have a positive effect on paraprofessional time, direct time with children with disabilities, and the social competence of children with disabilities (Janney, Snell, Beers, & Raynes, 1995; Kamps et al., 1998; Wolery, Werts, Caldwell, Snyder, & Lisowski, 1995).

Studies of teacher's interactions in inclusive classrooms indicate that teachers interact in a more directive manner with children with disabilities than with children who develop typically (Brophy & Hancock, 1985; Stipek & Sanborn, 1985). However, File (in contrast, 1994) observed that interactional frequencies between the two groups of children and their teachers were very similar.

Teacher training can be a factor, as can specific teaching behaviors that support play. Teachers with more training in early childhood education are more involved in supporting cognitive and social play (Arnett, 1989; File & Kontos, 1993; Whitebrook, Howes, & Phillips, 1990). However, teachers were found to be more likely to encourage cognitive skills rather than social skills (Clarke-Stewart, 1987).

Other factors can affect how successfully inclusion can benefit children with disabilities. The number of children in the classroom can make all the difference. Teachers with fewer children tend to be more involved in the social and cognitive play of children with disabilities (File & Kontos, 1993; Sontag, 1997). The number of children in the play group can also be a factor (Belsky, 1984, 1990; Kontos & Fiene, 1987).

## Adapted Play Environments

Designing play environments that include children with disabilities is a challenge for playground developers. Each disability presents unique considerations, and environments that serve large numbers of children must include modifications for all types of disabilities (Doctoroff, 2001). Children with hydrocephalus need protective headgear, and those with spina bifida need special mobile equipment and consideration for urine bags used for incontinence. Blind or partially sighted children need time to explore the environment to become familiar with its features. The environment needs to be predictable so they can play with confidence. Children with cerebral palsy are best served when they can have the playground to themselves to prevent abnormal reflex patterns of movement. They might also need physical assistance until they can relax and enjoy both the environment and the play actions of their playmates with normal physical development (London Handicapped Adventure Playground Association, 1978, as cited in Frost, 1992).

In the United States, there has been an interest for several decades in developing play environments that can serve children with disabilities. In 1976, the New York City Department of Planning and U.S. Department of Housing and Urban Development conducted a design competition to encourage play environments that would include children with disabilities. Suggestions were given for meeting that goal (Frost, 1992). In 1986, Play and Learning in Adaptable Environments (PLAE) conducted a series of sessions at Stanford University to develop guidelines for playgrounds that would address the needs of children with disabilities. The work of this group culminated in the publication of *Play for All Guidelines: Planning Design and Management of Outdoor Play Settings for All Children* (Moore, Goltsman, & Iacofano, 1987). This document was the first comprehensive guide to the development of outdoor play environments that would serve all children, including those with disabilities (Frost, 1992).

In 1990, developing play environments that include children with disabilities gained further momentum with the passage of ADA, which aims to "ensure that people with disabilities

have access to employment, public accommodations, commercial facilities, government services, transportation, and telecommunications" (Lindemann, 1992, p. 48). Covered in this law are institutions serving children, including play environments. The Architectural and Transportation Barriers Compliance Board (Access Board) was made responsible for developing accessibility guidelines relevant to ADA, to include the construction of new facilities (Recreation Access Advisory Committee, 1994). The ADA Accessibility Guidelines were revised in 2000 (Architectural and Transportation Barriers Compliance Board, 2000).

The Play Settings Subcommittee of the Access Board developed preliminary accessibility guidelines for play areas that the committee defined as:

> a designated play and learning environment with a range of settings carefully layered on the site. A play area may be inside or outside and contains one or more of the following elements: entrances, pathways, fences and enclosures, signage, play equipment, game areas, landforms and topography, trees and vegetation, gardens, animal habitats, water play, sand play, loose parts, gathering places, stage areas, storage, and ground covering and surfacing. (Recreation Access Advisory Committee, 1994, p. 89)

Subsequently, in 1997, the Regulatory Negotiation Committee on Accessibility Guidelines for Play Facilities, also a subgroup of the Architectural and Transportation Barriers Compliance Board, issued a final report about play environments that include children with disabilities. The guidelines suggest accessibility standards for play facilities addressed by ADA, Titles II and III (Americans with Disabilities Act Accessibility Guidelines [ADAAG], 1991). They are consistent with the ASTM Public Playground Equipment Standard F 1487-95, issued in 1995 and revised in 1998 (American Society for Testing of Materials, 1998). The most recent revision of Standard F 1487 was in 2007 (American Society for Testing of Materials, 2007). The expectation is that children with disabilities will play in the same environment as children without disabilities and that modifications will permit all children to enjoy playing together.

The Regulatory Negotiation Committee on Accessibility Guidelines for Play Facilities; see Architectural and Transportation Barriers (Compliance Board, 1997, p. 3):

- Be based on children's anthropometric (human physical) dimensions and other resource information.

- Be based on children with disabilities using a variety of assistive devices.

- Provide opportunity for use by children who have a variety of abilities.

- Support social interaction and encourage integration.

- Create challenge, not barriers.

- Provide advisory information to assist designers, operators, and owners, to effectively incorporate access into their designs. Information should be in an understandable format.

- Maintain safety consistent with ASTM requirements.

- Be reasonable in terms of cost relative to benefit.

- Address access for parents and caregivers.

- Provide access to elevated structures. Additional ground-level accessible play

components may be required, depending on the type of vertical access provided to elevated structures.

The guidelines focus on accessing various components of the play environment, specifically, ground-level and elevated play components, as well as how to access them.

**Ground-Level Play Components** Ground-level play components are the different types of play components that can be entered and exited at ground level (e.g., swings, climbers, spring rockers, natural features). Children with disabilities should have a choice of at least one of each of the different types of play components. In addition, the number of ground-level components should be one-third of the number of elevated play components. Ground-level components should offer different types of play experiences.

**Elevated Play Components** Elevated play components are part of a composite play structure and are entered above or below grade. Slides, climbers, and activity panels that are part of a composite play structure are categorized as elevated play components. At least 50% of all elevated play components should be accessible to children with disabilities. This guideline allows all children to play together. Although children with disabilities would not be able to access all components of a composite

---

**NATIONAL CENTER FOR BOUNDLESS PLAYGROUNDS**

Jean Schappet and Amy Jaffe Barzack designed a playground for children of all abilities in Bloomfield, Connecticut, to comply with ASTM standards for play equipment and playgrounds. Jean Schappet has worked with ASTM standards since 1985. Schappet said, "Children who have either sensory disabilities or sensory-integration issues, or children who are cognitively delayed need huge amounts of sensory input." The developers worked to provide similar play experiences focused on removing sociological and architectural barriers that keep some children from playing outdoors. The new playground is characterized as a universal playground.

Source: C. Coppa. (2003, March). A Playground for All Abilities. ASTM People Page. Retrieved September 20, from *http://www.astm.org/SNEWS/MARCH_2003/people_mar03.html*

play structure, they would be able to play on at least half of the play components. In the 2000 revision of the guidelines, it was recommended that ramps rather than transfer systems be used for elevated play components because it is the preferred means of access for many children with disabilities. However, the guidelines recognized that some children with some disabilities can use transfer systems.

**Accessible Routes**   Children who use a wheel-chair, crutches, or other assistive equipment for mobility have special needs when accessing the playground, as well as the play components within the play area (Doctoroff, 2001). The guidelines requires constructing pathways from a material that is suitable for wheelchairs and other mobility aids. Guidelines recommend that at least one **accessible route** be provided within the boundary of the playground. In addition, "the accessible route is required to connect accessible play components, including entry and exit points" (Regulatory Negotiation Committee on Accessibility Guidelines for Play Facilities; see Architectural and Transportation Barriers Compliance Board, 1997, p. 6). Entry and exit points can be at ground level or elevated. When accessibility is provided for elevated play components, ramps and transfer systems provide accessibility. Expectations for accessible routes for small composite play structures (fewer than 20 play components) are lower than expectations for larger structures (20 or more play components).

**Ramps, Decks, and Stationary Bridges**
Children with physical disabilities are given access to elevated play components by way of ramps, decks, and stationary bridges. Landings where wheelchairs can be parked are also needed so children can leave their wheelchairs to play. ADAAG recommends ramp widths of 60 inches or greater. Minimum criteria are as follows:

a.  Minimum width of 36".

b.  Cross slope not to exceed 1:50.

c.  Running slope not to exceed 1:12.

d.  Ramp run or length not to exceed 12'.

e.  Landings at bottom and top of ramp run shall be a minimum of 60" in diameter (Recreation Access Advisory Committee, 1994, p. 93)

Additional guidelines specify recommendations for handrails and transfer points where children can transfer themselves onto play equipment or be assisted by an adult to make the transfer. Figure 10.2 shows specifications for ramps, landings, and parking spaces. Figure 10.3 provides information on turning spaces for wheelchairs.

Children with disabilities also need to be provided access to sand and water play areas and other play opportunities. Although elevated sand, water play, and gardening components may be provided through elevated equipment that can accommodate a wheelchair space underneath, ground-level components are preferable, with transfer points providing access. In the 2000 ADA guidelines, play tables with wheelchair access were preferred to tables without it.

Children with disabilities need the same types of play experiences as children without disabilities. The ADA guidelines (ADAAG Standards) and ASTM Safety Performance Specifications suggest how playgrounds can be adapted to include both safety and appropriate play features. Inclusive schools, child-care centers, and other settings need to follow the example of the PLAE organization and involve adults and children with disabilities as well as parents, playground specialists, and representatives of local and state organizations and agencies when preparing designs. Planners are urged to consult the following resources before beginning the planning process:

*Regulatory Negotiation Committee on Accessibility Guidelines for Play Facilities: Final Report*

U.S. Architectural and Transportation Barriers Compliance Board

1331 F Street, NW, Suite 1000

Washington, DC 20004-1111

**FIGURE 10.2** Playscape Wheelchair Ramp

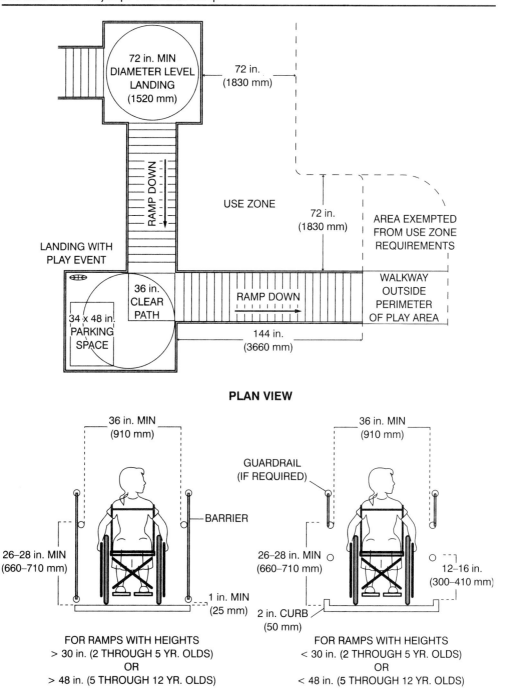

Source: From *Standard Consumer Safety Performance Specifications for Playground Equipment for Public Use* (p. 47) by American Society for Testing and Materials (ASTM), 1998, West Conshohocken, PA: ASTM. Reprinted by permission.

**FIGURE 10.3**   Platform Wheelchair Transfer Point

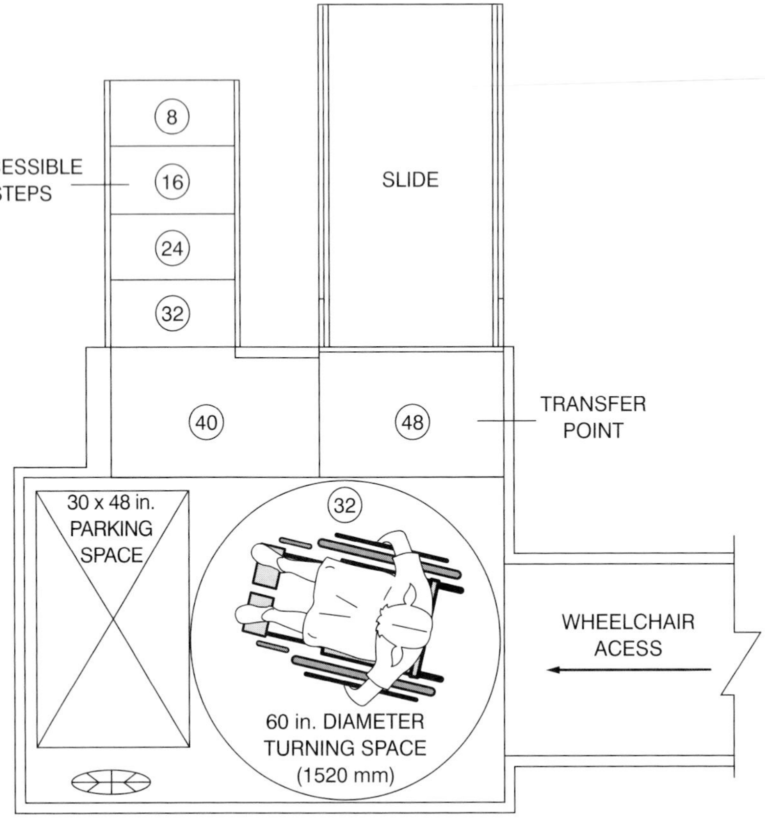

Note 1—Turning space and parking space may not overlap.
Note 2—⊗ denotes the height of the designated play surface in inches.

*Source:* From *Standard Consumer Safety Performance Specifications for Playground Equipment for Public Use* (p. 49) by American Society for Testing and Materials (ASTM), 1998, West Conshohocken, PA: ASTM. Reprinted by permission.

*Standard Consumer Safety Performance Specification for Playground Equipment for Public Use*

www.access.board.gov/play/assess/pdf

American Society for Testing of Materials

100 Barr Harbor Drive

West Conshohocken, PA 19428

www.astm.org

*Recommendations for Accessibility Guidelines: Recreational Facilities and Outdoor Developed Areas*

Recreation Access Advisory Committee

U.S. Architectural and Transportation Barriers Compliance Board

1331 F Street, NW, Suite 1000

Washington, DC 20004-1111

www.access-board.gov/play

## MORGAN'S WONDERLAND

Morgan's Wonderland is a large, nonprofit play park for children with disabilities in San Antonio, Texas.

The park is designed into many large areas such as the Sensory Village; The Wharf, with a pirate ship; and Water Works. A traditional carousel with several types of adaptations includes places for wheelchairs. A large area holds swings of various sizes and adaptations. On our visits a child in a wheelchair was swinging on a swing with a special platform for the chair. There is a miniature train ride and several different play structures of various sizes and play choices. The multitude of play and learning experiences throughout the park attract siblings of children with disabilities, and the adults accompanying children with severe disabilities also enjoy participating. Children with disabilities and their parent or adult companion are admitted to the park free of charge.

The day that we visited the park, the Water Works section was the most popular area. The area is wheelchair accessible, and levers required for some of the activities are also at wheelchair level. The entire park has beautiful landscaping, a large picnic area, and offers a guide to the other park areas.

 ## THE ROLE OF TECHNOLOGY

### Assistive Technology

Technological advances in recent years have enhanced possibilities for children with disabilities to be able to communicate, participate, and play with their peers. The Individuals with Disabilities Education Act Amendments of 1991 (IDEA) require school districts to provide assistive technology services to children who need them. These assistive services can be as simple as a drinking straw or as complex as adaptations to computers so they can be used for both communication and learning. Assistive devices are provided after evaluating the technological needs of individual children and selecting the most appropriate devices that can be acquired or devised.

Assistive technology, then, can involve low or high technology and can be described using 10 categories (Parette & Murdick, 1998):

1. Mobility (e.g., wheelchairs and scooters);
2. Electronic communication (i.e., devices which produce artificial or real life speech for talking with others);
3. Visual (e.g., magnification devices for reading tasks);
4. Assistive listening (e.g., hearing aids);
5. Environmental access (e.g., infrared control unit for manipulating a TV or stereo);
6. Computers (e.g., game software enabling cooperative play with others);
7. Leisure/recreation (e.g., handheld electronic toys used for independent play);

Children with disabilities need the same types of experiences as children without disabilities.

8. Independent living (e.g., buttoning or reaching devices for children with physical disabilities);

9. Positioning (e.g., vinyl-covered rolls and bolsters used to maintain proper body alignment);

10. Adaptive toys (e.g., battery-powered toys which are switch-controlled by the child). (p. 194)

Although some of the devices listed affect the play of children with disabilities indirectly, many of them have a direct impact on the child's ability to play. The term *technology* generally brings computers to mind, but actually, assistive technology includes a broad range of simple to complex devices (Parette & Murdick, 1998; Raver, 2009). Figure 10.4 shows examples of such devices.

## Adapted Toys

Assistive technology can be used to adapt toys for children with disabilities. Specially designed switches, control units, battery device adapters, and mounting systems can be used with available toys to make them interesting

**FIGURE 10.4** Low and High Assistive Technology Devices

**Low Technology**

Velcro closures
Suction cups
Adaptive eating utensils
Simple adaptive switches
Picture communication boards
Talking clocks and calculators
Adapted books

**High Technology**

Computerized communication devices
Powered mobility devices
Speech synthesizers
Advanced switches such as universal remote
  controls to open doors and turn on lights
Braille reader

and accessible. Battery-powered toys can be adapted for external switch control so the child can control the on-and-off operation of the toy. Switch control adaptations can be used for battery-powered kitchen appliances, action toys such as train sets, and cassette players (Locke & Levin, 1998).

Games can also be adapted with a control switch. The action of rolling dice can be simulated using a switch and special overlay. The child with disabilities can then actively participate in such games as Chutes and Ladders, Monopoly, and Clue (Locke & Levin, 1998).

The St. Agnes Hospital Children's Rehabilitation Center in White Plains, New York, uses adapted toys for children being treated for spina bifida, cerebral palsy, and other physical disabilities. Engineers, technicians, and occupational therapists study available toys to determine how they can be adapted for children who have impairments. They use a variety of types of switches and sip-and-puff devices to activate toys (Anonymous, 1997).

Stone and Sagstetter (1998) have specific suggestions for how adapted toys can be used for play. Children with disabilities can engage in bubble play using a battery-operated bubble maker with a battery device adapter and switch attached. Likewise, children can blow streamers or a mobile by using an adapted battery-operated fan.

## Interactive Video

Research has been conducted on whether interactive video can benefit children with special education needs. Interactive video combines interactive video machines with computers as an adapted learning tool. Blisset and Adkins (1993) found that interactive video benefits low-ability learners. In addition, reality-based interactive games can be used to change a child's learning environment. Using interactive video machines with keyboards and a mouse as input devices for math problems, Chambers (1997) found that interactive video could help raise self-esteem, provide equal opportunities for learning, and foster collaborative learning. Reduction of anxiety, language development, and a sense of ownership that result from using interactive video can translate into better play .

## Computer Technology

Like interactive video, computer skills permit children with disabilities to engage in socialization that may not be available to them in other classroom and play activities. Researchers in this area described computer learning games as play. Students also engaged in free-play activities. Usually, children were paired with another student without disabilities. In a study of preschool children's problem-solving activities using computers, Muller and Perlmutter (1985) found that they engaged in more social interaction than when working on a jigsaw puzzle. Toddlers and preschoolers with disabilities exhibited more positive interactive social behaviors when engaged in computer-based activities (Howard, Greyrose, Kehr, Espinosa, & Beckwith, 1996). Children without disabilities who had developed friendships with children with disabilities increased interactions with their friends when engaged in computer activities. Moreover, children with disabilities used turn-taking skills and increased socialization when engaged in free-play activities on the computer (Goodman, 1981; Zippiroli, Bayer, & Mistrett, 1988).

Children with disabilities typically need assistive technology in order to participate in computer activities. A touch screen, attached to the front of the computer monitor, can be activated by the touch of a finger. Expanded keyboards and trackballs also permit access for children with limited physical abilities (Dell & Newton, 1998). Students with sight limitations and other disabilities might need to use software that reads what is entered from a keyboard and vocalizes it back to the writer (Beigel, 1996).

Adaptive communication refers to the application of computer technology to permit children who are unable to speak or write to communicate with others. A portable computer equipped with speech output can be used by a nonspeaking child to talk with others. These children can type or press on the screen to express themselves. Likewise, children who cannot use their hands can use computers for writing or drawing. Both strategies enhance interactions with teachers and peers and facilitate social and language development. Blind children can use large print or Braille key labels for writing purposes (Burgstahler, 1998).

## Accessible Electronic and Information Technology

All types of people can use accessible electronic and information technology. It is either directly accessible or can be used with standard assistive technology. It incorporates universal design, meaning that users are able to use it according to how it works best for them. The National Center on Accessible Information Technology in Education (University of Washington, 2010) provides information on accessible software applications, multimedia products, and websites.

**Accessible software applications**  This type of application gives the user more than one way of completing a task. The user can use the mouse alone, the keyboard alone, or a combination of both. Established standards are followed for menus and prompts that can be accessed by assistive technology. Installation instructions, user guides, and documentation are available in large print, Braille, and electronic text formats.

**Accessible multimedia products**  Accessible multimedia products include synchronized text captions for spoken information and synchronized audio descriptions for visual content. They may be distributed on videotapes, CDs, DVDs, or the World Wide Web. They offer more than one way to input commands and respond to prompts. Captioning and alternative ways of navigating provide possibilities for students to use the technology independently.

**Accessible websites**   Accessible websites are designed so that all users can navigate the site. They provide a description for all nontext elements, such as audio, video, graphical buttons and image maps. Those who cannot see can access information with a screen reader that can read a description of a picture.

 ## CREATIVITY AND PLAY

Assistive technology makes it possible for children with some types of disabilities to engage in creative activities, as we discussed in the previous section. Other types of adaptations make it possible for children with disabilities to enjoy creative play. If children have the ability to hold crayons and other art materials, they can engage in creative art activities. Children with mental retardation can participate at their own developmental level. Those with hearing impairments can also participate in expressive arts activities.

However, children with severe hearing disabilities find it difficult to enjoy music. They can be taught to feel the beat of music through vibrations in the floor. They might need to learn to sign or be able to lip-read to enjoy books. They can engage in dramatic play when guided and assisted by adults and peers who give them cues and model the play theme.

Children with visual impairments can enjoy finger painting and other art activities that permit them to use the sense of touch to express themselves. They enjoy hearing stories, especially if sensory materials are used to help them experience story content. They readily engage in sociodramatic play when the environment is arranged so they can find their way around in the dramatic play center.

With careful planning, children with disabilities can be encouraged to engage in creative activities. Many of the materials are the same, but adults must determine what kinds of adaptations need to be made so individual children can participate.

 ## PLAY-BASED ASSESSMENT

Much attention was given in earlier sections to the differences between the play of children with disabilities and their peers without disabilities. Each disability can be unique in the way it affects play. Although understanding play variations resulting from disabling conditions can be helpful in intervention, the appearance of, or a delay in, play behaviors can also be used to assess children. Information in this section focuses on the use of play to assess children for possible delays and disabilities and to plan intervention programs when needed. We discuss the background of how play assessment came to be, followed by why and how it is applied with young children with disabilities. We also discuss research on the usefulness of play-based assessment.

Observing children's play in order to assess them is not new. Teachers and caregivers have observed play to measure young children's developmental progress for many decades. In addition, the use of play as an intervention strategy was promoted in the 1960s and 1970s to prevent developmental delay for children who were at environmental risk. Nevertheless, the use of play-based assessment for children with disabilities has gained in popularity only recently. Identification of children with delays or disabilities traditionally has been conducted mainly through standardized assessments. Instruments such as the Bayley Scales of Infant Development (Bayley, 1993) and Stanford-Binet Intelligence Scale (Thorndike, Hagen, & Sattler, 1986) have been commonly used to assess young children.

### Why Play-Based Assessment Is Used

A growing concern about the limitations of standardized tests has led psychologists and special educators to look for alternative methods that will be more effective (Linder, 1990, 1994, 2008). Limitations of standardized tests include the examiner's inability to modify items, resulting in assessments that are biased against young children with some disabilities, particularly children with language deficits (Bailey, 1989; Brooks-Gunn & Lewis, 1981). Other limitations to standardized tests are that they provide no information about learning styles, problem-solving strategies, or contextual skills at school and home (Bailey, 1989). Finally, tests assess developmental skills as separate domains, whereas children use the skills in combination in their environment (Fewell & Rich, 1987).

Assessment of play activities, then, provides information about domains of development that are correlated with other domains—specifically, cognitive, social, and language development (Belsky & Most, 1981; Fenson, 1986; Linder, 1994, 2008). Play assessment is nonthreatening, and it can be done unobtrusively (Fewell & Kaminski, 1988). Observing children's play can also reveal how children initiate and carry out play schemes, as well as what a child can do with play materials (Fewell & Rich, 1987). Raver (2009) has listed some benefits of play-based assessments:

1. Play-based assessments offer a typical sample of a child's behavior.

2. Play-based assessments provide an example of a child's interaction with an adult and materials, and occasionally with another child.

3. Play-based assessments may produce a more comprehensive sample of behavior for children who are noncompliant or slow to establish rapport (p. 55).

## How Play-Based Assessments Are Conducted

People disagree about how play-based assessments should be conducted. Three approaches to play observations are being used currently: nonstructured assessments, structured assessments, and transdisciplinary assessments.

Nonstructured assessments attempt to identify all behaviors that occur during a play session, whereas structured assessments focus on a previously designed set of play behaviors. In structured play observations, procedures are established, as are the toys to be used and tech-

niques employed by adults to initiate the play activities. Spontaneous play is observed in nonstructured play assessments, and play may be initiated by either the child or the caregiver (Segal & Webber, 1996).

Transdisciplinary play-based assessment includes a team of evaluators who concurrently observe the child at play. Each member of the team observes a different domain of development or for a different purpose. These play observations are generally structured, and they may include planned adult interactions (Bergen, 1991; Linder, 1998, 2008).

The transdisciplinary team observes how the interplay of domains in child development as well as individual differences in development characteristics are revealed in play opportunities. The makeup of the team, which includes parents, is based on the nature of the assessment, the needs of the child, and the purposes of the intervention plan. Structured observations include the presentation of selected tasks and play materials to elicit higher skills than are present in free-play activities (Linder, 1994).

## Research and Play-Based Assessment

Because observing play for assessment is relatively new, research evidence is scarce about its validity for screening children with developmental delay and making diagnoses for intervention programs (Eisert & Lamorey, 1996; Myers, McBride, & Peterson, 1996). Studies have been conducted to measure play-based assessment as compared to assessment using standardized tests. Myers et al. (1996) used transdisciplinary assessment to determine whether this type of play observation can supply useful information for intervention. Researchers also sought information on the efficiency of the method and to find out whether professionals and parents are satisfied with play-based assessment results.

Play-based assessment has been used to determine play differences between children with ADHD and children with both mental retardation and ADHD. Structured play observations were conducted to define the quality of play, the amount of time the two groups were able to play, the appropriateness of conduct during play, and impulsivity. Although the results of behaviors used by the two groups were inconclusive, these types of play observations might help in discriminating between children with mental retardation who have or do not have ADHD (Handen, McAuliffe, Janosky, Feldman, & Breaux, 1998).

## SUMMARY

Children can experience a variety and/or combination of disabilities that can affect their ability to play. Disabilities can be physical, intellectual, or emotional, and they can range in severity from mild to profound; nevertheless, all of these children have some capacity to engage in play. Their play abilities are different from, and of a lower sophistication than, those of their peers without disabilities. But with adaptations provided by adults and interventions to help them experience a broader range of play activities, these children can benefit from opportunities to play.

It is difficult to categorize the play needs of children with disabilities because the nature of the disability and the children's abilities are unique to each individual child. Children with multiple disabilities present more challenges because the interaction of disabilities impacts different developmental domains in play.

Adults play an important role in facilitating play for children with disabilities. They need to be aware of the challenges faced by each child with a disability and need to know how to adapt the environment and encourage the child to explore possibilities for play. In addition, they must ensure that the child has chances to self-initiate play, even though adult modeling and guidance may be needed before the child is able to play independently or with peers. Children without disabilities can become helpful play partners when they are knowledgeable about the nature of their friends' disabilities and how to interact with them. With the advent of inclusion or integrated classrooms, children are more likely to share a classroom with one or more children with disabilities and accept them as play partners. However, they, too, might need adult guidance on how to include a child with disabilities in their play activities.

The environment is key to play accessibility for children with disabilities. The indoor environment needs to be modified to accommodate children with different disabilities. Especially important are modifications of space and accessible location of materials for children using wheelchairs and other mobility aids.

More extensive adaptations must be made in outdoor environments. In the last two decades, much progress has been made in in adapting the outdoor environment to provide access to play components and maintain safety at the same time. Although there are no standards with the force of law, guidance on designing playscapes have been provided by the U.S. Architectural and Transportation Barriers Compliance Board and American Society for Testing and Materials.

Assistive technology has made it possible for children with disabilities to engage in more types of play. Through the use of different levels of technology, ranging from wheelchairs to infrared control units, children with disabilities are able to access physical environments and technological devices such as computers and interactive videos. Toys can be adapted through switches and adaptations so children can activate them when their manual dexterity is severely limited, thus enabling them to participate with their peers with typical development.

In recent decades, professionals who diagnose and plan intervention programs have been using play-based assessment to determine the abilities and needs of children with disabilities. The common method of assessment has been the administration of standardized tests; however, these instruments have limitations when applied to individual children with varying types of disabilities. Moreover, play-based assessment provides a more integrated perspective of developmental domains rather than the assessment of skills in isolation. Because children can display more advanced skill development in play activities than in clinical testing play-based assessment is being researched for its usefulness in diagnosis and intervention.

Play is important for all children. In the past, the perception has been that children with disabilities, especially children with cognitive delay, are not interested in play. Although play research on children with disabilities is lacking in some areas, much has been learned about how children with disabilities play and how their play possibilities can be expanded. As more is learned and newer advances are made in all types of play environments, more opportunities will be possible for children with disabilities to participate in childhood play.

## KEY TERMS

Abused children
Accessible route
Asperger's syndrome
Attention deficit
　hyperactivity
　disorder (ADHD)
Autism
Autism spectrum
　disorder
Behavioral disorders
Biological risk factors
Cerebral palsy
Cognitive delay
Elevated play
　components

Emotional disorders
Environmental risk
Ground-level play
　components
Hearing impairments
Hydrocephalus
Language delay
Motor impairments
Muscular dystrophy
Pervasive
　developmental
　disorder
Positioning equipment
Spina bifida
Visual impairments

## STUDY QUESTIONS

1. Why is it important to understand an individual child's disability or disabilities when planning for play?
2. Explain how play might be affected in children with visual impairments, motor impairments, and emotional disorders.
3. Children can be at risk for developmental delay because of biological or environmental factors. Explain how these life factors can affect children.
4. What are some causes of behavioral disorders?
5. Compare the play behaviors of children who have been sexually abused with children who have been physically abused.
6. Why is language an important component of play with peers? How does language delay affect social play?
7. Why do autistic children fail to engage in symbolic play? Explain.
8. How do inclusion classrooms generally benefit play behaviors in children with disabilities? Give examples.
9. Define ground-level components, elevated play components, and accessible routes in outdoor playscapes. How do these components provide access for children with disabilities?
10. Why are ramps, decks, and stationary bridges important for children who use wheelchairs?
11. What are transfer points? Where are they needed on adapted playgrounds?
12. Define assistive technology and describe some examples.

13. How do adapted computers encourage play between peers with disabilities and those without disabilities?
14. Is play-based assessment beneficial helpful for diagnosis and plans for intervention? Describe some advantages of using play-based assessment.

## REFERENCES

Alessandri, S. M. (1994). Play and social behavior in maltreated preschoolers. *Development and Psychopathology, 3,* 191–205.

American Society for Testing of Materials. (1996a). *Standard consumer safety specification on toy safety.* West Conshohocken, PA: American Society for Testing of Materials.

American Society for Testing of Materials. (1996b). *Standard specification for impact attenuation of surface systems under and around playground equipment.* West Conshohocken, PA: American Society for Testing of Materials.

American Society for Testing of Materials. (1998). *Standard consumer safety performance specifications for playground equipment for public use.* West Conshohocken, PA: American Society for Testing of Materials.

American Society for Testing of Materials. (2007). *ASTM FI47-07ae1 Standard Consumer Performance Specifications for Playground Equipment for Public Use.* Retrieved September 28, 2010 from http://www.astm.org/Standards/F1487.htm

Architectural and Transportation Barriers Compliance Board. (1997). *Regulatory negotiation committee on accessibility guidelines for play facilities: Final report.* Washington, DC: Architectural and Transportation Barriers Compliance Board.

Architectural and Transportation Barriers Compliance Board. (2000). *ADA Accessibility guidelines for play areas.* Washington, DC: Architectural and Transportation Barriers Compliance Board.

Arnett, J. (1989). Caregivers in day-care centers: Does training matter? *Journal of Applied Developmental Psychology, 10,* 541–552.

Atlas, J. A., & Lapidus, L. B. (1987). Patterns of symbolic expression in subgroups of the childhood psychoses. *Journal of Clinical Psychology,43,* 177–188.

August, R. L., & Forman, B. D. (1989). A comparison of sexually abused and non-sexually abused children's responses to anatomically correct dolls. *Child Psychiatry and Human Development, 20,* 39–47.

Bailey, D. (1989). Assessment and its importance in early intervention. In D. Bailey & M. Wolery (Eds.), *Assessing infants and preschoolers with handicaps* (pp. 1–21). Upper Saddle River, NJ: Merrill/Prentice Hall.

Barren-Cohen, S., Leslie, A. M., & Frith, U. (1985). Does the autistic child have a theory of mind? *Cognition, 21,* 37–46.

Bayley, N. (1993). *Bayley Scales of Infant Development (BSID-II)* (2nd ed). San Antonio, TX: Psychological Corporation.

Beigel, A. R. (1996). Developing computers competencies among special needs educations. *Learning and Leading with Technology, 23*, 69–70.

Belsky, J. (1984). Two waves of cay care research: Developmental effects and conditions of quality. In R. Ainslie (Ed.), *The child and the day care setting* (pp. 1–34). New York: Praeger.

Belsky, J. (1990). Parental and nonparental child care and children's socioemotional development. A decade in review. *Journal of Marriage and Family, 52*, 885–903.

Belsky, J., & Most, R. (1981). From exploration to play: A cross-sectional study of infant free play behavior. *Developmental Psychology, 17*, 630–639.

Bergen, D. (1991). *Play as the vehicle for early intervention with at-risk infants and toddlers.* Paper presented at the annual conference of the American Educational Research Association (ED 335 115).

Blasco, P. M., Bailey, D. B., & Burchinal, M. A. (1993). Dimensions of mastery in same-age and mixed-age integrated classrooms. *Early Childhood Research Quarterly, 8,* 193–206.

Blisset, G., & Adkins, M. (1993). Are they learning? A study of the use of interactive video. *Computers and Education, 21,* 31–39.

Brooks-Gunn, J., & Lewis, M. Assessing young handicapped children: Issues and solutions. *Journal of the Division for Early childhood, 2,* 84–95.

Brophy, K., & Hancock, S. (1985). Adult-child interaction in an integrated preschool programme: Implications for teacher training. *Early Child Development and Care, 22,* 275–294.

Burgstahler, S. (1998). Focus on technology. Retrieved April 27, 2006 from *http://stuff.Washington.edu/sherylb/haring/html*

Burkour, C. K. (1998). We want to play too! *The Exceptional Parent, 28,* 72–74.

Burlingham, D. (1961). Some notes on the development of the blind. *Psychoanalytic Study of the Child, 16,* 194–198.

Burlingham, D. (1965). Some problems of the ego development in blind children. *Psychoanalytic Study of the Child, 20,* 194–208.

Burlingham, D. (1967). Developmental considerations in the occupation of the blind. *Psychoanalytic Study of the Child, 22,* 187–198.

Burlingham, D. (1972). *Psychoanalytic studies of the sighted and the blind.* New York: International Universities Press.

Burlingham, D. (1975). Special problems of blind infants: Blind baby profile. *Psychoanalytic Study of the Child, 30,* 3–14.

Casby, M. W. (1997). Symbolic play of children with language impairment: A critical review. *Journal of Speech, Language, and Hearing Research, 40,* 468–479.

Chambers, P. (1997). IV and SEN: Using interactive video with special education pupils. *British Journal of Educational Technology, 28,* 31–39.

Clarke-Stewart, K. A. (1987). Predicting child development from child care forms and features: The Chicago Study. In D. Phillips, (Ed.), *Quality in child care: What does research tell us?* (pp. 21–41). Washington, DC: National Association for the Education of Young Children.

Cohn, D. (1991). Anatomical doll play of preschoolers referred for sexual abuse and those not referred. *Child Abuse and Neglect, 15,* 455–466.

Coppa, C. (2003). A playground for all abilities. Retrieved September, 28, 2010 from http://www.astm.org/SNEWS/MARCH_2003/people_mar03/html

Dell, A. G., & Newton, D. (1998). Software for play and active early learning. *The Exceptional Parent, 28,* 39–43.

Doctoroff, S. (2001). Adapting the physical environment to meet the needs of all young children for play. *Early Childhood Education Journal 29,* 105–109.

Dunlap, L. L. (2009). *An introduction to early childhood special education.* Upper Saddle River, NJ: Pearson.

Eisert, D., & Lamorey, S. (1996). Play as a window on child development: The relationship between play and other developmental domains. *Early Education and Development, 7,* 221–235.

Erin, J. N. (1990). Language samples from visually impaired 4- and 5-year-olds. *Journal of Childhood Communication Disorders, 13,* 181–191.

Esposito, B. G., & Koorland, M.A. (1989). Play behavior of hearing impaired children: Integrated and segregated settings. *Exceptional Children, 55,* 412–419.

Fagot, B. I., Hagen, R. Youngblade, L. M., & Potter, L. (1989). A comparison of the play behaviors of sexually abused, physically abused, and non-abused children. *Topics in Early Childhood Special Education, 9,* 88–100.

Fenson, L. (1986). The developmental progression in play. In A. Gottfried and C. C. Brown (Eds.), *Play interactions: the contribution of play materials and parental involvement to children's development.* Lexington, MA: Heath.

Fewell, R., & Kaminski, R. (1988). Play skills development and instruction for young children with handicaps. In S. Odom & M. Karnes (Eds.), *Early intervention for infants and children with handicaps* (pp. 145–158). Baltimore, MD: Brookes.

Fewell, R., & Rich, J. (1987). Play assessment as a procedure for examining cognitive, communication, and social skills in multihandicapped children. *Journal of Psychoeducational Assessment, 2,* 107–118.

Fewell, R., & Wheedon, C. A. (1998). A pilot study of intervention with adolescent mothers and their children: A preliminary examination of child outcomes. *Topics in Early Childhood Special Education, 18,* 18–25.

File, N. (1994). Children's play, teacher-child interactions, and teacher beliefs in integrated early childhood programs. *Early Childhood Research Quarterly, 9,* 223–240.

File, N., & Kontos, S. (1993). The relationship of program quality to children's play in integrated early intervention settings. *Topics in Early Childhood Special Education, 13,* 1–18.

Fraiberg, S. (1968). Parallel and divergent patterns in blind and sighted infants. *Psychoanalytic Study of the Child, 23,* 264–300.

Fraiberg, S., (1977). *Insights from the blind: Comparative studies of blind and sighted children.* New York: Basic.

Fraiberg, S., & Adelson, E. (1973). Self-representation in language and play: Observations of blind children. *Psychoanalytic Quarterly, 42*, 539–562.

Freeman, R. D., Goetz, E., Richards, P., Groenveld, M., Blockberger, S. Jan, J. E., & Skylanda, A. M. (1989). Blind children's early emotional development: Do we know enough to help? *Child Care, Health and Development, 15*, 3–28.

Frost, J. L., & Klein, B. L. (1979). *Children's play and playgrounds*. Boston: Allyn & Bacon.

Ganz, J. B., & Flores, M. M. (2010, May). Implementing visual cues for young children with autism spectrum disorders and their classmates. *Young Children, 65*, 78–83.

Gitlin-Weiner, K. (1998). Clinical perspectives on play. In D. P. Fromberg & D. Bergen (Eds.), *Play from birth to twelve and beyond. Contexts perspectives and meanings* (pp. 77–92). New York: Garland.

Gleason, J. J. (1990). Meaning of play: Interpreting patterns in behavior of persons with severe developmental disabilities. *Anthropology & Education Quarterly, 21* 59–77.

Goodman, F. (1981). *Computers and the future of literacy*. Proceedings of the National Computer Conference.

Gross, M. U. M. (2002). *The Seng Newsletter, 2*, 1–3. Retrieved April 27, 2006, from www.sengifted.org.

Guralnick, M. J. (1990). Social competence and early intervention. *Journal of Early Intervention, 14*, 3–14.

Guralnick, M. J., Conner, R. T., Hammond, M. A., Gottman, J. M., & Kinnish, K. (1996). The peer relations of preschool children with communication disorders. *Child Development, 67*, 1556–1572.

Guralnick, M. J., & Groom, (1987). The peer relations of mildly delayed and nonhandicapped children in mainstream playgroups. *Child Development, 58*, 1556–1572.

Guralnick, M. J., & Groom, J. (1988). Friendships of preschool children in mainstreamed play groups. *Developmental Psychology, 24*, 595–604.

Guralnick, M. J., & Weinhouse, E. M. (1984). Peer–related social interactions of developmentally delayed young children: Development and characteristics. *Developmental Psychology, 20*, 815–827.

Hadley, P. A., & Rice, M. L. (1991). Conversational responsiveness of speech- and language-impaired preschoolers. *Journal of Speech and Hearing Research, 34*, 1308–1317.

Handen, B. L., McAuliffe, S., Janosky, J., Feldman, H., & Breaux, A. M. (1998). A playroom observation procedure to assess children with mental retardation and ADHD. *Journal of Abnormal Child Psychology, 4*, 269–277.

Harper, J. (1991). Children's play: the differential effects of intrafamilial physical and sexual abuse. *Child Abuse and Neglect, 15*, 89–98.

Helm, J. M., Comfort, M., Bailey, D. B., & Simeonsson. R. J. (1990). Adolescent and adult mothers of handicapped children: Maternal involvement in play. *Family Relations, 39*, 432–437.

Hess, K., & Sexton, S. (2002). An uncommon friendship. *Young Children, 57*, 26–28.

Hill, P., & McCune-Nicolich, L. M. (1981). Pretend play and patterns of cognition in Down's syndrome children. *Child Development, 52*, 611–617.

Howard, J., Greyrose, E., Kehr, K., Espinoza, M., & Beckwith, L. (1996). Teacher-facilitated microcomputer activities: Enhancing social play and affect in young children with disabilities. *Journal of Special Education Technology, 13*, 36–47.

Hughes, E. P. (1998). Play in special populations. In O. N. Saracho & B. Spodek (Eds.), *Multiple perspectives on play in early childhood education*. Albany: State University of New York Press.

Hughes, M., Dote-Kwan, J., & Dolendo, J. (1998). A close look at the cognitive play of preschoolers with visual impairments in the home. *Exceptional Children, 64*, 451–462.

Hupp, S. C., Boat, M. B., & Alpert, A. S. (1992). The impact of adult interaction on play behaviors and emotional responses of preschoolers with developmental delays. *Education and Training in Mental Retardation, 27*, 145–152.

Jampole, L., & Weber, M. K. (1987). An assessment of the behavior of sexually abused victims in anatomically correct dolls. *Child Abuse and Neglect, 11*, 187–192.

Janney, R. E., Snell, M. E., Beers, M. K., & Raynes, M. (1995). Integrating students with moderate and severe disabilities into general education classes. *Exceptional Children, 61*, 425–439.

Kamps, D. M., Kravits, T., Lopez, A., Kemmerer, K., Potucek, J., & Harrell, L. G. (1998). What do the peers think? Social validity of peer-mediated programs. *Education and Treatment of Children, 21*, 107–134.

Kearney, K. (1996). *Highly gifted children in full inclusion classrooms*. The Hollingworth Center for Highly Gifted Children. Retrieved April 27, 2006 from www.hollingworht.org/fullincl.html

Kontos, S., & Fiene, R. (1987). Child care quality compliance with regulations, and children's development: The Pennsylvania Study. In D. A. Phillips (Ed.), *Quality and childcare: What does research tell us?* (pp. 57–79). Washington, DC: National Association for the Education of Young Children.

Kontos, S., Moore, S., & Gioretti, K. (1998). The ecology of inclusion. *Topics in Early Childhood Special Education, 18*, 38–48.

Kozub, F. M., & Porretta, D. (1996). Including athletes with disabilities: Interscholastic athletic benefits for all. *Journal of Physical Education, Recreation, & Dance, 67*, 19–24.

Lewis, V., & Boucher, J. (1988). Spontaneous instructed and elicited play in relatively able autistic children. *British Journal of Developmental Psychology, 6*, 325–339.

Lindemann, P. (1992). The Americans with Disabilities Act (ADA) is now law. *ASTM Standardization News*, pp. 48–51.

Linder, T. (1990). *Transdisciplinary play-based assessment: A functional approach to working with young children*. Baltimore: Brookes.

Linder, T. (1994). The role of play in early childhood education. In P. L. Stafford (Ed.), *Year-book in Early Childhood Education* (Vol. 5). New York: Teachers College Press.

Linder, T. (Ed.). (2008). *Transdisciplinary play-based assessment and transdisciplinary play-based intervention* (2nd ed.). Baltimore, MD: Brookes.

Locke, P. A., & Levin, J. (1998). Creative play...begins with fun objects, your imagination, and simple-to-use technology. *The Exceptional Parent, 28*, 36–40.

Lombardino, L., Stein, J., Kricos, P., & Wolfe, M. (1986). Play diversity and structural relationships in the play and language of language-impaired and language-normal preschoolers: Preliminary data. *Journal of Communication Disorders, 19*, 475–489.

Lovell, K., Hoyle, H., & Siddall, M. (1968). A study of some aspects of the play and language of young children with delayed speech. *Journal of Child Psychology and Psychiatry, 9*, 41–50.

Moore, R. B., Goltsman, S. M., & Iacofano, D. S. (Eds.), (1987). *Play for all guidelines: Planning design, and management of outdoor play settings for all children.* Berkeley, CA: MIG.

Moucha, S., Crawford, S., Drause, J., & Stein, J. V. (1997). Can students with disabilities be adequately accommodated in today's physical education classes? *Journal of Physical Education, Recreation & Dance, 68*, 7–14.

Muller, A. A., & Perlmutter, M. (1985). Preschool children's problem-solving interactions at computers and jigsaw puzzles. *Journal of Applied Developmental Psychology, 6*, 173–186.

Myers, C. L., McBride, S. L, & Peterson, C. A. (1996). Transdisciplinary play-based assessment in early childhood special education: An examination of social validity. *Topics in Early Childhood Special Education, 16*, 102–126.

National Institutes Health, Eunice Kennedy Shrive National Institute of Child Health & Human Development. (2010, July). Autism Spectrum Disorders. Retrieved September 28, 2010 from http://www.nichd.nih.gov/health/topics/asd/cfm

National Institutes of Mental Health (NIMH). (2010, September). Autism Spectrum Disorders (Pervasive Developmental Disorders). What are autism spectrum disorders? Retrieved September 28, 2010 from http://www.nimh.nih.gov/health/topics/autisum-spectrum-disorders

O'Brien, J., Boatright, T., Chaplin, J., Geckler, C., Gosnell, D., Holcome, J., & Parrish, K. (1998). The impact of positioning equipment on play skills of physically impaired children. In S. Reifel (Ed.), *Play and culture studies: Vol. 1, diversions and divergences in field of play* (pp. 249–159). Greenwich, CT: Ablex.

Olson, M. R. (1981). Enhancing the exploratory behavior of visually impaired preschoolers. *Journal of Visual Impairment & Blindness, 75*, 375–378.

Osborn, J. B. (2006, April). Gifted children: Are their gifts being identified, encouraged, or ignored? New York Child Study Center. Retrieved April 7, 2006, from www.about our kids.org/aboutour/articles.

Parrette, H. P., Jr., & Murdick, N. L. (1998). Assistive technology and IEPs for young children with disabilities. *Early Childhood Education Journal, 25i*, 193–196.

Parsons, S. (1986). Function of play in low vision children: Part 2, Emerging patterns of behavior. *Journal of Visual Impairment & Blindness, 80*, 777–784.

Porter, L. (2001). *Social skills of gifted children.* Retrieved April 27, 2006, from *www.tasgifted.org/au2/2-01/porter.htm.*

Preisler, G., & Palmer, C. (1989). Thoughts from Sweden: The blind child at nursery school with sighted children. *Child Care, Health and Development, 15*, 45–52.

Quinn, J., & Rubin, K. (1984). The play of handicapped children. In T. D. Yawkey and A. Pellegrini (Eds.), *Child's play: Developmental and applied.* Hillsdale, NJ: Erlbaum.

Raver, S. A. (2009). *Early childhood special education-0-8 years.* Upper Saddle River, NJ: Pearson.

Recchia, S. L. (1987). *Learning to play—Common concerns for the visually impaired preschool child.* Los Angeles Blind Children's Center (ERIC Document Reproduction Service Number ED292249).

Recreation Access Advisory Committee. (1994). *Recommendations for accessibility guidelines: Recreational facilities and outdoor developed areas.* Washington, DC: U. S. Architectural and Transportation Barriers Compliance Board.

Rescorla, L., & Goosens, M. (1992). Symbolic play development in toddlers with expressive specific language impairment. *Journal of Speech and Hearing Research, 35*, 1290–1302.

Rettig, M. (1994). The play of young children with visual impairments: Characteristics and interventions. *Journal of Visual Impairment and Blindness, 88*, 410–420.

Rothschild, J. (1960). Play therapy with blind children. *New Outlook for the Blind, 54*, 329–333.

Ruff, H. A., Lawson, K. R., Parniello, R. & Weissberg, R. (1990). Long-term stability of individual differences in sustained attention in the early years. *Child Development, 61*, 60–76.

Rutter, M. (1983). Cognitive deficits in the pathogenesis of autism. *Journal of Child Psychology and Psychiatry, 24*, 512–531.

Sale, P., & Carey, D. M. (1995). The sociometric status of students with disabilities in a full inclusion school. *Exceptional Children, 62*, 6–19.

Sandler, A. M. (1963). Aspects of passivity and ego development in the blind infant. *Psychoanalytic Study of the Child, 18*, 343–360.

Sandler, A. M., & Wills, D. M. (1965). Some notes on play and mastery in the blind child. *Journal of Child Psychotherapy, 1*, 7–19.

Schneekloth, L. H. (1989). Play environments for visually impaired children. *Journal of Visual Impairment and Blindness, 83*, 196–201.

Schneider, J. (1997). *Developmental stages of chase play: A proposal.* Unpublished manuscript.

Schnorr, R. F. (1990). "Peter? He comes and goes...": First graders' perspectives on a part-time mainstream student. *Journal of the Association for Persons with Severe Handicaps, 15*, 231–240.

Segal, M., & Webber, N. T. (1996). Nonstructured play observations: Guidelines, benefits, and caveats. In S. J. Meisels, & E. Fenichel (Eds.), *New visions for the developmental assessment of infants and young children* (pp. 207–230). Washington, DC: Zero to Three: National Center for Infants, Toddlers, and Families.

Shatz, M., & Gelman, R. (1973). The development of communication skills: Modifications in the speech of young children as a function of listener. *Monographs of a Society for Research in Child Development, 38,* Serial No. 152.

Skellenger, A. C., & Hill, E. W. (1994). Effect of a shared teacher-play intervention on the play skills of three young children who are blind. *Journal of Visual Impairment and Blindness, 91,* 433–445.

Skellenger, A. C., Rosenblum, L. P., & Jager, B. K. (1997). Behaviors of preschoolers with visual impairment in indoor play settings. *Journal of Visual Impairment and Blindness, 91,* 519–530.

Sontag, J. C. (1997). Contextual factors influencing the sociability of preschool children with disabilities in integrated and segregated classrooms. *Exceptional Children, 63,* 389–404.

Stahmer, A. C., & Schreibman, L. (1992). Teaching children with autism appropriate play in unsupervised environments using a self-management treatment package. *Journal of Applied behavior Analysis, 25,* 447–459.

Stipek, D. J., & Sanborn, M. E. (1985). Teacher' task-related interactions with handicapped and nonhandicapped preschool children. *Merrill-Palmer Quarterly, 31,* 285–300.

Stone, M. & Sagstetter, M. (1998). Simple technology—It's never too early to start. *The Exceptional Parent, 28,* 50–51.

Tait, P. E. (1972a). Behavior of young blind children in a controlled play situation. *Perceptual and Motor Skills, 34,* 963–969.

Tait, P. E. (1972b). A descriptive analysis of the play of young blind children. *Education of the Visually Handicapped, 4,* 12–15.

Tait, P. E. (1972c). The implications of play as it relates to the emotional development of the blind child. *Education of the Visually Handicapped, 4,* 52–54.

Tamis-Lemonda, C. S., & Bornstein, M. H. (1991). Individual variation, correspondence, stability and change in mother and toddler play. *Infant Behavior and Development, 14,* 143–162.

Terrell, B., & Schwartz, R. (1988). Object transformations in the play of language-impaired children. *Journal of Speech and Hearing Disorders, 53,* 459–466.

Thorndike, R. L., Hagen, E. P., & Sattler, J. P. (1986). *Stanford-Binet Intelligence Scale* (4th ed.). Chicago: Riverside.

Tilton, J. R., & Ottinger, D. R. (1964). Comparisons of the toy play and behavior of autistic, retarded, and normal children. *Psychological Reports, 15,* 967–975.

Troster, H., & Bambring, M. (1992). Early social-emotional development in blind infants. *Child Care, Health and Development, 18,* 207–227.

Troster, H., & Bambring, M. (1993). Early motor development in blind infants. *Journal of Applied Developmental Psychology, 14,* 83–106.

Troster, H., & Bambring, M. (1994). The play behavior and play materials of blind and sighted infants and preschoolers. *Journal of Visual Impairment and Blindness, 88,* 421–432.

University of Washington The National Center on Accessible Information Technology in Education. (2010). What is accessible electronic and information technology? Retrieved September 28, 2010 from http://www.washington. edu/accessit/articles?110

U. S. Consumer Product Safety Commission. (n.d.). *Which toy for which child? A consumer's guide for selecting suitable toys.* Washington, DC: Author.

Waniganayake, M. (2001). From playing with guns to playing with rice: The challenges of working with refugee children. *Childhood Education, 77,* 289–294.

Warren, D. (1984). *Blindness and early childhood development.* New York: Foundation for the Blind.

WebMD. (2008, April). Autism Spectrum Disorders Health Center-Asperger's Syndrome-Symptoms. Retrieved September 28, 2010 from http:// Webmd.com/brain/autism/tc/.asbergers-syndrome

Wheatley, M. (1992). *Leadership and the new science.* San Francisco: Berrett-Koehler.

Whitebrook, M., Howes, C., & Phillips, D. (1990). *Who cares? Child care teachers and the quality of care in America.* Oakland, CA: Child Care Employee Project.

Wing, L., Gould, J., Yeats, S. R., & Brierly, L.M. (1977). Symbolic play in severely mentally retarded and autistic children. *Journal of Child Psychology and Psychiatry, 18,* 167–178.

Wills, D. M. (1965). Some observations on blind nursery school children's understanding of their world. *Psychoanalytic Study of the Child, 20,* 344–364.

Wills, D. M. (1968). Problems of play and mastery in the blind child. *British Journal of Medical Psychology, 41,* 213–222.

Wills, D. M. (1970). Vulnerable periods in the early development of blind children. *Psychoanalytic Study of the Child, 25,* 461–480.

Wills, D. M. (1972). Problems of play and mastery in the blind child. In E. P. Trapp & P. Himmelstein (Eds), *Readings on the Exceptional Child* (pp. 335–349). New York: Meredith.

Wills, D. M. (1979). The ordinary devoted mother and her blind baby. *Psychoanalytic Study of the Child, 34,* 31–49.

Wills, D. M. (1981). Some notes on the application of the diagnostic profile to young blind children. *Psychoanalytic Study of the Child, 36,* 217–237.

Wolery, M., Werts, M. G., Caldwell, N. K. Snyder, E. D., & Lisowski, L. (1995). Experienced teachers' perceptions of resources and supports for inclusion. *Education and Training in Mental Retardation and Developmental Disabilities, 30,* 15–26.

Wolfberg, P. J., & Schuler, A. L. (1993). Integrated play-groups: A model for promoting the social and cognitive dimensions of play in children with autism. *Journal of Autism and Developmental Disorders, 23,* 467–489.

Zippiroli, S., Bayer, D., & Mistrett, S. (1988). *Use of the microcomputer as a social facilitator between physically handicapped and non-handicapped preschoolers.* N.p: Handicapped Children's Early Education Program.

# 11 Computers and Technology as Emerging Toys

*This game—and this turned out to be true of video games more generally—requires the player to learn and think in ways at which I was not then adept. Suddenly all my baby-boomer ways of learning and thinking, for which I had heretofore received ample rewards, did not work.*

(Gee, 2007, p. 2)

By the time this chapter reaches you, there will be something new in the world of computers and technology play. In the years since the last edition of this book was written, we have seen many new play technology opportunities appear for children. We have also seen technology play that has in the past been enjoyed only by older children and adults, now being played by younger children. This part of the universe of play is changing very quickly for adults and for children. And the changes can be disorienting. Computers and other gaming platforms are evolving, opening new doors of possibility for play. These changes raise red flags for some, who worry about the sedentary and anti-social aspects of some technology play (e.g., Carr, 2010; Collins, 2009; Elkind, 1996; Fertig, 2008; Greenfield, 2009; Oppenheimer, 2003; Raley, 2008). Others see new opportunities for development in these forms of play that did not exist 10 to 20 years ago. The rapid change means that research is not keeping up with what is new in play.

This chapter will survey the current status of technology play, report what research can tell us about it, and situate play in the various debates about what technology is doing for, or to, children. With this information, teachers and parents can monitor children's engagement with play technology and make decisions about how technology should become a part of young children's developmental experiences. Adults may find themselves scrambling to keep up with new play, as new ways to play appear. Teachers will need to partner with parents to keep track of the new devices, programs, and social opportunities that were not part of our lives when we were young. The chapter will also point to areas where new forms of supervision are necessary; adults need to know what devices children have access to, as well as where those devices lead them.

The history of play shows us how our thinking about play has changed during different eras (Frost, 2010). The materials we play with are part of that thinking. In terms of technology, over the past 200 years, we can see how technology allowed children to play in new ways. Industrial technology created mass manufacturing, allowing for hands-on play with toys that cost little and became widely available. Electronic technology contributed to the invention of electronic media, creating new forms of recreation and play related to media characters. Computer technology created more compact and mobile gaming, bringing into the home games that had been enjoyed only by older players outside of the home. The Internet multiplied play options synergistically, bringing together all earlier forms of play in new, previously unknown versions. We will begin by tracing how play with a mouse has changed through this span of technological history. We shall see how play transformed from one type of hands-on engagement with real objects, into a very different sort of play that brings players into a play world of virtual playmates and objects. We shall also see how the words we use to describe play are taking on new meanings in this technologically created play world.

##  AN EVOLVING DEFINITION OF PLAY TECHNOLOGY: MOUSE, TO MOUSE, TO MOUSE, TO . . .

### From Play with Real Objects to Mass-Produced Toys

> Some small animals—rabbits, white mice, guinea pigs and the like—were considered good playmates for children, who were also expected to learn responsibility from caring for them. (Grier 2006)

Play pre-dates most technology. You do not need technology to play with pet white mice or rabbits; you just play with them. You could feel their furriness, smell them, and feel as they wiggled in your hands; they are real. Technology has altered this hands-on world of play with real objects. To understand the rapidly evolving world of play and technology, it is important to understand what we mean by terms such as technology, media, and synergy. (See Table 11.1.) **Technology**, in one form or

**TABLE 11.1**    Media and Technologies Related to Play (examples)

| Media | Technology | Synergy | Play (e.g.'s) |
|---|---|---|---|
| Toys | Industrial manufacturing | Froebel's writing | Tinkertoys |
| Print (e.g., books, comics) | Printing press | Action, imaginary stories | Superman |
| Phonograph | Sound recording | Children's theater | Kids Corner |
| Film (e.g., at theaters, DVD) | Motion photography, projection, animation | Children's literature | Willy Wonka, Cinderella |
| Radio | Broadcast engineering | Children's theater | *Roy Rogers* Show |
| Television (broadcast, cable, recorded) | Broadcast and cable engineering | Film<br>Comic books<br>Literature<br>Education | *Mickey Mouse Club*<br>Looney Tunes<br>Baby-Sitters Club<br>Sesame Street |
| Computers (e.g., PCs, handheld, game boxes) | Microprocessors/chips, batteries, Internet<br>Electronic music | Arcade games<br>Sports<br>Fantasy literature<br>Education/reality<br>Records | Pong<br>Wii Tennis<br>Tomb Raider<br>Sims<br>Downloads |
| Telephone (cell phones) | Chips, batteries, applications | Games<br>Music<br>Fantasy/Literature | Scrabble®<br>Rock Band<br>Harry Potter: Spells |

another, has a long history in childhood play. If we think of technology in dictionary terms, as "a capability given by the practical application of knowledge or a manner of accomplishing a task using technical processes, methods, or knowledge," then we can see a range of technical solutions to problems (such as digging canals to bring water to arid fields, allowing farms to exist where there had been none in the past; solving the problem of getting from one place to another using automobiles). For play, industrial technology allowed toys to be manufactured for the masses, rather than being crafted by hand for individuals. To this we must add an understanding of **media** (plural of medium), or the go-betweens or intermediaries that allow us to connect one thing to another. Media often help us to communicate with one another, as when a telephone serves as a medium to allow us to talk with one another from a distance. Vinyl records (whether singles or albums) were a common technology

for distributing music and other entertainment to homes and schools, where they could be played by means of the technology built into phonographs; digital (electronically represented) technology replaced vinyl records with CDs that could be played on a variety of electronic technologies that replaced phonographs. Visual digital technology replaced older television and computer screen cathode ray tubes with high definition digital screens, allowing for flatter, smaller screens with sharper images for viewing programs and games.

Toys and games are media for play, just as television is a medium for receiving programs transmitted into our homes, and personal computers are a medium for connecting us to the Internet (and the Internet is a medium for connecting us to online chat, e-mail, and other resources). As we will discuss next, there is **synergy** (a combination of different media and technology that creates something totally new) that is creating novel ways of engaging in play. Technology and media are part of our culture, so we often take them for granted; we just live with them, and we probably wouldn't dream of living without a telephone, a television, or a personal computer.

As we presented in Chapter 1, there is a long history of using industrial, technological methods to produce playthings (Cross, 1997). Froebel created some of his gifts and occupations to give children the capability to explore technical processes (e.g., building with peas and sticks) to gain understanding of the spatial world; industrial technology allowed many of those gifts and occupations to be manufactured as toys for home play (Brosterman, 1997). Other technological things from our growing 19th century economy, such as locomotives and skyscrapers, captured the imaginations of toy manufacturers and children; manufactured toy trains and building sets allowed children to play with their knowledge of the world of transportation and urban living. Mass production of erector sets allowed children to play with technical methods related to architectural construction. We have many examples of manufacturing technology that was used to create toys, with which children could play their way to technological understandings. Play changed accordingly, although it was still a hands-on form of play: toy trains and construction sets allowed for play with real play objects made of metal, wood, cloth, and fabric.

When children played with their pets, they were playing with real mice or kittens that they could feel. Nineteenth century manufacturing technology brought toys that simulated real pets: teddy bears. You felt simulated fur and, possibly, heard mechanical animal sounds, but they were not real pets. Children could play with toy animals as if they were real animals, just as they could play with real toy trains as if they were real trains. Manufacturing technology brought us real things that we could hold and manipulate, to enhance our play.

## Media Technologies Influence Play

*Walt Disney's Comics and Stories*, the magazine that reprinted Mickey Mouse and Donald Duck newspaper comic strips, found itself running out of strips. The editors suddenly needed a new source of page-filling material . . . Mickey Mouse was already being used extensively . . . (Barks, 1978, p. 11)

For more than a century, we have had machines (i.e., technology, "practical applications of knowledge") that were part of our fun and recreation. Radio, film, and television, all media built with electronic technology, have been tied to children's play, long before personal computers entered our homes and schools. Listening to the radio was a play interest of children 80 years ago (Jersild, 1933). Beginning nearly at the same time, from the silver screen, comic strips, and mass-manufactured books, Buck Rogers and many other characters served as models for children's role play, just as other book characters like Tarzan and the Rover Boys had done before; those media heroes and others eventually scaffolded play by means of radio and television broadcasts. Mickey Mouse and Snow White made the leap from the big screen to the television screen, and eventually to comic books and the toy store, as technology stimulated the larger consumer culture that was built on play (Bogart, 2000).

Technology supported play in new ways. Children (or their parents) could become consumers of play that began as recreation that was broadcast or projected through what were at the time new technological media. Children learned about Mickey Mouse from going to the movies, then from comic books. A child could play by listening to the radio, watching TV, reading "the funnies" or by playing with toys based on characters that appeared in the media. By the 1950's, children could play with Mickey Mouse from their experiences at the movies, on television (with *The Mickey Mouse Club*), and by visiting Disneyland with their families, where they could buy related toys. There is a clear synergy

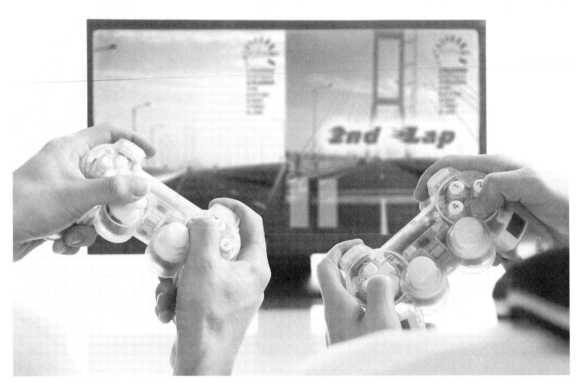

Arcade-type games enter the home on familiar TV screens.

among play, play's media sources, and new technology that broadcasts them; more media, and media connections, combined with toys to support Disney mouse play. Mickey Mouse board games and art play were encouraged by the popularity of television programming.

Older players also participated in all of these forms of play. At the same time, they participated in sports, music and dancing, and arcade games. Arcade gaming deserves mention, as it serves as one source of play that transitioned into computer games. Although there is no research documenting young children participating in arcade games when they were played in arcades, there is ample evidence that computer games have become a common experience for the younger players, as technology brought

arcade-like games (such as Pong and Frogger) into the home (Kaiser Family Foundation, 2010).

In the 1950s, television became a major cultural influence, for relaxation, education, and recreation. Television was essentially a technological medium for providing content (news, drama, comedy, children's programming) to the masses (Winston, 1998). Children's programming was often playful, providing viewers with recreation. It also, as movie viewing had done before, provided sources for pretend role play. Cartoons, *The Howdy Doody Show* (Davis, 1987), *Daniel Boone, The Mickey Mouse Club* and other programs became a resource for children's role play, and for toys that were marketed in association with those programs. (Related to the *Daniel Boone* television program, toy replicas of

Boone's coonskin cap were a major play fad in the 1950s as a role-play prop. There are reports from that time of sales in excess of 5,000 coonskin cap replicas per day; Johnson, 2002.) By the 1970s, television had become an accepted source for children's education, with programs as varied as *Mister Rogers' Neighborhood* and *Sesame Street* (Fisch & Truglio, 2001). Play was tied to those programs synergistically, by means of toys related to television characters and activities (e.g., Mr. Rogers's Trolley, *Sesame Street*'s Elmo doll; see end of chapter for related URL links). (See Table 11.2.) When children played with these toys, they played with real objects that made reference to what they were exposed to through movie, television, and print media. Technology provided children not only with real objects for play; it gave them media characters to serve as a basis for role play.

## Personal Computers Expand the World of Play at Home and Beyond

> Physically, a mouse consists of an object held under one of the user's hands, with one or more buttons. . . . The mouse's motion typically translates into the motion of a cursor on a display, which allows for fine control of a graphical user interface. (Wikipedia, 2010)

By the 1970s, personal computers, a technology to solve problems for scientists and engineers, were appearing and were becoming less expensive and more versatile. Computers themselves tended to be synergistic, reflecting thinking about how to solve a range of problems; they needed to merge electronics, linguistics, logic, and game theory to solve their computational problems. Computer scientists found that gaming provided one good way of making computers work for people; they used simple games, such as table tennis, as models for developing their technology. Because these computer games were engaging, there was a market for them. One of the first ways that many people encountered computer technology was in the form of games, such as Pong and Tetris. (Many adults

may have obtained a personal computer (PC) for word processing or data management, but they often included games on their computers to provide a break from work. For some, the break overtook the work (Young, 2004). As computers became more affordable, they became fixtures in more homes either in the form of a PC or a gaming device that was connected to a television (Kushner, 2004). Younger children were exposed to computers and acquired skills using them.

Eventually, the market for games expanded to include younger computer users. How children understand technology is mediated by how technology intersects with toys and games. Computer linked play, with its joysticks and mice for controlling the play, became part of the culture. Children learned how to manipulate computer games as part of a shared peer experience, with players teaching each other about the technology (Greenfield, 1984; Gee, 2007). Play became interactive in a new way; players were interacting with each other, around computers (or electronic gaming devices) and by means of computers. Virtual play settings like *Imbee.com* websites, where children as young as preschoolers can "visit with friends," "write a blog," and "share pictures" become new playgrounds for children (Industrious Kids, 2006). Personal computers and the technologies that support them have altered this synergy. What children can do with the objects has changed. How play relates to other media and playmates has changed. And it continues to change rapidly.

Technology became less about ways of manufacturing toys and allowing children to pretend to be engineers; it was more about media, such as television and computer play, competing for children's play interests (Kaiser Family Foundation, 2010). Instead of having a hands-on play experience with a pet mouse or a manufactured toy for pretend, children were becoming familiar with manipulating a joystick or computer mouse so they could participate in gaming.

The synergistic interaction between play for young adults and technology development

**TABLE 11.2**  Play in the Synergy of Emerging Technologies

| Manufacturing Technologies | Mass Production | Toys |
|---|---|---|
| Engineering toys (like Froebel's occupations) | allowed children to play with ideas about | Technology/construction e.g, Tinker Toys |
| Toy trains | allowed children to play with ideas about | Transportation Technology e.g., Lionel Trains |
| Arcade games | allowed older children to play | e.g., Pong |
| **Media Technologies** | **Media Mass Produced** | **Role Play** |
| Books, newspapers, comics (sometimes influenced by play) | provided children with popular characters for | e.g., Nancy Drew, Dick Tracy, Huck Finn, river rafting |
| Moving pictures, radio (sometimes influenced by print) | provided children with popular characters for | e.g., Hardy Boys, superheroes |
| Television (sometimes influenced by print or movies) | provided children with popular characters for | e.g., Superman, *Mickey Mouse Club* |
| **Computers (with varying platforms)** | **Gaming and Pretend** | **Toys/Games** |
| PC's (developed with gaming models associated with arcade games) | provided PC based games | e.g., Pong |
| PC role playing games (developed with digital animated technology) | provided PC based role playing/action | e.g., Tomb Raider, Dungeons and Dragons |
| Game players (connected to TV or mobile) | provided all of the above, with the comfort of TV | e.g., Wii, Gameboys |
| **Internet/Telephone Technologies** | **All of the Above** | **Toys/Games/Role Play** |
| Online gaming | with Internet connections, players can play solitary or with others | e.g., Pokemon, |
| Create games | players can make their own games | e.g., Mickey's Soccer Fever, Fashion Time |
| Texting | friends can hang out, whether present or not | e.g., American Girl Doll Games, Boys' Life |

**Current Synergies:**

As of late 2010, children who have access to Internet connections (either through a computer or a cell phone) can find solitary or multiple-player online games that relate to books (e.g., The Baby-sitters Club), dolls (e.g., Kit Kittredge), cartoon characters (e.g., Mickey Mouse), television personalities (e.g., Miley Cyrus), arcade games (e.g., Brilliant Blocks/Tetris), board games (e.g., Battleship), pet care (e.g., Virtual Pet Game), movies (e.g., Mulan), educational programs (e.g., *Sesame Street*) and other cultural activities. Many are free; some must be purchased.

Websites where gaming and play are provided may be sponsored by toy companies (e.g., Lego, Mattel), media conglomerates (e.g., Walt Disney), publishers (e.g., Harper Collins), personalities (e.g., Miley Cyrus), or unaffiliated producers.

New platforms have made gaming mobile, in and out of the home.

opened the door to new toys that merged old game playing (from arcades) with new ways of playing them (computerized first for gaming in arcades and then for playing at home). Cheaper technology allowed the games to go from the arcade to the home, where different **platforms**, such as PlayStation and Wii, could be connected to the television. (A platform is the hardware, or device, on which particular software programs can be played.) Electronic gaming with computer technology, combined with the familiarity of television, escalated players' interest in computer games (Greenfield, 1984). And with games such as Pong and Super Mario Brothers at home, younger players were

exposed and attracted to them. Children would use their joysticks and computer mice to play games that starred Mickey Mouse and other characters.

Novelty and lowering prices of the technologies that are basic to these new electronic toys contributed to the number of different platforms that players could buy. Some platforms are small and self-sufficient for play (such as Game Boys, and more recently iPods, e-books, and smartphones). Other platforms required a television connection for play (such as Play Station, GameCube, Xbox, and Wii). Game software for each platform could be purchased and inserted into the gaming platform. Games were initially designed for adolescents and young adults, but game developers for most platforms began to develop games for children as young as 3 years.

At this same time, there were efforts to bring the power of computer technology playfully to young children's education. Software was applied to classroom purposes, and small computers that individuals can use became common fixtures in children's classrooms. Classroom computers became a tool where children could experience the full range of academics and development that they had experienced prior to the appearance of this technology. Children playing (or relating playfully) at PCs could be seen to write (Dickinson, 1986; Jones & Pellegrini, 1996), be creative (Clement, 1995; Escobedo, 1992), problem solve (Muller & Perlmutter, 1985), and use game software for practicing skills, writing, social relationships, and art (e.g., Beaty & Tucker, 1987; Hamilton, 2007; Haugland, 1999, 2000). In addition to using PCs as a tool for teaching, many were noticing that fairly typical play and play relationships occur as children interact with computers in classrooms (Anderson, 2000; Dickinson, 1986: Genishi, McCollum, & Strand, 1985; Shade, 1994; Wang & Ching, 2003). While there were concerns about the appropriateness of PCs for young children, a consensus was forming that they have a useful, developmentally appropriate place in classrooms (Clements & Nastasi,

1993; Clements & Sarama, 2003; Shade, 1994; Wang & Hoot, 2006).

One approach to technology use by young children reflected the unique possibilities of computer play. Rather than using the computer to pass on information or to focus on long-established school subjects such as writing and art, Papert (1980) found a way to turn children into computer programmers with his LOGO programming language. He wanted to empower children to use computer technology to create their own toys, to serve their own purposes. By giving children power over simple computer technology, Papert let children discover their own ways to explore, draw, and challenge themselves, with toys that they constructed themselves. This work leads directly to robotics, a form of play that allows children to fully control the content of their technology play without having to play with adult-created software. Children construct their own computerized toys. All the while, they are learning about technology and about the content that interests them (Bers, 2008; Resnick, 1994, 2006; Resnick, Bruckman & Martin, 1996; Resnick, Ocko & Papert, 1988).

As electronic gaming became more common, the industry and its game developers agreed to a rating system, overseen by the Entertainment Software Rating Board (ESRB). To receive a rating, a game manufacturer must provide accurate information about each game's age appropriateness—from age 3 to adult—and about its content, such as "Comic Mischief," "Blood and Gore," "Strong Language," or "Violence." Age ratings and content descriptors appear on game packaging. (See the end of this chapter for related URL links.)

As new play technologies became more a part of the culture, the range of content increased. Simple games, such as Pong and Super Mario Brothers, became more complex, and new content appeared. Games were developed from other cartoon and children's television characters (e.g., Looney Tunes, Disney Games), from educational television programs (e.g., *Sesame Street*), and from film (such as *Alice in Wonderland* and *Toy Story*). (See the end of this chapter for related URL links.) The synergy between familiar media, such as television programming and movies, and electronic play is strong. That synergy influenced older media as well, with games such as Pokemon and Super Mario Brothers generating television programs, movies, toys, and collectibles. Media create games, and games create media. (See Table 11.2.)

Contemporary technology (i.e., toy manufacturing, computer electronics, more powerful batteries) and various media (print, film, television) found their synergy, and play related to these technologies grew quickly over the past 20 years (Kaiser Family Foundation, 2010). Some media, such as radio, faded, while new electronic play devices became much more popular for children of all ages. Many new platforms emerged just for children, for viewing DVDs, listening to music, creating art, and make-believe animal care. These changes were clearly part of popular culture (Edwards, 2005; Kalliala, 2005); they are especially a part of a growing commercial culture that is tied to technology. Playing with a mouse in the 21st century is a technological activity. A computer or some other computer-like platform has become a toy. Players with these technologies no longer have to physically touch the objects they are playing with; they play with images on a screen, images that they manipulate with a joystick or a mouse. The images on the screen may relate to other screen media like television or movies, or they may be images of games that had in the past been played by moving plastic, wooden, or cardboard pieces. Whether an image of a real mouse or an image of Mickey Mouse appears on screen, technology creates play with images rather than with hands-on objects. The play universe has been translated onto a flat screen.

As technology evolves, newer forms of scrolling on computer screens might replace the computer mouse, whether on PCs, smartphones, e-books, or other platforms, for play and recreation. In any case, technology creates

Younger players have access to smaller technology.

synergy with older forms of play and other familiar media. New home and school influences have changed play from an experience with real objects to an experience on a screen. Some platforms, such as Wii, are attempting to bridge the play world with real-world play actions, with bodily action translated into a screen effect. At the same time, new technologies providing easier access to the Internet are taking technology play in new directions that expand on recent computer play.

## THE INTERNET AND NEW TECHNOLOGY PLATFORMS: VIRTUAL PLAY WORLDS

Very quickly in the recent past, technology allowed children to log on to the Internet from their home and school computers. The **Internet**, a network web (the World Wide Web) of computers, had originally been available only for adults, to communicate, store, and share information. New Internet access technologies, such as search engines, allowed children to locate online information and play opportunities. The Internet's potential for education and development was apparent (e.g., Harris & Reifel, 2002; Yan & Greenfield, 2006), as was its synergistic connection to play. An Internet player goes

online when connecting a computer to the World Wide Web, often by means of a search engine. With access to the Internet, by means of smartphone or other handheld device, younger children have additional access to all the games, role play, and information that only older players previously had. With an increasing number of younger users going online, game developers began to include more online play content for them. These play opportunities are adding to, and in some cases replacing, older forms of play.

As of this writing, the Internet provides access to play content intended for children as young as 3. (We have little data to tell us whether even younger children are participating in this play, other than anecdotes about parents who play with their toddlers by using hand-held devices such as smartphones.) We often refer to this play as "**virtual**" or "analog," in the sense that the player is engaged with a game that is in the technology, rather than with concrete objects that are manipulated by hand. We call something virtual when it has some qualities of a real thing (e.g., appearance, action, sound), but is not real (i.e., it appears only as a flat-screen representation of the real thing). Rather than playing with wooden blocks or game pieces that are made out of cardboard and plastic, children play with electronic analogs of those physical world objects that appear on a screen. That content may be a virtual game that is an online version of a game (such as Battleship) that children might play without technology. It could be a game involving characters from a television program, movie, or book. It could be a game involving a popular toy, such as a doll or toy car, or school skills, such as counting or letter recognition. Instead of playing with a toy car, children drive a virtual car on a screen. Instead of counting real objects, children count virtual objects.

It is important to remember that all pretend play is virtual, in the sense that children who pretend are acting as if their actions mean what those actions mean in reality (Bateson, 2000).

When children enact family routines in a play-house, the playhouse is a virtual house (it is not a real house; it is a toy house) and the players are virtual moms, dads, and babies (they are not really parents or infants; they are children). In a computer game, the virtual house and player actions are transferred to a computer screen. Online pretend can be a virtual version of activity that is virtual to begin with. Yet, we can justly use the term virtual for both, adding some confusion to our understanding and description of play.

Some of these play activities need to be downloaded from an Internet source, as applications (or "apps") that can be played on the platform where they have been downloaded. Many downloads are free, but many others must be purchased (perhaps with parental assistance). Other Internet play is possible without downloading simply by clicking the mouse (or scrolling and tapping) on the appropriate screen image; the click opens the play world in the Internet. Children are increasingly engaged with the Internet. The Kaiser Family Foundation (2010) reports an increase in children's (8 to 18 year olds) reports of home Internet access from 47% in 1999 to 84% in 2009; the increase in Internet access in their own bedrooms was from 10% to 33% during that same time. We can only guess how this increase is making the Internet available for younger players. Adding to Internet connections and play is the appearance of more technology-rich cell phones or smartphones for younger children. The Kaiser Family Foundation reports that phone ownership for this age group has increased from 39% to 66%, making communications and Internet connections more available for children, and possibly less supervised by adults. There appears to be a broad range of parental supervision and restriction of all sorts of media and technology use, including Internet play.

The growth of Internet play and its synergy with other popular culture media raise many questions about what we can know from research about how children are playing and

A variety of mobile platforms allow online play.

what their play tells us about their development. While earlier descriptive studies of children's play relied on observations of real-life activities or interviews about play interests, researchers of contemporary technology play have to rethink what it means to observe play (because so much of the action takes place on the screen and in the players' heads) and interview children about technology play (because they can do so much more technologically than they can verbally describe). The addition of online social play made possible by the Internet creates new challenges for understanding social play, where we cannot see the players physically interacting and we may not have a good idea who the online players are. The real-world things that were once the setting for children's play (e.g., the dollhouses, the block centers, the game boards) are virtual on computers and the Internet, and playmates may be located just down the street or halfway around the world.

James Gee (2007) is an educational researcher who has studied technology gaming as it relates to literacy learning. He tells us that most adults are not "adept: at doing this play, or studying it; "our ways of learning and thinking" do not work in the culture of new online technology (p. 2). We have to approach the Internet and play as a slightly alien culture, a culture that we know only a little about. We do not know as much about it as the child players and game developers do. One reason for this is that many adults are not as familiar with the online context as younger players may be; older adults did not grow up with the technology and play that children have. Children know things about their play, and can do things in their play, that were not available to those who are older. A second reason is that online technology allows players to create their play, in ways analogous to those in which sociodramatic players create their play worlds in the playhouse or on a jungle gym. The big difference with online created play is that players can participate in creating their *virtual* environment, their *virtual* characters, and the story that they will enact. Children can play house online, but they must decide what the house looks like, what is in it, what the players will look like, and how they will act. Once there was imaginary play. Now there is virtual imaginary play. Technology and its play possibilities are changing so quickly that adults often do not have the time to keep up. The Internet site for an online game can appear, become the rage, and then disappear before most adults know it is there. A new, necessary part of virtual online play is engaging with computer technology to create the world where online pretend will take place.

Given these major differences in technology-assisted play (especially on the Internet), it is up to researchers and child development specialists to describe the new technological context of play. As this chapter has pointed out, technology and its associated play have changed over 200 years. How we use words to describe play must be contextualized in new ways. To play with a mouse now means something very different, depending on the era and the technology we are using. Computer play means something different on the Internet than it does with a 1980s-era handheld device. Role playing means something different in the context of television, movies, and online pretend. Social play may be meaningfully different when we are playing face to face, as opposed to playing virtually. We must describe play in new ways that take into account the particular technologies that make children's play meaningful

for them. We will look in more detail at attempts to describe these technology play contexts.

## Playing in Virtual Contexts: Synergy and Commercialism

Girls' play is more social, and boys' is more physical (Ramsey, 2001). As we discuss in Chapter 7, it remains typical to see girls playing with dolls and boys pushing cars and trucks down building-block roads. Now, both boys and girls are including more electronic media in their lives, including computers and computer play (Kaiser Family Foundation, 2010). How do media, in particular going online with the Internet, alter how we can think about children's play contexts? The relative novelty of this kind of play means we have little research on this question, in particular for younger children. We do have some insights into this new technology play world that can help us understand play in new ways.

Research on play and the Internet reveals how much synergy there is for play, with combinations of new and old media all supported by online resources. Reifel (2009) explored the multiple contexts (real world, virtual, and ideological) that a commercial doll manufacturer can build into girls' doll play. These play options go far beyond what was possible when girls played with dolls that were handcrafted individually for them (Frost, 2010). For example, Mattel's American Girl Dolls®, originally sold in a small number of specialized, big-city stores, became available for purchase online with the technology for online purchasing. The dolls were planned to have synergy with related toys, such as doll clothes, furniture, outfits for girls that matched the dolls' outfits, other play props, and related media, such as books, magazines, videos, and big-screen movies that elaborated the background story for each doll, all marketed both in stores and online. With technology allowing online gaming, this doll play began to include fun activities for girls, including interactive online games, e-cards for sending to friends, and at various times, opportunities for girls and adults to comment via blog about their play experiences with dolls. Girls with an interest in a particular doll could form an online community of like-minded players, a kind of virtual doll play.

One important aspect of the technology of this kind of doll play is that it is commercial; one reason for the technology is to enable players to buy more play products. (The doll manufacturer provides a gift registry and wish list online, so individuals can indicate which play objects they want.) Technology is a tool for play commerce (Lamb & Brown, 2006). Online play exposes players to new play products, from the comfort of their own homes. Another aspect of technology is that it creates a global play culture that is available to anyone who can go online (and who can afford it). Children have access to toys, games, and play activities that are not available to them in local stores or by means of commercial media such as television. Children's play world is no longer geographically bound. This means that their online playmates will not necessarily be from local neighborhoods or schools, where parents might physically monitor them. Finally, a child playing online might be one mouse click away from a game that presents views that are contrary to what a parent might approve for a child. Online play sites, beyond their commercial influence, might lead children to influences that adults might find controversial (Reifel, 2009).

Barbie, Bratz, and many other dolls have their own websites with related products and play activities, and the same goes for TONKA, Lego, Transformers, and other toys for boys and girls. Likewise, television franchises (e.g., *Sesame Street*), television networks (e.g., Nickelodeon, Cartoon Network), media conglomerates (e.g., Walt Disney), and children's books (e.g., the Harry Potter series) have an online presence where children can play games. Some of the sites include clubs and social networking for children, in addition to free games and games that can be purchased related to online experiences. The synergy of play may begin with a toy, lead to an online game and a movie, and then include a game that can be purchased in a toy store. A major context of play and technology is commercial, marketing toys to children, often with the support of online games that motivate children to play more with a particular toy or character.

As mentioned earlier, there are numerous online games that are free. The websites that offer those free games often function like a commercial television station; the games are the programming, and there are commercials (in the margins of the screen, or pop-up ads) that support the website. Such sites are not synergistic with a brand toy or character, but they are still commercial, a source of advertising directed at players.

## Creating Play by Means of Technology

LOGO and robotics allow children to program their own toys. The Internet opened a world of child programming play in new ways. A form of technology play that has grown vastly over the past decade is online role playing (sometimes called multiplayer online role-playing games—MORGs, or massively multiplayer online role-playing games—MMORGs). Some of these games may be online versions of games that appeared earlier on different platforms. Others have been designed specifically for online play, and for player interaction. The games originated for older players, but now many are designed for young children who are beginning to read and write. Some are free online; others require a fee and must be downloaded to a platform. Some are rated and have parental controls, while others do not (Beck & Wade, 2004; Berger, 2002).

MORGs are interesting for a number of reasons. First, they appear to be a technology version of the kinds of role play (or sociodramatic play) that is familiar to observers of young children; the player assumes the role of a character in a pretend setting, where objects are often used to support the player's actions to further a make-believe plot. There is an aspect to MORGs that is like playing house or playing superheroes in real life: the virtual environments may be prepared (the way classrooms are set up with play kitchens), the player might choose a costume (the way child role players put on capes or high heels) and pretend powers (the way a child says "I can fly!"), and there can be negotiations about who will be what, and what players will do and say (the way children do when they agree on their cooperative pretend-play purposes). There are also differences. The play setting is virtual (on a screen), rather than being comprised of real physical props for play. Other participants may be physically present, or they may participate by means of online communication, using chat technology rather than face-to-face speech. There are no (or few) facial cues or signals from other players to guide participation. Online chat requires writing and typing skills, whereas sociodramatic play can be arranged with spoken words and physical actions that can be viewed (e.g., pointing, an outreached hand). Sociodramatic play allows players to alter their imaginary world to something entirely different on the whim of the players, whereas most online games are constrained by a virtual play world that players opt for.

Second, it is difficult to know who is playing online in MORGs, as the real-world identity of each player is masked by the identity of the **avatar** (the game manifestation, appearance, or incarnation of the real-world player) that is acting for the player in the game world. As most MORGs are anonymous play spaces, it is often never clear who the other players really are, unless friends from the real world agree to play the game and then inform one another of their avatars in the game world. Anonymity means that it is impossible to know for sure the age, gender, or any other characteristic of players. For this reason, it is nearly impossible for researchers to know who really plays MORGs.

It is assumed that such play is the province of adolescent and young adult males, but the content of many of the games is designed to include females, and in some cases children as young as five or six. Our knowledge is also confounded by the fact that any one player might have two or more avatars in any game, so that it may seem that there are five or six MORG players when there are really only two or three.

Third, the social world of MORGs, while anonymous in some senses, is complicated by the synergy of real world and virtual world social relationships. Friends may agree to play a MORG game, where they interact through chat with other players they may or may not know in real life. In real life, players may monitor, coach, and support one another; strangers who get to know one another in the game may do the same. Friendship and related social relationships can be both real and virtual in their play world. Players must learn the circumstances where they can trust other players and what it means to get to know playmates. (Gee, 2007; Greenfield, 1984) This raises an issue of how we think about relationships that are formed online: Are online friends like pen pals of the recent past that exchanged letters via post, or are they something different, more immediate, and yet more anonymous? How should we think about social relationships that are formed virtually? (There are also legitimate concerns about predatory social actions that may transfer from the game world to the real world.)

There is an additional form of social relationship online that is not available to children who participate in real-life sociodramatic play: online social exchanges for cheat codes. Online players establish websites where they can share information about games, including short cuts, tricks, and ways to cheat. They create a virtual play community, where they can ask questions and find answers about games. There is nothing comparable to this social play community for non-virtual players.

These issues and others are raised in one of the most extensive contemporary analyses of video gaming. Gee (2007) presents 36 principles of learning, with a particular emphasis on how youth acquire literacy understandings from video games. From a social constructivist theoretical perspective, these principles call attention to how active game participants learn through social influences, game design, cultural meanings, textual content, and the symbol systems built into games. For example, games are designed to allow players to easily acquire basic information needed to play, leading to success so that players are motivated to acquire more information; there is ample practice using basic information in the game setting where it is meaningful, allowing more competent performance later on. The many "sign systems (images, words, actions, symbols, artifacts, etc.)" (p. 221) give players ways to understand the game and to follow different routes to progress in the game. Many of the principles described by Gee provide a good way to make connections between online games such as MORGs and our less technological understandings about play, including how we use the same words for both while meanings something fairly different. While his discussion is based mostly on observation of players in the teen years, the principles he describes appear to be appropriate for understanding what young players experience online.

Cognitively, players have a great deal to learn in order to play online games. They must learn how to navigate the virtual play world. They must figure out strategies for advancing and winning. They must learn all the visual signs that make the game meaningful. They must learn the rules. In other words, in online gaming, children must function with all the cognitive challenges that Piaget (1965) tells us children develop during the concrete operational stage. Beyond this, children must learn to function with the technology itself, mastering the skills needed to maneuver in a virtual world. We have no evidence yet, but some have argued that child players must acquire adaptive cognitive skills that are unfamiliar to those of us who did not grow up with technology play (Gee, 2007; Greenfield, 1984). Children need to be able to reflect about their play (metacognitive skills, being aware of how we are thinking) and to reflect about how they are using technology. (See Table 11.3.)

Emotionally, children are very motivated to engage with online games. Their friends play them. The games include content that appeals to children. The way the games are constructed

**TABLE 11.3**   Online Role Playing

| Developmental Domain | Traditional Role Play | Online Play |
| --- | --- | --- |
| Cognition | Moral and strategic thinking, metacognition (thinking about play) | Moral and strategic thinking, and technical thinking and metacognition about play and technology |
| Emotional | Expression, empathy, identity, intrinsic motivation | Expression, empathy, identity, intrinsic motivation |
| Social | Peer interaction skills, social awareness | Peer interaction skills, virtual peer interaction |
| Creativity | Imagination, play narrative | Imagination, technical expression of imagination and play narrative |
| Language | Oral communications with players, expressing play narrative | Oral and written communication with players, expressing play narrative, communicating with cheat sites |

challenges children, allowing them to build on what they know and move on to more challenging levels. Children are highly motivated when they play on computers (Lepper & Gertner, 1989). Children also may select or create their own online identities, providing them with a personally crafted sense of power or strength that they can sense only in play.

Socially, children participate in technology in some ways that are traditional. They may convene and decide what to play. They may comment on one another's participation. There may be leaders and followers; they may support players who need it and follow those who are excellent. They help their friends and undermine their enemies. They may enjoy each other's company during play, just as players often have done. Online gaming adds to this

social world, by opening the social world to non-present players, who participate in the virtual world and communicate with other players by means of chat. Players are also in the virtual world with strangers, who can be friendly or not. There are also other social supports for play, for example, online in cheat sites.

Creatively, online gaming offers a palette of opportunities for making a world according to the player's design. Players can decide what to include and what it will look like. They can decide the appearance of characters and create story lines for them. Gee (2007) points out that players build on our cultural notions of story and character as they play, so that online gaming becomes a new way to experience literacy.

In terms of language, online players must read and write to put words into the mouths of

New technology forces us to re-think the meaning of social play.

their avatars. Beyond this, they must use literacy to chat with other online players and to participate in other web-based communication about a game. Again, creating stories online involves many levels of language and literacy, as players contribute to a game's narrative.

Online gaming resembles children's role play in many ways, and we can use many of the terms we use to describe sociodramatic play, as we describe MORG play. One major difference is that online role playing is virtual in a way that sociodramatic play is not; online role playing occurs on a screen. As we think about how children are participating in online play, we need to take into account all the ways that technology adds to the demands of play. Children must communicate with the technology, in addition to communicating with other players. They must think about the technology in addition to play, in order to achieve their desired play goals. They are engaged motivationally with influences that are simultaneously present (other players, a technology platform) and virtual (other players, a virtual world of their own construction). We can use a short cut for describing online role play, saying it is like the kind of social role play that is familiar to us, but we need to remember that there are real differences in how children are engaged with technology as they play online. Those differences are unfamiliar to those of us who have not grown up with this kind of play.

## PERSPECTIVES ON VIABILITY OF CHILDREN'S MEDIA PLAY

Research on the health and development consequences of media play for young children focuses on both the potential benefits and the negative effects of misuse and overuse. A study organized by the Kaiser Foundation and the University of Texas in 2005 was among the first to examine the extent of very young children's media use (Vandewater et al., 2007). The survey included more than a thousand parents of children aged 6 months to 6 years. On a typical day, 75% of children aged 0 to 6 watched television, and 32% watched videos/DVDs for about 1 hour and 20 minutes. One fifth of 0- to 2-year-olds and more than a third of 3- to 6-year-olds have a television in their bedroom. During a typical day, 68% of the 0- to 3-year-olds watched television. Data from a nationally representative data set show that children before age 3 engage in an average of 2.2 hours a day viewing television and 3.3 hours for ages 3 to 5 years (Zimmerman, & Christakis, 2005). They found modest adverse effects of television. Very young children are growing up in a media saturated environment and use of media has become part of the fabric of their daily lives. There are many unknowns about the impact of media usage on young children's health, learning, and development, but usage appears to be increasing.

The Kaiser Foundation Report (2010) adds extensive evidence for older children and teens, showing that 8- to 18-year-olds devote an average 7 hours and 38 minutes to using entertainment media in a typical day. This increases to 10 hours and 45 minutes when multitasking is packed into those 7½ hours. This indicates that for many, media entertainment is the chief activity, surpassing time for sleep or schoolwork and keeping children indoors to engage in sedentary activity. Coupled with contemporary emphasis on high-stakes testing and loss of physical education, recess time, and free neighborhood play, the stage is set for increased levels of obesity and related health and development consequences. The heaviest media users get lower grades, with half getting Cs or lower. Black and Latino children spend far more time using entertainment media than White children—about 13 hours a day for Black and Latino children versus about 8½ hours for White children.

Dorothy and Jerome Singer (2005) examined the long studied and debated effects of electronic media on children's cognitive and moral development, concluding that the toxic effects of media violence are as real as many have believed. They argue, however, that with appropriate guidance from teachers and parents, electronic media can contribute positively to creativity, imagination, empathy, and school readiness. Pretend play with traditional play materials such as blocks, dolls, and soft toys, combined with incentives of television, computers, stories, and songs, can lead to increased imagination and the love of play. When teachers and parents become active in children's play, they can prompt the child to construct and elaborate, and thus encourage play and learning. Such scaffolding of the child's play with electronic media contributes to their learning to use media in constructive ways.

The voluminous evidence about the upsides and downsides of electronic media for children is sufficient for major professional organizations such as the National Association for the Education of Young Children to produce guidelines for teachers and parents for young children's entertainment media usage. (See Salonius-Pasternak & Gelfond, 2005 for a review of studies of positive and negative influences). The American Academy of Pediatrics (AAP) recommends that children older than 2 should watch no more than 1 to 2 hours of quality entertainment media per day, and children younger than 2 years not watch television. They also recommend that parents set consistent rules about media use. The APA 2009 Policy Statement holds that exposure to violence in media represents a significant risk to the health of children and adolescents. Media violence can contribute to aggressive behavior, desensitization to violence, fear, and other media-related health risks.

Television viewing before age 3 years can have negative effects on the subsequent cognitive development of children. A Dana Foundation briefing paper (Patoine et al., 2008) reviews cautionary flags raised by prominent neuroscientists about the long-term consequences of cognitive overload. In general, technology can be good for children's cognitive development if it is used judiciously, but, if used in a non-judicious fashion, it will shape the brain in a negative way. Judicious thinking is among the important skills developing in the frontal lobe of the brain well past the teen years and is the seat of executive function (see Chapter 3). Repeated multitasking, common to those using electronic devices, dividing the brain between two or more tasks simultaneously, has its cost both in performance and in time. Nicholas Carr's (2010) book length synthesis of recent cognitive research charts how the technologies we use can reroute neural pathways, so we become ever more adept at scanning and skimming but reduce our capacity for concentration, contemplation, and reflection. Todd Oppenheimer's (2003) earlier book, *The Flickering Mind*, paints a similar, compelling portrait of the "culture of the flickering mind," meaning a generation poised between becoming confident, creative problem solvers and becoming victims of computerization and commercialization. The rapidly emerging evidence points to technology play and work as a two-edged sword, offering unprecedented insight into the world's knowledge and pleasurable activity on the one hand and potential negative consequences for health, learning and development on the other. We need balance.

As we consider how children are being affected by technology and play, we need to remember the speed of advancing technology. New discoveries and applications of technology will probably contribute to new forms of play and new ways of participating in play. Remote access to wireless hotspots (a hotspot is a site that offers Internet access over a wireless network through a router connected to a link to an Internet service) might allow players to be more mobile; younger players with easy access to wireless hotspots through handheld devices might roam and congregate wherever they choose in order to participate in games that are

## WHAT PARENTS AND CAREGIVERS CAN DO RELATED TO NEW PLAY TECHNOLOGY

1. Consider the appropriateness of particular platforms and software for individual children, beyond ESRB ratings.

2. Be sure to balance children's play, to ensure that more sedentary technology play does not replace healthy physical play.

3. Be vigilant of the software and Internet connections on a child's play device; undesired material may pop up.

4. When children and adults share a technology device, be sure that adult materials are blocked for children.

5. Monitor the suitability of games and websites for individual players' interests and maturity levels.

6. Remember that new technology may broaden a child's social world; know both actual and virtual playmates.

7. Children may have access to friends' technology devices; keep up with emerging technology and how your children have access to it.

both proximally social and interactive online. Natural user interface (technological refinements for tactile/fingertip manipulation of images on platform screens) might become popular for play with younger children who are not yet able to read directions. Voice activated screen response, where a computer can respond to a player's verbal directions, might bring play devices to even younger children. Smaller, more powerful chips and batteries may make computer games cheaper, faster, and more available to player communities that presently have lower incidents of technology play. Play technology and play culture will be altering rapidly, as research races to describe it.

Technology is changing quickly. It is important to remember that much of what we know about technology play is based on how older players play. It is also important to remember that many of these forms of play have not been with us for long, meaning that we cannot be sure what influence they have on adults or children. New research is showing both positive benefits

and negative effects of computer play for adults. For example, gaming appears to improve probabilistic inferential thinking for adults, allowing them to think better about decision making (a metacognitive skill) (Green, Pouget, & Bavelier, 2010). Alternatively, computer gaming can be addictive and impair adults' daily living (Young, 2004). Many have concerns about possible negative influences on children's social relationships, learning, physical health, and attention span (e.g., Carr, 2010; Collins, 2009; Elkind, 1996; Fertig, 2008; Greenfield, 2009; Oppenheimer, 2003; Raley, 2008). We do not know the long-term effects of technology play on children. All we know is that the prevalence is increasing (Kaiser Family Foundation, 2010). These forms of play deserve continued scrutiny, and this chapter suggests a range of things to look for. It is difficult to imagine that this common form of play is not having significant influences on young children and their development.

Research on children's play and technology will change, too. In addition to existing studies that have used observational, interview, and printed evidence of children's play activities, new technologies will allow insight into newer forms of play. Screen image capture, where software can record the images that players generate on their computer screens, will allow us to analyze more about children's thinking, relationships, and communication in that virtual world. Eye scan devices will let us understand more about how players perceive their computer screens and attend to what is generated in that virtual setting. These technologies can be research tools that allow adult researchers to understand more about play experiences that children are growing up with, but are in many ways currently beyond adult understanding.

 ## SUMMARY

*A colleague's 3-year-old granddaughter has grown up in a family with smartphones. She has played games with her family on the smartphones that operate with digital scrolling. One day she approached a flat screen television. Apparently not liking the program that was on, she moved her hands in a sweeping motion across the screen, attempting to scroll to another program.*

Play has been supported by technology for hundreds of years, but in the past few decades we have seen how a synergy of old play forms and new play platforms has altered the world of play for adults and for children. Play that began as children manipulated and imagined with real objects or animals became play with manufactured objects; those manufactured objects were influenced by content from popular culture and media, broadcast to us by technological media such as cinema and television. Computational technology, influenced by play (such as arcade games), entered our homes and schools, where younger children become familiar with a variety of gaming platforms, such as PCs, as they play on them. Internet connections make possible all of these forms of play to younger audiences, whether players are attracted by the technology itself, the popular culture it draws on, or the social and cultural world that is represented by these new forms of play. With

faster and smaller play devices connected to the Internet, children's play is changing faster than adults can keep track of it. Adults, who are not as active in this new social and cultural play world, need to catch up with young players and their technology toys.

Although we may continue to use traditional play words to describe play on computers and the Internet, technology play itself may be significantly different from its origins in a material world. As ping-pong (with at least two players, positioned on opposite sides of a net-equipped table, holding paddles and swinging at a small white ball) differs physically and perceptually from Pong (with perhaps only one player, facing a screen, manipulating by hand a mouse or joystick used to direct a ball icon across the screen), so does Wii Ping Pong differ from both. They all are the same game, yet they are not the same. These differences become more pronounced and difficult to describe with online role-playing games, where social relationships, imaginary worlds, perceptible play objects, and story line may be described as role play, but differ in important ways from how children pretend with dolls and toy heroes. The words we use to talk about play are taking on new meanings, as children become involved in play that requires computer skills and an understanding of relationships in a technologically virtual world.

We know children are playing more with computers and devices that allow them to go online. We know that research has identified traditional aspects of play as children interact with computers; children imagine and create symbols, they relate to one another playfully, and they participate in organized games. We do not yet know whether scholarly speculations about the effects of this new technology play are true: Are children learning to think differently as they play by means of technology, possibly on higher or different levels? Are they relating to one another in new ways or thinking about play relationships differently? Are the new platforms and games children play creating a different motivational system that will alter how children view work and play? As younger children play more with new devices and become more a part of the Internet, are they changing developmentally in fundamental ways? We need research to understand what all these rapidly changing forms of play mean for children's development.

**KEY TERMS**

| | |
|---|---|
| Avatar | Platform |
| Internet | Synergy |
| Media | Technology |
| On line (or online) | Virtual |

 **STUDY QUESTIONS**

1. How does the technology of the 21st century differ from the technology of the 19th century? How do those differences make a difference in how children play, in terms of the toys they use and the content of their play?

2. What is the difference between players being consumers of media and players playing with media?

3. Think about play that occurs outside the home (or classroom). How might that play be transferred into the home (or classroom)? What are some examples from earlier eras of play that has moved from out of the home to into the home?

4. Think about play that began as activity for older people, such as adults or teens. How does that play become part of younger children's play worlds?

5. Locate a computer game (perhaps online). What connection does that game have to other media (such as movies, television, music, books), or other games (real or virtual)? What synergy can you identify? Was the game generated from the media, or did the game serve as a basis for the media?

6. What thinking skills are necessary for players of online games? What do they need to know, and how does the technology enable them to learn?

7. How is the social world of technology play different for contemporary players? How does it differ from traditional, interactive play? What new layers of social relationships are part of the online play world?

8. Use a search engine to locate one of your favorite childhood toys. Is that toy still available? What connections can you find between that toy and online play? What connections can you find with other media, such as movies or television?

9. Locate online a role-playing game for a young child. What skills must the player have to begin playing the game? What online resources support those skills? Could a child play the game without adult assistance?

10. Play a free online role playing game. How do you feel when you begin? After an hour? Do you turn to friends for assistance? How do you feel about the character/avatar that is standing in for you during the game? How do you feel when something happens to that character/avatar?

11. Interview a young child. Ask what technology play devices (e.g., platforms) she has in her home and which ones she plays with. Which ones does she no longer play with? Why? Which ones does she like now? Why? What games does she play on them?

12. Ask a child to describe what is going on while he plays an online game. Is the child telling a story? What story elements are present: character, setting, motivation, plot, and so on?

13. What play platforms were available when you were a child? Do children still play with these technology toys? What has replaced them?

14. Observe young children playing together in a classroom. What in their play is virtual and what is real? Now observe an online player. What is virtual?

 **CITED URLS**

Mr. Roger's Trolley: http://www.sears.com/shc/s/p_10153_12605_SPM103108678P

*Sesame Street*'s Elmo doll: http://store.sesamestreet.org/

Entertainment Software Rating Board (ESRB): http://www.esrb.org/ratings/ratings_guide.jsp.

Looney Tunes: http://looneytunes.kidswb.com/games

Disney Games: http://www.bing.com/shopping/search?q=disney games

*Sesame Street:* http://store.sesamestreet.org/Dept.aspx?cp=21415_21456_21465_21524

 **REFERENCES**

Anderson, G. (2000). Computers in a developmentally appropriate curriculum. *Young Children, 55*(2), 90–93.

Barks, C. (1978). Forward to *Donald Duck* (Walt Disney best comic series). New York: Abbeville Press.

Beaty, J. J., & Tucker, W. H. (1987). *The computer as a paintbrush: Creative uses for the personal computer in the preschool classroom*. Columbus, OH: Merrill.

Bers, M. U. (2008). *Blocks to robots: Learning with technology in the early childhood classroom*. New York: Teachers College Press.

Bogart, L. (2000). *Commercial culture: The media system and the public interest* (Rev. Ed.). New Brunswick, NJ: Oxford University Press.

Campbell, P. H., McGregor, G., & Nask, E. (1994). Promoting the development of young children through the use of technology. In P. L. Safford, B. Spodek, & O. Saracho (Eds.), *Early childhood special education: Yearbook in early childhood education* (Vol. 5, pp. 193–217). New York: Teachers College Press.

Carr, N. (2010). *The shallows: What the Internet is doing to our brains*. New York: W. W. Norton.

Clements, D. H. (1995). Teaching creativity with computers. *Educational Psychology Review, 7*(2), 141–161.

Clements, D. H., & Nastasi, B. K. (1993). Electronic media and early childhood education. In B. Spodek (Ed.), *Handbook of research on the education of young children* (pp. 251–275). New York: Macmillan.

Clements, D. H. & Samara, J. (2003). Young children and technology: What *does* the research say? *Young Children, 58*(6), 34–40.

Collins, A. (2009). *Rethinking education in the age of technology: The digital revolution and schooling*. New York: Teachers College Press.

Davis, S. (1987). *Say, kids! What time is it?* New York: Little Brown.

Dickinson, D. K. (1986). Cooperation, collaboration, and a computer: Integrating a computer into a first-second grade writing program. *Research in the Teaching of English, 20*, 357–378.

Edwards, C. P. (2005). *Children's play in cross-cultural perspective: A new look at the six cultures study*. Lincoln, NB: University of Nebraska (http://digitalcommons.unl.edu/famconfacpub/1).

Elkind, D. (1996). Viewpoint. Young children and technology: A cautionary note. *Young Children, 51*(6), 22–23.

Fatouros, C. (1995). Young children using computers: Planning appropriate learning experiences. *Australian Journal of Early Childhood, 20*(2), 1–6.

Fertig, R. E. (Ed.). (2008). *Handbook of research on effective electronic gaming in education* (Vol. 2. pp. 876–892). Hershey, PA: Information Science Reference.

Fisch, S. M., & Truglio, R. T. (Eds.). (2001). *"G" is for growing: Thirty years of research on Sesame Street*. Mahwah, NJ: Lawrence Erlbaum Publishers.

Frost, J. L. (2010). *A history of children's play and play environments*. New York: Routledge.

Gee, J. P. (2007). *What video games have to teach us about learning and literacy* (Rev. Ed.). New York: Macmillan.

Genishi, C., McCollum, P., & Strand, E. B. (1985). Research currents: The interactional richness of children's computer use. *Language Arts, 62*(5), 526–532.

Gentile, D. A. (Ed.), (2003). Media violence and children. Westport, CT: Praeger Publishing.

Gentile, D. A., Anderson, C. A., Yukawa, N., Saleem, M., Lim, K. M., Shibuya, A., Liau, A. K., Khoo, A., Bushman, B. J., Huesmann, L. R., & Sakamoto, A. (2009). *The effects of prosocial video games on prosocial behaviors: International evidence from correlational, longitudinal, and experimental studies. Personality and Social Psychology Bulletin, 35,* 752–763.

Green, C. S., Pouget, A., & Bavelier, D. (2010). Improved probabilistic inference as a general learning mechanism with action learning games. *Current Biology, 20*(17), 1573–1579.

Greenfield, P. M. (1984). *Mind and media: The effects of television, video games, and computers*. Cambridge, MA: Harvard University Press.

Greenfield, P. M. (2009). Technology and informal education: What is taught, what is learned. *Science, 323*(5910), 69–71.

Hamilton, B. (2007). *IT's elementary! Integrating technology in the primary grades*. Washington, DC: International Society for Technology in Education.

Harris, J., & Reifel, S. (2002). Children should be seen and heard on the Web. *Learning & Leading with Technology, 29*(7), 50–53, 59.

Haugland, S. W. (1999). What role should technology play in young children's learning? *Young Children, 54*(6), 26–31.

Haugland, S. W. (2000). What role should technology play in young children's learning? Part 2. Early childhood classrooms in the twenty-first century: Using computers to maximize learning. *Young Children, 55*(1), 12–18.

Johnson, J. (2002). *Coonskin Cap Clings to 'Crockett', Los Angeles Times*, August 23, p. A-1.

Jones, I., & Pellegrini, A. D. (1996). The effect of social relationships, writing media, and microgenetic development on first-grade students' written narratives. *American Educational Research Journal, 33*, 691–718.

Kaiser Family Foundation. (2010). *Generation M2: Media in the Lives of 8- to 18-Year-Olds*. Menlo Park, CA: Henry J. Kaiser Family Foundation. (http://www.kff.org/entmedia/mh012010pkg.cfm)

Kalliala, M. (2005). *Play culture in a changing world*. Columbus, OH: Open University Press.

Kushner, D. (2004). *Masters of doom: How two guys created an empire and transformed pop culture*. New York: Random House.

Lamb, S. & Brown, L. (2006). *Packaging girlhood: Rescuing our daughters from marketers' schemes*. New York: St. Martin's Press.

Lepper, M. R., & Gurtner, J. (1989). Children and computers: Child development and education approaching the twenty-first century. *American Psychologist, 44*, 170–178.

Muller, A. A., & Perlmutter, M. (1985). Preschool children's problem solving interactions at computers and jigsaw puzzles. *Journal of Applied Developmental Psychology*, 6, 173–186.

Oppenheimer, T. (2003). *The flickering mind: The false premise of technology in the classroom*. New York: Random House.

Papert, S. (1980). *Mindstorms: Children, computers, and powerful ideas* (1st Ed.). New York: Harper Collins.

Patoine, B., Whitman, A., & Goldberg, J. (2008). *Brain development in a hyper-tech world: Briefing Paper*. The Dana Foundation.

Ratey, J. J. (2008). *Spark: The revolutionary new science of exercise and the brain*. New York: Little, Brown.

Reifel, S. (2009). Girls' doll play in educational, virtual, ideological, and market contexts: A case analysis of controversy. *Contemporary Issues in Early Childhood*, 10(4), 343–352.

Reifel, S., & Sutterby J. (2009). Play theory and practice in contemporary classrooms. In S. Feeney, A. Galper, & C. Seefeldt (Eds.), *Continuing Issues in Early Childhood Education* (3rd ed., pp. 238–257). Upper Saddle River, NJ: Prentice Hall/Merrill.

Resnick, M. (1994). *Turtles, termites, and traffic jams: Explorations in massively parallel microworlds*. Cambridge, MA: MIT Press.

Resnick, M. (2006). Computer as paintbrush: Technology, play and the creative society. In D. Singer, R. M. Golinkoff, & K. Hirsh-Pasek (Eds.), *Play = learning: How play motivates and enhances children's cognitive and social-emotional growth* (pp. 192–208). New York: Oxford University Press.

Resnick, M., Bruckman, A., & Martin, F. (1996). Pianos not stereos: Creating computational construction kits. *Interactions*, 3(5), 40–50.

Resnick, M., Ocko, S., & Papert, S. (1988). LEGO, Logo, and design. *Children's Environments Quarterly*, 5(4), 14–18.

Salonius-Pasternak, D. E., & Gelfond, H. S. (2005). The next level of research on electronic play: Potential benefits and contextual influences for children and adolescents. *Human Technology*, 1(1), 5–22.

Shade, D. D. (1994). Computers and young children: Software types, social contexts, gender, age, and emotional responses. *Journal of Computing in Childhood Education*, 5(2), 177–209.

Singer, D. G., & Singer, J. L. (2005). *Imagination and play in the electronic age*. Cambridge, MA: Harvard University Press.

Vandewater, E. A. Rideout, V. J., Wartella, E. A., Huang, X., Lee, J. H., & Shim, M. (2007). Digital childhood: Electronic media and technology use among infants, toddlers, and preschoolers. *Pediatrics, 119*, 1006–1015.

Wang, X. C. & Ching, C. C. (2003). Social construction of computer experience in a first-grade classroom: Social processes and mediating artifacts. *Early Education and Development*, 14(3), 335–361.

Wang, X. C., & Hoot, J. L. (2006). Information and communication technology in early childhood education. *Early Education and Development*, 17(3), 317–322.

Wikipedia. (2010). Mouse (computer). http://en.wikipedia.org/wiki/Mouse_%28computing%29.

Winston, B. (1998). *Media technology an society. A history: From the telegraph to the Internet*. New York: Routledge.

Young, K. S. (2004). Internet addiction: A new clinical phenomenon and its consequences. *American Behavioral Scientist*, 48(4), 402–415.

Zimmerman, F. J., & Christakis, D. A. (2005). Children's television viewing and cognitive outcomes: A longitudinal analysis of national data. *Archives of Pediatrics and Adolescent Medicine, 159*, 619–625.

# 12 Introduction to Play Therapy

*Ultimately, what determines how children survive trauma, physically, emotionally, or psychologically, is whether the people around them . . . stand by them with love, support and encouragement.*

(Perry & Szalavitz, 2006, p. 5)

*Play Therapy is the systematic use of a theoretical model to establish an interpersonal process wherein trained play therapists use the therapeutic powers of play to help clients prevent or resolve psychosocial difficulties and achieve optimal growth and development.*

(Board of Directors of the Association for Play Therapy, 1997, p. 14)

*The play therapy room is good growing ground. (In this room) . . . the child is the most important person . . . no one tells him what to do, no one criticizes what he does, no one nags, or suggests, or goads him on, or pries into his private world, he suddenly feels that here he can unfold his wings . . . for this is his world.*

(Axline, 1947b, p. 16)

*". . . play therapy research dates back more than 45 years, providing empirical support for even the harshest of critics. There are few interventions that can claim such a lengthy research history as well as thriving body of current research."*

(Ray & Bratton, 2010, p. 3)

Principles of play therapy are informally applied by sensitive teachers whenever and wherever children play, and children benefit from the natural therapeutic powers of play during their normal, self-selected, spontaneous play. All adults who provide for or participate in children's play in either formal or informal contexts will find the material to follow of value in shaping and supporting their interest and involvement. However, play therapy for children under special stresses, e.g., trauma or abuse, is a specialized field, requiring professional training.

The belief that play is therapeutic and healing is fundamental to understanding the delicate dance among child, playthings, and therapist in the play therapy relationship. Throughout the 20th century, child developmentalists, psychologists, and other behavioral scientists recognized the therapeutic power of play for young children (Adler, 1927; Axline, 1947b; Erikson, 1950; Freud, 1928, 1946, 1961, 1965; Kottman, 2001, 2003; Landreth, 1991, 2001; O'Connor, 2000; Rogers, 1942; Schaefer, 1993; Webb, 1999). Play therapy is now a rapidly growing and respected profession, applicable to a wide range of children's problems. Establishment of the Association for Play Therapy (APT) in 1982 marked play therapy's acceptance as a specialized field within the mental health profession. In 1992 *the International Journal of Play Therapy* was launched to promote and disseminate play therapy research. In 2008 the APT reported more than 5,600 members, representing 27 nations. Credentialed play therapists are licensed or certified, with master's degrees or higher and with substantial clinical and play therapy experience. In 2009, the

University of North Texas was designated the first Approved Center for Play Therapy Education.

The growing interest in play therapy coincided with the acceleration of fragmented parenting, divorce, school and neighborhood violence, media violence, child abuse, high-stakes testing, and drug abuse during the latter quarter of the 20th century (Frost, 1986, 2010). These and other factors, including natural disasters such as earthquakes, tsunamis and hurricanes, accidental injuries, war, genocide, and resulting physical, mental, and emotional disabilities, create an ever-growing need for therapeutic intervention (Frost, 2005a). *Lest one assumes that knowledge of play therapy is important or relevant only for professional therapists, bear in mind that play by its very nature is therapeutic. Whenever and wherever children play, they are reaping its therapeutic benefits. Consequently, whenever adults make provisions for developmentally appropriate play environments, provide time for children's play, and support their play through sensitive interactions, play is reaping its natural therapeutic benefits. The all-too-frequent scenario of teachers sitting at a table, discussing non-play related matters during outdoor play does not result in deeper understanding of play and its meanings, nor does it offer clues for interacting with children during play. In order to do this, teachers must observe play carefully, listen to children, interact about play on occasion, and get involved when the need is clear.*

Principles of play therapy can serve both as a specialized process for helping alleviate the consequences of trauma and as a guide for parents, teachers, and other significant adults for preventing or healing children's emotional trauma. Psychoanalysis should be conducted only by highly skilled professional therapists. Untrained parents, teachers, and other adults should not attempt to conduct formal play therapy with disturbed or traumatized children.

Scientists have now demonstrated that extreme stress or trauma floods the brain with neurochemicals, which over time can change the nature of the brain, sometimes permanently (Begley, 1996, 1997, 2007; Frost, 1998; Shore, 1997; Bronson, 2009; Amen, 2010; see also Chapter 3). Prolonged stress, neglect, or abuse disrupt **bonding** between child and caregivers (DeAngelis, 1997), damage memory and learning, and negatively impact the functioning of affect, empathy, and emotions (Lowenthal, 1999; Nash, 1997; Neuberger, 1997: Bronson, 2009).

In the formal sense, play therapy is a supportive relationship between a child and a therapist who allows the child to play out or express her feelings and emotions in a context of supportive play materials and positive relationships. Play is the child's natural medium of expression. In play therapy the child plays out her feelings and problems just as in certain therapeutic contexts, adults talk out or express themselves through language (Axline, 1949). Play therapy can be *directive*, in which the therapist guides and interprets, or it may be *nondirective*, in which responsibility and direction are left to the child. Play therapy may also be individual (i.e., between a therapist and a child in a play setting), or it may be in a group, in which a child plays with other children and must consider the reactions and feelings of others in the group. Children may not fully understand the source of their problems leading to play therapy and may not have the language to express problems, frustrations, hurts, or abuses. Play is children's language and has therapeutic powers that allow children to play out their problems and, potentially, to heal.

Play is the major therapeutic approach for individual and group therapy with children for several reasons:

- Play is the child's natural medium for self-expression, experimentation, and learning.
- The child can readily relate to toys and play out concerns with them because she feels at home in a play setting.
- Play facilitates the child's communication and expression.
- Play allows for a cathartic release of feelings and frustrations.

- Experiencing play is renewing, wholesome, and constructive in the child's life.

- Observing the child at play allows the adult therapist to understand the child's world.

- The therapist can more readily relate to the child through play activities than through verbal discussion. (Schaefer, 1985, pp. 106–107)

The primary focus in this chapter is on the origins, development, and approaches of client-centered or child-centered play therapy, with lesser emphasis on the more structured approaches. How did we arrive at a child-centered approach to therapy for children? How has play therapy been used to treat maladjusted children? What is the appropriate context and process for play therapy? How successful is play therapy? This chapter introduces play therapy by tracing its history across various approaches, theorists, and practitioners; explaining how play acts as a therapeutic agent; describing the nature and importance of play therapy; and reviewing research on effectiveness of play therapy.

## HISTORY AND THEORIES OF PLAY THERAPY

### Psychoanalysis: Roots of Play Therapy

The following brief discussion introduces a sampling of the rudimentary elements of psychoanalysis. Traditional psychoanalysis per se was not conducted in a play setting. However, play therapy has foundations in psychoanalysis, and modern approaches to play therapy, especially structured approaches, still rely on psychoanalytic traditions.

**Sigmund Freud**  Modern play therapy is rooted in the psychoanalytical method pioneered by Sigmund Freud and associates during the early 1900s. Although Freud is widely

credited with founding psychotherapy, the approach was developed and refined by a number of scientists. Freud (1938, p. 933) himself stated in a public lecture that "it was not I who brought psychoanalysis into existence," crediting Josef Breuer for doing so while Freud was still a student. However, Freud's associates declared that Breuer's "cathartic procedure" was a mere preliminary to psychoanalysis that began when Freud rejected the hypnotic technique (some people cannot be hypnotized) and introduced free association.

Freud's repression technique depended on the expression of experiences that could be observed by the therapist during analysis. Freud traced back the morbid symptoms of neurotic people to sources in their life history by uncovering unconscious experiences and explaining transference and resistance demonstrated by the patient.

**Transference** refers to attitudes transferred by the client to the therapist that were originally transferred to the parent or other significant person. In transference, the patient perceives the therapist as the representative of his original repressed reactions. The patient creates, in relationship to the therapist, new editions of early conflicts during which the patient behaves as he originally behaved.

**Resistance** is the defensive striving against painful memories or experiences that can lead to forgetting and keeping experiences repressed and out of consciousness. It is the unconscious process of rejecting or attempting to discard unwelcome impulses or unconscious neuroses.

The basic concepts underlying Freudian psychoanalysis are broad and complex, some requiring a book in themselves for explanation. The unconscious is that highly active self within us of which we are essentially unaware. The **id**, the **ego**, and the **superego** can be broadly understood as, respectively, the unconscious, the conscious, and the conscience functions of the self. Freud's **Oedipus complex** refers to the feelings surrounding the natural impulse of children to crave exclusive love, usually from the parent of the opposite sex (Freud, 1946, pp. v, vi).

Freud attempted to explain and confirm his discoveries by observation and analysis of very young children, focusing on infantile sexuality, which he believed was the ultimate source of neurotic symptoms. He later developed techniques for interpreting dreams, integrated dream interpretation into his practice of psychoanalysis, and even conducted an analysis of his own dreams that "led me through all the happenings of my childhood years" (1938, p. 942). Jung (1954, pp. 23–24) later declared that Freud's interpretation of dreams was the decisive step that made modern psychotherapy a method of individual treatment.

**Carl Jung**   By 1911, psychoanalysis was championed and carried out in several countries. In 1908, the first private congress of psychoanalysts was held, with Sigmund Freud presiding. In 1909, Freud and Carl Jung, a Swiss psychiatrist, were invited to North America by Clark University president Stanley Hall to give lectures at that institution. Freud soon transferred leadership of the congress of psychoanalysts to Jung, and the International Psychoanalytic Association was formed in 1910, with Jung the elected president, and the first American group was formed as the New York Psychoanalytic Society. By this time Freud had become disappointed with Jung's leadership and believed that the theories of both Jung and Alfred Adler, another rising star in psychoanalysis, were rife with contradictions and misconceptions. Freud (1938) stated, "Any analysis carried out in accordance with the rules [Freud's rules] . . . repudiates the new interpretations of Adler's and Jung's systems" (p. 976).

Because individuality is unique and unpredictable, Jung (1954) proposed that the therapist must abandon preconceptions about psychotherapy and engage in a dialectical procedure. In such, the therapist is no longer the agent of treatment but a fellow participant in the therapeutic process, entering into the relationship as both questioner and answerer. He is no longer the superior or judge as in traditional psychotherapy but a fellow participant who is as deeply involved as the patient.

## Psychoanalytic Play Therapy

Freud was not credited with developing play therapy for children, but his description of work with "Little Hans and The Rat Man" (Freud, 1909/1955) was the first published case describing a psychological approach to working with a child. He believed that play has a cathartic effect, allowing children to purge themselves of negative feelings associated with traumatic events. Play rids the child of the constraints and sanctions of reality and provides a sanctuary for venting unacceptable or aggressive impulses. In play, the child can assume the role of the punisher and transfer negative feelings to a substitute object (doll, puppet) or person (sibling, classmate).

Hermine Hug-Hellmuth (1921) was among the first therapists to propose that play is central in child analysis and to use play materials for play expression, but Melanie Klein (1932) and Anna Freud (1946) built on the psychoanalytic tradition to construct approaches to play therapy. Both continued the tradition of seeking to uncover past experiences of the child and strengthening the ego.

**Melanie Klein**   Melanie Klein (1932) gained access to the minds of young children and developed play therapy procedures by applying Freud's findings and procedures. She concluded that the criteria of psychoanalysis for adults could be applied to children and lead to the same results. However, for children she substituted play for Freud's free verbal association. She believed that children suffer from more acute degrees of anxiety than adults do, so it is important to establish therapy quickly and gain access to their anxieties and guilt as early as possible. To Klein, children live through and work out their anxieties and phobias when the therapist treats those anxieties and phobias as transference situations (making connections between original experiences or fantasized ones and the actual situation). In response to continued interpretation by the therapist of the meaning of a child's play, the scope of play widens and the child's inhibitions are reduced.

Through uncovering the child's infantile experiences, Klein's analysis ostensibly corrects "errors of development" (1932, p. 18) and resolves fixations. She saw symbolic sexual meanings, frequently involving sexual behaviors of the mother or father, in virtually all play episodes and interpreted these for the child.

Ruth (4 years) exhibited excessive reliance on her mother, disliked strangers, and could not make friends with children—all leading to anxiety attacks and other neurotic symptoms. Ruth drew a picture of a tumbler with several small round balls inside and a lid on top. She stated that the lid was to keep the balls from rolling out. She had previously shut a purse and a bag tightly to keep items from falling out.

The therapist [Klein] immediately sought to bring about a positive transference by interpreting these actions. She explained (interpreted) to Ruth that the balls in the tumbler and the items in the purse and bag "all meant children in her Mummy's inside, and that she (Ruth) wanted to keep them safely shut up so as not to have any more brothers and sisters." Whereupon [Klein wrote], "The effect of my interpretation was astonishing. For the first time Ruth turned her attention to me and began to play in a different, less constrained, way" (Klein, 1932, pp. 26–27).

Despite her apparent excessive reliance on the significance of infantile sexual anxieties, Klein advanced the practice of play therapy well beyond its earlier state. Her therapy setting was simple, containing a low table holding a number of small, simple toys—carts, trains, animals, bricks and houses, carriages, little wooden men and women, paper, scissors, and pencils. The child soon began to play freely with these toys, offering the therapist insight into her complexes by the manner of play and

attitude toward the toys. Interpretation followed promptly during the first session, carrying the negative transference back to its roots in reality, reducing the child's resistance, and eventually resulting in diminished anxieties.

**Anna Freud**    Anna Freud, a contemporary of Klein's and Sigmund's daughter, disagreed with Klein on several major points regarding play therapy. She maintained that Klein's play method was almost indispensable with small children who are not capable of verbal self-expression or free association as adults are in psychotherapy (Freud, 1946). But whereas Klein saw underlying symbolic meanings in virtually all play, Anna Freud believed that instead of a particular play activity being invested with symbolic meaning, there may be a simple, harmless explanation. For example, the child who shuts a bag or purse tightly is not necessarily symbolically shutting up her mother's womb to ensure she will have no new brothers or sisters but may merely be playing out some previous experience with such objects.

Unlike Klein, who followed the procedures of adult analysis strictly, Anna Freud sought to develop positive emotional relationships and positive transference from the child to the therapist and to avoid negative relationships and negative transference. She believed that a child only believes a loved person. Negative impulses or transference toward the therapist should be dealt with promptly, for the really fruitful work takes place in the context of positive attachments and transference.

In spite of the difficulties in child therapy, Anna Freud identified several advantages of child therapy over adult therapy. The neuroses of the child must be traced only a short distance in time to arrive at normal behavior; in child therapy one deals with living, usually accessible people; and the child's needs are simpler and easier to fulfill or oversee because the therapist can deal with the child's actual environment rather than relying on an adult's memories of times long past.

Anna Freud extended her knowledge of play therapy by observing children's play and interviewing their parents. She used play and art to form alliances with children, then proceeded to interpret the child's unconscious motivations. Having developed positive emotional relations with a child (the "wooing period"), she encouraged the child to verbalize fantasies and daydreams or to sit quietly and "see pictures." She also pioneered storytelling in the therapeutic setting. As the child verbalized, she helped her understand her feelings, and the emphasis shifted from play to verbal interaction. Such informal approaches hold potential for teacher and positive parent interaction with children during play. Structured approaches to play therapy, on the other hand, should be employed by trained therapists.

**Structured Play Therapy**   Several **structured play therapy** approaches grew out of the psychoanalytic school. The basic tenets of psychotherapy were retained, but major differences in therapeutic procedures emerged. In general, the structuralists assumed the major role in therapy, believing the therapist is more aware, than the child, of the child's needs. Consequently, the therapist designs the activity, selects the medium, and makes the rules.

**David Levy**   During the 1930s, David Levy (1939) formulated **release therapy**, a structured approach for children ages 2 to 10. In release therapy, Levy determined the cause of a child's difficulty by studying his case history, then controlled the play by providing selected toys expected to assist in working out the child's problem. If, for example, the child was experiencing nightmares about monsters, the therapist provided toy monsters for play. The therapist then asks questions about the child's feelings and thoughts and observes the child's verbal and nonverbal behaviors during play. At times, the therapist plays with the child or even models play for the child.

Three forms of release therapy were developed: (1) release of aggressive behaviors by throwing objects or bursting balloons; (2) release of feelings in a common setting that would simulate sibling rivalry, such as presenting a baby doll at a mother's breast; and (3) release of feelings by presenting in play the child's stressful experiences.

An example of Levy's release therapy is the case of a 2-year-old girl who suffered from night terrors resulting from a fish merchant holding her up to see a fish in his display. A clay fish was introduced during therapy, and the therapist asked the child why she was afraid of the fish. The child replied that the fish would go "in here," pointing to her eye, ears, and vagina. The fish was introduced in various parts of a 10-session play therapy experience in which the chief process was facilitating the child's own types of play. Fear of the fish left after the third or fourth session, and improvement was judged to be maintained 7 months later (Levy, 1939, p. 720).

**Gove Hambridge**   Structured play therapy was further developed by Gove Hambridge (1955). He developed a thorough history of the child from parents and observations of the child at play, developed hypotheses about the sources of her stress, then recreated the stressful situation through dramatic play. He disapproved of the common practice of flooding, or pushing the child to release strong, massive negative feelings. Rather, he started slowly with less threatening materials and progressed to more threatening materials. He stressed that parents should be assisted in learning to help structure the child's recovery process.

Hambridge advocated the development of strong positive supportive relationships between the therapist and the child. He identified repetition as the most important factor in structured or release therapy. Repetition of a stressful event allows release of tension and assists the child in assimilating and mastering stressful feelings and experiences. This basic repetition, **catharsis**, or emotional purging, approach, was not unique to 20th-century therapists but was discovered by Josef Breuer more than a century ago when found to be effective with mental patients (Schaefer, 1985, p. 100). A major advantage of release therapy is that it increases specificity of treatment, saving hours of time by avoiding diffuse and haphazard therapy (Schaefer, 1985).

## Nondirective Therapy

**Carl Rogers**    The work of relationship therapists (Allen, 1942; Taft, 1933) was synthesized and expanded by Carl Rogers (1942) as *non-directive therapy,* later called **client-centered therapy** (Rogers, 1951). Rogers's and Virginia Axline's works were influential in modifying relationship play therapy (Moustakas, 1953) and establishing group play therapy (Ginott, 1961) and **child-centered play therapy** (Landreth, 1991; Moustakas, 1953).

According to Rogers (1951), therapy is "a process, a thing-in-itself, an experience, a relationship, a dynamic . . . therapy is the essence of life" (pp. ix, x). Such descriptive conceptual underpinnings are light-years apart from the structured conceptions of psychoanalysis and place virtually unlimited faith in the striving of all individuals to seek **self-actualization**, or self-fulfillment—to become the best they can become (Rogers, 1962). The emphasis is on the well person rather than the sick person.

Rogers broke with the tradition of promoting therapy primarily for adults and adolescents. He recognized that Axline's play therapy for problem children was effective and that client-centered play therapy is appropriate for a wide variety of people, problems, and contexts, including the military, industry, and schools.

According to Rogers, the client-centered therapist should give up subtle directiveness and concentrate on understanding the client. If the therapist can help the client understand the way the client seems to himself, he can do the rest. The therapist must give up his preoccupations with professional evaluations, diagnoses, and prognoses and concentrate on one purpose:

help the client understand and accept conscious attitudes held at that moment while exploring the dangerous areas denied to consciousness.

The setting for therapy must be one of safety and acceptance in which the client is free to explore without guilt the hostile meanings and purposes of his behavior. The client is able to do this because another person, the therapist, has adopted his frame of reference and perceives his problems with acceptance and respect. The client must come to be loved—that is, deeply understood and accepted. Such outcomes do not depend merely on verbal exchange but on the experiences in the relationship. Unlike psychotherapists, Rogers contended that transference attitudes of the client toward the counselor occur only in a small percentage of cases. In most cases, attitudes toward the counselor reflect reality rather than the unconscious.

**Virginia Axline**    Axline's nondirective approach—and other child-centered approaches to be discussed—have much to offer teachers and all those who engage with children during play. Virginia Axline (1947b) studied with Carl Rogers and worked with him in exploring the possibilities of nondirective therapy. She based her nondirective counseling technique on Rogers's work, proposing, as he had, that therapy principles for adults (e.g., the individual's striving for growth and self-realization) could be applied to play therapy for children (p. 27). She believed that "[a] play experience is therapeutic because it provides a secure relationship between the child and the adult, so that the child has the freedom and room to state himself in his own terms, exactly as he is at that moment in his own way and in his own time" (p. 68). The child expresses herself naturally through play, and a child playing out during therapy is equivalent to the adult's talking out (p. 9). The relatively immature child may not have the words, as do adults, for expressing her deeper conscious or unconscious conflicts. Such expression is possible, however, through play.

Axline's nondirective therapy is based on the assumption that the individual has within herself the ability to solve her own problems and the drive to mature behavior. The therapist must accept the child completely, without pressure to change, to be herself and to chart her own course. Play allows the child to play out accumulated feelings of anxiety, aggression, frustration, and fear. By so doing, she learns to abandon or control such impulses, to make her own decisions, and to become more mature.

The therapist must see the child as the most important person in the therapeutic process. There are no diagnostic interviews and few interpretations. There is no criticism, nagging, directing, or prying into the child's private world. The past is history. The child is allowed to express herself fully. The therapist is sensitive to the child's feelings and reflects them back to her in a way that aids understanding. The therapist conveys the attitude that she is understanding and accepting of her at all times. Consequently, the child digs deeper into her inner world to bring out her real self and begins to direct her own growth. She is psychologically free.

## Relationship and Child-Centered Play Therapy

The field of play therapy grew dramatically over the 20th century, and the sheer number of contributors and approaches defies discussing each within the scope of this work (see Table 12.1). Presently, every approach previously discussed—psychoanalysis, structured, nondirective, client centered—and more, is alive at the beginning of the 21st century and practiced in a wide range of contexts. The approach chosen for elaboration here is nondirective, or child-centered, play therapy as developed by Rogers (1942, 1951), Axline (1950), Moustakas (1953),

**TABLE 12.1**   Approaches to Play Therapy

| Approaches | Techniques | Contexts |
|---|---|---|
| Psychoanalytic | Puppets | Playrooms |
| Release | Sand play | Hospitals |
| Relationship | Costume play | Schools |
| Nondirective | Board games | Psychiatric settings |
| Filial | Storytelling | University laboratories |
| Group | Water play | Homes |
| Structured | Block play | |
| Child centered | Role play | |
| Ecosystem | Telephone play | |
| Existential | Mud and clay | |
| Gestalt | Drawing | |
| Developmental | Painting | |
| Jungian | Squiggle drawing | |
| Adlerian | Computer play | |
| Cognitive-behavioral | | |
| Cognitive-developmental | | |
| Theraplay | | |
| Eclectic | | |

Ginott (1961); Landreth (1991, 2002); Cochran, 2010).

Among these authorities on nondirective therapy, all devoted to child-centeredness in the therapeutic process, certain commonalities and differences in theoretical premises and therapy practices are evident. Each theorist borrowed heavily from other prominent theorists and modified his or her views through extensive practice. The theoretical constructs of Rogers were decidedly influential in subsequent child-centered approaches. He, more than any therapist in the group, is responsible for shifting the focus of therapy from the therapist to the client and highlighting the self-worth of the individual. His nondirective counseling is more a philosophy of human capacities than a set of techniques. The power for growth lies within the client.

Axline offered perhaps the clearest, simplest, yet most profound approach to play therapy for children. Her techniques of play therapy were built from Rogers's principles of self-realization and self-direction. Collectively, Rogers and Axline are preeminent scholars and visionaries in shifting focus from the therapist to the child.

Haim Ginott (1961), Clark Moustakas (1953), and Garry Landreth (2002) were influenced by Rogers and Axline and were also principal figures in establishing contemporary nondirective or child-centered play therapy.

Ginott gave credit to his "great teacher" Virginia Axline in combining relationship principles with psychotherapy to show that group therapy as well as individual therapy can benefit children and that no one method is effective with all persons. Moustakas (1953, 1998) became interested in play therapy from reading the works of Rogers and Axline. He is credited with framing major portions of the theory and technique used in modern play therapy (James, 1997, p. 140). Landreth was influenced by the work of Axline, Ginott, and Moustakas as well as that of Rogers. Yet he gradually strengthened the theoretical and research bases for his approach and made it uniquely his own. By the turn of the 21st century, the Center for Play Therapy that Landreth developed at the University of North Texas was the largest such center in the world, including programs for training master's and doctoral students and housing classroom facilities for workshops and seminars, an extensive collection of play therapy materials (Landreth, Hohmeyer, Bratton, & Kale, 1995; Baggerly, et al, 2010), and playrooms for therapy sessions with children.

 ## CONDUCTING PLAY THERAPY

### Setting Up the Playroom

The child-centered play therapist works from the position that play is the language of the child and toys are the child's words. The playroom is a special place used for one specific purpose—play therapy—and it is carefully arranged with toys or play materials to accommodate a range of children's play. Different therapists have different views about which play materials to provide and why they are important. Consequently, playrooms differ according to the theoretical views of the therapist and the nature of the child's needs. Special arrangements may be needed for children who are abused, hospitalized, or blind or who have other types of disabilities. The play materials need not be manufactured or expensive, for children can use simple raw materials to represent almost anything. Children's symbolic powers are usually quite remarkable.

Generally, for a given child, the playroom should always be the same when she enters. It should be carefully planned, prepared, cleaned, organized, restocked with disposable materials, and predictable after the first visit. The size of the room varies with availability in different settings, but typically the desired size is about 12 to 14 feet by 14 to 16 feet, or about 150 to 250 square feet. Although specially designed playrooms are desirable, effective therapy can be conducted in a child's hospital room, using play materials carried in by the therapist, or in an equipped section of an unused room (e.g., office, classroom, workroom).

Materials, too, differ with the views of the therapist. Typical materials and arrangement include a sink with cold water; a child-sized bathroom opening to the therapy room; cabinets, counter (child size), and shelves for storing materials; clear plastic containers for toys; a child-size table and chairs; dress-up clothes; multiethnic dolls; a doctor's bag; one or more doll- or playhouses; playhouse materials; building blocks; clay; toy animals; toy soldiers and army equipment; a dart gun that shoots (safe) rubber darts and a target; rubber knife; small cars, trucks, and airplanes; a sandbox with sand tools; finger paints and other art materials; puppets and a stage; a broom and mop; and a table and easel with drawing and painting supplies. For conducting research and observation, parent viewing, or videotaping for training programs, an observation room with one-way mirror and remote speakers are needed. The room should be well lit, safe, and easily cleaned.

Ginott (1961) groups the desired materials for a playroom, with each category containing multiple play materials: climbing equipment, dollhouse, toy animals, transportation toys, water play, easel painting and water coloring, finger painting, clay play, block play, puppets, aggressive toys, housekeeping equipment, and sand. Landreth (1991) includes toys not mentioned earlier: a pacifier and plastic nursing bottle; pots, pans, and dishes; an all-terrain vehicle for riding; a pounding bench and hammer; musical instruments; a "Bobo bag" (stuffed bag) for hitting; handcuffs; a toy machine gun; blunt scissors; construction paper; and Tinkertoys.

Play materials should be developmentally appropriate and usable in independent or solitary play. Landreth (1991, p. 116) suggests several criteria for selection. Toys and play materials should engage the child's interest; facilitate creative expression, emotional expression, and exploratory play; allow success without prescribed structure and verbalization; allow for noncommittal play; and be sturdily

constructed. In addition, the materials and the child–therapist relationship should remain stable (Moustakas, 1953). That is, the playthings should always be arranged the same way when the child enters the room, and the therapist's attitudes must remain consistent. In the playroom, the child is the guide. She makes the changes.

## Beginning Play Therapy

**Axline's eight basic play principles** (1947b) underlie modern child-centered play therapy and are perhaps the best known and most frequently referenced. They follow in revised form:

- The therapist quickly establishes a warm, friendly relationship.
- The therapist accepts the child exactly as she is.
- The therapist creates a permissive relationship in which the child is free to express her feelings completely.
- The therapist recognizes and reflects back the child's feelings to help her understand her behavior.
- The therapist respects the child's ability to solve her own problems. Responsibility for decisions and change is left to the child.
- The therapist does not attempt to direct the child's actions or conversation. The child leads the way; the therapist follows.
- The therapist does not attempt to hurry therapy. It is a gradual process.
- The therapist sets only the limitations necessary to help the child accept responsibility in the relationship.

Although individual therapists have unique approaches, Axline's basic principles remain the primary guides for child-centered play therapy. Her 1964 book, *Dibs in Search of Self*, is a detailed account of her methods.

The initial contact with the child is of great importance to the success of therapy. Rapport and structure must be established. This is done through words and through building relationships between the child and the therapist.

## Establishing Rapport

The playroom is established, the therapist is on hand, and the child arrives. The initial contact is a time for communicating warmth and friendliness. The therapist greets the child, showing a genuine interest in him. He is the most important person in the room. After the warmup, the therapist invites the child to go to the playroom with her and see all the toys. During this time, the therapist must accept the child exactly as he is, and her language should reflect the child's feelings (Axline, 1947b, pp. 77–78). This is not a time to be dominated by the parent relating the child's history, the therapist directing her attention to the mother. This is the child's time.

Following a brief introduction, the therapist says to the child, "We can go to the playroom now. Your mother will wait here so she will be here when we come back from the playroom" (Landreth, 1991, p. 159). "It is especially important at this time that the child himself decides whether or not he wishes to come to the playroom. Whatever decision the child makes is accepted by the therapist" (Moustakas, 1953, p. 13). Although most children readily go to the playroom, if the child is reluctant, the mother may be invited to walk to the playroom with them and separate at the door or as soon into the session as the therapist judges appropriate.

## Structuring the Playroom Experience

**Structuring** is the process therapists use to convey to the child the special nature of the therapeutic relationship. The child and the therapist enter the playroom, and the therapist structures the situation verbally:

> "You may play with any of the toys in here any way that you want to, Jean. There are paints, clay, finger paints, puppets." (Axline, 1947b, p. 88)

Moustakas (1953) structures the experience this way:

> "You may use these [toys] in any way that you want," "It can be anything you want it to be," "I can't decide that for you; the important thing is that you decide for yourself what you want to do," "You want me to do that for you Janey, but here you do things for yourself." (p. 14)

Landreth (1991, p.162) points out that there are boundaries on freedom in the playroom and the therapist should not communicate that the child can play "any way you want." This could result in withdrawal of approval for play (e.g., being hit with a toy or shot with a dart gun) that threatens the safety of the child or the therapist. He suggests instead saying, for example, "Melissa, this is our playroom, and this is a place where you can play with the toys in a lot of the ways you would like to."

As soon as the child is introduced to the playroom, the therapist sits on a chair (with rollers to facilitate movement) and directs her full attention to the child. The whole body is oriented toward the child as the therapist conveys interest, involvement, and total absorption in the child (see the videotape by Landreth, 1998).

## The Playroom Relationship

Following the initial steps of establishing rapport, introducing the child to the playroom, and structuring the relationship, several additional factors influence success in the playroom relationship: (a) accepting the child as she is; (b) making the child safe and comfortable; (c) establishing permissiveness within limits; (d) recognizing and reflecting the child's feelings; (e) maintaining a listening/supportive attitude; (f) facilitating emotional expression; (g) facilitating decision making, responsibility, and control. The overall behaviors and language of the therapist convey these principles of freedom, respect, and responsibility.

The **therapy hour** (often 45 minutes) is a time for children to use the materials in the playroom as they wish, within limits. As the child initially explores the materials in the playroom, the therapist conveys permissiveness and support through her whole being—tone of voice, facial expressions, and actions. The child is given the freedom to play or not to play, to select play materials and to choose how she will play. Even silence is respected. For the reluctant child, the therapist might say, "It's sort of hard to get started. You don't know just what you would like to do. Or maybe you would rather just sit here and not do anything?" (Axline, 1947b, p. 93).

Pressuring the child to talk or play ignores his feelings, removes a degree of freedom, and obviates his role in making decisions. Every behavior, even reluctance to talk or to play, says something about the child.

Therapy cannot be hurried. Taking time for the child to feel comfortable with the playroom and the therapist helps reduce anxiety and allows the child to feel comfortable and supported.

> *Angela:* (stands right in front of therapist, twisting hands, looking at therapist, and then looks at toys on shelf)
>
> *Therapist:* I see you're looking at the toys over there. (pause)
>
> *Angela:* (looks at observation mirror, sees herself and grins)
>
> *Therapist:* And you saw yourself in the mirror there. (pause) I guess sometimes, maybe . . . it's just hard to decide what to do first (pause). (Landreth, 1991, p. 166).

In a similar manner, the therapist continues to respond to the child's actions in a friendly, accepting, and supporting way. Eventually, emotional barriers come down, and the child begins to communicate verbally with the therapist, explore the playroom, and play. The therapist must remember that the child's behavior at any given time is symbolic of the child's feelings. When the child feels safe and secure with the therapist and the playroom, she may begin

to express and explore, through play, emotionally or physically traumatic experiences. Play itself, not the therapist, is the primary therapeutic vehicle. The therapist is a facilitator.

## Establishing Limits

Important as freedom is, limits are necessary for learning decision making, self control, and responsibility. Most prominent play therapists (Axline, 1947b; Bixler, 1949; Ginott, 1961; Glasser, 1975; James, 1997; Klein, 1955; Kottman, 2001, 2003; Landreth, 1991, 2002; Moustakas, 1953; O'Connor, 2000; Cochran, 2010) advocate *establishing limits.* Some advocate more clearly defined restrictions than others, but all see limits as essential to the therapeutic process and to learning to act responsibly.

No one is truly free without certain limitations. However, limits should be accompanied by trust and confidence. James (1997, p. 22) explains: Her 7-year-old son, Hunt, was at a friend's house for a sleepover. A tree branch scratching against a window frightened his young friend, and Hunt explained, "in our house, you don't ever have to be afraid. Even if a lion comes to the door, my mom would stop it." Such trust helps the child cope with scary situations.

Confidence in the therapist and the safety of the playroom is established by the limits that protect the sanctity of the playroom and make it safe. Limits are established as the need arises and are designed to:

1. Enhance the child's feeling of security.
2. Prevent the destruction or loss of property.
3. Protect the physical safety of the child and the therapist.
4. Promote consistent behavior.
5. Facilitate the development of self-control, responsibility, and decision making.
6. Prevent harm to the child.
7. Establish time parameters for the therapy session.

8. Define the boundaries of the therapy relationship and

9. Establish both psychological and physical limits.

Limits help form secure relationships and link them to reality. The therapist must attend to certain basic principles (limitations) in therapeutic practice to establish rapport and support the child's development. Similarly, the child needs limits to guide her emotional growth and to ensure her physical safety. Reasonable limits are essential for healthy growth. Possible alternatives are guilt, anxiety, irresponsibility, barriers in relationships, and threatened health and safety.

## Progress in Play Therapy

The therapist has prepared the playroom and materials; the relationship between the child and the therapist has been initiated; the child has been introduced to the playroom; the relationship in the playroom has been structured; limitations are being established. The therapist and child settle in for a series of playroom interactions that gradually free the child to sort out negative feelings, to feel safe, to accept herself as a person of worth, to learn to trust the therapist, and to establish a caring, respectful, and responsible relationship. The successful therapeutic process results in growth in the child, the therapist, and the relationship.

In nondirective therapy, toys are used to develop the relationship between child and therapist and to allow the child to play out her fears and conflicts. There is no pattern of diagnosis or tracing the origins of the child's phobias or conflicts. The successful conclusion of therapy is the child gaining confidence to "go ahead on [her] own" and to be comfortable in expressing her feelings openly and honestly (Axline, 1947b).

The success of play therapy is directly related to the degree to which the therapist is able to establish an atmosphere of safety and acceptance in the child's mind. The learning is not so much cognitive as it is a "developing experiential, intuitive learning about self that occurs over the course of the therapeutic experience" (Landreth, 1991, p. 82). Landreth identifies

The play therapy room may take many forms to accommodate the play needs of children and the perspectives of therapists.

Group therapy is effective for helping children cope during and after natural disasters such as earthquakes and hurricanes.

expected outcomes of the therapeutic experience: Children learn self-control, responsible freedom of expression, respect for self, ability to control their feelings, responsibility for self, creativity and resourcefulness in confronting problems, self-direction, acceptance of self, and responsibility for choices.

The climate created by the therapist and the unconditional acceptance and support provided by the therapist make these changes possible. They are primarily accomplished within the child, by the child, and do not depend on analysis or instruction. Child-centered play therapy is an experience to be lived, not a set of principles to be taught and learned.

## SETTINGS AND APPLICATIONS

Our focus has been on play therapy in a prepared playroom with one therapist and one child. However, play therapy can be used effectively in many other settings and applications. Only a selected few are discussed here.

### Group Play Therapy

Group play therapy is growing in popularity. The basic concepts in Ginott's (1961) group approach are derived from psychoanalytical theory. He believed that group therapy applies equally well to individual therapy, and his procedures are applicable to the needs of individual children.

Initially, the presence of two or three other children of her age group may help allay a child's anxiety about going to the play therapy room with an adult therapist. In the group playroom, the individual child may gain comfort in identifying with other children. There are no group goals. Each child has the freedom to engage in individual or group play experiences, and there are two media for catharsis: play and verbalization. Each child learns from the other children and from both giving and receiving. Ginott (1961) illustrates:

> Barbara, age 8, had not seen her father in two years. She missed him keenly. During one of the therapy sessions, while handling a gun, she hurt her finger. It was a minor injury, but she reacted with much emotion. She cried bitterly and pleaded with the therapist.
>
> *Barbara:*    Please let me go. My finger hurts, and I need my mother.
>
> *Therapist:*  It's not only your finger that hurts. Something hurts inside.
>
> *Barbara:*    Yes.
>
> *Therapist:*  You miss your Dadd?
>
> *Barbara:*    My Daddy went away and I don't have a Daddy. He never comes home, and I need my Daddy.

Barbara stood close to the therapist and cried.

Shirley, age 9, came over, put her arm around Barbara and said: "I don't have a Daddy either. My parents are divorced, and my father is far away in California."

The two girls stood close to each other, sharing their common sorrow. (p. 6)

A number of specialists have raised concerns about the appropriate focus in group play therapy. The focus of treatment in group play therapy is always the individual child. No group goals are set and no group cohesion is looked for (Baggerly, et al., 2010). Later writers had different views, maintaining that to comprehend fully the nature of child group therapy, it is necessary to clarify the constructs of group dynamics (Hansen & Cramer, 1971). Dies and Riester (1986) conducted a comprehensive review of research and concluded that researchers had yet to identify specific mechanisms of group dynamics or mechanisms of change explaining the contributions of group therapy to children's progress.

Researchers and practitioners seek answers to concerns about criteria for selecting or rejecting children for group therapy (Brady, 1991; Celano, 1990; Schaefer, Johnson, & Wherry, 1982). Some favor homogeneous grouping (similar areas of dysfunctionality); others favor heterogeneous grouping (different personalities, different symptoms). Following natural disasters such as earthquakes and floods, play therapists are sent to assist children. Group therapy may be essential because of the large numbers of traumatized children and the small number of therapists. The result can be quite positive. Group therapy can result in significant decrease in anxiety and suicidal risk with children who experience massive earthquakes (Shen, 2010). The multifaceted results of such disasters include cognitive, affective, somatic, behavioral, and neurobiological. Such therapy is also effective for children experiencing domestic violence (Tyndall-Lind, 2010).

## Interdisciplinary Teams

Interdisciplinary teams work together in school and hospital settings to assist with behavior problems and learning disabilities. In schools, the team may consist of a parent, teacher, play therapist, nurse, and remedial personnel. In hospitals, nurses, doctors, play therapists, and diagnosticians are team members. Collectively, such teams make plans for the child's total learning environment and experiences. In schools, the play therapist receives and contributes information about the child's total developmental needs and makes recommendations for enhancing emotional, social, and academic progress. Learning disabilities affect the *whole child.*

In hospitals, the team members work to make the initial hospital experience positive and as comfortable as possible. They understand that play assists recovery from illness or injury, not only emotionally but also physically. The return to normal play following a traumatic experience is a primary marker for such progress.

## Filial Therapy

As focus in the therapeutic profession shifted from intrapsychic concerns (e.g., psychoanalysis) to sociocultural concerns, a number of approaches emerged that involve parents in their children's play therapy. Including children in family therapy allows the clinicians to work from observed patterns of communication, roles, and coalitions rather than working from assumptions based on self-reports of a few individuals (Sweeney & Rocha, 1999).

Louise Guerney (1964) developed a model of **filial therapy** for training parents to conduct weekly home play therapy sessions with their children (Andronico, Fidler, Guerney, & Guerney, 1967). This model substitutes a trained parent for the traditional therapist. During parent training sessions, the parents may observe or join the sessions. Observing, sometimes with interpretations by the therapist, helps the parent understand what their children are doing. Parents participation may be highly structured, with the therapist assigning parents tasks to accomplish with the child. Common outcomes of this approach are both changed behavior of the child and changed parental perceptions of the child.

Filial therapy sessions may be supplemented with a "special time" (O'Connor, 2000) that gives the child 15 to 20 minutes of daily contact with parents. During this time, the parent focuses exclusively on the child's needs without waiting for the child to display symptoms. Getting the parent's attention and gaining a sense of control make these sessions valuable for the structured therapy sessions and help develop understanding and rapport between parent and child. Parents, like teachers and others responsible for the care and development of children, can secure training in physical therapy that equips them to assist "problem" children and also other children between the ages of 3 and 12 (Cochran, et al, 2010).

Yet another approach, **theraplay** (Jernberg, 1979), uses structured play for problem families.

The delicate interplay of the early bonding ritual between mother and child form the basis for theraplay. The therapy is purposefully physical, sensorimotor play intended to engage the senses and to replicate earlier child–parent bonding rituals. With roots in psychoanalysis, developmental psychology, and nursery school practice, the theraplay process is a mix of empathy and adult authority with the goal of treating troubled children and reducing mental illness.

The principles underlying theraplay rely on the basics of bonding between mother and infant. What does a normal mother do for her baby, and how does the baby respond? The normal actions of the mother—singing, whispering, playing, rocking, washing, rubbing, nuzzling, and protecting—and those of the infant—cooing, imitating, gurgling, staring, and smiling—are essential to the bonding process. Jernberg (1979) groups these reciprocal nurturing and responding behaviors into *structuring, challenging, intruding,* and *nurturing* interactions—all in the context of empathy, authority, and fun. Those deprived of such behaviors may well grow up incapable of bonding with their own babies or forming healthy love relations (Stringer, 1971). Prescott (cited in Hoover, 1976) links such childhood deficits to later violence and drug abuse, and Jernberg (1979) stresses, "Since abusing parents generally are under stress, were never properly parented, are friendless and isolated, and are depressed, dependent, deprived, and need care as much as their children do, Theraplay is often indicated" (p. 32).

Theraplay is used in individual, group, and family therapy. In individual therapy, the child enters a virtually bare room, and play materials are brought in to bolster planned activities. Sessions are designed to be fun, action oriented, and therapist directed. Group theraplay is based on the same principles and assumptions as individual theraplay but is structured for children having difficulty relating to peers.

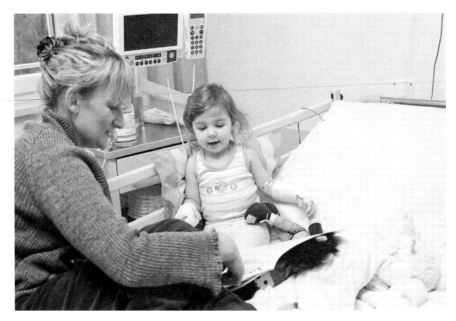

Medical play is used in the outpatient Cancer and Blood Disorder Center.

Jernberg believes the most effective theraplay is that which simultaneously treats the child and her parents. The treatment is enhanced by training all adults who interact with the child regularly—mother, father, grandparents, teacher, principal, and classroom aides.

## Medical Play

Children often react to medical visits or hospitalization with fear and stress because they are in a strange place where invasive procedures are common. Their perceptions are distorted because of their immature reasoning and active imaginations. Confused by their fantasies, perhaps linked to viewing medical and horror programs on TV and lacking accurate information, they may view medical procedures as punitive and threatening. For example, 5-year-old Kent has been told by his doctor that he will have to have an operation on his stomach to make him well. No one has told Kent that he will be asleep during the operation or that the

hole in his stomach will be sewn up after the surgery. Kent believes that he will feel pain during the operation and that all the "things" inside him will fall out (Jessee, 1991, p. 23).

Professionals need not wait until children are hospitalized to help them cope with impending stays. Teachers can employ simple therapy practices with children during classroom play (Jessee, Wilson, & Morgan, 2000) by talking with the child about her fears, providing medical play props, reinforcing the child's accurate perceptions, and gently guiding the child to explore medical events through play.

Following World War II, the medical profession's focus shifted from disease-oriented to patient-oriented pediatric care, and the Association for the Care of Children's Health (ACCH) developed the **Child Life Program**. The intent of ACCH was to minimize stress and anxiety and promote self-esteem and independence for children and adolescents facing medical care. The American Academy of Pediatrics and the Accreditation Council for Graduate Medical

Education acknowledge the importance of child life programs and promote the thorough preparation of medical professionals, including child life specialists (Thompson, 1990). Child life specialists work in a variety of healthcare settings to help alleviate stress and anxiety of children preparing, entering, or recovering from medical treatment. There are more than 400 child life programs in the United States and Canada in numerous health care settings including hospitals, pediatric physician and dental offices and other medical facilities. Play can make medical experiences less stressful and help both the child and her family understand the medical treatment and be more comfortable during procedures (Patte, 2010).

**Child life specialists** are trained in child development, counseling, education, and family studies. They help children cope with the stress and anxiety of hospital experiences both in the hospital and after returning home (Jessee, 1991). Their work includes the following:

- Preparing children for hospitalization and medical procedures.
- Providing guidance and materials for play.
- Advocating the child's point of view with medical personnel.
- Providing emotional support to parents and siblings.
- Maintaining a positive, receptive environment for children and their families. (Thompson & Stanford, 1981)

Hospitalized children need space to play in a natural, active way and appropriate materials for their play. This may be in a playroom exclusively for that purpose, or it may be a designated area in a corner of a room, end of a hall, or even a covered outdoor play area (Azarnoff & Flegal, 1975). The playroom should be readily accessible to children so those whose health allows can go there on their own (Brooks, 1970).

The playroom may be organized as follows:

- A large central activity table, offering structured play, such as handcrafts.

- A sink and work counter for painting and clay play.
- Interest centers such as block corner and housekeeping center for construction and make-believe.
- A medical center with play instruments, doctor bags, and expendable supplies such as tape, bandages, face masks, tongue blades, and stethoscope.
- A convenient storage area with puppets, cloth dolls and animals, medical supplies, and other materials. (Azarnoff & Flegal, 1975)

Therapists sometimes take materials for play therapy directly to children confined in hospital rooms. When choosing materials, the therapist must consider the physical limitations of the child, possible physical harm to the child, and possible damage to medical equipment in the room. A nondirective or child-centered relationship is appropriate, allowing the child to take the lead. The therapist must avoid overwhelming the child with too many play materials and must be alert to avoid overtiring the child. James (1997, p. 95) includes the following materials when planning a hospital room session:

- Small paint pots, brushes, and bed easel
- Puppets and dolls, including nurses, parents, children, and doctors
- Doctor bag stocked with medical toys
- Clay when appropriate
- Small animals
- Folding dollhouse
- Bed tray for small toy play
- Sand tray with lid and small objects
- Books

Medical play is a frequent playroom activity, with the children assuming the roles of doctors and nurses. Children release anxieties and emotions by treating one another, sometimes evidenced by violent, relentless shot giving. This play communicates their perceptions, often inaccurate, of examinations and treatments and gives the therapist opportunities to offer accurate, age-appropriate information. The therapist may use doctor play with dolls to model step-by-step procedures for the child to imitate.

## Preschools and Elementary Schools

Among professional groups, *play therapy* typically refers to play intended to accomplish specific therapeutic outcomes. However, play at any level may be therapeutic in many ways, including improvement in play skills, interpersonal skills, self-confidence, and reduction of stress. The basic principles of play therapy can be adapted by parents, child caretakers, and teachers. Adults who deal with children see a growing array of conflict and stress factors (violence, abuse, physical and emotional disabilities) that far exceed those seen as recently as the 1960s. Children can be assisted in playing out their feelings and phobias in drama, music, storytelling, water play, drawing, painting, clay, puppets, and spontaneous play, both indoors and outdoors. Researchers are even exploring the possible applications of computer play in therapy (Johnson, 1993). Play therapy and its emulation by semiskilled parents, caretakers, and teachers is more than just messing around.

Just as the mental health of teachers is linked to the relationship established with administrators and coworkers, the relationship between the child and the teacher is essential for the child's mental health. Furthermore, good mental health is essential for learning. The teacher should establish rich environments for play, model skills, and help children clarify and deal with fears and disturbing feelings. The teacher should create conditions for enhancing self-reliance, decision making, and initiative, with a focus on preventing problems.

Techniques used in play therapy are effective in helping children settle disputes and improve social behavior and, consequently, reduce discipline problems. Rather than assume a strict

authority role, the teacher can use reflective listening, feedback children's feelings and ideas, and reflect a consistent code of values. He can treat the child with respect and honesty and create a warm, friendly climate for living and learning. In so doing, the mental health of the teacher himself can be improved.

East Carolina University developed a model based on Landreth's work for training preschool teachers to use play therapy techniques in their classrooms (Clark, 1995). The model, based on Landreth's (1991) principles, includes the following elements:

- Emotional sharing of feelings
- Being attentive but letting children make decisions
- Basing responses on careful observation
- Allowing children to take the lead
- Making therapeutic responses brief and interactive
- Returning responsibility to the child
- Avoiding interrupting the natural flow of play
- Focusing on the child's efforts rather than the product

Group and filial play therapy work in schools in a variety of contexts and applications, across age levels, and for a wide range of problems such as depression and anxiety. Group activity therapy with learning disabled preadolescents has a positive effect on total behavior, and coping and interaction skills. Group activity allows one counselor or therapist to meet the needs of more students in less time.

Parents. Teachers, parents and researchers agree that behavior is improved. (Packman & Lebeauf, 2010). Group therapy in schools increases the benefits because the children are learning with children they have relationships with and already know. Such therapy may use a combination of semi-structured activities designed to facilitate practice cohesion in group cooperation and cohesion. And self and group-directed times for testing

Creativity, coping, and expression thrive in setting where adults provide rich play materials and support for play.

limits, practice decision-making skills, and explore their world. (Landreth, 2002; Paone, et al., 2008: Ginott, 1975).

## Links to Creativity

Even among practicing play therapists, the positive effects of play therapy on creativity are largely unexplored. Yet the linkages are everywhere. Consider the settings in which play therapy is conducted. They include specially prepared rooms stocked with a wide variety of creative materials: dolls, puppets, paints, water, sand, musical instruments, building materials, blocks, Tinkertoys, and clay. The play bags carried into hospital rooms by therapists contain an assortment of creative materials. Even the techniques or applications of therapy reflect engagement in creative activity—puppet therapy, sand play therapy, storytelling therapy, role play therapy, art therapy, squiggle-drawing therapy, and telephone play therapy.

Indeed, the child's creative impulse may be at the roots of successful play therapy. Essentially,

influences from adults and the outside world stifle the child's natural expression, creating phobias and disturbances that result in the need for play therapy. Lowenfeld (1947a) seemed to understand that children's creative impulses can be defeated but can also be rekindled:

> [T]he child's creative expression during specific stages of his mental and emotional growth can only be understood and appreciated if the general causal interdependence between creation and growth is understood . . . what civilization has buried we must try to regain by recreating the natural base necessary for such free creation. (Lowenfeld, 1947a, pp. vi, l)

A body of research demonstrates that the processes that occur in play are involved in creativity (Russ, 2005). These studies explore major categories of play important for creativity including divergent thinking, transformational abilities, sensitivity to problems, problem finding, multiple qualities of imaginative play, and other cognitive abilities important in creative thinking.

Play therapy may be considered as a necessary antidote for outside interference with the child's natural growth. We still find creative confidence in remote areas or developing countries where children are not yet deeply affected by technology and unwitting efforts to impose guidelines and restrictions on the child's creative experience. We also see extraordinary levels of creative confidence and expression among children in industrialized countries who live and play with adults who value play and creativity and provide the necessary conditions for their expression. Child-centered play therapy is consistent with Lowenfeld's contention that play and creative activity are therapeutic, but growth is linked to freedom of expression.

Creative activity can become a means of overcoming this isolation (physical and mental disabilities) through improving those sensory experiences that deal with the establishment of communications by relieving tensions and inhibitions that stand in the way of sound development (Lowenfeld, 1947a, p. 282). "[In creative activity,] don't impose your own images on a child! We should neither influence nor stimulate the child's imagination in any direction which is not appropriate to his thinking and perception. The child has his own world of experiences and expression" (Lowenfeld, 1947a, p. 3).

## RESULTS OF PLAY THERAPY

The research on both processes and outcomes of play therapy is limited but expanding. The existing studies are marked by methodological inadequacies, lack of conceptual models of how play therapy benefits children, the wide range of techniques used, the wide range of problem areas treated, and failure of the academic community to take play therapy seriously (Phillips, 1985). The available studies cover a wide range of hypotheses and outcome measures. The results, overall, are positive, supporting the efficacy of play therapy for disturbed children and children with problems.

Research has concluded that play therapy is effective for the following:

- Overall functioning (Holloway, Myles-Nixon, & Johnson, 1998; Kaduson, Cangelosi, & Shaefer, 1997; Paul, 1993; Webb, 1999)
- Personality outcomes (Dorfman, 1958)
- Social and emotional adjustment (Andriola, 1944; Burroughs, Wagner, & Johnson, 1997; Conn, 1952; Cox, 1953; Johnson, McLeod, & Fall, 1997; King & Ekstein, 1967; Moustakas, 1951; Smith, 1984; Ude-Pestel, 1977; Ray, 2010; Schottelkorb, 2010)
- Self-concept (Bleck & Bleck, 1982; Cowden, 1992; Crow, 1989; Pelham, 1971; Quattlebaum, 1970; Wick, Wick, & Peterson, 1997)
- Healing through storytelling (Henderson-Dickson, 1991)
- Temper tantrums, self-control, and aggression (Barlow, Strother, & Landreth, 1986; Stiber, 1991; Trostle, 1984; Willock, 1983)
- Phobias (Mendez & Garcia, 1996)
- Coping with grief (chronic illness, death) (Jones, & Carnes-Holt, 2010; Le Vieux, 1999)
- Progress in reading (Axline, 1947a, 1964; Bills, 1950; Bixler, 1945; Carmichael, 1991; Pumfrey & Elliott, 1970; Winn, 1959)
- Intelligence (Heinecke, 1969; Mundy, 1957)
- Academic performance (Bills, 1950; Guerney, 1983; Moustakas, 1951; Seeman & Edwards, 1954; Blanco, 2010)
- Child abuse (Beezley, Martin, & Kempe, 1976; Berkeley Planning Associates, 1978; Davoren, 1979; Frazier & Levine, 1983; Friedrich & Reams, 1987; Green, 1978; Mann & McDermott, 1983)
- Creativity, emotional adjustment (Lowenfeld, 1939, 1947; Van Fleet, Lilly, & Kaduson, 1999)
- Recovery from sexual abuse (Costas & Landreth, 1999; Johnston, 1997)

• For additional research on benefits of play therapy, see Carmichael, 2006; Bratton, Ray, & Rhine, 2005; Ogawa, 2004; Landreth, Sweeney, Ray, Homeyer, & Glover, 2005; Baggerly, et al., 2010).

Overall, the results of play therapy research are positive, demonstrating the efficacy and power of play for therapy and healing. Consequently, interest in play therapy is growing rapidly, and novel applications continue to emerge. The growing patterns of child-against-child violence and adults abusing children pose ever-greater challenges to develop therapeutic as well as preventive measures. There is a continuing need for in-depth process studies and controlled outcome studies, especially for preschool children. Fortunately, a comprehensive overview of play therapy research over 70 years, reaching through the first decade of the 21st century, is now available in a single source (Baggerly, J. N., and others, 2010). The detailed analyses of single cases continue to be invaluable to scholars and practitioners.

Consider Axline's (1964) classic book, *Dibs: In Search of Self,* is an account of the clinical play therapy treatment of a 6-year-old boy enrolled in an exclusive private school. The therapy for child and mother resulted in profound changes in the feelings, attitudes, and behaviors of both child and family.

#### BEFORE (CHAPTER ONE)

Dibs seemed determined to keep all people at bay. . . . When he started to school, he did not talk and he never ventured off his chair. He sat there mute and unmoving all morning. After many weeks he began to leave his chair and to crawl around the room, seeming to look at some of the things about him. When anyone approached him he would huddle up in a ball on the floor and not move. He never looked directly into anyone's eyes. He never answered when anyone spoke to him. . . . He was a lone child in what must have seemed to him to be a cold, unfriendly world. . . . "He's a strange one," the pediatrician had said. "Who

knows? Mentally retarded? Psychotic? Brain-damaged? Who can get close enough to find out what makes him tick?" (pp. 2–4)

#### AFTER (CHAPTER TWENTY)

Yep, I [Dibs] was afraid, but I'm not afraid any more. . . . I guess I am growing up. . . . As Dibs stood before me now his head was up. He had a feeling of security deep inside himself. He was building a sense of responsibility for his feelings. His feelings of hate and revenge had been tempered with mercy. . . . He could hate and he could love. He could condemn and he could pardon. . . . Yes, Dibs had changed. He had learned how to be himself, to believe in himself, to free himself. Now he was relaxed and happy. He was able to be a child. . . . They left together—a little boy who had had the opportunity to state himself through his play and who had emerged a happy, capable child, and a mother who had grown in understanding and appreciation for her very gifted child. (A week after play therapy ended, Dib's tested IQ was 168.) (pp. 156, 161, 176, 181, 185)

#### DIBS AT AGE 15

He is a brilliant boy. Full of ideas. Concerned about everybody and everything. Very sensitive. A real leader. (p. 184)

 **SUMMARY**

Play therapy, the supportive relationship between a child and a therapist in a play context, allows a child to play out feelings and emotions and, ideally, to heal. This is possible because play by its very nature is therapeutic and healing. The consequences of playing and not playing or playing in bizarre ways, as in excessive violence themes, are profound and lasting. Just as adults talk out their feelings and phobias with a therapist, children play out theirs. Play is the language of children, and healthy play is essential for healthy development.

Play therapy had its roots in the psychoanalytic tradition of Sigmund Freud and his associates and peers. Over the years, it has evolved from the psychoanalytic tradition into a multifaceted treatment option for a wide range of problems, phobias, and disabilities. Currently, play therapy approaches developed by therapists are being integrated into the repertoires of classroom teachers.

Overall, the reports of success for play therapy include improvement in physical, mental, and emotional disabilities; problems in speech; reading and general academics; abused children; phobias; children with attachment problems; hospitalized children; and children who have experienced trauma. Play therapy is carried out successfully in elementary schools, homes, hospitals, child-care centers, university laboratories, and psychiatric settings. It also is conducted successfully in individual, group, and family contexts and includes the age ranges from preschool through adolescence.

 ## KEY TERMS

| | |
|---|---|
| Axline's eight basic play principles | Oedipus complex |
| Bonding | Release therapy |
| Catharsis | Resistance |
| Child-centered play therapy | Self-actualization |
| Client-centered therapy | Structured play therapy |
| Child life program | Structuring |
| Ego | Superego |
| Filial therapy | Theraplay |
| Id | Therapy hour |
| Medical play | Transference |

## STUDY QUESTIONS

1. What is play therapy? Why is play therapy needed?
2. What is the evidence indicating that play is therapeutic?
3. How did play therapy originate and expand over the 20th century? Who were the major players, and what were the major approaches? What were the philosophical similarities and differences?
4. What were the major principles of Freudian psychoanalysis?
5. What individuals are most responsible for modifying psychoanalysis into play therapy? What modifications did they make to psychoanalysis?
6. What are the fundamental reasons for the emergence of client-centered or child-centered play therapy?

7. How should the playroom be set up? What materials are needed? Why are these materials appropriate? Are there toys you would not place in the playroom? Why?
8. What are the major roles of the therapist in child-centered play therapy? How would you introduce the child to the playroom? How would you establish rapport with the child? How would you conduct the therapy session?
9. Should limitations be placed on children in therapy? If so, describe the limitations and defend your answer. If not, explain why.
10. Select the individual whom you believe has been the leading play therapist. Why did you select this individual? Compare his or her contributions to other leading therapists.
11. How have Axline's eight basic principles of play therapy influenced the field of play therapy?
12. For which disabilities or problems is play therapy effective?
13. What does research say about the effectiveness of play therapy? What are the present limitations of play therapy research?
14. Can and should play therapy be successfully conducted in elementary school classrooms? By classroom teachers? By play therapists? In hospitals? In playgrounds? By playground supervisors, play leaders, or play workers? Why or why not?
15. In your opinion, what is the future of play therapy? Defend your answer.

 ## REFERENCES

Adler, A. (1927). *Understanding human nature* (W. B. Wolfe, Trans.). Garden City, NY: Garden City Publishing.

Allen, F. H. (1942). *Psychotherapy with children*. New York: Norton.

Amen, D. G. (2010). *Change your brain: Change your body*. New York: Harmony Books.

Andriola, J. (1944). Release of aggressions through play therapy for a ten-year-old patient at a child guidance clinic. *Psychoanalytic Review, 31*, 71–80.

Andronico, M., Fidler, J., Guerney, G., & Guerney, L. (1967). The combination of didactic and dynamic elements in filial therapy. *International Journal of Group Psychotherapy, 17*, 10–17.

Axline, V. (1947a). Nondirective play therapy for poor readers. *Journal of Consulting Psychology, 11*, 61–69.

Axline, V. (1947b). *Play therapy: The inner dynamics of childhood*. Boston: Houghton Mifflin.

Axline, V. (1950). Entering the child's world via play experiences. *Progressive Education, 27,* 68–75.

Axline, V. (1964). *Dibs:In search of self.* Boston: Houghton Mifflin.

Azarnoff, P., & Flegal, S. (1975). *A pediatric play program: Developing a therapeutic play program for children in medical settings.* Springfield, IL: Thomas.

Baggerly, J. N., Ray, D. C., & Bratton. S. C. (2010). *Child-centered play therapy research: The evidence base for effective practice.* Hoboken, NJ: John Wiley & Sons:

Barlow, K., Strother, J., & Landreth, G. (1986). Sibling group play therapy: An effective alternative with an elective mute child. *School Counselor, 34,* 44–50.

Beezley, P., Martin, H. P., & Kempe, R. (1976). Psychotherapy. In H. P. Marrin & C. H. Kempe (Eds.), *The abused child: A multidisciplinary approach to developmental issues and treatment.* Cambridge, MA: Ballinger.

Begley, S. (1996, February 29). Your child's brain. *Newsweek,* pp. 55–58.

Begley, S. (1997, Spring-Summer). How to build a baby's brain. *Newsweek Special Edition,* pp. 28–32.

Begley, S. (2007). How the brain rewires itself. *Time, 169(5),* 72–79.

Berkeley Planning Associates. (1978). *Evaluation of child abuse and neglect demonstration projects, 1974-1977* (Vols. 1 and 22). (DHEW Report No. 79-3217-1). Washington, DC: National Center for Health Services Research.

Bills, R. C. (1950). Nondirective play therapy with retarded readers. *Journal of Consulting Psychology, 14,* 140–149.

Bixler, R. (1945). Treatment of a reading problem through nondirective play therapy. *Journal of Consulting Psychology, 9,* 105–118.

Bixler, R. (1949). Limits are therapy. *Journal of Consulting Psychology, 13,* 1–11.

Blanco, P. J. (2010). Impact of school-based child-centered play therapy on academic achievement, self-concept, and teacher-child relations. In J. N. Baggerly, D. C. Ray, & S. C. Bratton, *Child-centered play therapy research: The evidence base for effective practice.* Hoboken, NJ: John Wiley & Sons.

Bleck, R., & Bleck. B. (1982). The disruptive child's play group. *Elementary School Guidance and Counseling, 17,* 137–141.

Board of Directors, Association for Play Therapy. (1997). Minutes. *Association for Play Therapy Newsletter, 16,* 14.

Brady, G. L. (1991). A group-work approach for sexually abused preschoolers. *Journal of Group Psychotherapy Psychodrama and Sociometry, 43(4),* 174–183.

Bratton, S., Ray, D., & Rhine, T. (2005). The efficacy of play therapy with children: A meta-analytic review of treatment outcomes. *Journal of Professional Psychology Research and Practice, 36,* 376–390.

Bronson, P., & Merryman, A. (2009). *Nurture shock: New thinking about children.* New York: Twelve-Hachette Book Group.

Brooks, M. M. (1970). Why play in hospitals? In E. C. Rothrock & E. Wesseling (Eds.), *The nursing clinics of North America.* Philadelphia: Saunders.

Burroughs, M. S., Wagner, W. W., & Johnson, J. T. (1997). Treatment with children of divorce: A comparison of two types of therapy. *Journal of Divorce and Remarriage, 27,* 83–99.

Carmichael, K. (1991). Play therapy: Role in reading improvement. *Reading Improvement, 4,* 273–276.

Carmichael, K. D. (2006). *Play therapy: An introduction.* Upper Saddle River, NJ: Pearson Prentice Hall.

Celano, M. P. (1990). Activities and games for group psychotherapy with sexually abused children. *International Journal of Group Psychotherapy, 40(4),* 419–429.

Clark, R. J. (1995). Research review: Violence, young children and the healing power of play. *Dimensions, 23,* 28–30, 39.

Cochran, N. H., Nordling, W. J., & Cochran, J. L. (2010). *Child-centered play therapy: A practical guide to developing relationships with children.* New York: John Wiley & Sons.

Conn, J. H. (1952). Treatment of anxiety states in children by play interviews. *Sinai Hospital Journal, 1,* 57–65.

Costas, M., & Landreth, G. (1999). Filial therapy with nonoffending parents of children who have been sexually abused. *International Journal of Play Therapy, 8,* 43–66.

Cowden, S. T. (1992). *The effects of client-centered group play therapy on self concept* (Masters Abstracts International 31/01). Unpublished master's thesis, University of West Florida, Pensacola.

Cox, F. E. (1953). Sociometric status and individual adjustment before and after play therapy. *Journal of Abnormal Psychology, 40,* 354–356.

Crow, J. (1989). *Play therapy with low achievers in reading.* Unpublished doctoral dissertation, University of North Texas, Denton.

Davoren, E. (1979). Low budget play therapy for very young children. *Child Abuse and Neglect, 3,* 199–204.

DeAngelis, T. (1997, June). Trauma at an early age inhibits ability to bond. *Monitor: American Psychological Association,* pp. 11–13.

Dies, R. R., & Riester, A. E. (1986). Research on child group therapy: Present status and future directions. In A. Riester & I. Kraft (Eds.), *Group child psychotherapy: Future tense* (pp. 173–220). Madison, CT: International Universities Press.

Dorfman, E. (1958). Personality outcomes of client centered play therapy. *Psychological Monographs, 72,* 1–22.

Erikson, E. H. (1950). *Childhood and society.* New York: Norton.

Foley, Y. C. (2010). A qualitative study of parents' perceptions of filial therapy in a public school. In J. N. Baggerly, D. C. Ray, & S. C. Bratton, *Child-centered play therapy research: The evidence base for effective practice.* Hoboken, NJ: John Wiley & Sons.

Frazier, D., & Levine, E. (1983). Reattachment therapy: Intervention with the very young physically abused child. *Psychotherapy: Theory, Research, and Practice, 20,* 90–100.

Freud, A. (1928). *Introduction to the technique of child analysis* (L. P. Clark, Trans.). New York: Nervous and Mental Disease Publishing.

Freud, A. (1946). *The psychoanalytical treatment of children.* London: Imago.

Freud, S. (1938). *The basic writings of Sigmund Freud* (A. A. Brill, Trans. & Ed.). New York: Modern Library.

Freud, S. (1955). Analysis of a phobia in a five year old boy. In *The standard edition of the complete psychological works of Sigmund Freud.* London: Hogarth. (Original work published 1909)

Freud, S. (1961). *Beyond the pleasure principle.* New York: Norton.

Freud, S. (1965). *The psycho-analytical treatment of children.* London: Imago.

Friedrich, W. N., & Reams, R. A. (1987). The course of psychological symptoms in sexually abused young children. *Psychotherapy: Research, Theory, and Practice, 24,* 160–170.

Frost, J. L. (1986). Children in a changing society. *Childhood Education, 62,* 242–249.

Frost, J. L. (1998). *Neuroscience, play and child development.* Paper presented at the American Association for the Child's Right to Play Conference, Longmont, CO.

Frost, J. L. (2005a). Lessons from disasters: Play, work and the creative arts. *Childhood Education, 82,* 2–8.

Frost, J. L. (2010). *A history of children's play and play environments: Toward a contemporary child saving movement.* New York & London: Routledge Publishers.

Ginott, H. G. (1961). *Group psychotherapy with children.* New York: McGraw-Hill.

Glasser, W. (1975). *Reality therapy.* New York: Harper & Row.

Green, A. H. (1978). Psychiatric treatment of abused children. *Journal of the American Academy of Child Psychiatry, 17,* 356–371.

Guerney, L. (1964). Filial therapy: Description and rationale. *Journal of Consulting Psychology, 28,* 304–310.

Guerney, L. (1983). Play therapy with learning disabled children. In C. E. Schaefer & K. L. O'Connor (Eds.), *Handbook of play therapy* (pp. 419–435). New York: Wiley.

Hambridge, G. (1955). Release therapy. *American Journal of Orthopsychiatry, 9,* 601–617.

Hansen, J. C., & Cramer, S. H. (1971). *Group guidance and counseling in the schools.* New York: Meredith.

Heinecke, C. M. (1969). Frequency of psychotherapeutic sessions as a factor affecting outcome: Analysis of clinical rating and test results. *Journal of Abnormal Psychology, 74,* 553–560.

Henderson-Dixon, A. S. (1991). The child's own story: A study of the creative process of healing in children in play therapy. *Dissertation Abstracts International, 52*(09A).

Holloway, P. J., Myles-Nixon, C., & Johnson, W. M. (1998). *Identification, differentiation and intervention of the demographically diverse four year old: Strategies for rural special education.* (ERIC Document Reproduction Service No. ED417917)

Hoover, E. (1976, January). Affection as an inoculation against aggression. *Human Behavior,* pp. 10–11.

Hug-Hellmuth, H. (1921). On the technique of child analysis. *International Journal of Psychoanalysis, 2,* 287.

James, O. O. (1997). *Play therapy: A comprehensive guide.* Northvale, NJ: Aronson.

Jernberg, A. (1979). *Theraplay.* San Francisco: Jossey-Bass.

Jessee, P. O. (1991, Fall). Making hospitals less traumatic: Child life specialists. *Dimensions,* 23–24, 37.

Jessee, P. O., Wilson, H., & Morgan, D. (2000, Summer). Medical play for young children. *Childhood Education, 76,* 215–218.

Johnson, L., McLeod, E. H., & Fall, M. (1997). Play therapy with labeled children in the schools. *Professional School Counseling, 1,* 31–34.

Johnson, R. G. (1993). High tech play therapy. In C. E. Schaefer & D. M. Cangelosi (Eds.), *Play therapy techniques* (pp. 281–286). Northvale, NJ: Aronson.

Johnston, S. M. (1997). The use of art and play therapy with victims of sexual abuse: A review of the literature. *Family Therapy, 24,* 101–113.

Jones, E. M., & Carnes-Holt, K. (2010). The efficacy of intensive individual child-centered play therapy for chronically ill children. In J. N. Baggerly, D. C. Ray, & S. C. Bratton, *Child-centered play therapy research: The evidence base for effective practice.* Hoboken, NJ: John Wiley & Sons.

Jung, C. G. (1954). *The practice of psychotherapy* (R. F. C. Hull, Trans.). New York: Pantheon.

Kaduson, H. G., Cangelosi, D. M., & Schaefer, C. E. (Eds.). (1997). *The playing cure: Individualized play therapy for specific childhood problems.* Northvale, NJ: Aronson.

King, P., & Ekstein, R. (1967). The search for ego controls: Progression of play activity in psychotherapy with a schizophrenic child. *Psychoanalytic Review, 54,* 25–37.

Klein, M. (1932). *The psychoanalysis of children.* London: Hogarth.

Klein, M. (1955). The psychoanalytic play technique. *American Journal of Orthopsychiatry, 25,* 223–237.

Kottman, T. (2001). *Play therapy: Basics and beyond.* Alexandria, VA: American Counseling Association.

Kottman, T. (2003). *Partners in play: An Adlerian approach to play therapy.* Alexandria, VA: American Counseling Association.

Landreth, G. L. (1998). *Child centered play therapy: A clinical session* [videotape]. Denton: University of North Texas Center for Play Therapy.

Landreth, G. L. (Ed.). (2001). *Innovations in play therapy: Issues, process, and special populations.* Philadelphia: Taylor & Francis.

Landreth, G. L. (2002). *Play therapy: The art of the relationship.* (2nd edition). Muncie, IN: Accelerated Development.

Landreth, G., Hohmeyer, L., Bratton, S., & Kale, A. (Eds.). (1995). *The world of play therapy literature: A definitive guide to authors and subjects in the field* (2nd ed.). Denton: University of North Texas Center for Play Therapy.

Landreth, G., Sweeney, D., Ray, D., Homeyer, L., & Glover, G. (2005). *Play therapy interventions with children's problems* (2nd ed.). Northvale, NJ: Jason Aronson.

Le Vieux, J. (1999). Group play therapy with grieving children. In L. E. Homeyer (Ed.), *The handbook of group play therapy: How to do it, how it works, whom it's best for*. San Francisco: Jossey-Bass.

Levy, D. M. (1939). Trends in therapy III: Release therapy. *American Journal of Orthopsychiatry, 9*, 713–736.

Lowenfeld, V. (1939). *The nature of creative activity*. New York: Harcourt, Brace.

Lowenfeld, V. (1947a). *Creative and mental growth*. New York: Macmillan.

Lowenthal, B. (1999). Effects of maltreatment and ways to promote children's resiliency. *Childhood Education, 75*, 204–209.

Mann, E., & McDermott, J. F. (1983). Play therapy for victims of child abuse and neglect. In C. E. Schaefer & K. L. O'Connor (Eds.), *Handbook of play therapy* (pp. 283–307). New York: Wiley.

Mendez, F. J., & Garcia, M. J. (1996). Emotive performances: A treatment package for children's phobias. *Child and Family Behavior Therapy, 3*, 19–34.

Moustakas, C. E. (1951). Situational play therapy with normal children. *Journal of Consulting Psychology, 15*, 225–230.

Moustakas, C. E. (1953). *Children in play therapy*. New York: McGraw-Hill.

Moustakas, C. E. (1998). *Reflections on relationship play therapy* [videotape]. Denton: University of North Texas Center for Play Therapy.

Mundy, L. (1957). Therapy with physically and mentally handicapped children in a mental deficiency hospital. *Journal of Clinical Psychology, 13*, 3–9.

Nash, J. M. (1997, February 3). Fertile minds. *Time: Special Report*, pp. 48–56.

Neuberger, J. J. (1997). Brain development research. *Young Children, 52*, 4–9.

O'Connor, K. J. (2000). *The play therapy primer: An integration of theories and techniques*. New York: Wiley.

Ogawa, Y. (2004). Childhood trauma and play therapy intervention for traumatized children. *Journal of Professional Counseling Practice, 32*, 19–29.

Packman, J., & Lebeauf, I. (2010). A school-based activity therapy intervention with learning-disabled preadolescents exhibiting behavior problems. In J. N. Baggerly, D. C. Ray, & S. C. Bratton, *Child-centered play therapy research: The evidence base for effective practice*. Hoboken, NJ: John Wiley & Sons.

Paone, T. R., Packman, J., Maddux, C., & Rothman, T. (2008). A school-based group activity therapy intervention with at-risk high school students as it relates to their moral reasoning. *International Journal of Play Therapy. 17*(2). 122–137.

Patte, M. (2010). The therapeutic benefits of play for hospitalized children. In E. E. Nwokah (Ed.), *Play as engagement and communication*. Play and Culture Studies, Volume 10. New York: University Press of America.

Paul, R. (1993). Background interpretation with a child placed under government protection by means of play therapy. *Masters Abstracts International, 32*(01).

Pelham, L. E. (1971). *Self-directive play therapy with socially immature kindergarten students*. Unpublished doctoral dissertation, University of Northern Colorado, Greeley.

Perry, B. D., & Szalavitz, M. (2006). *The boy who was raised as a dog*. New York: Basic Books.

Phillips, R. D. (1985). Whistling in the dark? A review of play therapy research. *Psychotherapy, 22*, 752–760.

Pumfrey, P. D., & Elliott, C. D. (1970). Play therapy, social adjustment and reading attainment. *Educational Research, 12*, 183–193.

Quattlebaum, R. F. (1970). *A study of the effectiveness of nondirective counseling and play therapy with maladjusted fifth-grade pupils*. Unpublished doctoral dissertation, University of Alabama, Tuscaloosa.

Ray, D. C. (2010). Play therapy with children exhibiting ADHD. In J. N. Baggerly, D. C. Ray, & S. C. Bratton, *Child-centered play therapy research: The evidence base for effective practice*. Hoboken, NJ: John Wiley & Sons.

Ray, D. C., & Bratton, S. C. (2010). What the research shows about play therapy: Twenty-first century update. In J. N. Baggerly, D. C. Ray, & S. C. Bratton, *Child-centered play therapy research: The evidence base for effective practice*. Hoboken, NJ: John Wiley & Sons.

Rogers, C. R. (1942). *Counseling and psychotherapy*. Boston: Houghton Mifflin.

Rogers, C. R. (1951). *Client-centered therapy*. Boston: Houghton Mifflin.

Rogers, C. R. (1962). Toward becoming a fully functioning person. In ASCD Yearbook Committee (Ed.), *Perceiving, behaving, becoming: Yearbook 1962*. Washington, DC: Association for Supervision and Curriculum Development.

Russ, S. W. (2005). Building an empirical foundation for the use of pretend play in therapy. In C. Schaefer, J. McCormick, & A. Ohnogi (Eds.), *International handbook of play therapy*. New York: Jason Aronson.

Schaefer, C. E. (1985). Play therapy. *Early Child Development and Care, 19*, 95–108.

Schaefer, C. E. (Ed.). (1993). *The therapeutic powers of play*. Northvale, NJ: Aronson.

Schaefer, C. E., Johnson, L., & Wherry, J. H. (1982). *Group therapy for children and youth: Principles and practices of group treatment*. San Francisco: Jossey-Bass.

Schottelkorb, A. (2010). Effectiveness of child-centered play therapy and person-centered teacher consultation on ADHD. In J. N. Baggerly, D. C. Ray, & S. C. Bratton, *Child-centered play therapy research: The evidence base for effective practice*. Hoboken, NJ: John Wiley & Sons.

Seeman, J., & Edwards, B. (1954). A therapeutic approach to reading difficulties. *Journal of Consulting Psychology, 18*, 451–453.

Shen, Y. (2010). Effects of post earthquake group play therapy with Chinese children. In J. N. Baggerly, D. C. Ray,

& S. C. Bratton, *Child-centered play therapy research: The evidence base for effective practice*. Hoboken, NJ: John Wiley & Sons.

Shore, R. (1997). *Rethinking the brain: New insights into early development*. New York: Families and Work Institute.

Smith, J. E. (1984). Non-accidental injury to children: 1. A review of behavioral interventions. *Behavior Research and Therapy, 22,* 331–347.

Stiber, J. A. (1991). The effect of play therapy on the temper tantrums of a seven-year-old-boy. *Masters Abstracts International 30*(01).

Stringer, L. (1971). *The sense of self: A guide to how we mature.* Philadelphia: Temple University.

Sweeney, D. S., & Rocha, S. L. (2000). Using play therapy to assess family values. In R. E. Watts (Ed.), *Techniques in marriage and family counseling* (Vol. 1, pp. 33–47). Family Psychology and Counseling Series. Alexandria, VA: American Counseling Association.

Taft, J. (1933). *The dynamics of therapy in a controlled relationship.* New York: Macmillan.

Thompson, R. J. (1990). From the president. *Child Life Council Bulletin, 7,* 2.

Thompson, R. J., & Stanford, G. (1981). *Child life in hospitals.* Springfield, IL: Thomas.

Trostle, S. L. (1984). An investigation of the effects of child-centered group play therapy upon sociometric, self-control, and play behavior ratings of three- to six-year-old bilingual Puerto Rican children. *Dissertation Abstracts International, 46*(05A).

Tyndall-Lind, A. (2010). Intensive sibling group play therapy with child witnesses of domestic violence. In J. N. Baggerly, D. C. Ray, & S. C. Bratton, *Child-centered play therapy research: The evidence base for effective practice.* Hoboken, NJ: John Wiley & Sons.

Ude-Pestel, A. (1977). *Betty: History and art of a child in therapy.* Palo Alto, CA: Science and Behavior.

Van Fleet, R., Lilly, J. P., & Kaduson, H. (1999). Play therapy for children exposed to violence. *International Journal of Play Therapy, 8,* 27–42.

Webb, N. B. (Ed.). (1999). *Play therapy with children in crisis: Individual, group, and family treatment* (2nd ed.). New York: Guilford.

Wick, D. T., Wick, J. K., & Peterson, N. (1997). Improving self-esteem with Adlerian Adventure Therapy. *Professional School Counseling, 1,* 53–56.

Willock, B. (1983). Play therapy with the aggressive, acting-out child. In C. E. Schaefer & K. L. O'Connor (Eds.), *Handbook of play therapy* (pp. 387–411). New York: Wiley.

Winn, E. V. (1959). *The influence of play therapy on personality change and the consequent effect on reading performance.* Unpublished doctoral dissertation, Michigan State University, Lansing.

# 13 Child Safety in Public Places

## INDOORS AND OUTDOORS

*"Kids should be allowed to experiment and try things. Otherwise when they grow up they'll make very stupid mistakes from not getting enough experience at childhood."*

(Tim Gill 2007, p. 19. Teenager quoted from BBC website, March 1, 2005)

*EVERY TIME someone gets accidentally injured, someone, somewhere made a mistake. God ain't doing this stuff—we are.*

(Dr. Red Duke, director of Trauma and Emergency Medical Services at Hermann Hospital in Houston, TX, quoted in Modern Maturity, July–August 1995)

*. . . Better to let kids be a hazard to nature than let nature be a hazard to them. . . . Learning what to fear, and what not to fear, is a large part of growing up.*

(Nabhan & Trimble, 1994, pp. 9, 152)

*SOME PEOPLE think that accidents just happen—that they are due to fate or bad luck and are unavoidable. . . . [I]njuries result from hazardous conditions, which can be corrected, and unsafe behaviors, which can be changed.*

(National Safety Council, 1999, p. iv)

The quotes above illustrate seemingly divergent views about control and freedom in children's play. Children's play is often over-regulated and children must be allowed—even encouraged—to meet and master challenges in play, yet they must be guided in developing good judgment to avoid serious hazards. Both a prominent emergency room physician (with years of experience piecing children's broken bodies back together) and the National Safety Council (drawing from voluminous safety data) point to the preventable features of accidents, especially those associated with manufactured materials. Those concerned about the power of risky play in building brains and bodies urge the loosening of adult reins, reducing conflicting activities, and turning children loose to explore and engage in natural outdoor learning and development. This chapter emphasizes a balanced approach. Certain minor remedial actions can reduce disabling injuries and fatalities without over-regulating children's outdoor play and damaging children's health, learning, and development. Yet, children must be free to engage in skinned-knee play and blistered-hands work in order to build brains, learn skills, and develop bodies for protecting themselves in challenging environments.

During the last two decades of the 20th century, continuing through 2011, a number of interrelated factors were contributing to the dissolution of outdoor play in the United States. Play and recess were disappearing from schools and neighborhoods (Pica, 2003, 2005). The International Play Association (Clements, 2005) reported that 40% of American public schools were abolishing or reducing recess time, and Marano (2004) reported that 40,000 schools no longer allowed play time. The contributing factors include parental concern about possible criminal activity at public playgrounds, growing popularity of indoor technology play, high-stakes testing, expanding, inconsistent safety standards, and lawsuits and threats of lawsuits.

This chapter outlines common safety issues and guidelines that all adults can employ to help prevent serious injuries (and lawsuits) to children and simultaneously help orient children to safe play practices. However, we have serious reservations about continuing trends to standardize and overregulate children's playgrounds, just as we have reservations about the effects of illogical and ill-founded high-stakes testing prevailing in American schools.

The national playground safety standards and guidelines—(**Consumer Product Safety Commission (CPSC)** and **American Society for Testing and Materials (ASTM)**)—are influential in promoting the safety of manufactured equipment (consumer products). We should now direct our attention to reducing the scope and inconsistencies of state and national guidelines, regulations and standards; reducing the technical and sometimes irrelevant portions; identifying safety standards of documented importance; making those standards simple and understandable to consumers; and addressing them to the developmental needs of children. This would require extensive collaboration between skilled practitioners and researchers from several disciplines. Presently, legal requirements and the threat of lawsuits mean that child-care centers, public schools, parks, and other affected agencies must comply with CPSC guidelines and ASTM standards.

This chapter illuminates the types of hazards and the nature of physical risks that children and their caretakers may encounter in public places. It also makes recommendations for improving child safety while preserving acceptable levels of risk and ensuring play value, challenge, diversity, and learning. It is unreasonable to expect that attention to safety will result in prevention of all injuries, particularly minor scrapes, abrasions, or bruises. However, it is reasonable to expect that careful, organized safety programs will reduce the probability of serious injuries.

In a safety context, **risk** refers to an action chosen by an individual that poses a chance of injury. The level of risk may vary widely, depending on the nature of the hazard, the abilities of the individual, and related factors such as weather, adult supervision, and maintenance. **Hazard** refers to a condition, seen or unseen, that is likely to cause injury, ranging from minor to serious, debilitating, or life threatening. Hazards are encountered during normal anticipated activity or as a result of reasonably foreseeable abuse or misuse of materials and equipment in the play environment.

**Risk management** is the systematic planned prevention and reduction of accidents by selecting safe materials and equipment, reducing hazardous conditions, and providing information and supervision that identifies potential hazards and advises how to avoid them. Safety specialists are concerned with levels of hazards. Level I, or **limited hazards,** are conditions likely to cause minor or non-disabling injuries. Level II, or **moderate hazards,** are conditions that are likely to cause serious injury resulting in temporary disability. Level III, or **extreme hazards,** are conditions likely to cause permanent disability or loss of life or body parts. When examining playgrounds, inspectors may identify levels of hazards and make recommendations for immediate and protracted corrections based on the level of hazard. For example, playground equipment posing extreme hazards is immediately removed from the playground or secured from use until the hazards are corrected. Limited hazards may be subject to immediate correction.

A reasonable risk level is necessary in play, but as in other life activities, there must be limitations on the degree of physical risk. We must ensure that children have access to play environments that challenge them and pose acceptable risks. By its very nature, spontaneous play is pleasurable, challenging, and, to a certain degree, risky. All healthy mammals play, and their fundamental play moves include leaping, defying gravity, climbing, jumping, horsing around—all activities that place the player at risk (Brown, 1997, 1998). Through experience with risk taking, adult and older peer **scaffolding** (presenting gradually increasing levels of risk and assisting children in developing skills), and

Taking reasonable risks at play builds physical and cognitive skills essential for playing safely.

exposure to increasingly complex materials and problems, levels of challenge and complexity are constantly expanded. Risk is essential for play and for healthy development.

There may be *physical risks,* as when exposed to challenges or hazards; *emotional risks,* as when expressing anger, trusting others, admitting fear; or *intellectual risks,* as when admitting error or trying to outwit a peer. These risks are often interconnected (S. J. Smith, 1998). Adults frequently engage in yet other types of risk—*financial risks* (investing in the stock market, gambling, overextending credit-card debt) and *supervisory risks* (standing back and observing children taking manageable risks, responding to them, considering what is good for them, and letting them grow and mature). Common sense is an admirable trait in this context.

The CPSC (www.cpsc.gov) makes available a huge range of safety resources to assist the public in evaluating and regulating the safety of approximately 15,000 types of consumer products (manufactured products), from coffeemakers to toys to lawn mowers to playground equipment. This independent regulatory agency of the U.S. government protects the public against unreasonable risks of injuries and deaths resulting from consumer products. Information on consumer product–related injuries and deaths, product recalls, and other CPSC activities are available over telephone, the Internet, letter, or messenger service. Contact numbers are included in the "General Information" section at the end of this chapter, and the news releases referenced are available from these same sources.

The home, the shopping mall, and the classroom are places where children encounter hazards and take risks, but these places are not always designed for taking physical risks during play, as are playgrounds. Failure to foresee that children tend to play in almost all contexts using anything that remotely resembles a toy or play device and failure to take preventive safety measures, is a frequent cause of child injury. Children are naturally attracted to water, equipment, or devices, including furniture and railings, that can be climbed or manipulated, and, even in public places not designed for play, children commonly engage in risk taking in hazardous settings. An important function of parenting and teaching is planning with children in advance about potential high-level hazards, for example, water, traffic, and extreme heights.

Specifically, one of the most common unacceptable—yet easily preventable—physical risks for young children occurs in grocery stores and shopping malls where young children are allowed to stand up, jiggle, jump, reach for merchandise, and play in shopping carts rolling over hard floors. Injuries resulting from shopping cart falls increased from 7,800 in 1985 to more than 16,000 in 1996. The number of injuries increased to 24,200 during 2005 (Smith, 2006). Two-thirds of the victims were treated in emergency rooms for head injuries, with more than half suffering severe injuries such as concussions and fractures (CPSC Press Release #97–116). Shopping carts should be designed to decrease the risk of injury. In 2004, the CPSC issued a voluntary standard that included using seat belts and preventing children from standing up in carts.

Most children should be walking with adults, gaining health and fitness benefits and learning through assisting in planning and shopping. Consider the pattern being established by placing children capable of walking into shopping carts thereby losing the benefits of walking: A growing number of obese adults drive motorized carts for shopping, having grown too fragile to walk due to a lifetime of taking shortcuts with their health. Many children needing to ride and those capable of walking can be instructed through talk and example rather than restrained in carts. Some adults engage in the onerous practice of leading/dragging their children around shopping venues with harness and leashes when walking.

Regardless of the setting, careful planning can reduce or eliminate extreme hazards while preserving challenge and acceptable levels of risk. On outdoor playgrounds, fast slides, challenging climbing equipment, supervised outdoor cooking over open fires, as well as building and gardening with tools can all be made available with reasonable levels of safety. For humans to grow in maturity, they must take reasonable risks and learn from their mistakes. Those deprived of such opportunities grow up fearful, timid, and brittle. Children of an earlier, more rural era learned to identify hazards and handle risks through extensive play and work activities. From an early age they interacted with animals, nature, tools, and farm equipment via the careful tutelage of adults and extensive practice. They learned to use tools, to appreciate heights, to plant and nurture gardens, and to sort out dangerous and wild animals from docile domesticated ones; doing so, they developed highly refined perceptual and motor skills (Frost, 2010).

## PLAYING FOR HEALTH, FITNESS, AND SAFETY

The typical pattern for preventing child injury is to protect, through standards, prohibitions, restricting play, and over-parenting, yet growing contemporary sentiment is to make kids safe for play by having many free, unstructured opportunities for taking reasonable risks in challenging outdoor environments. Contemporary kids, perhaps because of fragmented parenting, latchkey living, television addiction, junk food, gangs, perceived and real neighborhood dangers, absence of places to play, elimination of recess, high-stakes testing, reduction of physical education, excessive safety standards, lawsuits, and a host of other modern pressures, have fewer opportunities to develop the motor and cognitive skills needed for safe play (Sutterby & Frost, 2002; Frost, 2006b). American children rank lowest among developed countries on measures of physical fitness (Dennison et al., 1988; Javernick, 1988;

Ross & Gilbert, 1985). A study of 2,205 adolescents by Northwestern University researchers, published in the *Journal of the American Medical Association* (*Austin American-Statesman*, December 21, 2005, p. A8) concluded that 34% of girls and boys ages 12 to 19 showed poor cardiovascular fitness on a treadmill test. This low fitness group was two to four times more likely to be overweight or obese. Similarly, on tasks involving use of overhead equipment by 3- to 5-year-olds, only the obese children were unable to traverse the equipment after 2 weeks of practice (Frost et al., 2004).

The benefits of play extend far beyond developing the skills needed for predicting and successfully avoiding injury at play. Both active structured and unstructured play engages the body in fine and gross motor development, the mind in negotiation, problem, imagination, and flexibility. Play that is active, creative, and social also encourages autonomous thinking and environment building, provides opportunities to practice new skills and functions, and develops creative and aesthetic appreciation, and problem solving. All these can be accomplished in play environments posing acceptable risks, coupled with both natural and built creations stimulating aesthetic appreciation (Cole-Hamilton et al., 2002; Frost, 2010). American Academy of Pediatrics studies support these conclusions and add benefits in creativity, development of multiple competencies, healthy brain development, developing social and leadership skills, and engaging in joyful imagination (Ginsburg, 2006). Studies by Stanford University (2007) and the American Heart Association (Marcus et al., 2006) add extensive health benefits—prevention of obesity, heart disease, high blood pressure, and diabetes—all implicated in related diseases and shortened life spans.

Children need daily physical activity at school and in neighborhoods. Such play carries developmental, academic, and health benefits not seen in structured play. Studies by the Robert Wood Johnson Foundation (2007) confirm that school recess is just as important as classroom work in compensating for such issues as depression, violence, and obesity. Only 36 percent of American schoolchildren meet physicians' recommendations for time in physical activity during the school year and recess offers the greatest opportunity to fill these needs. Loss of free, outdoor play and recess resulted in the need for trained play leaders or playworkers because growing numbers are not learning how to engage in creative, spontaneous, active play and games. Modern children are developing disorders such as ADHD and autism that create the need for play therapy and medical attention. Trained adults can help children express themselves through play, guide them initially and letting go as they develop physical, cognitive, and social skills.

Sedentary lifestyles and consumption of junk food are seen by pediatricians as contributing to obesity (Deitz & Gortmaker, 1985), diabetes (Thompson, 1998), and early symptoms of later heart disease (Centers for Disease Control, 2005). Overweight and obesity are associated with hypertension, cardiovascular disease, diabetes, depression, and some types of cancer (Malik, Schulze, & Hu, 2006). During the last two decades, obesity has escalated to epidemic proportions. In the United States, 64% of the population is overweight, and 30% of these are obese. The pattern is spreading throughout the industrialized world where 300 million are obese (Malik et al., 2006). Obesity and early signs of such diseases are seen earlier and earlier during childhood. The *Chicago Tribune* (August 10, 2006) reported on a study of 120,000 children by Matthew Gillman, a Harvard professor, and associates, concluding that the incidence of overweight infants increased by 73% during the past two decades. This appears to have resulted from mothers being overweight during pregnancy, with possible contributions of overfeeding during infancy.

The solution to the fitness and obesity dilemma for most children is not complicated. Ensure that children (and their parents), both at home and at school, receive a balanced diet of nutritious food and engage in regular, sustained physical activity. Evidence is accumulating that children's 1 hour per day of regular active play is needed to provide adequate exercise. The weight of epidemiologic and experimental evidence indicates that consumption of sugar-sweetened beverages is a contributor to weight gain and obesity (Malik et al., 2006). The National Association for Sport and Physical Education recommends (Fukushima, 1998) that elementary-school-age children have at least 1 hour of vigorous physical activity each day. Vigorous activities should last 15 minutes or more with brief rest periods, and children should engage in a variety of activities of various intensities.

A national online survey of more than 800 mothers in the United States (Clements, 2003) found that children play outdoors on a daily basis less often than did children a decade ago—declining from 70% then to 31% today. Children's current engagement in television viewing, playing computer and video games, reading, and playing board games helps account for this decrease. Concerns about crime and safety coupled with lack of adult supervision also contributed to the decline in outdoor play. The results indicated that 71% of parents do not have adequate time to spend outdoors with their children.

Children are naturally drawn to challenging environments rich with play materials—free or expensive, natural or manufactured. Construction sites, adventure playgrounds, swimming pools, ice skating areas, zoos, and wilderness areas invite and challenge children, but all pose unseen hazards, particularly for very young children who have not developed logical thought (reflective, evaluative, cause-and-effect thinking) and for those with poorly developed motor skills (clumsy, uncoordinated). Children must be exposed to managed levels of hazards, learn to identify hazards, evaluate hazards, and cope with or master hazards. This is best done through experiencing challenges from an early age, under the watchful eyes and helpful hands of adults. Many children are unsafe in any play

**FIGURE 13.1** Examples of Very Serious Hazards

- Exposed electrical outlets can cause severe shock, unprotected floors around climbing equipment can result in serious fall injuries, furniture unattached to walls can fall on children, small parts can strangle children and window blind cords can choke children,

- Cords on children's clothing, jewelry around necks, and jump ropes can catch on playground apparatus, in car or bus doors, and choke children.

- Openings on playground apparatus between 3.5 inches and 9 inches can entrap children's heads and lead to strangulation.

- Falls onto concrete, asphalt, and hard-packed earth under and around playground equipment can result in fractures, paraplegia, quadriplegia, brain damage, damaged internal organs, and death. Wherever children climb, hard surfaces, indoors or outdoors—including homes, child-care centers, and commercial establishments—are hazardous. ASTM standards address these hazards and how to prevent them.

- Heavy wood, plastic, or metal swings, especially those with protruding bolts, can cause serious or fatal injury to children upon impact.

- Excessive heights on playground equipment or other climbing equipment can result in serious injury or death from falls, particularly for very young children.

- Wearing jewelry (rings, earrings, necklaces) on playgrounds can result in hang-ups on protruding equipment parts, causing finger amputation or injury to neck or ear.

- Open S-hooks and protruding elements on playground and sports equipment can entangle children's clothing or jewelry and lead to suffocation.

- Exposed sheet metal apparatus (e.g., playground slides and decks, sewer covers, black or heat-absorbing padded surfaces) can result in severe burns, especially to toddlers who tend to "freeze" or "stick" to hot surfaces.

- Swimming pools, improperly protected by fences, secure gates, and alarms, are the sites of many drownings each year, especially of toddlers. Toddlers should never be left alone or unsupervised near water, even for a minute. *Be paranoid about this!*

- Improperly designed or improperly anchored soccer goals can and do collapse on children, resulting in serious injuries and deaths.

- Beginning ice skaters, in-line skaters, roller skaters, and skiers are at high risk of head injury in falls. Helmets would prevent most of these injuries.

- Riding bicycles without a helmet can result in serious injury and fatalities in collisions and falls. Helmets dramatically reduce such results.

- Unsupervised children can gain access to dangerous animals in zoos by crossing barriers, inserting fingers and hands into animal containment areas, and falling into animal containment pits and moats. Many existing barriers at zoos do not prevent such access.

- Trampolines are frequently poorly designed and maintained, leading to the risk of serious injuries in falls onto unpadded frames of trampolines or onto unprotected surrounding floor or ground.

- In many states, carnival and theme park rides are poorly regulated or unregulated and many are involved in serious injuries and deaths. This is especially true of traveling carnivals.

- Many car trunks, abandoned refrigerators, storage boxes, and toy chests have doors or lids that can be opened and closed by children, allowing them to become entrapped and suffocate.

- Window guards should be installed in multifloor apartments and homes to prevent young children from falling out. Window screens do not protect from falling.

- Loose cords such as those used for window blinds should be secured so that they cannot form a loop around a child's head and lead to strangulation.

- Standing up in shopping carts is very hazardous because children can easily lose their balance and the carts are unstable and tilt over easily. Falls from the height of a shopping cart onto a concrete floor covered with vinyl can be fatal.

- Young children can pull out heavy furniture drawers, and cause furniture to topple or appliances and television sets to topple from tables or chests onto them. This can result in serious injury or death.

- Fireworks cause many serious burns to children each year. Many fireworks entering the United States do not meet U.S. federal standards. Young children should not be allowed to use fireworks in any manner.

- Toddlers must be given extra protection from water in buckets, toilets, pools, and streams because they are attracted to water, do not realize the dangers of water, and cannot easily extricate themselves from falls into water. Drowning is the number-two cause of death for young children.

- Children should be properly secured in car seats taking into account type of air bags, quality of car seats, and age of child. Auto accidents are the number-one cause of accidental death for young children.

- Extreme caution should be used to protect children against exposure to pesticides, prescription drugs, housekeeping products, and other toxic materials.

- Firearms should be kept locked away and unloaded.

- Adults and children should get up-to-date recall and product safety information from the Consumer Product Safety Commissions Website (www.cpsc.gov) so they will know which products are causing injuries and deaths.

- Adults who care for children—parents, grandparents, teachers, caretakers, and others—should secure federal and state safety guidelines for classroom safety, toys, playground equipment, swimming pools, and other potentially hazardous consumer products used by children.

---

environment because they spend too little time in challenging, complex settings to develop perceptual-motor and safety skills, because they are too heavy (obese) to manage their excess weight in challenging activities (Frost & Henniger, 1979; Frost et al., 2004; Sutterby & Frost, 2002; Frost, 2010), or they receive little or no guidance on safety from adults.

## HAZARDS IN PUBLIC PLACES

Throughout this chapter, we use injury data from the National Electronic Injury Surveillance System (NEISS) to illustrate the scope of injuries, type of injuries, and consumer products implicated in injuries. NEISS is a federal agency that collects injury data associated with 15,000

consumer products from hospital emergency departments across the United States. The examples of very serious hazards in Figure 13.1 were selected from personal litigation documents, CPSC data that include NEISS data, Safe Kids data, personal communication with specialists in child safety, inspection of injury/fatality sites, and safety conferences. These examples represent very serious play-related hazards that are likely to result in permanent disability, loss of body parts, or loss of life.

## CHILD DEVELOPMENT AND SAFETY

The ages and developmental abilities of children must be taken into account in formulating a safety program. The following sections consider the unique characteristics of toddlers, preschoolers, and early-school-age children, and how those characteristics affect safety concerns.

## Toddlers

As children grow into the toddler stage (ages 1–3 years), beginning with the onset of walking, they become increasingly mobile. During the toddler period, cognitive, social, motor, and emotional development is rapid and leads to a growing sense of independence. Toddlers are avid explorers, trying out everything in the immediate environment, but their curiosity frequently threatens their safety. They will walk into pools of water, touch hot surfaces, step off high places, or run into the paths of cars. They may be unaware of the consequences of their actions and must be carefully protected by adults.

As toddlers learn to understand and accept common rules of behavior, adults must supervise them closely and take steps to reduce hazards they may encounter, indoors and outdoors. This is frequently called childproofing, but proofing is not really possible under normal conditions. Toddlers must take acceptable risks to learn how to protect themselves. Adults attempt to reduce hazards to a reasonably acceptable level, focusing on avoiding or removing those hazards that could result in loss of life or debilitating injury. Even animals take care to protect their young from extreme hazards. Such care by human adults need not extend to overprotection, paranoia, or interference with creativity. As toddlers experience challenges and think about steps for solving problems, they gradually learn to anticipate the consequences of their actions and are better able to protect themselves from previously unrecognized hazards. Adults should encourage experimentation in reasonably safe environments, for trying on for size is essential to toddler's learning and safety.

Toddlers are sometimes referred to as the terrible twos. Their curiosity and extreme activity can cause considerable anxiety for caretakers, especially in public play and entertainment environments such as playgrounds, pools, zoos, and amusement parks. In such places, the caretaker must stay in visual and auditory range at all times and attempt to stay in range for physical restraint when necessary. With toddlers, there will be breakdowns or lapses in supervision, including the time when they run out of auditory or visual range. This is especially true when a single adult is responsible for supervising more than one child. Consequently, both child supervisors and sponsors of play sites should carefully evaluate the environments they allow toddlers to enter. In extremely hazardous places, such as along busy streets or adjacent to steep drop-offs, adults must hold toddlers by the hand because they can move quickly and unexpectedly. Those responsible for operating public play and entertainment places must meet or exceed common regulations and standards for child safety.

Children are most active at ages 2 and 3, and their activity levels decrease during the preschool years. Because of their high activity levels and their relatively immature motor and cognitive skills, toddlers are at greater risk of accidental injuries than preschoolers and must be supervised more closely. This is graphically and tragically illustrated by a wide range of data: toddlers walking or running into the path of cars, climbing through gates and fences and drowning in pools, standing up in shopping carts or other wheeled devices and falling onto concrete floors, locking themselves in refrigerators and car trunks, sitting down or placing hands on hot metal and sticking to the surface, and walking into the path of swings on the playground.

## Preschoolers and Early-School-Age Children

Preschoolers (ages 3–5) and early-school-age children (ages 5–7) have generally developed beyond toddlers in physical appearance, height and weight, levels of activity, refinement of motor skills, thinking processes, knowledge of events, language and communication, social skills, and emotional maturity. Their motor skills allow them to gain access to previously forbidden or inaccessible places such as pools, high places, trees, walls, deck railings, and fences, and they are motivated to play on such challenging devices. The conceptual development of these age groups is progressing rapidly, but most are still engaging in pre-logical thought and lack high levels of skill in recognizing and evaluating potentially hazardous conditions. Furthermore, they are increasingly influenced by peers and may participate in motor challenges beyond their abilities to impress or compete with them. Such risks often lead to injury, particularly on playgrounds but also in other public places.

Preschoolers experience an increase in fears and anxieties. They have vivid imaginations, engage frequently in symbolic (make-believe) play, and may have difficulty distinguishing reality from fantasy. The fears of some children are specific to certain events. The child who has been mauled by a dog or burned on a hot surface may generalize her fears to other animals or to other surfaces. Some children may show little fear in most contexts, even in very hazardous situations. They may approach vicious animals as though they were docile pets; they may display little fear of heights, water, or automobiles in streets. They may play hangman in realistic fashion ("like on television") by actually forming a noose, placing it around one's head, and jumping off a deck or chair. Learning the crucial concepts "injuries can cause severe pain" and "death is permanent" is a task that takes time, experience, and adult guidance.

## GUIDELINES/STANDARDS FOR SAFETY

Because of a variety of related factors (including young children's vulnerability to hazards, growing numbers of child injuries, and mushrooming litigation) safety guidelines, standards, regulations, and laws are being developed to help ensure that play equipment and environments are reasonably safe. These range from guidelines prepared by schools and child-care centers relevant to their own contexts; to mandatory regulations of state departments of health, human services, and education; to voluntary standards prepared and distributed by national standards organizations and U.S. government agencies such as the CPSC (see Figure 13.2).

The safety standards established by organizations such as ASTM and by agencies of the U.S. government are usually recognized as national standards of care, meaning that they usually prevail in litigation. In other words, if a child is injured or killed in an accident on a playground or other public place where national standards apply and a lawsuit is filed, the winner is often, but not always, determined by compliance or noncompliance with the state and/or national standard. Compared to national playground and play equipment standards, state playground standards or regulations were typically sterile and extremely limited in scope and clarity until recently. Consequently, many child-care providers, unwittingly relying on compliance with state regulations to protect themselves in litigation, find themselves facing huge liability settlements because they fail to meet national standards of care (e.g., ASTM, CPSC).

## History of Playground Equipment Standards

The section to follow traces the development of safety guidelines and standards for public playground equipment—that is, equipment designed for parks, schools, child-care facilities, multiple-family dwellings, restaurants, resorts and recreational developments, and other areas of public use. These guidelines and standards cover children ages 2 to 12. ASTM standards for toddlers were under development as of July 2006.

In the early 20th century, manufactured playground equipment was constructed primarily of

**FIGURE 13.2** Overview: CPSC *Handbook for Public Playground Safety*

**Scope of *Handbook***

- *Handbook* specifies separate play areas for 2- to 5-year-olds and 5- to 12-year-olds.

**Source of Guidelines**

- Guidelines are based on injury data from NEISS, expert opinion, public commentaries, and research data.

**Supervision**

- Supervisors should understand the basics of play safety.
- Preschool children require more attentive supervision than older children.
- Supervisors should be aware of age appropriateness of equipment (look for posted signs).

**Selecting, Purchasing, and Installing Equipment**

- Confirm that equipment meets CPSC guidelines (e.g., select equipment approved by the International Play Equipment Manufacturers Association, IPEMA).
- Select experienced installers. Require CPSC compliance and insurance.
- Check equipment for durability and finish.
- Follow manufacturer's assembly and installation instructions.
- Have equipment and play area inspected by a qualified playground inspector during and after installation.

**Surfacing**

- Concrete, asphalt, soil, hard-packed earth, and grass are not acceptable.
- Properly tested rubber materials—unitary and loose fill—are acceptable.
- Properly selected loose-fill materials—wood chips, engineered wood chips, sand, pea gravel, and shredded tires—are acceptable.
- Depth of material depends on potential fall height, type of material, and scientific tests (see CPSC critical height tables).
- Extreme cold and hot climates require special attention to type of surface. Sand freezes solid, but pea gravel and some manufactured surfaces are less prone to freezing (not in CPSC *Handbook for Public Playground Safety*).
- Loose-fill surfacing should not be installed over concrete or asphalt.
- Surfacing should be kept in place under and around equipment according to specified dimensions and maintained regularly.
- The use zone of stationary equipment (area to receive resilient surfacing) should extend a minimum of 6 feet in all directions. Check *Handbook* regarding use zones for swings, slides, moving equipment, and overlap zones.
- The guidelines do not address indoor equipment, but a CPSC Safety Alert dated May 1995 (available at www.cpsc.gov) warns consumers never to put children's climbing gyms on hard surfaces, including wood or carpeted floors, indoors or outdoors.

**Safety and Maintenance**

- Develop a comprehensive maintenance program.
- Inspect all equipment and play areas frequently.
- Follow the CPSC *Handbook* and manufacturer's recommendations for maintenance.
- Use inspection checklists, repair promptly, and keep records.

- Check protective surfacing for reduced depth, compacted areas, and foreign material.
- Check for head entrapment (most components should not form openings between 3.5 and 9 inches; check the *Handbook for* details). CPSC guidelines do not address extreme climate conditions, but ice may form in a manner that could create head entrapments. Ice may also fall from play structure roofs when thawing.
- Check for suspended hazards.
- Check for ropes or cables that can form loops around neck.
- Check all equipment for CPSC-prescribed dimensions (height, width, diameter, elevation, transition, guardrails, protective barriers, etc.).
- Check for sheet metal (e.g., slides and decks) exposed to in direct sunlight.
- Check for sharp points, missing or damaged parts, protrusions, potential clothing entanglement hazards (open S-hooks and bolts), shearing points, trip hazards.
- Check for rust, rot, cracks and splinters, and termites (probe underground).
- Check for broken or missing play components, fences, benches, and signs.
- Check that all equipment are securely anchored.
- Check for loose fasteners and worn connections.
- Check for worn swing hangers and bearings of moving devices.
- Check area for drainage, especially in heavy-use areas (e.g., under swings).
- Check for lead paint and cracked, chipped, and peeling paint.
- Check for toxic materials (wood preservatives, insecticides, pesticides, and herbicides).
- Check entire area for litter.
- Check entire area for damaged or missing parts, signs, and fence components.
- Check all equipment for structural stability, excessive wear, and damage.

---

heavy-duty steel and wood. The most common devices were swings, slides, jungle gyms, teeter-totters, and giant strides (a circular device mounted on a support post and swivel with chains hanging down for grasping and circular movement). They featured fast rotation and extreme heights, accommodated large numbers of children, and the surface underneath equipment was commonly hard-packed earth, packed cinders, or asphalt. As early as 1917, concern about injuries was evident, and a lawsuit, resulting from an injury to a child who fell from a swing, was successfully litigated against a school board in Tacoma, Washington. During the 1920s, the design, selection, installation, and use of playground equipment was debated in professional publications (Playground and Recreation Association of America, 1928). Concerns about playground injuries led the National Recreation Association (NRA) to form the Committee on Standards in Playground Apparatus for the purpose of developing a guide for communities in selecting playground equipment (NRA, 1931). The resulting document included essential elements for playground success: location, arrangement, and erection of equipment; supervision; apparatus zones; care of ground under equipment; instructions for use of equipment; age designations; and types of equipment.

Even during this early period, park professionals recognized the hazards of hard surfacing under equipment, and, in 1932, the NRA published a two-part report on problems in surfacing children's playgrounds in its periodical

*Recreation.* Based on his knowledge of law and of lawsuits, Jacobson (1940) made specific recommendations for playground safety. He emphasized purchasing the best equipment, observing equipment in use, setting up inspection systems, creating printed inspection and repair forms, recording all inspections and work, employing careful supervision by trained professionals, and posting warning signs for unsafe conditions. Ironically, over a half-century later, professionals are still debating similar recommendations.

By the 1950s, injuries and fatalities on the school playgrounds of Los Angeles (Brashear, 1952; Zaun, 1952, 1955) resulted in public protest about asphalt surfaces under and around play equipment. With 190 school playgrounds surfaced with asphalt, several children suffered fatal injuries in falls onto the hard surfaces. Following citizen action and a lawsuit, Los Angeles installed rubber surfacing under playground equipment and had no additional fatalities over the following decade.

Systematic efforts to collect scientific data on playground injuries were initiated in 1972, resulting in a report by the Bureau of Product Safety, U.S. Food and Drug Administration (1972). It drew from NEISS data to reveal a dismal picture of playground injuries and hazards, and ranked playground equipment eighth in number of injuries on the Consumer Product Safety List. A University of Iowa report (McConnell, Parks, & Knapp, 1973) used data from NEISS, the National Safety Council, in-depth studies by the CPSC, and anthropometric data. Yet another study (CPSC, 1975) explored playground injuries in depth and estimated from NEISS data that 117,951 playground injuries were treated in emergency rooms in 1974. During this same period, the Playground Equipment Manufacturer's Association and the National Recreation and Park Association (NRPA) were working with the CPSC to develop preliminary safety standards for playground equipment.

Spurred by this activity and petitions by Butwinick (1974), endorsed by the Americans for Democratic Action and the Consumers Union and by a second petition by Sweeney (1974), the stage was set for the CPSC to contract with the NRPA to develop a standard for public playground equipment (NRPA, 1976). The National Bureau of Standards revised the standards and published them as two handbooks in 1978. On October 4, 1979, commentaries on the handbooks were requested by the CPSC in the *Federal Register,* and, following revisions, the reports were published and made available to the public by the CPSC in two handbooks (CPSC, 1981a, 1981b). These handbooks, with periodic revisions (revised in 1991, 1993, and 1997) and combined with the ASTM standards published in 1993 (revised in 1995 and 2005), would be argued as the national standard of care in play equipment safety litigation.

By 2006, several states had passed legislation addressing playground safety with a common requirement to meet all or specified CPSC guidelines (voluntary in Connecticut) and, in some states, ASTM standards. See Chapter 9 for information on playground standards and regulations for children with disabilities.

**Playground Safety Surveys** During the period when the early CPSC guidelines were being developed, three national surveys of playground safety were conducted by teams of professionals (child development, architecture, physical education, recreation, and playground design) and published by the American Alliance for Health, Physical Education, Recreation, and Dance (AAH-PERD). An initial survey of elementary school playgrounds (Bruya & Langendorfer, 1988) was followed by a survey of public park playgrounds (Thompson & Bowers, 1989) and a survey of preschool playgrounds (Wortham & Frost, 1990). Collectively, these surveys revealed an overall pattern of antiquated design, hazardous conditions, and poor or absent maintenance. The worst playgrounds of the lot were judged accidents waiting to happen, sterile in play value, and essentially unfit for children's play (Frost, Bowers, & Wortham, 1990, p. 21).

Overall, the surveys concluded that the safety of American public playgrounds was unconscionably bad. Common hazards included head entrapment areas, open-base merry-go-rounds, crushing rotating mechanisms, open S-hooks, protruding bolts, excessive heights, poor or absent resilient surfacing, rigid and heavy swing seats, and very little evidence of maintenance. Statistical analyses are available in each of the reports. These surveys were influential in the work of standards committee groups in developing and revising national playground standards.

National surveys conducted by the U.S. Public Interest Research Group and the Consumer Federation of America (Mierzwinski, Fise, & Morrison, 1996; Sikes, Fise, & Morrison, 1992; Wood, Fise, & Morrison, 1994) reinforced the earlier national surveys' findings of neglect in playground safety. Later, national surveys of playgrounds were conducted by the National Program for Playground Safety (1999) (see General Information, pp. 505–506) and the Consumer Federation of America (2000). Even more recent surveys by these same groups showed that compliance has improved over time (Olsen, Hudson, & Thompson, 2004; Weintraub & Cassady, 2002), yet puzzling statistics remain; the rate of injuries reported to NEISS at emergency rooms grew from about 117,000 in 1974 to well over 200,000 in 2010.

## PROMOTING SAFETY WHERE CHILDREN PLAY

Annually, 20% to 25% of all children are injured badly enough to require medical attention, missed school, or bed rest. Unintentional injury is the leading cause of death for children under age 21. The leading causes of fatal injuries are motor vehicles, fires/burns, drowning, falling, and poisoning (National Center for Injury Prevention and Control, 2003a).

Children encounter hazards wherever they play, and they play wherever they happen to be—whether their bedroom, a classroom, a

The Houston Parks and Recreation Department trains workers and equips vans for playground maintenance.

theme park, or a shopping center. The large numbers of children's accidents are not merely a natural consequence of growing up. This is a particularly pernicious view, for virtually all fatal and permanent accidental injuries are preventable. Numerous safety measures have demonstrated success in reducing injuries and fatalities—for example, seat belts in cars, bicycle helmets, proper barriers around pools, resilient surfacing around play equipment, even removing cords from children's clothing and small parts from infant and toddler toys (no toddler has ever been choked by the absence of a cord or strangled by the absence of an object).

A second common misconception is that requiring playground equipment to conform to national safety standards must result in sterile, unimaginative, unchallenging playgrounds. Interpretations of CPSC and ASTM guidelines/standards can and often do result in such playgrounds, but that may be the choice or fault of the designer or sponsor. CPSC guidelines and ASTM standards deal essentially with consumer products—that is, manufactured equipment. They barely touch natural features—gardens, woodlands, tools, building or construction materials, living things, shelters, cooking facilities, wheeled-vehicle paths, sand and water play areas, streams, hills, and vegetation. However, in overzealous lawsuits such natural features are sometimes treated as playground equipment, subject to playground equipment safety standards. Gardens, animal habitats, and natural areas are the stuff of creative, imaginative, magical playgrounds and should be integrated into playgrounds.

## Playground Safety

Data from NEISS show a rising incidence of playground injuries from a level of about 117,000 annually from 1974 through 1984; to about 200,000 annually from 1984 through 1988; and another jump to almost a quarter million annually from 1991, continuing through the

remainder of the decade and into the 21st century. About 45% of playground injuries are severe; 75% occur on public playgrounds; girls sustain slightly more injuries than boys; children ages 5 to 9 are the most frequently injured (National Center for Injury Prevention and Control, 2003a). Reasons for the growing number of injuries are somewhat speculative, but improved reporting, neglected maintenance, absence of adult supervision, and declining fitness levels of children are all probable contributing factors. A growing number of children are unsafe on any playground because they are deprived of active outdoor play by overemphasis on high-stakes testing and high-tech sedentary play, and affected by poor diets, soaring obesity, and a decline in fitness. Although conclusive data are not available, physically fit children may have significantly fewer injuries on playgrounds.

**Limitations of CPSC Guidelines and ASTM Standards**    A growing number of experts, including the author, believe that the CPSC guidelines and the ASTM standards are unduly restrictive and tend to influence cookie-cutter, or standardized, playgrounds. This is indeed the case, particularly in schools and parks where sponsors tend to limit their playgrounds to an array of commercial equipment, fixed in concrete, and devoid of loose materials, natural features, and children's creations. The safety specifications of the guidelines/standards are heavily influenced by play equipment manufacturers who initially resisted regulations but later came to embrace them as old outmoded, out-of-compliance equipment was destroyed and sales of new equipment skyrocketed.

Through continuing revision, the ASTM standards grew to 55 pages by 2006 and were excessive in scope and detail, contradictory, and burdensome to playground sponsors (see Frost, 2005b, 2006). As state safety regulations are revised, we see growing numbers of discrepancies between these and national

Both installation and design are important for play equipment safety.

standards. Equipment acceptable to ASTM may be rejected by state regulations, causing confusion and excessive expense among all concerned parties, and diminished play opportunities for children.

Consider, for example, that a range of equipment is deemed "not recommended" for preschool-age children, including vertical sliding poles and overhead apparatus. Extensive research shows that preschool children can and do use such equipment when it is available (Frost et al., 2004). The decision to not recommend is based on injury data arising from preschoolers using equipment designed for elementary schools—excessively tall, lacking protective resilient surfacing, and often having exposed concrete footings. The issue of height of equipment is of particular importance in determining safety parameters of equipment, especially for preschool and early primary school children (Frost et al., 2002; 2004). Safety specifications prescribe narrow diameters

(less than 1.9 inches) for sliding poles. Very young children like to hug broad sliding poles (3 to 4 inches in diameter) for their short descent. Much of the prohibited equipment can be used with reasonable safety if it is scaled to children's abilities. The playground manufacturing industry is beginning to sponsor limited research on children's play and play environments.

All too frequently, playgrounds are merely selections of purchased equipment arranged in standardized form. Such playgrounds are neat and tidy, but they lack child appeal, creative function, challenge, and diversity. In addition to using safety guidelines and standards, designers and consumers should seek information on integrating manufactured equipment with more creative play materials and opportunities. These include most portable materials or loose parts, trike paths, wheeled vehicles, sand, water and dirt, construction materials and tools, gardening and gardening materials, nature areas and materials, provision for pets, art materials, storage, hand tools, and special places. Many potential purchasers assume that such materials and activities are hazardous, unimportant, and frivolous.

## Water Safety

Nationwide, drowning is the second most frequent cause of injury-related deaths among children ages 1 to 14, despite a 40% decline in drownings from 1987 to 2001 (Safe Kids USA, 2004, 2010). The decline appears to have resulted from growing numbers of states developing and enforcing pool safety standards. Safe Kids USA (2010) reports that each year 830 children under age 14 drown and many more nearly drown. Children who survive near drownings commonly suffer brain damage after 4 to 6 minutes under water. Requiring child-proof fencing around pools is a major preventive step. In some states, including California, Texas, and Arizona, drowning was the top killer of young children in 1992 (CPSC, 1992). The National Center for Injury Prevention and Control (NCIPC, 2003b) reported that in 2000, 943 children ages 0 to 14 years died from drowning. For every child who drowns, six receive emergency room care for near-drowning which may result in brain damage. Children under age 1 most frequently drown in buckets, bathtubs, and toilets. Children ages 1 to 4 most frequently drown in residential swimming pools. As children get older, they are more likely to drown in lakes, ponds, and rivers (NPIPC, 2003b). Toddlers are at great risk around water for they are attracted to water, have limited cause-and-effect thinking ability, usually cannot swim, are poorly coordinated, and may walk or jump into pools or streams and drown without a sound. When around water they must receive unfaltering supervision. Even momentary lapses in supervision such as answering a phone or stepping inside can result in disaster.

Growing awareness of the scope of drowning is leading communities, cities, and states to implement laws and regulations for child protection. Existing national regulations/ guidelines include those by the National Spa and Pool Institute (1991, 1992), the Southern Building Code Congress (1992), the American Public Health Association (1981), and the CPSC (1996). These regulations and guidelines typically specify barriers (fences, walls) around pools at least 4 feet high with self-closing, self-latching gates. The authors and some municipalities recommend that barriers be 6 feet tall because many preschool-age children can scale 4-foot fences, particularly those of chain-link construction. Barriers should have openings no greater than 4 inches wide; they should be difficult to climb, and gate latches should be out of reach of young children. If the home or adjacent house forms one side of the pool barrier, doors leading to the pool should be equipped with alarms as well as locking devices that cannot be operated by young children. During the off-season, pools should be covered with durable covers that support a child's weight and cannot collapse under a child's weight into the water. The CPSC (1992) offers free publications available by calling its hotline (800–638–2772) or visiting its website (www.cpsc.gov). ASTM provides updates at www.astm.gov.

Young children can drown in a few inches of water in bathtubs, spas, hot tubs, creeks, wading pools, ponds, toilets, and buckets. With a toddler in the house or child-care center, bathrooms must be secured, buckets stored empty, and multiple levels of protection installed between indoor places and pools. Pools should be secured against entry by children when home owners are absent or when child-care centers or schools are closed. This requires tall, difficult-to-climb fences (6-foot minimum height) and secure locks on all entrances.

## Noise

**Noise** is commonly described as unwanted sound and has adverse effects on people of all ages. The effects are cumulative and more severe for children than for adults. The extent of damage resulting from high levels of noise depends on the duration of the noise, its intensity or volume, and the individual's relative susceptibility. The damage includes stress, hearing loss, psychiatric disorders, cardiovascular disease, and decline in school performance (Kryter, 1994; Center for Hearing and Communication, 2010). The effects of noise are cumulative; long-term exposure can result in permanent damage to the inner ear and central nervous system.

The opportunities for damage from noise are perhaps greatest in large urban areas of congregated living where airports (Kryter, 1994), trains (Bronzaft & McCarthy, 1975), expressways (Glass & Singer, 1972), rock music (Danenberg, Loos-Cosgrove, & LoVerde, 1987), and other noise-producing sources, such as factory and construction activity, are concentrated. Concentrations of children at schools and apartment buildings with unprotected noise sources result in large numbers being exposed regularly. Many such concentrations are present throughout the world, particularly in flight paths of airports and adjacent to expressways. Damaging levels of noise may be present both indoors and outdoors, so steps should be taken to reduce or eliminate exposure.

Solutions and partial solutions to noise include (a) avoidance of noise, (b) reduction or elimination of noise at its source, and (c) reduction or elimination of noise by installing sound-reducing materials (Frost, 1996a). The solution begins at home and is carried over to child-care centers and schools. Adults should review noise conditions when selecting homes and schools, spending time indoors and outdoors and observing and listening to types and levels of noise. They should also restrict children from participating in excessive noise-producing activities, such as most rock concerts, and instruct them on safe use of earphones and acoustical equipment.

Noise can be reduced indoors by replacing sound-reflecting materials (e.g., highly reflective tiles, walls, ceilings) with sound-absorbing materials (e.g., carpets, draperies, acoustic materials), installing sound barriers, and sealing cracks or openings. Excessive noise at musical events should be limited to Occupational Safety and Health Act (OSHA) regulations (Beranek, 1996; Hodge & Price, 1978). Outdoor noise may be a more serious problem than indoor noise because the protection of walls and insulation is not present there. The first step in outdoor noise control is locating playgrounds away from noise sources or locating them on the opposite side of the school building from the source. That failing, landscape architects can assist in buffering and redirecting noise with hills, fences, and dense vegetation. It is cheaper and more effective to design and construct quiet facilities and equipment than to attempt remedies later.

## Toy Safety

In 2003, 11 children ages 14 and younger died from toy-related injuries and 155,400 were treated at emergency rooms for toy-related injuries (www.safekids.org). At least 25 children under age 12 died, and about 202,500 were treated in hospital emergency rooms from toy-related injuries in 2000 (National Safe Kids Campaign, 2003). Slipshod manufacture and importation of toys from foreign countries represent a major risk to children because the large volume reaching American entry points cannot be thoroughly evaluated by customs inspectors. Consequently, the CPSC and other government agencies are constantly recalling dangerous products after they have been placed in the hands of children and resulted in injuries. Wise caretakers of children inspect all toys intended for children upon purchase and periodically thereafter. The CPSC report, *Age Determination Guidelines* (Therrell, Brown, Sutterby, & Thornton, 2002) is an extensive analysis of toy characteristics and developmental guidelines, and Figure 13.3 summarizes some safety points for toys for various ages.

**FIGURE 13.3**   Safety in Toy Play

## Ages 0–3

- Select toys appropriate to the child's age. Toddlers put objects in their mouth, creating choking hazards.
- Avoid objects including balls, marbles, buttons, pea gravel on playgrounds, pellets from bean bag chairs, and removable toy parts that are less than 1.75 inches in diameter. Check all toys carefully to ensure that parts cannot be torn off.
- Never allow children to play with uninflated balloons because they pose a choking hazard.
- Never allow children to play with plastic bags, including dry cleaning bags and bags that package merchandise, because of the suffocation hazard. Any material that covers the entire head can be hazardous.
- Check toys for parts that active children can pull off and put in their mouths.
- Check toys for sharp edges and points.

## Ages 3–5

- Instruct older children to keep toys that are hazardous for younger children away from them.
- Select art materials marked "ASTM D-4236," which means they have been reviewed for toxic content.
- Avoid toys constructed of brittle material that might break into small pieces with jagged edges.

## All Ages

- Review age designations and safety warnings on toys before purchasing or giving them to children.
- Check toys regularly for breakage, excessive wear, and potential hazards.
- Require children to wear helmets when riding bicycles and when learning to roller skate, ice skate, or ski in snow.
- Teach children to put toys away when not in use and not leave them where others can fall over them.
- Be sure that toy guns are brightly colored and cannot be mistaken for a real gun.
- Never allow young children to play with fireworks. Fireworks displays are best conducted by experts for the entertainment of all ages.
- Avoid purchasing toys, such as dart guns, that fire projectiles.
- Check areas where children play with chests and trunks that can close on them, leading to suffocation. Some automobile trunks can be opened without a key. Presently, automobile trunks cannot be opened from the inside.
- Never allow children to play with automatic garage door openers. Ensure that safety reversal systems are installed and operational.
- Secure a copy of American Society for Testing and Materials (ASTM, 1996), *Standard Consumer Safety Specification on Toy Safety* (phone [610] 832-9585; Website: www.astm.org).
- Check Web pages of the CPSC (www.cpsc.gov) to secure safety alerts and related data on hazardous toys and devices.
- Get involved with the National Safe Kids Campaign (www.safekids.org), a nonprofit organization that conducts efforts to prevent unintentional deaths and injuries to children. Read its literature.

The U.S. Public Interest Research Group (enter US PIRG 2009 Toy Safety Survey) focused on three categories of toy hazards: choking hazards, excessively loud toys, and toys that contain toxic chemicals, especially lead and phthalates. During the early months of 2009, more than 5 million toys and other children's toys were removed from store shelves due to choking hazards. Adults should look for warnings against choking and suffocation hazards and check for loose parts that could lead to choking when selecting toys for young children. Almost 15 percent of children ages 6 to 17 show signs of hearing loss. The Consumer Product Safety Commission (CPSC) adopted voluntary acoustics standards for toys in 2007, but toys are available that exceed the prescribed 85 decibels or 65 decibels at close range.

Lead and certain other toxins can affect almost every organ and system in the body, including the brain, in young children. During the early months of 2009 the CPSC recalled about 1.3 million toys and other children's products for levels of lead violating Federal standards. The CPSC does not test all toys some toys on store shelves violate do not meet their standards. Scientists are finding levels of phthalates in humans high enough to cause adverse health effects but manufacturers are not required to label products that contain known toxic products. For example, Bisphenol A (BPA) is a chemical used in the epoxy lining of many canned foods and beverages and also used in polycarbonate, a hard, clear plastic commonly used to contain food and water. BPA has been found to link with health problems including diabetes, heart disease, cancer, and metabolic disorders. This chemical has been found in the urine of 90 percent of Americans tested. A few food companies are conducting research on alternatives to BPA and some states and federal legislators have moved to ban or regulate BPA. Third party testing and vigorous enforcement of safety rules are sorely needed. In addition to toxic chemicals in food, enormous quantities of toxic chemicals are released in the air, water, and soil of certain areas of the nation.

## Other Hazards

**Fireworks**   In 2000, 10 people were killed and 11,000 were treated in hospital emergency rooms from fireworks-related injuries (National Safety Council, 2002). During 2005, fireworks were involved in injuries to 10,800 people and there were four fatalities. Because of the extreme hazards associated with igniting fireworks, they are best left to professionals. Every year fireworks, frequently illegal ones imported from Asia, and their improper use result in deaths, blindings, amputations, and severe burns. Most of these occur around the Fourth of July. From 1988 to 1998, the CPSC enforcement program prevented over 400 million hazardous fireworks from reaching consumers by stopping them at import docks.

The National Safety Council (2009) (enter National Safety Council Fireworks) recommends that young children never be allowed to play with or in close proximity to fireworks. Adults who decide to use them should read the warnings and instructions and follow them carefully. They should never attempt to relight misfired fireworks, and all fireworks activities should take place well away from flammable materials. The American Academy of Pediatrics (AAP) and the National Fire Protection Association urge that private use of fireworks be banned (2003).

**Head Injuries and Helmets**   Proper helmets, approved by CPSC, ASTM, and/or the American National Standards Institute (ANSI), should be worn by children in a number of play and recreational activities. In 1998, 275 deaths and 430,000 visits to emergency rooms resulted from bicycle-related injuries to children under age 21. About 23,000 children sustained a traumatic brain injury while bicycling (www.aap.org). Helmets, if used, can reduce head injuries by up to 85% and deaths from head injuries by 75 percent (Safe Kids USA, 2010). Evidence is accumulating that young children, especially beginners, should wear helmets for all types of skating, including in-line, roller, and ice, as well as skateboarding and snow skiing.

Some child-care centers use helmets for tricycle riders. Powell, Tanz, and DiScala (1997) determined from the National Pediatric Trauma Registry (NPTR) and CPSC data that injuries related to bicycle use are far more common than injuries associated with the use of tricycles or wheeled toys. As an alternative to using helmets, replacing concrete and asphalt tricycle tracks with discarded (or new, if affordable) rubber/fiber conveyor belts would provide a much more resilient surface for tricycles. Discarded conveyor belts can often be obtained free of charge from sand and gravel companies, airports, factories, and other places that use them.

**Cords, Clothing, Strangulation, and Sudden Infant Death Syndrome**   Loops on window blind cords at homes, schools, and child-care centers should be cut and separate tassels attached to prevent entanglement and strangulation. The CPSC (1998, News Release #98–157) reported that about one child a month dies from strangulation with window-blind cords, but a study by the American Medical Association and CPSC found that about half of the deaths were not reported to CPSC. Children's clothing should not have cords attached. Between 1985 and 1998, 21 children died when drawstrings caught on school buses, playground equipment, and other products. The entry to playground slides may contain openings or protrusions that can entangle cords in coat hoods.

Adults should examine play equipment for protruding parts that can entangle clothing. The mesh on some playpens may unravel, creating choking hazards, and some playpens have top rails that can collapse, trapping children at the neck. Cribs and bunk beds should also be examined for head entrapment hazards. Infant swings and carriers should be examined for straps that can entangle the head and leg openings through which infants can slip, trapping the head.

Sudden infant death syndrome (SIDS) is the leading cause of infant death beyond the neonatal period (AAP, 2000). SIDS is described as the sudden death of an infant under 1 year of age. The risk factors include prone (on stomach) sleeping position, soft or loose sleeping surfaces, overheating, exposure to smoking, and bed sharing. Comprehensive guidelines for preventing SIDS are available from CPSC and AAP.

**Poisons and Preservatives**   Each year, approximately 50 children under age 5 die from poisoning, and more than a million consumers call poison control centers about child poisonings from medicines, pesticides, or household chemicals (CPSC, 1997, News Release #97–077). More than 700 children were saved between 1970 and 1997 because of child-resistant packaging for aspirin and oral prescription medicines. Many school districts and park systems use toxic pesticides and herbicides to control insects and weeds on and around children's playgrounds. This is a hidden hazard that can threaten the health of young children.

Using preservatives in wood playground equipment is a subject of ongoing controversy. The CPSC tests and approves certain types of preservatives for playground equipment use, but consumer groups increasingly push for toxin-free, totally inert products. If contemplating the purchase of wood equipment, the purchaser should determine the type of preservative used and ensure that it has been judged acceptable for children's play by a federal agency such as the CPSC. See www.cpsc.gov for action taken by the Environmental Protection Agency to ban common preservative chromated copper arsenate (CCA) from all residential uses. The lumber industry and playground equipment manufacturers are phasing out CCA-treated wood, and consumers should avoid its use.

**Baby Walkers**   More children are injured with baby walkers than with any other nursery product. In 1997, about 14,300 children less than 15 months of age were treated at emergency rooms for baby-walker injuries, most from falling down stairs. Walkers were involved in 34 deaths between 1973 and 1998 (CPSC News Release #98–142). A baby walker certified by the Juvenile Products Manufacturers

Association must meet one of two require-ments: It must be too wide to fit through a stan-dard doorway, or it must have a feature, such as a gripping mechanism, to stop the walker at the edge of a step. Some child development spe-cialists recommend against use of baby walkers for their possible interference with normal motor development.

## Field Trips and Safety: Zoos

Every year hundreds of thousands of school-children take field trips to special places of edu-cational and recreational value. These trips are often under the care of teachers, child-care center caretakers, or parents. The scope of this chapter does not allow discussion of all the popular field trip destinations. A trip to a zoo is used as an example of the nature and extent of plan-ning for safety that should be a part of every field trip. Zoos are among the popular choices and appear to be among the safer public enter-tainment/educational places for children, but, as in all field trip destinations, hazards exist and precautions should be taken. Perhaps the most common errors by child supervisors on trips to zoos involve failing to prevent children from climbing on objects in the zoo or failing to appreciate the danger posed by wild ani-mals. Children must be taught that wild ani-mals are not pets and, with certain exceptions, can cause great bodily harm if approached or touched.

Zoos generally do a good job of containing animals but face a very difficult task of keeping children from accidental, deliberate, or mischie-vous intrusion into animal containment spaces. The behavior of wild animals is not predictable, especially by children. For certain animals (e.g., wolves), merely inserting fingers through a mesh fence has resulted in the loss of children's fingers. Some barriers are so poorly constructed that very young children can easily gain access or fall into animal containments (e.g., gorilla habitats). Alligators in their native habitats (swamps) may be separated from visitors

merely by bridge railings spanning the habitats. Some zoos install nets to catch children who fall from bridges before they enter the water.

There are various levels of hazards and risks associated with zoo animals (Frost & Griffith, 1997). Those posing minimal danger to humans if humanely treated include animals commonly found in petting zoos (e.g., guinea pigs, rab-bits). Those posing moderate danger, especially to young children who contact them directly, include small-hoof stock (goats, sheep, calves) under 100 pounds. Those posing greater dan-ger include large-hoof stock (cows, horses, deer) and large wild animals in general (lions, tigers, wolves, alligators, elephants).

Zoos routinely construct barriers of various types, depending on the type of animal, to keep animals contained and to keep visitors from contacting animals. This must be done without compromising views of the habitat and the ani-mals' natural behavior. The total zoo experience includes interaction with some animals, obser-vation of animals, visitor education, animal preservation, and research. These experiences must be preserved while ensuring reasonable degrees of safety. See Figure 13.4 for the special play/nature area in the San Antonio Zoo.

Visitors and animals are separated by barri-ers according to the type of animal. Types of barriers include **primary barriers** (solid impen-etrable barriers, deep pits, moats, and partially solid barriers such as fences), **setback zones** (several feet of vegetation between primary and public barriers to hamper access), and **public barriers** (low fences adjacent to visitor trails) to reduce accessibility, particularly by young children. Adult supervisors should never allow children to violate any of these barriers.

Zoos vary widely from city to city in the degree of safety they provide for visitors. Adults who take children to zoos should plan with children in advance and maintain contact with them throughout the zoo visit. Figure 13.5 lists safety precautions for field trips to zoos and other general destinations with children.

## ⌐ CHILD INJURIES
## AND LITIGATION

CPSC and NEISS data describe thousands of injuries, but depth of analysis is limited. Frost and Sweeney (1996) report data from 190 lawsuits on child injury and fatalities in public places, including swimming pools, carnivals, ice-skating rinks, amusement parks, wilderness camps, fast-food restaurants, indoor entertainment complexes, and playgrounds at city parks, public and private schools, and child-care centers. These lawsuits were spread over 38 states, from Alaska to Florida and from Hawaii to Washington, D.C. The sources of data were personal inspection of injury sites, depositions, police reports, private investigator reports, safety standards, regulations and laws, photographs of injury sites, medical records, interviews with children and caretakers, and autopsies. These data were supplemented by personal safety inspections of playgrounds, zoos, theme parks, and entertainment centers for children, personal interaction with safety specialists, and the vast array of data available from safety organizations. Most litigation data are not available to the public because about 90% of child injury/fatality cases settle out of court and records remain private.

Injuries to children in this study were serious, ranging from serious limb fractures to brain trauma, quadriplegia, and death. The leading cause of injuries, 113 of 190 cases, was falling onto hard ground surfaces—concrete, asphalt, or hard-packed earth. Falling onto equipment accounted for 21 additional cases, with 71% of all cases resulting from falling onto hard surfaces. Entrapments, shearing mechanisms, heavy, battering ram-type swings, protrusions, and open S-hooks accounted for an additional 41 injuries (22%), and a range of factors accounted for the remaining 15 injuries (7%) (Figure 13.6). The injuries to 13 children were fatal—6 asphyxiated by entrapment, entangled clothing, and a jump rope; 2 from being struck by heavy swings; and 1 each from

hitting a concrete culvert, falling onto concrete, falling onto rocks, being hit by a car (unfenced playground), and being hit by a motorcycle (on the playground).

The equipment most frequently implicated in serious injuries was slides (38 cases) and swings (38 cases), followed by climbers (24 cases), merry-go-rounds (16), horizontal ladders (14), fire poles (sliding poles) (8), superstructures (7), chinning bars (6), and jungle gyms (6). The three types of equipment most often implicated in injuries—slides, swings, and climbers—are the types most frequently found on playgrounds (see Figure 13.6). Although the height of equipment and design of safety features are frequently implicated in injuries, including falls, the most common direct cause of injuries is falling onto hard surfaces under and around the equipment.

Public school playgrounds, which were identified by national surveys of playgrounds (AAH-PERD) as the most hazardous among three groups—public schools, public parks, and preschools—were also the most common sites for injuries leading to lawsuits. Seventy of the 190 cases (37%) were at public schools, 48 involved public parks, 25 were at child-care centers, 15 at fast-food restaurants, 13 at backyards, 7 at apartment complexes, and the others at camps, drive-in theaters, state schools, zoos, swim clubs, retail stores, private schools, and theme parks.

Children in the early childhood range were the most often injured, with 2- to 8-year-olds accounting for 137 of the 190 injuries and fatalities, or 72%. This statistic appears to be related to immature physical skills, extensive time on playgrounds, hazardous playgrounds, and poor supervision (Frost, 1997). Boys were more frequently injured than girls (57% vs. 43%). As children enter the primary grades, their playground time is supplanted by organized sports activities and physical education.

One of the most compelling findings was that 179 of the 190 injuries and fatalities (94%) involved violations of CPSC playground safety

**FIGURE 13.4**   Kronkosky's Tiny Tot Nature Spot, San Antonio Zoo.

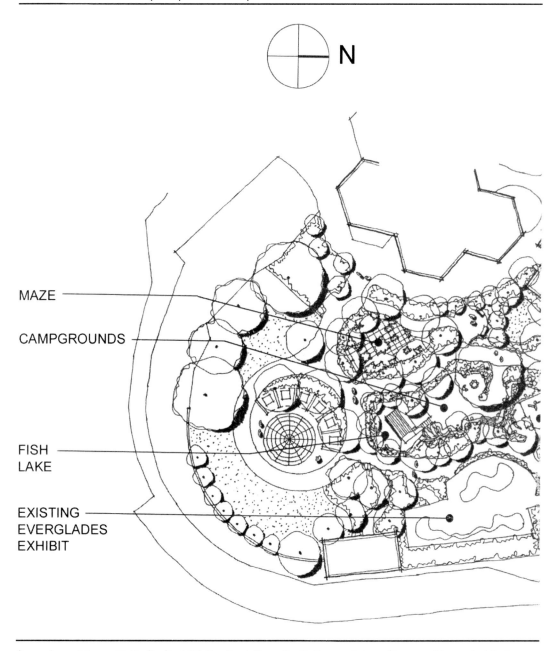

MAZE

CAMPGROUNDS

FISH
LAKE

EXISTING
EVERGLADES
EXHIBIT

*Source:* Jones & Jones, Riatto Studio, MIG (Joe Frost, Consultant). By permission of Jones and Jones, Architects, Seattle, Washington.

*(continued)*

**FIGURE 13.4** *Continued*

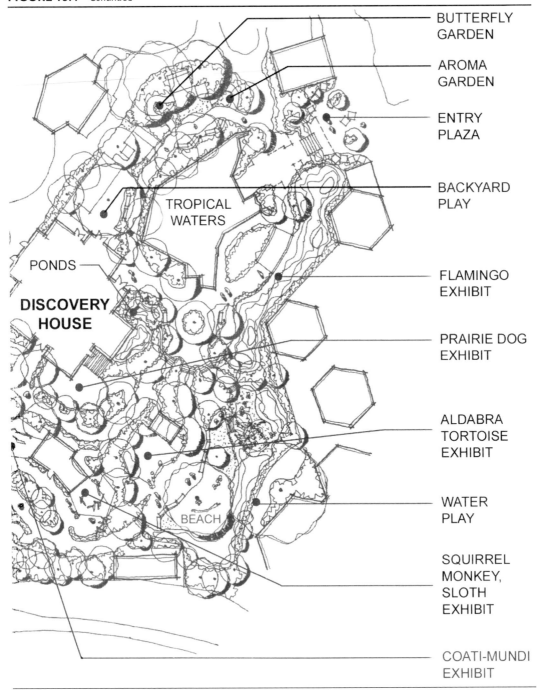

BUTTERFLY
GARDEN

AROMA
GARDEN

ENTRY
PLAZA

BACKYARD
PLAY

TROPICAL
WATERS

PONDS

DISCOVERY
HOUSE

FLAMINGO
EXHIBIT

PRAIRIE DOG
EXHIBIT

ALDABRA
TORTOISE
EXHIBIT

WATER
PLAY

BEACH

SQUIRREL
MONKEY,
SLOTH
EXHIBIT

COATI-MUNDI
EXHIBIT

**FIGURE 13.5**   Zoos and Field Trips

- Visit field trip site in advance. Check access for children with disabilities.
- Get permission forms from parents.
- Send information to parents regarding schedule, clothing, food, and transportation.
- Increase the normal adult-to-child ratio for field trips.
- Check liability insurance for drivers and vehicles. Check maintenance and fuel for vehicles.
- Plan all steps well in advance, including safety procedures, with children and supervisors before reaching the site.
- Plan with supervisors where and when entire group will meet in the event they become separated.
- Check carefully the location of transportation vehicles before leaving parking lots. Inform driver(s) of plans for departure.
- Take advantage of orientation provided by zoo personnel.
- Read and heed all warning signs throughout the zoo.
- Check locations of water fountains, toilets, first-aid stations, and food concessions upon entry to zoo.
- Do not assume that all zoos have high-quality safety programs. Look for obvious and hidden hazards.
- Young children should never be left unsupervised. Toddlers are generally unaware of hazards and must be supervised closely. Many zoos do not have sufficient protective devices to prevent toddlers and very young children from gaining access to animals or pools of water during momentary lapses of supervision.
- Children should not be allowed to engage in horseplay in zoos.
- Never touch animals unless allowed by zoo personnel.
- Avoid climbing over or through barriers.
- Never place small children on top of fences or barriers for better views of animals.
- Be alert to changing circumstances (weather, obstacles, etc.).
- Avoid teasing animals or throwing objects at animals.
- Avoid feeding animals unless expressly invited. Certain foods are not good for animals.
- Carry a portable phone and emergency phone numbers.
- Notify zoo personnel if you see safety conditions that need attention.
- Falls onto hard surfaces appear to be the chief cause of injuries at field trip destinations. Do not allow children to climb or play on structures not intended for climbing—railings, tables, strollers or rolling devices, fences, safety barriers, water fountains, or statues.
- Ensure that children scrub hands with soap and water after visiting a zoo or a farm, especially if they have been to a petting zoo or had contact with animals.

guidelines and ASTM safety standards. Falls and failure to install and maintain resilient surfacing under and around equipment dominated these findings, involving 101 of the 190 cases. Concrete, asphalt, and hard-packed earth accounted for almost all of these data. Does this mean that the injuries would not have happened if recommended surfacing practices had been followed? The answer is somewhat speculative, for children do sustain injuries from falling onto approved surfaces, but the injuries are less serious and less frequent. For example, children sometimes suffer broken arms when falling onto resilient surfacing, but they are unlikely to suffer brain damage or death. These differences are worth the effort and expense of installing and maintaining resilient surfacing. For detailed information on selecting, installing,

**FIGURE 13.6**    Avoiding Serious Playground Injuries and Lawsuits

- Develop a carefully documented safety inspection and maintenance program.
- Adopt the CPSC and ASTM playground safety guidelines and standards as minimum requirements for playgrounds. Do not depend on limited state safety regulations for protection from liability.
- Replace hard surfaces with approved resilient surfacing.
- Destroy all outmoded equipment such as battering ram-type swings and vintage open-base merry-go-rounds.
- Ensure that very young children do not use overhead apparatus designed for school-age children.
- Replace bare metal slides and decks that can cause serious burns.
- Ensure that concrete footings, especially at the base of fire or sliding poles, are recessed well under base ground and then covered with recommended resilient surfacing.
- Do not allow children to wear jewelry (rings, necklaces, earrings) or loose cords on playgrounds.
- Replace all S-hooks with permanently closed hooks.
- Fence playgrounds for young children from streets, cliffs, and water hazards.
- Require manufacturers and installers to certify in writing that their equipment and installation conform to CPSC guidelines, ASTM standards, IPEMA regulations, and ADA regulations.
- Require manufacturers and installers to provide evidence of liability insurance ($5 million minimum).
- Provide NPSI training and certification for one or more maintenance personnel.
- Provide annual safety training for all adults who supervise playgrounds.
- Document and keep records for all the above.

and maintaining resilient surfacing on playgrounds, see CPSC (1997), ASTM (1996b, 2005), and Frost (1996b).

The case profile resulting from data in the Frost and Sweeney (1996) study is a seriously injured boy between the ages of 2 and 8 years, who fell from a slide, swing, or climber onto concrete, asphalt, or hard-packed earth while playing at a public school, public park, or childcare center playground. The child suffered a broken limb or head injury resulting in litigation that endured for 2 to 4 years before being settled out of court in an agreement negotiated by attorneys and favoring the plaintiffs (p. 14).

By 2006, lawsuits resulting from playground injuries in the United States were essentially out of control, with suits ranging from obviously justified cases of callous disregard for safety, to such extremely frivolous cases as suing because a child fell over a stump in a miniature forest. Such abuse of the legal system is influencing some public schools to eliminate recess and/or playground equipment. The

pattern of spiraling actual and punitive damages in American courts is influencing the design and use of playground equipment, resulting in what we earlier designated the standardized era in playgrounds. In the United States, those who depend on manufactured equipment as a central feature in playgrounds have little choice but to comply with safety guidelines and standards that frequently (not always) prevail in litigation. Case studies from litigation are instructive for preventing some of the most serious playground injuries that are likely to result in lawsuits (see Figure 13.6).

During the early 21st century, the reduction and deletion of outdoor play and playgrounds, triggered by lawsuits, high-stakes testing, parental fear of injuries and predators, and substitution of indoor cyber play for free, spontaneous play were resulting in a growing national movement to get kids back outdoors. Adults finally awakened to the links between faltering health, fitness, and well-being of their children and began taking action to bring back risky play.

Children needed daily, active, challenging outdoor play in order to develop cognitive, social, and physical skills to protect themselves from injuries, obesity, and related health problems. (Frost, 2010).

## Standards and Lawsuits: The United States Versus Europe

"The notion of a riskless society is a peculiarly American one" (Andrews, 1998, p. D–1). Playgrounds in much of Europe are more challenging, more hazardous, and more fun than typical American playgrounds. These conditions may change because the European safety standards (European Committee for Standardization, 1998), prepared by representatives of 18 European countries, are stringent and similar in most respects to American standards. The Europeans wisely exclude adventure playgrounds— "fenced, secured playgrounds, run and staffed according to pedagogical principles, that encourage children's development and often use self-build equipment" (p. 4)—in their draft standard. In Europe, staffing "according to pedagogical principles" frequently means that a trained play leader or play worker is available to play and work with children on playgrounds (see Chapter 14). American standards contain no such exclusion, and self-build adventure playgrounds are a threatened phenomenon.

European children typically swing from greater heights, play on more challenging equipment, depend less on adult directives than American children, and, if injured, are unlikely to collect huge damage awards in lawsuits. Until recently European courts offer little financial compensation for injuries and virtually no punitive damages for negligence. Even for very serious injuries, plaintiffs may not recover damages from careless manufacturers, operators, and doctors. This is balanced by generous European systems of government health care.

One factor accounting for these differences between the American and European systems is their views of responsibility and risk. The Europeans place greater responsibility on children and allow greater freedom to take risks because risk taking is essential to development. Too much supervision or inappropriate supervision can hinder opportunities for development. The adventure playgrounds of Scandinavian countries, Germany, the United Kingdom, and the Netherlands are clear testimony to the efficacy of such beliefs, practices, and results (see Chapter 13). In recent years, countries around the world, developed and developing, are experiencing growing threats to children's traditional play, including lawsuits, parental fear, poverty, spread of technology, and indoor cyber play (Ohanian, 2002; Stearns, 2003; Frost, 2007; Gill 2007; Singer & Singer, 2009; Frost, 2010). All these factors contribute to a changing culture of childhood and deleterious consequences of play deprivation.

## SUMMARY

Striking a balance between allowing healthy development through play and managing risk of serious physical harm is a prevailing dilemma in promoting the play of children. Risk is inherent in all human behavior and, indeed, is essential to survival in mammals, especially the smarter ones (Brown, 1997, 2009). Play enhances risk, and the more adventuresome the child, the greater the risk may be. The roles of adults are to be smart (get educated) about what constitutes excessive risk, that is, risk likely to result in serious injury or death; to see that children have extensive daily opportunities to play in challenging, stimulating places that promote creativity, learning, fitness, and motor development; to check carefully all consumer products that children play with and help children examine them for safety, without encouraging paranoia; to spend time with children ensuring that they develop both motor and cognitive skills that make them smarter, safer players; and to intervene on behalf of children against distribution and use of slipshod manufactured products and hazardous play places. Take reasonable precautions, exercise common sense about the risks, then stand back and *let children play.*

#  KEY TERMS

American Society for
 Testing and Materials
 (ASTM)
Consumer Product
 Safety Commission
 (CPSC)
Extreme hazards
Hazard
Limited hazards

Moderate hazards
Noise
Primary barriers
Public barriers
Risk
Risk management
Scaffolding
Setback zones

# STUDY QUESTIONS

1. What are the meanings of the following terms: *risk, risk management, hazard, limited hazards, moderate hazards,* and *extreme hazards?* What is the importance of risk for child development? How should risk at play be balanced with children's need to play?

2. How can the Consumer Product Safety Commission be helpful to children's teachers and caretakers in reducing play hazards?

3. Identify key elements in managing risk (risk management). That is, how can play hazards be managed to reduce physical risk to reasonable levels?

4. In what ways does a contemporary lifestyle (e.g., TV, fast food, busy schedules, pay-for-play) contribute to making kids unsafe?

5. What steps would you take to help ensure safety for young children you are taking to a mall? On a field trip? To a playground?

6. How do safety needs of infants and toddlers differ from those of preschoolers? Of school-age children?

7. Why are standards, regulations, and codes important for play safety? What are their limitations and problems? How do consumer products threaten children's safety? Should standards, regulations, and codes be applied to natural features of playgrounds? Why?

8. What steps should be taken to improve safety in classrooms? What are the most common serious hazards in classrooms for young children?

9. How safe are American playgrounds? Are they developmentally appropriate? Why or why not?

10. Identify the 10 to 12 major safety hazards on playgrounds. How can these be corrected? Must correction of these hazards reduce the play value of the playground? Why or why not?

11. What is the general state of safety at pay-for-play places such as amusement parks, video arcades, carnivals, museums, swimming pools, and water parks?

12. What steps would you take to protect infants and toddlers against hazardous toys?

13. When should safety helmets be used? Cite evidence. Should tricycle riders wear helmets? Why or why not?

14. How is litigation affecting the safety of American playground equipment and toys? How is it influencing their design and distribution? How is it affecting challenge, creativity, and diversity in play? How does this situation differ from European conditions? Which do you prefer, the American or the European system? Why?

# REFERENCES

Brown, S., with Vaughan, C. (2009). Play: *How It Shapes the Brain, Opens the Imagination, and Invigorates the Soul.* New York: Penguin.

Center for Hearing and Communication (2010). *Noise and Children's Health, Learning, and Behavior.* New York: Center for Hearing and Communication.

Cole-Hamilton, I., Harrop, A., and Street, C. (2002). *The value of children's play and play provision: A systematic review of the literature.* London: New Policy Institute.

Frost, J. L. (2010). *A History of Children's Play and Play Environments: Toward a Contemporary Child-Saving Movement.* New York: Routledge.

Gill, T. (2007). *Growing Up in a Risk Averse Society.* London: Calouste Gulbenkian Foundation.

Ginsburg, K. R. (2006). Clinical report: The importance of play in promoting health child development and maintaining strong parent-child bonds. *American Academy of Pediatrics.* Retrievd February 28, 2010 from www.aap.org/pressroom/play-public.htm

Marcus, B. H. Williams, D. M., Dubbert, P. M., Sallis, J. F., King, A. C., Yancey, A. K., Franklin, B. A., Buchner, D., Daniels, S. R., and Claytor, R. P. (2006). What we know and what we need to know. A scientific statement from the American Heart Council on Nutrition Physical Activity, and Metabolism. *Circulation, 114,* 2739–52.

Mercogliano, C. (2007). *In Defense of Childhood: Protecting Kids' Inner Wildness.* Boston: Beacon Press.

National Safety Council (2009). Fixed-site Amusement Ride Injury Survey, 2009 Update. Itasca, IL: National Safety Council.

Ohanian, S. (2002). *What Happened to Recess and Why are Our Children Struggling in Kindergarten?* New York: McGraw-Hill.

Robert Wood Johnson Foundation. (2007). *Recess rules: Why the undervalued playtime may be America's best investment for healthy kids and healthy schools.* Princeton, NJ: The Foundation.

Safe Kids USA (2010). *Weekly News Digest* / Retrieved December 2010 from www.safekids.org/

Singer, D., & Singer. (2009). Children's pastimes and play in sixteen nations: Is free play declining? *American Journal of Play. 1, 3, 283–312.*

Stearns, P. N. (2003). *Anxious Parents: A History of Modern Childrearing in America.* New York: New York University Press.

American Academy of Pediatrics (AAP). (2000). *Changing concepts of sudden infant death syndrome.* Policy statement RE9946. Elk Grove Village, IL: The Academy. Retrieved March 29, 2004, from *http://www.aap.org*

American Academy of Pediatrics and National Fire Protection Association. (2003). AAP and NFPA urge ban on private use of fireworks. News release. Elk Grove Village, IL: The Academy. Retrieved March 29, 2004, from *http://www.aap.org*

American Public Health Association. (1981). *Public swimming pools: Recommended regulations for design and construction, operation and maintenance.* Washington, DC: Author.

American Society for Testing and Materials. (1996b). *Standard specification for impact attenuation of surface systems under and around playground equipment.* West Conshohocken, PA: Author.

American Society for Testing and Materials. (2005). *Standard consumer safety performance specification for playground equipment for public use.* West Conshohocken, PA: Author.

Andrews, E. L. (1998, March 15). Where a lawsuit can't get any respect. *New York Times.*

Beranek, L. (1996). *Concert and opera halls: How they sound.* Woodbury, NY: Acoustical Society of America.

Brashear, E. (1952). "But suppose she falls": Safety education. *National Safety Council, 32(1),* 2, 5, 26.

Bronzaft, A. L., & McCarthy, D. P. (1975). The effects of elevated train noise on reading ability. *Environmental Behavior, 7,* 517–527.

Brown, S. (1997). *Discovering the intelligence of play: A new model for a new generation of children* [videotape]. (Available from Touch the Future, 4350 Lime Ave., Long Beach, CA, 90807.)

Brown, S. (1998). Play as an organizing principle: Clinical evidence and personal observations. In M. Bekoff & J. Byers (Eds.), *Animal play: Evolutionary, comparative, and ecological perspectives* (pp. 243–259). Cambridge, MA: Cambridge University Press.

Brown, S., with Vaughan, C. (2009). *Play: How it shapes the brain, opens the imagination, and invigorates the soul.* New York: Penguin.

Bruya, L. D., & Langendorfer, S. J. (Eds.). (1988). *Where our children play: Elementary school playground equipment.* Reston, VA: American Alliance for Health, Physical Education, Recreation, and Dance.

Butwinick, E. (1974). *Petition requesting the issuance of a consumer product safety standard for public playground equipment.* Washington, DC: Consumer Product Safety Commission.

Center for Hearing and Communication (2010). *Noise and children's health, learning, and behavior.* New York: Author.

Centers for Disease Control. (2005). Preventing obesity and chronic diseases through good nutrition and physical activity. Retrieved June 25, 2006, from *www.cdc.gov/need-php/publications/factsheets/prevention/obesity.htm*

Clements, R. (2003, June). New research finds a decrease in USA outdoor play. *PlayRights, 25(1-2),* 11–13.

Clements, R. (2005). *Elementary school recess: Selected readings, games and activities for teachers and parents.* Boston: American Press.

Cole-Hamilton, I., Harrop, A., & Street, C. (2002). *The value of children's play and play provision: A systematic review of the literature.* London: New Policy Institute.

Consumer Federation of America. (2000). *Fifth nationwide investigation of public playgrounds.* Washington, DC: Consumer Federation of America.

Consumer Product Safety Commission (CPSC). (1975). *Hazard analysis of injuries relating to playground equipment.* Washington, DC: Author.

Consumer Product Safety Commission (CPSC). (1981a). *A handbook for public playground safety: Vol. I. General guidelines for new and existing playgrounds.* Washington, DC: Author.

Consumer Product Safety Commission (CPSC). (1981b). *A handbook for public playground safety: Vol. II. Technical guidelines for equipment and surfacing.* Washington, DC: Author.

Consumer Product Safety Commission (CPSC). (1992). *Barriers for residential swimming pools, spas, and hot tubs.* Washington, DC: Author.

Consumer Product Safety Commission (CPSC). (1996). *Pool safety guidelines.* Washington, DC: Author.

Consumer Product Safety Commission (CPSC). (1997). *A handbook for public playground safety.* Washington, DC: Author.

Danenberg, M. A., Loos-Cosgrove, M., & LoVerde, M. (1987). Temporary hearing loss and rock music. *Language, Speech and Hearing Services in Schools, 18,* 267–274.

Deitz, W. H., & Gortmaker, S. L. (1985). Do we fatten our children at the television set? Obesity and television viewing in children and adolescents. *Pediatrics, 75,* 807–812.

Dennison, B., Strans, J. H., Mellits, E. D., & Charney, E. (1988). Childhood physical fitness tests: Predictor of adult physical activity levels? *Pediatrics, 82,* 3.

European Committee for Standardization. (1998). *European standard for playground equipment.* Brussels: Central Secretariat.

Frost, J. L. (1996a). The effects of noise on children. *International Journal of Early Childhood Education, 1*(1), 21–35.

Frost, J. L. (1996b). *Protective surfacing for playgrounds.* Report prepared for the U.S. Air Force. (ERIC Document Reproduction Service No. PS024092)

Frost, J. L. (1997). Child development and playgrounds. *Parks and Recreation, 32*(4), 54–60.

Frost, J. L. (2005b). How playground regulations are messing up children's play. *Today's Playground, 5,* 14–18.

Frost, J. L. (2006b). Revisit the safety rules: Part II. *Today's Playground, 6,* 28–35.

Frost, J. L (2010). *A history of children's play and play environments: Toward a contemporary child-saving movement.* New York & London: Routledge.

Frost, J. L., Bowers, L. E., & Wortham, S. C. (1990). The state of American preschool playgrounds. *Journal of Physical Education, Recreation and Dance, 61*(8), 18–23.

Frost, J. L., Brown, P. S., Sutterby, J. A., & Thornton, C. D. (2004). *The developmental benefits of playgrounds.* Olney, MD: Association for Childhood Education International.

Frost, J. L., & Griffith, L. (1997). *Visibility, accessibility and safety assessment.* Houston, TX: Houston Zoological Gardens.

Frost, J. L., & Henniger, M. L. (1979). Making playgrounds safe for children and children safe for playgrounds. *Young Children, 34*(5), 23–30.

Frost, J. L., Sutterby, J. A., Therrell, J. A., Brown, P., & Thornton, C. D. (2002). Does height matter? *Parks and Recreation, 37*(4), 74–83.

Frost, J. L., & Sweeney, T. B. (1996). *Cause and prevention of playground injuries and litigation: Case studies.* Olney, MD: Association for Childhood Education International.

Fukushima, R. (1998, December 29). Study: Kids need an hour of exercise. *Austin American-Statesman,* p. E-3.

Gill, T. (2007). *Growing up in a risk averse society.* London: Calouste Gulbenkian Foundation.

Ginsburg, K. R. (2006, January). Clinical report: The importance of play in promoting health child development and maintaining strong parent-child bonds. *Pediatrics, 119*(1), 182–191.

Glass, D. C., & Singer, J. E. (1972). *Urban stress: Experiments on noise and social stressors.* New York: Academic Press.

Hodge, D. C., & Price, G. R. (1978). Hearing damage risk criteria. In D. M. Lipscome (Ed.), *Noise and audiology* (pp. 167–191). Baltimore: University Park Press.

Jacobson, W. (1940). Safety versus lawsuits. *Recreation, 34*(2).

Javernick, E. (1988). Johnny's not jumping: Can we help obese children? *Young Children, 43,* 18–23.

Kryter, K. D. (1994). *The handbook of hearing and the effects of noise: Physiology, psychology, and public health.* New York: Academic.

Malik, V. S., Schulze, M. B., & Hu, F. B. (2006). Intake of sugar-sweetened beverages and weight gains: A systematic review. *American Journal of Clinical Nutrition, 84,* 274–288.

Marano, H. E. (2004). *A nation of wimps.* Retrieved April 25, 2006 from http://psychologytoday.com/articles/pto-20041112-000010.html

Marcus. B. H., Williams, D. M., Dubbert, P. M., Sallis, J. F., King, A. C., Yancey, A. K., Franklin, B. A., Buchner, D., Daniels, S. R., & Claytor, R. P. (2006). What we know and what we need to know. A scientific statement from the American Heart Council on nutrition, physical activity, and metabolism. *Circulation, 114,* 2739–52.

McConnell, W. H., Parks, J. T., & Knapp, L. W. (1973). *Public playground equipment (The Iowa Study).* Washington, DC: Consumer Product Safety Commission.

Mercogliano, C. (2007). *In defense of childhood: Protecting kids' inner wildness.* Boston: Beacon Press.

Mierzwinski, E., Fise, M. E., & Morrison, M. (1996). *Playing it safe: A third nationwide safety survey of public playgrounds.* Washington, DC: U.S. Public Interest Research Group and the Consumer Federation of America.

Nabhan, G. P., & Trimble, S. (1994). *The geography of childhood: Why children need wild places.* Boston: Beacon Press.

National Center for Injury Prevention and Control (NCIPC). (2003a). *Playground injuries.* Atlanta, GA: Retrieved March 29, 2004, from http://www.cdc.gov/ncipc/

National Center for Injury Prevention and Control (NCIPC). (2003b). *Water-related injuries.* Atlanta, GA: Retrieved March 29, 2004, from http://www.cdc.gov/ncipc/

National Program for Playground Safety. (1999). *Playground safety.* Cedar Rapids, IA: Author.

National Recreation Association. (1931). *Report of Committee on Standards in Playground Apparatus* (Bulletin 2170). New York: Author.

National Recreation and Park Association. (1976). *Proposed safety standard for public playground equipment.* Washington, DC: Consumer Product Safety Commission.

National Safe Kids Campaign. (2003). Retrieved January 19, 2004 from www.safekids.org

National Safety Council. (1999). *Injury facts.* Itasca, IL: Author.

National Safety Council. (2002). *National Safety Council fireworks advisory.* Itasca, IL: National Safety Council. Retrieved May, 2002, from http://www.nsf.org

National Safety Council. (2009). *Fixed-site amusement ride injury survey, 2009 update.* Itasca, IL: The Council.

National Spa and Pool Institute. (1991). *American national standard for public swimming pools*. Alexandria, VA: Author.

National Spa and Pool Institute. (1992). *American national standard for aboveground/onground residential swimming pools*. Alexandria, VA: Author.

Ohanian, S. (2002). *What happened to recess and why are our children struggling in kindergarten?* New York: McGraw-Hill.

Olsen, H., Hudson, S., & Thompson, D. (2004, October). Do playgrounds make the grade? *National School Boards Journal*, pp. 40–43.

Pica, R. (2003). *Your active child: How to boost physical, emotional, and cognitive development through age-appropriate activity*. New York: McGraw-Hill.

Pica, R. (2005). Reading, writing, 'rithmetic, recess! *Linkup Parents Newsletter*. Retrieved August 12, 2006, at http://www.linkupparents.com/education.html

Playground and Recreation Association of America. (1928). *Play areas: Their design and equipment*. New York: Barnes.

Powell, E. C., Tanz, R. R., & DiScala, C. (1997). Bicycle-related injuries among preschool children. *Annals of Emergency Medicine, 30*(3), 260–265.

Robert Wood Johnson Foundation. (2007). *Recess rules: Why the undervalued playtime may be America's best investment for healthy kids and healthy schools*. Princeton, NJ: The Foundation.

Ross, J., & Gilbert, G. (1985). The national children and youth fitness study: A summary of the findings. *Journal of Health, Physical Education, Recreation and Dance, 56*, 45–60.

Safe Kids USA. (2004). *Clear danger: A national study of childhood drownings*. Retrieved July 16, 2006, from http://www.usa.safekids.org/nskw.cfm

Sikes, L., Fise, M. E., & Morrison, M. (1992). *Playing it safe: A nationwide survey of public playgrounds*. Washington, DC: Public Interest Research Group and the Consumer Federation of America.

Singer, D., & Singer, J. L. (2009). Children's pastimes and play in sixteen nations: Is free play declining? *American Journal of Play, 1*(3), 283–312.

Smith, G. A. (2006). Shopping cart-related injuries to children. *Pediatrics, 118*, e540–e544.

Smith, S. J. (1998). *Risk and our pedagogical relation to children: On the playground and beyond*. Albany: State University of New York Press.

Southern Building Code Congress. (1992). *Standard swimming pool code*. Birmingham, AL: Author.

Stearns, P. N. (2003). *Anxious parents: A history of modern childrearing in America*. New York: New York University Press.

Sutterby, J. A., & Frost, J. L. (2002). Making playgrounds fit for children and children fit on playgrounds. *Young Children, 57*(3), 36–42.

Sweeney, T. (1974). *Petition to develop safety standards for playground equipment*. Washington, DC: Consumer Product Safety Commission.

Therrell, J. A., Brown, P., Sutterby, J. A., & Thornton, C. D. (2002). *Age determination guidelines: Relating children's ages to toy characteristics and play behavior*. Washington, DC: U.S. Consumer Product Safety Commission.

Thompson, D., & Bowers, L. (Eds.). (1989). *Where our children play: Community park playground equipment*. Reston, VA: American Alliance for Health, Physical Education, Recreation and Dance.

Thompson, G. (1998, December 14). More diabetes cases found in obese children. *Austin American-Statesman*, pp. A-1, A-3.

Weintraub, R., & Cassady, A. (2002). *Playing it safe: The sixth nationwide survey of public playgrounds*. Washington, DC: Consumer Federation of America.

Wood, B., Fise, M. E., & Morrison, M. (1994). *Playing it safe: A second nationwide safety survey of public playgrounds*. Washington, DC: U.S. Public Interest Research Group and the Consumer Federation of America.

Wortham, S. C., & Frost, J. L. (Eds.). (1990). *Playgrounds for young children: American survey and perspectives*. Reston, VA: American Alliance for Health, Physical Education, Recreation, and Dance.

Zaun, C. G. (1952). It's not what you fall on: It's how you land. *Safety Education, 32*(1), 3–4.

Zaun, C. G. (1955). Four conclusions. *Safety Education, 34*(5), 8.

# 14 Playwork in American and European Playgrounds

*FIRST AND FOREMOST . . . play is a voluntary activity. . . . It is never a task. . . . Second, play is not "ordinary" or "real" life. It is rather a stepping out of "real" life into a temporary sphere of activity. . . . Third, play is distinct from "ordinary" life both as to location and duration. It is "played out" within certain limits of time and space. . . . It plays itself to an end.*

(Johan Huizinga, 1938/1950, pp. 7–9)

*A CERTAIN supervision and guidance will, of course, be necessary but I am firmly convinced that one ought to be exceedingly careful when interfering in the lives and activities of children. The object must be to give the children of the city a substitute for the rich possibilities for play which children in the country possess.*

(Lady Allen of Hurtwood, 1968, p. 55)

*Play is a process, not a product. We have to learn to trust in the innate wisdom of children and allow them to get on with it.*

(Penny Wilson, 2010, p. 5)

The influences of history and theories of play permeate this textbook. Initially, we explained that over the centuries, philosophers and scholars held different views about the nature of play and its importance in social, cognitive, motor, and cultural aspects of development. In this chapter, we draw from various leading theories, research, and accounts of experience to focus on the role of adults in children's outdoor play environments or playgrounds. Bear in mind that the concept and reality of "playground" is rapidly broadening to reflect (a) the need to reintroduce natural features, (b) the rapid introduction of technology into children's lives, (c) a growing emphasis on safety, (d) the introduction of new equipment designs and materials, and (e) the appearance of playgrounds in a broadening context (e.g., backyards, neighborhood spaces, public parks, schools, child development centers, shopping malls, children's museums, children's wilderness camps, theme parks, and vacation destinations).

The roles of adults in most dimensions of teaching and caring for children are carefully prescribed and protected by bodies of theory. Teachers do not all teach the same way, but many can point to theory that supports their behavior. Play therapists identify several alternate, sometimes conflicting, theories to support their practice. Theory is available for behavior management, language teaching,

reading, and a host of other child development tasks faced daily by adults, but the foundations for playground supervision have yet to rise beyond the level of fragmented research and theory. Despite such shortcomings, common practice is to apply these classroom theories and resulting methods to children's outdoor play and play environments. We visit indoor play intervention views and theories in this chapter, but the major emphasis is on playwork principles emerging in Europe, which are rooted in a century of extensive attention to children's play and play environments, and to the appropriate roles of playworkers, formerly called play leaders.

Some of the most thoughtfully developed and highly respected early childhood programs (e.g., High/Scope, Head Start, Reggio Emilio, Bank Street; see Chapter 8) integrate play into virtually all aspects of classroom environment, materials and equipment, teaching techniques, and curricula. These programs draw from the work of such noted scholars as Friedrich Froebel, Jean Piaget, John Dewey, Jerome Bruner, and Lev Vygotsky. All of these prominent figures valued and described the processes and benefits of play, but among these, only Froebel provided extensive application of his views to outdoor play in public settings. Consequently, leaps of faith are taken when adults apply their theories to practical applications.

The role of adults in young children's classroom play has been extensively studied, carefully explained, and applied in programs throughout the United States (discussed in Chapter 8). However, with limited exceptions, only minimal attention has been directed to the role of adults in American children's out-of-classroom or outdoor play environments during recent decades. Consequently, a common pattern on school and child-care center playgrounds across America is adult supervisors sitting in the shade talking with their peers—taking a break—while their young charges play, or attempting to insert academic-related strategies used during indoor play to outdoor play contexts. The pattern of supervision in American city park playgrounds is even less planned. Many cities employ out-of-school teenagers to oversee park play during the summer months and provide no adult supervision for the remainder of the year. Shortage of funds is a primary reason for lack of full-time play leaders in public parks.

In the following sections, we review the history of adult roles in outdoor play, summarize theories and research on adult roles, and describe the practices of select programs in the United States and Europe. Finally, we make recommendations for application in child-care centers, schools, and other organized public playgrounds. The emphasis is on outdoor play environments, but many of the principles are applicable to all contexts where children play. We draw from personal views and experiences, from American and European research and practice in play leadership or playwork in playgrounds, and from extensive on-the-job experiences of playwork in European playgrounds. We believe these sources are all relevant in building and conducting playwork programs in playgrounds. Across countries and even within countries, the terms "playworkers" and "play leaders" denote the roles of adults who assist children in playgrounds. They will be used interchangeably here.

Play professionals in the United States and other countries, notably the Scandinavian countries, the United Kingdom, and other developed countries, struggle to find language that clearly describes the preferred roles of adults on playgrounds. The concept of supervisors is seen as inconsistent with the desired freedom, independence, and creativity of children at play. **Play leaders** was a popular label for many years but has been replaced with **playworkers** in some European countries, notably the United Kingdom and is increasingly used in the United States. The United Kingdom is experiencing a vibrant, growing playwork program involving extensive training resources (see Bonel & Lindon, 1996; Brown, 2003; Davy, 2001; Wilson, 2010). The roles of adults in children's outdoor play changed periodically over the past century as children abandoned their centuries-old playgrounds of the wilderness, fields, barnyards, village streets, and vacant places.

## THE EMERGENCE OF PLAYWORK IN AMERICA

The history of American play leadership and playwork is erratic and spread across various play contexts. Major contexts for play include urban parks, public and private schools, child development centers, and both rural and urban neighborhoods. Adults responsible for play leadership across these contexts hold differing views about the nature and importance of children's play, play environments, and the appropriate roles and training of play leaders or playworkers. These views also differ across countries, particularly the United States versus the United Kingdom, Germany, the Netherlands, and Scandinavia.

### History of Play Leadership in Public Parks and Playgrounds

During the early 1900s, organized city park playgrounds in the United States were developed in unprecedented numbers (Frost, 1992). Soon the public came to believe that without trained leadership, playgrounds fostered idleness, immorality, and vandalism (Lee, 1927). Consequently, the *Playground Association of America (PAA)* developed guidelines for training play leaders, often called *play directors,* and courses were established in normal (teacher training) schools (Cavallo, 1976; Curtis, 1917). The initial goals established for these training programs focused on physical education and recreation but included courses in sociology, social psychology, biology, industrial arts, and civic relationships. In 1914, the Russell Sage Foundation identified 50 high schools, colleges, or normal schools offering training course for play leaders. In 1915, there were 774 full-time and 5,000 part-time directors in the United States, and by 1916 approximately 100 institutions were offering training courses with about half in normal schools. Harvard and one or more universities in Pennsylvania offered courses and 42 towns in Kansas, influenced by the University of Kansas, employed trained directors of play. In Gary, Indiana, girls and boys were employed to work as apprentices in playgrounds and gymnasiums. The initial goals established for these training programs focused on physical education and recreation but included courses in sociology, social psychology, biology, industrial arts, and civic relationships. The normal course, outlined in a manual (Playground and Recreation Association of America, 1925) was broad in scope, including program planning, play leadership, play facilities, organization, history of community recreation, the nature and function of play, and history of the community recreation movement.

The recreation emphasis was reinforced during the 1930s when the name of the Playground Association of America was changed to the National Recreation Association and eventually to the present name, National Recreation and Park Association (NRPA). Due, in part, to crises such as the Great Depression and World War II, the important role of play leader during the 1920s and 1930s was gradually deemphasized to become a subcategory of workers under the recreation supervisor, and the emphasis on trained play leaders shifted from playground play to organized recreation and sports (Butler, 1950). The early ideals of training play leaders have not regained their importance in the structure of American public park playgrounds. By the turn of the 21st century, the NRPA was reemphasizing the role of play in their publications, conferences, websites, and other organizational activities (Frost, 2010).

## Play Leadership in Preschools

Early 20th-century views held by preschool professionals—child care, nursery school, and kindergarten—about the roles of adults in children's play were founded on radically different premises than were those of public park and public school personnel. Rather than focusing primarily on physical development and recreation, preschool professionals adopted the views of Friedrich Froebel, John Dewey, Jean Piaget, leaders of the early child development research centers and evolving research in child development (Frost, 2010; Smuts & Hagen, 1985; Sears, 1975). Froebel (1902) viewed play as important for developing the mind, body, and character. College and university training programs and the best preschool programs promoted context (providing space and a wide range of materials), the "whole child" (social, cognitive, emotional, and physical), emphasis on process over product, experiential learning, and a general hands-off policy, but with specific steps for adult intervention (Iowa Child Welfare Research Station, 1934).

- Expose the child to materials.
- Explain correct uses when materials are misused.
- Support the child in using new materials.
- Praise the child for accomplishing difficult tasks.
- Give slow, timid children time; then encourage use of materials.

- Encourage reluctant but capable children to "Try it yourself."
- Support the child's inclinations to try new or difficult materials or equipment.
- Redirect the child when he overuses materials or equipment.
- If the child throws materials, ask her to pick them up before playing with anything else.
- If the child continues to abuse materials or use a toy unsafely, remove it until she is willing to comply.
- The child should use large equipment properly and safely.

Early leaders in the nursery-kindergarten movement promoted adults' role in shaping the development of children during play (Palmer, 1916). They were aided in this effort by the training of preschool teachers in college and university programs that emphasized child development. This contrasted sharply with the typical training of elementary school teachers, including limited attention to supervising playground play, a difference that prevails today and continues to shape play leadership across the two contexts.

## Play Leadership in Public and Private Elementary Schools

The views and practices of elementary school professionals concerning the roles of adults in children's play roughly parallel those of public park professionals. Throughout most of the 20th century, public and private elementary school playgrounds were equipped to promote exercise, organized games, and sports. Play rested on old "excess energy" theory rather than developmental foundations; equipment for play was antiquated, hazardous, and limited in function; and loose or portable materials were virtually nonexistent. Teacher education institutions rarely devoted attention to play or play leadership beyond the early childhood period and play time was widely viewed as

trivial and inconsequential. These patterns are slowly improving.

The role of adults in elementary school playgrounds has been subjected to limited study. Available studies include those by Block and King (1987), Evans (1989, 1990), Finnan (1982), Frost (1992), (Frost et al., 2004), Moore (1974), Sluckin (1981), and Wilson (2010). Because playground play in elementary schools typically takes place during recess, also see Pellegrini (1995) on school recess and playground behavior.

Evans's (1990) studies in American and Australian schools are among the most insightful for understanding the roles assumed by teachers on playgrounds during recess. Teachers generally view recess as an activity break or a time for children to let off steam, but many children, especially those in upper elementary grades, use recess to talk with peers, sit on equipment, wait in line for equipment, or wander around. Children do not always return to the classroom relaxed and attentive but may be agitated or excited about events that transpired.

Teachers may use recess as a time to take a break, have coffee, or converse among themselves. Many school systems hire parents or unskilled workers to supervise recess while teachers have lunch, prepare lessons, or simply spend time alone. Recess is commonly seen as an unpleasant duty, especially by teachers of older children who may engage in confrontations with the teacher and require policing.

Evans (1990) found that teachers' assumed roles on playground duty varied widely. Some stood or sat near the school building; some wandered around the playground; others joined in games or talked with children. Some teachers avoided contact with the children, remained aloof, and discouraged children from bringing grievances to them. Younger children sought out teachers more frequently than older ones did. Teachers basically saw their roles as supervisory, ensuring a safe environment and alternately acting as police officer, referee, counselor, or coplayer.

The roles of playworkers are varied and sometimes complex but should contribute to close, warm relationships with children, as evident here.

Despite teachers assuming multiple roles on playgrounds, they are generally given little or no advice by school administration for performing their roles and are unclear as to the value of recess. Little wonder that some abhor the role, many try to avoid it, and few feel competent doing it. Teachers do believe that supervision is necessary, and that children, even older children, should not be left unsupervised, in part because of legal concerns. Those who understand play's value for child development believe children should be supervised and by adults who know the children and have been trained for the role.

Our research and personal experiences reveal that appropriate adult roles on children's playgrounds are varied and complex, extending well beyond enforcement of rules. Roles should also include ensuring that children have rich, challenging, and ever-changing environments for play. As playgrounds are improved, behavior problems decline. Good playgrounds breed good behavior. Some rules are needed—but only necessary ones established *with* the children.

One of the most pressing issues in recess supervision remains: How much intervention by adults? Evans (1990) concludes that "there are sound moral and legal reasons why adult presence is required when children are at recess, but . . . the more we can leave them to their own devices in the playground the better" (p. 233). During recess, children have unique opportunities not available in the classroom to learn organization, negotiation, and physical and social skills. Qualified, well-trained teachers can assist without excessive intervention. See www.ipausa.org/recess.htm (2006) and Zygmunt-Fillwalk & Bilello (2005) for research on the benefits of recess.

 ## THEORETICAL BASES FOR ADULT INTERVENTION IN CHILDREN'S PLAY

Play leadership takes place in many physical contexts, and play takes many forms, so no one theory or philosophy taps the conceptual depth and range necessary to establish a scientific basis for play leadership for all children in all settings. For example, both Piaget and Vygotsky seemed to realize that play had emotional and therapeutic components, but neither gave these critical factors much attention. One could hardly rely on either of these theorists to explain the appropriate roles of adults in play therapy. The work of Anna Freud, Carl Rogers, and Virginia Axline (see Chapter 10) are far more significant for assisting children in dealing with serious problems of neglect, abuse, conflict, and trauma. This examination of theory and practice identifies appropriate roles for adults in children's play in typical home, child-care center, and school contexts.

In *The Republic*, Plato wrote that children from the earliest ages must take part in the more lawful forms of play if they are to grow up to be well-conducted and virtuous citizens. He stressed that adults should learn about children by observing their play. In the 1st century, Quintilian thought that play could be arranged by adults to develop children's intellects. In the 16th century, John Amos Comenius considered playgrounds to be essential to a well-ordered school and encouraged adults to provide objects, pictures, and puzzles in lower schools to encourage the play interests of children (Caplan & Caplan, 1973; Frost & Kissinger, 1976). Jean-Jacques Rousseau, in the 18th century, emphasized the value of play and the vast differences in the interests and values of adults and children. Rousseau believed the child should receive no kind of verbal instructions, and his learning should come from direct experience. Growth was to be natural and unfettered by society.

Johann Pestallozi, in the late 1700s, also attacked the harsh rote instruction of his era, emphasizing instead learning through direct experiences. The adult or teacher was not to adopt the tone of an instructor, Pestallozi thought, but should gently help children engage in real-life activities such as setting up a business and making use of nature. The older children should teach the younger children. However, no system of educational play was to be followed until Froebel's time.

Froebel, a student of Pestallozi's, established the first kindergarten (literally "garden of children") in Blankenburg, Germany, in 1837. These were seen as enclosures in which human plants were nurtured. Schools for very young children existed before Froebel's kindergarten, but they focused on the mothers more than on the children (Quick, 1896). To Froebel, the children's employment (activity) was play, and any occupation in which children gained delight was play to them. In Froebel's kindergarten, work or learning activities were infused with the pleasure of play and became **play/work**, with the intent that pleasurable activities would have an educational object. Learning from simple playthings (gifts and occupations) in the classroom was further strengthened by extensive creative self-activity with games and nature in the outdoors.

Froebel's outdoor gardens combined practical work with the literary school and served to assist physical health. Children tended a patchwork of plants, vegetables, shrubs, and meadows and modeled mountain chains, river valleys, canals, and ponds complete with fishes and frogs (Von Marenholz-Bulow, 1897). Nothing lay closer to Froebel's heart than the study of animals and plants, and the outdoors in general (Kilpatrick, 1916, p. 187). Consider his views of the garden:

> The kindergarten . . . necessarily requires a garden. . . . Personal responsibility is fixed by the provision that in their own little beds the children can plant what and how they will, also deal with the plants as they will, that they may learn from their own judicious treatment. . . . This will be shown to them by the plants in the common bed [a separate garden planned by the group], which they must observe carefully. The seeds and plants should be so compared and discussed that the children may learn to recognize them readily. Seeds preserved for the next planting should be kept in little paper boxes previously made by the

children themselves. The beds should be so labeled as to name plant and child. Through this the child is not only carried along the road towards reading, but receives the merited silent praise or blame, according as his work has been. (Kilpatrick, 1916, pp. 193–194)

Froebel believed that not only kindergartens but every town should have its common playground where the games of children could be carried out. The adult (teacher) was to watch the children at play and recast their games to form the habit of "association with comrades" (Kilpatrick, 1916, p. 153). The true kindergarten teacher "will listen to the suggestion of children and will be guided by circumstances" (p. 154). Froebel did not propose to do away with free play. He understood that there was much time for free play outside the 3 hours of the kindergarten. (In the 21st century, however, kindergarten and child care may occupy most of a child's waking hours.) In Froebel's school, traditional and instinctive games furnish the material that may be transfigured into truly educative play. Through insight into the ideal, the adult (teacher) can help children select games that form a logically related sequence and develop the child into the chosen game's image. As each new generation gains experience, fresh images are added to the children's dramatic reproductions of the vital and formative facts of their own lives (Blow, 1909). (Consider the images that are introduced into contemporary children's play via television and the Internet.) As you will see, the views and practices of contemporary play leaders on Europe's adventure playgrounds have much in common with Froebel's outdoor kindergarten activities.

John Dewey acknowledged that Froebel was perhaps the first to consciously set forth that children's play is not only essential to their growth but that their games and activities "are the foundational stones of educational method" (Tanner, 1997, p. 30). However, Dewey believed that elaborate **symbolism** (sweeping a make-believe room with a make-believe broom, for example), perhaps essential in the Germany of Froebel's time, was not essential in early 20th-century America. Societal change justified making kindergarten activities more natural and representative of current life. Dewey's children, like Froebel's, worked in gardens in their school yard, applied principles learned in classrooms in cooperatively building clubhouses outdoors, learned to use tools in shops, planned and prepared meals using natural grains, studied elementary biology in natural outdoor settings, and built models of their community while studying community life. The classroom was extended, through both play and work, into the community.

Dewey's teachers used a range of approaches including **cooperative planning** with children, group discussion, writing about experiences, laboratory experiments, practical and fine arts experiences, and reproduction of home and family life. The school must be a community in which children work and play in a social context and in which the subject matter of formal instruction is integrated with the subject matter of life experiences. Formal instruction easily becomes "remote and dead." The danger of improper balance increases as societies become more complex in structure and resources. Learners must test their ideas through applications. "Only by wrestling with the conditions of the problem at first hand, seeking and finding his own way out, does he [the child] think" (Dewey, 1916, p. 160).

What, then, are the conditions for balancing formal instruction with life experiences? For balancing play and work? What is the role of the teacher? First, he provides the context—a rich blend of classrooms, playgrounds, laboratories (indoor and outdoor), and workrooms. Second, he ensures opportunity for interaction—the social context. Playgrounds, for example, involve intercourse, communication, and connection (Dewey, 1916, p. 358). Third, cooperative planning and acting occur to develop a spirit of companionship and shared activity. Fourth, there is carryover of social concern and understanding into the broader community outside the school, lest the "social life of the school . . . no more represent or typify that of the world beyond the school walls than that of a monastery" (p. 359). Fifth, the teachers strive to keep a proper balance between the informal and the formal, the abstract and the practical. Gardening, for example, is more than the preparation of future gardeners or an agreeable way of passing time. It allows for the study of growth, soil chemistry, animal life, and human relations. Playing in sand and water or engaging in chase games or symbolic housekeeping play carries similar advantages beyond the sheer joy and delight experienced by the player. Finally, the teacher ensures that the joy and delight of play permeates the work experience.

"From a very early age . . . there is no distinction of exclusive periods of play activity and work activity, but only one of emphasis . . . both involve ends consciously entertained and the selection and adaptations of materials and processes designed to effect the desired ends" (Dewey, 1916, pp. 202–203). "The defining characteristic of play is not amusement nor aimlessness. . . . Work which remains permeated with the play attitude is art-in-quality if not in conventional designation" (pp. 205–206).

During the early 1900s, psychoanalysis was integrated into play therapy for children and two schools of thought developed (see Chapter 10), each advocating a particular form and frequency of intervention. The **directive school** emphasized directed play and prescribed materials, and it interpreted play to determine the source and nature of phobias and conflicts. The **nondirective school** confirmed, repeated, and clarified the child's play acts, emphasizing the importance of nonintervention by adults in children's play. Play itself, aside from the adult's direction or interpretation, was seen as the critical factor in fostering the child's social and intellectual development. Today, scholars continue to debate the relative importance of these approaches to adult intervention in children's play (see Chapter 8).

## Piaget and Constructivism

Piaget's cognitive theories of play and implications for the roles of adults in children's play were dominant among early childhood educators from the 1960s until the late 1980s. Now, growing numbers of scholars recommend specific roles for adults in children's play and visionary programs are shifting from a constructivist to a social-constructivist approach. The Piagetian "watching and waiting" approach is tempered by the Vygotskian view that children do not merely construct their knowledge but that their performance can be assisted by others. Following the translation of Vygotsky's work and its dissemination and interpretation throughout the English-speaking world, growing numbers of early childhood educators modified their views to place greater emphasis on the social context of children's play, especially with respect to the role of adults (teachers and parents).

## Vygotsky and Social Constructivism

Vygotsky (1966) broke with the views of Piaget (1962) about play in several ways that have implications for adults' role in play. For example, Vygotsky maintained that there is no such thing as play without rules laid down in advance by real-life behavior. If the child is nurturing a baby, she is obeying rules of maternal behavior. Unlike Piaget, who held that rules emerge after the preschool period, primarily in organized games, Vygotsky believed that children younger than age 3 engage in imaginary play and that all imaginary play contains rules. Piaget focused only marginally on sociocultural dimensions of development and the roles of adults in development, maintaining that education was the "American question," yet he included **social transmission** as one of four fundamental factors influencing children's development.

For Piaget, make-believe play emerges spontaneously with the onset of representational thought, and cognitive construction takes place largely through interaction with physical objects. Vygotsky and his followers contend that from its beginnings, make-believe play is a social activity, a product of **social collaboration** (Haight & Miller, 1993; Smolucha, 1992).

Vygotsky identified a **zone of proximal development (ZPD)**, a range of tasks between those the child can handle independently and those at the highest level he can handle with the help of adults or more competent peers, which placed adults in a prominent role in the child's play and educational life. He identified play as the "highest level of preschool development" (Vygotsky, 1966, p. 16). His followers maintained that adults and more competent peers could effectively **scaffold** intervention to match the child's learning ability (introduce tasks more complex than the child's independent level but not beyond his potential level), helping him achieve higher levels of development than possible by working independently. Thus the constructivism of Piaget's followers was tempered by the co-constructivism of Vygotsky's followers.

Following the Vygotskian approach, the child engages in joint problem solving with a more skilled partner (teacher or parent), who introduces the intellectual tools of the society to the child within the manageable ZPD (Rogoff et al., 1993). This reciprocal relationship between child, teacher, and social environment promotes movement through the ZPD as knowledge is continuously reconstructed (Wertsch & Hickman, 1987) or co-constructed (Rogoff, 1990; Winegar, 1989). Teaching is assisted performance (Tharp & Gallimore, 1988), and a social environment is essential for cognitive development (Newman, Griffin, & Cole, 1989).

## Chaos Theory

The rationale for **chaos theory** draws from the growing national, and to some degree international, paradox that postmodern families and institutions—indeed, societies—are experiencing a transformation from traditional predictable structures to ever more complex and interdependent ones. Chaos theory holds that social systems are nonlinear, interdependent, and unpredictable. Workers must now have portable skills allowing them to move from job to job. The traditional intact nuclear family is declining. Global interests and concerns touch everyone's community (Naisitt, 1994; VanderVen, 1998). The reality of the world is essentially chaotic (Goerner, 1994). Consequently, an essential question arises: What kinds of persons will be needed to survive in such a world, and how can parents and educators help children cope in a chaotic world?

Despite growing knowledge of the prevailing creeping chaos in society, those parents and teachers most directly responsible for helping children adapt to chaos cling to outmoded, antiquated views about teaching, parenting, and the role of play as a legitimate educational enterprise. In resolution, VanderVen (1998) proposes a chaotically oriented approach to education that incorporates play at every developmental level, an approach that unifies play and school curriculum. Her views are based on two basic principles: (1) Play is a complex adaptive system that embraces and generates other complex adaptive systems, and (2) play is essential for young children to experience pervasive chaos and to identify themselves as complex adaptive beings. When children play, they seek chaotic experiences—novelty, surprise, loss of control, and disequilibrium—the very experiences that adults avoid (Wheatley, 1992). Many of the underlying principles of chaos theory were discovered through free play with computers and computer games (Peitgen, Jurgens, & Saupe, 1992, p. 35; Whitton, 1998, p. 480).

Unfortunately, the current emphasis on high-stakes testing and the creeping national curriculum emanating from preformed limited criteria—the so-called basics—essentially denies children rich opportunities to reflect and learn about the complexities of an ever more chaotic or complex world. Preparing for complexity and change, understanding the present and developing the creativity and imagination essential for dealing with profound societal changes, is not accomplished by drilling on a single set of concepts and skills to be tested. Consider, for example, the emerging research initiatives explored in the compelling book, *Imagining the Impossible: Magical, Scientific, and Religious Thinking in Children* (Rosenberg et al., 2000) and the exciting emerging theory about change and learning in *Presence: An Exploration of Profound Change in People, Organizations, and Society* (Senge et al., 2004). The reader can hardly deny that helping children learn beyond the ordinary boundaries of understanding, going beyond what initially seems impossible, is perhaps cultivated early through the seemingly boundless reflections of children in their imaginative play.

> As long as our thinking is governed by habit—notably by industrial, machine-age concepts such as control, predictability, standardization, and "faster is better"—we will continue to re-create institutions as they have been, despite their disharmony with the larger world and the need of all living systems to evolve. (Senge et al., 2004, p. 9)

Many parents, politicians, child caretakers, and educators resist the ideas that play is an essential component of parenting, child-care programs, and school curricula and that adults should have an active role in supporting play. VanderVen (1998), following the leads of Smilansky and Shefatya's (1990) research and Berk and Winsler's (1995) interpretations of Vygotsky, contends that adult facilitation of play is essential for children's development and for adaptation to a chaotic world. She proposes a number of chaos theory concepts of play facilitation:

- *Determinism.* A system or process can be predetermined *and* have unpredictable outcomes. Adults need not resist play facilitation strategies (e.g., suggesting a theme) simply because the outcomes may be unpredictable.

- *Weak chaos.* Any play facilitation strategy by an adult injects weak chaos (a change in the dynamic) and keeps it changing, evolving, and dynamic.

- *Bifurcation.* The adult facilitator may introduce a bifurcation or transition into a new form or state by scaffolding, as suggested by Vygotsky's followers.

- *Attractor.* As play runs down, adult facilitators may introduce novel "attractors" to reengage the child's attention and energy by, for example, introducing a new toy or material.

Following chaos theory, the play leader of young children would abandon prescriptive curricula focusing on memorization, prescriptive thinking, and linear instruction and implement a play-based curriculum focusing on flexibility, extended options, divergent thinking, risk taking, learning through error, flexible planning, and magical qualities. VanderVen playfully proposes that **supersymmetry** (Freedman, 1991; Weinberg, 1992), a concept embracing both symmetry and chaos, will be the new worldview beyond chaos. Games, play, and highly skilled adults can help children adapt to change and meet the complex challenges of a chaotic world.

## RESEARCH BASES FOR ADULT INTERVENTION IN CHILDREN'S PLAY

Since 1960, a number of researchers have studied the effects of intervention, commonly referred to as **play tutoring** or training, on children's play. In these studies, adults participated in children's play through such activities as discussing topics that might be used in play, encouraging use of nonstructured materials, encouraging children to invite others to join their play, helping elaborate themes, making imaginative uses of play materials, encouraging invention, helping create pretend episodes, and taking children on trips to community centers (fire stations, doctor's office, grocery store, etc.) and encouraging reenactment in dramatic play. The terms *training* and *tutoring* are misleading because the adult interventions were generally informal and consisted of adults unobtrusively suggesting, questioning, supporting, and encouraging rather than teaching, telling, directing, or requiring.

Positive correlations were found between parents' verbal behavior (e.g., discussing topics that could be used in the child's dramatic play) and the amount of nursery school children's dramatic play (Marshall, 1961). Doll play training increased the frequency of dramatic play for nursery school children (Marshall & Hahn, 1967). Imaginative training sessions for "ghetto school" kindergarten children resulted in significant improvement in imaginativeness and concentration (Freyberg, 1973). Kindergarten children from working-class families exposed to play tutoring made significant gains in combinatory play and creativity. There were no significant gains for nontutored children in the same play environment (Feitelson & Ross, 1973). Kindergartners from low socioeconomic groups who received sociodramatic play tutoring showed significantly higher gains than a control group on measures including manipulation of objects, interaction with coplayers, use of verbal descriptions, problem-solving tasks, and perceptual role taking (Rosen, 1974). More recent research paints even more comprehensive benefits of play in early childhood and further reveals the appropriate roles of adults (Ratey, 2008; Hirsh-Pasek et al., 2009; Miller & Almon, 2009; Wilson, 2010).

Additional positive results of play intervention for young children include:

- enhanced imaginative play (Feitelson & Ross, 1973; Smilansky, 1968; Smilansky & Shefatya, 1990);
- improvement in cognitive tasks, impulse control, verbal intelligence, story interpretation, and spontaneous engagement in sociodramatic play (Saltz et al., 1977);
- creativity, group activity, attention span, cognitive ability, and amount of group activity (Smith & Sydall, 1978);
- perspective taking (Burns & Brainerd, 1979);
- verbal comprehension and cognitive tasks (Dansky, 1980);
- cognitive complexity (Sylva, Roy, & Painter, 1980);
- conservation tasks (Golomb & Bonen, 1981);
- verbal fluency, amount of imaginative play, social interaction, reduced aggression, social adjustment (Udwin, 1983);
- associative fluency (Dempsey, 1985);
- attention span (Hutt, Tyler, Hutt, & Christopherson, 1989);
- language development (Levy et al., 1992);
- attachment to adults and peer interaction (Howes & Smith, 1995);
- play enrichment (Bennett et al., 1997);
- school readiness (Zigler, Singer, & Bishop-Josef, 2004),
- brain development and emotional and cognitive health (Ratey, 2008).

Play takes on many functions and is engaged in many levels of activity—from sedentary thought and reflection when playing with toys to prolonged aerobic activity when engaging in such play as chase games, ball games, and rough-and-tumble play. Aerobic play or exercise is as effective as antidepressants for some people, sparks new brain growth, and transforms brains for improved performance in academics (Ratey, 2008). Moving the body produces proteins that travel through the bloodstream and into the brain where they exert powerful influence on the development of our highest thought processes. Active, outdoor play is an essential ingredient and must be encouraged, provided for, supported, and modeled by the adults in children's lives. The signs of sedentary activity coupled with poor diets and its results are frequently seen in entire schools and families as they gorge on junk food in school cafeterias and in fast food and all-you-can-eat restaurants. Adults set the patterns for good health when they teach and practice regular physical activity and guide children to participate. These are the playworkers we need.

Smilansky (1968) conducted studies of low-income immigrant children in Israel and concluded that they engaged in less sociodramatic play than did middle-income Israeli children. The preschool and kindergarten children were assigned to four treatments: direct or preparatory experiences (guided visits and discussions), teaching how to play, a combination of direct experiences and teaching, and control. She concluded that direct teaching and a combination of teaching and provision of direct experiences were effective in increasing the extent and quality of sociodramatic play.

Although the most compelling conclusion from play intervention studies is that play tutoring or training results in academic and developmental outcomes, a central concern remains: What form of intervention for which children? Gains in developmental indexes among earlier studies were questioned by Smith and Sydall (1978), who concluded that advantages in language and cognitive skills ascribed to play tutoring may have been related to lack of adult contact with children in the non-play tutored or control groups. Christie and Johnsen (1985) questioned whether the cognitive and social benefits of play training are caused by children's social interaction during play or by the adult play component. Failure to control experiments for effects of peer interaction and adult tutoring are seen as methodological weaknesses in the research. Which is the major factor in determining effectiveness of adult intervention, play per se or adult contact? However, "If the tutors playing with children produce important scholarly results, this is an important finding regardless of the exact nature of the antecedents" (Sutton-Smith, 1993a, p. 23). Researchers are still divided as to *how* adults should play with children.

The approaches used in experimental studies ranged from informal to directive, and the subjects included a range of ages, developmental abilities, and ethnic groups. Those children who do not engage in play have different intervention needs than those who are skilled and secure in their play. Unwitting or unskilled adults can interrupt the flow of children's play, discourage certain types of play (e.g., rough-and-tumble), inhibit play activities, reduce problem solving and peer interaction, interfere with learning during play, stifle imagination, or even prohibit play (Frost, 1992; Frost, 2004; Johnson, Christie, & Yawkey, 1998; Jones & Reynolds, 1992; Miller, Fernie, & Kantor, 1992; Ohanian, 2002; Pellegrini & Galda, 1993; Sutton-Smith, 1992; Wood, McMahon & Cranstoun, 1980; Wilson, 2010). Overall, research indicates that an increase in wise involvement by adults in adult–child play would benefit children's play and development. The key element appears to be not whether, but *how*, adults intervene. Intervention need not and should not mean interference.

 ## PRACTICING PLAY LEADERSHIP

We conclude that decisions about the nature, type, and timing of intervention into children's play involves a complex mix of approaches:

1. Providing natural and designed spaces for play
2. Scheduling extensive time for play
3. Providing a challenging mix of natural and manufactured play materials and equipment
4. Individualizing play intervention through observation and study of children
5. Deciding what strategies to use during personal interactions with children

These approaches are explained in detail in Chapter 11, "Creating Play Environments" (outdoors), and Chapter 8, "Play and the Curriculum" (indoors).

## Pacific Oaks College Perspectives on Practice

For many years, the faculty of Pacific Oaks College in Pasadena, California, has operated one of the most visionary and creative sets of play yards in the United States. There children spend many hours playing and learning in well-designed and skillfully managed outdoor play yards. These play yards contain many imaginative do-it-yourself play structures; exciting linkages between indoor curricula and outdoor play; storage and loose parts; an abundance of natural materials, including sand, dirt, vegetation, and even fire for cookouts; and involve adults trained in enhancing children's spontaneous play. The success of the Pacific Oaks faculty and its long-term studies of children at play deserves special recognition and offers a model to emulate.

The Pacific Oaks program was developed over many years at Pacific Oaks College but was influenced by the developmental approaches of Bank Street College and the High/Scope curriculum and refined in collaboration with the Pasadena Unified School District. Its theoretical bases reside in both cognitive and interactionist theory, especially Piaget's constructivism (Jones & Reynolds, 1992). "Young children learn the most important things not by being told but by constructing knowledge for themselves in interaction with the physical world and with other children—and the way they do this is by playing" (Jones & Reynolds, 1992, p. 1). The Pacific Oaks program emphasizes the importance of language, construction with materials, and bodies in action during both fantasy and reality play themes (scripts) (p. 9). They break with scholars who believe that Piaget ignores or deemphasizes the socioemotional benefits of play and with educators who see the role of adults as teller or interrupter of children's play—as one who merely teaches (p. 1). They acknowledge the work of Vygotsky, stressing the cognitive challenge that play offers children (p. 5), and they identify intervention strategies for teachers to assume during children's play.

Because becoming a master player represents a high level of development for preschool children and has high educational significance (Jones & Cooper, 2006; Jones & Reynolds, 1992; Reynolds & Jones, 1997), the teacher pays attention to play; that is, she carefully observes children at play to take their perspectives and to answer such questions as these: What is happening to this child in his play? What is the child's agenda? Does he have the skills and materials he needs to accomplish his intent? How can I support the child's play? Using observation as a guide, the teacher takes steps to make play possible. These steps include assuming the roles of stage manager, mediator, player, scribe, assessor and communicator, and planner.

## Vygotskian Perspectives on Practice

Bodrova and Leong (1996, 1998a), and Berk and Winsler (1995) conducted extensive analyses of Vygotsky's work, resulting in recommendations for the roles of adults in children's play. Just as many other play scholars have done, Bodrova and Leong (1998a, p. 279) recognize that adults have indirect influences on children's play, including preparing the environment, choosing toys and materials, and encouraging children to play together. Vygotskians reach beyond indirect influences to exert direct influences on play, especially for infants, toddlers, and preschoolers. These include providing experiences that can become play themes, modeling how to play with a toy, taking turns, settling disputes, and describing sequences.

As children mature in their play, adult intervention should change and decline. Adults help infants establish attachment with adults and provide for interaction with other people, toys, books, and objects. Toddlers are helped to use language to describe actions and interact socially with peers, and to see roles, implicit rules, and imaginary situations. Preschoolers are assisted by offering props for play, organizing activities, planning with children before and after play, expanding pretending and role taking, and providing for scaffolding by older children and adults. Fantasy play is encouraged well into elementary school, but adults assume a minor role in play, and adult domination is avoided. Interaction with slightly older peers is encouraged, and self-regulation is promoted (Bodrova & Leong, 1998a).

Working independently, numerous individuals and groups have identified strategies for adult intervention in children's play (Figure 14.1). These strategies resulted from study of children on playgrounds, analysis of research literature, and practical experience. The contexts were primarily indoor classrooms, but the findings are adaptable to some degree in outdoor playgrounds, bearing in mind that most outdoor play should basically be free of academic motives. Such outdoor skills as basic gardening, animal care, and other work/play activities do require sensitive, skillful adult involvement.

## Adventure Play and Play Leadership in Europe

Play professionals everywhere have noticed the excitement and energy of children playing in construction sites, vacant lots, and natural areas. In 1943, the first of many junk playgrounds, later named building playgrounds or **adventure playgrounds**, was developed by C. T. Sorensen, a Danish landscape architect, in Emdrup, Denmark. John Bertelson, a nursery school teacher and former seaman, was named as the first play leader. Adventure playgrounds start with basically nothing. A fenced space is provided within walking distance of many children's homes, and one or more play leaders are assigned to the space and the children. Within this space, children are free to play almost any way they choose (Lambert, 1992). The playground is essentially a place for building with scrap materials. Children build dens, huts, and secret places. They play with water and mud.

**FIGURE 14.1**    Adult Intervention

| | |
|---|---|
| *Smilansky (1968)* | *Bennett, Wood, and Rogers (1997)* |
| Observer | Observer |
| Outside intervention | Provider |
| Inside intervention | Participant |
| Coplayer | Model |
| *Jones & Reynolds (1992)* | Review and feedback |
| Observer | *Van Hoorn, Scales, Nourot, and Alward (1999)* |
| Stage manager | Observer |
| Mediator | Stage manager |
| Player | Scaffolder |
| Scribe | Peacemaker |
| Assessor and communicator | Gate guardian |
| Planner | Parallel player |
| *Johnson, Christie, and Yawkey (1999)* | Spectator |
| Observer | Participant |
| Stage manager | Matchmaker |
| Oonlaver | Storyplayer |
| Play leader | Play tutor |
| Provider | Assessor |

Children in European adventure playgrounds enjoy a wide range of challenging play under the direction of trained play leaders.

They care for animals, tend gardens, construct play equipment, and build fires for warming and cooking.

The American Adventure Playground Association was formed in California in 1976, and 16 adventure playgrounds were identified in the United States by 1997. The association later succumbed to lack of support. Americans object to adventure-type playgrounds because of their untidy appearance, ignorance concerning the nature of children's play, and misplaced fear of injury and liability (Frost & Klein, 1979). By 2006, the dissolution of adventure playgrounds was almost total. The Houston Adventure Playground Association had closed its doors because of lack of support, and only three adventure playgrounds remained in California.

Unlike in the United States, where most playgrounds are basically standardized, limited in play function, and either unstaffed or staffed by supervisors or baby-sitters, playgrounds in Denmark and some other countries "are recognized as so important they are provided by law" (Lambert, 1992, p. 14). **Playwork,** or play leadership, is a nationally recognized profession in some countries, and training programs range from on-the-job to university programs. Playwork as a profession is active in the United Kingdom, Scotland, Scandinavian countries, the Netherlands, and Australia, and it is gaining momentum in Japan and Hong Kong (Jacobs, 1998).

Bonel and Lindon's (1996) strategies (Figure 14.2) were prepared as a text for playwork students in four National Centres for Playwork Education in England, underpinning the system of National Vocational Qualifications for playworkers. The contexts for implementation are adventure playgrounds, play centers, school play centers, and after-school clubs. Playwork strategies are based on the experiences of playworkers or play leaders since the early 1940s and do not appear to be tied to a particular

**FIGURE 14.2** Playwork Strategies: Adventure Playgrounds

| | |
|---|---|
| Friendly companion | Impartial referee |
| Source of ideas and suggestions | Gatekeeper of boundaries |
| Model of behavior | Assessor of risks |
| Balancer—joining play and standing back | Balancer—initiating play or follower |
| Resource to children | Encourager of older to coach younger children |
| Reviewer and planner with children | Confidence builder |

*Source*: Information from Bonel and Lindon (1996).

scientific theory. Playwork training is alive and well in the United Kingdom (Brown, 2003; Davy, 2001; Wilson, 2009, 2010).

Jack Lambert (1974), a former adventure playground leader, quotes John Bertelsen (the first adventure playground play leader) regarding the appropriate roles of the play leader:

> The children are sovereign and the initiative must come from them. The leader can make suggestions but must never demand. He must obtain the tools and material needed or requested by the children but must at any time be prepared to give way to new activities. To organize and arrange programmes is to stifle imagination and initiative and preclude children whose lively curiosity and interests constantly demand new outlets. (p. 18)

This basic philosophical intent, adopted informally but widely throughout European adventure playgrounds, is rejected in American playground contexts, where the practices of adults are basically laissez-faire or didactic. Marjory Allen, Lady Allen of Hurtwood (1968, p. 56), who introduced adventure playgrounds to the United Kingdom and established the London Handicapped Adventure Playground Association, helped explain this: "Only rarely do the . . . school teachers feel at home in so unorthodox a situation. Perhaps they have too much to unlearn before they can begin." She quotes a personal letter from Sorensen, the famous Danish landscape architect mentioned earlier:

> A certain supervision and guidance will, of course, be necessary but I am firmly convinced that one ought to be exceedingly careful when interfering in the lives and activities of children. The object must be to give the children of the city a substitute for the rich possibilities for play, which children in the country possess. (Allen, 1968, p. 55)

Functionally, adventure play leaders perform many roles:

- They nurture play in an unrestrictive setting (Bengtsson, 1972).
- They act as referees when a situation is getting out of hand (Allen, 1968).
- They maintain order but are friends to the children (Benjamin, 1974; Nicholson, 1971).
- They ensure that the playground is well staffed, equipped, and safe (Jacobs, 1998).
- They attract voluntary workers to the playground and involve families (Allen, 1968).
- They scrounge for tools and materials needed by the children (Lambert, 1992).
- They make suggestions but do not demand. They are never too busy to talk (Lambert, 1992).
- They don't interfere in play but teach an interesting skill if asked (Lambert, 1992).
- They accept a wide range of ages and individual differences (Frost & Klein, 1979).
- They support the work and play of children with minimum interference (Frost & Klein, 1979).
- They create opportunities that allow children to pursue their own play agendas (Brown, 2003).

- They help children create environments that address the negative effects of play deprivation and play bias (Brown, 2003).
- They introduce flexibility and adaptability into play environments (Brown, 2003).

The secret is to learn from children, to listen to them, and to understand what they are saying. Play leadership is being among children with a mind free of preconceptions (Lambert, 1992).

Personal observations of play leaders at work in several European countries and Japan confirm that the best of the group meet these criteria and support children's play at a level rarely seen in the United States. Some of the most memorable observations were children in Stockholm consoling a sow giving birth; children in Denmark feeding and cleaning burros in preparation for a ride; children in Birmingham, England, cultivating vegetable and flower gardens; children in Tokyo creating beautiful pieces of pottery; children in London bringing scraps of food from home to cook over open fires; children in Copenhagen organizing volunteers to help them build their own wading pool; children near Ringe, Denmark, planning, creating, and running their own operational village, built to child scale—all under the watchful yet unobtrusive tutelage and support of trained play leaders.

Today, playworkers frequently work with regional and national play associations and help develop play policies. They are well trained and can earn vocational certificates or diplomas in playwork at the bachelor's, master's, or doctoral level. The term playwork is deliberately oxymoronic. It is a craft filled with paradoxes. The playworkers are aware that in an ideal world they should not need to exist. They manage the spaces for children's play, but this work needs to be as invisible and unobtrusive to children as possible. The ideal playworker

Good playworkers observe children, listen, and learn from them.

leaves the children free to play for themselves but intervenes in carefully measured ways to support the play process. She is aware of her own playfulness, but does not impose it upon the children. She must necessarily be devoted to the playing of the children but shun the popular role of pied piper. Play is the children's business. (Wilson, 2010).

For additional information and photos of adventure playgrounds in London and Tokyo, see www.arunet.co.uk/fairplay/facts/adplay.htm and http://efcf.vgc.be/. See also www.cityfarms.org.

## CONCLUSIONS AND RECOMMENDATIONS

The initial tendency is to assign the same playwork roles to adults regardless of whether the context is classroom play or playground play. However, even in the better play-oriented classrooms for young children, a mix of academic pursuits is integrated with play activities; the degree of integration depends on the ages and developmental levels of the children and the nature of the topic or problem under consideration. Space in the classroom is limited and unsuitable for the free, active, unfettered play of the playground. Applying the same intervention strategies in the playground that are used in the classroom may restrict play opportunities, flow and enthusiasm of play, and the spontaneity, creativity, and independence of playing children. Much playground play should be essentially free—free to make choices for self, free to choose play materials, free to create topics and themes, free to choose play partners, free to play themes to an end without undue interference from adults.

In the outdoors, compared to indoors, children have more space, larger equipment, a greater variety of natural materials and features, real tools, more challenge and flexibility, higher activity levels, less structure and constraint, fuller expression, messier and louder activities, a wider range of sensory experiences, a greater range of social behaviors, uncontrolled movement, greater range of gross motor activities, more assertive play—all conducive to free, unfettered, spontaneous play. Although some adult roles are appropriate wherever children play, it does not follow that the same adult-imposed constraints,

directives, rules, admonitions, requirements, and expectations extant indoors should be operable in the outdoor play environment. What, then, are the appropriate roles of adults on playgrounds?

**First, the playworker studies children** to understand whether intervention into their play is needed. In simplest terms, this means getting to know children. One does not get to know merely through observing or applying a checklist of behaviors. Knowing a child requires a degree of intimacy resulting from a two-way process of sensitive relating—talking, listening, planning, sharing, negotiating, helping, and trusting.

Children whose play is consistently outside a broad normal range may indeed benefit from direct prompting, modeling, scaffolding, refereeing, or even tutoring (direct support or instruction) by adults (e.g., children who are abnormally shy, withdrawn, or overly aggressive). A few children are too damaged (traumatized, abused, disabled) to play in a healthy manner, and an occasional child does not know how to play. Damaged or unhealthy children or children who engage in unhealthy play (cruel teasing, demeaning others, behaving violently) need direct help from adults. "There is sufficient data correlating the lack of play competence with various forms of pathology to support the value of amplifying play opportunities just for their own sake" (Sutton-Smith, 1993a, p. 23). Times have changed since children settled disagreements with brief fisticuffs. Some disabled or frightened children now take real guns to school, and adults must constantly be alert to bizarre patterns of behavior that might signal impending violence. Most children, given rich natural or prepared play environments, need only minimal intervention by adults to engage in a wide range of healthy play—play that is fun, intense, creative, but not likely to inflict serious damage to others.

**Second, the playworker ensures that children have access to challenging playscapes** that integrate multiple levels of complexity, using both natural and built materials (see Chapter 11). The provision of exciting, magical, natural playscapes is perhaps the most formidable task facing teachers and play leaders at public playgrounds, and perhaps the most important. Over the past half-century, many American children have lost contact with wilderness areas and wild places (see Frost et al., 2004; Louv, 2005; Nabhan & Trimble, 1994). They have lost contact with the land—the rivers, forests, and native animals—and, consequently, their ability to cope in the wild and to understand and value nature. They have, in sum, lost important parts of their souls and senses. This was recognized by prominent educators a century ago.

> In the child's best playground, the country, he can climb trees and fences, hang from a branch, swing from the apple tree, make a wreath of leaves or flowers or a basket of burrs, seesaw across the watering trough or a fallen log, wade in the brook, dig in the earth, slide down the haymow, skip stones on the water, or skate on the pond. (Palmer, 1916, p. 252)

Even earlier, Tsanoff (1897), reputed to be the author of the first book about playgrounds published in America, extolled the value of the countryside for children's play:

> "[T]he children of the small towns and villages do not need playgrounds, because they have enough open country places in which to play. . . . [P]laygrounds are needed only in the large cities. (Tsanoff, 1897, p. 11)

How can adults compensate for the loss of play spaces in inner cities and in crowded schools? The selection of teachers should include searching for individuals who not only teach the typical subject matter but who also have special skills in motor development, gardening, conservation, animal care, horticulture—people who know about tools, rocks, dirt, pollution, clear-cutting, minerals, hills, hollows, cliffs, reefs, volcanoes, hurricanes, tides, salamanders, snakes, rabbits, and pigs; people who have childhood memories about special places and games like dens, tree houses, spinning tops and shooting marbles, kick-the-can, stick hockey, working in fields and shops; adults who remember how children express their fantasies in creative and wonderful ways. Such people are needed to help children shape small sterile spaces into growing, blooming, mysterious, challenging places. They are needed to move children beyond the classroom, to take children back to the land, to build with scrap and inexpensive materials, and to introduce traditional games that many, even adults, have forgotten or never known.

**Third, the playworker prepares the child for risks, challenges, and hazards.** Children must take risks to grow. During the early years, the child can be prepared by gradually introducing more complex challenges. Small climbing equipment makes way for larger, more complex, equipment. Ever more complex tools and tasks are introduced. Young children must learn to negotiate and to respect and yield to the rights of others. Even during the early 20th century, leading early educators recognized the need to let go and to limit their interference in children's play:

> In these [playgrounds] he should learn two things—to take care of himself while playing, and to respect the rights of others. . . . Even with little children the frequent "Don't, you will hurt yourself," should be changed to "Do, but be careful." A few falls and bruises will teach a child more than much caution and advice, but the adult must use judgment in allowing the child to endanger himself—always guarded but seldom interfered with. (Palmer, 1916, p. 253)

If adults are to help children counter the loss of nature and wildness, they must pay more attention to preserving and planting and less to building monolithic-like plastic and steel jungle gyms. They must be prepared to create a *compact countryside* in the playground or to take the children to the countryside.

> At the very moment that the bond is breaking between the young and the natural world, a growing body of research links our mental, physical, and spiritual health directly to our association with nature—in positive ways. (Louv, 2005, p. 2)
>
> [I]t is clear that we need to find ways to let children roam beyond the pavement, to gain access to vegetation and earth that allows them to tunnel, climb, or even fall. . . . Better to let kids be a hazard to nature than let nature be a hazard to them. . . . Learning what to fear, and what not to fear, is a large part of growing up. (Nabhan & Trimble, 1994, pp. 9, 152)
>
> [E]xtremely safe tends to equate with extremely boring. . . . Learning anything new will also bring some level of risk—social, psychological or physical—and children can cope with adult support along with their own personal resources. (Bonel & Lindon, 1996, p. 96)

*If we refuse our children the chance to play because they may get a bump, or a cut, or a scrape, or get into an argument, if we try to make sure that nothing in the world upsets them, if we stop kids from having the chance to experience the perilous range of human experience, then we are not protecting them. We are endangering them. They will develop no coping mechanisms for themselves. They will have no resilience, no depth of character. They will not understand how to come at the world. They will consider themselves to be precocious little gods and goddesses, probably inclined to tyranny.*

*That is what mollycoddling does to a child. (Wilson, 2010)*

None of this should mean that the play leader is a pushover or overly permissive, nor is he or she overly authoritarian. Play leaders explain their perspectives and listen to those of the children. They establish friendly relationships but are not just one of the kids. They can be both firm and kind, strict and fun, capable of stepping in and taking charge when situations get out of hand. They sometimes mediate disputes or impose consequences for ignoring ground rules. They help children understand the importance of maintaining their own play areas and raise their awareness of health and safety hazards.

**Fourth, playworkers prepare children for play.** The wise play leader engages children in planning before play and after play as needed. Planning for play is not to restrict places, opportunities, and materials for play but to allow children opportunities to learn to plan, to consider safe and unsafe play, to examine the play needs of all the players, and to determine how to secure and use materials for play projects. Learning to plan results from planning. As children's planning skills develop, they can assume the role of planning leader from the play leader who gradually becomes an adviser and consultant. The perspectives of children must be seriously considered in planning for play.

Initially, the play leader conducts a tour of the playground, discussing safety issues, asking open-ended questions of children, and establishing written ground rules necessary to avoid serious injury and to protect rights of others. These are best established as positive (dos) rather than negative (don'ts). Before outdoor playtime, the group comes together to jointly lay plans. For example, one subgroup is building an aboveground wading pool with materials donated by a local contractor, another subgroup has chosen today to plant and tend the garden, and yet another will continue the organized game begun the day before. Many play times are simply free choice—doing whatever one chooses to do.

After-play planning takes place whenever unresolved conflicts remain, either conflicts between players or conflicts resulting from frustration in the projects undertaken. Group A will not share building materials and tools with group B. Ryan and Lisa are throwing gravel at one another. The water continues to leak from the new wading pool despite best efforts. Clearly, the play leader needs to step in at times to resolve disputes on the spot or to stop activities that threaten children's safety. Negotiating and arguing may be constructive and are necessary for growth; bitter conflicts and physical violence are destructive.

**Fifth, the playworker focuses on creative aspects of play.** Creativity refers to "mental processes that lead to solutions, ideas, conceptualization, artistic forms, theories or products that are unique and novel" (Reber, 1995, p. 172). The spontaneous play of children is freely chosen, takes place within a given space and time span, is linked to materials, carries opportunities for divergent thinking and problem solving, and supports the creation of new images, ideas, products, and artistic forms. In sum, spontaneous play *is* a creative process. Play loses these qualities when there is a paucity of resources, when there is not enough time for play to take form and gain power and intensity, or when play is directed or oversupervised. Many forms of play, including organized sports and video games, and entertainment, including television, have limited creative benefits. Such activities should be carefully selected and supervised and should not be allowed to substitute for opportunities for spontaneous, creative play. Playful learning and teaching foster creative expression through music, movement, and the visual arts, whether indoors or outdoors (Kieff & Casbergue, 2000).

**Sixth, the playworker extends the child's world.** Children need extensive experiences to produce mental images for imaginative play and to support their growth in problem solving. These experiences should take them outside the playground to visit points of interest in the community: museums, factories, botanical gardens, and farms. They also include reading great children's books, storytelling, and interacting with grandparents, community artists, and leaders. Now children can take virtual tours of faraway places—Indian reservations, theme parks, even other countries—via the medium of computerized virtual-reality equipment. Such equipment promises to offer positive, growth-enhancing opportunities to balance the negative influences of much television and Internet play.

Extending the child's world also refers to providing opportunities for children from different cultures to interact with one another and for children with disabilities to have equal access to all the activity areas on the playground. Children learn from one another. When children are allowed to play in mixed-age groups, older children can assume some of the roles often left to adults—teach traditional games to younger children, support them in learning play skills, and show them how to deal with safety hazards. Generally, children should be free to choose their own friends, but the play leader makes exceptions for children who are ignored or excluded from play and helps them develop positive relationships.

**Seventh, playworkers help children cope in an increasingly chaotic world.** In a culture of fragmented and absent families, play leaders carry responsibilities once assumed by parents. They interact with growing numbers of children who are alienated, abused, traumatized, and disabled—kids who are dependent on drugs to help them cope, who are shifted from caretaker to caretaker, who have little security and support, or who move from place to place. Helping these kids within a mix of kids with no such problems is a constant and growing challenge to contemporary teachers and play leaders. Many simply need an understanding adult who recognizes and expresses appreciation for work well done and trusts them to assume growing responsibility. Others need help in securing special professional assistance to cope with their problems and disabilities. Some need adults who recognize the signs of child abuse, communicate with other professionals, and promptly report their findings to the proper authorities.

Providing for extensive time in healthy play, under the guidance of skilled adults who integrate flexible indoor and outdoor curricula (work and play), is a profound challenge for 21st-century teachers and play leaders. Schools must come to understand that recess is a critical component of the educative process.

**Eighth, playworkers step aside and let children play.** Adults step aside and let children play when their joint consciousness is riveted to a powerfully satisfying theme, enveloped with intensity and ecstasy, and functioning freely and creatively. Consider Ackerman's deep play (1999), Csikszentmihalyi's flow (1990), Maslow's self-actualization (1962), and Rogers's fully functioning person (1962). **Deep play,** a concept Ackerman borrowed from Jeremy Bentham (1748–1832), is characterized by rapture, ecstasy, risk, obsession, pleasure, distractedness, timelessness, and a sense of the holy or sacred:

> In those rare moments of deep play, we can lay aside our sense of self, shed time's continuum, ignore pain. . . . No mind or heart bobbles. No analyzing or explaining. No questing for logic. No promises. No goals. No worry. . . . What is the difference between simple play and deep play? Simple play can take many forms and have many purposes, but it goes only so far. When it starts focusing one's life and offering ecstatic moments, it becomes deep play. . . . [I]n deep play's altered mental state one most often finds clarity, revelation, acceptance of self, and other life affirming feelings. (Ackerman, 1999, pp. 23, 24)

For many years, Csikszentmihalyi (1990; Csikszentmihalyi & Csikszentmihalyi, 1995) studied states of **optimal experience,**—those times when people report heightened, more intense states of enjoyment, concentration, and absolute absorption in an activity. He calls those times "flow experiences." **Flow** is most consistently experienced in sports, games, art, hobbies, and play. The characteristics of flow recognizable in play include the merging of action and awareness, a centering of attention, a narrowing of consciousness to an immediate activity as in a play theme, a loss of ego and self-consciousness, a sense of being in control, an integration of one's activities with those of another, motivated by the activity itself, and the existence of a *spirit of play.*

**Self-actualizing people** (Maslow, 1962) are those who accept and express the inner self and who have minimal presence of ill health or loss of capacities. There are requirements for controls as capacities are organized and higher forms of expression are sought, but there must be a balance between controls and spontaneity. Education and healthy development are directed by both the cultivation of inner controls by the child and the cultivation of spontaneity, expression, and creativity. In the playground culture, spontaneity should rule over controls. To be strong, a child must develop frustration tolerance—that is, experience frustration in a helping context, grapple with it, win or cope, and survive to play again. For self-actualizing people, work can be playful, having its qualities of spontaneity, expression, and creativity. The highest levels of self-actualization have childlike qualities of fun, humor, silliness, whimsicalness, and craziness. The ultimate experience during play is those peak experiences in which time disappears.

The **fully functioning person** (Rogers, 1962) is a person in flow, in process, rather than one who has achieved some state. He is a creative being who permits himself to experience freely, to delve into the unique, to explore the mysterious, to stretch and grow, to express himself in his own unique way. Is it any wonder that children's playgrounds must possess matching qualities of mystery, uniqueness, wildness, and magic?

Frost (2003) sums the transcendental experiences described by these scholars as **transcendental play**—play that *transcends* the real and the make believe—a state of intensity and being in which the child loses contact with the outside world, places herself into mental oneness with the activity, loses inhibitions, revels in physical risk and mental challenge, and creates a profound play world of magic and intrigue.

Transcendental play, deep play, or flow are perhaps understandable only to those who have experienced such phenomena as children. When school recess was long, adult supervision was casual, and natural materials were abundant, such experiences were regular and profound. One of us recalls one such experience that permeated school recess for a week following a rain that gorged a small stream running through the school grounds. Void of any adult supervision except for curious observation near the end of the intense activity, a group of children built a mud dam across the stream and backed up the water, forming an increasingly deep pond. This eventually captured the attention of a second group, who went upstream to build their own dam and later released the water to wash out the downstream dam. This led to several days of intense experimentation with various materials—mud, clay, sticks, limbs, boards, rocks, scrap iron—to strengthen new dams in efforts to entrap more water or to prevent washout by the opposing group's dam. The sight of 20-plus children sloshing through classrooms in dripping clothing could easily have drawn reprimands and closure on dam building. Fortunately, the teachers allowed the activity to continue until it ran its course (the water dried up), and the children experienced those rare levels of intensity, creativity, loss of self, pushing limits, and ecstasy described as deep play or flow. Such is the stuff from which joy, creativity, learning, and development are formed. Such play as that described here is rarely seen during a typical 15-minute recess period at a typical standardized playground.

For even keener insight into the nature or meaning of transcendental play, deep play, and flow as they relate to children's play, absorb the wonderful book for children *Roxaboxen* (McLerran & Cooney, 1991), powerfully but simply written by Alice McLerran and sensitively illustrated by Barbara Cooney. *Roxaboxen* is a celebration of children's play and special play places enjoyed by the author's mother during her childhood. On a hill in Arizona exists the remains of the magical town of Roxaboxen—a simple scattering of rocks, plants, broken glass, and an old car chassis—a place never forgotten by the children who played there.

 ## KEY TERMS

| | |
|---|---|
| Adventure playgrounds | Playground Association of America (PAA) |
| Chaos theory | Playwork |
| Cooperative planning | Playworkers |
| Deep play | Scaffold |
| Directive school | Self-actualizing people |
| Flow | Social collaboration |
| Fully functioning person | Social transmission |
| Nondirective school | Supersymmetry |
| Optimal experience | Symbolism |
| Play leaders | Transcendental play |
| Playwork | Zone of proximal development (ZPD) |
| Play tutoring | |

 ## STUDY QUESTIONS

1. How is the concept of "playground" changing? What are the implications for changing the nature of playground supervision or play leadership?

2. How did play leadership in the United States change during the 20th century? Compare play leadership in city park and school playgrounds.

3. What do major theorists believe are adults' primary roles in playgrounds for children? How do these beliefs compare to your personal beliefs?

4. What challenges does Vygotsky's work pose for proponents of Piaget's theories, particularly in regard to adult roles in children's play?

5. What general conclusions do you draw from research regarding adult roles in children's play? How do conclusions from research compare with views of early theorists?

6. What are the qualities of adventure playgrounds? How do they differ from typical American playgrounds? What are the advantages and disadvantages of each? Would you propose establishing adventure playgrounds at American parks and schools? Why or why not?

7. How does the content of the "Conclusions and Recommendations" section of this chapter differ from theoretical and research perspectives discussed earlier in the chapter? How are they consistent?

8. Reflecting on your own childhood play, describe one or more play experiences that you would characterize as "flow," "deep play," or "transcendental play." How do you believe that these experiences would contribute to self-actualization or becoming fully functioning?

9. How does high-stakes testing or the No Child Left Behind Act interfere with children's play? What are the consequences of such interference?

10. What is the preferred length of a school recess period? Why?

## ◠ REFERENCES

Ackerman, D. (1999). *Deep play.* New York: Random House.

Allen, Marjory, Lady Allen of Hurtwood. (1968). *Planning for play.* Cambridge, MA: MIT Press.

Bengtsson, A. (Ed.). (1972). *Adventure playgrounds.* New York: Praeger.

Benjamin, J. (1974). *Grounds for play: In search of adventure.* London: Bedford Square.

Bennett, N., Wood, L., & Rogers, S. (1997). *Teaching through play: Teachers' thinking and classroom practice.* Philadelphia: Open University Press.

Berk, L. E., & Winsler, A. (1995). *Scaffolding children's learning: Vygotsky and early childhood education.* Washington, DC: National Association for the Education of Young Children.

Block, J., & King, N. (1987). *School play: A source book.* New York: Guilford.

Blow, S. E. (1909). *Symbolic education: A commentary on Froebel's "mother play."* New York: Appleton.

Bodrova, E., & Leong, D. J. (1996). *Tools of the mind: The Vygotskian approach to early childhood education.* Upper Saddle River, NJ: Merrill/Prentice Hall.

Bodrova, E., & Leong, D. J. (1998a). Adult influences on play. In D. P. Fromberg & D. Bergen (Eds.), *Play from birth to twelve and beyond: Contexts, perspectives, and meanings* (pp. 277–282). New York: Garland.

Bonel, P., & Lindon, J. (1996). *Good practice in play-work.* Cheltenham, England: Thornes.

Brown, F. (Ed.). (2003). *Playwork: Theory and practice.* Philadelphia: Open University Press.

Burns, S., & Brainerd, C. (1979). Effects of constructive and dramatic play on perspective taking in young children. *Developmental Psychology, 15,* 512–521.

Butler, G. D. (1950). *Playgrounds: Their administration and operation.* New York: Barnes.

Caplan, F., & Caplan, T. (1973). *The power of play.* New York: Anchor.

Cavallo, D. J. (1976). *The child in American reform: A psychohistory of the movement to organize children's play, 1880–1920.* Unpublished doctoral dissertation, State University of New York, Stony Brook.

Christie, J., & Johnsen, P. (1985). Questioning the results of play training research. *Educational Psychologist, 20,* 7–11.

Csikszentmihalyi, M. (1990). *Flow: The psychology of optimal experience.* New York: Harper & Row.

Csikszentmihalyi, M., & Csikszentmihalyi, I. S. (Eds.). (1995). *Optimal experience.* New York: Cambridge University Press.

Curtis, H. S. (1917). *Education through play.* New York: Macmillan.

Dansky, J. L. (1980). Cognitive consequences of sociodramatic play and exploration training for economically disadvantaged preschoolers. *Journal of Child Psychology and Psychiatry, 21,* 47–58.

Davy, A. (2001). *Playwork: Play and care for children 5–15.* London: Thomson.

Dempsey, J. D. (1985). *The effects of training in play on cognitive development in preschool children.* Unpublished doctoral dissertation, University of Texas, Austin.

Dewey, J. (1916). *Democracy and education.* New York: Free Press.

Evans, J. (1989). *Children at play: Life in the school playground.* Victoria, Australia: Deakin University Press.

Evans, J. (1990). The teacher role in playground supervision. *Play & Culture, 3,* 219–234.

Feitelson, D., & Ross, G. S. (1973). The neglected factor—play. *Human Development, 16,* 202–223.

Finnan, C. (1982). The ethnography of children's spontaneous play. In G. Spindler (Ed.), *Doing the ethnography of schooling: Educational anthropology in action* (pp. 356–380). New York: Holt, Rinehart & Winston.

Freedman, D. (1991). The new theory of everything. *Discover, 12,* 53–61.

Freyberg, J. T. (1973). Increasing the imaginative play of urban disadvantaged kindergarten children through systematic training. In J. L. Singer (Ed.), *The child's world of make-believe* (pp. 129–154). New York: Academic Press.

Froebel, F. (1902). *Education of man* (W. N. Hailmann, Trans.). New York: Appleton. (Original work published 1826)

Frost, J. L. (1992). *Play and playscapes.* Albany, NY: Delmar.

Frost, J. L. (2003). Bridging the gaps: Children in a changing society. *Childhood Education, 80,* 29–34. Olney, MD: Association for Childhood Education International.

Frost, J. L. (2004a). How adults enhance or mess up children's play. *Archives of Pediatrics and Adolescent Medicine, 158,* 16.

Frost, J. L. (2010). *A history of children's play and play environments: Toward a contemporary child-saving movement.* New York and London: Routledge.

Frost, J. L., Brown, P. S., Sutterby, J. A., & Thornton, C. D. (2004). *The developmental benefits of playgrounds.* Olney, MD: Association for Childhood Education International.

Frost, J. L., & Kissinger, J. B. (1976). *The young child and the educative process.* New York: Holt, Rinehart & Winston.

Frost, J. L., & Klein, B. L. (1979). *Children's play and playgrounds.* Boston: Allyn & Bacon.

Gill, T. (2007). *No fear: Growing up in a risk averse society.* London: Calouste Gulbenkian Foundation.

Goerner, S. (1994). *Chaos and the evolving ecological universe.* Langhorne, PA: Gordon & Breach.

Golomb, C., & Bonen, S. (1981). Playing games of make-believe: The effectiveness of symbolic play training with children who failed to benefit from early conservation training. *Genetic Psychology Monographs, 104,* 137–159.

Haight, W. L., & Miller, P. J. (1993). *Pretending at home: Early development in a sociocultural context.* Albany: State University of New York Press.

Hirsh-Pasek, K., Golinkoff, R. M., Berk, L. E., & Singer, D. G. (2009). *A mandate for playful learning in preschool: Presenting the evidence.* New York: Oxford University Press.

Howes, C., & Smith, E. (1995). Relations among child care quality, teacher behavior, children's play activities, emotional security, and cognitive activity in child care. *Early Childhood Research Quarterly, 10,* 381–404.

Huizinga, J. (1950). *Homo ludens: A study of the play-element in culture.* Boston: Beacon. (Original work published 1938).

Hutt, S., Tyler, S., Hutt, C., & Christopherson, H. (1989). *Play, exploration, and learning: A natural history of the preschool.* London: Routledge.

Iowa Child Welfare Research Station. (1934). *Manual of nursery school practice.* Iowa City: State University of Iowa.

Jacobs, P. J. (1998). *A constructivist inquiry into the issues in the contemporary practice of playwork in England.* Unpublished doctoral dissertation, University of Texas, Austin.

Johnson, J. E., Christie, J. F., & Yawkey, T. D. (1999). *Play and early childhood development* (2nd ed.). New York: Longman.

Jones, E., & Cooper, R. M. (2006). *Playing to get smart.* New York: Teachers College Press.

Jones, E., & Reynolds, G. (1992). *The play's the thing: Teacher's role in children's play.* New York: Teachers College Press.

Kieff, J. E., & Casbergue, R. M. (2000). *Playful learning and teaching.* Boston: Allyn & Bacon.

Kilpatrick, W. H. (1916). *Froebel's kindergarten principles: Critically examined.* New York: Macmillan.

Lambert, J. (1992). *Adventure playgrounds: A book for play leaders.* N.P.: Out of Order Books.

Lambert, J., & Pearson, J. (1974). *Adventure playgrounds.* Baltimore: Penguin Books.

Lee, J. (1927). Play, the architect of man. *The Playground, 21,* 460–463.

Levy, A., Wolfgang, C., & Koorland, M. (1992). Sociodramatic play as a method for enhancing language performance of kindergarten age students. *Early Childhood Research Quarterly, 7,* 245–262.

Louv, R. (2005). *Last child in the woods: Saving our children from nature-deficit disorder.* Chapel Hill, NC: Algonquin.

Marshall, H. R. (1961). Relations between home experiences and children's use of language in play interaction with peers. *Psychological Monographs, 75*(5, Serial No. 509).

Marshall, H. R., & Hahn, S. (1967). Experimental modification of dramatic play. *Journal of Personality and Social Psychology, 5,* 119–122.

Maslow, A. H. (1962). Some basic propositions of a growth and self-actualization psychology. In *A.S.C.D. Yearbook: Perceiving, behaving, becoming* (pp. 34–49). Washington, DC: Association for Supervision and Curriculum Development.

McLerran, A., & Cooney, B. (1991). *Roxaboxen.* New York: Penguin.

Miller, E., & Almon, J. (2009). *Crisis in the kindergarten: Why children need to play in school.* College Park, MD: Alliance for Childhood.

Miller, S. M., Fernie, D., & Kantor, R. (1992). Distinctive literacies in different preschool contexts. *Play & Culture, 5,* 107–119.

Moore, R. (1974, October). Anarchy zone: Encounters in a school yard. *Landscape Architecture,* pp. 364–369.

Nabhan, G. P., & Trimble, S. (1994). *The geography of childhood: Why children need wild places.* Boston: Beacon Press.

Naisitt, J. (1994). *Global paradox.* New York: Avon.

Newman, D., Griffin, P., & Cole, M. (1989). *The construction zone: Working for cognitive change in school.* Cambridge: Cambridge University Press.

Nicholson, M. (1971). *Adventure playgrounds.* London: National Playing Fields Association.

Ohanian, S. (2002). *What happened to recess and why are our children struggling in kindergarten?* New York: McGraw-Hill.

Palmer, L. A. (1916). *Play life in the first eight years.* Boston: Ginn.

Peitgen, H., Jurgens, J., & Saupe, D. (1992). *Chaos and fractals.* New York: Springer.

Pellegrini, A. D. (1995). *School recess and playground behavior: Educational and developmental role.* Albany: State University of New York Press.

Pellegrini, A. D., & Galda, L. (1993). Ten years after: A reexamination of symbolic play and literacy research. *Reading Research Quarterly, 28,* 162–177.

Piaget, J. (1962). *Play, drama and imitation in childhood.* New York: Norton.

Playground and Recreation Association of America. (1925). *The normal course in play.* Washington, DC: McGrath Publishing Co., and the National Recreation and Park Association (reprint).

Quick, R. H. (1896). *Essays on educational reformers.* New York: D. Appleton.

Ratey, J. J., & Hagerman, E. (2008). *Spark: The revolutionary new science of exercise and the brain.* New York: Little, Brown and Company.

Reber, A. S. (1995). *Dictionary of psychology.* New York: Penguin.

Reynolds, G., & Jones, E. (1997). *Master players: Learning from children at play.* New York: Teachers College Press.

Rogers, C. R. (1962). Toward becoming a fully functioning person. In ASCD Yearbook Committee (Ed.), *Perceiving, behaving, becoming: Yearbook 1962.* Washington, DC: Association for Supervision and Curriculum Development.

Rogoff, B. (1990). *Apprenticeship in thinking: Cognitive development in social context.* New York: Oxford University Press.

Rogoff, B., Mistry, A., Goncu, A., & Mosier, C. (1993). Guided participation in cultural activity by toddlers and caregivers. *Monographs of the Society for Research in Child Development, 58,* (Serial No. 236).

Rosen, C. E. (1974). The effects of sociodramatic play on problem-solving behavior among culturally disadvantaged preschool children. *Child Development, 45,* 920–927.

Rosenberg, K. S., Johnson, C. N., & Harris, P. L. (2000). *Imagining the impossible: Magical, scientific and religious thinking in children.* New York: Cambridge University Press.

Saltz, E., Dixon, D., & Johnson, J. (1977). Training disadvantaged preschoolers on various fantasy activities: Effects on cognitive functioning and impulse control. *Child Development, 48,* 367–380.

Sears, R. R. (1975). Your ancients revisited: A history of child development. In E. M. Hetherington (Ed.), *Review of Child Development Research, 5,* 1–73.

Senge, P., Scharmer, C. O., Jaworski, J., & Flowers, B. S. (2004). *Presence: An exploration of profound change in people, organizations and society.* New York: Doubleday.

Sluckin, A. (1981). *Growing up in the playground: The social development of children.* London: Routledge & Kegan Paul.

Smilansky, W. (1968). *The effects of sociodramatic play on disadvantaged preschool children.* New York: Wiley.

Smilansky, S., & Shefatya, L. (1990). *Facilitating play: A medium for promoting cognitive, socioemotional and academic development in young children.* Gaithersburg, MD: Psychosocial & Educational Publications.

Smith, P. K., & Sydall, S. (1978). Play and non-play tutoring in preschool children: Is it play or tutoring which matters? *British Journal of Educational Psychology, 48,* 315–325.

Smolucha, F. (1992). The relevance of Vygotsky's theory of creative imagination for contemporary research in play. *Creativity Research Journal, 5,* 69–76.

Smuts, A. B., & Hagen, J. (1983). *History and research in child development.* Monographs of the Society for Research in Child Development. *50*(4–5, Serial No. 211).

Sutton-Smith, B. (1992). Foreword. In J. Frost (Ed.), *Play and playscapes* (pp. vii–viii). Albany, NY: Delmar.

Sutton-Smith, B. (1993a). Dilemmas in adult play with children. In K. MacDonald (Ed.), *Parent-child play: Descriptions and implications* (pp. 15–40). Albany: State University of New York Press.

Sylva, K., Roy, C., & Painter, M. (1980). *Childwatching at playgroup & nursery school.* Ypsilanti, MI: High/Scope Press.

Tanner, L. N. (1997). *Dewey's laboratory school: Lessons for today.* New York: Teachers College Press.

Tharp, R. G., & Gallimore, R. (1988). *Rousing minds to life: Teaching, learning, and schooling in social contexts.* New York: Cambridge University Press.

Tsanoff, S. V. (1897). *Educational value of the children's playgrounds.* Philadelphia: Author.

Udwin, O. (1983). Imaginative play training as an intervention method with institutionalized preschool children. *British Journal of Educational Psychology, 53,* 32–39.

VanderVen, K. (1998). Play, Proteus, and paradox: Education for a chaotic and supersymmetric world. In D. Fromberg & D. Bergen (Eds.), *Play from birth to twelve and beyond: Contexts, perspectives, and meanings* (pp. 119–132). New York: Garland.

Von Marenholz-Bulow, Baroness. (1897). *Reminiscences of Friedrich Froebel.* Boston: Lee & Shepard.

Vygotsky, L. S. (1966). Play and its role in the mental development of the child. *Soviet Psychology, 12*(6), 62–76.

Weinberg, S. (1992). *Dreams of a final theory.* New York: Pantheon.

Wertsch, J. V., & Hickman, M. (1987). Problem solving in social interaction: A microgenetic analysis. In M. C. Hickmann (Ed.), *Social and functional approaches to language and thought* (pp. 251–266). San Diego: Academic Press.

Wheatley, M. (1992). *Leadership and the new science.* San Francisco: Berrett-Koehler.

Whitton, S. (1998). The playful ways of mathematicians' work. In D. P. Fromberg & D. Bergen (Eds.), *Play from birth to twelve and beyond: Contexts, perspectives, and meanings.* New York: Garland.

Wilson, P. (2009). The cultural origins and play philosophy of playworkers: An interview with Penny Wilson. *American Journal of Play.* 1(3), 269–282.

Wilson, P. (2010). *A playwork primer.* College Park, MD: Alliance for Childhood.

Winegar, L. T. (1989). Organization and process in the development of children's understanding of social events. In L. T. Winegar (Ed.), *Social interaction and the development of children's understanding* (pp. 45–65). Norwood, NJ: Ablex.

Wood, D., McMahon, L., & Cranstoun, Y. (1980). *Working with under fives.* Ypsilanti, MI: High/Scope Foundation.

Zigler, E. F., Singer, D. G., & Bishop-Josef, S. J. (2004). *Children's play: The roots of reading.* Washington, DC: Zero to Three Press.

Zygmunt-Fillwalk, E., & Bilello, T. E. (2005). Parents' victory in reclaiming recess for their children. *Childhood Education, 82,* 19–23.

# Appendix

# Playground Checklist

Most child-care centers and elementary schools have limited spaces and budgets for outdoor play. Many loose parts, both natural and built, are inexpensive and readily available. Research (Frost & Klein, 1997; Frost, 2002; Frost, et al., 2004; Frost, 2010) demonstrates that such materials are among the top choices of children. Many types of large, built equipment are also developmentally valuable for complementing loose parts and ensuring provision for the full range of children's natural play initiatives. Every child-care center and school for young children, preschool and elementary, should create and maintain with children integrated natural/built outdoor play environments and ensure daily recess for free, creative, unstructured, challenging play.

*Note:* This checklist is not intended as a research tool but as an aid to planning and evaluating playgrounds.

© 2011 Joe L. Frost (revised)

| CHECK | SECTION I. What does the playground contain? |
|---|---|
| | 1. An open area with marked spaces for games, and goals for such activities as basketball and soccer. A network of marked paths or rubber conveyor belts for wheeled toys, linked to key play zones. |
| | 2. Sand and sand play equipment including a variety of loose parts—toys, blocks, scoops, and containers. |
| | 3. Water-play areas with fountains, pools and sprinklers, and water-play materials. |
| | 4. Dramatic play structures (playhouses, cars or boats with complementary loose parts such as adjacent sand and water, and housekeeping equipment). |
| | 5. A built (naturalized) manufactured superstructure with room for many children at a time and with a variety of challenges and exercise options (entries, exits, climbing, and levels). |
| | 6. Mound(s) of earth for climbing, rolling, sliding, and digging. |
| | 7. Trees and natural areas for shade, animal habitats, nature study, and play. |
| | 8. Continuous challenge, linkage of areas, functional physical boundaries, vertical and horizontal treatment (hills and valleys). |
| | 9. Construction area with junk materials such as tires, crates, planks, boards, bricks, and nails; tools should be provided and demolition and construction allowed. |
| | 10. A purchased or built vehicle, airplane, boat, or car that has been made safe but not stripped of its play value (should be changed or relocated after a period of time to renew interest). |
| | 11. Equipment or natural features for active play: a variety of overhead apparatus, climbers, slides, balancing devices, and swings. |
| | 12. A large, open, sandy or grassy area for organized games. |
| | 13. Small semiprivate spaces at the child's own scale: tunnels, niches, playhouses, private or special places partially enclosed by trellises, plants, trees, and berms. |
| | 14. Fences, gates, walls, and windows that provide security for young children and are adaptable for learning/play. |
| | 15. Gardens for flowers, vegetables, and herbs located so they are protected from active play and games but with easy access for children to tend them. Special nature areas such as butterfly gardens. Gardening tools are available. A greenhouse and rainwater barrels for plants greatly enhances nature study. |
| | 16. Provisions for housing of pets. Pets and supplies. Special areas to attract birds and insects. Storage for supplies. |
| | 17. A covered outdoor space (outdoor classroom) for art, music and nature study. This can be a covered play area linked to the playroom, which will protect children from the sun and rain and extend indoor activities to the outdoors. |
| | 18. Storage building for outdoor play equipment, such as tools for construction and garden areas, maintenance tools, wheeled toys linked to the track, sand play equipment, and tools for children's building. Storage can be next to the building or fence and should not block view of children. Storage should aid children's picking up and putting away equipment at the end of each play period. |
| | 19. Easy access from outdoor play areas to coats, toilets, and drinking fountains. Shaded areas, benches, tables, and support materials for group activities (art, reading, etc.). |
| | 20. Accessibility, materials, and equipment for children of all abilities/disabilities. |

| CHECK | SECTION II. Is the playground in good repair and relatively safe per ASTM, CPSC, and ADA?* |
|---|---|
| | 1. A protective fence (with lockable gates) next to hazardous areas (busy streets, deep ditches, deep water, etc.). |
| | 2. Eight to 12 inches of noncompacted sand, wood mulch, or equivalent manufactured surfacing under all climbing and moving equipment, extending through fall zones and secured by retaining barriers. |
| | 3. Size of equipment appropriate to age and skill levels served. Special attention to reduced heights for preschool children. |
| | 4. Area free of litter (e.g., broken glass), electrical hazards, high-voltage power lines, toxic hazards. See CPSC for toxic hazards in wood products. |
| | 5. Moving parts free of defects (e.g., no pinch and crush points, bearings not excessively worn). |
| | 6. Equipment free of sharp edges and broken, loose, and missing parts. |
| | 7. Swing seats constructed of soft or lightweight material (e.g., rubber, plastic). Basketball goalposts padded. Soccer goals secure in ground. |
| | 8. All safety equipment in good repair (e.g., guardrails, padded areas, protective covers). |
| | 9. No openings that can entrap a child's head (approximately 3.5" x 9"). See CPSC/ASTM for measurements and tests. |
| | 10. Equipment structurally sound. No bending, warping, breaking, sinking, missing parts, Heavy fixed and moving equipment secured in ground and concrete footings recessed underground at least 4 inches. |
| | 11. Adequate space between equipment—typically 6 feet, depending on type and location of equipment (see CPSC/ASTM). |
| | 12. No signs of underground rotting, rusting, or termites in wood support members (probe underground). |
| | 13. No metal slides or decks exposed to sun. Use plastic components or place in permanent shade. |
| | 14. Guardrails and protective barriers in place that meet CPSC/ASTM height and other requirements. |
| | 15. No loose ropes, suspended ropes, or cables in movement area. No jewelry (rings or necklaces) on children. |
| | 16. All balance beams, cables, and chains at heights prescribed by CPSC/ASTM. |
| | 17. Signs at entry alerting to appropriate ages of users, need for adult supervision, and any hazards. |
| | 18. No protrusion or entanglement hazards. |
| | 19. No tripping or fall hazards in equipment use areas. For example, exposed concrete footings. |
| | 20. Check water hazards—access to unsupervised pools, creeks. Check traffic hazards—streets, parking lots, delivery areas. |

*For details, refer to current issues of the United States Consumer Product Safety Commission's (CPSC's) *Handbook for Public Playground Safety* (*www.cpsc.gov*), the American Society for Testing and Materials (ASTM's) *Standard Consumer Safety Performance Specification for Playground Equipment for Public Use*, and the Americans with Disabilities Act (*ADA*) *Guidelines for Playgrounds.*

| CHECK | SECTION III. How should the playground and/or the play-leader function? |
|---|---|
| | 1. Encourages play: <br> • Inviting, easy access. Natural walking trails bordered by natural ecosysems. <br> • Open, flowing, and relaxed space <br> • Clear movement from indoors to outdoors <br> • Appropriate equipment for the age group(s) |
| | 2. Stimulates the child's senses: <br> • Changes and contrasts in scale, light, texture, and color <br> • Flexible equipment, both natural and built <br> • Diverse experiences for free play, games, and outdoor learning |
| | 3. Nurtures the child's curiosity: <br> • Materials that the child can change <br> • Materials for experiments and construction <br> • Plants and animals |
| | 4. Supports the child's social and physical needs: <br> • Comfortable to the child <br> • Scaled to the child <br> • Physically challenging |
| | 5. Allows interaction between the child and the resources: <br> • Systematic storage that defines routines <br> • Semi-enclosed spaces to read, work a puzzle, talk or plan with friends, or be alone |
| | 6. Allows interaction between children: <br> • Variety of spaces <br> • Adequate space to avoid conflicts <br> • Materials that invites socialization |
| | 7. Allows interaction between the child and adults: <br> • Organization of spaces to allow general supervision <br> • Rest areas for adults and children |
| | 8. Supports functional, imaginative, exercise, rough-and-tumble, gross motor, active play. Include natural or built, challenging swings, overhead equipment, and climbing equipment scaled to age and skill levels of children. |
| | 9. Supports creative, constructive, building play. Children are taught safe ways of using tools and materials for construction. |
| | 10. Supports dramatic, pretend, make-believe play. Sufficient time is given during recess or playtime for children to generate and engage fully in pretend play themes. |
| | 11. Supports organized games and games with rules. Adults and older children teach traditional games, then step out of the way and provide equipment for sports activities. |
| | 12. Supports special play (e.g., nature play, chase games, rough-and-tumble, sand and water play). Chase and rough-and-tumble are unobtrusively supervised. |

| CHECK | SECTION III. How should the playground and/or the play-leader function? |
|---|---|
| | 13. Promotes solitary, private, meditative play. Children assist in preparing nature areas, habitats, and small built spaces (e.g., gazebos) for semi-privacy. |
| | 14. Promotes group, cooperative, sharing play. Children are encouraged to include new and reticent peers in their play groups. |
| | 15. Involves children in care and maintenance of playground. Adults model and teach maintenance skills—tool use, hazard identification, etc. |
| | 16. Involves adults in children's play—regular adult/child planning and evaluation. Adults help children learn to solve playground problems through cooperative planning and analysis of problems. |
| | 17. Integrates indoor/outdoor play and work/play activities—art, music, science, and language into nature play and work. |
| | 18. Promotes interaction between children and nature—plants, animals, weather stations, fish ponds, Knowledgeable adults are identified to lead field trips, provide direct instruction, and interact with children. |
| | 19. Adults are trained in play values, playground maintenance and safety, emergency procedures. Play leaders receive annual workshops to maintain skills. |
| | 20. The play environment is constantly changing—growing in appeal, challenge, and complexity. Good playgrounds are never finished. |

## REFERENCES AND SOURCES

Danks, G. D. (2010). *Asphalt to Ecosystems: Design Ideas for Schoolyard Transformation.*

Frost, J. L., & Klein, B. L. (1979) *Children's Play and Playgrounds.* Boston: Allyn Bacon.

Frost, J. L. (1992). *Play and Playscapes.* Albany, NY: Delmar.

Frost, J. L, Brown, P. S., Sutterby, J. A., & Thornton, C. (2004). *The Developmental Benefits of Playgrounds.* Olney, MD: Association for Childhood Education International.

Frost, J. L. (2010). *A History of Children's Play and Play Environments: Toward a Contemporary Child-Saving Movement.* New York: Routledge.

Keeler, R. (2008). *Natural Playscapes: Creating Outdoor Play Environments for the Soul.* Redmond, WA: Exchange Press.

Tai, L., Hague, M. T., McLellan, G. K., & Knight, E. J. (2006). *Designing Outdoor Environments for Children: Landscaping Schoolyards, Gardens, and Playgrounds.* New York: McGraw-Hill.

# Name Index

# Subject Index